S0-BPR-505

Advances in
Local Area Networks

FRONTIERS IN COMMUNICATIONS

Amos E. Joel, Jr., *Series Editor*

Advisory Committee
Paul Green
Masao Kawashima
Maurizio Decina
William H. Tranter
John O. Limb

OTHER IEEE PRESS BOOKS

Undersea Lightwave Communications, *Edited by P. K. Runge and P. R. Trischitta*
Phase-Locked Loops, *Edited by W. C. Lindsey and C. M. Chie*
Spread-Spectrum Communications, *Edited by C. E. Cook, F. W. Ellersick, L. B. Milstein, and D. L. Schilling*
Electronic Switching: Digital Central Office Systems of the World, *Edited by A. E. Joel, Jr.*
Satellite Communications, *Edited by H. L. Van Trees*
Phase-Locked Loops & Their Application, *Edited by W. C. Lindsey and M. K. Simon*
Spread Spectrum Techniques, *Edited by R. C. Dixon*
Electronic Switching: Central Office Systems of the World, *Edited by A. E. Joel, Jr.*
Waveform Quantization and Coding, *Edited by N. S. Jayant*
Communications Channels: Characterization and Behavior, *Edited by B. Goldberg*
Computer Communications, *Edited by P. E. Green and R. W. Lucky*

FRONTIERS IN COMMUNICATIONS

Advances in Local Area Networks

Edited by

Karl Kümmerle
IBM Research Laboratory, Zurich, Switzerland

Fouad A. Tobagi
Stanford University

John O. Limb
Hewlett Packard Laboratories, Great Britain

Published for the IEEE Communications Society by the IEEE PRESS

The Institute of Electrical and Electronics Engineers, Inc., New York

IEEE PRESS

1987 Editorial Board

R. F. Cotellessa, *Editor in Chief*

J. K. Aggarwal, *Editor, Selected Reprint Series*

Glen Wade, *Editor, Special Issue Series*

James Aylor	J. F. Hayes	A. C. Schell
F. S. Barnes	W. K. Jenkins	L. G. Shaw
J. E. Brittain	A. E. Joel, Jr.	M. I. Skolnik
B. D. Carrol	Shlomo Karni	P. W. Smith
Aileen Cavanagh	R. W. Lucky	M. A. Soderstrand
D. G. Childers	R. G. Meyer	M. E. Van Valkenburg
H. W. Colborn	Seinosuke Narita	John Zaborsky
	J. D. Ryder	

W. R. Crone, *Managing Editor*
H. P. Leander, *Technical Editor*
Laura Kelly, *Administrative Assistant*

Carolyne Tamney, *Publications Manager*
Valerie Cammarata, *Associate Editor*

Copyright © 1987 by

THE INSTITUTE OF ELECTRICAL AND ELECTRONICS ENGINEERS, INC.
345 East 47th Street, New York, NY 10017-2394

All rights reserved

PRINTED IN THE UNITED STATES OF AMERICA

IEEE Order Number: PC02105

Library of Congress Cataloging-in-Publication Data

Advances in local area networks.

(Frontiers in communications)
Includes index.
1. Local area networks (Computer networks)
I. Kümmerle, Karl. II. Limb, J. O. (John O.)
III. Tobagi, Fouad A. IV. IEEE Communications
Society. V. Series.
TK5105.7.A38 1987   004.6'8   87-4220
ISBN 0-87942-217-3

The Contributors

J. L. Adams
British Telecom Research Laboratories

A. Albanese
Bell Communications Research, Inc.

Flaminio Borgonovo
Politecnico di Milano

Peter I. P. Boulton
University of Toronto

Thomas H. Brunner
Swiss Federal Institute of Technology

Werner Bux
IBM Corporation

H. Che
Dana Computer, Inc.

Felix H. Closs
IBM Corporation

Ronald C. Crane
3Com Corporation

Yogen K. Dalal
Metaphor Computer Systems

John D. DeTreville
Digital Equipment Corporation

Jeremy Dion
Cambridge University

Robert A. Donnan
IBM Corporation—Consultant

Ken-Ichi Donuma
Toshiba Corporation

R. M. Falconer
British Telecom Research Laboratories

Marion R. Finley, Jr.
University of Montreal

Lois E. Flamm
Bell Communications Research, Inc.

C. Flores
AT&T Bell Laboratories

Alexander G. Fraser
AT&T Bell Laboratories

Luigi Fratta
Politecnico di Milano

Yohji Fujii
Nippon Telegraph and Telephone Corporation

Timothy A. Gonsalves
Worcester Polytechnic Institute

Larry Green
Communication Machinery Corporation

Davide Grillo
Fondazione Ugo Bordoni

J. P. Haggerty
AT&T Bell Laboratories

Bill Hawe
Digital Equipment Corporation

Jeremiah F. Hayes
Concordia University

Peter L. Heinzmann
Swiss Federal Institute of Technology

Gregory T. Hopkins
Ungermann-Bass, Inc.

Andrew Hopper
University of Cambridge

Daniel E. Huber
Swiss PTT

Willi Huber
Swiss Federal Institute of Technology

V. Bruce Hunt
Forthright Systems, Inc.

Takao Ito
Toshiba Corporation

Dittmar Janetzky
Siemens AG

J. Richard Jones
FiberLAN, Inc.

Heinz J. Keller
IBM Corporation

Yukio Kimura
Nippon Telegraph and Telephone Corporation

Alan Kirby
Digital Equipment Corporation

P. A. Kirslis
AT&T Bell Laboratories

Felix Kugler
Swiss Federal Institute of Technology

Karl Kümmerle
IBM Research Laboratory

Chin-Tau A. Lea
Georgia Institute of Technology

E. Stewart Lee
University of Toronto

John O. Limb
Hewlett-Packard Laboratories

G. W. R. Luderer
AT&T Bell Laboratories

W. T. Marshall
AT&T Bell Laboratories

James S. Meditch
University of Washington

Norman B. Meisner
Linkware Corporation

Heinrich Meyr
Technical University of Aachen

James G. Mitchell
Xerox Corporation

Hans R. Mueller
IBM Corporation

Shigeru Ohshima
Toshiba Corporation

Yoshinori Oikawa
Nippon Telegraph and Telephone Corporation

David L. Oster
Communication Machinery Corporation

Daniel Avery Pitt
IBM Corporation

David D. Redell
Digital Equipment Corporation

Jeffrey W. Reedy
FiberLAN, Inc.

Martin Reiser
IBM Corporation

John F. Shoch
Asset Management Company

W. David Sincoskie
Bell Communications Research, Inc.

Walter Steinlin
Swiss PTT

Bob Stewart
Xyplex Corporation

Hisayoshi Sugiyama
Nippon Telegraph and Telephone Corporation

Kian-Bon K. Sy
IBM Corporation

Dale Taylor
Communication Machinery Corporation

Fouad A. Tobagi
Stanford University

Nobuyuki Tokura
Nippon Telegraph and Telephone Corporation

Kym S. Watson
Fraunhofer-Institute of Information and
Data Processing

Peter J. Wild
Hasler Ltd.

Robin C. Williamson
IBM Corporation

Willy Zwaenepoel
Rice University

Contents

Part IV: Performance

Part V: Integrated Traffic

Part VI: Bridges and Gateways

Part VII: Software and Applications

Preface
Advances in Local Area Networks

LOCAL AREA NETWORKS (LAN's) are still evolving rapidly. While rings were first invented in the late 1960's it was not until the mid to late 1970's that local area networks became anything more than a laboratory curiosity. First-generation LAN's operating at speeds up to 10 Mbits/s are widely deployed in office environments today. Second-generation LAN's and metropolitan area networks (MAN's) operating at about 100 Mbits/s are the subject of current standardization efforts, and third-generation LAN's operating in the Gbit/s region are the object of current research.

LAN's can take many forms, so that at times it becomes difficult to define just what constitutes a LAN. Indeed, it is not infrequently suggested that a digital PABX handling voice and data is a form of LAN. We have taken a somewhat more restricted definition. We believe local area networks differ from classical communications channels in that firstly, the transmission medium is shared by a number of users and, secondly, that at least some of the information is sent in packets containing a destination address. These two properties are also shared by many MAN's. LAN's and MAN's exploit similar concepts, the primary difference being in the geographical coverage provided.

The aim of this volume was to collect in one place a description of the most important principles of LAN's, and to emphasize some of the new directions that LAN technology is taking. In selecting contributions for the volume, we placed emphasis on concepts rather than accurately reflecting the current state of the technology; there are a number of available books that guide the data communications manager in his/her search for an appropriate network.

As part of COMSOC's Frontiers in Communications Series, the source of our material was primarily from the JOURNAL ON SELECTED AREAS IN COMMUNICATIONS. Where appropriate, other sources have been tapped. The chapters presented herein are not just reprints of the original papers, corrections have been made, repetitive sections have been deleted, and, where appropriate, new material has been added.

Part I provides an introduction to the subject for readers who have no previous knowledge of the area. This chapter provides a good foundation for understanding any of the chapters in Part II. In Part II an attempt is made to describe the most common types of LAN's. Bus, star, and ring topologies are presented; token, slotted, and buffer insertion rings and CSMA/CD are covered; coaxial cable, twisted pair, and optical fiber are referenced.

Optical fiber is a medium with many desirable characteristics on which to build a LAN, particularly where very high speeds are required. However, obtaining optical access to a fiber presents some problems and the chapters in Part III explore this. While the logical operation of a LAN may frequently be described in a handful of well-crafted sentences, they are very difficult to analyze in detail. In Part IV we present some landmark results describing the performance of some types of LAN's. It is still necessary to make some approximations in order to get solutions, but the models being analyzed are coming close to real systems.

One of the exciting aspects of LAN's is that they can be used for transmitting not just computer data but voice, facsimile, graphics, video, and visual information. Part V describes three studies in combining multiple types of traffic; however, there is still much work to be done in this area. The only commercial systems that we are aware of that combine voice, video, and data traffic do so using separate frequency bands—scarcely integration.

In order to expand the size of a LAN, to accommodate more users, or to get from one type of network to another requires a bridge or a gateway; a whole new set of problems is encountered with gateways and bridges and some discussion of these takes place in Part VI.

The purpose of LAN's, of course, is to provide the interconnection necessary to support distributed processing and resource sharing. In many cases, the multiple access property of shared-medium LAN's and the inherent broadcast capability permit approaches to supporting these applications that are very different from those permitted by more classical communications systems. Examples presented in Part VII describe distributed computing applications, servers providing simultaneous access from many clients, and distributed call processing for an integrated data and voice system.

We would particularly like to acknowledge the contributions of the authors. To an individual they worked conscientiously to maintain a high quality. Finally, we thank Reed Crone, Carolyne Tamney, and Valerie Cammarata of the IEEE Press for their committed support.

Part I
Introduction

1
Local Area Networks—Major Technologies and Trends

KARL KÜMMERLE AND MARTIN REISER

In this chapter, we first review the origins of local area networks, discuss the major factors characterizing them, and outline the driving application scenarios. Particular emphasis is put onto bus and ring systems with both standardized and other medium-access control mechanisms. Specifically, we discuss the delay-throughput characteristic of carrier-sense multiple access with collision detection and token passing, and review the relevant engineering considerations for CSMA/CD baseband and broadband systems and for token rings. Finally, we summarize several new concepts and standardization efforts which aim at higher data rates than the IEEE 802 LAN's, and use optical-fiber media.

I. INTRODUCTION

During the early 1960's two developments took place which proved to be important for the later emergence of distributed local area networks (LAN's): the introduction of packet switching [1] and the realization of the ALOHA packet-radio network [2].

For a better understanding of the unique characteristics of the local area network, let us take a look at a typical cluster of terminals attached to a data-processing machine, also called a host. Figure 1(a) shows the structure of a local cluster. A set of terminals, typically up to 32, is attached to a control unit which at its backend connects to the I/O channel of the host. The necessary control functions are performed in the control unit and shared among the terminals. At the time when the cost of logic was a substantial factor of the overall system cost, this shared logic design obviously improved the economy.

Figure 1(b) depicts the case of remote terminals attached via modems and leased TP lines. Often, several terminals (or groups of terminals) share the line forming a so-called multidrop configuration. To avoid interference through multiple simultaneous transmissions, access to the multidrop line must be controlled. This is typically achieved through polling. The host, called the primary station, polls the terminals, the secondary stations. A terminal ready to send has to wait for its poll signal until allowed to initiate the data transmission. Note that control of the system is centralized and executed in the processor of the primary station.

The centralized polling mechanism used in the TP world was questioned by Abramson, who was faced with the task of interconnecting various terminals dispersed in a wide geographical area to a central computer via a radio network [2]. This network, known as

2

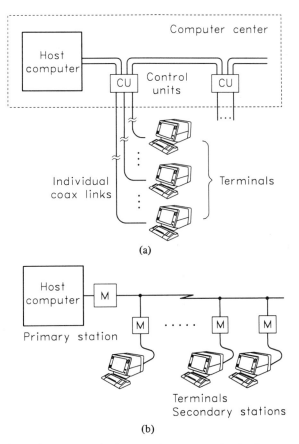

Fig. 1. Terminal-to-host communication. (a) Star system for local data communication. (b) TP cluster on multidrop link.

the ALOHA system, uses the simplest form of random access. A terminal ready to send simply sends its message, disregarding the state of the channel. Clearly, collisions may take place, in which case the terminals affected retransmit after a randomly chosen time-out.

The ALOHA system had a significant impact, especially on the academic community. The major benefits envisioned by the inventors were elimination of the access delay owing to waiting for the poll signal and simplicity of the system. There was no central control needed, the stations operated in a purely distributed fashion. However, simulation studies and analytical analysis showed that the elegance of random access was tarnished by a reduction of the usable bandwidth (18 percent in the case of ALOHA). A great deal of effort to improve the efficiency of random access commenced [2], [3].

During the late 1960's, R. Metcalfe was faced with the task of constructing a fast network linking small computers. He drew on the ideas of random access thus far discussed in the domain of packet radio and satellite communication. Metcalfe envisaged a "packet-radio network" on a coaxial cable, which he termed suggestively "Ethernet." One of Metcalfe's major contributions was carrier sensing, a technique which significantly improved the achievable performance of random-access systems. Running at 3 Mbits/s, a prototype "Ethernet" was implemented at the Xerox Palo Alto Research Center and used in the distributed office system prototype [4]. From this highly influential research into systems composed of intelligent workstations and specialized servers [5], the notion was lodged that the LAN was a key component of future office systems.

A substantial amount of research and development work aiming at the optimal LAN was launched and a rich body of literature developed, both advancing theory of access protocols as well as describing research prototypes [6], [7]. Alternatives to the original "Ethernet" design emerged. Re-examination of the theory of more traditional telecommunication systems revealed that there were designs which could be adopted to fit the new requirements of the distributed LAN. For example, a group of researchers at Cambridge University generalized the slotted-system approach, well known in PCM systems, and arrived at the slotted ring, also known as the "Cambridge Ring" [8].

Within the theory of polling systems, there is a symmetric version called hub-polling [9]. The token-access method was derived from the hub-polling scheme. Token rings were investigated independently and implemented at M.I.T. [10] and at IBM [11].

The mid-1970's and the early 1980's were characterized by vigorous research activities at universities and in industry, leading to a great number of competing system designs. Now, small companies, semiconductor vendors, and major providers of data-processing equipment offer local area network products and components. However, it is fair to say that the market explosion predicted by some analysts has not yet occurred.

II. TAXONOMY AND APPLICATION SCENARIOS

A. Definition

The object of this survey is the local area network, more precisely the distributed version of such networks which is schematically depicted in Fig. 2, and consists of the following elements:

1) a transmission medium shared among the attaching stations, and providing a broadcast capability,

2) a distributed protocol, the medium-access protocol, which controls access to the transmission system and prevents simultaneous transmissions, or recovers from collisions,

3) a set of cooperating adaptors through which stations attach to the network and which execute the access protocol, provide necessary data buffers, and interface with the processors of the station.

The service offered by such a LAN is packet switching, i.e., data blocks contain an explicit address recognized by the system, and used to deliver the data block to its destination.

B. Taxonomy

Local area networks may be characterized by the following factors:

1) Transmission medium:
   - coaxial cable
   - twisted-pair wire (unshielded and shielded)
   - optical fiber
2) Modulation scheme:
   - baseband transmission
   - carrier-modulated transmission termed "broadband" in the LAN literature

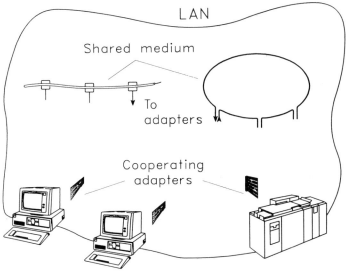

Fig. 2.   LAN definition.

3) Wiring scheme or wiring topology:
- bus or tree of buses
- ring
- star or set of connected stars

4) Logical topology:
- bus
- ring
- star

5) Medium-access control:
- random-access schemes, most importantly carrier-sense multiple access with collision detection (CSMA/CD) on bus topology
- controlled access schemes, most importantly token passing on both bus and ring topologies; in addition, slotted ring and buffer/register insertion ring.

Some major system design points are the following:

- baseband bus with CSMA/CD, wiring: tree of bus segments, coaxial cable. This system is widely known as "Ethernet" [12], [13] [see Fig. 3(a)],
- broadband bus with token passing, wiring: tree, coaxial cable [14] [see Fig. 3(b)],
- baseband ring with token passing, star wiring from distribution frames to wall outlets, twisted-pair cable [15], [16] [see Fig. 3(c)],
- slotted ring, baseband transmission on twisted pairs [8].

These systems will be discussed in more technical detail in subsequent sections.

C. Driving Applications

1) Distributed Office System: Historically, the distributed office system was the first major application foreseen for the LAN [6]. Each user is provided with a workstation with a powerful microprocessor. The high function version of such a workstation is equipped with

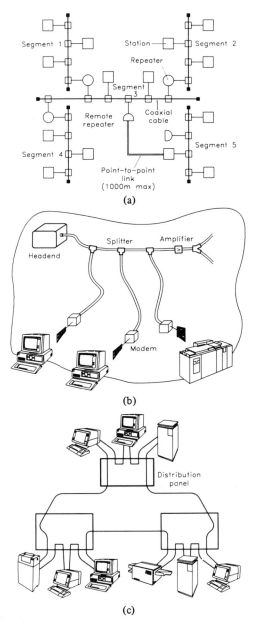

Fig. 3.   Typical LAN's. (a) "Ethernet." (b) Broadband bus. (c) Token ring.

an all-points addressable full screen display, a pointing device such as a mouse, and a local hard disk. The user interface (e.g., editors, graphics spreadsheets, etc.) is executed on the local processor. However, there are expensive resources such as laser printers which must be shared for cost reasons. Also, users may prefer a reliable central storage facility which will alleviate the need for data security and management.

In [5], the term clients was introduced for workstations and servers for shared resources, e.g., file server, printer server, communication server, mail server. The local area network is the glue which holds the distributed system together (see Fig. 4). From the need for favorable human factors, the data rate of such a local area network needs to be high, i.e., 1 to 10 Mbits/s.

2) Terminal to Host Communications, Front-End Network: The local cluster design of Fig. 1(a) served the industry well and is widely used by mainframe manufacturers. The cost advantages which accrued from the shared logic design were vital in the 1960's and early 1970's, and only now lose importance owing to the low cost of VLSI microprocessors of suitable power.

However, leading establishments witness growing problems in maintaining their terminal or front-end networks (see Fig. 5).

1) The number of terminals approaches the number of employees. Terminals are installed and frequently moved.

2) The fact that controllers need to be placed in close proximity to the data hosts since I/O channels are of limited length (typically 200 ft.). Space is at a premium in the machine room, and placement of a few tens of controllers may become difficult.

3) Cables converge in the machine room, and may crowd cable ducts and cable termination racks.

4) There are different hosts and a variety of smaller machines; a variety of types and grades of cables are in use.

5) Terminals are physically bound to one processor. If the user needs services from another host, he has to go to a different terminal or he needs more than one cable strung to his office, thus aggravating the duct crowding mentioned above.

Various tactical fixes are in use, such as link multiplexors, channel extenders, and wideband circuit switches. It is the local area network, however, which may lead to a truly

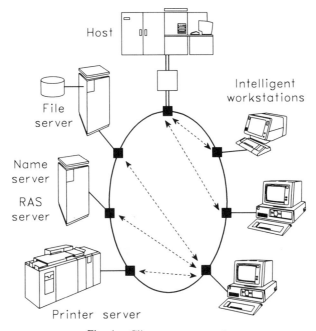

Fig. 4.   Client-server network.

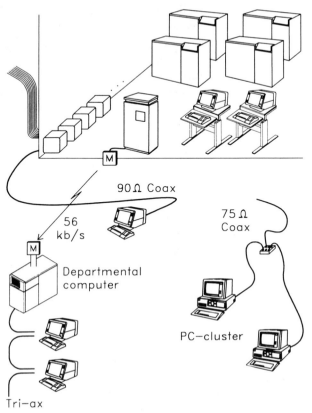

90 Ω Coax

56 kb/s

75 Ω Coax

Departmental computer

PC-cluster

Tri-ax

Fig. 5.   The cabling problem.

integrated solution. It addresses cable crowding through the shared medium and the need to access various resources through its packet-switched service. A consolidated network with network management tools is given to the system administrator.

3) Extension of the I/O Channel, Back-End Network: A situation not unlike the one described for the terminal-to-host network exists in the machine room proper. I/O devices are bound to processors through multidrop channels of limited drive distance. The resulting system structure lacks easy dynamic reconfigurability. A LAN of suitably high data rate would address both the need for flexibility and extended range.

4) Factory Automation: Fast progress is witnessed in the area of computer-aided design and computer-aided manufacturing. Numerically controlled machine tools abound and need to be provided with manufacturing data. The scheduling of work and control of part flow require massive use of computers. The ultimate system requires links between design data bases, manufacturing information data bases, and cells of machine tools on the plant floor.

It is evident that a manufacturing system is highly distributed and composed of heterogeneous equipment. A LAN is the key link between all these resources. In addition, an open systems network architecture is required to allow equipment from many sources to exchange data [17], [18].

5) Campus Networks: A problem which first appeared on university campuses was the need for connecting a large number of terminals, minicomputers, and hosts. This equipment is spread over a relatively large area (up to a few miles). Terminals are usually ASCII and the equipment is heterogeneous. Therefore, there is no teleprocessing network which would connect all the devices.

Special LAN's which provide flexible point-to-point connectivity for ASCII terminals are marketed. They typically use the broadband technology based on cable television componentry, which allows spanning of the distances required [19].

6) Clusters of Personal Computers: During the last few years, we have witnessed fast growth of the personal computer in small and large establishments, many of which have multiple machines, and numerous opportunities to share file storage and printing devices exist.

A large number of products to link personal computers through LAN's is on the market. These products must meet two key specifications: low cost and ease of installation, whereas universality and extensibility beyond a few tens of nodes are no issues. This market segment is characterized by a large number of different systems, offered by both the original manufacturer of the personal computer as well as by third parties.

III. MEDIUM-ACCESS CONTROL AND STANDARDS

A. LAN Standards

Local area network standards have been developed by the Institute of Electrical and Electronics Engineers (IEEE), the European Computer Manufacturers Association (ECMA), and various other national bodies. Some of these standards are becoming international through the International Organization for Standardization (ISO). LAN standards apply to the data link and physical layers of the OSI reference model (see Fig. 6).

Three medium-access control standards exist and their associated physical layer standards: CSMA/CD bus [13], token bus [14], and token ring [15]. A brief discussion of the medium-access control schemes based on the standard documents and on [20] follows in the next subsections.

1) CSMA/CD Bus: CSMA/CD was described in [4] as the access protocol of Ethernet [21]. The CSMA/CD protocol can be divided conceptually into a transmission and a reception part.

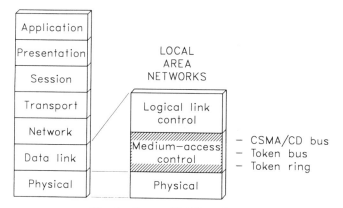

Fig. 6.   Scope of LAN standards.

Transmission: When a station has a frame ready for transmission, it monitors the cable to determine whether any transmissions take place. When the medium is found utilized, transmission is deferred. When the medium is clear, frame transmission is initiated.

If multiple stations attempt to transmit at the same time, interference can occur. Overlap of different transmissions is called a collision. In this case, each transmitting station enforces the collision by transmitting a bit sequence called the jam signal. This ensures that the duration of the collision is sufficient to be noticed by all other stations involved in the collision. Then stations schedule a retransmission attempt for a randomly selected time in the future. Retransmission is attempted repeatedly in case of subsequent collisions. Repeated collisions indicate a heavily utilized medium; therefore, stations adjust their retransmission activity to the traffic load perceived. This is accomplished by expanding the mean of the random retransmission time on each retransmission attempt.

Reception: All active stations synchronize with the preamble of an incoming frame and then decode the signal received. The destination-address field of the frame is checked to decide whether the frame should be received by this station. If so, the relevant parts of the frame will be copied. The station also checks the validity of the frame received by inspecting the frame check sequence.

The standards specify 10 Mbit/s operation on coaxial-cable segments at a distance of 500 m using baseband transmission.

Three other varieties of CSMA/CD standards are in preparation. A standard for shorter distance, which should allow lower cost, specifies 10 Mbits/s on coaxial cable at a distance of 200 m using baseband transmission. Another baseband scheme is proposed to operate on unshielded twisted-pair cable at a speed of 1 Mbit/s and a distance of 500 m. Finally, there is a standard for broadband transmission at 10 Mbits/s over distances of 3600 m; this scheme is intended to be compatible at the attachment-unit interface with devices designed for baseband.

2) Token Ring: A token ring consists of a set of stations connected serially by a transmission medium. Information is transferred sequentially from one active station to the next. A given station (the one having access to the medium) transfers information onto the ring. All other stations repeat each bit received. The addressed destination station copies the information as it passes. Finally, the station which transmitted the information removes it from the ring.

The basic token access protocol is very simple. A station gains the right to transmit when it detects a free token passing on the medium. The token is a control signal that circulates on the medium following each information transfer. Any station, upon detection of a free token, may capture the token, set it to busy, and then append appropriate control and address fields, data proper, the frame check sequence, and the frame ending delimiter. On completion of its information transfer, and after appropriate checking for proper operation, the station generates a new free token which provides other stations the opportunity to gain access to the ring.

A token-holding timer controls the length of time a station may occupy the medium before passing the token.

Multiple levels of priority can be provided on a token ring through an efficient priority mechanism. This mechanism is based on the principle described in [11] where higher priority stations can interrupt the progression of lower priority tokens and frames by making "reservations" in passing frames. When a frame with a priority reservation is received at the station currently transmitting, this station issues a free token with the priority requested instead of the priority previously used. The station requesting can subsequently transmit at the higher priority.

To guarantee reliable operation, the circulating token has to be protected against loss, permanent busy condition, or duplication. As shown in [11], this problem has been solved by introducing a monitor function available in each ring adapter and which can perform token supervision and recovery either in a fully distributed fashion [10], i.e., all active adapters are involved at all times, or in a centralized fashion with one monitor function active and the others monitoring the health of the active monitor function.

The token ring standard defines data signaling rates of 1 and 4 Mbits/s.

3) Token Bus: The token-bus technique is the third standardized medium-access control scheme. The intention behind developing this technique was to combine attractive features of a bus topology, e.g., use of broadband transmission, with those of a controlled medium-access protocol, e.g., good efficiency under high traffic load, speed-distance insensitivity, fairness of access.

The essence of the token-bus access method can be characterized as follows. A token controls the right to access the medium; the station which holds the token has momentary control over the medium. The token is passed among the active stations attached to the bus. As the token is passed, a logical ring is formed. Since the bus topology does not impose any sequential ordering of the stations, the logical ring is defined by a sequence of station addresses.

Steady-state operation simply requires the sending of the token to a specific successor station when a station has finished transmitting. The maximum transmission time of any station is controlled by a token-holding timer. A more difficult task is establishing and maintaining the ring (initialization, station insertion in, or removal from, the original ring). Each participating station knows the addresses of its predecessor and its successor. After a station has completed transmitting data frames, it passes the token to its successor by sending a so-called "token" MAC-control frame.

After having sent the token, the station monitors the bus to make sure that its successor has received the token and is active. If the sender detects a valid frame following the token, it will assume that its successor has the token and is transmitting. If the sender does not sense a valid frame from its successor, it must assess the state of the network and, if necessary, take appropriate recovery actions to re-establish the logical ring.

The standards provide three transmission options, all on 75 Ω coaxial cable. A single-channel phase-continuous frequency-shift-keying scheme is defined at 1 Mbit/s. For multiple channels on the same cable, phase-coherent frequency-shift keying is defined with a variety of signaling options. These include 5 Mbits/s in 5 or 10 MHz channels or 10 Mbits/s in 10 or 20 MHz channels. Finally, the standard defines multilevel, duobinary, amplitude-modulation phase-shift keying at three data rates. These rates are 1 Mbit/s in a 1.5 MHz channel, 5 Mbits/s in a 6 MHz channel, and 10 Mbits/s in a 12 MHz channel. A standard for quadrature partial-response signaling allowing 20 Mbits/s transmission in a 12 MHz channel is in preparation.

B. Performance Characteristics of Medium-Access Protocols

Two performance aspects are of primary interest: the delay-throughput characteristic of the medium-access control schemes, and system behavior when the load approaches the saturation point. There exists a large body of performance analyses of bus and ring

systems; some examples are given in [23]–[25]. In the following, we use some of the
results reported in [20] and [22] to compare the performance of CSMA/CD buses and token
rings.

Figure 7(a)–(c) shows the delay-throughput relation of token ring and CSMA/CD bus for
two data rates: 1 Mbit/s and 10 Mbits/s. The general conclusions we can draw from these
results are:

1) at a data rate of 1 Mbit/s, both systems perform equally well;

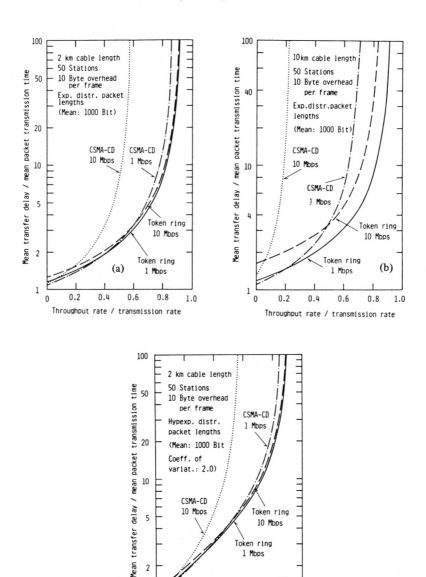

Fig. 7.   Delay-throughput characteristic for CSMA/CD bus and token ring.

2) when the data rate is increased to 10 Mbits/s, the token ring has better performance characteristics over a wide range of parameters.

In Fig. 7(a), the frame-length distribution is negative exponential with an average value of 1000 bits. A frame represents the entity transmitted by a station when it has access to the medium. The critical parameter that determines the performance of the CSMA/CD bus is the ratio of propagation delay to mean frame transmission time. Since the propagation delay is independent of the data rate, this ratio increases with the data rate. Theory shows [22] that a CSMA/CD bus behaves ideally as long as this ratio is sufficiently low. If, for reasonable traffic loads, it exceeds 2–5 percent, the increasing collision frequency will cause significant performance degradation.

The general validity of the conclusions drawn above is supported by Fig. 7(b) and (c). In Fig. 7(b), all parameters are the same as before except for the length of the cable, which is now 10 km instead of 2 km. The curve for the CSMA/CD bus at 10 Mbits/s illustrates the impact of the propagation delay, and confirms the importance of the ratio propagation delay and average frame transmission time. As a practical consequence, all CSMA/CD systems being discussed specify a maximum distance less than 10 km. Finally, Fig. 7(c) further demonstrates the robustness of the results. There, the frame-length distribution has a coefficient of variation of 2.

How the maximum throughput depends on the transmission speed is shown in Fig. 8(a) and (b) for the CSMA/CD bus and the token ring, respectively. Figure 8(a) shows, for different values of the mean information-field length, the maximum throughput. It can be seen that the efficiency of the CSMA/CD protocol decreases significantly with increasing speed and decreasing information-field lengths. Measurements performed on an Ethernet showed a mean frame length of 976 bits [26]. Figure 8(b) shows the maximum information throughput for the token ring. Several observations can be made.

1) The efficiency of the token protocol is much less sensitive to increased transmission rates and decreasing information-field lengths compared to CSMA/CD.

2) The single token operation, i.e., the standard medium-access protocol described in Section III-A-2, performs reasonably well even at 32 Mbits/s and for short frames (1000 bits).

3) Multiple-token operation, i.e., a mode when the free token is generated at the end of a transmission (see [11]) instead of when the frame header has returned to the sender, is very efficient at high data rates. These facts demonstrate that token access on rings is open to significantly higher transmission rates than the ones currently standardized and in use.

C. Other Medium-Access Control Schemes

In addition to the standard medium-access control schemes described in Section III-A, there exists a great number of other principles either employed in existing prototype systems and products, or proposed in the literature. In the following, we describe two of these methods.

1) Slotted Ring: In a slotted ring [27], [28], a constant number of fixed-length slots circulates continuously around the ring. A full/empty indicator within the slot header is used to signal the state of a slot. Any station ready to transmit occupies the first empty slot by setting the full/empty indicator to "full," and places its information in the slot. When the sender receives back the busy slot, it changes the full/empty indicator to "free." This prevents hogging of the ring, and guarantees fair sharing of the bandwidth among all stations.

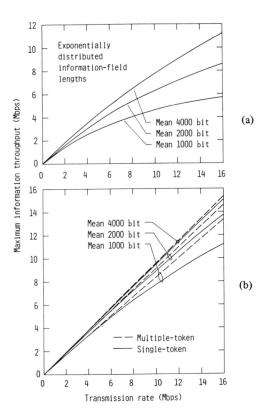

Fig. 8. Maximum information throughput versus transmission rate. (a) CSMA/CD. (b) Token ring.

2) Buffer Insertion Ring: In buffer insertion rings, the contention between the traffic to be transmitted by a station and the data stream already flowing on the ring is resolved by dynamically inserting sufficient buffer space into the ring at each ring adapter [29]–[31]. In contrast to the token ring where the sender is responsible for removal of the frame it transmitted, this function is performed by the receiver. With regard to the point in time when a station is allowed to transmit one of its pending messages, we can distinguish between two operational modes: station priority and ring priority [32].

IV. Engineering Considerations, Wiring, and Transmission

A large volume of literature exists on the medium-access control aspect of local area networks, particularly on performance. However, in choosing a particular system for implementation, considerations stemming from electrical engineering, wiring, transmission, reliability, availability, and serviceability play an equally important role [33], [34].

In Sections IV-A and IV-B, we shall discuss some of these issues for systems with baseband transmission, i.e., where data are transmitted as electrical pulses without prior modulation of a frequency carrier. In Section IV-C, broadband systems will be addressed, where the available frequency spectrum is subdivided into different frequency bands through frequency multiplexing techniques.

A. CSMA/CD Baseband Bus

The CSMA/CD bus protocol described in Section III-A-1 looks quite simple to the protocol designer. This simplicity, however, causes difficult problems for the transmission engineer. In particular, the following problems have to be solved in order to obtain reliable and efficient operation: tapping of the main cable, reliable collision detection, electrical separation of the transceiver, and fault location.

Several technical approaches are conceivable to solve the tap problem [12], e.g., pressure taps or T-connectors. From the tap, the signal is fed to the transceiver circuits. To avoid reflections on the coaxial cable, the stub between tap and transceiver must be short.

Since the main cable is most likely installed in cable ducts or in ceilings, the adapter is partitioned into the transceiver which is in close physical proximity to the main cable and the protocol handler which is located in the attaching station. Transceiver and station are connected via an interface cable which consists of multiple-twisted pairs for power, data, and controls (see Figs. 3(a) and 9).

To lower attachment costs, the so-called Cheapernets [35] place the transceiver inside the attaching station and, thus, have the station connected directly to the primary cable which in this case consists of a less expensive, thinner, and more flexible coaxial cable. The overall system performance is reduced in terms of both maximum cable length and number of stations to be interconnected.

For its reliable operation, the CSMA/CD protocol requires that a transceiver must be capable of detecting the weakest other transmitter during its own transmissions, and of distinguishing the signals from the other transmitter from the echoes of its own transmitter. Furthermore, for its efficient operation, collisions have to be detected at the earliest possible moment to abort transmission. Even the best collision-detection circuits developed thus far limit the attenuation allowable to a value significantly smaller than for a point-to-point transmission without collisions. Consequences are the need to use high-quality cable and a limitation of the distance which can be covered by a single segment between repeaters.

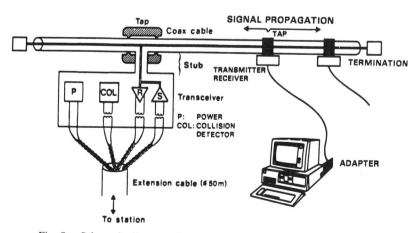

Fig. 9.   Schematic diagram of transceiver in baseband CSMA/CD system.

As shown in Fig. 9, the transceiver circuits are galvanically coupled with the coaxial cable. To avoid ground-loop problems, the entire transceiver must be carefully isolated from the attaching station. In Fig. 9, this is schematically indicated by the transformer symbols. In practice, other devices such as electrooptical couplers can be used. The galvanic coupling of the transceiver to the coaxial cable causes reliability exposures which require additional protective components. A short circuit in one transceiver, for example, would bring the network down. Circuits requiring multicomponent failures to short the cable have been proposed. An additional consequence of the galvanic coupling is that a segment can only be grounded at one point.

The number of stations which can be attached is limited by the residual reflections caused by the taps. To keep the noise from reflections low, the placement of taps must be controlled. A typical 10 Mbit/s system [13] allows segments with a length of 500 m and requires a minimum distance between taps of 2.5 m. Also, the number of transceivers per segment should be less than 100.

In addition to reliability aspects of the transceivers discussed above, it should be emphasized that the system is insensitive to power failures or to damage to the extension cable. However, if the main coaxial cable is mutilated or otherwise shorted, e.g., through a malfunctioning transceiver or a tap not properly installed, transmission on the afflicted segment will break down because of the reflections which occur at the point of failure. Time-domain reflectometry (TDR) has been proposed to locate such faults. In TDR, the time between sending of a pulse and arrival of its echo is correlated to the distance of the problem point on the cable. However, even with the addition of TDR circuits to each adapter, the problem of correlating linear distance measured on the cable with a location in a building is not solved in practice.

B. Token Ring

The monitor function discussed in Section III-A-2 ensures reliable token operation from a protocol point of view. To achieve reliability and stability at low cost, two engineering problems require special attention:

1) ring synchronization, and

2) the development of a wiring system which allows bypassing of inoperative or malfunctioning stations, and elimination of faulty cable segments from the ring.

A ring network consists of a closed sequence of individual point-to-point links. For its efficient operation, the token protocol requires minimal delay per station, and the ability to change a single bit, e.g., the token, "on-the-fly." To achieve minimum delay, the individual links are synchronized to a temporary master clock as discussed in [11] and [34]. In such a design, station delays of half-a-bit time can be achieved, except for the station providing the clock. In this station, an elastic buffer of a few bits is used to equalize the accumulated timing jitter. Other approaches to coordinate the clock are mentioned in [33] and [36]. Since the ring consists of point-to-point segments, mixing of different media (including optical fibers) in one system is easily achieved.

Engineering of optimized sender and receiver circuits for point-to-point links is well understood. Because reflections are controlled, high attenuations can be accepted, and hence long distances reached. One problem, however, required careful study: the design of the clock extraction circuits. The solution described in [34] uses a phase-locked loop (PLL) in each repeater which tracks the next active repeater upstream. The design of the PLL filter has to meet two criteria. First, to limit the accumulation of timing errors in the PLL

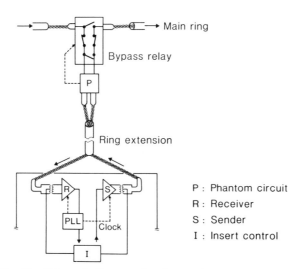

Fig. 10. Schematic diagram of station attachment to a token ring.

(called jitter) and, thus, allow interconnection of an adequate number of stations through a single ring; secondly, to provide fast resynchronization after station insertion or removal. Optimized PLL circuits which meet both requirements are available, and details can be found in [34] and [37]. Analysis and measurements show that up to 300–400 stations can be attached to a single ring, a number which is considered fully satisfactory for all practical purposes.

Attachment of a station to the ring is schematically shown in Fig. 10. Sender and receiver circuits, together with the protocol handler, can be packaged on the same card, located in, and powered from, the station. This is a significant advantage with respect to the LSI/VLSI integration and low-cost packaging. Direct current-free (DC-free) coupling of in- and outbound links and balanced transmission, e.g., via transformers, makes the system immune to ground-loop problems.

Physical reliability can be achieved by using distribution panels with bypass relays (Fig. 11) [10], [11]. A main-ring cable linking distribution panels is installed in conduits or ceilings. Wall outlets are connected to the distribution panels through extension wires or local lobes. If the relays, activated by phantom circuits, remain unpowered, the local lobe will not be inserted into the ring. Thus, power failure of the station or breakage of the extension wire will automatically remove the station from the active ring which will resume proper operation after a short resynchronization interval.

A failure of the main-ring cable, however, will bring the system down. Such a failure is detected by the next adapter downstream from the breakage. Since communication in the sequence of downstream links is unaffected, the adapter which detects the failure can locate the faulty link.

One can test a station before it is inserted through a wrap-around circuit (Fig. 10). In such a test, the station sender is connected to its receiver through the local lobe cable. Only if proper operation of both the adapter and the extension cable are diagnosed, will permission for relay activation and station insertion be granted. In its simplest form, the distribution panels are passive boxes which house the relays. If desired, prewiring of a building is possible, and rings can be configured later, as needed, at the distribution panels.

At the expense of adding a power supply and a microprocessor to the distribution box,

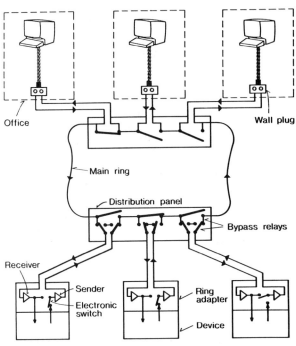

Fig. 11.   Ring with distribution panels.

further reliability of the main ring can be achieved through backup cables automatically activated to bypass a breakage.

C. Broadband Systems

Broadband systems use frequency division multiplexing (FDM) to divide the frequency spectrum of the cable into bands which can be used independently of one another, e.g., one band for CSMA/CD or token access, a band for voice, and other bands for video. Figure 12 schematically shows the principle.

The following two driving forces fostered the development of broadband LAN's:

1) the possibility to use standard CATV components such as 75 Ω coaxial cable, connectors, splitters, and amplifiers, and

2) the potential to support multiple channels on a single cable. Physically, broadband systems can be implemented either as single-cable systems or as dual-cable systems [38]–[40] [see Fig. 13(a) and (b)].

In the single-cable case, the two directions of transmission are realized by defining a backward channel or inbound path used by all attached stations to transmit, and a forward channel or outbound path on which all stations receive. These split systems are categorized by the frequency allocation to the two paths. Most widely used in LAN's is the midsplit, which provides an inbound range of 5–116 MHz and an outbound range of 168–300 MHz on a 350 MHz cable. Translation of the frequency of the return channel into the frequency of the forward channel is performed at the headend. In a dual-cable configuration, the inbound and outbound paths are on separate cables joined at the midpoint by a passive connector. In this case, frequency translation in a headend is not required since stations send and receive on the same frequency.

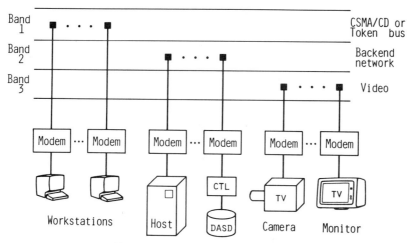

Fig. 12.   Principle of broadband system.

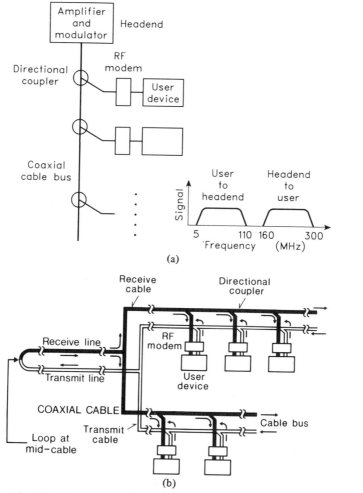

Fig. 13.   Broadband systems. (a) Single-cable system. (b) Dual-cable system.

Regarding the modems in use, we can differentiate between fixed-frequency and agile-frequency modems. The first type is used either for point-to-point connections in a certain frequency band or for multiple-access applications, e.g., CSMA/CD or token passing, in a band. The latter type allows provision of switched services, and requires adjustment of the modem frequency to a value allocated by a controller to two communicating devices.

For the access to shared bands, both CSMA/CD and token passing are employed. Carrier sensing and collision detection are performed differently in baseband and broadband systems. With the use of Manchester phase encoding, the carrier is conveniently indicated in a baseband system by the presence of transitions on the channel, whereas in the broadband case the RF carrier is detected. A collision in a baseband system is detected through the presence of higher DC levels than those produced by a single transmitter. The most common approach to collision detection in broadband systems is to perform a bit-by-bit comparison between transmitted and received data. When a station transmits on the inbound channel, it starts—after some propagation delay—to receive its own transmission on the outbound channel. The problem is the danger that differences in signal level between colliding signals will cause the receiver to treat the weaker signal as noise, and fail to detect the collision. Therefore, to avoid this problem, the cable system with its taps, splitters, and amplifiers must be carefully tuned and re-tuned after configuration changes.

V. New Concepts, Fiber Optics

Local area networks operating at 1–10 Mbits/s are being commercially offered and appear to adequately meet current demands for both the office and the manufacturing application environments discussed in Section II. However, future needs such as high-capacity backbone networks, multimedia communication supporting data, voice, facsimile, image and video traffic in a single digital system, the provision of backend networks, and the application of LAN technology to metropolitan area networks stimulate research, development, and standardization activities in LAN's of significantly higher speeds, e.g., 100 Mbits/s or more. Apart from modified or new medium-access control protocols tailored to cope with the higher data rates, these developments frequently also aim at making use of optical-fiber media.

In Section V-A, we shall outline the basic ideas of unidirectional broadcast bus systems. They have to be seen as an attempt to overcome the limitations of CSMA/CD systems by employing unidirectional transmission and avoiding collisions. Therefore, they are open to higher speeds, a variety of transmission media including optical fibers, and, by virtue of their capacity, to handling multimedia traffic. Section V-B deals with the most prominent effort to extend the token-ring technology into a speed range an order of magnitude higher compared to the IEEE 802 LAN's. Finally, Section V-C contains some general considerations on the use of fiber optics in LAN's and some examples of system approaches.

A. Unidirectional Broadcast Bus Systems

The performance limitations of CSMA/CD-type contention systems [see Section III-B, Fig. 8(a)], and the fact that these systems do not easily scale up to significantly higher speeds, led to new approaches, the so-called unidirectional broadcast bus systems. Two prominent examples, Expressnet and Fasnet are described in [41] and [42]; the outline provided below follows [43]. Similar to two-cable broadband systems, unidirectional broadcast bus systems comprise two channels.

Broadcast communications is achieved in two ways. The first approach is to fold a unidirectional cable onto itself so as to create two channels, an outbound channel onto which the users transmit packets and an inbound channel from which users receive packets; all signals transmitted on the outbound channel propagate on the inbound channel, as shown in Fig. 14(a). This is referred to as the folded bus structure. Another way to achieve broadcast communications is to provide two unidirectional buses with signals propagating in opposite directions as shown in Fig. 14(b). This is referred to as the dual bus structure. Given a unidirectional bus to which stations are connected, an implicit ordering exists among the stations of which the access control schemes under consideration make use. These schemes also require that on every unidirectional bus segment, each station is to be given the ability to sense activity owing to stations on the upstream side of its transmit tap. In the dual bus structure, the receive taps provide this function while in the folded bus structure, as shown in Fig. 14(a), additional sense taps are needed.

The basic operation of the access protocol for Expressnet works as follows.

1) A station ready to transmit waits for the next end of the carrier on the outbound channel.

2) This station immediately begins to transmit the packet, and at the same time, senses the outbound channel for activity from the upstream side.

3) When activity is detected from upstream, the transmission is aborted otherwise completed. If the transmission had to be aborted, go back to 1), otherwise wait for the next packet arrival.

The whole operation is cyclic, and each station has the opportunity to transmit once in a cycle.

In Fasnet, a station ready to transmit a packet will first sense the line by means of the nondirectional read tap to determine when to transmit, and then write signals using the

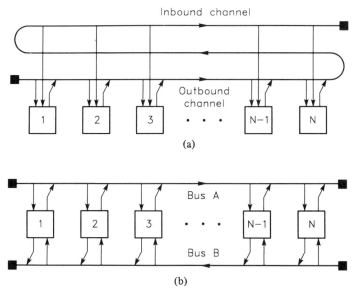

Fig. 14.   Unidirectional broadcast bus systems. (a) Folded bus structure, Expressnet. (b) Dual bus structure, Fasnet.

directional write connection. The receiving stations read the signals by means of the nondirectional tap. Access to the link is controlled by the first and last stations on the link. By means of timing provided by these end stations, a station is able to read any bit or group of bits from a passing slot of fixed length. A station ready to transmit inspects a busy bit associated with each slot to see whether the slot has already been used. If the slot is free, the station will set the busy bit and write a packet into the slot. If the slot has already been used, a station must wait for the next free slot to arrive.

B. Ring Systems

The American National Standards Institute (ANSI) is working towards a new standard known as Fiber Distributed Data Interface (FDDI) [36]. It is a 100 Mbit/s token ring using fiber-optic cable. Originally, FDDI was conceived as a backend network (see Section II-C-3) to provide high-speed packet communications among processors and fast storage devices. More recently, FDDI is also viewed as a high-performance backbone LAN to interconnect lower speed LAN's such as IEEE Standards 802.3, 802.4, or 802.5. In addition, work within ANSI on FDDI-II is addressing the requirements for synchronous services such as real-time voice.

The medium-access control protocol used in FDDI is largely based on the token-ring standard, IEEE 802.5. Some of the major differences follow.

1) To achieve efficient utilization of the 100 Mbit/s bandwidth, a multiple-token operation has been defined as opposed to the single-token operation in the IEEE standard, see also Fig. 8(b). This means that a station issues a free token immediately after it has terminated transmitting.

2) FDDI uses timer-based priorities instead of the IEEE scheme where reservation events cause the ring to operate at different priority levels.

Similar to the token bus standard, FDDI uses a timed token rotation protocol to control access to the medium. Under this protocol, each station measures the time that has elapsed since a free token was last received. The initialization procedures establish the target token rotation time as that of the lowest bidding station. Two classes of service are defined: synchronous and asynchronous. Synchronous operation allows seizing of a token whenever synchronous frames are queued for transmission. The asynchronous class gets serviced only when the time elapsed since the last token was received has not exceeded the established target token rotation time. If required, multiple priority levels can be provided within this class by specifying additional time thresholds for token rotation.

An FDDI ring may consist of two independent, counterrotating rings, called the primary and secondary rings in Fig. 15. Two node types have been defined to allow users to tailor the network to a broad spectrum of needs and to meet cost objectives. Class-A nodes may connect to both the primary and secondary rings simultaneously, and represent stations or wiring concentrators. The payoff for the additional hardware required is a higher level of fault tolerance because stations can continue to operate on the healthy ring should one of them fail. Class-B stations, on the other hand, can only be connected to the primary ring via a wiring concentrator. The rationale for having a wiring concentrator is the same as discussed in Section IV-B.

The major differences in the transmission system between FDDI and the IEEE Standard 802.5 are the use of a block code (4/5) instead of Manchester encoding, and the independent clocking of individual ring segments with elastic buffers to compensate for frequency offsets as opposed to synchronizing individual links to a master clock.

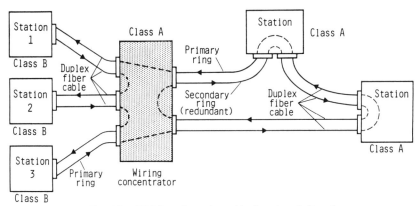

Fig. 15.   FDDI configuration with class-A and -B nodes.

C. Fiber-Optic LAN's

In this subsection we shall briefly review some of the activities using optical-fiber media in LAN's. The fact that the FDDI ring will employ optical-fiber links was mentioned in the previous section. Also, even though not specified to exclusively make use of optical fibers, it is stated explicitly that unidirectional broadcast bus systems such as Expressnet or Fasnet [41], [42] could support fiber links. A recent publication [43] reports on first attempts to use optical transmission media for Expressnet.

The well-known characteristics of fiber links which make them attractive for use in LAN's are subsequently summarized as follows.

- Large bandwidth distance product, i.e., the capability to allow very high data rates over distances required in real systems.
- Immunity to electromagnetic interference. This makes optical fibers very desirable in harsh environments such as production plants.
- Small physical dimensions, a fact which facilitates installation.

Despite these very desirable features, there are still unresolved problems and debates pertaining to the optical components to be used which have prevented a pervasive use of optical fibers in LAN's. Issues such as optical tap losses (bus systems) or losses in optical bypass relays (ring systems) still deserve much attention and innovation and at least partially account for the tight attenuation budgets. In addition, there are the debates regarding the use of LED's or laser diodes in optical sources and, respectively, p-i-n diodes, or avalanche photodiodes (APD) in receivers. Furthermore, users seem to be uncertain as to what size fiber will be used predominantly in the future, and seem to be somewhat reluctant to invest in fiber-optic cabling systems right now.

In the remaining part of this section, we shall summarize the features of some commercial systems and the effort of the IEEE 802.3 Committee to standardize a fiber link.

Several examples of token-ring networks operating at 32 Mbits/s exist [44], [45]. The C&C-Net loop 6770 [44] built by NEC, for example, represents a system with fault-tolerance mechanisms for ring interface bypassing in case of a ring interface failure and alternate path selection if a fiber is broken. The ring consists of two optical-fiber loops transmitting in opposite directions. Under normal circumstances, one loop is idle and on standby, whereas the other is active. Since the ring interfaces are active, bypassing is achieved by electronic, as opposed to optomechanical, switching.

There exists a variety of efforts to introduce optical fiber into CSMA/CD systems. The basic problem is that the optical equivalent of the high-impedance electrical tap does not yet exist. There are two ways to approach the problem: the use of active or passive stars.

Fibernet II [46], for example, uses an active star repeater to create the equivalent of the IEEE 802.3 coaxial-shared medium channel. Collision detection is performed on a backplane of the star repeater which behaves like a short IEEE 802.3 bus and which is electrically compatible with the 10 Mbit/s standard. Another approach is to use passive star couplers, and has been reported in [47]. Other than in Fibernet II, the collision detection mechanism is distributed and implemented in the attaching stations.

To conclude the discussion on attempts to introduce fiber optics into CSMA/CD LAN's, it should be mentioned that the IEEE 802.3 Committee is close to completing a standard for a fiber-optic inter-repeater link [48]. It represents a point-to-point optical link which enables the interconnection of CSMA/CD coaxial-cable segments separated by distances of up to 1 km.

VI. SUMMARY

Local area networks are a new technology expected to play an important role. The field has reached a certain level of maturity, and a large number of vendors offers LAN's and LAN components. All technologies discussed in this chapter have their adherents and are being used in practice. However, it is fair to say that the market explosion predicted by some analysts has not yet occurred.

Scientific and engineering analysis reveals significant technical differences among the various system approaches. The delay-throughput characteristic of the medium-access control schemes and system behavior under high traffic loads represent one important aspect for existing systems and with respect to their potential of being scaled up to higher data rates. Other relevant differences are to be found in wiring schemes, transmission media, transmission problems which had to be solved, and of providing maintenance and reconfiguration facilities.

Today, there is scant information on how different local area network products perform on user premises. It will be such experience rather than scientific and engineering analysis which will eventually resolve the continuation for the one or few predominant local area network technologies.

ACKNOWLEDGMENT

The authors gratefully acknowledge the help of W. Bux in providing performance results, and of H. R. Müller for reviewing part of the manuscript.

REFERENCES

[1] L. G. Roberts and B. D. Wessler, "Computer network development to achieve resource sharing," in *Proc. SJCC,* 1970, pp. 543–549.
[2] N. Abramson, "The ALOHA system—Another alternative for computer communications," in *Proc. 1977 Fall Joint Comp. Conf.,* Arlington, VA, 1977, pp. 117–128.
[3] L. Kleinrock and S. S. Lam, "Packet-switching in a multiaccess broadcast channel: Performance evaluation," *IEEE Trans. Commun.,* vol. COM-23, pp. 410–423, Apr. 1975.

[4] R. M. Metcalfe and D. R. Boggs, "Ethernet: Distributed packet switching for local computer networks," *Commun. Ass. Comput. Mach.*, vol. 19, pp. 395–404, 1976.

[5] J. E. Israel, J. G. Mitchel, and H. Sturgis, "Separating data from function in a distributed file system," in *Proc. Workshop on Operating Systems*, Paris, France, 1978, pp. 17–22.

[6] D. D. Clark, K. T. Pogran, and D. P. Reed, "An introduction to local-area networks," *Proc. IEEE*, vol. 66, pp. 1497–1517, 1978.

[7] K. Kümmerle and M. Reiser, "Local-area communication networks—An overview," *J. Telecommun. Networks*, vol. 1, pp. 349–370, 1982.

[8] M. V. Wilkes and D. J. Wheeler, "The Cambridge digital communication ring," in *Proc. Symp. Local Area Commun. Networks*, Boston, MA, 1979, pp. 47–61.

[9] W. W. Chu and A. G. Konheim, "On the analysis and modeling of a class of computer communication systems," *IEEE Trans. Commun.*, vol. COM-20, pp. 645–660, June 1972.

[10] J. H. Saltzer and K. Pogran, "A star-shaped ring network with high maintainability," in *Proc. Local Area Commun. Network Symp.*, Mitre Corp., 1979, pp. 179–190.

[11] W. Bux, F. Closs, K. Kümmerle, H. Keller, and H. R. Müller, "Architecture and design of a reliable token-ring network," *IEEE J. Select. Areas Commun.*, vol. SAC-1, pp. 756–765, Nov. 1983; see also this volume, ch. 5.

[12] J. F. Shoch, Y. K. Dalal, D. D. Redell, and R. C. Crane, "Evolution of the Ethernet local computer network," *Tutorial Local Network Technology*, W. Stalling, Ed. IEEE Computer Society, pp. 49–66.

[13] "IEEE standards for local area networks: Carrier sense multiple access with collision detection (CSMA/CD) access method and physical layer specifications," ANSI/IEEE Standard 802.3-1985 (ISO DIS 8802/3, ECMA 80-82, 1982), 1985.

[14] "IEEE standards for local area networks: Token-passing bus access method and physical layer specifications," ANSI/IEEE Standard 802.4-1985 (ISO DIS 8802/4, ECMA 90, 1983), 1985.

[15] "IEEE standards for local area networks: Token ring access method and physical layer specifications," ANSI/IEEE Standard 802.5-1985 (ISO DP 8802/5, ECMA 89, 1983), 1985.

[16] R. C. Dixon, N. C. Strole, and J. D. Markov, "A token-ring network for local data communications," *IBM Syst. J.*, vol. 22, pp. 47–62, 1983.

[17] "Information processing systems, open systems interconnection, basic reference model," ISO 7498-1984, 1984.

[18] R. S. Crowder, "MAP, PROWAY, and IEEE 802: A marriage of standards for automation," in *Proc. IEEE Infocom '86*, Miami, FL, Apr. 1986, pp. 337–342.

[19] M. A. Dineson and J. J. Picazo, "Broadband technology magnifies local networking capability," *Datacommun.*, pp. 61–79, Feb. 1980.

[20] W. Bux, "Performance issues in local-area networks," *IBM Syst. J.*, vol. 23, no. 4, pp. 351–374, 1984.

[21] Digital, Intel, and Xerox, "The Ethernet—A local area network data link layer and physical layer specifications," 1980.

[22] W. Bux, "Local-area subnetworks: A performance comparison," *IEEE Trans. Commun.*, vol. COM-29, pp. 1465–1473, 1981; see also this volume, ch. 22.

[23] A. G. Konheim and B. Meister, "Waiting lines and times in a system with polling," *J. Ass. Comput. Mach.*, vol. 21, pp. 470–490, 1974.

[24] S. S. Lam, "A carrier sense multiple access protocol for local networks," *Comput. Networks*, vol. 4, pp. 21–32, 1980.

[25] F. A. Tobagi and V. B. Hunt, "Performance analysis of carrier sense multiple access with collision detection," Comput. Syst. Lab., Stanford Univ., Stanford, CA, Tech. Rep. 173, 1979; see also this volume, ch. 20.

[26] J. F. Shoch and J. A. Hupp, "Measured performance of an Ethernet local network," *Commun. Ass. Comput. Mach.*, vol. 23, pp. 711–721, 1980.

[27] B. K. Penney and A. A. Baghdadi, "Survey of computer communication loop networks, Parts 1 and 2," *Comput. Commun.*, vol. 2, pp. 165–180 and pp. 224–241, 1979.

[28] A. Hopper, "Data ring at Computer Laboratory, University of Cambridge, Computer Science and Technology: Local area networking," Washington, DC, National Bureau of Standards, NBS Special Publication 500-31, pp. 11–16, 1977.

[29] "Local communication controller description," IBM Publication GA 34-0142, 1981.

[30] C. C. Kearnes and M. T. Liu, "A loop network for simultaneous transmission of variable length messages," in *Proc. 2nd Annual Symp. on Comput. Architecture*, Houston, TX, 1975, pp. 7–12.

[31] E. R. Hafner, Z. Nenandal, and M. Tschanz, "A digital loop communications system," *IEEE Trans. Commun.*, vol. COM-22, pp. 877–881, 1974.

[32] W. Bux and M. Schlatter, "An approximate method for the performance analysis of buffer insertion rings," *IEEE Trans. Commun.*, vol. COM-31, no. 1, pp. 50–55, 1983.

[33] J. H. Saltzer and D. D. Clark, "Why a ring?," in *Proc. 7th Data Commun. Symp.*, Mexico City, Mexico, 1981, pp. 211–217.

[34] H. R. Müller, H. Keller, and H. Meyr, "Transmission in a synchronous token ring," in *Proc. Int. Conf.*

Local Computer Networks, Florence, Italy, Apr. 1982, pp. 125–147.

[35] A. V. Flatman, "Low-cost local network for small systems grows," IEEE 802.3 Standard Electronic Design, pp. 185–188, July 1984.

[36] F. E. Ross, "FDDI-fiber, farther, faster," in *Proc. IEEE Infocom '86,* Miami, FL, Apr. 1986, pp. 323–330.

[37] H. Keller, H. Meyr, H. R. Müller, and L. Popken, "Synchronization failures in a chain of repeaters," in *Proc. Globecom 82,* Miami, FL, vol. 2, 1982, pp. 859–869.

[38] E. Cooper and P. Edholm, "Design issues in broadband local networks," *Data Commun.,* vol. 12, pp. 109–122, Feb. 1983.

[39] G. T. Hopkins and N. B. Meisner, "Choosing between broadband and baseband local networks," *Mini-Micro Syst.,* vol. 16, June 1983; see also this volume, ch. 4.

[40] M. Stahlmann, "Inside Wang's local net architecture," *Data Commun.,* vol. 11, pp. 85–90, Jan. 1982.

[41] F. A. Tobagi, F. Borgonovo, and L. Tralta, "Expressnet: A high-performance integrated-services local area network," *IEEE J. Select. Areas Commun.,* vol. SAC-1, pp. 898–913, Nov. 1983.

[42] J. O. Limb and C. Flores, "Description of Fasnet—A unidirectional local-area communications network," *Bell Syst. Tech. J.,* vol. 61, pp. 1413–1440, Sept. 1982; see also this volume, ch. 12.

[43] M. E. Markic and F. A. Tobagi, "Experimentation with a fiber-optic implementation of Expressnet," in *Proc. EFOC/LAN 86,* Amsterdam, The Netherlands, June 1986, pp. 244–254.

[44] M. Kigono, M. Tada, K. Yasue, K. Takumi, and Y. Narita, "C&C netloop 6670—A reliable communication medium for distributed processing systems," in *Proc. LAN' 82,* Sept. 1982, pp. 47–50.

[45] H. Watanabe, "An overview of Hitachi's fiber optic transmission technology and products," *Hitachi Rev.,* vol. 31, no. 3, pp. 107–108, 1982.

[46] E. G. Rawson and R. V. Schmidt, "Fibernet II: An Ethernet compatible fiber-optic local area network," in *Proc. LAN '82,* Sept. 1982, pp. 15–17.

[47] J. R. Jones, J. S. Kennedy, and F. W. Scholl, "A prototype CSMA/CD local network using fiber optics," in *Proc. LAN '82,* Sept. 1982, pp. 86–90.

[48] S. Moustakas, "IEEE 802.3 draft standard for the fibre optic interrepeater link: A technical description and its application in fiber optic CSMA/CD active star LANs" in *Proc. EFOC/LAN 86,* Amsterdam, The Netherlands, June 1986, pp. 136–139.

Part II
Evolution of Local Area Networks

Local area communications networks can be viewed as an extension to data networks for making high-speed packet-switching services available within a building complex or plant. Among the major driving forces are the availability of data rates in the range of 1–10 Mbits/s at low cost, the fact that VLSI technology permits the implementation of network adapters with the necessary network access control functions at reasonably low cost, the need for a consolidated wiring system, and the explosive growth of personal computers and intelligent workstations which require efficient ways for peer-to-peer communication and for accessing shared resources.

The introductory paper in Part I provides the background on LAN's and contains an outline of the major technologies, application scenarios, and trends. Part II builds on the introduction and contains selected examples of a broad class of LAN's without aiming at completeness.

Among the various technical considerations for the design of a LAN, the issue of open systems, i.e., systems with standardized medium access control protocols and interfaces is considered to be very important both from the user and the vendor points of view. Therefore, it can be stated that the local area networks which are most widely used are the ones for which the Institute of Electrical and Electronics Engineers (IEEE), the European Computer Manufacturers Association (ECMA), and various other national bodies have developed standards. LAN standards apply to the data link and physical layers of the OSI reference model and comprise the carrier sensing multiple access with collision detection bus, the token bus, and the token ring.

In addition to the standard systems there exists a great number of other principles either employed in existing prototype systems and proprietary products, or proposed in the literature. It should be noted that not all systems employ shared transmission media with distributed access control but that there are systems available which favor a centralized packet switching approach.

Local area networks operating at 1–10 Mbits/s are being commercially offered and appear to adequately meet current demands. However, future needs such as high-capacity backbone networks, multimedia communication supporting data, voice, facsimile, image and video traffic in a single digital system, the provision of backend networks, and the application of LAN technology to metropolitan area networks stimulate research, development, and standardization activities in LAN's of significantly higher speeds, e.g., 100 Mbits/s or more. In addition to using modified or new medium-access control protocols tailored to cope with the higher data rates, these developments frequently also aim at making use of optical-fiber media.

2
Ethernet

JOHN F. SHOCH, YOGEN K. DALAL, DAVID D. REDELL, AND
RONALD C. CRANE

I. INTRODUCTION

One of the most successful designs for a local area network is the Ethernet [1]–[4]. In general terms, Ethernet is a multiaccess, packet-switched communications system for carrying digital data among locally distributed computing systems. The shared communications channel in an Ethernet is a passive broadcast medium with no central control; packet address recognition in each station is used to take packets from the channel. Access to the channel by stations wishing to transmit is coordinated in a distributed fashion by the stations themselves, using a statistical arbitration scheme.

The Ethernet strategy can be used on many different broadcast media, but our major focus has been on the use of coaxial cable as the shared transmission medium. The Experimental Ethernet system was developed at the Xerox Palo Alto Research Center starting in 1972. Since then, numerous other organizations have developed and built ''Ethernet-like'' local area networks [5]. In 1980 a cooperative effort involving Digital Equipment Corporation, Intel, and Xerox produced an updated version of the Ethernet design, generally known as the Ethernet Specification [6]. This lead to the IEEE Standards 802.2 and 802.3 [7], [8].

One of the primary goals of the Ethernet Specification is compatibility—providing enough information for different manufacturers to build widely differing machines in such a way that they can directly communicate with one another.

Meeting the Ethernet Specification is only one of the necessary conditions for intermachine communication. There are many levels of protocol, such as transport, name binding, and file transfer, that must also be agreed upon and implemented in order to provide useful services [9]–[11]. This is analogous to the telephone system: the common low-level specifications for telephony make it possible to dial from the U.S. to France, but this is not of much use if the caller speaks only English while the person who answers the phone speaks only French. Specification of these additional protocols is an important area for further work.

The design of any local area network must be considered in the context of a distributed system architecture. Although the Ethernet Specification does not directly address issues of high-level network architecture, we view the local network as one component in an *internetwork* system, providing communication services to many diverse devices connected to different networks [9], [12], [13]. The services provided by the Ethernet are influenced by these broader architectural considerations.

As we highlight important design considerations and trace the evolution of the Ethernet from research prototype to industry standard, we use the term Experimental Ethernet for the former and Ethernet or Ethernet Specification for the latter. The term Ethernet is also used to describe design principles common to both systems.

II. GENERAL DESCRIPTION OF ETHERNET-CLASS SYSTEMS

A. Theory of Operation

The general Ethernet approach uses a shared communications channel managed with a distributed control policy known as *carrier sense multiple access with collision detection,* or CSMA/CD. With this approach, there is no central controller managing access to the channel, and there is no preallocation of time slots or frequency bands. A station wishing to transmit is said to "contend" for use of the common shared communications channel (sometimes called the Ether) until it "acquires" the channel; once the channel is acquired the station uses it to transmit a packet.

To acquire the channel, stations check whether the network is busy (that is, use *carrier sense*) and defer transmission of their packet until the Ether is quiet (no other transmissions occurring). When quiet is detected, the deferring station immediately begins to transmit. During transmission, the transmitting station listens for a collision (other transmitters attempting to use the channel simultaneously). In a correctly functioning system, collisions occur only within a short time interval following the start of transmission, since after this interval all stations will detect carrier and defer transmission. This time interval is called the *collision window* or the *collision interval* and is a function of the end-to-end propagation delay. If no collisions occur during this time, a transmitter has acquired the Ether and continues transmission of the packet. If a station detects collision, the transmission of the rest of the packet is immediately aborted. To ensure that all parties to the collision have properly detected it, any station that detects a collision invokes a *collision consensus enforcement procedure* that briefly jams the channel. Each transmitter involved in the collision then schedules its packet for retransmission at some later time.

To minimize repeated collisions, each station involved in a collision tries to retransmit at a different time by scheduling the retransmission to take place after a random delay period. In order to achieve channel stability under overload conditions, a controlled retransmission strategy is used whereby the mean of the random retransmission delay is increased as a function of the channel load. An estimate of the channel load can be derived by monitoring the number of collisions experienced by any one packet. This has been shown to be the optimal strategy among the options available for decentralized decision and control problems of this class [14].

Stations accept packets addressed to them and discard any that are found to be in error. Deference reduces the probability of collision, and collision detection allows the timely retransmission of a packet. It is impossible, however, to guarantee that all packets transmitted will be delivered successfully. For example, if a receiver is not enabled, an error-free packet addressed to it will not be delivered; higher levels of protocol must detect these situations and retransmit.

Under very high load, short periods of time on the channel may be lost due to collisions, but the collision resolution procedure operates quickly [1], [15]–[17]. Channel utilization under these conditions will remain high, particularly if packets are large with respect to the collision interval. One of the fundamental parameters of any Ethernet implementation is the length of this collision interval, which is based on the roundtrip propagation time between the farthest two points in the system.

B. Basic Components

The CSMA/CD access procedure can use any broadcast multiaccess channel, including radio, twisted pair, coaxial cable, diffuse infrared, and fiber optics [18]. Figure 1 illustrates a typical Ethernet system using coaxial cable. There are four components.

Station: A station makes use of the communication system and is the basic addressable device connected to an Ethernet; in general, it is a computer. We do not expect that ''simple'' terminals will be connected directly to an Ethernet. Terminals can be connected to some form of terminal controller, however, which provides access to the network. In the future, as the level of sophistication in terminals increases, many terminals will support direct connection to the network. Furthermore, specialized I/O devices, such as magnetic tapes or disk drives, may incorporate sufficient computing resources to function as stations on the network.

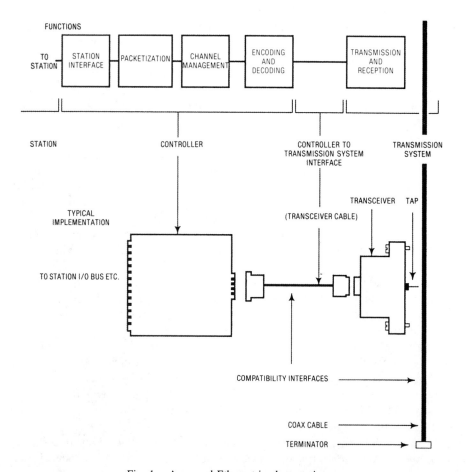

Fig. 1.   A general Ethernet implementation.

Within the station there is some interface between the operating system environment and the Ethernet controller. The nature of this interface (often in software) depends upon the particular implementation of the controller functions in the station.

Controller: A controller for a station is really the set of functions and algorithms needed to manage access to the channel. These include signaling conventions, encoding and decoding, serial-to-parallel conversion, address recognition, error detection, buffering, the basic CSMA/CD channel management, and packetization. These functions can be grouped into two logically independent sections of each controller: the transmitter and the receiver.

The controller functions are generally implemented using a combination of hardware, microcode, and software, depending on the nature of the station. It would be possible, for example, for a very capable station to have a minimal hardware connection to the transmission system and perform most of these functions in software. Alternatively, a station might implement all the controller functions in hardware. Most controller implementations fall somewhere in between. Several semiconductor manufacturers already have Ethernet chip sets. As many of the functions as possible should be moved into the chip set, provided that this preserves all of the flexibility needed in the construction and use of system interfaces and higher level software.

Our description of the controller is functional in nature and indicates how the controller must behave independent of particular implementations. There is some flexibility in implementing a correct controller, and we will make several recommendations concerning efficient operation of the system.

Transmission System: The transmission system includes all the components used to establish a communications path among the controllers. In general, this includes a suitable broadcast transmission medium, the appropriate transmitting and receiving devices—transceivers—and, optionally, repeaters to extend the range of the medium. The protocol for managing access to the transmission system is implemented in the controller; the transmission system does not attempt to interpret any of the bits transmitted on the channel.

The broadcast transmission medium contains those components that provide a physical communication path. In the case of coaxial cable, this includes the cable plus any essential hardware—connectors, terminators, and taps.

Transceivers contain the necessary electronics to transmit and receive signals on the channel and recognize the presence of a signal when another station transmits. They also recognize a collision that takes place when two or more stations transmit simultaneously.

Repeaters are used to extend the length of the transmission system beyond the physical limits imposed by the transmission medium. A repeater uses two transceivers to connect to two different Ethernet segments and combines them into one logical channel, amplifying and regenerating signals as they pass through in either direction [19]. Repeaters are transparent to the rest of the system, and stations on different segments can still collide. Thus, the repeater must propagate a collision detected on one segment through to the other segment, and it must do so without becoming unstable. A repeater makes an Ethernet channel longer and as a result increases the maximum propagation delay of the system (delay through the repeater and propagation delay through the additional segments). To avoid multipath interference in an Ethernet installation, there must be only one path between any two stations through the network. (The higher level internetwork architecture can support alternate paths between stations through different communications channels.)

Controller-to-Transmission-System Interface: One of the major interfaces in an Ethernet system is the point at which the controller in a station connects to the transmission system. The controller does much of the work in managing the communications process, so this is a fairly simple interface. It includes paths for data going to and from the transmission system. The data received can be used by the controller to sense carrier, but the transmission system normally includes a medium-specific mechanism for detecting collisions on the channel; this must also be communicated through the interface to the controller. It is possible to power a transceiver from a separate power source, but power is usually taken from the controller interface. In most transmission systems, the connection from the controller is made to a transceiver, and this interface is called the transceiver cable interface.

C. Two Generations of Ethernet Designs

The Experimental Ethernet confirmed the feasibility of the design, and the dozens of installations that have been in regular use since then have been the subject of extensive performance measurements confirming the predicted behavior [16], [17].

Based upon that experience, a second-generation system was designed at Xerox in the late 1970's. That effort subsequently led to the joint development of the Ethernet Specification and the IEEE Standards 802.2 and 802.3.

The two systems are very similar: they both use coaxial cable, Manchester signal encoding, and CSMA/CD with dynamic control. Some changes were made based on experience with the experimental system or in an effort to enhance the characteristics of the network. Some of the differences between the systems are summarized in Table I.

III. TRANSMISSION SYSTEM DESIGN

A number of design issues and tradeoffs emerged in the development of the Ethernet transmission system, and several lessons were learned from that experience.

A. Coaxial Cable Subsystem

In addition to having favorable signaling characteristics and the ability to handle multimegabit transmission rates, a single coaxial cable can support communication among many different stations. The mechanical aspects of coaxial cable make it feasible to tap in at any point without severing the cable or producing excessive RF leakage; such considerations relating to installation, maintenance, and reconfigurability are important aspects in any local network design.

There are reflections and attenuation in a cable, however, and these combine to impose some limits on the system design. Engineering the shared channel entails tradeoffs involving the data rate on the cable, the length of the cable, electrical characteristics of the transceiver, and the number of stations. For example, it is possible to operate at very high data rates over short distances, but the rate must be reduced to support a greater maximum length. Also, if each transceiver introduces significant reflections, it may be necessary to limit the placement and possibly the number of transceivers.

The characteristics of the coaxial cable fix the maximum data rate, but the actual clock is generated in the controller. Thus, the station interface and controller must be designed to match the data rates used over the cable. Selection of coaxial cable as the transmission medium has no other direct impact on either the station or the controller.

Cable: The Experimental Ethernet used 75-Ω, RG-11-type foam cable. The Ethernet

TABLE I
COMPARISON OF ETHERNET SYSTEMS

	Experimental Ethernet	Ethernet Specification
Data rate	2.94 Mbits/s	10 Mbits/s
Maximum end-to-end length	1 km	2.5 km
Maximum segment length	1 km	500 m
Encoding	Manchester	Manchester
Coax cable impedance	75 Ω	50 Ω
Coax cable signal levels	0 to +3 V	0 to −2 V
Transceiver cable connectors	25- and 15-p-i-n D series	15-p-i-n D series
Length of preamble	1 bit	64 bits
Length of CRC	16 bits	32 bits
Length of address fields	8 bits	48 bits

Specification uses a 50-Ω, solid-center-conductor, double-shield, foam dielectric cable in order to provide some reduction in the magnitude of reflections from insertion capacitance (introduced by tapping into the cable) and to provide better immunity against environmental electromagnetic noise. Belden Number 9880 Ethernet Coax meets the Ethernet Specification.

Terminators and Connectors: A small terminator is attached to the cable at each end to provide a termination impedance for the cable equal to its characteristic impedance, thereby eliminating reflection from the ends of the cable. For convenience, the cable can be divided into a number of sections using simple connectors between sections to produce one electrically continuous segment.

Segment Length and the Use of Repeaters: The Experimental Ethernet was designed to accommodate a maximum end-to-end length of 1 km, implemented as a single electrically continuous segment. Active repeaters could be used with that system to create complex topologies that would cover a wider area in a building (or complex of buildings) within the end-to-end length limit. With the use of those repeaters, however, the maximum end-to-end length between any two stations was still meant to be approximately 1 km. Thus, the segment length and the maximum end-to-end length were the same, and repeaters were used to provide additional flexibility.

In developing the Ethernet Specification, the strong desire to support a 10 Mbit/s data rate—with reasonable transceiver cost—led to a maximum segment length of 500 m. We expect that this length will be sufficient to support many installations and applications with a single Ethernet segment. In some cases, however, we recognized a requirement for greater maximum end-to-end length in one network. In these cases, repeaters may now be used not just for additional flexibility but also to extend the overall length of an Ethernet. The Ethernet Specification permits the concatenation of up to three segments; the maximum end-to-end delay between two stations measured as a distance is 2.5 km, including the delay through repeaters containing a point-to-point link [6].

Taps: Transceivers can connect to a coax cable with the use of a *pressure tap,* borrowed from CATV technology. Such a tap allows connection to the cable without cutting it to insert a connector and avoids the need to interrupt network service while installing a new station. One design uses a tap-block that is clamped on the cable and uses a special tool to penetrate the outer jacket and shield. The tool is removed and the separate tap is screwed into the block. Another design has the tap and tap-block integrated into one unit, with the tap puncturing the cable to make contact with the center conductor as the tap-block is being clamped on.

Alternatively, the cable can be cut and connectors fastened to each piece of cable. This unfortunately disrupts the network during the installation process. After the connectors are installed at the break in the cable, a T-connector can be inserted in between and then connected to a transceiver. Another option, a connectorized transceiver, has two connectors built into it for direct attachment to the cable ends without a T-connector.

Experimental Ethernet installations have used pressure taps where the tap and tap-block are separate. Installations conforming to the Ethernet Specification have used all the options.

B. Transceiver

The transceiver couples the station to the cable and is the most important part of the transmission system.

The controller-to-transmission-system interface is very simple, and functionally it has not changed between the two Ethernet designs. It performs four functions: 1) transferring transmit data from the controller to the transmission system, 2) transferring receive data from the transmission system to the controller, 3) indicating to the controller that a collision is taking place, and 4) providing power to the transmission system.

It is important that the two ground references in the system—the common coaxial cable shield and the local ground associated with each station—not be tied together, since one local ground typically may differ from another local ground by several volts. Connection of several local grounds to the common cable could cause a large current to flow through the cable's shield, introducing noise and creating a potential safety hazard. For this reason, the cable shield should be grounded in only one place.

It is the transceiver that provides this ground isolation between signals from the controller and signals on the cable. Several isolation techniques are possible: transformer isolation, optical isolation, and capacitive isolation. Transformer isolation provides both power and signal isolation; it has low differential impedance for signals and power, and a high common-mode impedance for isolation. It is also relatively inexpensive to implement. Optical isolators that preserve tight signal symmetry at a competitive price are not readily available. Capacitive coupling is inexpensive and preserves signal symmetry but has poor common-mode rejection. For these reasons transformer isolation is used in Ethernet Specification transceivers. In addition, the mechanical design and installation of the transceiver must preserve this isolation. For example, cable shield connections should not come in contact with a building ground (e.g., a cable tray, conduit, or ceiling hanger).

The transceiver provides a high-impedance connection to the cable in both the power-on and power-off states. In addition, it should protect the network from possible internal circuit failures that could cause it to disrupt the network as a whole. It is also important for the transceiver to withstand transient voltages on the coax between the center conductor and shield. While such voltages should not occur if the coax shield is grounded in only one place, such isolation may not exist during installation [1].

Negative transmit levels were selected for the Ethernet Specification to permit use of fast and more easily integrated NPN transistors for the output current source. A current source output was chosen over the voltage source used in the Experimental Ethernet to facilitate collision detection.

The key factor affecting the maximum number of transceivers on a segment in the

Ethernet Specification is the input bias current for the transceivers. With easily achievable bias currents and collision threshold tolerances, the maximum number was conservatively set at 100 per segment. If the only factors taken into consideration were signal attenuation and reflections, then the number would have been larger.

IV. CONTROLLER DESIGN

The transmitter and receiver sections of the controller perform signal conversion, encoding and decoding, serial-to-parallel conversion, address recognition, error detection, CSMA/CD channel management, buffering, and packetization. Postponing for now a discussion of buffering and packetization, we will first deal with the various functions that the controller needs to perform and then show how they are coordinated into an effective CSMA/CD channel management policy.

A. Signaling, Data Rate, and Framing

The transmitter generates the serial bit stream inserted into the transmission system. Clock and data are combined into one signal using a suitable encoding scheme. Because of its simplicity, Manchester encoding was used in the Experimental Ethernet. In Manchester encoding, each bit cell has two parts: the first half of the cell is the complement of the bit value and the second half *is* the bit value. Thus, there is always a transition in the middle of every bit cell, and this is used by the receiver to extract the data.

For the Ethernet Specification, MFM encoding (used in double-density disk recording) was considered, but it was rejected because decoding was more sensitive to phase distortions from the transmission system and required more components to implement. Compensation is not as easy as in the disk situation because a station must receive signals from both nearby and distant stations. Thus, Manchester encoding is retained in the Ethernet Specification.

In the Experimental Ethernet, any data rate in the range of 1–5 Mbits/s might have been chosen. The particular rate of 2.94 Mbits/s was convenient for working with the first stations. For the Ethernet Specification, we wanted a data rate as high as possible; very high data rates, however, limit the effective length of the system and require more precise electronics. The data rate of 10 Mbits/s represents a tradeoff among these considerations.

Packet framing on the Ethernet is simple. The presence of a packet is indicated by the presence of carrier, or transitions. In addition, all packets begin with a known pattern of bits called the *preamble*. This is used by the receiver to establish bit synchronization and then to locate the first bit of the packet. The preamble is inserted by the controller at the sending station and stripped off by the controller at the receiving station. Packets may be of variable length, and absence of carrier marks the end of a packet. Hence, there is no need to have framing flags and ''bit stuffing'' in the packet as in other data-link protocols such as SDLC or HDLC.

The Experimental Ethernet used a one-bit preamble. While this worked very well, we have, on rare occasions, seen some receivers that could not synchronize with this very short preamble [20]. The Ethernet Specification uses a 64-bit preamble to ensure synchronization of phase-lock loop receivers often used at the higher data rate. It is necessary to specify 64 bits to allow for 1) worst-case tolerances on phase-lock loop components, 2) maximum times to reach steady-state conditions through transceivers, and 3) loss of preamble bits owing to squelch on input and output within the transceivers. Note that the presence of repeaters can add up to four extra transceivers between a source and destination.

Additional conventions can be imposed upon the frame structure. Requiring that all packets be a multiple of some particular byte or word size simplifies controller design and provides an additional consistency check. All packets on the Experimental Ethernet are viewed as a sequence of 16-bit words with the most significant bit of each word transmitted first. The Ethernet Specification requires all packets to be an integral number of 8-bit bytes (exclusive of the preamble, of course) with the least significant bit of each byte transmitted first. The order in which the bytes of an Ethernet packet are stored in the memory of a particular station is part of the controller-to-station interface.

B. Encoding and Decoding

The transmitter is responsible for taking a serial bit stream from the station and encoding it into the Manchester format. The receiver is responsible for decoding an incoming signal and converting it into a serial bit stream for the station. The process of encoding is fairly straightforward, but decoding is more difficult and is realized in a *phase decoder*. The known preamble pattern can be used to help initialize the phase decoder, which can employ any of several techniques including an analog timing circuit, a phase-locked loop, or a digital phase decoder (which rapidly samples the input and performs a pattern match). The particular decoding technique selected can be a function of the data rate, since some decoder designs may not run as fast as others. Some phase decoding techniques— particularly the digital one—have the added advantage of being able to recognize certain phase violations as collisions on the transmission medium. This is one way to implement collision detection, although it does not work with all transmission systems.

The phase decoders used by stations on the Experimental Ethernet included an analog timing circuit in the form of a delay line, an analog timing circuit in the form of a simple one-shot-based timer, and a digital decoder. Stations built by Xerox for the Ethernet Specification use phase-locked loops.

C. Carrier Sense

Recognizing packets passing by is one of the important requirements of the Ethernet access procedure. Although transmission is baseband, we have borrowed the term "sensing carrier" from radio terminology to describe the detection of signals on the channel. Carrier sense is used for two purposes: 1) in the receiver to delimit the beginning and end of the packet, and 2) in the transmitter to tell when it is permissible to send. With the use of Manchester phase encoding, carrier is conveniently indicated by the presence of transitions on the channel. Thus, the basic phase decoding mechanism can produce a signal indicating the presence of carrier independent of the data being extracted. The Ethernet Specification requires a slightly subtle carrier sense technique owing to the possibility of a saturated collision.

D. Collision Detection

The ability to detect collisions and shut down the transmitter promptly is an important feature in minimizing the channel time lost to collisions. The general requirement is that during transmission a controller must recognize that another station is also transmitting.

There are two approaches:

1) Collision Detection in the Transmission System: It is usually possible for the transmission system itself to recognize a collision. This allows any medium-dependent technique to be used and is usually implemented by comparing the injected signal to the received signal. Comparing the transmitted and received signals is best done in the transceiver where there is a known relationship between the two signals. It is the controller, however, that needs to know a collision is taking place.

2) Collision Detection in the Controller: Alternatively, the controller itself can recognize a collision by comparing the transmitted signal with the received signal, or the receiver section can attempt to unilaterally recognize collisions, since they often appear as phase violations.

Both generations of Ethernet detect collisions within the transceiver and generate the collision signal in the controller-to-transmission-system interface. Where feasible, this can be supplemented with a collision detection facility in the controller. Collision detection may not be absolutely foolproof. Some transmission schemes can recognize all collisions, but other combinations of transmission scheme and collision detection may not provide 100 percent recognition. For example, the Experimental Ethernet system functions, in principle, as a wired OR. It is remotely possible for one station to transmit while another station sends a packet whose waveform, at the first station, exactly matches the signal sent by the first station; thus, no collision is recognized there. Unfortunately, the intended recipient might be located between the two stations, and the two signals would indeed interfere.

There is another possible scenario in which collision detection breaks down. One station begins transmitting and its signal propagates down the channel. Another station still senses the channel idle, begins to transmit, gets out a bit or two, and then detects a collision. If the colliding station shuts down immediately, it leaves a very small collision moving through the channel. In some approaches (e.g., DC threshold collision detection) this may be attenuated and simply not make it back to the transmitting station to trigger its collision detection circuitry.

The probability of such occurrences is small. Actual measurements in the Experimental Ethernet system indicate that the collision detection mechanism works very well. Yet it is important to remember that an Ethernet system delivers packets only with high probability—not certainty.

To help ensure proper detection of collisions, each transmitter adopts a *collision consensus enforcement* procedure. This makes sure that all other parties to the collision will recognize that a collision has taken place. In spite of its lengthy name, this is a simple procedure. After detecting a collision, a controller transmits a *jam* that every operating transmitter should detect as a collision. In the Experimental Ethernet the jam is a phase violation, while in the Ethernet Specification it is the transmission of 4–6 bytes of random data.

Another possible collision scenario arises in the context of the Ethernet Specification. It is possible for a collision to involve so many participants that a transceiver is incapable of injecting any more current into the cable. During such a collision, one cannot guarantee that the waveform on the cable will exhibit any transitions. (In the extreme case, it simply sits at a constant DC level equal to the saturation voltage.) This is called a *saturated collision.* In this situation, the simple notion of sensing carrier by detecting transitions would not work anymore. In particular, a station that deferred only when seeing transitions would think the Ether was idle and jump right in, becoming another participant in the collision. Of course, it would immediately detect the collision and back off, but in the extreme case (everyone wanting to transmit), such jumping-in could theoretically cause the saturated collision to snowball and go on for a very long time. While we recognized that this form of instability was highly unlikely to occur in practice, we included a simple enhancement to the carrier sense mechanism in the Ethernet Specification to prevent the problem.

We have focused on collision detection by the transmitter of a packet and have seen that the transmitter may depend on a collision detect signal generated unilaterally by its receiving phase decoder. Can this receiver-based collision detection be used just by a receiver (that is, a station that is not trying to transmit)? A receiver with this capability could immediately abort an input operation and could even generate a jam signal to help ensure that the collision came to a prompt termination. With a reasonable transmitter-based collision detection scheme, however, the collision is recognized by the transmitters and the damaged packet would come to an end very shortly. Receiver-based collision detection could provide an early warning of a collision for use by the receiver, but this is not a necessary function and we have not used it in either generation of Ethernet design.

E. CRC Generation and Checking

The transmitter generates a cyclic redundancy check, or CRC, of each transmitted packet and appends it to a packet before transmission. The receiver checks the CRC on the packets it receives and strips it off before giving the packet to the station. If the CRC is incorrect, there are two options: either discard the packet or deliver the damaged packet with an appropriate status indicating a CRC error.

While most CRC algorithms are quite good, they are not infallible. There is a small probability that undetected errors may slip through. More importantly, the CRC only protects a packet from the point at which the CRC is generated to the point at which it is checked. Thus, the CRC cannot protect a packet from damage that occurs in parts of the controller, as, for example, in a FIFO in the parallel path to the memory of a station (the DMA), or in the memory itself. If error detection at a higher level is required, then an end-to-end software checksum can be added to the protocol architecture.

In measuring the Experimental Ethernet system, we have seen packets whose CRC was reported as correct but whose software checksum was incorrect [18]. These did not necessarily represent an undetected Ethernet error; they usually resulted from an external malfunction such as a broken interface, a bad CRC checker, or even an incorrect software checksum algorithm.

Selection of the CRC algorithm is guided by several concerns. It should have sufficient strength to properly detect virtually all packet errors. Unfortunately, only a limited set of CRC algorithms is currently implemented in LSI chips. The Experimental Ethernet used a 16-bit CRC, taking advantage of a single-chip CRC generator/checker. The Ethernet Specification provides better error detection by using a 32-bit CRC [21], [22]. This function will be easily implemented in an Ethernet chip.

F. Addressing

The packet format includes both a source and destination address. A local network design can adopt either of two basic addressing structures: *network-specific* station addresses or *unique* station addresses [23]. In the first case, stations are assigned network addresses that must be unique on *their* network but may be the same as the address held by a station on another network. Such addresses are sometimes called *network relative* addresses, since they depend upon the particular network to which the station is attached. In the second case, each station is assigned an address that is unique over all space and time. Such addresses are also known as absolute or universal addresses, drawn from a flat address space.

To permit internetwork communication, the network-specific address of a station must usually be combined with a unique network number in order to produce an unambiguous address at the next level of protocol. On the other hand, there is no need to combine an absolute station address with a unique network number to produce an unambiguous address. However, it is possible that internetwork systems based on flat (internetwork and local network) absolute addresses will include a unique network number at the internetwork layer as a "very strong hint" for the routing machinery.

If network-specific addressing is adopted, Ethernet address fields need only be large enough to accommodate the maximum number of stations that will be connected to one local network. In addition, there must be a suitable administrative procedure for assigning addresses to stations. Some installations will have more than one Ethernet, and if a station is moved from one network to another it may be necessary to change its network-specific address, since its former address may be in use on the new network. This was the approach used on the Experimental Ethernet, with an 8-bit field for the source and the destination addresses.

We anticipate that there will be a large number of stations and many local networks in an internetwork. Thus, the management of network-specific station addresses can represent a severe problem. The use of a flat address space provides for reliable and manageable operation as a system grows, as machines move, and as the overall topology changes. A flat internet address space requires that the address space be large enough to ensure uniqueness while providing adequate room for growth. It is most convenient if the local network can directly support these fairly large address fields.

For these reasons the Ethernet Specification uses 48-bit addresses [24]. Note that these are station addresses and are not associated with a particular network interface or controller. In particular, we believe that higher level routing and addressing procedures are simplified if a station connected to multiple networks has only one identity which is unique over all networks. The address should not be hardwired into a particular interface or controller but should be able to be set from the station. It may be very useful, however, to allow a station to read a unique station identifier from the controller. The station can then choose whether to return this identifier to the controller as its address.

In addition to single-station addressing, several enhanced addressing modes are also desirable. *Multicast* addressing is a mechanism by which packets may be targeted to more than one destination. This kind of service is particularly valuable in certain kinds of distributed applications, for instance the access and update of distributed data bases, teleconferencing, and the distributed algorithms that are used to manage the network and the internetwork. We believe that multicast should be supported by allowing the destination address to specify either a physical or logical address. A logical address is known as a *multicast ID*. *Broadcast* is a special case of multicast in which a packet is intended for all active stations. Both generations of Ethernet support broadcast, while only the Ethernet Specification directly supports multicast.

Stations supporting multicast must recognize multicast ID's of interest. Because of the anticipated growth in the use of multicast service, serious consideration should be given to aspects of the station and controller design that reduce the system load required to filter unwanted multicast packets. Broadcast should be used with discretion, since all nodes incur the overhead of processing every broadcast packet.

Controllers capable of accepting packets regardless of destination address provide *promiscuous* address recognition. On such stations one can develop software to observe all of the channel's traffic, construct traffic matrices, perform load analysis, (potentially) perform fault isolation, and debug protocol implementations. While such a station is able to read packets not addressed to it, we expect that sensitive data will be encrypted by higher levels of software.

V. CSMA/CD CHANNEL MANAGEMENT

A major portion of the controller is devoted to Ethernet channel management. These conventions specify procedures by which packets are transmitted and received on the multiaccess channel.

A. *Transmitter*

The transmitter is invoked when the station has a packet to send. If a collision occurs, the controller enforces the collision with a suitable jam, shuts down the transmitter, and schedules a retransmission.

Retransmission policies have two conflicting goals: 1) scheduling a retransmission quickly to get the packet out and maintain use of the channel; and 2) voluntarily backing off to reduce the station's load on a busy channel. Both generations of Ethernet use the *binary exponential back-off algorithm* described below. After some maximum number of collisions the transmitter gives up and reports a suitable error back to the station; both generations of Ethernet give up after 15 collisions.

The binary exponential back-off algorithm is used to calculate the delay before retransmission. After a collision takes place the objective is to obtain delay periods that will reschedule each station at times quantized in steps at least as large as a collision interval. This time quantization is called the *retransmission slot time.* To guarantee quick use of the channel, this slot time should be short; yet to avoid collisions it should be larger than a collision interval. Therefore, the slot time is usually set to be a little longer than the roundtrip time of the channel. The real-time delay is the product of some retransmission delay (a positive integer) and the retransmission slot time.

To minimize the probability of repeated collisions, each retransmission delay is selected as a random number from a particular retransmission interval between zero and some upper limit. In order to control the channel and keep it stable under high load, the interval is doubled with each successive collision, thus extending the range of possible retransmission delays. This algorithm has very short retransmission delays at the beginning but will back off quickly, preventing the channel from becoming overloaded. After some number of back-offs, the retransmission interval becomes large. To avoid undue delays and slow response to improved channel characteristics, the doubling can be stopped at some point, with additional retransmissions still being drawn from this interval, before the transmission is finally aborted. This is referred to as *truncated binary exponential back-off.*

The truncated binary exponential back-off algorithm approximates the ideal algorithm where the probability of transmission of a packet is $1/Q$, with Q representing the number of stations attempting to transmit [25]. The retransmission interval is truncated when Q becomes equal to the maximum number of stations.

In the Experimental Ethernet, the very first transmission attempt proceeds with no delay (i.e., the retransmission interval is [0-0]). The retransmission interval is doubled after each of the first eight transmission attempts. Thus, the retransmission delays should be uniformly distributed between 0 and $2^{min(retransmission\ attempt,\ 8)} - 1$. After the first transmission attempt, the next eight intervals will be [0-1], [0-3], [0-7], [0-15], [0-31], [0-63], [0-127], and [0-255]. The retransmission interval remains at [0-255] on any subsequent attempt, as the maximum number of stations is 256. The Ethernet Specification has the same algorithm with ten intervals, since the network permits up to 1024 stations; the maximum interval is therefore [0-1023]. The back-off algorithm restarts with a zero retransmission interval for the transmission of every new packet.

This particular algorithm was chosen because it has the proper basic behavior and because it allows a very simple implementation. The algorithm is now supported by empirical data verifying the stability of the system under heavy load [16], [17]. Additional attempts to explore more sophisticated algorithms resulted in negligible performance improvement.

B. Receiver

The receiver section of the controller is activated when the carrier appears on the channel. The receiver processes the incoming bit stream in the following manner.

The remaining preamble is first removed. If the bit stream ends before the preamble completes, it is assumed to be the result of a short collision, and the receiver is restarted.

The receiver next determines whether the packet is addressed to it. The controller will accept a packet in any of the following circumstances:

1) The destination address matches the specific address of the station.

2) The destination address has the distinguished broadcast destination.

3) The destination address is a multicast group of which the station is a member.

4) The station has set the controller in promiscuous mode and receives all packets.

Some controller designs might choose to receive the entire packet before invoking the address recognition procedure. This is feasible but consumes both memory and processing resources in the controller. More typically, address recognition takes place at a fairly low level in the controller, and if the packet is not to be accepted the controller can ignore the rest of it.

Assuming that the address is recognized, the receiver now accepts the entire packet. Before the packet is actually delivered to the station, the CRC is verified and other consistency checks are performed. For example, the packet should end on an appropriate byte or word boundary and be of appropriate minimum length; a minimum packet would have to include at least a destination and source address, a packet type, and a CRC. Collisions on the channel, however, can produce short, damaged packets called collision fragments. It is generally unnecessary to report these errors to the station, since they can be eliminated with a fragment filter in the controller. It is important, however, for the receiver to be restarted promptly after a collision fragment is received, since the sender of the packet may be about to retransmit.

C. Packet Length

One important goal of the Ethernet is data transparency. In principle, this means that the data field of a packet can contain any bit pattern and be of any length, from zero to arbitrarily large. In practice, while it is easy to allow any bit pattern to appear in the data field, there are some practical considerations that suggest imposing upper and lower bounds on its length.

At one extreme, an empty packet (one with a zero-length data field) would consist of just a preamble, source and destination addresses, a type field, and a CRC. The Experimental Ethernet permitted empty packets. However, in some situations it is desirable to enforce a minimum overall packet size by mandating a minimum-length data field, as in the Ethernet Specification. Higher level protocols wishing to transmit shorter packets must then pad out the data field to reach the minimum.

At the other extreme, one could imagine sending many thousands or even millions of bytes in a single packet. There are, however, several factors that tend to limit packet size, including: 1) the desire to limit the size of the buffers in the station for sending and receiving packets; 2) similar considerations concerning the packet buffers that are sometimes built into the Ethernet controller itself; and 3) the need to avoid tying up the channel and increasing average channel latency for other stations. Buffer management tends to be the dominant consideration. The maximum requirement for buffers in the station is usually a parameter of higher level software determined by the overall network architecture; it is typically on the order of 500 to 2000 bytes. The size of any packet buffers in the controller, on the other hand, is usually a design parameter of the controller hardware and thus represents a more rigid limitation. To ensure compatibility among buffered controllers, the Ethernet Specification mandates a maximum packet length of 1526 bytes (1500 data bytes plus overhead).

Note that the upper and lower bounds on packet length are of more than passing interest, since observed distributions are typically quite bimodal. Packets tend to be either very short (control packets or packets carrying a small amount of data) or maximum length (usually some form of bulk data transfer) [16], [17].

The efficiency of an Ethernet system is largely dependent on the size of the packets being sent and can be very high when large packets are used. Measurements have shown total utilization as high as 98 percent. A small quantum of channel capacity is lost whenever there is a collision, but the carrier sense and collision detection mechanisms combine to minimize this loss. Carrier sense reduces the likelihood of a collision, since the acquisition effect renders a given transmission immune to collisions once it has continued for longer than a collision interval. Collision detection limits the duration of a collision to a single collision interval. If packets are long compared to the collision interval, then the network is vulnerable to collisions only a small fraction of the time and total utilization will remain high. If the average packet size is reduced, however, both carrier sense and collision detection become less effective. Ultimately, as the packet size approaches the collision interval, system performance degrades to that of a straight CSMA channel without collision detection. This condition only occurs under a heavy load consisting predominantly of very small packets; with a typical mix of applications this is not a practical problem.

If the packet size is reduced still further until it is less than the collision interval, some new problems appear. Of course, if an empty packet is already longer than the collision interval, as in the Experimental Ethernet, this case cannot arise. As the channel length and/ or the data rate are increased, however, the length (in bits) of the collision interval also increases. When it becomes larger than an empty packet, one must decide whether stations are allowed to send tiny packets that are smaller than the collision interval. If so, two more problems arise, one affecting the transmitter and one the receiver.

The transmitter's problem is that it can complete the entire transmission of a tiny packet before network acquisition has occurred. If the packet subsequently experiences a collision farther down the channel, it is too late for the transmitter to detect the collision and promptly schedule a retransmission. In this situation, the probability of a collision has not increased, nor has any additional channel capacity been sacrificed; the problem is simply that the transmitter will occasionally fail to recognize and handle a collision. To deal with such failures, the sender of tiny packets must rely on retransmissions invoked by a higher level protocol and thus suffer reduced throughput and increased delay. This occasional performance reduction is generally not a serious problem, however. Note that only the sender of tiny packets encounters this behavior; there is no unusual impact on other stations sending larger packets.

The receiver's problem with tiny packets concerns its ability to recognize collision fragments by their small size and discard them. If the receiver can assume that packets smaller than the collision interval are collision fragments, it can use this to implement a simple and inexpensive fragment filter. It is important for the receiver to discard collision fragments, both to reduce the processing load at the station and to ensure that it is ready to receive the impending retransmission from the transmitter involved in the collision. The fragment filter approach is automatically valid in a network in which there are no tiny packets, such as the Experimental Ethernet. If tiny packets can occur, however, the receiver cannot reliably distinguish them from collision fragments purely on the basis of size. This means that at least the longer collision fragments must be rejected on the basis of some other error detection mechanism such as the CRC check or a byte or word alignment check. One disadvantage of this approach is that it increases the load on the CRC mechanism, which, while strong, is not infallible. Another problem is that the CRC error condition will now be indicating two kinds of faults: long collisions and genuine line errors. While occasional collisions should be viewed as a normal part of the CSMA/CD access procedure, line errors should not. One would therefore like to accumulate information about the two classes of events separately.

The problems caused by tiny packets are not insurmountable, but they do increase the attractiveness of simply legislating the problem out of existence by forbidding the sending of packets smaller than the collision interval. Thus, in a network whose collision interval is longer than an empty packet, the alternatives are as follows.

1) Allow Tiny Packets: In this case, the transmitter will sometimes fail to detect collisions, requiring retransmission at a higher level and impacting performance. The receiver can use a partial fragment filter to discard collision fragments shorter than an empty packet, but longer collision fragments will make it through this filter and must be rejected on the basis of other error checks, such as the CRC check, with the resultant jumbling of the error statistics.

2) Forbid Tiny Packets: In this case, the transmitter can always detect a collision and perform prompt retransmission. The receiver can use a fragment filter to automatically discard all packets shorter than the collision interval. The disadvantage is the imposition of a minimum packet size.

Unlike the Experimental Ethernet, the Ethernet Specification defines a collision interval longer than an empty packet and must therefore choose between these alternatives. The choice is to forbid tiny packets by requiring a minimum data field size of 46 bytes. Since we expect that Ethernet packets will typically contain internetwork packet headers and other overhead, this is not viewed as a significant disadvantage.

VI. CONTROLLER-TO-STATION INTERFACE DESIGN

The properties of the controller-to-station interface can dramatically affect the reliability and efficiency of systems based on Ethernet.

A. Turning the Controller On and Off

A well-designed controller must be able to: 1) keep the receiver on in order to catch back-to-back packets (those separated by some minimum packet spacing) and; 2) receive packets a station transmits to itself. We will now look in detail at these requirements and the techniques for satisfying them.

Keeping the Receiver On: The most frequent cause of a lost packet has nothing to do with collision or bad CRC's. Packets are usually missed simply because the receiver was not listening. The Ethernet is an asynchronous device that can present a packet at any time, and it is important that higher level software keep the receiver enabled.

The problem is even more subtle, however, for even when operating normally there can be periods during which the receiver is not listening. There may, for instance, be turnaround times between certain operations when the receiver is left turned off. For example, a receive-to-receive turnaround takes place after one packet is received and before the receiver is again enabled. If the design of the interface, controller, or station software keeps the receiver off for too long, arriving packets can be lost during this turnaround. This occurs most frequently in servers on a network, which may be receiving packets from several sources in rapid succession. If back-to-back packets come down the wire, the second one will be lost in the receive-to-receive turnaround time. The same problem can occur within a normal workstation, for example, if a desired packet immediately follows a broadcast packet; the workstation gets the broadcast but misses the packet specifically addressed to it. Higher level protocol software will presumably recover from these situations, but the performance penalty may be severe.

Similarly, there may be a transmit-to-receive turnaround time when the receiver is deaf. This is determined by how long it takes to enable the receiver after sending a packet. If, for example, a workstation with a slow transmit-to-receive turnaround sends a packet to a well-tuned server, the answer may come back before the receiver is enabled again. No amount of retransmission by higher levels will ever solve this problem!

It is important to minimize the length of any turnaround times when the receiver might be off. There can also be receive-to-transmit and transmit-to-transmit turnaround times, but their impact on performance is not as critical.

Sending to Itself: A good diagnostic tool for a network interface is the ability of a station to send packets to itself. While an internal loop-back in the controller provides a partial test, actual transmission and simultaneous reception provide more complete verification.

The Ethernet channel is, in some sense, half duplex: there is normally only one station transmitting at a time. There is a temptation, therefore, to also make the controller half duplex—that is, unable to send and receive at the same time. If possible, however, the design of the interface, controller, and station software should allow a station to send packets to itself.

Recommendations: The Ethernet Specification includes one specific requirement that helps to solve the first of these problems: there must be a minimal interpacket spacing on the cable of 9.6 μs. This requirement applies to a transmitter getting ready to send a packet and does not necessarily mean that all receivers conforming to the Specification must receive two adjacent packets. This requirement at least makes it possible to build a controller that can receive adjacent packets on the cable.

Satisfying the two requirements described earlier involves the use of two related features in the design of a controller: full-duplex interfaces and back-to-back receivers. A full-duplex interface allows the receiver and the transmitter to be started independently. A back-to-back receiver has facilities to automatically restart the receiver upon completion of a reception. Limited back-to-back reception can be done with two buffers; the first catches a packet and then the second catches the next without requiring the receiver to wait. Generalized back-to-back reception can be accomplished by using chained I/O commands; the receiver is driven by a list of free input buffers, taking one when needed. These two notions can be combined to build any of the following four interfaces: 1) half-duplex interface, 2) full-duplex interface, 3) half-duplex interface with back-to-back receive, and 4) full-duplex interface with back-to-back receive.

Our experience shows that any one of the four alternatives will work. However, we strongly recommend that all interface and controller designs support full-duplex operation and provide for reception of back-to-back packets (chained I/O).

B. Buffering

Depending upon the particular data rate of the channel and the characteristics of the station, the controller may have to provide suitable buffering of packets. If the station can keep up with the data rate of the channel, only a small FIFO may be needed to deal with station latency. If the station cannot sustain the channel data rate, it may be necessary to include a full-packet buffer as part of the controller. For this reason, full compatibility across different stations necessitates the specification of a maximum packet length.

If a single-packet buffer is provided in the controller (a buffer that has no marker mechanism to distinguish boundaries between packets), it will generally be impossible to catch back-to-back packets, and in such cases it is preferable to have at least two input buffers.

C. Packets in Memory

The controller-to-station interface defines the manner in which data received from the cable are stored in memory and, conversely, how data stored in memory are transmitted on the cable. There are many ways in which this parallel-to-serial transformation can be defined [26]. The Ethernet Specification defines a packet on the cable to be a sequence of 8-bit bytes, with the least significant bit of each byte transmitted first. Higher level protocols will in most cases, however, define data types that are multiples of 8 bits. The parallel-to-serial transformations will be influenced by the programming conventions of the station and by the higher level protocols. Stations with different parallel-to-serial transformations that use the same higher level protocol must make sure that all data types are viewed consistently.

D. Type Field

An Ethernet packet can encapsulate many kinds of client-defined packets. Thus, the packet format includes only a data field, two addresses, and a type field. The type field identifies the special client-level protocol that will interpret the data encapsulated within the packet. The type field is never processed by the Ethernet system itself but can be thought of as an escape, providing a consistent way to specify the interpretation of the rest of the packet.

Low-level system services such as diagnostics, boot-strap, loading, or specialized network management functions can take advantage of the identification provided by this field. In fact, it is possible to use the type field to identify all the different packets in a protocol architecture. In general, however, we recommend that the Ethernet packet encapsulate higher level internetwork packets. Internetwork router stations might concurrently support a number of different internetwork protocols, and the use of the type field allows the internetwork router to encapsulate different kinds of internetwork packets for a local network transmission [27]. The use of a type field in the Ethernet packet is an instance of a principle we apply to all layers in a protocol architecture. A type field is used at each level of the hierarchy to identify the protocol used at the next higher level; it is the bridge between adjacent levels. This results in an architecture that defines a layered tree of protocols.

The Experimental Ethernet design uses a 16-bit type field. This has proved to be a very useful feature and has been carried over into the Ethernet Specification.

VII. CONCLUSIONS

We have highlighted a number of important considerations that affect the design of an Ethernet local area network and have traced the evolution of the system from a research prototype to an industry standard by discussing strategies and tradeoffs between alternative implementations.

The Ethernet is intended primarily for use in such areas as office automation, distributed data processing, terminal access, and other situations requiring economical connection to a local communication medium carrying bursts of traffic at high peak data rates. Experience with the Experimental Ethernet in building distributed systems that support electronic mail, distributed filing, calendar systems, and other applications has confirmed many of our design goals and decisions [28]–[31].

Questions sometimes arise concerning the ways in which the Ethernet design addresses (or chooses not to address) the following considerations: reliability, addressing, priority, encryption, and compatibility. It is important to note that some functions are better left out of the Ethernet itself for implementation at higher levels in the architecture.

All systems should be reliable, and network-based systems are no exception. We believe that reliability must be addressed at each level in the protocol hierarchy; each level should provide only what it can guarantee at a reasonable price. Our model for internetworking is one in which reliability and sequencing are performed using end-to-end transport protocols. Thus, the Ethernet provides a "best effort" datagram service. The Ethernet has been designed to have very good error characteristics, and, without promising to deliver all packets, it will deliver a very large percentage of offered packets without error. It includes error detection procedures but provides no error correction.

We expect internetworks to be very large. Many of the problems in managing them can be simplified by using absolute station addresses that are directly supported within the local network. Thus, address fields in the Ethernet Specification seem to be very generous—well beyond the number of stations that might connect to one local network but meant to efficiently support large internetwork systems.

Our experience indicates that for practically all applications falling into the category "loosely coupled distributed system," the average utilization of the communications network is low. The Ethernet has been designed to have excess bandwidth, not all of which must be utilized. Systems should be engineered to run with a sustained load of no more than 50 percent. As a consequence, the network will generally provide high throughput of data with low delay, and there are no priority levels associated with particular packets. Designers of individual devices, network servers, and higher level protocols are free to develop priority schemes for accessing particular resources.

Protection, security, and access control are all system-wide functions that require a comprehensive strategy. The Ethernet system itself is not designed to provide encryption or other mechanisms for security, since these techniques by themselves do not provide the kind of protection most users require. Security in the form of encryption, where required, is the responsibility of the end-user processes.

Higher level protocols raise their own issues of compatibility over and above those addressed by the Ethernet and other link-level facilities. While the compatibility provided by the Ethernet does not guarantee solutions to higher level compatibility problems, it does provide a context within which such problems can be addressed by avoiding low-level incompatibilities that would make direct communication impossible. We expect to see standards for higher level protocols emerge during the next few years.

Within an overall distributed systems architecture, the two generations of Ethernet systems have proven to be very effective local area networks.

REFERENCES

[1]   R. M. Metcalfe and D. R. Boggs, "Ethernet: Distributed packet switching for local computer networks," *Commun. Ass. Comput. Mach.,* vol. 19, pp. 395–404, July 1976.

[2]   R. M. Metcalfe, D. R. Boggs, C. P. Thacker, and B. W. Lampson, "Multipoint data communication system with collision detection," U.S. Patent 4,063,220, Dec. 13, 1977.

[3]   J. F. Shoch, Y. K. Dalal, D. D. Redell, and R. C. Crane, "Evolution of the Ethernet local computer network," *IEEE Computer Mag.,* pp. 10–26, Aug. 1982.

[4]   R. C. Crane and E. A. Taft, "Practical considerations in Ethernet local network design," in *Proc. 13th Hawaii Int. Conf. Syst. Sci.,* Jan. 1980, pp. 166–174.

[5]   J. F. Shoch, "An annotated bibliography on local computer networks," 3rd ed., Xerox Parc Tech. Rep. SSL-80-2, and IFIP Working Group 6.4 Working Paper 80-12, Apr. 1980.

[6]   *The Ethernet, A Local Area Network: Data Link Layer and Physical Layer Specifications,* Version 1.0, Digital Equipment Corporation, Intel, Xerox, Sept. 30, 1980; Version 2.0, Nov. 1982.

[7]   "IEEE standard for local area networks. Logical link control," ANSI/IEEE Standard 802.2-1985.

[8]   "IEEE standard for local area networks. Carrier sense multiple access with collision detection (CSMA/ CD) access method and physical layer specification," ANSI/IEEE Standard 802.3-1985.

[9]   D. R. Boggs, J. F. Shoch, E. A. Taft, and R. M. Metcalfe, "PUP: An internetwork architecture," *IEEE Trans. Commun.,* vol. COM-28, pp. 612–624, Apr. 1980.

[10] H. Zimmermann, "OSI reference model—The ISO model of architecture for open systems interconnection," *IEEE Trans. Commun.,* vol. COM-28, pp. 425–432, Apr. 1980.

[11] Y. K. Dalal, "The information outlet: A new tool for office organization," in *Proc. On-Line Conf. Local Networks and Distributed Office Syst.,* London, England, May 1981, pp. 11–19.

[12] V. G. Cerf and P. K. Kirstein, "Issues in packet-network interconnection," *Proc. IEEE,* vol. 66, pp. 1386–1408, Nov. 1978.

[13] Y. K. Dalal, "Use of multiple networks in the Xerox network system," *IEEE Computer Mag.,* pp. 82–92, Oct. 1982.

[14] F. C. Shoute, "Decentralized control in computer communication," Division of Eng. Appl. Phys., Harvard Univ., Cambridge, MA, Tech. Rep. 667, Apr. 1977.

[15]   R. M. Metcalfe, "Packet communication," Thesis Harvard University, Project MAC Rep. MACTR-114, Mass. Inst. Technol., Cambridge, MA, Dec. 1973.

[16]   J. F. Shoch and J. A. Hupp, "Performance of an Ethernet local network—A preliminary report," in *Proc. Local Area Comm. Network Symp.*, Boston, MA, May 1979, pp. 113–125; revised version in *Proc. Compcon Spring 80*, San Francisco, CA, 1980, pp. 318–322.

[17]   J. F. Shoch and J. A. Hupp, "Measured performance of an Ethernet local network," *Commun. Ass. Comput. Mach.*, vol. 23, pp. 711–721, Dec. 1980.

[18]   E. G. Rawson and R. M. Metcalfe, "Fibernet: Multimode optical fibers for local computer networks," *IEEE Trans. Commun.*, vol. COM-26, pp. 983–990, July 1978.

[19]   D. R. Boggs and R. M. Metcalfe, "Communications network repeater," U.S. Patent 4,099,024, July 4, 1978.

[20]   J. F. Shoch, *Local Computer Networks.*   New York: McGraw-Hill, to be published.

[21]   J. L. Hammond, J. E. Brown, and S. S. Liu, "Development of a transmission error model and an error control model," Rome Air Development Center, Tech. Rep. RADC-TR-75-138, 1975.

[22]   R. Bittel, "On frame check sequence (FCS) generation and checking," ANSI working paper X3-S34-77-43, 1977.

[23]   J. F. Shoch, "Internetwork naming, addressing, and routing," in *Proc. Compcon Fall 78*, 1978, pp. 430–437.

[24]   Y. K. Dalal and R. S. Printis, "48-bit internet and Ethernet host numbers," in *Proc. 7th Data Commun. Symp.*, Oct. 1981.

[25]   R. M. Metcalfe, "Steady-state analysis of a slotted and controlled ALOHA system with blocking," in *Proc. 6th Hawaii Conf. Syst. Sci.*, Jan. 1973; reprinted in *Sigcom Review,* Jan. 1975.

[26]   D. Cohen, "On holy wars and a plea for peace," *J. Computer,* vol. 14, pp. 48–54, Oct. 1981.

[27]   J. F. Shoch, D. Cohen, and E. A. Taft, "Mutual encapsulation of internetwork protocols," *Comput. Networks,* vol. 5, pp. 287–301, July 1981.

[28]   A. D. Birrell *et al.*, "Grapevine: An exercise in distributed computing," *Commun. Ass. Comput. Mach.,* vol. 25, pp. 260–274, Apr. 1982.

[29]   H. Sturgis, J. Mitchell, and J. Israel, "Issues in the design and use of a distributed file system," *ACM Operating Syst. Rev.,* vol. 14, pp. 55–69, July 1980.

[30]   D. K. Gifford, "Violet, an experimental decentralized system," Xerox Palo Alto Res. Center, Palo Alto, CA, CSL-79-12, Sept. 1979.

[31]   J. F. Shoch and J. A. Hupp, "Notes on the 'worm' programs—Some early experiences with a distributed computation," *Commun. Ass. Comput. Mach.,* vol. 25, pp. 172–180, Mar. 1982.

3
VLSI Node Processor Architecture for Ethernet

DALE TAYLOR, DAVID L. OSTER, AND LARRY GREEN

The VLSI Ethernet controller chips are discussed from a designer's viewpoint. Their method of operation is explained and design tradeoffs are presented with concentration placed on memory response requirements, memory location options relative to the VLSI devices, and the effects of FIFO depth on performance. A "common sense" architecture for an Ethernet node processor with application to many classes of Ethernet nodes is suggested to conclude the chapter.

I. INTRODUCTION

Over the past few years we have developed several controllers for Ethernet with various architectures and different controlling processors, including an emulator for the DEC/AMD/Mostek/Motorola LANCE VLSI controller. In studying the behavior of these devices, several design tradeoffs have become apparent in designing an interface for Ethernet. This chapter presents some of our findings.

Another level of design tradeoffs exists as well, of a more global nature. These considerations concern the nature of the device, or node, to be interfaced to the network, with its attendant data throughput requirements and performance parameters. These issues are addressed and concluded by a "common sense" Ethernet node processor architecture.

II. NODE PERFORMANCE CLASSES

Many types of nodes will benefit from an industry-wide-standard LAN connection. Performance classes can be differentiated according to representative data rate demands. Table I shows four performance classes with examples of typical nodes.

Clearly, the different performance classes will have different requirements for an Ethernet connection. Even within a given class, performance requirements will vary because of considerations such as the burstiness or steadiness of data flow and the nature of the processing aside from communications which must be performed. If a graphics processor, for instance, uses 80 percent of the CPU time continually updating its display memory and performing video processing, placing communications processing responsibilities on it as well will impact its ability to perform its primary task of graphics. The node

TABLE I

High Performance	Data Rate, Kilobits per second
Host at 5 MIPS	1000
Communications server	1000
Video (compressed)	400
Laser printer	256
Graphics (not compressed)	256
File server	100
Medium Performance	
Host at 0.5 MIPS	100
Mail server	100
Graphics (compressed)	64
Voice (real time)	64
Video (freeze frame)	64
Line printer	20
Voice (store and forward)	16
9600 Baud	
Word processor	9.6
Data entry terminal	9.6
Facsimile	9.6
Information server/calendar	9.6
Low Performance	
Optical character reader	2.4
Heat/alarm/security	0.1

requirements and processing responsibilities are key design parameters to consider when designing its Ethernet interface.

III. ETHERNET INTERFACE DESIGN TRADEOFFS

The elements of an Ethernet interface can be roughly separated into physical layer and link layer functions, using terms from the open systems interconnection (OSI) communications model. The physical layer Ethernet functions are Manchester encoding and decoding, preamble generation and detection, CRC-32 generation and validation, and serialization/deserialization of data. The link layer functions are those which could be handled by ancillary hardware and/or software support and deal with the temporary storage and buffering of incoming and outgoing packets of data: direct memory access support, runt packet rejection on received messages, retry interval calculation upon collision detection on transmit, ability to store closely spaced incoming messages, and the ability to utilize multiple noncontiguous data buffers to store a message (intramessage buffer chaining). We will consider this latter class of elements and expose some tradeoffs and considerations which have become apparent in deciding upon architectures for Ethernet interfaces.

Prime considerations for node architecture are the costs of development, manufacturing, field support, and form factor constraints driven by the amount of available power and board real estate. Folded in here also is the difficulty of implementation; i.e., how long will it take to design, build, and check the device out? This will be a function of the number of

IC's used, the test features built in, and the difficulty and complexity of test software both to write and for a technician to comprehend. How difficult will it be to produce and check out on the production line? In general, VLSI devices have distinct advantages over discrete implementations, such as ease of assembly, board test, and field repair. All these tradeoffs must be confronted early in the development phase, providing guidelines for a successful design.

With the various VLSI Ethernet controller devices available, the designer has a broad selection to choose from. There were, as of July 1986, five such devices available: LANCE from AMD/Mostek/Motorola, i82586 LAN Controller from Intel, the DP8390 Network Interface Controller from National, the 8001 Ethernet Data Link Controller, EDLC, from SEEQ, and the MB61301 Data Link Controller, DLC, from Ungermann-Bass/Fujitsu. These can be grouped by performance: LANCE, the DP8390, and the i82586 manage multiple transmit or receive data buffers, and the SEEQ and Fujitsu devices manage one transmit or receive buffer at a time. The SEEQ and U-B/Fujitsu devices perform the physical layer Ethernet controller functions as defined in the "Blue Book" Specification 1.0/2.0 for Ethernet, and the IEEE Local Area Network Standard 802.3, leaving multiple buffer management design to the user. LANCE, the DP8390, and i82586 provide for all the link layer functions mentioned above using sophisticated buffer management techniques as well as the physical Ethernet protocol functions.

The way these Ethernet interface devices work is as follows. For transmit, the chip is given a memory address for the transmit data, which it uses to read the data from memory into its FIFO for temporary buffering until it is time to serially encode the data for transmission on the Ethernet cable; for receive, a FIFO is used to buffer the data temporarily until it can be written into memory at the buffer address supplied by the user. The translation of data between its serial form on the Ethernet and its parallel form in memory is the physical layer function of the OSI seven layer communications model. As more intelligence is added to the memory interface portion of the device, more link layer functions can be performed by the device. The SEEQ and U-B/Fujitsu devices provide for one memory address at a time for receive and one for transmit, and this address is directly supplied to the device by the user. The LANCE and i82586 devices provide one level of indirection between the device and the data because the user supplies the address of a buffer descriptor which in turn provides the memory address of the data. Provisions are made for multiple buffer descriptors in both devices. Thus, with one command, multiple buffers can be supplied to these devices. The National device requires a set of contiguous 256-byte buffers for transmit and receive. These buffers are dedicated to their respective functions, and are fixed in memory. There can be an arbitrarily large number of each (up to 64K bytes total for both).

When the design for an Ethernet node is in preliminary stages, one of the first decisions to be made involves the very crucial area of memory management. With the SEEQ and Fujitsu chip sets, the memory arrangement and DMA capabilities must be designed and built by the designer. This approach has the benefit that it may be designed to exactly fit the needs of the node being interfaced, and for low-performance and low-demand nodes, a simple Ethernet interface can be implemented using these devices. However, when the total parts and implementation costs are compared to the chips which do buffer management, there may be no benefit to this approach (see Table II).

For high performance node applications, the memory arrangement must provide continuous memory accessibility for back-to-back or sequential incoming messages and/or rapid sequential transmit buffers for outgoing messages. The LANCE, the Intel i82586,

TABLE II
VLSI SUPPORT CHIP TABLE

Ethernet Chip	Approximate Number of Support Chips	Estimated Parts Cost @ 100 qty.
SEEQ 8001	25	$250
LANCE	5	50
i82586	5	50

This table provides estimates of parts needed and their costs to illustrate the tradeoffs involved in implementing a direct Ethernet-to-memory interface. Costs of the Ethernet chips are not included. The "memory interface" is assumed to have multibuffer DMA capability with intelligence adequate to handle minimal real-time link layer functions. These include receiving back-to-back packets (>2) with no processor intervention and posting status in memory. Assume that with chips not capable of the above functions, the LSI/MSI to implement the functions will be provided externally.

and the DP8390 include provisions which allow controlling software to satisfy requirements for both sequential receive buffers and sequential transmit buffers. The LANCE has implemented a contiguous ring arrangement of buffer descriptors which is configurable at initialization time to allow up to 128 active buffers on both the transmit and the receive side. Once the LANCE device has been initialized, the fixed number of buffer descriptors are always located in the same fixed area of memory, so the LANCE device computes the location of the next buffer descriptor as required. This arrangement requires the software to track the circular queue of descriptors as they are activated (receive) or deactivated (transmit) by the device. The Intel device has implemented a linked list arrangement, which allows the software to provide as many or as few buffers as required for each side. This arrangement requires the i82586 to perform a word memory fetch to fetch the address of the next buffer descriptor from the link field of the previous descriptor. The controlling software must handle linking in new buffers, unlinking old buffers, and traversing the linked list. Both devices provide for using multiple buffers within a single transmit or receive frame, which leaves buffer size management up to the software; an important consideration where an operating system memory management scheme is involved. The DP8390 implements a memory arrangement where the transmit and receive buffer memory is dedicated to the device; the host is not allowed to directly access this memory. The host must provide a DMA capability, which feeds words to the DP8390 DMA, which in turn fills its transmit buffers, and conversely for receive. This allows for contiguous message transmittal and reception, at the expense of a separate memory dedicated only to the Ethernet.

There are several important considerations when designing the memory arrangement to be used with an Ethernet controller. The most important one is the decision of where to place the memory: is it local to the controller and dedicated to it, does it have a memory which it shares with a local network-dedicated microprocessor, or must the controller attempt to use memory on the shared bus of a computer system? The 10 Mbit data rate used on Ethernet dictates that the lower limit of the memory bandwidth be 1.25 Mbytes/s, continuously. In reality, it may have to significantly exceed this rate if sequential buffer access is required because message length and status must be stored, and the next buffer descriptor must be fetched in time for the next message, which can be as little as 9.6 μs (the minimum intermessage gap time, as defined in the Ethernet 2.0 specification). In the case of buffer chaining, the memory bandwidth requirements are greater because the next buffer descriptor must be fetched and previous buffer status stored while a message is arriving or being transmitted without running out of FIFO (see Fig. 1). Memory interleaving schemes may be useful here but the designer must bear in mind that when buffer chaining is performed, the controller must access the next buffer descriptor, which will not be a sequential memory access with the data buffer, determine if another buffer is available, read the buffer address from memory, and store the buffer status for the previous buffer before beginning to access the next data buffer. The smaller the buffers in the chain are, the more often this descriptor access must take place relative to data accesses, requiring higher memory bandwidth. The DP8390 does not have to fetch descriptors between each message, but some status must be stored for each 256-byte buffer used, which requires a nonsequential memory access, since the status is stored at the beginning of each buffer. The

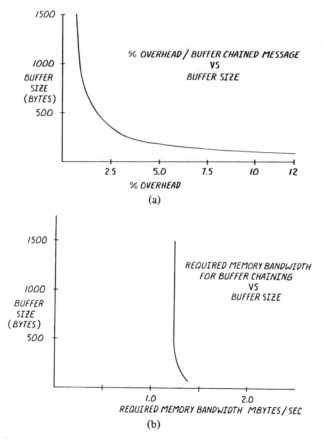

Fig. 1. Buffer chaining graphs. (a) The graph on the top shows the percentage of overhead to perform buffer chaining plotted against the buffer size. The overhead is calculated by dividing the number of memory accesses required to store the previous buffer status and find the next buffer by the number of memory accesses to fetch or store the data. (b) The graph on the bottom shows the minimum memory bandwidth required in the steady state to perform all memory accesses for buffer chaining plotted against buffer size.

device performs an internal check to determine if the user has removed data from the next 256-byte "page" using the internal DMA (on receive), or if the user has filled the next page on transmit. This scheme has the advantage of providing the Ethernet device direct and total control over its own memory access times, providing the host can remove or provide data in a timely manner.

If a dedicated memory approach to an Ethernet controller interface is used, a dual port memory is required. It must be interfaced to the host bus and the Ethernet controller, as well as provide memory access arbitration, host interrupts, and supervisory access to the controller from the host. Although cycle time and latency can be minimized, the network protocol processing must still be handled externally.

If the designer chooses not to provide dedicated local memory for the controller, but rather uses memory accessible over a shared I/O bus, several issues must be confronted. If the shared bus is the main system bus, can the additional bus loading be tolerated by other devices on the bus? Do these other devices require continuous, uninterrupted data access over the bus or can they tolerate higher latency while the Ethernet controller is accessing memory over the common bus? Conversely, how much bus latency can the Ethernet controller tolerate? Generally, some amount of local transient data buffering such as first-in first-out (FIFO) is provided by the Ethernet controller. The depth of the FIFO in a controller must be considered with the related factors of memory cycle time, average and peak latency, and the number of words/bytes transferred in a single bus acquisition sequence (burst length). The FIFO depth determines the latitude of memory and bus design parameters allowed when incorporating a controller into a system. (See the Appendix for the effects of FIFO depth.)

The simplest interface for a buffer managing controller with no dedicated memory is a direct bus interface to the host system bus. Although this approach is only a host bus interface with no local memory, this style of interface is likely to have the greatest impact on system performance because of bus loading and processing requirements. The bus loading effect can approach 100 percent in a system where the controller accesses memory on the main system bus and the latency or effective memory cycle time are stretched to the limits. An example of this bus hogging effect was observed when a controller was transferring data across a system bus to a dual port RAM with 400 ns access time out of which the controlling host processor was executing code. Effective memory cycle times approached 1.5 μs, due to contention for the memory between the LANCE and the CPU.

Memory response time cannot be overemphasized in importance as a design issue. The more throughput is required of the Ethernet controller, the more important the issue becomes. In one implementation, we observed that when two nodes of an Ethernet were attempting to transmit continuously, with one node able to access its next transmit frame instantly while the other node required over 10.6 μs (a time greater than the maximum allowable intermessage gap time on Ethernet) to store previous buffer status, acquire its next transmit buffer, and get data actually ready to serially transmit on the Ethernet media; the first node always sent its message on the first try while the second node always had to defer on its first try. Furthermore, when the second node attempted to transmit after this first deferral, the first node always had its next message ready to send and a collision occurred. If the first node happened to send its message because of a shorter backoff time, it again had another message to send when the other one was gone, resulting in ongoing collisions and deferrals for the node with the slower sequential message acquisition.

A possible alternative to the dedicated memory controller interface and the direct bus interface approaches is a dedicated network microprocessor with RAM sharing its bus with the Ethernet controller and a host interface. In addition to having the advantages offered by a dedicated memory interface, this approach offloads the real-time processing burden of the network from the host. Since the local microprocessor field interrupts and arbitrates memory usage, the additional real estate required for the microprocessor may actually result in a lower parts count than a dedicated memory controller interface. Also, since the controller only transfers over the system bus at the request of the system CPU, and since these transfers do not require the 10 Mbit continuous transfer rate of Ethernet, the system impact of this architecture is minimal.

Factors other than memory response time enter into a node's ability to successfully transmit and receive sequential messages. The interaction of the Ethernet controller with its controlling software is a very important issue as well. The goal is to have the style of the controller mesh well with the style of I/O handling and memory management used by the controlling operating system. If software can be written to merge well with an efficient controller, rather than attempting to tailor controller hardware to an operating system, the chances of a successful implementation are increased. Both the Intel i82586 and the LANCE device provide flexible memory arrangements which allow operating system interfaces with a minimal amount of software effort, while the SEEQ, Fujitsu, and National devices require the hardware designer to design a memory access arrangement which fits in well with the local software environment, at the expense of added board real estate. LANCE requires contiguous 8 byte aligned buffer descriptor rings, which localize all the buffer descriptors at any properly aligned location in a 24 bit address space, and requires three word memory accesses to acquire the next buffer address and length for either transmit or receive. The Intel device allows the flexibility of buffer descriptors anywhere within a 64 kbyte address range, with a linked list arrangement which requires at least four word memory accesses to obtain the next buffer address. Because the linked list arrangement places the address of the next buffer descriptor in the current buffer descriptor, the software designer has the capability of either separating the descriptors and spreading them throughout memory or placing them all together in a block as LANCE does. The Intel device, however, requires one more memory access to find the next buffer than LANCE does, which can be a very critical factor in sequential message handling as described.

Other memory arrangements are possible with all the Ethernet controllers by simply declaring certain constraints on usage or designing them into the controller, such as disallowing buffer chaining within a message. While lessening the response time requirements placed on the memory, this approach requires larger memory buffers to be allocated for messages which may or may not use the entire buffer. Memory is wasted with this approach because of the unused space in the large buffers. In some operating systems, it may ease the burden on the memory management software to use larger buffers and accept the fact that some memory space goes unused. If the RAM is shared with the software of a dedicated network microprocessor, the space wasted with a large number of maximal length (1518 bytes) receive buffers may result in space contention with the network protocol software in RAM. The National device does not allow the use of large buffers, so these comments do not apply to it.

The Ethernet specification defines three types of address: station, multicast, and broadcast. Station addresses are unique to one station, so messages with a station address as their destination are recognized by only one device, or station, on the Ethernet. Multicast addresses require a hashing capability by the receiving controller and allow sending a message to a group of stations on the Ethernet. The broadcast address is recognized by all stations on the Ethernet. Some Ethernet controller designs may require software address recognition on all or some incoming addresses. While the Intel, National, and LANCE controllers all have complete station, multicast, and broadcast address recognition capabilities, the SEEQ device requires external multicast address recognition. Placing the burden of address recognition on the software takes valuable CPU execution cycles, and the controller's memory can easily become clogged up with potential receive messages awaiting screening by the CPU. It is important to place the address recognition logic in the controller hardware for virtually any nontrivial controller implementation.

Due to delays caused by long cable lengths on Ethernet (up to 500 m/segment), it is possible to receive message fragments caused by collisions which occur after a small amount of data has been transmitted (see Fig. 2). This type of message is referred to as a "runt" message, and its byte count can be up to 64 bytes maximum.

While runt filtering (ignoring messages shorter than 64 bytes) is of a lower frequency of occurrence and therefore less of a strain on the controlling processor than the address recognition, it is easy enough to place in the hardware that it should be done. Another more important area, however, is the random backoff calculation for retrying on a transmit message for which a collision occurred. While LANCE, the DP8390, and the i82586 all perform the binary exponential backoff algorithm required for Ethernet with no intervention, the SEEQ device performs only part of the task. The SEEQ EDLC notifies the controlling CPU that a collision has occurred and waits for the computed backoff interval without intervention, but it is up to the CPU or surrounding hardware to place the beginning bytes of the message into the SEEQ's transmit FIFO before the interval has expired. This can be as soon as 9.6 μs, which far exceeds the interrupt response time of most microprocessors. This dictates a hardware solution where the first bytes of a message are placed into the chip's transmit FIFO immediately upon collision detection. Since LANCE, the DP8390, and the i82586 handle all the retry functions by themselves, they must be regarded as superior in this function.

Each node should be capable of reporting the amount of time it spent idling, transmitting, backing off (awaiting the expiration of a retry interval), and receiving. Furthermore, accumulated statistics such as the number of times the controller was forced to defer because when it was ready to send, another message was on the media, the number of retries required, the number of retry failures, and the number of receive errors of each type which occurred (runt messages, CRC errors, FIFO overruns, framing errors, and resource errors) should be available. The more complete the set of available statistics is, the more precisely a system manager can evaluate the network characteristics. Including a microprocessor in the design of the controller facilitates gathering these values without burdening the main system CPU with the task. Ultimately, the system manager would like a set of statistics indicating the time the Ethernet media spent in various states as well as the information from the individual nodes.

Fig. 2.   Runt message illustration. To show how runt messages occur, suppose node 1 and node 2 both begin transmitting simultaneously. Since node 3 is nearer to node 2 than node 1, it will begin to receive node 2's message before node 1's. The portion of the message received at node 3 before the collision is detected is called a runt message.

IV. Common Sense Node Processor Architecture

With emerging higher level protocol standards such as Xerox Network Systems (XNS) and the International Standards Organization (ISO), memory bandwidth constraints imposed by Ethernet's 10 Mbit data rate, and the availability of VLSI controllers, an intelligent processor with dedicated memory provides a general solution for attaching node devices to Ethernet (see Fig. 3). While capable of buffering Ethernet traffic and offloading protocol processing from very busy nodes such as high and medium performance devices, it can be compact and inexpensive enough to effectively complement the 9600 Bd and low performance devices as well. With intelligence gravitating out to the nodes of a network, these nodes are generally busy performing the functions they were designed for, such as graphics or data processing. Placing the added burden of communications processing upon the nodes detracts from their effectiveness. Consequently, the architecture proposed here is an effective solution for interfacing a wide spectrum of node devices to Ethernet.

Basic elements of the node processor include a CPU, RAM, VLSI Ethernet controller and host interface.

V. CPU

The CPU performs supervisory functions, host interaction, and network management. Added benefits are as follows.

- Higher-level protocols can be offloaded from the host, allowing it to perform applications-level processing.
- The CPU will be responsive to the VLSI Ethernet controller, providing higher performance than if it had other operating system responsibilities. This also relieves the host CPU from the complexities and real-time demands of network traffic.
- A memory management scheme can be optimized for the VLSI controller, adding to the performance of the node. This scheme can be unrelated to the host memory management scheme.

Any microprocessor of the designer's choice can be used for the CPU of an Ethernet node processor.

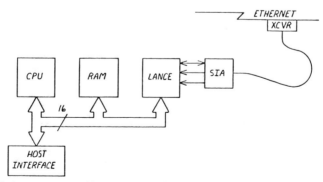

Fig. 3. Node processor architecture. This illustrates the node processor architecture. The host interfaces with the node processor RAM via the host interface to access send and receive data. The node processor CPU performs protocol processing on the data in RAM and interacts with both the LANCE and the host. LANCE uses the RAM for message buffering and interacts with the serial interface adapter (SIA), which performs Manchester encoding/decoding and interacts with the Ethernet transceiver.

VI. RAM

The dedicated RAM on a node processor must provide adequate bandwidth to support the required Ethernet data rate. For low to medium performance nodes 32 kbytes of RAM are adequate in most cases. Considering an average required throughput rate of 64 kbits/s and assuming the network protocol software on the node processor occupies 20 kbytes of code space, with another 2 kbytes for connection management, there are 10 kbytes of buffering available. This affords about 1 s worth of buffering for incoming messages at the average data rate, leaving some space for transmitting acknowledgments and other outgoing traffic. Assuming that for these performance classes there is a single network connection active at a time, the protocol software can use flow control effectively to minimize data burstiness and to allow the host to process the messages at its own pace. More buffer space can be made available by placing protocol software in ROM on the node processor if required. For these lower performance classes of nodes, 32 kbytes of volatile memory should be adequate for most applications.

For higher performance nodes, however, much more memory is required for code and buffer space. If we assume 30 kbytes of code space for a multiple connection implementation, including connection management variables, we see quickly that 32 kbytes of RAM is not enough. For a 256 kbit/s average throughput rate, and assuming multiple simultaneous virtual circuits on a host which can transfer and process 800 kbits/s, a 64 kbyte RAM would be sufficient for the steady-state case, where data are always flowing at the average data rate. However, considering that in reality data will come in bursts of high rate intermixed with periods of inactivity, it may not suffice. At five times the average throughput rate, with the host emptying data out of the node processor at its maximum rate of 800 kbits/s, in 0.72 s the node processor runs out of buffer space in the best case (perfect buffer usage, no transmit buffers) for a 64 kbyte implementation. Flow control cannot be as effective in controlling the problem in a multiconnection situation, besides which more flow control adds more traffic to the network. Clearly there are many variables to weigh in deciding on the RAM size, including the nature of the node, the loading on the network, the number of simultaneous connections to support, the required code space for the protocol, etc. It is safe to say that the more buffer space available on the node processor, the greater its throughput capabilities will be and the less its impact on the network.

VII. VLSI CONTROLLER

Now that the VLSI controllers are becoming available, it is quite difficult to justify a hardware implementation of an Ethernet interface. Both cost and real estate analyses will result in significant savings using VLSI.

VIII. HOST INTERFACE

The host interface architecture will vary according to the performance class and nature of the host, or node, being considered. With the modular architecture of the proposed node processor, different types and styles of host interfaces can be designed according to requirements of the particular host.

The high performance nodes will require higher performance DMA-style host interfaces, medium and low performance nodes may perform adequately with slower parallel bus interfaces, and some lower performance nodes will be adequately served by a serial host interface. This is an area which requires some work towards standardization; meanwhile, it provides ample opportunity for creativity.

APPENDIX

EFFECTS OF FIFO DEPTH

The FIFO buffer in an Ethernet controller provides two valuable functions: more efficient bus/memory usage through multiple transfers for each bus acquisition (bursts) and more tolerance to long bus latencies. The deeper a FIFO is, the larger a burst transfer may be and the longer peak latency will be.

Quantifying FIFO buffer size requires considering memory cycle time, combined bus controller average and peak latency to a burst transfer, and the number of words per burst transfer. [1] For the sake of brevity we will consider the FIFO to be 16 bits wide and some as yet unspecified number of words deep. The analysis is for receive but applies equally to transmit. The FIFO input rate Ri during Ethernet receive is

$$Ri = (10 \text{ Mbits/s})(16 \text{ bits/word}) = 0.625 \text{ Mwords/s}. \tag{1}$$

The input period

$$Pi = 1/Ri = 1.6 \text{ } \mu\text{s/word}. \tag{2}$$

The FIFO output period Po must average out to less than or equal to the FIFO input period to avoid overflowing the FIFO during receive

$$Po \leqslant Pi. \tag{3}$$

The average output rate is the sum of the average latency L and the product of the burst size N and the memory cycle time T, all divided by the burst size

$$Po = \frac{L + N*T}{N} \leqslant 1.6. \tag{4}$$

Thus,

$$L/N + T \leqslant 1.6 \tag{5}$$

and

$$T \leqslant 1.6 - L/N. \tag{6}$$

A family of curves (see Fig. 4) can be drawn showing the relation between three variables T, N, and L. These curves represent the outside limits of average performance

---

[1] In this discussion it will be assumed that we have a fixed number of words per burst transfer and that a minimum burst is in the FIFO before a bus acquisition. Some controllers will not release the bus until the FIFO is empty, which can result in bus hogging in systems with slower memory.

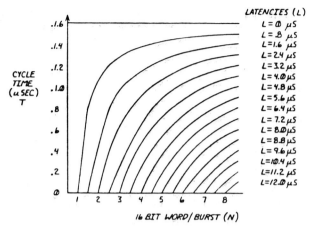

Fig. 4. Memory performance versus burst size graph. This graph shows required memory cycle time and bus latency for different burst sizes (number of words transferred from FIFO to RAM per bus acquisition) in an Ethernet controller.

for a choice of the three variables. In practice, chosen performance parameters must be practical and well inside the limits. There is no such thing as a 0 μs memory time, and the 1.6 μs memory cycle time would require 100 percent utilization of the memory bus.

It can be seen from the graph that for a given memory cycle time, the allowed average latency increases with the burst size. Thus, for a given latency and cycle time, the longer bursts give a greater margin against FIFO overruns which might occur during peak latency periods. Also, since there is usually some time penalty for bus acquisition and release, larger bursts will consume less total bus bandwidth.

It is clear from the above discussion that the FIFO depth has a direct effect on the maximum allowable burst size and thus the maximum average latency. If the average latency is less than the maximum we can define a peak latency based on the FIFO depth. The peak latency Lp is the product of the FIFO depth D and the data input period Pi less the time to unload a single word from the FIFO, T

$$Lp = Pi*D - T. \tag{7}$$

Let us now apply these results to two different FIFO lengths: 8 words (as used by the Intel i82586) and 24 words (as used by the LANCE). For the sake of simplicity we will choose two different memory cycle times for the above FIFO lengths. Burst length for the 8 word FIFO will be 4 words, and 8 words for the 24 word FIFO. (See Table III.)

TABLE III
FIFO LENGTH TABLE

FIFO Length	Cycle Time	Burst Length	Average Latency	Peak Latency
8	0.6	4	4.0 μs	12.2 μs
8	1.0	4	2.4 μs	11.8 μs
24	0.6	8	7.2 μs	37.8 μs
24	1.0	8	4.8 μs	37.4 μs

Clearly the 24 word FIFO gives a better average latency because of the larger burst size. However, the real benefit of the 24 word FIFO can be seen in the peak latency. This parameter is of great importance in any system where the worst-case latency delays due to system bus contention are several times larger than the average bus latency. The larger the allowable peak latency of an Ethernet controller is, the less likely it will suffer a FIFO overrun/underrun in a system with a heavily utilized bus.

ACKNOWLEDGMENT

R. Bryan of Advanced Computer Communications was very helpful in the formulative aspects of this work.

REFERENCES

[1] "Internet transport protocols," Xerox Corp., XS1S 028112, Dec. 1981.
[2] "The Ethernet—A local area network—Data link layer and physical layer specifications," Version 2.0, Digital Equipment Corp., Intel Corp., and Xerox Corp., Nov. 1982.
[3] "Standard ECMA-72 Transport Protocol," ECMA, 2nd ed., Sept. 1982.
[4] "The AM7990 family Ethernet node," Advanced Micro Devices Corp., Nov. 1982.
[5] "Ethernet protocol chip specification," Revision 1.0, Digital Equipment Corp., Feb. 1982.
[6] "i82586 LAN controller data sheet," Intel Corp.
[7] "8001 Ethernet data link controller, EDLC data sheet," SEEQ Corp.

4
Choosing Between Broadband and Baseband Local Networks

GREGORY T. HOPKINS AND NORMAN B. MEISNER

I. INTRODUCTION

Local area network developers, who have traditionally focused on two communications media—baseband and broadband—may have placed too much emphasis on which medium is the ultimate solution rather than on which better supports a user's application. To understand the applications of baseband and broadband local area networks, system design, performance, electrical characteristics, maintenance, and installation for both media must be understood.

II. BASEBAND VERSUS BROADBAND

Baseband local networks typically use a bidirectional signal path on which signals are encoded onto the cable using Manchester encoding or other baseband methods which occupy the entire spectrum in the cable to support a single channel. A variety of packet-mode-media access techniques can be used, but the most common implementation and IEEE Standard 802.3 is carrier sense multiple access with collision detection (CSMA/CD), in which all subscribers share a channel. Subscribers decide to transmit after sensing that a channel is free. If collisions of data packets occur, subscribers retransmit after a randomized delay. This is an effective way to allocate capacity on a channel to "bursty," or low-duty cycle, devices in which the channel capacity is matched to the aggregate demand of many subscribers. The 802.3 local area network, for example, is a baseband CSMA/CD channel that operates on a 50 Ω coaxial cable at a system data rate of 10 Mbits/s or on a twisted pair at 1 Mbit/s.

Broadband local networks use the media technology developed by the CATV industry. Because CATV amplifiers, taps, splitters, and cable can support up to a 450 MHz bandwidth, the same cable using frequency division multiplexing can support several channels. Any channel can serve as a video, data, or voice system, depending on the equipment connected.

Because CATV systems are unidirectional, a transmit and a receive path must be provided. This is accomplished either by splitting the available 450 MHz bandwidth into transmit and receive channels on the same cable or by providing separate cables for signal transmission and reception. As with baseband systems, a variety of media-access techniques can be used independently of the CATV system. CSMA/CD systems are also popular for CATV-based local networks and are standardized by the IEEE 802.3

Committee although token passing (an IEEE 802.4 Standard), polling, and reservation schemes have also been used as media-access techniques.

There are several system considerations when comparing baseband and broadband local-network implementations. One is the total geographic coverage of the network. Broadband networks have greater distance capability while retaining full bandwidth because they use active amplifiers to distribute and extend the signaling range. Baseband networks can be extended beyond their usual 2.5 km range at 10 Mbits/s, but reduced data rate from the effects of dispersion results.

Deciding on broadband just for distance is somewhat shortsighted because inefficiencies are inherent in multichannel operation, the media-access technique efficiency is a function of propagation delay, and store-and-forward bridges can be used to extend overall distance. However, even with these factors, broadband delivers significantly greater bandwidth over longer distances than baseband networks.

Another advantage of broadband is the support of multimode communications, including audio, video, and data, on one cable pathway. This is accomplished by frequency division multiplexing or channelization in the same manner that the RF spectrum is divided. The diversity of communications available within the 450 MHz CATV spectrum is enough to satisfy the most ambitious office-of-the-future designer.

Baseband systems must be supplemented with other forms of wiring to provide nondata-communications needs. If video is required, a CATV network must coexist with the baseband network. It could be argued that all communication can be digitized and transmitted as data, but real-time digitized voice and video would overwhelm a single baseband channel. Counterbalanced against the logistical convenience of using a broadband pipeline for a company's voice, video, and data communications requirements is the potential of accidental or intentional catastrophic failure and vulnerability to professional eavesdroppers. A single source of wideband noise at low power applied to a CATV outlet can interfere with many channels. While baseband systems are similarly susceptible, only one channel of data communications is destroyed by such problems.

III. Performance Characteristics

The collective mythology of local area networks greatly confuses the issue of network performance in baseband and broadband systems. Performance is more closely related to access technique than to medium. The same constraints apply to baseband and broadband systems, and performance levels differ according to differences in scale of data rate and distance.

The performance of a technique such as CSMA/CD depends on the ratio of message length to propagation delay. The higher the ratio, the better the performance because the propagation delay is the interval during which the packet is vulnerable to collision. After that interval, all users will have "heard" the transmission and deferred.

With baseband, all data must be carried on a single channel, necessitating use of a high data rate network such as the IEEE Standard 802.3. For a given data-packet size in bits, this implies a short packet, which demands a short propagation delay to maintain superior performance. Hence, the IEEE 802.3 specification limits total propagation delay leading to a maximum allowable distance for 10 Mbit/s baseband systems of 2.5 km.

This distance limitation for baseband systems based on performance is alleviated by broadband techniques that can be extended to 10 km and more. But it is impossible to extend geographic coverage without sacrificing something. In some cases, it is channel data rate. A lower data rate CSMA/CD channel, say 1 Mbit/s, would result in 10 times the packet duration than for 10 Mbits/s and would permit 10 times the propagation delay or total layout extension. The concomitant sacrifice is the potential lack of total connectivity promised by a bus network. A 1 Mbit/s channel provides total connectivity only with complex additions. A between-channel bridge that filters packets via media access control (MAC) addresses and rebroadcasts the data on the appropriate other channel is the usual solution. This invokes additional overhead, bridge delay, throughput, and reliability penalties to achieve greater distance.

Increased overhead is evident when users are randomly assigned to channels in a multichannel situation. Half the traffic on a two-channel system would have to be rebroadcast channel-to-channel via the bridge. This repetition of packets lowers the combined throughput of the two channels. Two 1 Mbit/s channels have a combined maximum data rate of 1.33 Mbits/s of new data, the remaining 0.67 Mbits/s being bridged, rebroadcast packets. Ten 1 Mbit/s channels can carry only 5.26 Mbits/s. This illustrates the law of diminishing returns when multiple fully connected channels are employed.

A counterargument is that devices can be carefully allocated to channels to minimize interchannel communication. This denies the demand that the office or plant of the future makes for full connectivity. Although yesterday's dumb terminals can be associated with specific devices, tomorrow's intelligent workstations will not flourish under such a restrictive architecture.

Another method of achieving greater distance is to use other time-division-multiplexing techniques such as static time-slot assignments or reservations. These access mechanisms are not performance-limited by propagation delay, and can be used with baseband or broadband channels. They suffer, however, from a nonresponsiveness to the bursty, low-duty cycle demand that characterizes local data communications.

One additional performance factor is the difficulty and potential uncertainty of broadband collision detection. A well-designed CATV network provides equal signal strength at each outlet and presumes equal signal strength delivered from each upstream transmitter. However, seasonal variations, component aging, or poorly designed extensions to the original CATV system can cause variations in received signal strength at drop locations. A strong signal colliding with a weak signal may not appear as a collision to all users. Similar reception problems exist for other media-access techniques. Broadband systems typically stress higher level protocols because the communications medium for large CATV networks is less reliable than baseband. Significant work has been done by the IEEE Committee on Broadband Collision Detection and Enforcement. These efforts are reflected in the current broadband IEEE Standard 802.3.

IV. PHYSICAL AND ELECTRICAL CHARACTERISTICS

CATV systems require power to operate the cable and use radio frequency modulation techniques to transmit signals on the cable. This power is typically supplied by a 30 V AC signal from the center conductor for use by the RF amplifiers in the system. Baseband systems use a passive medium, and digital techniques based on voltage differences are used to transmit data.

The simplicity of the baseband-signaling scheme precludes use of the cable for multiple simultaneous channel operation. This is because the baseband signal is unfiltered and generates harmonics throughout the cable spectrum.

Because broadband systems impress the signal modulation on a carrier, no spectral components lower than about 2 MHz are generated. This allows easy grounding procedures, whereas baseband cables must be grounded at only one point on the cable. Multiple-channel operation, however, is not without its problems. Care must be taken in the design and maintenance of all RF equipment to assure that noise and intermodulation (interference between channels) do not degrade system performance. Rigid specifications do not exist for RF equipment to assure that services on different channels can coexist and that keyed-off noise from a large transmitter population can be controlled. Further, interoperability of different manufacturers' equipment on a single RF channel may be difficult to achieve. For large CATV systems, cumulative noise from keyed-off transmitting equipment, packet collisions, improperly terminated taps, or poorly installed components can interfere with other cable services. The baseband IEEE 802.3 system benefits in this respect because it has been jointly and tightly specified by a large number of engineering organizations. This specification assures interoperable equipment on the limited geography of the baseband channel.

CATV component technology has been developed with protection from stray signal ingress and egress. Metropolitan CATV operators follow strict Federal Communications Commission radiation regulations to ensure that no interference occurs with on-the-air services, especially in the Federal Aviation Administration and the navigation band areas of the signal spectrum. While the regulations do not generally apply to CATV systems used exclusively within a company, a local-network installer should adhere to the intent of these regulations. The CATV industry has developed connector technology that supports this signal-protection capability.

The status of CATV and baseband cables with respect to fire codes is unclear. Teflon coverings for some baseband systems are available. CATV components contain flammable dielectric material within an aluminum sheath, and their ability to pass fire codes for internal building use from state to state is also unclear.

V. DESIGN AND INSTALLATION

In evaluating local networks, relative performance and price of interface units are usually studied in great detail, but substantial cost may reside with the design and installation of the medium. This is especially true when the mobility of office and plant workers is considered. Frequent reorganization and rounds of ''musical chairs'' can lead to significant wiring cost without additional local-network hardware or software expenses. Hence, broadband and baseband media must be compared not just for initial purchase price, but for probable reconfiguration costs during the life of the equipment.

A significant cost differential exists between the two media. The layout of a baseband cable plant is simple: there are rules for trunk layout in the IEEE 802.3 specification. The rules delimit individual segment lengths, number of repeaters in cascade, and overall cable length. Using these guidelines, a novice local-network engineer can lay out a baseband cable plant. Similar guidelines exist for other baseband implementations.

Contrasting with the fundamental simplicity of baseband is the design of a broadband cable plant. The engineering involved is similar in difficulty to designing a layout for a small town. The signal strength is equalized at all tap locations, necessitating care in the positioning of amplifiers, splitters, and taps, as well as calculating tap values. This is not an exercise for a novice: it requires an experienced CATV design engineer. Similarly, the care needed in selection of components forces reliance on an experienced CATV designer.

Installation parallels this difference in design complexity. A baseband cable can be installed and maintained by plant engineers and electricians. However, broadband demands RF engineering skills not usually present in an end user's workforce.

VI. OPERATION AND MAINTENANCE

Because of the analog nature and geographic coverage of CATV systems, companies considering large broadband local networks must staff RF technicians and acquire test equipment for periodic alignment and maintenance (amplifiers, for instance, must be adjusted for gain and slope). Attention must be given to each service placed on the cable to ensure that it does not overlap in frequency with or affect the operation of other channels. Frequency management, equipment acceptance testing, configuration and control, and periodic maintenance are critical tasks for CATV networks. Placing all communications on a single CATV cable increases the importance of network monitoring and control. Media components and modem equipment that degrade performance must be quickly isolated and replaced.

Because of the limited distance and passive nature of baseband systems, operation and media maintenance procedures are simpler. Transceivers, the devices that transmit and receive data on the cable, are the critical element of baseband systems. If the transceiver fails in the ON state, the channel jams. However, most transceiver designs to date have addressed this problem.

VII. MIXING BROADBAND AND BASEBAND

While baseband and broadband local networks meet local environment needs, there is no clear winner. Each has its advantages. An architecture which takes advantage of the best features of each medium is a CATV system used as an internetwork for a number of limited distance baseband networks. Baseband networks would be dedicated to groups within an organization for their data-communications services. When data must move between local networks, a channel of the CATV system serves as the internetwork.

In such a scheme, the CATV system serves as a trunk running between all buildings or floors in a building to teleconferencing centers, but not indiscriminately dropped to each office. This simplifies the CATV system, thus reducing design, installation, operation, and maintenance costs as well as cumulative system noise. In areas in which CATV installation and design are difficult, a simpler baseband medium can be employed. This hierarchical structure is less subject to catastrophic failure and allows individual groups to control their own networks. If significant traffic is anticipated between baseband networks (that is, terminals in building A to computers in building B), the performance of the internetwork bridge is critical.

Different baseband systems can be interconnected if they follow a fixed internetworking scheme. Thus, a variety of baseband systems incorporating coaxial cable or fiber optics and using appropriate access mechanisms can be individually selected and tailored for each group interfacing to the broadband CATV trunk.

5

Architecture and Design of a Reliable Token-Ring Network

WERNER BUX, FELIX H. CLOSS, KARL KÜMMERLE,
HEINZ J. KELLER, AND HANS R. MUELLER

Architecture, performance, transmission system, and wiring strategy of a token-ring local area network implemented at the IBM Zurich Research Laboratory are described. In the design of the system, particular emphasis was placed on high reliability, availability, and serviceability. To ensure robustness of the token-access protocol, we employ the concept of a monitor function which is responsible for fast recovery from access-related errors. Our protocol supports asynchronous transmission of data frames concurrently with full-duplex synchronous channels, e.g., for voice services or other applications requiring guaranteed delay. The delay-throughput performance of the token ring is shown to depend very little on data rate and distance. The transmission system of the ring is fully bit synchronous and allows insertion/removal of stations in/from the ring at any time. A mixed ring/star wiring strategy is used which provides the means for both fault detection and isolation, and system reconfiguration, and allows systematic wiring of a building.

I. INTRODUCTION

Local communication systems for data employing various topologies have been used for a long time [1], [2]. The current activities in the field of local area communication networks can be viewed as an expansion to data networks to make high-speed packet-switching services available to the in-house domain.

This chapter describes the major aspects pertaining to architecture, wiring, transmission, and performance of a local area ring system with token-passing access designed and implemented at the IBM Zurich Research Laboratory [3]–[9]. For a detailed description of the design criteria for the token-ring transmission system, we refer to [10].

One of the first accounts of the basic token-access mechanism was presented by Farmer and Newhall [11]; some other references are [12]–[15]. Our contributions focus on system reliability, availability, and serviceability. In particular, our investigations demonstrate that a local area network based on a token ring has the following attractive features:

1) robustness and efficiency of the access protocol, i.e., quick recovery from token errors and excellent delay-throughput characteristics compared to other access control schemes employed on bus and/or ring systems,

2) physical reliability and the potential for systematic wiring through the concept of wiring concentrators to which stations are connected in a radial fashion and which are interconnected by the main ring cable,

3) electrical stability of a ring consisting of a chain of several hundred repeaters, and

4) the potential to provide synchronous channels in addition to the asynchronous (packet-oriented) data operation for applications requiring guaranteed delay or throughput. Examples are process control and real-time voice services.

In the next section, we describe the data format on the ring, the access method, and a monitor function through which we achieve a reliable ring operation. Section III discusses the wiring scheme, Section IV presents an outline of the ring transmission system, and, finally, we consider the delay-throughput behavior of the token ring in Section V.

II. TOKEN-ACCESS PROTOCOL

The design of the access method and the frame format was led by the consideration that the ring has to fit into the framework of a general architecture, e.g., SNA [16], without requiring changes in higher level protocols. This has two basic consequences.

1) Protocols related to the ring access have to be confined to the bottom layers, physical and data link layers. In particular, the mechanisms for access-related error detection and recovery must also be embedded in these layers.

2) Access method and data link control functions should be clearly separated in order to be open-ended for the use of the most appropriate data link control procedures.

In addition to these architectural requirements, the desire to provide synchronous channels on the ring had a major impact on our ring architecture.

A. Frame Format

Transmission on the ring is in the form of variable-length frames, the structure of which is shown in Fig. 1. A frame is delimited by start- and end-delimiters (DELs, DELe) and consists of an access-control field (AC), TO- and FROM-link addresses (AT, AF), the information field (I), and the frame check sequence field (FCS). For ease of description, we subsequently refer to the combination of start delimiter, access-control field, and the two link addresses as "frame header" (FH) and the combination of the FCS field and end delimiter as "frame trailer" (FT). The meaning of the above frame elements is defined as follows.

Delimiters consist of four bit patterns representing violations of the differential (polarity-insensitive) Manchester code (see Section IV-A), followed by two unused bits and two "qualifier bits" which serve to distinguish between start and end delimiters.

Access-Control Field serves the following purposes: access control, multiplexing of asynchronous and synchronous traffic, ring supervision, and recovery. It consists of the following eight bits.

1) Priority Indicator (PI) which serves to distinguish between a frame carrying asynchronous traffic (PI = 0) and synchronous traffic (PI = 1).

2) Reservation Indication (RI) needed to guarantee timely access for stations with synchronous traffic.

3) Token (TK) which controls access to the ring and can be in either of two states: "free" (TK = 0) or "busy" (TK = 1).

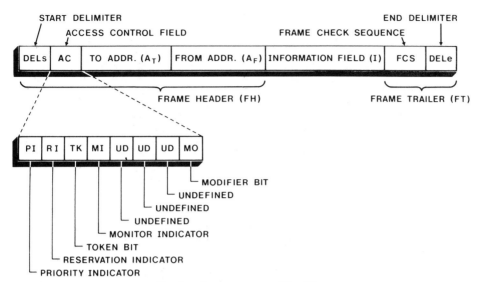

Fig. 1.   Frame structure. After [5].

4) Monitor Indicator (MI) is manipulated by the ring monitor for ring supervision/ recovery purposes. For details, see Section II-C.

5) Undefined Bits (UD) of which the meaning is not defined.

6) Modifier (MO) allows the distinction between normal "user frames," i.e., the *I* field contains user data, and "access-control" frames, i.e., the *I* field contains well-defined control information related to the ring operation.   ˙

Link Addresses: The address space is based on the notion of a local network consisting of several interconnected subnetworks (rings). To simplify the routing function in the interconnecting units, we use structured TO- and FROM-addresses each four bytes long. The first two bytes of the link address denote the ring number (unique in the entire local network), the second two bytes are the station number (unique at least on one ring, possibly within the entire network).

Information Field contains higher level data; it may contain any sequence of bits. The architecture does not impose any restrictions on the maximum frame size. It should be noted, however, that the setting of timers (see Section II-C) in an actual implementation does depend on the maximum frame length selected.

Frame Check Sequence Field is two bytes long and generated according to the standard HDLC/SDLC generator polynomial of degree 16. A two byte FCS was chosen because of readily available chips performing this function. The FCS protects the MO bit, the TO- and FROM-addresses, and the *I* field. Thus, the frame check sequence guarantees correctness of a frame received in a ring adapter (Fig. 2) and to be passed across the system interface into the station memory. Other errors, such as faulty transmission between ring adapter and station or lost frames, are detected by parity bits or by detection and recovery functions provided above ring access control, e.g., in the logical link control sublayer.

The frame structure shown in Fig. 1 is simpler than the one in the standards of ECMA [17] and IEEE 802 [18]. This is due to various features which the standards groups added to the ring protocol, such as more priority levels, larger address space, four byte frame check sequence, and various indicators, e.g., the "address-recognized" and the "frame-copied"

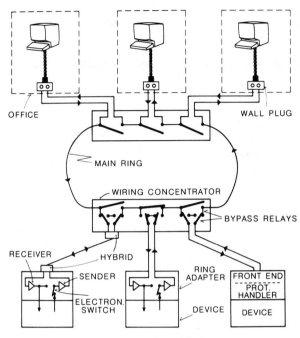

OFFICE

WALL PLUG

MAIN RING

WIRING CONCENTRATOR

BYPASS RELAYS

RECEIVER HYBRID

SENDER

ELECTRON. SWITCH

RING ADAPTER

DEVICE

FRONT END
PROT. HANDLER

DEVICE

DEVICE

Fig. 2.   Ring wiring.

indicators. It should be noted that the key elements necessary for reliable token operation are basically the same in the standards and in our architecture.

B. Access Control

In this section, we describe the basic ring-access protocol for both asynchronous and synchronous operation. Token supervision and recovery which are also part of the token-access protocol are discussed in Section C.

Basic Ring Protocol/Asynchronous Operation: Access to the ring is controlled by passing a token contained in the AC field around the ring. The token can be in either of two states: busy or free. A busy token is always associated with a full frame according to Fig. 1, whereas a free token is contained in an AC field preceded by a start delimiter and followed by idles.

Stations are attached to the ring via a ring adapter. If a station has a frame pending for transmission, then its adapter will turn an arriving free token to a busy one on the fly, leave the REPEAT mode, and transmit its frame (see Fig. 3). When the adapter has finished transmission, it generates a start delimiter followed by an AC field in which all bits (including TK) are set to zero, provided that:

1) the adapter has received back the entire FH including both addresses,

2) the received FROM-address equals the station's own address, and

3) the RI bit is still zero, i.e., the reservation indicator has not been changed (compare synchronous operation).

The reasons for imposing these conditions on the generation of a free token are as follows.

• Receipt of a FROM-address different from the station's address indicates that an error

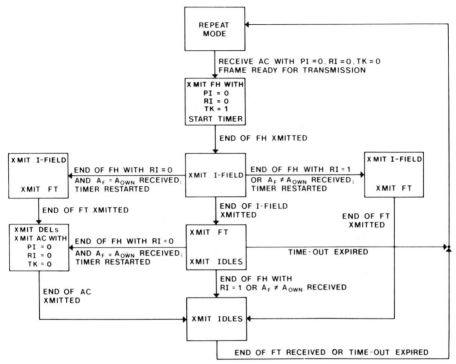

Fig. 3.   Ring-access protocol. After [5].

in the access protocol has occurred. Consequently, the transmitting adapter refrains from issuing a free token. (Recovery from this and other access-related errors is described in the next section.)

- As will be presented in detail later, the ring is switched into synchronous operation in regular time intervals. To guarantee a timely start of the synchronous-access intervals, the synchronous bandwidth manager, explained below in the paragraph on synchronous operation, is allowed to set the RI bit in any AC field passing through with a busy token. This indicates to the transmitting adapter, which receives back the header of its frame, that it must not issue a free token.

Following transmission of the frame (and usually of a free token), the adapter keeps transmitting idles until it receives the next end delimiter which is the end of its own frame provided no access error has occurred. Upon detection of the end delimiter, the adapter enters the REPEAT mode. In the REPEAT mode, a ring adapter simply retransmits all data on the ring with a short latency, typically one bit time. It also monitors the TO-address fields of the frames passing through. When it detects its own address, it copies the frame, but does not modify the passing frame.

Rationale of Protocol Design: Two basic elements of a token-ring protocol have a major impact on its overall characteristics.

1) The repeater switching strategy, i.e., the rule according to which the adapter enters the REPEAT mode following the transmission of a frame.

2) The token-generation strategy, i.e., the rule determining when and under which conditions the adapter issues a new free token. We subsequently give the motivation for choosing our particular solutions regarding these two issues.

Repeater Switching Strategy: There are two natural points in time when the adapter returns to the REPEAT mode after transmission:

1) immediately after the end delimiter of a frame has been transmitted, or

2) after the end delimiter has been received back.

Our major reason for preferring the second method is to guarantee that under error-free conditions, no garbage (i.e., fragments of previously transmitted frames) is left on the ring.

Token-Generation Strategies: Based on our repeater switching strategy, three approaches are conceivable regarding the point in time when an adapter generates a free token following the transmission of a frame.

1) "Single-frame operation" in which the sender of a frame issues the new token when it has completely received its entire frame and, hence, erased it from the ring.

2) "Single-token operation" in which the sender of a frame does not issue a new token before it has received back the header of its frame including the busy token. This rule becomes effective in cases where a frame is shorter than the ring latency.

3) "Multiple-token operation" in which a new free token is generated immediately after the end delimiter of a frame has been transmitted. This implies that depending on ring latency and frame transmission times, multiple tokens can exist on the ring; at most one of them, however, is in the free state.

Since the priority operation described below requires that a free token is not issued before the frame header has returned to the sender, and since performance analysis shows nearly ideal delay-throughput characteristic for realistic speeds and distances [4], we decided in favor of the single-token operation. This decision is further backed up by the fact that token supervision and recovery will be greatly facilitated if the protocol ensures that only one token (free or busy) exists on the ring.

It has been mentioned above that the latency of a ring adapter in REPEAT mode is typically one bit time. Figure 4 shows the sensitivity of the delay-throughput behavior of a token ring operating under the single-token rule at 4 Mbits/s with respect to adapter latency. The figure demonstrates that 1) there is a significant performance degradation when the latency is increased from 1 to 8 bits, 2) this effect strongly depends on the number of active stations, and 3) the delay-throughput behavior is fairly insensitive to the number of stations, provided the latency is 1 bit. Therefore, our design decision was to select a latency of 1 bit per adapter (station).

Synchronous Operation: Our ring protocol offers two priority levels and thus allows provision of priority access for selected stations. The token-ring standards [17], [18] provide eight priority levels through three bit priority and reservation indicators. One important application of priority access is for synchronous operation requiring guaranteed bandwidth, e.g., 64 kbits/s in the case of PCM voice channels. Another application of the synchronous capability is to use it as a vehicle to attach data devices requiring guaranteed bandwidth and delay.

Stations desiring to establish a synchronous connection have to go through a call-setup procedure which involves a central control station, called the synchronous bandwidth manager (SBM). The SBM station will grant or reject a request for a synchronous connection, depending on the number of synchronous connections already established and on the bandwidth required for asynchronous data traffic. The assignment of bandwidth to the two traffic types is completely flexible, as will become clear from the subsequent description, which focuses on the mechanism of how synchronous full-duplex connections and asynchronous types of transmissions are concurrently provided on the same ring. It is assumed that the synchronous connections have already been established and all stations

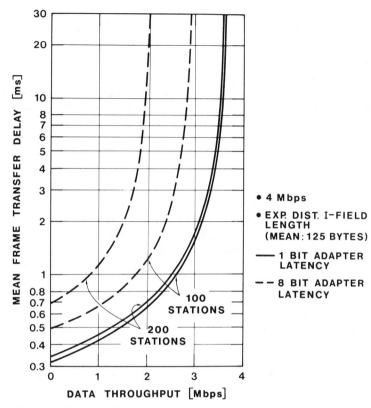

Fig. 4. Impact of adapter latency on delay-throughput characteristic. © 1983 World Telecommunication Union (I.T.U.).

holding a synchronous connection are designated either as "calling" or as "called" stations. This property is defined during connection setup and is used to avoid ambiguities.

The SBM prepares switching of the ring into synchronous operation by making priority reservations at such points in time that it is possible to periodically issue priority tokens (PI = 1). To achieve this, the SBM uses the reservation indicator to interrupt the asynchronous operation. When the reservation indicator gets set (RI = 1) in a frame being currently transmitted, the transmitting station does not issue a free token but transmits idles until it receives the end delimiter of its own frame (see Fig. 2). It also remembers that it was the last one in the asynchronous cycle. When the SBM detects the end delimiter of the frame, it releases a free priority token (PI = 1, RI = 0, TK = 0). Subsequently, the first calling station A downstream from the SBM changes the token to busy, appends TO-address B and FROM-address A, and puts its synchronous data into the information field. Station B, like every called station, monitors for its own address in the TO-address field. Upon detection of its own address, it copies the information field and puts its own synchronous data, destined to A, in the information field of the same frame. As in the asynchronous mode, adapter A removes its own frame from the ring but instead of discarding the information field, A copies it since it contains synchronous data from its partner B. Issuing of a new priority token follows exactly the same rules as for asynchronous operation, i.e., A sends a free token at the end of its frame but not before it has received its own FROM-address. When all synchronous stations have had exactly one transmission opportunity, the SBM will receive the free priority token. It then issues a start delimiter followed by an AC field with PI = 0, RI = 1, TK = 0, which cannot be used by any station but the last one in the previous asynchronous cycle. This station will flip the RI bit to zero, and thus issue the next free asynchronous token. It should be noted that this mechanism preserves the fairness of access among all stations operating in the asynchronous mode.

A performance analysis studying the tradeoff between number and bandwidth of synchronous channels, and the bandwidth left, or delay achievable for the asynchronous operation has been made [19].

C. Token Supervision and Recovery

Our approach to achieve reliable operation is to have a monitor function responsible for supervising the proper token operation and performing fast recovery in case of errors. Implementation showed that both hardware and microcode necessary to provide the monitor function in addition to the token-access protocol only slightly increased the complexity of a ring adapter. Therefore, the monitor function is provided in each ring adapter, however, it is active in only one adapter at any one time.

Adapters in the REPEAT mode play a passive role in token recovery. Transmitting adapters enter the REPEAT mode upon detection of a protocol error and do not issue a free token. All active recovery measures are taken by the monitor itself.

Access to the ring is exclusively controlled by the token. Particular supervisory functions are therefore embedded in the protocol to invoke recovery actions when the token is mutilated. We classify the token-related error situations into three different types.

1) Lost-Token Situation when during a certain critical time interval, neither a free nor a busy token is transmitted over the ring. This can occur, for example, if a start delimiter is mutilated and also during ring initialization.

2) Circulating Busy-Token Situation when a start delimiter and an AC field with a busy token continuously circulate around the ring. This may be caused by noise hitting the free-token bit.

3) Duplicate-Token Situation when two (or more) stations transmit simultaneously because both have received a free token. Such an error situation can occur, e.g., if a free token is generated by noise hitting a busy token.

How the ring recovers from these error situations is subsequently described.

Recovery from Lost-Token Error: One of the basic tasks of the monitor is to constantly check the data stream passing through for tokens. From the above description of the access protocol, it becomes clear that the time interval between subsequent observations of a free or busy token (or equivalently of a start delimiter) is upper bounded by the maximum frame transmission time plus the ring latency. Therefore, the monitor can detect a lost-token situation with the aid of an appropriately adjusted timeout $T1$ started whenever it observes a start delimiter. Upon expiration of the timeout, the monitor clears the ring from possible garbage by transmitting idles for a time interval longer than the ring latency, and eventually issues a new free token.

Recovery from Circulating Busy-Token Error: A permanently circulating busy token can be detected by the monitor with the aid of the monitor indicator bit (MI) in the AC field. Any adapter transmitting a frame sets MI to "zero." When the frame passes through the monitor, it changes MI to "one." In this way, the monitor is able to detect any AC field with a busy token circulating more than once around the ring by checking the MI bit.

Recovery is again performed by the monitor through clearing the ring, and then transmitting a start delimiter followed by an AC field with a free token.

Recovery from Duplicate-Token Error: Duplication of a free token can lead to a situation where multiple stations are transmitting simultaneously. Two mechanisms in the access protocol are provided to recover from this error situation. The first mechanism is that a transmitting adapter checks the FROM-address field which it receives back. A second recovery mechanism is needed for those cases where a transmitting station does not receive back any intact FH at all. In such a case, the timeout $T1$ shown in Fig. 3 will expire. As shown in the state diagram of Fig. 3, the reaction of an adapter to either of these situations is to finish the transmission of the current frame and afterwards to enter the REPEAT mode without generating a free token. Thus, the error is converted into a lost-token situation and recovered accordingly.

As described above, the ring is supervised by *one* adapter which, in addition to its normal access-control functions, acts as an active monitor. All adapters are identical, therefore, any adapter can assume the role of the active monitor. This allows automatic replacement of a failing active monitor, triggered by either of the following two events:

1) ''watchdog'' circuits sensing loss of synchronization of the bit stream, and

2) the absence of a free token for a period longer than the maximum free-token cycle time, detected by timeout. It should be noted that this situation is different from the lost-token condition described above.

The replacement process is split into two phases. In phase 1, all passive monitors continuously broadcast a ''monitor-recovery'' message. Upon receipt of such a message from another passive monitor which carries a FROM-address greater than its own address, a passive monitor terminates competition mode and enters the REPEAT mode. Eventually, the monitor-recovery message which carries the largest FROM-address will succeed in traveling around the ring.

Phase 2 starts when a passive monitor has received its own monitor-recovery message. It first enters the active-monitor mode and then informs all other adapters of this by broadcasting an ''end of monitor replacement'' message. Upon receipt of this message, the new active monitor generates a free token, thus restoring the ring operation.

The procedure described above is not only used for monitor recovery, but also to resolve contention when several adapters with monitor capability simultaneously connect to an inactive ring, i.e., to a ring which does not yet carry any signal.

There are, of course, alternative approaches to provide a reliable token operation. For example, it is possible to distribute the recovery functions among all active stations. This excludes use of the monitor indicator as described above, but requires recovery protocols entirely based on timeouts. Such an approach is viable but leads to significantly slower recovery. For this reason, the standards groups abandoned it in favor of a monitor-recovery solution very similar to ours [17], [18].

III. Ring Wiring

The installation of a local area network (LAN) in a building or on a campus requires a wiring strategy designed to offer sufficient flexibility for a wide variety of building structures. The LAN wiring plan must be open to reconfiguration and expansion. It must meet high standards of reliability, availability, and serviceability on a wide scale of environments ranging from office systems to more EMI-exposed plant control systems.

In our ring network, we use a two-level wiring hierarchy [7]. The main ring interconnects a set of wiring concentrators which can be placed at strategic and protected locations in a building (Fig. 2). Offices are wired to concentrators in a radial fashion. This hybrid ring/star wiring strategy allows wiring of a building in a systematic way without having to loop the main-ring cable through every office and to every outlet.

Wiring concentrators are centralized points for maintenance and reconfiguration. In its simplest form, a concentrator contains bypass relays for each lobe (Fig. 2). It is a passive device in the sense that it does not amplify data signals. Lobe cables, wall outlets, and ring adapters can be isolated from the main ring. Bypass relays are operated by the station for inserting/removing itself into/from the ring. Powering down a station leads to automatic disconnection of the station's lobe from the main ring. Breakage of a lobe has the same effect. All other parts of the ring network remain operational without the need for manual intervention.

The concept of passive wiring concentrators can be extended by introducing an active element such as a signal amplifier. It allows increasing of the maximum distance between concentrators. In our prototype, we developed an active concentrator with electrooptical transducers. With these devices, some sections of the main ring were implemented with optical fibers.

Figure 2 shows additional relay contacts for configuring a "local-wrap" ring which consists of the lobe cable and the ring adapter. The wiring concentrator allows testing of ring-adapter hardware, the lobe cable, and significant parts of the ring access protocol prior to inserting a station in the ring.

IV. The Transmission System

A ring adapter comprises two functional entities, the front end which implements the transmission system, and the protocol handler which executes the token protocol discussed in Section II, and supports the system's interface. Here, we first review the design decisions for the transmission system, and then address the key issues and findings of the ring synchronization method. For details, refer to the companion paper, Chapter 6, of this volume.

A. Design Decisions

1) Clocking of the ring matches the principle employed with the monitor function. Each adapter contains a quartz oscillator; the actual ring clock, however, is provided by the adapter with the active-monitor function. The other adapters derive clocking information from the data stream with phase-locked loops (PLL). Switchover of the monitor function to another adapter (Section II-C) also causes a transfer of the ring clock.

2) Stations are inserted in and removed from the ring randomly, i.e., these actions can be initiated at any time. Station insertion/removal leads to a momentary loss of synchronism, and requires a fast resynchronization method. It should be noted that this does not trigger monitor switchover.

3) We use differential Manchester code because it provides good clocking information, allows a simple and low cost implementation, is polarity insensitive, and allows transformer coupling. The frame delimiters can then be defined as violations of this code.

B. Transmission Media

Transmission in a ring system is unidirectional and point-to-point. As a consequence, transmission media can be different in the various sections of the ring depending on

requirements. In our ring prototype, we use the following media:
- shielded dual twisted-pair cables between wiring concentrator and stations,
- shielded twisted-pair cable for the main ring which interconnects wiring concentrators, and
- optical fibers between some wiring concentrators. In this case, the wiring concentrator needs a power supply for the optical drivers.

C. Ring Synchronization

The front end of each adapter derives clocking information from the received data stream. Clock recovery is impaired by signal distortion and noise. Zero crossings of the received signal and of the derived clock do not coincide precisely; they deviate in a random fashion called timing jitter. A detailed analysis of jitter sources is presented in [10]. As each adapter uses the clock derived for receiving and transmitting data, timing jitter accumulates along the chain of adapters on the ring.

Timing jitter limits the number of stations which can be placed on a single ring. The design of the synchronization scheme must, therefore, be guided by the objective to minimize jitter accumulation. Analytic and measurement results [9], [10] have shown that more than 250 stations can be supported by a single ring without noticeable degradation of the transmission error performance.

The monitor derives its receive clock from data signals impaired by accumulated jitter (relative to its crystal-oriented transmit clock). A small elastic buffer is used in the monitor to compensate for accumulated jitter. It was shown analytically and by measurements [10] that 8–10 bits are sufficient for a chain of more than 250 adapters.

D. Station Insertion and Removal/Detection of Signal Loss

Stations are inserted in and removed from the ring by relays in the wiring concentrators. Relay operation interrupts the data signal on the ring for about 1–2 ms. Special care was taken to prevent this error burst from propagating through the entire ring and, as a consequence, insertion/removal does not cause loss of synchronization in the whole ring.

Each adapter is equipped with an energy detector to detect loss of the received signal. As above, the repeater prevents signal loss from propagating through the ring. Instead, it broadcasts a beacon message which allows identification of the location of the signal loss by analyzing the source address field of the beacon message.

V. Performance Characteristics

In a performance analysis [4], it was shown that the delay-throughput characteristic of a token ring compares very favorably to other access disciplines used on rings and media access-control procedures employed on bus systems. The most relevant performance features of a token ring, no speed and distance limitations over the range of parameters which is of practical interest, and fairness of access, will be explained below.

Figure 5(a) and (b) shows the mean frame transfer time in ms versus the total data throughput in Mbits/s, i.e., throughput due to information carried in the I field. The mean transfer time is defined as the time interval from the generation of a frame at the source station until its reception at the destination, and includes the queueing and access delay at the sender, the frame transmission time, and the propagation delay. In Fig. 5(a), the

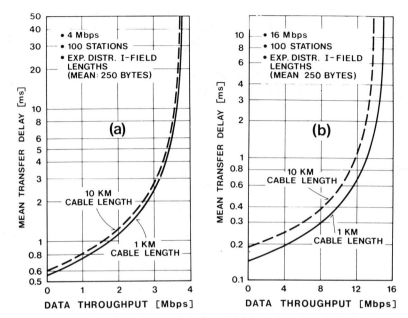

Fig. 5. (a) Delay-throughput characteristic for a 4 Mbit/s token ring. (b) Delay-throughput characteristic for a 16 Mbit/s token ring.

transmission rate is 4 Mbits/s and the ring lengths are 1 and 10 km. The rings are assumed to operate according to the single-token rule. The curves clearly show that:

1) the maximum achievable utilization is very high, and

2) the performance of the token protocol is practically insensitive to the length of the transmission medium.

Figure 5(b) confirms this characteristic of the access protocol for a transmission rate of 16 Mbits/s, and also shows that maximum utilization will be only degraded insignificantly if we increase the transmission speed from 4 to 16 Mbits/s. We consider these performance characteristics as important advantages of a token-ring protocol compared to CSMA/CD on a bus (baseband or broadband); see [4].

Finally, Fig. 6 illustrates that the token protocol provides fair access in case of asymmetric traffic load. It is assumed that two of the 20 active stations, 1 and 8, each generate about 40 percent of the total traffic, the other stations each contribute 1.1 percent. The results show that stations generating a small amount of traffic experience a much smaller transfer delay than heavy traffic stations, and do not get penalized by them. Furthermore, it can be seen that this property is preserved when the throughput approaches the saturation point. It should be noted that fair access in the above sense is only guaranteed when the transmission time per token is upper bounded for each station, e.g., to one frame, as assumed in Fig. 6.

VI. CONCLUSIONS

This chapter has presented architecture, wiring, transmission, and performance of a token-ring local area network. A 4 Mbits/s prototype has been implemented and is operational at the IBM Zurich Research Laboratory. The prototype provides communication between a variety of devices like terminals, workstations, printers, and mainframe

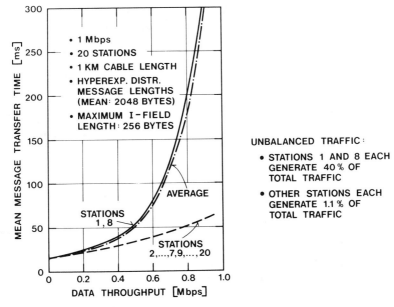

Fig. 6.   Fair sharing of bandwidth in a token ring.

computers. File and printer server applications were implemented together with an electronic mail service. Recently, the prototype ring was enhanced to support synchronous voice traffic concurrently with asynchronous data transfer.

The key features of our token-ring network are as follows.

1) Reliable token operation is achieved through a monitor function present in each ring adapter, but active in only one adapter to perform detection of and recovery from token-error situations.

2) Since the token-access scheme is a deterministic access protocol, it can, in addition to asynchronous data traffic, support applications requiring guaranteed delay or throughput.

3) The hybrid ring/star wiring scheme with wiring concentrators is the key to physical ring reliability, error isolation, system maintenance, and reconfiguration. It also allows prewiring of a building systematically.

4) The ring network allows the use of different media in different sections, and thus can be adapted to different environments, and is open to advances in transmission technology.

5) From a performance point of view, the token-access protocol compares very favorably to other major access-control schemes. Its key features are insensitivity with respect to speed and distance, and fair sharing of the bandwidth.

ACKNOWLEDGMENT

The authors express their gratitude to L. Recknor for implementing and testing of the ring adapter, to P. Zafiropulo for designing significant parts of the adapter microcode and the ring operation software, and to P. Dill for supporting experimentation and replication of the adapter hardware.

REFERENCES

[1] K. Kümmerle and M. Reiser, "Local-area communication networks—An overview," *J. Telecommun. Networks*, vol. 1, pp. 349–370, 1982.

[2] R. J. Cypser, *Communication Architecture for Distributed Systems*. Reading, MA: Addison-Wesley, 1978.

[3] H. Meyr, H. R. Müller, U. Bapst, and H. Bouten, "Manchester coding with predistortion: An efficient and simple transmission technique in local digital ring networks," in *Proc. Nat. Telecommun. Conf.*, Houston, TX, 1980, pp. 65.4.1–65.4.7.

[4] W. Bux, "Local-area subnetworks: A performance comparison," *IEEE Trans. Commun.*, vol. COM-29, pp. 1465–1473, Oct. 1981; see also this volume, ch. 22.

[5] W. Bux, F. Closs, P. Janson, K. Kümmerle, and H. R. Müller, "A reliable token-ring system for local-area communication," in *Proc. Nat. Telecommun. Conf.*, New Orleans, LA, 1981, pp. A2.2.1–A2.2.6.

[6] W. Bux, F. Closs, P. Janson, K. Kümmerle, H. R. Müller, and E. H. Rothauser, "A local-area communication network based on a reliable token-ring system," in *Local Computer Networks*, P. C. Ravasio, G. Hopkins, and N. Naffah, Eds. Amsterdam, The Netherlands: North-Holland, 1982, pp. 69–82.

[7] H. R. Müller, H. Keller, and H. Meyr, "Transmission in a synchronous token ring," in *Local Computer Networks*, P. C. Ravasio, G. Hopkins, and N. Naffah, Eds. Amsterdam, The Netherlands: North-Holland, 1982, pp. 125–147.

[8] H. Rudin, "Validation of a token-ring protocol," in *Local Computer Networks*, P. C. Ravasio, G. Hopkins, and N. Naffah, Eds. Amsterdam, The Netherlands: North-Holland, 1982, pp. 373–387.

[9] H. Meyr, L. Popken, H. Keller, and H. R. Müller, "Synchronization failures in a chain of repeaters," in *Conf. Rec. GLOBECOM*, Miami, FL, vol. 2 of 3, pp. 859–869.

[10] H. Keller, H. Meyr, and H. R. Müller, "Transmission design criteria for a synchronous token ring," *IEEE J. Select. Areas Commun.*, vol. SAC-1, pp. 724–733, Nov. 1983; see also this volume, ch. 6.

[11] W. D. Farmer and E. E. Newhall, "An experimental distributed switching system to handle bursty computer traffic," in *Proc. ACM Symp. Problems Optimization Data Commun.*, Pine Mountain, GA, Oct. 1963, pp. 31–34.

[12] D. J. Farber, J. Feldman, F. R. Heinrich, M. D. Hopwood, D. C. Loomis, and A. Rowe, "The distributed computer system," in *Proc. 7th IEEE Comput. Soc. Int. Conf.*, pp. 31–34, 1973.

[13] B. K. Penney and A. A. Baghdadi, "Survey of computer communications loop networks: Parts 1 and 2," *Comput. Commun.*, vol. 2, pp. 165–180, 224–241, 1979.

[14] D. D. Clark, K. T. Pogran, and D. P. Reed, "An introduction to local-area networks," *Proc. IEEE*, vol. 66, pp. 1497–1517, 1978.

[15] J. H. Saltzer and K. T. Pogran, "A star-shaped ring network with high maintainability," *Comput. Networks*, vol. 4, pp. 239–244, 1980.

[16] "Systems network architecture, Technical overview, IBM Pub. GC 30-3073-1, 1985.

[17] "Local area networks token ring," Standard ECMA-89, Sept. 1983.

[18] "Token ring access method and physical layer specifications," ANSI/IEEE Standard 802.5, 1985.

[19] P. Zafiropulo, H. R. Müller, and F. Closs, "Data/voice integration based on the IEEE 802.5 token-ring LAN," in *Proc. 4th Annual European Fibre Optic Commun. and Local Area Networks Conf.*, Amsterdam, The Netherlands, June 25–27, 1986.

6

Transmission Design Criteria for a Synchronous Token Ring

HEINZ J. KELLER, HEINRICH MEYR, AND HANS R. MUELLER

This chapter discusses the transmission design criteria and limiting factors of an experimental synchronous token ring implemented at the IBM Zurich Research Laboratory. The following key aspects are addressed: 1) ring topology and wiring, 2) transmission, and 3) ring synchronization with phase-locked loops. Wiring of a ring is based on a two-level hierarchy with passive wiring concentrators placed at convenient locations in a building. Data are transmitted with differential Manchester code. Special emphasis is placed on the synchronization methods and on the parameters and tolerances which limit distance and number of stations that can be attached to a ring. An analysis of the behavior of a chain of repeaters under growing jitter is given. Also, the various procedures for guaranteeing high reliability are outlined. An experimental token ring has been running since 1981, and has been tested extensively under extreme jitter and noise conditions.

I. INTRODUCTION

This chapter describes the transmission system of a token ring local area network (LAN) implemented at the IBM Zurich Research Laboratory (for usage scenarios, see [1]–[3]).

A prototype token ring has been operational since 1981, and offers reliable data transmission at 4 Mbits/s. A detailed description of the architecture of the ring and its access protocol is given in [1]. A monitor function, active in one station, is responsible for token recovery. Any station adapter on the ring can replace the active monitor automatically should it become inoperational. For details, refer to [4].

The major goal of our effort was to achieve high reliability at all functional levels of the LAN.

In this chapter, we first discuss the ring-wiring structure and fault-isolation techniques by which inoperational stations and faulty cable sections can be automatically bypassed without affecting the operational parts of the system. Then, signal encoding and transmission media will be discussed with the objective of deriving an attenuation budget for cable selection. In the next section, station insertion into and removal from the ring will be discussed. Both actions are permitted at any time. The network will recover within a few milliseconds. Special attention will be given to ring synchronization and, in particular, the timing jitter. In this context, the timing jitter behavior of a long chain of repeaters will be analyzed to obtain figures for the maximum number of stations which can be supported by a single ring without the risk of synchronization failures. This limit will be related to various design parameters of the transmission system.

The following performance figures summarize experimental and theoretical results.

1) Our transmitter/receiver design and the cables selected tolerate a maximum distance of 700 m.

2) Proper design of phase-locked loop-synchronization circuits permits the support of up to 260 stations on a single ring.

3) Fast ring resynchronization within 4000 bit times can be achieved.

II. Ring-Wiring Structure

The wiring of a building to interconnect CPU's, workstations, displays, and other stations is a substantial expenditure for the data processing customer. A local area network must address these cost concerns and allow for systematic prewiring of a facility and for system growth.

Systematic prewiring of a facility with a common media should reduce or eliminate the expense of rewiring when a terminal is moved from one office location to another. Today's common practice is to run a new cable from the computer room to the office location where the new attachment is required, leading to crowded raceways and trays with unused and untraceable cables.

Two objectives must be considered when developing a wiring strategy. The first is to keep the total length of wire small to achieve low system installation cost and to minimize overall transmission distance. The second objective is to provide concentration points in the network to facilitate configuration and maintenance of the network. To keep wire lengths to a minimum, a pure serial interconnection of stations would be appropriate. However, the costs associated with installing, maintaining, and reconfiguring such a network would be intolerable. On the other hand, a purely star-radial wiring scheme, where all stations are cabled to a single concentration point, only solves the maintenance problem. It also requires a prohibitive amount of cable. A hybrid solution combining the key advantages of both approaches was chosen for our wiring strategy; see Fig. 1. A similar solution was proposed in [5].

The main-ring cable interconnects wiring concentrators placed at strategic locations in a building. They facilitate configuration and maintenance. In its simplest form, a wiring concentrator is a passive device containing switching elements which provide for bypassing of each lobe selectively. This lobe bypass function is remotely controlled by circuits in the ring adapter. A ring adapter contains all circuitry necessary to allow attached devices, as described above, to communicate over a ring network. Powering of the switching elements is achieved via phantom circuits [6]. A station is only connected to the ring via the wiring concentrator when the station is active. With this approach, the worst-case ring distance is given by twice the lobe length plus the main-ring length. Lobes can be tested by a station without being connected to the main ring (wrap test).

The use of ring-wiring concentrators to configure a network offers an additional level of availability. Faults in the lobe-wiring elements can be effectively isolated from the ring network since sensors in the ring adapter indicate a short or open-wire condition in the lobe [7].

Reconfiguration of the main ring is possible by use of an alternate ring that parallels the path of the principal ring through a (lobe bypass) wrap-around function. It may be

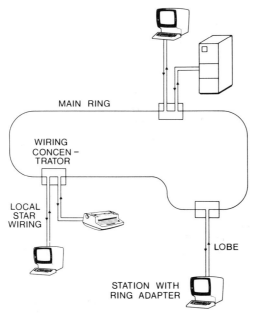

Fig. 1. Ring topology. © 1980 IEEE.

implemented with manual switches, automatic switching logic, or be command-initiated from a remote-control facility [8], [9].

III. TRANSMISSION

A. Coding and Equalization

The objective is to find a transmission scheme resulting in a simple and low cost transceiver design. Baseband technology exhibits the best potential to meet these goals.

Codes with two amplitude levels allow for the simplest transceiver circuit since they avoid adaptation to different attenuation and automatic gain control. The decision threshold can be made insensitive to input level variations. To achieve a simple timing recovery circuit at the receiver, codes with high transition density are preferable. Scramblers were ruled out to reduce cost and to simplify word synchronization.

A code without dc component is desired to allow for ac (transformer) coupling. An important requirement in a token ring is a small delay per station for coding and decoding to achieve high ring utilization. This makes word-organized block codes less attractive.

The above requirements leave us with two codes: the Manchester [10] and the Miller [11] codes. The latter was ruled out because it has a small dc component, which adds to signal distortion and jitter when ac coupling is used. The differential Manchester code, in particular, permits the interchange of wires of a twisted pair without leading to data errors. The maximum transmission distance employing a Manchester code can be improved at no substantial increase in hardware complexity if coarse equalization is implemented. Equalization compensates signal distortion by the cable manifested by intersymbol interference. Distortion reduces the signal amplitude at the receiver; it is also the main source of timing jitter which impairs ring synchronization. The latter effect will be discussed in Section VI. Two equalization methods were explored: 1) equalization by a fixed, two-tap transversal filter in the transmitter (predistortion) [10] and 2) nonlinear, signal amplitude-dependent equalization in the receiver. The basic idea behind the second method is that only small signals, attenuated by a long cable section, require equalization [12].

Comparing both approaches, we found that nonlinear equalization produces less jitter for small cable lengths, however, since it relies on the signal amplitudes it is sensitive to transmitter signal level variations, insertion losses of connectors, decoupling transformers, and switching elements in the wiring concentrators. Predistortion produces more power dissipation in the transmitter, but it is less sensitive to circuit tolerances.

B. Cable Characteristics

Four parameters determine the selection of transmission cables; crosstalk, attenuation, signal distortion, and susceptibility to EMI. The lobe cable, between a station and the wiring concentrator, is exposed to crosstalk. The transmitter signal couples into the receive-signal wire pair. This noise signal and cable attenuation limit the maximum distance between stations on the ring. Crosstalk can be minimized by providing additional shielding around each pair, and by combined twisting [13], [14]. This technique has proven to be successful in long-haul transmission systems, however, for in-house applications, the cables become two expensive and too bulky. In Section IV, it will be shown that low signal distortion, the third cable parameter mentioned above, is important for jitter reduction.

Symmetric media, such as shielded twisted-pair or twin-axial cables, are significantly less susceptible to electromagnetic interference (EMI) and electrostatic discharges (ESD) than conventional coaxial cables. For our prototype, therefore, we chose twisted-pair cables.

Cable attenuation in the MHz transmission range is mainly determined by skin effect, and is, therefore, proportional to the square root of the frequency [15], [16]. Table I shows a simplified transmission system attenuation budget with realistic margins for implementation losses and tolerances (values are based on 4 Mbit/s transmission). The extreme scenario is basically given with only one station (monitor) in the system. The attenuation

TABLE I

Minimum required signal level at receiver input (before equalizer) 50 mV peak sender level 2 V peak	− 32 dB
260 relays (multistation access unit)	5.2 dB
Wiring concentrator jumper cable attenuation (32 × 2.4 m)	2.5 dB
Cable connectors (32 wiring concentrators × 2)	3.2 dB
4 transformers	0.5 dB
Eye-pattern degradation (by delimiters)	1.0 dB
3 σ value for loss variations	2.0 dB
System margin	1.5 dB
	15.9 dB
Budget for cable attenuation (22 dB/km) corresponding to 700 m ring length	16.1 dB
	32 dB

budget plan is given in Table I. The budget plan must guarantee a minimum signal level of 50 mV at the receiver, or 25 mV after the equalizer stage (-6 dB) to allow for a worst-case of 10 mV hysteresis in the decision circuit. It must also guarantee a peak crosstalk of 10 mV, as well as a maximum clock offset of 24 ns, with respect to the center of the data-eye pattern, to allow for PLL imperfections and alignment jitter. The crosstalk signal is not attenuated by the equalizer since it has only high-frequency components. Extensive measurements showed that worst-case crosstalk does not grow in direct proportion to network complexity. Crosstalk is not time-varying in the manner of Gaussian noise, instead it has signal-dependent characteristics and a finite peak value. It is basically inversely proportional to the rise and fall times of the transmitted signal, hence, care must be taken to limit it. In the worst case, the crosstalk peak falls together with the data signal detection timing. 99.9 percent of all worst-case networks with 260 stations will have a 1.5 dB margin for aging and higher temperatures of the cable, without producing transmission errors. For a cable with 22 dB/km attenuation at 4 Mbits/s, a worst-case distance of 700 m can be supported, given by the main-ring length and twice the local lobe length, if no regenerators are used. Note that unidirectional transmission on a ring allows increasing of this distance by a simple repeater, preferably located in a wiring concentrator.

Sections of the main ring can be implemented with optical fibers. They are especially attractive since they avoid crosstalk and radiation, and are immune to noisy environments (e.g., elevator shafts) [18].

C. Transceiver Structure

The basic structure of the transceiver is shown in Fig. 2. It consists basically of four units: sender, receiver with energy detector, phase-locked loop (PLL), and control logic. The receiver provides amplification for the incoming signals. The energy detector indicates loss of energy. Energy outage will be indicated if the cable has a short/open, or if a station is inserted or removed. The sender is of the current-source type and is impedance matched to avoid reflections. The control logic controls station insertion/removal and the local-wrap (testing of lobe section) function. It also holds or freezes the PLL clock at its existing frequency during energy outages. The insert control and synchronization will be discussed further in the next subsection.

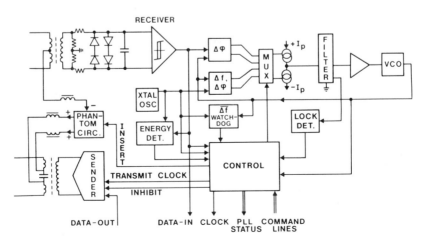

Fig. 2.   Transceiver structure.

The sender consists basically of a single current source fed positively or negatively to the transformer depending on the polarity of the signal element. To reduce crosstalk, the rise times are increased. The receiver consists of a low-pass filter and a high-speed comparator.

To determine an energy outage properly, a transition-count averager is used. The number of input transitions must reach at least 80 percent of the guaranteed bit transitions of the Manchester code. The data signal must exceed at least a certain threshold to ensure that noise causes no problem at small signal levels.

IV. SYNCHRONIZATION CONCEPT

A. Synchronization Methods

There are several methods to achieve synchronization on a ring. In a first possible solution, no master clock is provided [19]. A chain of phase-locked loops (PLL) operates at a frequency at which the ring cable propagation delay is an integer multiple of a bit time. Therefore, the exact bit rate of the system, stability, and synchronization time depend on the ring length.

In a second method, all stations use their own quartz oscillators for transmission and derive timing information for receiving with a phase-locked loop. The frequency differences between stations are compensated by inserting or deleting fill bits in the data stream. This is accomplished with an elastic buffer in each station holding a few bits. Bits will be inserted or deleted when the buffer tends to underflow or overflow, respectively [20].

A third approach uses a similar concept with two PLL's, one to receive and a second narrow-band PLL to transmit. The frequency of the latter PLL is changed, depending on the actual filling of the elastic buffer.

The elastic buffers required for each station in the latter two solutions increase ring latency. In systems with a large number of stations, this added delay considerably degrades delay-throughput performance [21].

In the fourth approach used in the token-ring, all the adopted standard stations are synchronized to a single master clock, which is provided by the ring adapter with the active monitor function [4]. As explained in [6], there is only one active monitor on the ring at any given time. However, any ring adapter can replace an inoperational monitor with all its functions including the master clock. In contrast to the above solutions, only one elastic buffer, also located in the active monitor, is necessary to compensate timing jitter introduced by a long chain of stations. The necessary length of the buffer, typically 10 bits, will be derived in Section VI. This approach has the advantage of smaller ring latency. Except for the active monitor, 2-bit delay in each ring adapter is sufficient.

B. Phase-Locked Loop Structure

The heart of the synchronization circuit is the phase-locked loop, Fig. 3, which extracts the timing information from the Manchester coded data.

To keep the jitter caused by intersymbol interference within limits, the bandwidth of the PLL must be kept small, namely, on the order of 1 percent of the data rate. Conventional PLL's have the disadvantage that reliable frequency acquisition is only possible within a narrow pull-in range, given approximately by the PLL bandwidth. With tolerances for temperature, voltage, capacitors, and resistors, the center frequency of the voltage-

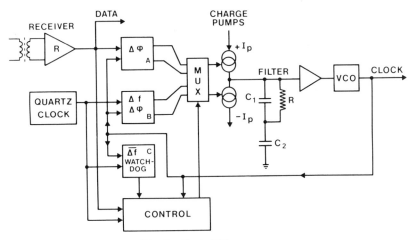

Fig. 3.   Basic PLL structure.

controlled oscillator (VCO) can deviate up to ± 20 percent from the reference clock given by the master oscillator in the active monitor. This frequency tolerance is much greater than the PLL's pull-in range. To guarantee fast and reliable frequency acquisition, we have added a frequency-sensitive detector to the conventional phase detector as shown in Fig. 3. With this circuit, the center frequency f_0 is already acquired with the aid of a local quartz oscillator before the station has been inserted into the ring. The frequency detector has a nonlinear characteristic and allows for fast frequency acquisition at startup and during automatic monitor (and master clock) replacement, see also Section IV-D. This method also has the great advantage of eliminating false-lock.

C. Phase Detector and Loop Filter Design

The phase detector must be designed with the objective of minimizing jitter. In Section VI we shall discuss the influence of PLL design parameters on jitter in detail.

The phase detector selected for our purposes is shown in Fig. 4. A sawtooth-edge-triggered phase detector is used: it is linear over a wide phase-error range. In our phase-detector implementation, a phase error is generated only for a positive data-signal transition. The phase-detector error signals are converted into analog pulses by means of current sources or "charge pumps." They can be built with a high degree of symmetry. Section VI-A shows that asymmetries create undesirable timing jitter. The loop filter in Fig. 3 is driven by a positive and a negative current pulse with a time difference between the positive and negative pulses proportional to the phase error. They give rise to transients in the voltage across the loop filter. In a second-order loop, these transients can easily be so large as to overload the VCO, thus creating a high amount of "frequency ripple"—an undesirable modulation of the voltage-controlled oscillator. An additional filter must, therefore, be added to reduce this ripple. The loop is then of order three. We used the filter configuration of Fig. 3 in our design. The filter function is

$$Z(s) = \frac{V(s)}{I(s)} = \frac{1 + s\tau_2\left(1 + \dfrac{1}{b}\right)}{sC_2(1 + s\tau_2/b)} \tag{1}$$

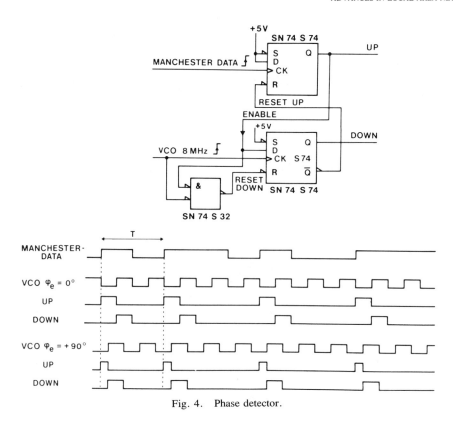

Fig. 4.   Phase detector.

with

$$\tau_2 = C_2 \cdot R \quad \text{and} \quad b = \frac{C_2}{C_1} . \tag{2}$$

An exact analysis of the charge-pump PLL has to take into account the time-varying nature of the circuit: the dynamic equations of the loop during the on-time of the charge pumps are different from those when the pumps are inactive. When the loop bandwidth is narrow enough with respect to the input frequency, an approximate analysis based on averaged response over a bit interval, time-continuous operation is permissible [22]. We start with an averaged response, time-continuous operation. The average current over a cycle of the input signal is

$$i_p = \frac{I_p \theta_e}{2\pi} \quad \theta_e = \text{phase error}$$

$$I_p = \text{charge-pump current}. \tag{3}$$

The loop filter of the PLL has an additional pole at $s = -b/\tau_2$, compared to a single-pole filter. The location of this pole must be chosen as a compromise between good frequency-ripple suppression and a small amount of "peaking." (A small maximum in the transfer function of the PLL equation (4) is called peaking.) The latter requirement is very important for jitter suppression in a large chain of repeaters [23], [24], Section VI. The closed-loop transfer function is found to be

$$H(x) = \frac{1 + j2\xi x \left(1 + \dfrac{1}{b}\right)}{1 - x^2 + j2\xi x \left(1 + \dfrac{1}{b} - \dfrac{x^2}{b}\right)} \qquad j = \sqrt{-1} \tag{4}$$

with $x = \omega/\omega_n$ where ω_n = natural frequency, ξ = damping factor, $b = C_2/C_1$. To compute ω_n and ξ, we have to take into account the probability for a phase-error event which depends on the code and the phase detector (Fig. 4).

The capacitor C_1 across the resistor R (see Fig. 3) smoothes the rectangular pulses into an exponential function for each pulse. Good frequency-ripple suppression requires a filter pole at the lowest possible frequency.

D. Clock Surveillance

As outlined in Section IV-A, the ring is synchronized to a master clock located in the active monitor. An active monitor failure leaves the ring without a master clock. The frequency of the remaining chain of PLL's will shift in an attempt to place an integer number of (half-) bits onto the ring. The potential frequency shift is largest for short ring lengths. Frequency shifts of ± 20 percent could be observed, whereas the pull-in range of the PLL is on the order of only 1 percent of the bit rate.

The clock frequency is supervised at each active station by the clock surveillance circuitry, also called "watchdog." Clock surveillance ensures that any excessive frequency shift, introduced by an active monitor failure or for any other reason, will automatically be corrected.

Detection of an average frequency shift of $\pm 0.3 \cdot B_L$ (B_L = loop bandwidth, $B_L = 80$ kHz in our prototype) initiates two corrective actions:

- monitor contention to establish a new monitor and master clock
- the PLL of the corresponding ring adapter is resynchronized to the local quartz oscillator by means of the frequency acquisition aid (Δf, $\Delta \varphi$) in Fig. 3.

The watchdog consists of a digital frequency difference detector with associated decision logic, and is insensitive to momentary frequency variations due to phase corrections.

E. Station Insertion/Removal

Station insertion into or removal from the ring can be executed at any time, and results in a temporary loss of synchronization. To allow fast resynchronization, we adopted a mechanism by which the phase-locked loops are slaved to a master clock located in the active monitor. Before a station can be inserted into the ring, the local lobe is tested in the wrap mode. After a successful test, the station activates an insert command to the ring adapter, which will initialize insert by impressing a dc current onto the local lobe (Fig. 2). Simultaneously, the sender of the inserting station is inhibited until the insert process has been completed. The current activates a relay in the wiring concentrator. To allow for sufficient relay settling time, the phase-locked loop is disabled for the first ms (in the prototype). After the 1 ms time interval, provided that energy is detected, phase synchronization starts and is accomplished in less than 40 μs provided no other resynchronization is in progress (for a PLL bandwidth of 1 percent of the bit rate). After 2 ms, given that phase-lock is achieved, the insert process is completed and the station inserted goes into the repeat mode, i.e., becomes a regenerative repeater.

Should acquisition not be achieved within 2 ms, due to a longer relay switch time, or some frequency deviation on the receive side due to a resynchronization process, caused by a simultaneous insert or remove event upstream, a time extension is granted. With termination of the insert process, the PLL is in the phase tracking mode and the frequency acquisition aid is disabled (see also the next section).

The station downstream of the inserting station senses this event by an energy outage, and disables the tracking mode of the PLL (''freeze''). From now on, its frequency acquisition aid is enabled to lock to the quartz clock of the station. This method ensures that the downstream link is operational after resynchronization. During minimum 3 ms freeze time, this station sends an idle pattern to ensure energy and synchronization. After the freeze period, normal operation is resumed given that energy is redetected.

Removal of a station requires no sequenced control; the downstream station will see an energy outage during relay switchover and also react with a freeze.

The introduction of active wiring concentrators with electronic control allows for the use of electronic gates instead of relays.

V. Analysis of Phase and Frequency Tracking

During insertion or removal of a station, the ring is inoperational for a few ms. Therefore, it is important to design the PLL to minimize the transient time required to correct phase variations and small frequency offsets. The latter can be caused by colliding insert/remove events of two neighbor stations or during active monitor replacement. Phase settling time is basically inversely proportional to the PLL bandwidth, therefore, one tends to make the PLL bandwidth B_L as large as possible, but this conflicts with increased jitter power (which is proportional to B_L). As a compromise we choose $B_L = 0.01 \cdot (1/T/2)$ where $1/T$ is the data rate (4 Mbits/s).

A. Phase Tracking

The phase of a repeater after insertion into the ring is completely arbitrary with respect to the downstream station since the latter was synchronized to its own quartz during freeze operation. Hence, if at time $t = 0$, repeater 1 is inserted, the next repeater sees a phase error $\Delta\theta$. The phase error

$$\varphi_K(t) = \theta_K(t) - \theta_{K-1}(t) \tag{5}$$

at the Kth repeater becomes (in the Laplace domain)

$$\varphi_K(s) = [H^K(s) - H^{K-1}(s)]\Delta\theta(s)$$

$$H(s) = \text{closed-loop transfer function.}$$

After some manipulation one finds (for first-order PLL's)

$$\frac{\varphi_K(t)}{\Delta\theta} = \frac{1}{(K-1)!} e^{-4B_L t}(4B_L t)^{K-1}: \qquad B_L = \frac{\omega_n \xi}{2} \qquad \omega_n: \text{ natural frequency.} \qquad (6)$$

The result is plotted for the increasing number of repeaters K in Fig. 5(a). Of particular interest is the time t_0 it takes until the phase error at the Kth PLL has decayed to 5 percent of a maximum phase step $\Delta\theta_{max} = 180°$ and the chain is again operational ($\varphi_K \leqslant 9°$). Figure 5(b) shows clearly that if the chain is equal to or longer than 65 repeaters, the phase error will never reach 5 percent after the 65th repeater. This corresponds to $B_L \cdot t_0 = 65$. The above analysis is highly simplified and breaks down for $K > 50$ at small ξ; see [25].

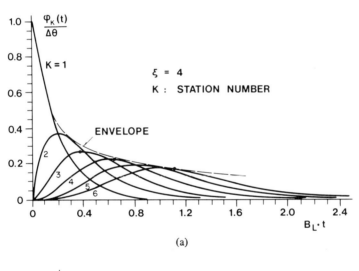

(a)

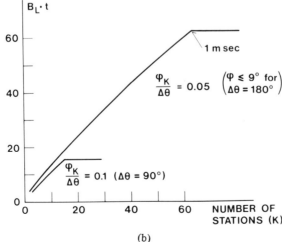

(b)

Fig. 5.   Phase tracking. (Fig. 6(a) © IFIP 1982).

B. Frequency Tracking

The phase error at the Kth repeater due to a frequency jump Δf is given by the following equation:

$$\varphi_K(t) = \frac{\pi}{2} \frac{\Delta f}{B_L} \left[e^{-B_L t/\xi^2} - e^{-4B_L t} \left(1 + 4B_L t + \cdots + \frac{(4B_L t)^{K-1}}{(K-1)!} \right) \right]. \qquad (7)$$

Equation (7) shows a strong dependence on the damping parameter ξ. The results are plotted in Fig. 6(a) and (b). The phase error φ_K has a maximum for $B_L t$ between 1 and 2, and then slowly diminishes, especially with large ξ. For a very large frequency jump $\Delta f = 0.5\, B_L$, the phase error will have decayed to $10°$ after 1 ms. Frequency jumps of this magnitude will only be experienced during monitor replacement. During normal insert/remove operations $\Delta f < 0.001 \cdot B_L$.

Figure 6(a) suggests choosing ξ as small as possible to achieve a small settling time of the phase error caused by a frequency jump. However, a large ξ is necessary for avoiding long oscillatory tails for $\varphi_K(t)$ [25].

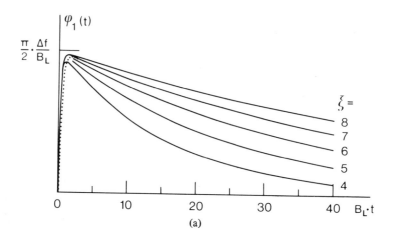

(a)

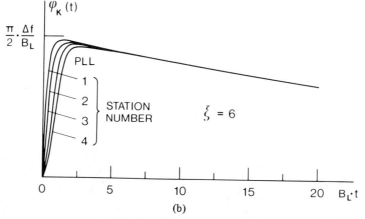

(b)

Fig. 6.   Frequency tracking.

VI. JITTER PERFORMANCE

A. Jitter Sources

In the basic mode of operation, the ring operates as a cascade of repeaters, with an elastic buffer at the end (active monitor) which compensates phase variations between the monitor quartz clock and the receive clock (see Fig. 7). The *accumulated jitter* at the end of the chain determines the elastic-buffer size. The elastic-buffer length must be chosen such that a probability of overflow is very small, in order to be negligible compared to errors caused by noise.

The alignment jitter is defined as the difference between the phase of the incoming signal and the phase of the recovered clock. It is responsible for potential synchronization failures called cycle slips. Since any cycle slip causes a burst of errors, the major design objective is to ensure that the probability of a cycle-slip event is much smaller than the probability of a bit error caused by additive noise. It is interesting to observe that for a very high signal-to-noise ratio, the transmission errors in a long chain of repeaters are almost solely caused by synchronization failures. This problem has been studied analytically and experimentally (see [27]).

The major contribution to jitter is caused by interpulse interference and PLL static phase offset; systematic jitter. Systematic refers to the fact that the same data pattern passes each repeater serially and the jitter generated by each cable section of the transmission path is the same (identical repeaters and cable sections are assumed). Therefore, systematic jitter accumulates from repeater to repeater.

Nonsystematic jitter is caused by PLL internal noise and additive noise at the repeater input. Experiments have revealed that PLL noise is small compared to systematic jitter. Since nonsystematic jitter is statistically independent from repeater to repeater, it accumulates much slower than systematic jitter. Based on the model of Fig. 7, the growth of systematic and nonsystematic jitter in a chain of repeaters can be computed (see, for example, [24]) for mathematical details. In Fig. 8, the variances $\sigma_{\theta N}^2$, $\sigma_{\varphi N}^2$, of both the accumulated jitter θ_N and the alignment jitter φ_N are plotted. Measurements by the authors

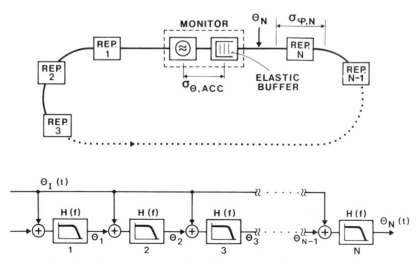

Fig. 7.   Chain of repeaters. Model for systematic jitter accumulation.

ACCUMULATED AND ALIGNMENT JITTER

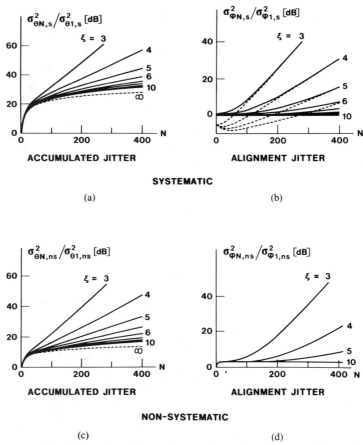

Fig. 8.   Growth of jitter variance with number of repeaters N.

on a chain of repeaters showed good agreement between theory and experiment; see [26]. The main parameter is the damping factor ξ. Nonsystematic accumulated jitter in a cascade of repeaters grows much slower with number of stations than the systematic jitter (-12 dB for 200 stations). Thus, it is well justified to neglect the nonsystematic accumulated jitter (see Fig. 8).

To compute the systematic-jitter power, we must know the basic jitter process. As mentioned above, two phenomena contribute to systematic jitter:

1) interpulse interference caused by signal distortion on the cable, and

2) static phase offset in the PLL can be caused by asymmetries of the charge pumps, VCO asymmetry, and leakage current.

The jitter contribution from a phase offset can dominate the first one. For conciseness, we omit a lengthy derivation and only present the final (approximate) expression for the normalized power spectral density of the jitter process at the frequency $f = 0$,

$$S(f=0) = \gamma_1 \bar{\varphi}^2 - \gamma_2 \bar{\varphi} + S_I. \tag{8}$$

Equation (8) is approximate in the sense that no exact model is available for the Manchester code and the particular phase detector used, to compute the coefficients γ accurately. For a lobe length of 300 m (assuming a cable attenuation of 22 dB/km at 4 MHz), γ_1 was experimentally determined to be approximately 0.13 and γ_2 is $1.3 \cdot 10^{-2}$. The maximum jitter power is obtained for a negative phase offset $\bar{\varphi}$.

S_I in (8) is the spectral power density of the jitter caused by intersymbol interference alone. Figure 9 shows power spectral density S_I versus *cable length* for predistorted signals and signals equalized at the receiver with a nonlinear equalizer. Nonlinear equalization reduces jitter. The improvement depends, however, on the transmitter signal level. Assuming a (relatively large) static phase offset of $\bar{\varphi} = 7$ percent ($25°$), we find that in (8)

$$\gamma_1 \bar{\varphi}^2 + \gamma_2 |\bar{\varphi}| \approx 2 S_I$$

which means that in this example, jitter by phase offset is considerably larger than jitter by intersymbol interference.

The variance $\sigma_{\theta 1}^2$ (after the first PLL) of the total systematic jitter caused by intersymbol interference and static phase offset is given by

$$\sigma_{\theta 1, \text{SYST}}^2 = 2 S \cdot B_L^1 \cdot (2\pi)^2 \ [\text{rad}^2] \tag{9}$$

where B_L^1 is the PLL bandwidth divided by twice the bit rate (8 MHz). The formula above is valid only when the spectrum is flat over the PLL bandwidth. The first two terms of (8) constitute a white noise process, whereas the third term S_I is due to intersymbol interference, and is not generally constant with frequency for well-equalized pulses. In our case with coarse equalization only, the spectrum can be assumed flat. This was verified by simulations and experiments.

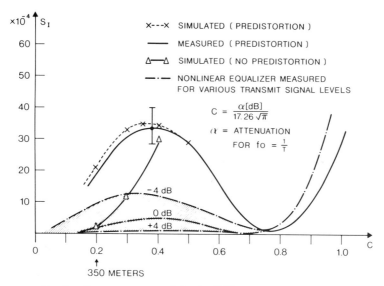

Fig. 9.   Jitter power spectral density $S_I(0)$ versus cable length.

B. Synchronization Failures

Large alignment jitter causes statistical, intermittent synchronization failures. Due to the statistical nature of the input phase to a PLL (caused by PLL phase offsets, intersymbol interference, and additive noise) the PLL can slip a cycle. This phenomenon was investigated in [27], [28]. Figure 8 shows that the systematic alignment jitter tends to grow along the chain of repeaters (after an initial decrease). The dotted line gives the result for a chain where all links produce exactly the same jitter. This is, of course, only the case when all links have exactly the same length and all PLL's have the same static offset. In order to account for variations, we have to take the worst case indicated by the nondotted lines. This result is obtained when neglecting the jitter source θ_I (Fig. 7) at the last repeater in a chain; thus, assuming

$$\varphi_N(s) = \theta_{N-1}(s)(H(s)-1) + \underbrace{\theta_I(s)H(s)}_{\text{neglected}}.$$

Figure 8 also shows the strong dependence of alignment jitter on the damping parameter ξ.

The normalized cycle-slip rate versus jitter power $\sigma_{\theta1}^2$ observed after the first repeater (see Fig. 7), and given by (9), is plotted in Fig. 10. To the left, we see theoretical and experimental results for a linear phase detector without noise and static phase offset. Since the latter two parameters are of utmost importance, experiments with noise and offset $\bar{\varphi}$ are included. The curve to the far right shows experimental results for a PLL with static phase offset $\bar{\varphi} = 8$ percent (30°) and additive noise ($S/N = 20$ dB).

Assuming a worst-case static phase offset $\bar{\varphi}$ of 7 percent, a spectral power density S_I of maximum 10^{-3}, and a PLL bandwidth of 80 kHz, we find from (8) and (9) that $\sigma_{\theta1}^2$ [dB] is -26 dB, see the vertical dotted line in Fig. 10. Thus, we see that an adequate margin is guaranteed. The results are based on a damping parameter $\xi \geqslant 6$.

The normalization of the cycle-slip rate is made with respect to four times the PLL

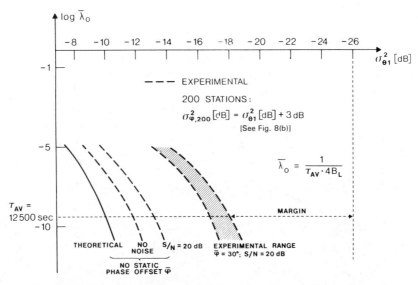

Fig. 10.   Mean cycle-slip interarrival time versus alignment jitter variance σ_φ^2.

bandwidth B_L which corresponds to $2\xi\omega_n$ [27]. The horizontal dotted line corresponds to our ring model operating at 4 Mbits/s, a PLL bandwidth of 80 kHz, an error probability $\leqslant 10^{-9}$, and a cycle-slip rate which is 100 times smaller than the error rate, resulting in a cycle-slip interarrival time of $\tau_{AV} = 12\ 500$ s. Since the cycle-slip rate is extremely sensitive to alignment jitter variations and phase offset, a safety margin of several dB should be provided in a realistic system. A static phase offset $\bar{\varphi}$ of $\leqslant 20°$ can be guaranteed for our design.

C. Optimization of Damping Parameter ξ

Accumulated jitter is compensated by an elastic buffer in the active monitor (Fig. 7). The size of this buffer depends on the amount of jitter, and will be discussed in Section VI-D. We have shown that the jitter growth depends strongly on the damping parameter ξ. The same is true, of course, for the alignment jitter. As a consequence, ξ has an influence on the cycle-slip rate and on the elastic-buffer size. Therefore, it is necessary to analyze the influence of PLL components on the damping parameter ξ. The variation of the damping parameter ξ with component tolerances is given by the expression

$$\left| \frac{\Delta\xi}{\xi} \right| = \left| \frac{\Delta R}{R} \right| + \frac{1}{2}\left(\left| \frac{\Delta k_0}{k_0} \right| + \left| \frac{\Delta I_p}{I_p} \right| + \left| \frac{\Delta C_2}{C_2} \right| \right) \qquad (10)$$

where k_0 is the VCO gain, R is the filter resistor (Fig. 4), I_p is the charge-pump current, and C_2 is the filter capacitor.

It is important to derive from (10) a lower tolerance limit for ξ for given component variations to obtain a bound for jitter growth (Fig. 8). Assuming that component tolerances (except R) are uniformly distributed over ± 20 percent of their nominal values, we find that 95 percent of all PLL's in a chain will still have $\xi \geqslant 0.8\xi_{nom}$ where ξ_{nom} is the nominal loop damping factor chosen without tolerances. Selecting ξ_{nom}, a compromise must be found between jitter build-up and phase/frequency tracking performance, Section V.

In Section IV-C, we mentioned that the PLL filter contains an additional capacitor (Fig. 3) parallel to the resistor R in order to reduce frequency ripple. The parameter $b = C_2/C_1$ must be chosen such that good frequency-ripple suppression is obtained, yet no significant additional peaking arises. Figure 11 shows accumulated and alignment jitter for a chain of 256 repeaters versus the damping parameter ξ, with b as parameter. We conclude that with $b \geqslant 2000$, a good compromise is found for $\xi_{nom} \geqslant 10$.

D. Elastic-Buffer Size

A formula was derived which gives the average interarrival time between overflow events as a function of accumulated jitter, buffer length, and PLL bandwidth B_L for random data patterns [26]. In the course of further investigations, it turned out that accumulated jitter caused by a repetitive data pattern is more critical. Bates [29] derived a formula which is given by

$$\phi_N = \{N + (N/2\xi)^2\}\phi_1$$

where N is the number of stations, ξ the damping parameter, and ϕ_1 = systematic phase

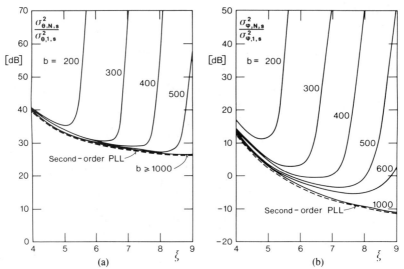

Fig. 11. Systematic jitter variance versus PLL damping parameter ξ, N = 256 stations.

excursion after a single station for the worst-case pattern change from $1111111 \cdots$ to $00000000 \cdots$, or vice versa.

The formula shows that in order to limit the jitter accumulation to a linear relationship with N, ξ must be chosen very large. In the final specification, ξ was chosen 25, N = 260, and the elastic buffer length is 12 bits.

VII. Conclusion

This chapter describes the implementation and performance of the transmission system of a token-passing local area network with ring topology. Stations can be inserted into and removed from the ring at any time. The system recovers from the short interruption by insertion/removal.

Differential Manchester code is used as the transmission format. An attenuation budget is presented which shows that the ring distance including one lobe can be approximately 700 m without the need of intermediate amplifiers. This is achieved with inexpensive shielded twisted-pair media. Data transmission is fully bit synchronous. The master clock is provided by that station in which the monitor function is active. Analysis and measurements of various sources of timing jitter have shown that 260 stations can be supported by one single ring without degradation of transmission system performance. This chapter describes design parameters of the phase-locked loop synchronization scheme, and their influence on timing jitter.

Timing jitter is compensated by an elastic buffer in the active monitor. The time between overflow/underflow of a buffer of given length is calculated as a function of the amount of jitter which has accumulated along the chain of repeaters.

In another test, more than one million station insertions/removals were made with extreme jitter and noise and with a large frequency offset of $0.2 \cdot B_L$ (where B_L = PLL bandwidth). As expected, the system always resynchronized. The synchronization and transmission concept described in this chapter has been adopted in the token-ring standard.

ACKNOWLEDGMENT

The authors are indebted to J. Hong and R. Bates (IBM–Raleigh) for their interest, feedback, and suggestions for improvement. Many thanks are also due to P. Dill for his continued support in experimentation, and to H. Thomas, for valuable support in analysis and computation.

REFERENCES

[1] W. Bux, F. Closs, P. A. Janson, K. Kümmerle, H. R. Müller, and E. H. Rothauser, "A local-area communication network based on a reliable token-ring system," in *Proc. IFIP TC 6th Int. In-Depth Symp. Local Comput. Networks,* Florence, Italy, 1982, pp. 69–82.

[2] R. C. Ravisio, G. Hopkins, and N. Naffah, Eds., *Local Computer Networks.* Amsterdam, The Netherlands: North-Holland, 1982.

[3] B. K. Penney and A. A. Baghdadj, "Survey of computer communications loop networks," *Comput. Commun.,* part I, vol. 2, Aug. 1979.

[4] W. Bux, F. Closs, K. Kümmerle, H. J. Keller, and H. R. Müller, "Architecture and design of a reliable token-ring network," *IEEE J. Select. Areas Commun.,* vol. SAC-1, pp. 756–765, Nov. 1983; see also this volume, ch. 5.

[5] J. R. Pierce, "How far can data loops go?," *IEEE Trans. Commun.,* vol. COM-20, pp. 527–530, June 1972.

[6] H. R. Müller, H. Keller, and H. Meyr, "Transmission in a synchronous token ring," in *Proc. IFIP TC 6th Int. In-Depth Symp. Local Comput. Networks,* Florence, Italy, 1982, pp. 125–149.

[7] "European Computer Manufacturers Association final draft on local-area networks (token ring) media access control layer," Dec. 1982.

[8] "IBM 8100 information system loop installation," in *Physical Planning Manual,* Ga-27-2878-0, File 8100-15.

[9] P. Zafiropulo, "Performance evaluation of reliability improvement techniques for single-loop communication systems," *IEEE Trans. Commun.,* vol. COM-22, pp. 742–751, June 1974.

[10] H. Meyr, H. R. Müller, U. Bapst, and H. Bouten, "Manchester coding with predistortion: An efficient and simple transmission technique in local digital ring networks," in *Proc. Nat. Telecommun. Conf.,* Houston, TX, 1980, pp. 65.4.1–65.4.7.

[11] R. H. Severt, "Encoding schemes support high-density digital data recording," *Comput. Design,* pp. 181–190, 1980.

[12] J. Hong, "Nonlinear equalizer," *IBM Disclosure Bulletin,* pp. 564–565, 1981.

[13] D. E. Setzer, "Low capacitance multipair cable for 6.3 megabit per sec transmission system," in *Proc. Int. Conf. Commun.,* 1972, pp. 19–19/19–23.

[14] K. Okamoto, H. Nods, and M. Onishi, "High-frequency crosstalk performance on Z-type shielded cable," in *Proc. Int. Conf. Commun.,* 1972, pp. 19–13/19–18.

[15] R. L. Wigington and N. S. Nahman, "Transient analysis of coaxial cables considering skin effect," in *Proc. IRE,* 1957, vol. 45, pp. 166–174.

[16] F. Braun, W. Steinlin, and H. Ryser, "Transmission in local digital loop communication," in *Zurich Seminar Digital Commun.,* Zurich, Switzerland, IEEE 78CH 1325-0, 1978, pp. C2.1–C2.6.

[17] H. Cravis and T. V. Craters, "Engineering of T1 carrier system repeated lines," *Bell Syst. Tech. J.,* vol. 42, pp. 481–482, 1963.

[18] P. Abramson and F. E. Nöel, "Local area network media," *Selection for Ring Topologies, Contribution to LAN Standards,* IBM Commun. Products Div., Raleigh, NC, 1982.

[19] M. V. Wilkes and D. J. Wheeler, "The Cambridge digital communications ring," in *Proc. Local-Area Commun.-Network Symp.,* Boston, MA, May 1979.

[20] IBM Series, "Local communications controller feature description," IBM Publ. GA34-0142, 3rd ed., 1982.

[21] W. Bux, "Local-area subnetworks: A performance comparison," *IEEE Trans. Commun.,* vol. COM-29, pp. 1465–1473, 1981; see also this volume, ch. 22.

[22] F. M. Gardner, "Charge-pump phase-lock loops," *IEEE Trans. Commun.,* vol. COM-28, Nov. 1980.

[23] D. L. Duttweiler, "The jitter performance of phase-locked loops extracting timing from baseband data waveforms," *Bell Syst. Tech. J.,* vol. 55, pp. 37–88, 1976.

[24] T. Schimamura and T. Eguchi, "An analysis of jitter accumulation in a chain of PLL timing recovery circuits," *IEEE Trans. Commun.,* vol. COM-25, pp. 1027–1032, Sept. 1977.

[25] E. Lutz and K. Tröndle, "Alignment in repeater chains with PLL," *Frequenz,* vol. 36, pp. 49–53, 1982.

[26] H. Keller and H. R. Müller, "Engineering aspects of token-ring design," in *Prints COMPINT,* Montreal, Canada, Sept. 1985, pp. 270–277.

[27] H. Meyr, L. Popken, H. Keller, and H. R. Müller, "Synchronization failures in a chain of repeaters," in *Conf. Rec. GLOBECOM,* Miami, FL, 1982, vol. 2, pp. 859–869.
[28] H. Meyr, L. Popken, and H. R. Müller, "Synchronization failures in a chain of repeaters," *IEEE Trans. Commun.,* vol. COM-34, p. 86, May 1986.
[29] R. J. S. Bates and L. A. Sauer, "Jitter accommodation in token-passing ring LAN's," *IBM J. Res. Develop.,* vol. 29, pp. 580–586, Nov. 1985.

7

SILK: An Implementation of a Buffer Insertion Ring

DANIEL E. HUBER, WALTER STEINLIN, AND PETER J. WILD

A LAN with ring/star topology is presented which is called SILK—system for integrated local communication (in German, "Kommunikation"). It was probably one of the first attempts to apply the distributed architecture of LAN's to voice communication as the primary service, today sometimes referred to as a fourth-generation PABX.

Sections of this chapter describe the synchronous transmission technique of the ring channel, the time-multiplexed access of eight ports at each node, the "braided" interconnection for bypassing defective nodes, and the role of interface transformation units and user interfaces, as well as some traffic characteristics and reliability aspects.

SILK's modularity, open system concept, and ability to serve different user groups are exemplified by implemented applications such as distributed data processing, PABX for telephony, telex and teletex, as well as process control.

I. INTRODUCTION

When surveys of LAN's [1] refer to the "buffer insertion" access method in ring topology networks, two early laboratory systems are sometimes mentioned. At the Research Laboratory of Hasler an experimental initial system using fixed length shift registers as insertion buffers was tested and the results were reported in 1974 [2]. At Ohio State University the "distributed loop computer network" (DLCN) was developed from 1975 onwards [3]. The subsequent development of SILK [4]–[10], "system for integrated local communication," with a considerably improved concept as compared to [2] aimed at service integration by using a LAN to replace conventional voice PABX's and to better serve the growing needs of on-site data communications with the same infrastructure. In order to fulfill these requirements, a ring with mesochronous baseband transmission was a good basis. However, the earlier experimental system [2] was improved as follows:

- higher ring transmission rate of approximately 17 Mbits/s [5],
- variable packet length of up to 16 bytes [6],
- removal of packets by the receiving node [6],
- multiaccess nodes with a resident monitor and up to seven user ports per node [6],
- multipacket insertion, reception, and transmission buffers dimensioned according to simulation results [6], [9],

- "braided" interconnection of nodes combined with sophisticated system supervision for higher availability [4], [10], and
- interface transformation units for different types of user interfaces [7], [9].

Details of these characteristics are presented in the following sections.

II. ARCHITECTURE

Normally a SILK ring is divided into several segments which are interconnected by repeaters to form a single unidirectional digital ring channel. Users have access to this channel only at repeater locations, which are the nodes of this LAN. On the ring, information is transferred in small packets which are transmitted in time-division multiplex. Packet switching is done by each node and thus is distributed. The only functions performed at one specific location are master clock generation, overall system supervision, and means for removing packets which are not removed elsewhere. These functions can be taken over by suitable standby nodes as explained in the section on braided interconnection.

The system can be considered to be divided into three hierarchical subsystems, the so-called "planes" (Fig. 1).

The lowest plane, called the transport plane, performs transmission and distribution of information. It represents the nucleus of every system realized with SILK. It is connected to the next higher plane, the connection plane, through a number of identical interfaces.

The connection plane consists of all devices that accomplish transformation between the identical interfaces of the transport plane and the various application-oriented interfaces,

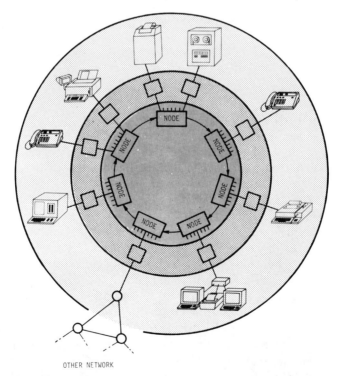

OTHER NETWORK

Fig. 1.   Hierarchical architecture of SILK. Transport, connection, and peripheral planes.

including gateways to other networks. This concept allows the integration of user groups with considerably different characteristics on the same system.

The peripheral plane, as the highest plane of this model, consists of terminal equipment such as communication terminals, servers, computers, and other networks attached to the connection plane.

III. TRANSPORT PLANE

Transmission

The nodes of the transport plane contain the circuitry for transmission and access to the ring (Fig. 2). The transmission sections between the nodes are of variable length with data regeneration and retiming in the nodes (Fig. 3). A serial bit stream is transmitted at a bit rate of 16.896 Mbits/s, which is an integer multiple of the commonly used data rates and a European PCM multiplex standard.

The design target of less than 10^{-9} bit error rate for each ring transmission section has been reached. The main sources of errors are impulsive noise and timing jitter in large systems. Signal levels will normally be far above any continuous noise levels.

Manchester coding is used for transmission [5]. Neither system architecture nor access strategy impose any restraint on the choice of a transmission medium and its propagation delay. In contrast to LAN's with CSMA/CD techniques, network size depends on attenuation and dispersion considerations only. The presently used nodes contain circuitry for baseband transmission with 75 Ω coaxial cable. To keep drivers and receivers simple, no equalizers are used. Transmission distance between the nodes is dispersion-limited with a cable parameter of $c = 0.5$ [5]. This corresponds to an attenuation of 15.4 dB at 17 MHz. With reasonable cable diameter a single section is therefore limited to approximately 500 m.

An add-on unit employing inexpensive optical modules (LED transmitter, p-i-n diode receiver) can extend the section length to 2000 m. With graded-index fibers, sections are limited by attenuation only. Transmitters using laser diodes would allow even greater distances.

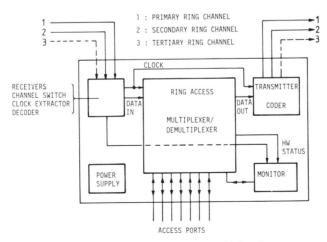

Fig. 2.   Block diagram of a node with multiplexed access.

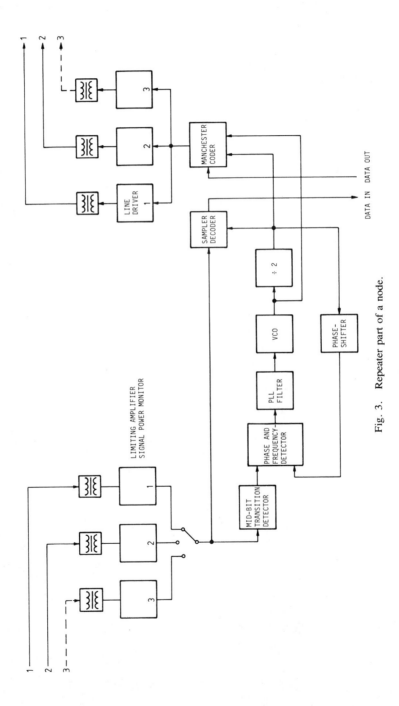

Fig. 3. Repeater part of a node.

Transmission around the ring is synchronous. A quartz oscillator in a special node, the so-called master clock node, generates the master clock. PLL's in subsequent nodes extract timing information from the incoming Manchester-coded bit stream, thus forming a chain. Second-order PLL's with PI loop filters are used. With a narrow relative bandwidth of 10^{-3} the probability of timing errors due to electromagnetic interference is kept low.

In order to use inexpensive wide-tolerance voltage-controlled oscillators (VCO) in this narrow-band PLL, a frequency acquisition aid has been incorporated [11]. A simple phase and frequency detector is used (Fig. 4). If the loop is unlocked its output voltage $V_{PF}(t)$ has an appropriate bias $\overline{V_{PF}}$ to make the loop integrator slew the VCO frequency f_2 towards the data frequency f_1. After frequency acquisition the detector behaves much like a linear phase detector, without disabling the acquisition aid. For reasons of noise performance of the PLL in lock, the frequency slewing rate is deliberately kept small. A single PLL and also the entire ring lock within less than 410 ms. This is sufficiently short since the ring stays locked under normal operating conditions. PLL frequency drift without input signal has been made very small by freezing the loop integrator upon signal loss detection. In case of a ring interruption, sections following the defective location up to the master clock node stay locked for at least 2 s, which still allows the sending of diagnostic messages.

A special problem is jitter accumulation along the chain of PLL's as known for PCM repeaters [12] and other ring systems [13] but with the added difficulty of varying delay in the nodes due to the buffer insertion technique. Using narrow-band media such as coaxial cables, jitter is mainly due to intersymbol interference and is therefore systematic, i.e., the jitter sources are correlated [12]. The power spectrum of the jitter sources is application-dependent and may even contain low-frequency discrete lines. Relevant timing parameters are the accumulated jitter ϕ_k (phase variation of the output of the kth PLL relative to master clock) and alignment jitter $\Delta\phi_k = \phi_k - \phi_{k-1}$.

The accumulated jitter, as well as the fraction of the ring delay which is not an integer multiple of a bit period, are compensated for in the master clock node. This compensation is not the limiting factor for system size.

Alignment jitter determines sampling at the receiver and the modulation of the phase detector of its PLL. Excessive jitter with $|\Delta\phi_k(t)| > \pi/2$ will first cause sampling errors

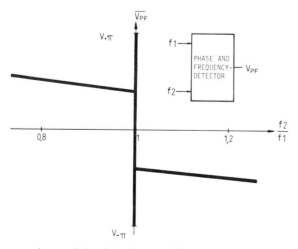

Fig. 4. Frequency characteristic of the phase and frequency detector. $V_{\pm\pi}:V_{PF}$ for $f_1 = f_2$ and a phase difference of $\pm\pi$ between the inputs.

and ultimately cycle slips. The variances of both the accumulated and the alignment jitter of the PLL's increase along a chain of repeaters [12]. Delay due to the insertion buffers may cause considerable additional amplification of certain jitter frequencies. Figure 5 depicts this effect.

A comprehensive analysis of the system limits due to timing errors has to consider the variable delay in the nodes as well as different data patterns and lengths of the individual ring sections. The simplified and pessimistic upper bound of Fig. 5, assuming $c = 0.3$, would limit the system to 150 sections for worst-case periodic data ($\sigma_{\phi j} = 5.2°$). For practical purposes a few hundred sections are reasonable.

The above considerations determined the PLL design: a high damping factor of 7 and a relatively small bandwidth tolerance of ± 6 percent reduce peaking of the alignment jitter transfer function, while the narrow relative bandwidth confines the possible spectrum of amplified jitter.

Data Structure

Data are processed in the nodes byte by byte. Each node periodically transmits a pair of synchronization bytes to which the next node synchronizes. Synchronization is performed independently on each ring section, which prevents propagation of byte-synchronization errors.

Four types of bytes exist in the transport plane:
- the already mentioned synchronization bytes, characterized by a unique bit sequence,
- header bytes containing packet format and control information,
- empty bytes containing no information but a special bit pattern that causes a minimum of jitter, and
- information bytes, whereof 7 bits contain addresses or user information.

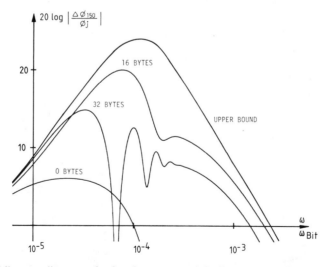

Fig. 5. Alignment jitter transfer functions computed for the case of 150 nodes. Simplified model with identical jitter excitation and insertion buffer filling for all sections. The upper bound assumes worst-case buffer filling for each node. ϕ_j: amplitude of jitter excitation of one section. $\Delta\phi_{150}$: amplitude of alignment jitter of the 150th node. Parameter: insertion buffer filling.

Packets on the ring consist of one header byte and information bytes and are of variable length so that transmission capacity is used optimally. Packet length is restricted to 16 bytes in order to allow real-time applications requiring short transmission delays. For telephone communication, packets of 8 bytes containing four PCM samples are used [Fig. 6(c)].

Packets are either broadcast to all users or sent to a particular physical address. The system strictly distinguishes the logical from the physical address so that users can be reached anywhere on the system as follows. Setting up a virtual circuit requires the exchange of the physical addresses of the participating users. Therefore, a caller sends a broadcast packet [Fig. 6(a)] containing the logical address of the called user (5 bytes) and his own physical return address (2 bytes for node and access port). Upon recognition of his logical address, the called user sends back an addressed packet (total of 10 bytes) to the caller containing his physical return address, thus establishing a virtual circuit between two particular access ports. The subsequent packets contain 3 bytes of overhead (header + physical address) and up to 13 bytes of information [Fig. 6(b)].

Access Scheme and Its Implementation

In addition to its repeater function, each node allows access of up to seven local users to the ring. As an eighth participant each node has its own monitor. Buffer insertion is used as the access strategy [2], [3]. In contrast to an earlier laboratory implementation using a shift register of fixed length [2], a FIFO buffer temporarily stores the incoming ring traffic in order to allow a local user to transmit a packet onto the ring. This strategy normally gives local users priority over ring traffic. In practice the insertion buffer is of limited capacity. To prevent packet loss on the ring, ring traffic is given priority as soon as the insertion buffer fills up. The filling of the insertion buffer can be reduced when empty or synchronization bytes between packets arrive on the ring channel or when packets are removed from the ring because they are addressed to this node.

Access to the ring involves three buffers (Fig. 7). As the node has to perform speed conversion as well as multiplexing and demultiplexing of user traffic, buffer memory is necessary in both the transmitting and receiving data paths.

An analytical model based on Markov chains [6] has shown that mean packet delay and packet loss probability in the transport plane depend on the sum of insertion and

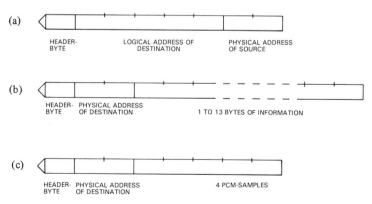

Fig. 6. Examples of packet formats. (a) Broadcast packet for establishing a virtual circuit. (b) Addressed data packet. (c) Addressed voice packet.

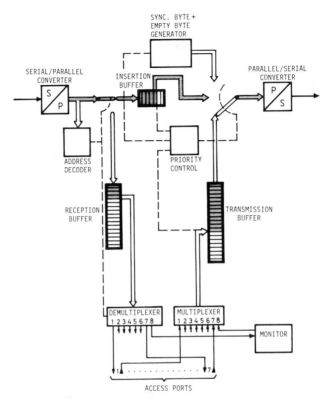

Fig. 7.   Access part of a node. Buffer insertion with priority switching.

transmission buffer capacity only (in this context, packet loss probability means the probability that a packet from a local user finds the transmission buffer already filled up). These results have been verified by computer simulations.

To keep the delay of ring traffic at a minimum in nodes with heavy traffic from the connection plane, the minimal capacity of the insertion buffer is chosen. It has to be able to store two full-sized packets of 16 bytes each. This FIFO buffer of 32 byte capacity can dynamically handle individual bytes.

Transmission and reception buffers are shared by all eight ports of a node. In contrast to the insertion buffer, they consist of blocks of 16 bytes each, which are dynamically assigned to users on request. The size of the transmission buffer has been chosen according to simulation results to be 32 blocks, an average of four blocks for each port. The size of the reception buffer is 16 blocks, which represents the minimal size.

The following behavior is observed. If there is no traffic from the connection plane to be sent onto the ring, the insertion buffer is empty. An average time interval of $1\frac{1}{2}$ bytes is needed for serial/parallel and parallel/serial conversion as well as byte synchronization. The time used for header or address decoding and temporary buffering of the incoming data is 2 bytes, which is necessary for the deletion of truncated packets as explained below. As a consequence, a minimal mean traffic delay of $3\frac{1}{2}$ bytes/node, i.e., 1.6 μs is required. When traffic from the connection plane increases, the insertion buffer can cause an additional packet delay to the incoming ring traffic. A maximum is reached when priority should be switched to ring traffic due to a half-filled insertion buffer, but the transmission buffer has just started transmitting a full-sized packet. The insertion buffer can be filled with up to 32 bytes, which determines the maximal delay of 35.5 bytes or 16.8 μs/node.

However, it has to be considered that the transmission time of a full-sized packet from a node to an interface transformation unit or vice versa is approximately 500 μs. The transmission between the interface transformation unit and the terminal equipment normally is even slower. For a virtual circuit under normal load conditions, this transmission time of more than 2×500 μs is much longer than the packet delay caused by the ring channel.

The header byte, possibly in conjunction with an address, defines whether a packet has to be removed from the ring channel at a specific node.

A particular bit of the header byte serves as a label which indicates whether a packet has passed the master clock node. If this label is true, the master clock node deletes the packet. Broadcast packets are only transferred to the access ports after this label has been set, i.e., after the first pass through the master clock node. They are removed at the second pass. This procedure ensures that broadcast packets reach each access port only once.

Another bit of the header byte indicates whether a packet contains a physical address. In this case the first two bytes after the header are interpreted as node and access port address. Addressed packets are removed from the ring channel at their destination. Up to the third byte it is unknown if an addressed packet has to be sent to a local port or forwarded on the ring. Therefore, it is possible that truncated packets are sent to the next node when transmission and insertion buffers are empty and the packet is addressed to a local port. These packet fragments are deleted at the following nodes without causing delay of any other packet.

The discussed procedures for removing regular packets are also effective in deleting packets that are corrupted by transient failures. Header bytes that are no longer recognizable as headers or headers with an erroneously reset label are taken care of in such a manner that no packet circulates more than twice.

In contrast to some other implementations of ring topology LAN's, there is no need for central regeneration of a control entity.

In case of node overload, the insertion buffer fills up first. Then ring traffic gets priority and the transmission buffer begins to fill up. Therefore, a node becomes overloaded if its transmission buffer overflows. As a consequence, overload occurs at individual nodes only. If a particular node is overloaded, the rest of the system still works as usual. In particular it is not possible that a single user can overload and paralyze the whole system by defective transmission of random data. Packet loss might occur, but only to users connected to the overloaded node.

To avoid packet loss due to overload, the node generates a busy signal when it can receive just one more packet from each local port. This busy signal is transmitted to all local users allowing packet flow control.

A hardware status word is generated in each node. It can be polled by a central supervisory terminal. Error events between polls are recorded by the monitor in the node.

Braided Interconnection

Common to most systems with ring or loop topology is their problematic reliability due to chaining of active repeaters. Several countermeasures have been proposed in the literature [1], e.g., bypassing of repeaters by relays [14], doubling of the ring channel [1],

[15], [16], or skipping of repeaters and ring sections by means of bypass transmission sections [4], [9], [10].

The braided structure of Fig. 8 has been chosen. A primary channel connects all nodes to form a ring. Each node is bypassed by a so-called secondary section. The secondary section that bypasses the master clock node contains a standby master clock node. Tertiary sections may be used as an option to protect the system against failures affecting groups of subsequent nodes such as power supply interruption in parts of a building.

Braid switching is under distributed control. All ring transmission sections originating at a given node carry the same signal. The monitor of the master clock node sends unaddressed test packets to all monitors, which therefore are able to measure the bit error rate of this test traffic. Depending on the results, switching to another transmission section is initiated. A special protocol prevents unintentional switching of subsequent nodes downstream. Switching causes an alarm which is indicated on a central alarm unit.

Another alarm is indicated if the bit error rate is higher than a preset level (typically 3 ×

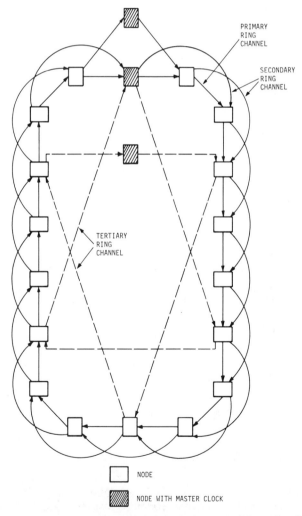

Fig. 8.   Braided interconnection of nodes to enhance ring channel availability.

10^{-6}). There is even a scheme to supervise proper operation of the node monitors. Total traffic load on the ring generated by these monitoring functions is about 20 kbits/s, a small fraction of 17 Mbits/s.

Hardware of the Nodes

Each node is contained in a unit that fits into a 19 in. rack. The housing measures 178 × 482 × 230 mm (Fig. 9). No forced-air cooling is required due to a sophisticated thermal concept based on thermal conduction. Extensive use is made of thick-film hybrid technology employing 4 × 4 in. substrates and automatic laser trimming. Different IC families are used depending on subsystem requirements. The high-speed bit stream is processed by ECL logic. To reduce chip count, LSI semicustom circuits are used.

IV. CONNECTION PLANE

The connection plane includes all equipment that translates the SILK-specific interface of the transport plane to the interfaces used in applications. Only a subset of the various characteristics of the transport plane interface is used for a given application. Therefore, the overall system characteristics are application-dependent and can be chosen accordingly. That is why different user requirements for file transfer, process control, or voice communication can be met on the same system.

At the interface to the transport plane, traffic is handled at a maximal data rate of 256 kbits/s with packets of variable length.

It is possible to supply power for connection plane devices from the node (e.g., for telephone handsets). However, data interface units are normally ac-coupled to prevent ground loops.

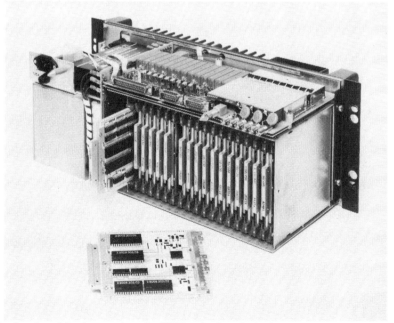

Fig. 9.   Actual implementation of a SILK node. Board with hybrid thick-film technology.

The interface transformation units contain microprocessors. As the hardware between transport plane interface and microprocessor bus is always identical, semicustom IC's are used.

An interface transformation unit always has a logical address assigned to it which remains unchanged when the unit is moved to another access port.

It was an important design goal to provide internationally standardized interfaces. The CCITT interface X.21 has been implemented for synchronous duplex traffic of up to 48 kbits/s or half-duplex operation up to 96 kbits/s. As many as 220 duplex links with 48 kbit/s data rate can be handled concurrently by the system.

For V.24/V.28 (RS 232) interfaces a front-end multiplexer with eight ports each has been made available. To make better use of the available bandwidth of node access ports and reduce cost per line, such multiplexers are used wherever a cluster of terminal equipment with V.24 interfaces is to be connected to SILK.

Physical integration of an interface transformation unit and the associated terminal equipment is possible as well. For a prototype system, a digital telephone handset has been developed which connects directly to the transport plane interface of a node [17]. Assuming no concurrent data traffic, 120 simultaneous telephone calls are possible on a single ring so that systems of more than a thousand subscribers (at 0.1 Erlang) are technically feasible.

Length and variation of delay for PCM samples is an important consideration for voice communications, especially for communication channels which include a satellite link or a long-haul international connection. As SILK does not provide isochronous channels similar to "slotted" rings, but is based on packet switching with variable packet delay according to traffic load, calculations have been carried out to determine delay by analysis and simulation.

The maximum packet jitter did not exceed approximately 500 bytes, i.e., approximately 250 μs assuming a system with 140 nodes and 980 subscribers, where 2×120 were chosen to be active (full-duplex 64 kbit/s channels). This corresponds to a load close to the maximum of 125 voice channels [6].

At a receiving telephone handset, PCM samples arrive in groups of four. If samples are not available on time as determined by the local 8 kHz sampling rate, the previous value is kept unchanged. With this method the loss of several subsequent PCM samples is not audible.

V. SYSTEM ASPECTS

Traffic Characteristics

Traffic characteristics of SILK are mainly influenced by variable filling and byte-wise organization of the insertion buffer. In particular, gaps between packets of the incoming data stream can be either closed or extended to insert packets from local users in order to efficiently use the common ring channel farther downstream.

Compared to other ring access schemes that remove packets at the transmitting node, average throughput is improved by a factor of two as addressed packets are already removed by the receiving node (destination removal). This has been taken into account for a full-duplex voice communication traffic analysis [6] assuming a packet pair occupying the whole ring during one packet transmission interval.

Another favorable characteristic of SILK is its flexible adaptation to varying traffic loads. Under low-load traffic conditions, overall packet delay is on the order of 1 ms, determined mainly by the transmission times on the 256 kbit/s interfaces between the transport and connection plane. Even under high-load conditions near the limit of system capacity, the user priority scheme allows fast access to the ring channel which behaves like a delay line with a delay that is artificially increased by the insertion buffers. As a consequence, a variable number of packets can be accommodated on the ring. Even close to the limit for continuous traffic, additional short-term load can be handled. This is in contrast to "slotted" rings, where the number of simultaneously circulating packets is mainly determined by cable propagation and, therefore, is constant.

Analysis and simulation results of the performance of the SILK transport plane are given in [6].

Major throughput limitations of implemented SILK systems are imposed by microprocessors and their software in sophisticated interface transformation units and in gateways to other networks. For the applications served by SILK so far, the performance of these units together with the characteristics of user terminals are the decisive factors of system throughput. Delay caused by buffers in the nodes can nearly be neglected when put into relation with the above-mentioned limitations.

Reliability and Maintenance

Availability is improved by the braided interconnection of ring sections. Localization and isolation of faults are performed automatically by the monitors as described above.

Alarm messages generated in the monitors of each node are displayed at the master clock node. In addition, a special supervisory terminal can be connected to any node of the system. This allows system supervision, initiation of additional tests, and manual control of reconfigurations of the braid. Messages generated automatically or upon request report system status and defects, so that preventive maintenance can be done. This supervisory terminal is optional. Small systems with few nodes do not require such a terminal.

As a result of the high system modularity, maintenance can be carried out by replacing faulty system units. Moreover, the braided system allows system expansion (such as introduction of additional nodes) without interrupting ring traffic.

Special consideration has been given to electromagnetic compatibility (EMC). The nodes are systematically shielded. All input and output lines are filtered. Transformer coupling is used in all transmission sections throughout the system. A special design using a proprietary shielding technique provides a common-mode transient immunity of 40 kV/μs [18]. During extended tests, external static discharges of up to 16 kV had no influence. Due to ac-coupling the system is insensitive to low-frequency potential differences.

To reduce maintenance to a minimum, no moving parts were used throughout the whole system. No forced-air cooling is required up to ambient temperatures of 50°C. To prevent damage, the internal temperature of the nodes is supervised and the nodes are switched off in case of overtemperature. Short power supply interruptions of approximately 100 ms duration do not affect operation.

Modularity

SILK was designed to accommodate a range of applications and system sizes. The smallest configuration consists of one master clock node with its ring output connected to the ring input. Up to seven users can be connected to a single node. The transport plane interface allows a distance of up to 300 m between a node and its remote interface transformation unit, depending on the cable used. A single node with its attached peripheral devices is a cluster configuration with star topology. Since there is no need for a supervisory terminal or any other type of additional network administrator, such a minimal configuration can be an interesting LAN solution by itself.

A network can grow by adding nodes with seven external access ports each. No modifications of the already installed equipment are required. In small systems with a few nodes only, it might not be necessary to have a braided ring interconnection.

Using the same system units, very large networks with over a thousand access ports in one ring can also be realized. Identical interfaces to all access ports are another reason for the high flexibility that allows easy configuration of such systems.

Due to the distributed monitoring and automatic braid reconfiguration technique with central indication and message recording for maintenance personnel, such large systems remain manageable.

VI. APPLICATIONS

Distributed Text Editing

A system with 33 nodes has been installed at a German broadcasting station [7]–[9]. It spans a distance of nearly 3 km and carries out transfers of text files between text editing workstations, data banks, and special communication processors that are linked to press agencies. External information exchange of the system is about three million characters per day. Internal traffic is much higher. On-site communications are carried out over synchronous 96 kbit/s half-duplex channels. They have circuit-switching characteristics. Interfaces conform to CCITT Standard X.21.

Process Control

A process control system has been installed in a large studio of an important German television network [9]. It includes 67 nodes and allows, among other tasks, remote computer control of complex technical studio equipment such as video tape recorders and film scanners. A reaction time of less than 20 ms (i.e., one video half-frame) is required in order to synchronize different video sources for ''live'' transmission of a television program. Communications are based on HDLC frames that are transmitted at a rate of 48 kbits/s across X.21 duplex interfaces. As every HDLC frame carries its destination address, it represents a datagram. This means that the terminal equipment has a multiplex connection to the SILK system. Such a requirement exists because some of the processors have to control more than one video source at the same time. Furthermore, a message containing the current time of day has to be distributed on the entire system every 40 ms. This problem has been solved with a broadcast type of packet. Besides excellent real-time performance, reliability, and availability are of major importance since television broadcasting quality depends heavily on the proper operation of the system, which has been in continuous use since 1984.

Local Teletex Exchange

In another type of application SILK is used as a private automatic branch exchange for teletex, a CCITT-defined public service. Message transfer is memory-to-memory at

2400 bits/s. The first implementation of such a teletex exchange with SILK is intended for countries which use a circuit-switched public data network and X.21 interfaces. An X.21 gateway is used to connect to the public network. Gateways can be operated in parallel to enhance throughput. Software facilities already developed for voice communications such as "group call" or "transfer on busy" have been adapted for this purpose. In order to allow local communications between teletex terminals, addressing with an alphanumeric prefix is necessary to differentiate internal and external calls. Prefixes for addresses are also used for calls to other SILK rings that are connected via internet gateways.

Integrated Services

Recent applications are characterized by more than one user group on a given SILK system. Combinations of distributed data processing configurations, word processor equipment, and data PABX's were integrated as separate closed user groups on a common system. Important advantages of LAN-type solutions in typical terminal/host environments are the concentrator function to make better use of a limited number of host ports and the improved connectability allowing access to different hosts from the same terminal.

The original intention of using SILK primarily as a voice PABX was abandoned due to the high cost of the technology employed at the time.

VII. CONCLUSION

It has been shown that ring topology LAN's characterized by a buffer insertion access technique have found practical application in various systems with demanding requirements. Very short delays in the active repeater and access nodes are not decisive for real-time performance, as shown by the process control tasks solved with SILK.

Braided interconnection with automatic bypassing of faulty ring transmission sections is a useful concept for maintaining high availability of the system.

The capability of using fiber-optic links between nodes, where required, and of operating at higher data rates is shared with other ring systems.

ACKNOWLEDGMENT

The authors wish to thank the many co-workers who contributed to this project. In particular they acknowledge valuable comments by Dr. F. Braun (especially for contributing the results of Fig. 5), J. Clavadetscher, and H. Ryser.

REFERENCES

[1] B. K. Penney and A. A. Baghdadi, "Survey of computer communications loop networks," *Comput. Commun.*, vol. 2, pp. 165–180, Aug. 1979, and pp. 224–241, Oct. 1979.
[2] E. R. Hafner, Z. Nenadal, and M. Tschanz, "A digital loop communication system," *IEEE Trans. Commun.*, vol. COM-22, pp. 877–881, June 1974.
[3] M. T. Liu, *Distributed Loop Computer Network* (Advances in Computing, vol. 17). New York: Academic, 1978.
[4] E. R. Hafner and Z. Nenadal, "Enhancing the availability of a loop system by meshing," in *Proc. Int. Zurich Sem. Digital Commun.*, Zurich, Switzerland, 1976, pp. D 4.1–D 4.5.
[5] F. G. Braun, W. Steinlin, and H. Ryser, "Transmission in local digital loop communication," in *Proc. Int. Zurich Sem. Digital Commun.*, Zurich, Switzerland, 1978, pp. C 2.1–C 2.6.
[6] F. G. Braun, E. R. Hafner, and E. Schultze, "System and traffic aspects in SILK: System for integrated local communications," in *Nat. Telecommun. Conf. Rec.*, 1980, vol. 3, pp. 65.1.1–65.1.6.

[7] I. Reibert, "IDA: A local digital information system for communication and data exchange in a German broadcasting station," in *Nat. Telecommun. Conf. Rec.,* 1980, vol. 3, pp. 65.2.1–65.2.5.

[8] W. Hack, W. Schott, and H. Schneeberger, "Software aspects of IDA: Principles and implementation," in *Nat. Telecommun. Conf. Rec.,* 1980, vol. 3, pp. 65.3.1–65.3.5.

[9] Special Issue on SILK, *Hasler Rev.,* vol. 14, no. 1, pp. 1–40, 1981.

[10] F. G. Braun, "Zuverlässigkeit von lokalen Kommunikationsnetzen," presented at Telecom 82 Deutschland, Köln, Germany, Oct. 27–29, 1982, Kongressdokumentation Bd 2, Workshopreihe D2, Seite 52–60.

[11] W. Steinlin, European Patent 60862.

[12] T. Shimamura and I. Eguchi, "An analysis of jitter accumulation in a chain of PLL timing recovery circuits," *IEEE Trans. Commun.,* vol. COM-25, pp. 1027–1032, Sept. 1977.

[13] H. R. Müller, H. Keller, and H. Meyr, "Transmission in a synchronous token ring," in *Proc. IFIP TC 6 Int. In-Depth Symp. Local Comput. Networks,* Florence, Italy, Apr. 19–21, 1982, pp. 125–147.

[14] W. Bux, F. Closs, P. A. Janson, K. Kümmerle, H. R. Müller, and E. H. Rothauser, "A local-area communication network based on a reliable token-ring system," in *Proc. IFIP TC 6 Int. In-Depth Symp. Local Comput. Networks,* Florence, Italy, Apr. 19–21, 1982, pp. 69–82.

[15] "Metropolitan area network, backbone ring," Draft Proposed IEEE Standard 802.6.

[16] "Fiber distributed data interface," Draft Proposed American Standard ASC X3T9.5.

[17] H. J. Matt and K. Fussgänger, "Integrated broad-band communication using optical networks—Results of an experimental study," *IEEE Trans. Commun.,* vol. COM-29, pp. 868–886, June 1981.

[18] H. Ryser, U.S. Patent 4342976, Aug. 1982.

8
Design and Use of an Integrated Cambridge Ring

ANDREW HOPPER AND ROBIN C. WILLIAMSON

The Cambridge ring is a local area network used both in universities and industry. It is based on the empty slot principle and data are transmitted using minipackets containing two bytes of data. This chapter describes the design process, decisions, and tradeoffs in implementing an integrated system which incorporates both analog and digital components. The technology chosen is a bipolar gate array. A number of options is provided for the implementor who can optimize network parameters such as minipacket size and transmission speed to his needs. He can also choose the style of interface between the communicating device and the network.

An important option provided by the integrated Cambridge ring is the ability to simultaneously transmit short control minipackets and long data packets. A system exploiting this feature has been built and is described. Its proposed uses are to interconnect telephones and other real-time systems as well as computers where the partitioning of bandwidth and precise performance specification are important.

I. INTRODUCTION

This chapter describes the design and use of an integrated version of the Cambridge ring and outlines some of the local area network structures that can be implemented with it. The initial impetus for an integrated ring was to reduce system cost, to increase the ease of constructing ring networks, and to gain experience of integrated circuit design techniques.

One of the most important parameters in any network design is the cost of connection. This can be divided into several levels. The first level is the cost of connection to the transmission medium which may involve looking at the costs of using a wide range of transmission media. Above this comes the cost of implementing the network architecture in either hardware or software. Most networks have a number of similar features which only vary in detail. These are framing, addressing, error checking, and maintenance. In general, these features are implemented in hardware for reasons of speed. Occasionally, to reduce cost, they may be performed in software, but such systems tend to be rather simple, and shifting problems to software does not always mean a lower total cost. Once a system for delivering data between nodes has been devised, the cost of interfacing machines can be considered. Here the problem is more general, as we may require both very simple and also sophisticated devices to be connected easily. For a simple device, it may be sufficient to ensure the network buffers at least the smallest unit the hardware delivers at full speed. For more sophisticated devices, appropriate interrupt or direct memory access (DMA) handling techniques are important.

II. THE CAMBRIDGE RING

The Cambridge ring (CR) [1]–[3] is a baseband mode local area network based on the empty slot principle. A CR consists of a set of *repeaters* connected by a communications medium, such as twisted pair or optical fiber cables, and a *monitor station* which has the responsibility for synchronizing and maintaining the network. Each repeater is connected to a ring *station* which controls the transmission and reception of data via the ring. The interface between the repeater and station is serial and consists of "data in," "data out," "clock out," and "gate new data" signals. The interface between the station and the user is parallel with 49 active signals. The station is connected to the target device through an *access box*. This is the logic required to interface the bus which is provided by the station with the host machine. The structure of the CR is shown in Fig. 1.

A CR repeater has a delay of 3 bits and a typical ring configuration with about 30 nodes and 1 km of wire operating at 10 Mbits/s has about 150 bits of delay. This delay is used to accommodate a whole number of 38 bit slots which are divided up into fields for source and

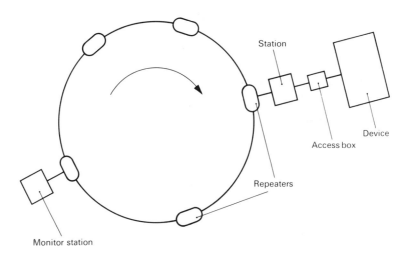

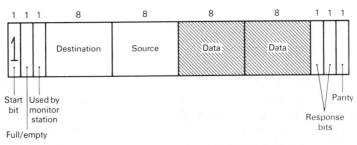

Fig. 1. Cambridge ring structure and minipacket format.

destination addresses, two bytes of data, and control information. Use of two bytes of data as the lowest level hardware transmission unit is the principal difference between a CR and most other local area networks. Each slot has a start of slot bit (always one) and a bit to indicate whether it is currently in use. When several slots exist on the ring at one time, they form a head-to-tail train. The delay remaining after the maximum number of slots has been inserted is called the gap, which always consists of zeros and is used for synchronization. The slot structure is set up initially by the monitor station. For transmissions to proceed correctly, stations have to be synchronized to the slot train. This is done by each station having two modes, in-slot and in-gap. When in-gap, a station waits for the next one, assumes this is the start of a slot, and counts 38 bits before repeating the algorithm. Because during synchronization slots leaving the monitor station are full and zero elsewhere, the first station downstream will synchronize, leaving an uninterrupted slot structure for the second station and so on.

To transmit, a station must wait until an empty slot arrives, then, having filled it with a *minipacket*, it waits until the slot returns and always marks it empty. When the slot has returned, two response bits, which are located after the data bytes, are inspected to see whether the minipacket was accepted, rejected, or marked busy by the destination station. Each station is provided with a unique address as well as information about the number of slots in the system so that it can mark empty slots it has used without increasing repeater delay.

For reception, each station looks at the destination addresses of all full minipackets circulating the ring and recognizes its own ring address. When this match takes place and the station is able to receive data, the source address and data fields are copied. Having recognized the destination address, the response bits of the minipacket are set according to whether it was accepted or not.

In order to diagnose breaks and parity faults on the ring, a self-maintenance system is provided [4]. The parity bit is inserted correctly for each slot leaving a repeater and is checked as it enters the next repeater. Thus, if a parity fault occurs, it is localized to a link which causes a special minipacket to be transmitted to destination zero (the error logger). A ring break generates a continuous train of minipackets to destination zero.

From the user's point of view, the CR provides a frequent opportunity to transmit a small amount of data. This can be used directly in simple systems, but often these minipackets are formed into longer variable length *packets*, similar to those in other networks [5]. However, in many other systems only one station can transmit at a time, while several transmissions can take place at once in the CR.

III. What Can Be Integrated?

When considering an LSI chip design, it is important to integrate as much of the system as possible so that the complexities of the design are hidden from the user, who has a simple and well-specified interface. We shall consider each layer of the architecture in turn.

The most common transmission medium is twisted pair wire. It is thus important to consider the design of line drivers and receivers for this medium. On the driving side, we must make sure that sufficient signal is injected into the wire to ensure that at the receiving end the data are decoded correctly with minimum distortion. With baseband signals and twisted pair wire, we would like to be able to transmit down several hundred meters of wire at up to 10 MHz, and in some systems also decode the clock. Normally, a 100 mV signal at the receiving end is sufficient to decode transitions correctly. With typical line impedances of around 100 Ω, a 20 mA TTL totem-pole output will give a satisfactory signal at the end of several hundred meters of wire. At the receiving end, an amplifier can be used to receive the signals and this may incorporate some hysteresis so that noise or a broken cable does not introduce erroneous data.

An important feature to be considered is the amount of jitter the transmission system introduces and how it can be minimized. Jitter can be made up of components from logic, drivers, the line, or receivers. Both the drivers and receivers may have different propagation delays for a positive edge and for a negative edge. The line itself may also introduce this effect, as well as attenuating signals for changing bit patterns in different ways.

In addition to the line driver and receiver, a chip design should also consider the clocking system. In some schemes, the clock is passed round on separate wires and can be regenerated easily. However, if the clock and data paths are shared, some form of clock extraction mechanism is required. If jitter has been introduced, some averaging may have to be performed. This can be done either digitally using a high-speed counter or gate delay chain, or in a more conventional way using analog phase-locked loop techniques [6], [7]. In summary, it is important that any chip design consider the line driving, receiving, and clocking systems, as often these are the most difficult or sensitive parts of the system and are typical of the kind of complexity that should be hidden from the user.

At the network design level, it is desirable that the chip perform the basic network functions of address recognition, framing, error checking, and maintenance. Such functions normally have to be done within one bit or minipacket time and are thus implemented in hard logic.

Once minipackets are addressed correctly, we can consider the buffers which store data to be transmitted or received. Such buffers can hold just one minipacket or they can be large enough to hold one or more packets. In some systems, the buffer is smaller than the smallest unit that can be transmitted, but this normally poses severe timing constraints on the user. If a simple 8 bit interface is permissible, then an integrated buffer is only constrained by chip space. However, in many applications, a wider bus is required and we are faced with pin-out problems.

DMA is a feature that is used on high-speed interfaces, and if provided in LSI may be used more widely. The requirement is usually for several DMA channels, some for transmit, some for receive, and some for control. It should be possible to perform scattered read and write operations with minimum delay when manipulating the DMA registers. Because of pin count constraints, these registers would normally only be available through shared pins and the resulting indirection may make rapid changes in DMA routes expensive.

On the CR, no error checking facilities are provided for the user who normally implements an external sumcheck over a packet. This error check could be implemented in hardware within the network chip. However, because the error rate is low (1 bit in 10^{11}), performing the error check close to the network may be unsatisfactory since there will be an unchecked path between the hardware error checker and the memory of the device, which may be as error prone as the ring itself. This poses a difficulty in that it may be impossible to perform the error check in hardware unless it is done in the memory itself.

At the next level, the interface has to be specified to the user in a way that is both convenient and allows high-speed data transfer. However, there is an overall constraint that the number of pins is minimized. An interface which is both easy to use and allows high-speed access logics to be built is one in which there is a general purpose data bus, and separate control signals for commands to the station logic. The CR interface is designed in this way. Access to the data and address buffers is through duplex 16 bit buses which can be folded to give 16 and 8 bit duplex or half-duplex systems and all of the control signals can be used independently. A reduction in the number of wires needed for control signals can be achieved using indirection and control registers. This means the control signals are allocated positions in registers, and since the registers are typically 8 bits wide, the number of pins is divided by eight. When a user wishes to perform some control function, he must identify which register he is using before writing into the appropriate position to specify the action to be performed. This can be duplex, but if further interface simplification is required, half-duplex operation permits a single 8 bit data bus to be used. By carefully arranging the position of bits within registers or only assigning one function per register, it is possible to ensure that the delay in manipulating registers is minimized.

Once the user interface is specified, it is possible to consider how much of the access logic can be placed in LSI. For the register-oriented interface, it is sufficient to add a chip enable signal and the network looks similar to any other peripheral chip. Once in LSI, this is probably the simplest way of interfacing a network.

A sophisticated access logic may require a microprocessor for control together with its own memory and buffer space. This is normally used to implement a stream protocol. Such protocols for local networks could be implemented in a modestly sized controller. Thus, it seems feasible that a stream protocol can be implemented in hardware.

IV. Design of the Integrated Cambridge Ring

A. Technology Choice and Partitioning

The design constraints for the integrated Cambridge ring (ICR) were to encapsulate as much of the design as possible in a chip, while enabling the implementor to have many options. It was not an original design goal to make the ICR system directly compatible with the TTL-based system at the wire level, although it was thought this would be desirable at the access box level.

The choice of technology was constrained by a number of factors. It was thought that the package size should not exceed 40 pins since larger sizes become prohibitively expensive. The target design speed of the system was 10 MHz, which suggested a typical gate delay of under 10 ns. At the time, easily available CMOS technology was not capable of providing this performance, particularly with 5 V power rails, which suggested a bipolar process. The technology would also have to provide facilities for analog circuits to enable the line drivers and receivers to be integrated. An estimate of the gate count indicated that the whole system would be integrated on several thousand gates and that a system with external minipacket buffers would require under 1000 gates. It was also a requirement that the design be completed rapidly, perhaps at the expense of the silicon area. For these reasons, the technology chosen was the Ferranti gate array current mode logic [8]. These arrays are uncommitted at the transistor level and thus can be used to construct analog structures as well as gates. Various sizes were available at the time; the largest provided about 500 gates for the designer.

On examining the original system, it was clear that some partitioning would have to take place to minimize the pin count. As access to the shift registers used for storing minipackets was through two 16 bit buses, a large reduction in pins could be achieved by retaining these shift registers in TTL. In addition, because the silicon area was limited, it was inappropriate to use it for such regular structures. It was thus decided to implement the shift registers externally. A design based on this structure was made, but the number of pins was still large and the gate count was too high for a single gate array. The logic was therefore partitioned into two sections: the repeater, which would perform the transmit and receive functions; and a station for decoding minipacket frames and transmitting and receiving user data. Because the gate utilization on the two chips was still uneven, some of the station logic was implemented on the repeater chip. This partitioning required duplication of logic and dedication of a number of pins for communication between the two chips. With this partitioning, most criteria of pin count, gate count, and cost were met.

B. Analog Design

For transmission media such as twisted pair wires, it is desirable to provide differential line drivers of sufficient power to cope with typical line impedances of 100 Ω. Attenuation is not a problem because of the short line lengths normally involved in local networks. With a typical twisted pair, it is sufficient to source and sink about 10–20 mA to provide satisfactory voltage swings at lengths up to several hundred meters. Also, if a modulation system with a restricted set of pulse widths is used, the differential attenuation with frequency is small at frequencies up to 10 MHz. On the repeater gate array, a single-sided drive has been provided to help maintain the pin count at 40. On short links, this can be used directly, but on long links it is preferable to use a transformer or similar means to convert to differential drive.

Line receivers must be optimized in terms of three parameters. These are gain, hysteresis, and the difference in propagation delay for positive and negative edges. The gain should be enough to reliably detect a signal down to several tens of mV. Hysteresis is used to prevent a partially or completely broken cable from apparently receiving spurious bit patterns. Such patterns may be interpreted as bits, which may upset maintenance transmissions. With no hysteresis, this happens because the inputs to the line receivers at the end of a broken link are likely to float to the most sensitive region. With a partially broken cable, some changes on the wire will be detected, but providing the other side is steady, this will be read as a string of zeros and the maintenance mechanism will operate properly. With this implementation, up to 300 m of standard twisted pair wire can be driven and decoded correctly at speeds up to 10 MHz.

The design of a phase-locked loop consists of three components. These are the voltage-controlled oscillator, the filter, and the phase comparator. The voltage-controlled oscillator should be implemented in such a way that noise in the chip does not cause arbitrary phase changes in the oscillation. In some oscillator designs, there may be a sensitive region in the cycle and noise at this time may make phase-locking difficult. With the ICR implementation, the oscillator has its own 5 V and GND supplies. The chip and oscillator GND supplies are internally connected although the extra pin improves decoupling. The phase comparator chosen is a sawtooth one based on EXCLUSIVE-OR gates. The delays through the various paths are matched to minimize jitter on the control waveform and the filtering and integration of the comparison signal is done by an external RC network.

C. User Options

A number of user options have been introduced during the design of the ICR. These may be used to implement a variety of systems and are described in the following.

1) The number of data bytes per minipacket now lies in the range from 1 to 8. The system designer defines this length by setting three static pins of the repeater chip. The performance changes with minipacket size in two ways. As the number of data bytes increases, the ring becomes more efficient in use of data and the effective system bandwidth improves. Increasing the number of data bytes also means that a single user can transmit more data each time he acquires a slot. However, as the slot size increases, the number of slots for any ring size will decrease, and thus the degree of sharing of bandwidth will tend to decrease. This means sharing will be at a coarser level and the upper bound on service time will increase. Another effect of changing the number of data bytes is on the design of the interface. However, as the shift registers for holding minipackets are external, the bus structure can be very wide because there is no direct limitation on the pin count. The ICR minipacket format is shown in Fig. 2.

2) The addition of two user control bits to the minipacket format is the main change which makes the ICR incompatible with the CR. The two extra control bits are available to the user who can load them and read them as required. The hardware treats these bits as an extension of the data field and does not change them in any way. Their primary use is to mark minipackets as belonging to some category, by higher level protocols, for instance. Another way of using the control bits is to allow hardware to interpret them in a specific way. For example, one could envisage a system where voice minipackets are marked as a special pattern of control bits.

Because the control bits are just an extension of the data field, it does not matter where they are in the minipacket structure. For compatibility reasons, however, they are normally implemented so that they precede the response bits.

3) A broadcast address has been implemented to permit a single minipacket to be recognized by every destination. It is characteristic of a ring that all minipackets pass all destinations. Thus, it is easy to reserve one address (255) which is detected by each station. Minipackets are then received in the normal way. There is a problem with responses, as it is difficult to inform the source what the response was at each station. To make this option more useful, the responses have been changed so that for broadcast minipackets only one bit is used. It is set by any station which accepts the minipacket. Thus, the response information available at the source indicates whether at least one station has received the minipacket.

4) One of the most important limitations of the transmission speed on the CR is that the transmit command cannot be issued until the previous minipacket has returned. Since this command is asynchronous to the network clock, by the time it has settled, the next full/empty bit has passed. To improve this, a transmit-on-accepted mode has been introduced in which two extra signals are provided. These are the transmit-on-accepted command and

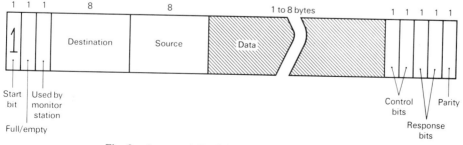

Fig. 2.   Integrated Cambridge ring minipacket format.

the buffer empty response. The transmit-on-accepted command is a conditional command and can only be issued while a previous minipacket is making its way round the ring. Its effect is to launch the next minipacket if the previous one was accepted. Because the transmit-on-accepted command can be early, synchronization can also take place early. The buffer empty response indicates when a minipacket has been shifted out and a new one can be loaded.

5) Another mode of operation has been provided in the ICR for use where either very high bandwidths are required or where the service times of the ring must have a very precise specification. This is called channel mode and allows a station to replenish data in a slot. Thus, once a station has acquired a slot, there is no compulsion for this slot to be released. The service time is deterministic and part of the ring bandwidth has been allocated to that station. To use this mode, the interface initially has to issue a normal transmit command which will use the next available slot. When the buffer empty response indicates that the minipacket has been moved out of the transmit shift register, a new minipacket is loaded and the channel-transmit command issued. The returning slot is not marked empty, the new data are inserted, and the next transmit command can be issued.

In channel mode there is difficulty in handling responses. Because new data are inserted into a slot before the responses are read, there is a possibility that minipackets are sent out of order. This happens whenever a minipacket is not accepted at a destination. Thus, in this mode it is important that either the destination can receive from the ring at full speed or that a protocol which deals with minipackets being received out of sequence is used.

D. LAN Implementations

Various board implementations of the ICR are possible. We shall discuss a number of these in the following.

Because of the extra control bits, it is impossible to design a ring node completely compatible with the TTL system. However, the control bits can be made transparent to the user and thus the access box interface can be made the same as the CR design. For this, the transmit and receive shift registers and a number of other components are required to implement echo signals, line buffers, etc. Like the TTL version, the integrated system can be based on a 16 bit transmit data bus and a 16 bit receive data bus. The access box interface has two extra lines which are used for access to the control bits. With the integrated system, the total chip count for a ring node can be reduced from the 80 used in the TTL implementation to 12.

The design is easily altered to increase the number of data bytes in a minipacket. This requires the appropriate buffering and the pins indicating minipacket length to be set correctly. The bus architecture can be arranged as required; in particular, a very wide structure can be used. This is attractive when an interface for a 32 or 64 bit machine is being constructed or when very high throughputs are required.

V. A HYBRID RING

A. Traffic Considerations

A recent survey [9] of the distribution of the size of packets transmitted on the CR suggests that while 79 percent of the packets contain less than 28 bytes of data, 96 percent of the total data are sent in the remaining 21 percent of the packets. The large packets mainly consist of data transfers to and from the file storage devices on the ring and a high proportion of these are the maximum length, 2048 bytes. The short packets are used to transmit mainly protocol control information. Figure 3 shows distributions of packet length and ring utilization measured under average traffic conditions on a 50 node ring.

As the slot utilization of the CR is relatively low, approximately 20 percent at peak times, these figures suggest that the delay in transmitting a large packet would be

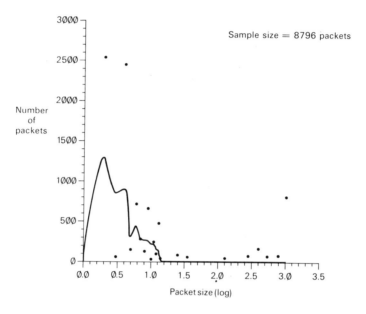

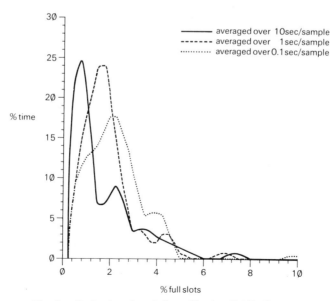

Fig. 3. Packet length and ring utilization distributions.

considerably reduced if the number of data bytes per minipacket were increased. Although the ring would then accommodate fewer slots, the additional delay in transmitting a minipacket is likely to be small because the number of devices using the ring at any one time is low. A further upgrade in the packet transmission time can be achieved by using the ICR channel mode. If the length of the ring were limited to one slot having an 8 byte data field, then the point-to-point bandwidth available to a user could be as high as 70 percent of the system bandwidth. Unfortunately, with ring traffic consisting predominantly of very short packets, the overall performance of the network would be severely degraded as the number of stations wanting to transmit increased. A solution to this problem would be to support a second type of slot for which retention was not allowed. If the length of this slot were short compared to the length of the channel mode slot, then the bandwidth available to channel users would still be high while access to the short slot would be rapid. A partitioning of the system bandwidth to various types of traffic in this way is possible with the integrated ring. This is achieved by changing the pins on the repeater chip which define the slot length at the appropriate time.

A system has been designed and built which incorporates these features using short minipackets holding one data byte and long minipackets with 8 bytes of data. The number of each type of slot is specified before synchronization of the ring is performed. The structure of the ring is similar to that of the CR, a cyclic network consisting of a number of repeaters. Attached to each repeater chip is a station chip and some extra logic, the combination of which is referred to as a ring *tap*. A host device may then be connected to the ring via an interface. One tap on the ring performs certain executive functions, which include synchronization, maintenance of the slot structure, and servicing errors. This special tap is called the *monitor station/logger* (MSL).

In a CR, a user can transmit once every $Q + 2$ slots where Q is the number of slots in the system. Thus, a typical CR with three slots, each of two data bytes, and a gap of 8 bits can support up to five users each transmitting 800 kbits/s. When slots can be replenished, this improves to once every Q slots for such channel mode transmissions. So, for a hybrid ring with one long slot, one short slot, and a gap of 4 bits operating at 10 Mbits/s, the point-to-point bandwidth for a station transmitting a large packet is 5.2 Mbits/s. The maximum bandwidth available to stations using the short slot is 325 kbits/s. Thus, for low traffic loads, there is a considerable reduction in the transmission delay of large packets, while the time to transmit a minipacket for other users will change little. It could be suggested that this type of network is similar to a token ring. Whereas this is true in that a long slot operates in the same way as a token, i.e., a user must wait until the empty slot arrives at the repeater and can then reserve it, when a channel mode slot is in use, it does not preclude all other traffic from the ring. Indeed, several channel mode slots and short slots can coexist with little interference. In allowing both short and long minipacket transmissions to be made simultaneously, the hybrid ring appears more flexible than the token ring. One particular area in which this facility would be most advantageous is in protocol control.

B. The Ring Tap

The ring tap is similar to the ICR node described above. As well as the repeater and station chips, there are minipacket buffers, in which minipackets are assembled and disassembled, bus buffers, and the analog components necessary to phase-lock and drive the ring. At each tap there is also the logic associated with detecting the slot structure (framing logic). This includes two 4 bit counters, one for each slot size, the values of which are used to switch the repeater chip control lines that define minipacket size. The contents of the counters may also be gated onto the data bus for inspection by the host. A diagram illustrating the structure of a ring tap is given in Fig. 4.

Since in channel mode the data transfer rate is potentially high, the shift registers of the conventional CR have been replaced by two sets of 16×16 FIFO registers, one each on the receive and transmit sides. The use of FIFO's on the transmit side enables data to be queued by a high-speed interface before the transmit command is given. The interface can then enter a wait state until an empty channel slot is received, possibly releasing a DMA hold over the host device. Once the transmisson is underway and the first data have been unloaded from the FIFO's, a line of the control bus will indicate that the FIFO is no longer full and the interface can resume transferring data from the host to the tap. The rate at which the rest of the data are transferred is then governed by the same FIFO-full control signal. On the receive side of the control bus, a similar signal (receive-FIFO-ready) indicates whether any data are waiting in the FIFO's and controls the rate at which the interface reads it. The receive and transmit buffers can easily be extended by connecting additional FIFO's in series with the existing buffers. If enough local storage is provided, entire packets could be assembled prior to transmission or reception, leaving the host free during the transfer of the packet.

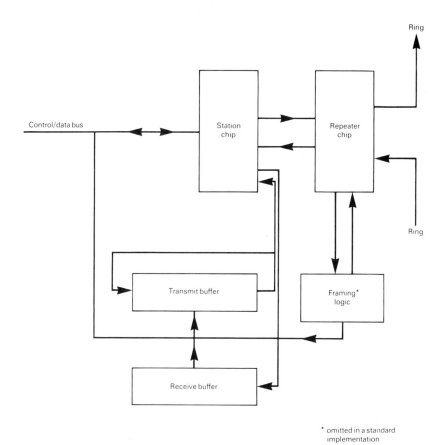

* omitted in a standard implementation

Fig. 4.   The structure of a hybrid ring tap.

C. The Monitor Station/Logger

The monitor station/logger is the central control node of the hybrid ring. Its main role as seen by the other taps is to set up and maintain the slot structure of the ring. The MSL can be functionally divided into two sections: a repeater with the external logic associated with setting up the slot structure and a ring tap similar to the other taps connected to the network which is used for error logging.

Overall control of the MSL is performed by a Z80-type microprocessor with which a network supervisor can communicate through a console. The control software continuously monitors the state of the ring and under some error conditions will attempt synchronization. The errors that can be detected by the MSL hardware are

1) lost start of minipacket bit,
2) incorrect parity bit in minipacket,
3) minipacket has already passed MSL, and
4) minipacket marked empty that should be full.

The network supervisor can, through a console, interrogate the MSL on the state of the ring. The information available describes the current number of each size of slot, the size of the gap, the number of each type of error detected, and the number of times that the ring has been resynchronized due to an error condition. The number of each size of slot and the gap length can also be updated at the console. The maximum number of slots that can be implemented on the ring is 16; this is dictated by the ICR specification, although the proportion of each size of slot is arbitrary. The MSL incorporates a long shift register so that if an addition is necessary to accommodate a particular slot train (because of insufficient total delay through repeaters and wire) a variable length extension can be provided. In the case where the supervisor does not know the physical length of the ring and therefore cannot calculate the length of shift register required for a minimum sized gap, the value is computed automatically.

A further facility contributing to the constant surveillance of the ring allows the insertion of random bit patterns into empty slots that are passing the MSL. Such slots are not marked full and can thus be used, but the maintenance mechanism is exercised with changing patterns. The error logging function is supported by the ring tap part of the MSL. The repeater in the tap is allocated ring address zero and so all maintenance minipackets generated by taps around the ring will be received by it. The source address of these packets can then be used to pinpoint the location of the error condition indicated by the data field so the MSL can take appropriate action.

On start-up or after errors which affect the frame structure the ring will be synchronized. Synchronization is the process by which all taps on the ring achieve a common view of the frame structure. For a ring with homogeneous slots, the number of slots is the only parameter required. However, for a ring with multiple slot sizes the position and number of each size must be determined. If the relative position of each group of similarly sized slots is kept constant, as in the hybrid ring, then this task is reduced to establishing the number of each size. As the format of a minipacket does not include a field indicating to which category it belongs, this information can be temporarily inserted during synchronization and each tap must retain a copy of the frame structure once synchronization is complete.

In a hybrid ring tap, the number of each size of slot is stored in a lockable counter which is unlocked at the beginning of synchronization by the MSL transmitting a train of zeros which is longer than the maximum permissible gap. The tap then enters a learning state in which it can interpret a stream of minipackets containing length markers which are issued by the MSL. It can be shown that the ring will be synchronized to the MSL after one complete frame structure has been transmitted and that the tap framing logic will take at most two complete frames to deduce the number of each of the sizes of slot. One gap later, the slot counters are locked. During the synchronization process, the taps will have their repeaters disabled so that no spurious transmissions can take place and so reduce the amount of garbage data on the ring. Once the slot counters are loaded and locked, transmissions are reenabled.

Resynchronization is only performed when certain errors occur, such as lost start of minipacket bit or when high numbers (a few hundred) of the other error types are detected. Fluctuations in the length of the gap, which probably mean that a tap has lost synchronization, can be detected by the MSL. If any change is noticed, reframing will be initiated.

The complete structure of the hybrid ring is shown in Fig. 5. At present, power is distributed on separate wires, although distribution through the transmission wires is possible as used in the original CR design. The ring is started by powering-on and booting the MSL program from an external source. It is planned that the MSL will also become a station in the ordinary way so that the control program can communicate with other nodes on the ring to collect and distribute traffic and error information.

VI. Conclusion

This chapter has shown the development process used to implement an integrated version of the Cambridge ring. The chips have been used to construct ring systems by a number of

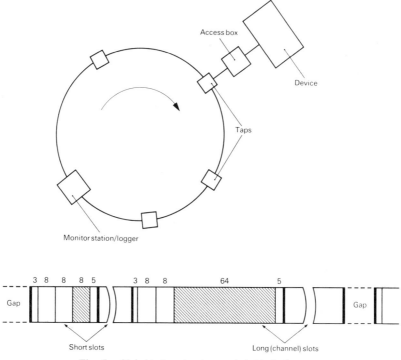

Fig. 5.   Hybrid ring structure and slot train format.

universities and commercial organizations. The design of a new type of local area network using many of the new features of the ICR was discussed. A hybrid ring partitions the system bandwidth by supporting two types of slot: long slots, which hold 8 bytes of data and which can be used in channel mode; and short slots with 1 byte data fields, which must be released after use. Different types of traffic such as voice, facsimile, and data can be allocated bandwidth in accordance with their traffic patterns. In advanced systems, the configuration of slots can be changed dynamically with needs. The traffic partitioning made possible by the hybrid ring makes the implementation of an integrated-services local network attractive.

Whereas the facilities of the hybrid ring were superimposed onto the ULA implementation of the more simple CR, the next step in the process of development would be to integrate the whole system. Recent advances in gate array technology suggest that a complete local area network chip could be produced incorporating the repeater/station functions, a ring monitor station, and internetwork bridges. With the availability of high-quality fiber-optic transmission cables, the new ring could operate at very high data rates, for example, above 50 Mbits/s. The system bandwidth could then be partitioned to provide slots which would support traffic ranging from interprocessor communication, high-quality video, and fast file transfer to protocol control information and voice traffic.

ACKNOWLEDGMENT

M. V. Wilkes, D. J. Wheeler, and R. M. Needham are responsible for numerous suggestions, ideas, and support related to the design. The idea of changing minipacket size on-the-fly is due to S. G. Zaky.

REFERENCES

[1] M. V. Wilkes and D. J. Wheeler, "The Cambridge digital communication ring," presented at Local Area Commun. Network Symp., Boston, MA, May 1979, sponsored by the National Bureau of Standards.
[2] A. Hopper, "Local area computer communication networks," Ph.D. dissertation, Cambridge Univ., Cambridge, England, Apr. 1978.
[3] Cambridge Ring 82, Interface Specifications, Science and Engineering Research Council, Sept. 1982.
[4] A. Hopper and D. J. Wheeler, "Maintenance of ring communication systems," *IEEE Trans. Commun.*, vol. COM-27, pp. 760–761, Apr. 1979.
[5] R. M. Needham, "System aspects of the Cambridge ring," in *Proc. 7th Symp. Opt. Syst. Princ.*, Pacific Grove, CA, Dec. 1979.
[6] I. M. Leslie, "Frequency stability in a unidirectional ring of phase locked loops," unpublished project note, Comput. Lab., Univ. Cambridge, Cambridge, England.
[7] ——, "A master clock repeater for the Cambridge digital communication ring," unpublished project note, Comput. Lab., Univ. Cambridge, Cambridge, England.
[8] *ULA Design Manual*, Ferranti Semiconductors Ltd., Ref. A/F00'2.
[9] N. J. Ody, "Monitoring ring traffic using a promiscuous station," unpublished project note, Comput. Lab., Univ. Cambridge, Cambridge, England, June 9, 1981.

9
Towards a Universal Data Transport System

ALEXANDER G. FRASER

It is anticipated that a ubiquitous data transport system will require integration of local area and wide area networks. The combined network will need to present a uniform appearance to the user, be effective as a transport mechanism for a great variety of traffic patterns, and be economically appropriate for a wide range of consumer products. Learning from telephony and from experiments with a local area network, we conclude that the transport system must seek a clean separation of function and protocol between the network and its users. This separation is achieved by a byte-stream architecture that carries control and data bytes over switched virtual circuits.

A DATAKIT® packet switch demonstrates how the byte-stream concept can integrate local area and wide area network objectives. This switch is an assembly of interface modules connected by a pair of short passive buses. Each type of interface module serves one type of remote equipment and, if need be, terminates the protocol of that equipment. There are interface modules for trunks that lead to other packet switches, for terminals, and for host computers. Other modules provide system timing, switching, network control, and maintenance support.

I. INTRODUCTION

After 35 years of cost and size reduction, computers now are found inside such diverse products as microwave ovens, electronic games, and sewing machines. Evidently microcomputers are to become the "electric motors" of future consumer products. Popular demand for data communications will surely soon follow. Thus, one can foresee a need for efficient and ubiquitous information transport that ultimately penetrates the majority of homes, offices, and factories in the nation.

Ubiquity in telecommunications suggests a standard wall socket distributed about as widely as electric power outlets are now. An appliance plugged into one of these sockets will be able to reach, by some simple and standard procedure, another appliance plugged into any other socket. Appliances will be purchased and installed with minimum formality. Once arrangements for billing and addressing have been established, the homeowner or proprietor of a business should be as free as possible to make rearrangements and additions

---

® DATAKIT is a trademark of AT&T.

to the installed equipment. When devices fail, the diagnostic procedures should be about as direct and easily carried out as they are for the power distribution system.

Thus, we are led to the technology of local area networks and the relationship that these have with networking in the large. Ring and bus systems allow statistical sharing of a wide-band circuit so that bursty data can be carried rapidly within a building or campus. These systems also perform a switching function that is distributed among the participating computers. Thus, small local area networks require relatively low initial capital investment and an informal administration. However, as local area networks expand, some of the informality must be replaced with planned development, particularly for building wiring and maintenance procedures. Expanding community of interest means that attachment to a wide area network becomes necessary; ultimately the service seen by a local network user is that provided by the integral of the local and wide area network parts. The service should be uniform enough that the same software and user interface can handle both short and long distance communications, and it is desirable that a similar service be seen by users of different local area networks that are in communication with one another. Thus, the challenge is to derive an adequate architecture for the combination of local and wide area networks that presents a uniform appearance to the user, is effective as a transport mechanism for a great variety of traffic patterns, and can be used economically by a wide range of consumer products.

The DATAKIT packet switch, network architecture, and design philosophy described in this chapter evolved from a desire to meet this challenge. It has been the subject of research in the Computing Science Research Center, Bell Laboratories, since the first components were designed in 1975. Universal service remains the architectural objective, although, currently, our experimental network primarily serves as a communications system for approximately 50 time-shared computers and 380 asynchronous terminals at four Bell Laboratories locations, three in New Jersey and one in Ohio. Figure 1 is a map of the network as of August 1983.

This chapter is in two main sections. First is a discussion of architectural strategy, and second is a description of the DATAKIT packet switch.

II. Architectural Strategy

The goal of universal service implies a consistency of purpose between the toll, access, and intrapremises components of the network. Whether one has access to the network

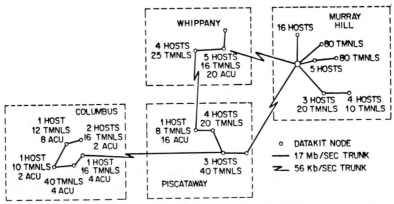

Fig. 1.   Experimental network (August 1983).

through a local area network or direct access to it from a business or residence, the perception of basic data communication service should be the same. That will encourage the development of communications equipment and appliances with the widest range of application. Without it, communication between devices in different environments is less likely to be successful.

Constancy of purpose is also important. The telecommunications network will grow and change through the use of new technology. Indeed, such change is essential if the network is to remain a vital and profitable enterprise. But the consumer requires a stable telecommunications environment within which to build new products and industries. From the points of view of both provider and consumer, it would be impractical to introduce new technology into the network if to do so required a compensating and coordinated change in the methods of network use.

Constancy and consistency seem incompatible with technical innovation and a rapidly developing new industrial order. The best hope seems to be for a very simple definition of data communications service that depends as little as possible on any particular technology. Thus, for the DATAKIT network, we have chosen two simple concepts as the basis for all of our networking experiments: all information is carried over switched virtual circuits, and the basic data structure is a single byte. Both of these are readily enough understood that users might easily learn what to expect from the service and entrepreneurs can easily see how they might exploit it.

Universal service for data communications is a challenging objective because of the great variety in terminal types, traffic patterns, and protocols. In order to accommodate interactive and bulk traffic, we must find a system design that allows low delay for small messages while giving reasonably good throughput when handling large messages. For voice and other synchronous sources that may one day pass over the data network, we desire a means of minimizing the variance of delay. Finally, since these various traffic sources may employ different protocols, we must find a system design that has the flexibility to represent data in many different ways.

Two types of information are allowed: an 8 bit byte of user data that is carried transparently through the network, and an 8 bit control byte which, depending upon its value, may be processed by the network. Experience so far suggests that these two information types are sufficient to allow the various network control and higher level protocol functions that users require. Since the network carries bytes asynchronously, it can use packet switching and statistical multiplexing as appropriate to minimize delay and/ or maximize transmission efficiency. But the network and users can nevertheless remain largely independent of the details of each other's protocols. It is, of course, necessary for a pair of communicating terminals to agree on a common protocol and, if the terminals use one of the de facto standard protocols, they must adopt an agreed upon way of representing the message structure of those protocols in terms of data and control bytes. If the data processing community can eventually agree on a single protocol standard, then all may benefit, but such is not a prerequisite for use of the network.

Universal service has been a goal of the telephone network and many of the technical, managerial, political, and economic forces that helped shape that network will continue to shape the telecommunications network of the future. Thus, the architecture of a DATAKIT network owes much to our heritage in telephony.

Telecommunications is an industry heavily dominated by capital investment that is tied up for long periods of time. Its future thus necessarily must evolve from its past. Early data networks used equipment developed for telephony, and the economics of scale in transmission will continue to cause voice and data to share at least the long-haul transmission system. Even though the volume of data traffic carried on the long-haul network is expanding rapidly, it will be a long time (if ever) before the volume of data exceeds that of voice.

While much of the Bell System continues to use analog transmission, the conversion to digital technology is well underway. Regenerative repeaters allow reduced error rates and make the digital system more attractive for data. In North America and Japan the dominant digital transmission system, called T1 [1], uses a 1.544 Mbit/s transmission rate and the world-wide standard for a single voice circuit is 64 kbits/s. At present, format constraints limit data users to about 7/8ths of this bandwidth, i.e., 1.344 Mbits/s and 56 kbits/s, respectively. These are, therefore, the speeds that have been used in calculating design tradeoffs for the DATAKIT network.

The 56 kbit/s transmission speed is considered particularly significant because of its presence in the access network. Local access, the means of linking a residence or business to the main network, accounts for a large part of the investment in any network. Thus, one must anticipate that, for some time to come, twisted wire pairs will be the dominant transmission medium. At present, these wires are used to carry analog signals, but digital line terminating equipment is becoming available. For example, time compression multiplexing [2] makes it possible to carry 56 kbit/s data full duplex on a single twisted pair over distances as great as 5 miles.

A. Rings, Buses, and Building Wiring

The building wiring for telephony is arranged as a tree with the possibility of several telephone attachment points along any one cable. However, two reasons for changing this distribution scheme to suit data communication are quite apparent. First, there is a need for greater flexibility in the installation and rearrangement of telecommunications equipment, and second, there is a need to handle bursty traffic at data rates higher than those now supported by voiceband modems.

We enjoy the flexibility to install and rearrange electrical appliances because a power distribution scheme has been developed which allows widespread deployment of an inexpensive wall socket. A similar arrangement would be attractive for telecommunications. Such would seem to be possible, even at high speed, if the wall socket were based upon shared use of a multiplexed transmission line.

Rings and bus systems provide such sharing and, at first glance, promise to be less expensive than a pure star-connected arrangement because fewer transmitters and receivers are required. Whereas there are $2N$ transmitters and receivers in a star-connected configuration with N terminals, only $N + 1$ transmitters and receivers are required when a ring or bus is used. (One pair is required for each terminal, and one pair is used to connect the ring or bus to the main network.) Furthermore, when all wall sockets are unoccupied the star-connected arrangement still has N transmitters and receivers while the ring or bus has just one pair. Of course, this argument does not necessarily imply that the star is always more expensive because the unit cost of transmitter, receiver, and transmission line might be less when the star topology is used. To understand why that might be so we note that, to a first approximation, for copper wire baseband systems the complexity of a transmission system increases with the number of bits stored in the transmission line. For example, a transmission line with EIA RS422 drivers and receivers operating at 1 Mbit/s over 1000 ft stores about 1 bit in the line, while the T1 system stores 8.2 bits in 1 mile of wire and Ethernet stores 10 bits in 1000 ft of wire. These last two systems are much more complex than the first. When there is more than 1 bit in the line, one must begin to worry about reflections, and as the density of transmitted symbols increases so does intersymbol interference.

Details of the DATAKIT network design grew out of the earlier experience with a ring network [3], [17]. In that experiment we learned, as others have, that the management of change and maintenance tends towards a star-like topology or, for large buildings, a tree formed by the interconnection of several stars. Faults are easier to find if the network can easily be partitioned, and one needs a systematic wiring plan if changes and rearrangements are not to slowly get out of hand. Many buildings, in fact, tend to naturally support a tree-structured wiring plan. Vertical wiring ducts in high-rise buildings efficiently feed each floor, and the corridor structure can usually be mapped into a tree topology. Additions and deletions on a tree are easily conceived and executed.

Small networks with totally distributed switching and control can be made with either ring or bus technology, but when such networks get large their administration tends to become a problem. Fault isolation, for example, can be assisted by suitable diagnostics in each ring node [4] or by special measuring equipment for buses, but it is not easy to reduce the repair/replacement procedure to the level of simplicity that most domestic circumstances will require. Saltzer [5], Bux *et al.* [6], and we have found that it is advantageous to route the cable for a ring in a star-like fashion so that there is a central point for maintenance and reconfiguration. The star topology avoids having to travel the corridors and climb over furniture with diagnostic equipment in hand. Rings usually employ regenerative repeaters whose clocks are recovered from the incoming signal and whose outgoing signal is clocked from the recovered clock. Clock jitter thus becomes a concern as the size of the ring grows. Ring, and bus systems also, pose a problem of privacy and vulnerability to mischief because the data for one user flow past many others. Such problems can be better contained and are certainly better understood when ring size is restricted.

Bus systems may also be better if kept short. The CSMA/CD discipline relies upon each node hearing the transmissions of another within a single packet transmission time [7]. Since signal propagation time increases with distance, the minimum acceptable packet size increases and/or slower transmission must be used even though small packets may be preferred for interactive traffic or voice communication. Another design constraint of a CSMA system is that every transmitter must be compatible with every receiver. That is in contrast to a ring or bus where each transmitter communicates with only one receiver. As the number of bits stored in a transmission line increases, it becomes necessary to use a receiver design that compensates for intersymbol interference [1]. Transmitter waveform, bus geometry, and the relative positions of transmitter and receiver are all relevant parameters to the design. With point-to-point transmission, these parameters remain constant and, if the system fails, it is more likely that the failure can be reproduced. With broadcast transmission, these parameters vary depending on which transmitter is communicating with which receiver, and identification of a transmitter/receiver incompatibility will not be so easily achieved. The probability and difficulty of this type of problem increase with increasing network size. Collision detection also poses a problem for an Ethernet bus receiver. In order to detect collisions, a node which is actively transmitting should be able to detect another's transmissions. But signal strength diminishes as the signal propagates along the bus, and it is not easy to reliably detect a weak signal in the presence of a strong one. This again is a problem that increases in severity with network size.

The building distribution arrangement for universal service must be based upon a technology that can be installed, modified, and repaired by electrical contractors, semiskilled labor, and do-it-yourself homeowners. Installation rules must be easy to understand, and the hardware design should be forgiving. The wall socket and wiring must be inexpensive, and the cost of a plug must not be such that it dominates the cost of a small electrical appliance. Aesthetics will also play a part. The plug and wiring, including extension cords and other conveniences, will have to share the living room and office without being offensive to the eye.

We conclude from these arguments that the intrabuilding distribution should be a star with short rings and/or buses at the periphery interconnected by a central switch. Point-to-point connection to the switch can be used where most economical or where special needs must be served.

Research on the DATAKIT packet switch started with a star architecture because in this way the bulk of existing terminals and hosts can be easily connected, and the switching technology needed to efficiently handle asynchronous traffic seemed, at the time, to require the most immediate attention. However, evolution towards wall sockets requires that in due course short buses or rings emanate from the star.

B. Functional Partitioning

The DATAKIT packet switch followed an earlier attempt to design a single switching machine that could be all things to all users. For simple terminals, the switch needs to be inexpensive and versatile. For large computers, the switch must exhibit high performance. These are conflicting objectives that we found difficult to resolve satisfactorily; a switch designed to handle high performance computers was too expensive for small terminal applications, and vice-versa. Resolution of this problem was finally inspired by a children's toy, an erector set consisting of many small plastic parts that could be plugged together to form a wide range of toy models. If it is impossible to design a universal packet switch, then perhaps, we can compromise with a kit of parts that can be configured on demand to meet particular requirements in an appropriate way. The kit would consist of software and hardware modules that could be used to build data networks of various types.

We have endeavored to assign logically distinct functions to separate modules. Switched virtual circuits are used when necessary to bring data to the module that must process it. For example, switching and the control of switching are separately implemented in distinct modules. A switch module concentrates on steering data to their proper destination while a control computer engages the user in a call setup protocol and chooses the route that each virtual circuit will take. The control computer communicates over a virtual circuit with one or more switch modules. As a natural extension of this arrangement, one control computer can manage several packet switches and, by switching virtual circuits appropriately, a second control computer can take over when the first has failed. Because these functions are separately implemented and the design of each is not encumbered by the environmental constraints of the other, we find that this functional organization is easier to understand and modify than it might otherwise have been.

Likewise, queueing has been separated from switching, and both of these are disengaged from the protocols used for error and flow control. A virtual circuit is a concatenation of very many parts, each of which needs error detection for maintenance purposes. Rather than try to guarantee end-to-end integrity by the concatenated integrity of many small parts, we treat end-to-end error control as an end-to-end function. The cost of that in terms of extra bandwidth used when retransmission must take place is small and is proportional to the transmission error rate. Cost savings arise in many small ways because extreme precautions do not have to be taken within the network to guard against data losses that result from rare failure modes. For example, parity error detected on data stored in a switch buffer memory can be handled by discarding the suspect data and by transmitting an error statistic to a central maintenance center. One does not need the complexity of identifying the affected virtual circuit and generating messages for the end user.

One can view the network as a large rearrangeable statistical multiplexor with queues to store data where there is a change of speed or traffic is concentrated. The switching machine is a flow-through device which rearranges traffic so that it travels to its appropriate destination. The switching function itself does not get involved in flow control. Queue overflow can only be allowed to occur infrequently and is avoided by using additional memory rather than by introducing a complex interlace of flow control mechanisms. Memory costs are already low and continue to reduce exponentially with each passing year. We believe that a memory-intensive approach to network design is simpler and will be increasingly cost competitive with one that involves extra protocols and high-speed processors.

User behavior cannot be predicted, yet most users prefer a predictable response from the network. This dilemma is resolved by doing as much as possible to prevent one user from interfering with the response experienced by another. While this is manifestly impossible to achieve perfectly in a statistically multiplexed system, we can queue separately the traffic for each virtual circuit and so serve users more even handedly than if the messages of one user were queued behind those of another.

The three lowest protocol levels in a DATAKIT network are denoted A, B, and C [8]. Level A corresponds to the physical level of the ISO reference model [9]. The functions of level B are those needed to implement switching and multiplexing of byte streams. Thus, level B handles the transport of bytes, checks for and discards defective data bytes as they are moved through the network, and provides for the necessary addressing to allow statistical multiplexing and switching. Level C functions are those that treat each virtual circuit separately and are performed end-to-end across the network. The level C functions include flow control and retransmission in case of error. Potentially, the interface between levels B and C could be quite complex, but since this is frequently the level of the interface between customer equipment and the network, we wish to keep it simple. One way of avoiding a coupling of protocols between these two levels is to ask the user at level C to limit to some agreed window size the volume of data stored in a virtual circuit. The transport system undertakes to accommodate that amount of data where necessary in queues and buffers within the network. Thus we avoid exchanging feedback signals between the center of the network and the level C user [10].

III. THE DATAKIT PACKET SWITCH

A DATAKIT network, such as that shown in Fig. 1, is an interconnected collection of nodes to which are attached computers and terminals. Asynchronous terminals connect to the network through an RS232C interface and host computers may employ either RS232C interfaces or a single multiplexed interface. The latter can accommodate up to 512 separate channels each of which can be connected by a switched virtual circuit to another host channel or RS232C interface.

A. Using the Network

When a terminal is idle the message "number please:" is displayed on its screen. By typing the name of a host or the word "dial", the terminal user obtains a virtual circuit which connects the RS232C interface through various nodes and trunks to a host computer channel or to a modem attached to the telephone network. If the connection is to a host, the terminal user may now log into that computer. If the connection is to a modem, the user must now type a telephone number and so obtain a connection through the telephone network. Subsequent exchanges of data are handled transparently and in full duplex over the established virtual circuit. Upon completion of the terminal session, the user either instructs the host to drop the connection (see below) or itself drops the terminal ready lead[1] in the RS232C interface with the network.

A host places a call by selecting an idle channel and sending a message containing the name of another host. After the network has exchanged messages over a previously idle channel on the remote host, the two channels are connected together by a virtual circuit. Subsequent data transmitted by either host are carried transparently through the network along the route of the virtual circuit. To drop the connection, either host sends a supervisory message to the network and the host at the other end of the connection receives a corresponding message indicating that the virtual circuit has been taken down.

In each case the virtual circuit defines a route for data passing between two end points (terminal or host channel). Information describing that route is stored in each packet switch en route. If the route includes transmission over a multiplexed trunk, one channel of the trunk is assigned to the virtual circuit and cannot be reassigned until the virtual circuit has been taken down. Unlike a time-division or frequency-multiplexed trunk, a channel of a DATAKIT trunk does not have any trunk bandwidth dedicated to it. Rather, the channel is simply denoted by a number (sometimes called an abbreviated address) and data are transmitted on the channel by means of packets that carry the channel number in an address field.

In some networks which implement virtual circuits, error detection and retransmission are performed separately on each trunk. In a DATAKIT network there is error detection at all points along a virtual circuit but retransmission, if required, must be done end-to-end over the virtual circuit. Flow control is also performed end-to-end when required. For asynchronous terminals the flow and error control protocol is handled at the RS232C/network interface while for hosts it is handled either in host software or in a front-end processor.

One or more of the hosts on the network has a special relationship with the hardware packet switch in each network node. That host is called a "control computer." It is this computer that communicates with a terminal or host during call setup and takedown. It is the control computer that chooses the route for a virtual circuit, performs any necessary accounting process, and monitors the health of the network. In theory, the control computer for a DATAKIT network can be any of the hosts attached to the network. In practice, a small computer is dedicated to this function for each separate network node.

---

[1] In some DATAKIT networks the break key is used to attract attention of the network control computer and a further key stroke is required to either drop the connection or send the break to the remote host.

B. A Network Node

A node is an assembly of modules with one module type for each type of attached equipment. Thus, there are modules for hosts, terminals, and trunk transmission lines. Other modules provide switching, timing, and protocol handling functions. The intention was to make all modules conform to a simple set of standards that would allow them to be assembled many different ways. This is achieved by defining a standard back plane and designing a bus protocol for use on that back plane. Figure 2 is a picture of the prototype node. In that node one can see several different types of circuit card, each being a different network module. From left to right are a switch module, two asynchronous terminal interface modules, a host interface module, a trunk interface, and the system clock module. A photograph of the fiber-optic trunk module is to be found in Fig. 3. The circuit board contains bus interface logic, buffer memory for data, and framing, error detection, and clock recovery logic for the transmission line.

A DATAKIT node consists of one or more equipment bins interconnected so that a pair of relatively short high-speed serial buses can span the entire node (Fig. 4). Every module interfaces to both of these buses. Most modules transmit on one bus, the contention bus, and listen on a second bus, the broadcast bus. The switch module is an exception to the rule since it listens on the contention bus and transmits on the broadcast bus. A passive contention resolution protocol is used to allow the various modules to share the contention

Fig. 2.   Prototype DATAKIT node.

Fig. 3.   Fiber trunk module.

bus. Thus, a module wishing to transmit a packet to another module first obtains access to the contention bus and then sends its packet over that bus, and through the switch onto the broadcast bus. From the broadcast bus the packet is picked up by the appropriate destination module.

The service is a byte stream carried over a virtual circuit. The encoding of this byte stream on any particular transmission medium depends upon economic tradeoffs that seem appropriate for that medium. On the back plane of a DATAKIT node the byte streams are broken up into short packets of fixed length. Each packet contains up to 16 bytes of user data padded out with null bytes if necessary. Each byte occupies 9 bits, with 1 bit designating data/control. Thus null is a control code that cannot be confused with an 8 bit

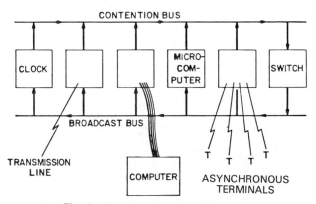

Fig. 4.   Data flow in a DATAKIT node.

byte of user data. At the beginning of each packet are a 9 bit module address and a 9 bit channel number. The module address on the contention bus identifies the module from which the packet came and on the broadcast bus identifies the module to which the packet is going. The 9 bit channel number allows each module to have up to 512 distinct circuits routed through that module at any instant.

C. Contention Resolution

The contention resolution protocol employed on the contention bus does not require any additional bus bandwidth beyond that needed to transmit a packet. It is similar to a scheme described by Mark [18].

A system-wide clock for the node indicates the start of a time slot that is exactly long enough to transmit one packet on the contention bus. A contending module first transmits its module address while simultaneously listening to the contention bus. An open collector bus driver is used so that the signal on the bus due to several contending modules is the logical OR of the several module addresses. Any module that detects a disparity between the address it is sending and the address seen on the bus, stops transmission immediately and tries again in the next time slot. It should be clear that only one module will still be active after the last module bit has been transmitted, and the address seen on the bus will be exactly the address of that module.

The module address is transmitted most significant bit first. Thus, the first modules to lose in the contention process will be those that have zero in the most significant address bit. The final effect is that of a priority contention protocol based upon the value of module address. Acampora *et al.* [11] have described a variation of this protocol that gives more equitable treatment to the contending modules. Such treatment may be important in nodes that are very heavily loaded. However, the present scheme also has an advantage. It is somewhat simpler to build a large node because the fixed priority based upon module address can be exploited to avoid the need for bidirectional transmission on the bus. In a DATAKIT node the modules are positioned along the contention bus in module address sequence starting with the largest address at the beginning of the bus. Since a module near the end of the bus cannot, because of its priority, prevail over a module near the beginning of the bus, we can use regenerative unidirectional repeaters to allow a long bus without the necessity of a reduced clock rate.

D. Virtual Circuit Implementation

All communication through DATAKIT is through virtual circuits. For example, such a circuit is shown in Fig. 5. It operates as follows. Computer A wishes to communicate with computer C. Computer A chooses one of the 512 channels available in its interface with the first DATAKIT node. Channel 3 is chosen in this case. The network common control assigns an unused trunk channel, in this case channel 15, and an unused channel, channel 2, to the destination computer C. If the incoming call is acceptable to C, data between A and C will pass over these assigned channels. To permit that, routing information is stored in each of the two packet switches. This information is similar in function to the permuter table information of a TYMNET switch [12]. In the first switch, routing information makes a connection between channel 3 of computer A and channel 15 of trunk T. In the second switch, the routing information makes a connection between channel 15 of trunk T and channel 2 of computer C.

Traffic passing through a DATAKIT node is routed in the manner just indicated by the

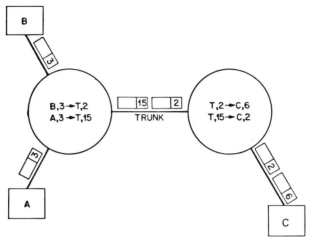

Fig. 5.   Virtual circuit example.

action of the switch module. Packets on the contention bus carry the source module address and channel number. These, in combination, address a control memory within the switch. From that memory are obtained a destination module address and a channel number that are inserted into the packet for its transmission over the broadcast bus. The packet is copied from the broadcast bus by the indicated module. Thus, the role of the switch module is quite simple and can be implemented as a pipe-lined processor that operates at bus speeds. Figure 6 is a photograph of the prototype switch module, and the control memory can be seen clearly in the photograph. The hardware shown is capable of handling approximately 42 000 16 byte packets/s. It has a control memory that can hold 2K 48 bit words where one word can contain routing information and a packet count for one-half of a full-duplex circuit.

E. Trunk Interface Module

In order that a DATAKIT packet switch could be both protocol transparent and efficient as a means of building a wide area network, we have experimented with design of trunk interface modules for 56 kbits/s and for line speeds in excess of 1.5 Mbits/s. The 56 kbit/s trunk is most suitable for use in the local access segment of a network and for long distance transmission in private networks that lack sufficient traffic to justify a high-speed trunk. Trunks that operate at the T1 speed or greater are appropriate for short distance transmission within a building or campus, and for the long-haul network.

The 56 kbit/s trunk interface module was designed to give low delay for certain types of data traffic. Experience indicates that short bursts of data generated by terminals and hosts should be transmitted as expeditiously as possible. For example, an asynchronous terminal communicating with the UNIX® operating system typically generates less than 10 characters/s, and is supported by a host program that echoes the characters typed at the terminal. The response time seen by the terminal operator should be less than about 0.1 s. More recently, screen editors and intelligent terminals have changed the pattern of terminal/host traffic, but the need for rapid response to short bursts of data remains. Hosts

---

® UNIX is a trademark of Bell Laboratories.

Fig. 6.   Switch module.

also generate short bursts of transmission when doing file transfer. For example, these short messages may be acknowledgments used for flow and error control or may be the administrative functions commonly used before and after the file itself is transferred.

For these reasons a network designer is tempted to assign high priority to acknowledgments and to the short bursts of information from asynchronous terminals. However, a priority scheme cannot simply be based upon message size for we wish to preserve data sequence on each virtual circuit. It is also desired, as indicated earlier, to make DATAKIT networks as transparent as possible to user protocol. Thus, we do not wish to build into the switching machines and trunk modules knowledge about particular user protocols. We prefer to design the trunk interface module around a queue service discipline that is as independent as possible of user protocol and traffic type.

When designing a statistically multiplexed trunk one must be concerned about the complexity of the trunk protocol and the interpacket arrival time that is available for implementation of that protocol. A design objective for the DATAKIT high-speed trunk interface module was to take advantage of VLSI by arranging that the required processing steps could be implemented in a pipe-line-like fashion with a series of special purpose mechanisms in place of a single, much faster, general purpose engine. To meet this objective and to be consistent with maintaining an uncluttered design for the basic transport mechanism, it was decided not to employ a flow control protocol on the trunk itself but to provide sufficient queue memory so that queue overflow does not occur when a higher-level protocol, level C, limits the volume of data in transmission separately for each virtual circuit. Consequently, we enjoy the benefits of per-channel flow control without the complexity of per-channel protocol handling in the high-speed trunk interface circuit. With sufficient queue space per virtual circuit to store a window of data, congestion on one virtual circuit does not block the flow on another circuit. The congestion control strategy for the network thereby is made simpler than it otherwise would have to be [10]. The price paid for streamlining the trunk module in this way is that more memory than might otherwise be necessary must be provided for queue storage. Thus, the design trades memory for high-speed logic and is judged to be more in harmony with current trends in integrated circuit design.

F. Queueing Delay

The trunk interface module multiplexes traffic from several virtual circuits on a single transmission line. While the data are waiting to be transmitted, they are stored in a queue memory. It is the algorithm used to serve these queues that determines how multiplexing occurs and the consequent delays experienced by the data. The queue service discipline used for the 56 kbit/s trunk was devised by G. G. Riddle. It is as follows. For each channel on the trunk there is a separate FIFO queue, and data wait in these queues until they can be sent over the trunk. The queues are served in a particular sequence as will be described. When served, up to 64 bytes of data are taken from the queue and these are transmitted with a very short header bearing the appropriate channel number. Several such short bursts are assembled for error detection purposes into a packet that bears a 16 bit frame check sequence and other administrative data. If there are more than 64 bytes of data in the queue, then the remainder must wait until the next time service is granted to that channel.

In addition to the per-channel queues, there are two lists of channel numbers (Fig. 7). Lists A and B are FIFO buffers that control the sequence with which the queues are serviced. When data are placed in a previously empty queue, the channel number for that queue is placed at the end of list A. The transmitter chooses which queue to service by first looking at list A. The channel number at the head of that list indicates which queue should next receive service. That queue is served, as indicated above, and the channel number is removed from list A. If data remain in the queue after service, then the channel number is placed on the end of list B. When the transmitter finds that list A is empty, it takes the next channel number from the head of list B. Again, after serving the queue the channel number is removed from the head of list B and, if data remain in the queue, the channel number is

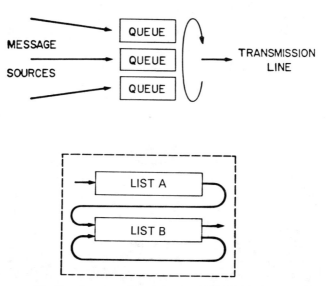

Fig. 7.   Queue service mechanism for 56 kbit/s trunk.

now placed at the end of list B. Thus, the queue service discipline gives priority to channels that have occasional short bursts of data and treats those with long bursts in a round-robin fashion.

Bursts of data from various channels are concatenated to form a single trunk packet. Bursts are added to a packet until the packet size following the addition of the last burst is not less than 256 bytes, or there are no more data waiting to be transmitted, or the last burst was obtained by serving list A and list A is now empty. The 256 byte packet size was chosen so that about 95 percent of the information transmitted when carrying bulk data is user message information. Termination of a packet when list A becomes exhausted was chosen to avoid long frame assembly delays when interactive traffic is being carried [13].

The queue service discipline has been analyzed and simulated by S. P. Morgan [13] to give the results shown in Fig. 8. The traffic used for these results was from an arbitrarily chosen mix of three different traffic types. The shortest delay was that experienced by single character messages such as acknowledgments or key strokes. The intermediate values of delay were for variable length messages with an exponentially distributed length having a mean of 40 characters. Such messages might be associated with computer output to a terminal. The longest delays were associated with variable length messages exponentially distributed with a mean length of 512 bytes. Such messages might arise in file transfer. The relative traffic intensities generated by these three types were in the ratio 10 percent: 40 percent: 50 percent, respectively, and the trunk utilization shown in Fig. 8 is the ratio of user data bytes carried (excluding overhead) to the trunk line speed in bytes/s. Delay is measured from the time of arrival for the last character of a message to the time when the frame carrying that last character has been assembled and checked at the far end of the trunk. It does not include any allowance for propagation delay on the trunk. The results show that expected delay experienced by single-character traffic with a nominal trunk load of 60 percent is less than 10 ms and that curve remains approximately linear up to saturation.

Queueing delay for a high-speed trunk operating at constant traffic intensity is reduced in proportion to trunk speed. If the trunks used in the long-haul segment of a network are more than an order of magnitude faster than the transmission lines used for local access, one would expect queueing delays for long-haul transmission lines to be an order of magnitude smaller than those experienced in the access network. Analysis by Anick *et al.* [14], and analysis and simulation by Morgan [13] suggest that there is an additional effect that further reduces queueing delay in the long-haul network. Traffic passing through the low-speed transmission lines of the access network is smoothed out so that statistical variations in its arrival rate at the queue for a high-speed trunk are less severe than might otherwise be the case. The result is a substantial reduction in queueing delay as shown in Fig. 9. That figure shows the queueing delay as a function of the ratio of access line speed to trunk line speed for constant trunk traffic intensity. For example, if access line speed is 56 kbits/s and trunk line speed is 1.344 Mbits/s, the speed ratio is 0.042 and the trunk queueing delay for messages with an average length of 512 bytes on a trunk carrying a 60 percent load is 7 percent of the queueing delay that would be experienced by the same messages had they arrived on a 1.344 Mbit/s access line. The traffic mix used in this particular case is the same as was described earlier in connection with Fig. 8. Of course, the time to transmit the message over a slow access line is greater, and in this case the two effects approximately cancel each other out.

The trunk queue service discipline was chosen for its simplicity when implemented by special purpose hardware, and for its independence of user protocol. However, the use of

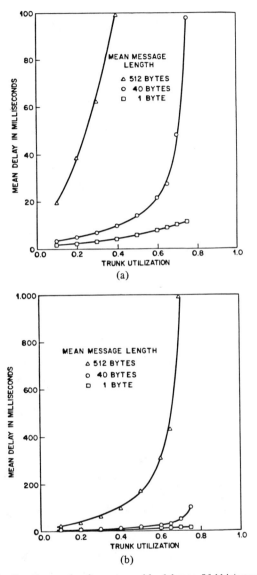

Fig. 8.   Queue plus frame assembly delay to 56 kbit/s trunk.

this queue service discipline further reinforces the byte-stream model of the data communications service supported by a DATAKIT network. Since the server only takes a small number of bytes from each queue before moving on to the next, the traffic on a trunk is quite highly multiplexed, and large blocks of data from a single source have interleaved among them the characters from other sources. Consequently, a host with a multiplexed network interface may receive data blocks simultaneously on several virtual circuits, and the characters from these blocks will be multiplexed in short bursts. Thus, it is necessary for the host interface to demultiplex the incoming byte stream into separate buffers per virtual circuit before any per-block processing can be completed. This block reassembly process in a host will be discussed again later, and it seems to be the primary burden

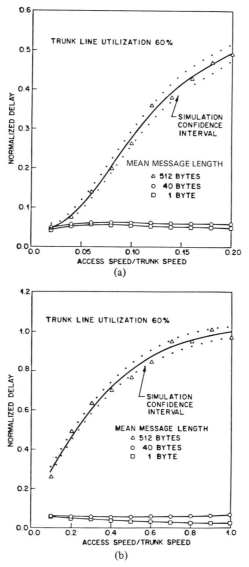

Fig. 9.   Queue plus frame assembly delay at various access line speeds.

incurred as a result of the byte-stream model implemented by a DATAKIT packet switch.

G. End-to-End Delay

The transmission delay end-to-end over a virtual circuit consists of four main parts: the time to move a message over an access line into the network, the time taken to transfer the message within a node, the queueing delay on trunks within the network, and propagation delay.

The transfer time for a packet within a lightly loaded node has been measured by Che and Marshall [16]. It is less than 100 μs. An estimate of the contention-induced addition to delay in a node carrying heavy traffic is given by Acampora *et al.* [11]. Using the contention bus protocol described earlier, delay depends upon the bus position of a module. The worst case at 80 percent traffic intensity is about 240 μs. However, Acampora *et al.* have studied an improved version of the contention protocol, also in [11], and demonstrate that the expected worst-case delay for 80 percent traffic intensity can be reduced to about 170 μs.

Queueing delay decreases with increased trunk speed so that the delay for interactive traffic, which is about 10 ms at 60 percent trunk utilization on a 56 kbit/s trunk, will be less than 500 μs if the trunk speed is increased to 1.344 Mbits/s and the traffic intensity is maintained at 60 percent. For this reason, and because there is economy of scale in transmission, it is recommended that T1 transmission rates, or greater, be employed where possible in the long-haul network.

The total delay for short messages depends upon the distance traveled and the number of packet switches en route. Over short distances employing only high-speed trunks, such as may be used in a building or campus, the delay for interactive traffic will be less than 1 ms/node. Short distances that involve a 56 kbit/s trunk will result in a delay that is dominated by the 10 ms trunk queueing time. For transcontinental communication involving one 56 kbit/s trunk and four high-speed trunks the total queueing delay plus node delay will be less than 20 ms. To that must be added propagation delay which, for coast-to-coast communication, brings the total to about 60 ms.

H. Terminal Interface Module

Our experimental network currently[2] serves about 380 asynchronous terminals. These are connected to the network by baseband connections using EIA RS232C signal levels. Experience indicates that this method of interconnection can be used to carry full-duplex asynchronous data as far as 500 ft at 9600 Bd.[3]

Asynchronous terminals connect to a DATAKIT interface module such as that illustrated in Fig. 10. It is constructed from an Intel 8085 microprocessor to which are attached four UART's that interface with four terminal access lines. The 8085 microprocessor proved to

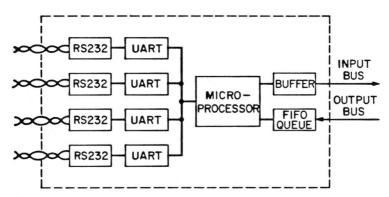

Fig. 10.   Asynchronous line interface module.

[2] August 1983.
[3] The EIA RS232C Standard recommends a maximum range of 50 ft which our experience indicates is very conservative.

be a practical experimental environment in which to develop the control procedures and protocols necessary for this type of line module. However, the long-term goal is to reduce the line interface to approximately one LSI chip per line. In this way we expect to substantially reduce the cost of the most numerous interface module in our network.

Figure 11 shows the information flow for one terminal within the asynchronous terminal interface module. There are five major logic functions performed in the module: packet assembly, packet disassembly, flow control, terminal timing control, and supervision. Data characters from a terminal are temporarily held in a buffer while a packet of data bytes is formed for transmission through the network. Since we wish the interface module to be transparent to user data, the packet assembly algorithm is to collect characters until either a 16 byte packet is full or until about 50 ms has elapsed since the arrival of the first character. In this way the characters from a keyboard are transmitted without noticeable delay, and characters from a host using this asynchronous interface module tend to be carried in full packets. Data from the network are also stored in a 256 byte buffer as it waits for transmission to the terminal. Flow and error control for traffic from a remote host are achieved by means of additional control characters interleaved with the user data. Other control characters may be transmitted by a remote host in order to effect necessary transmission delays. For example, some mechanical terminals require that delivery of further data is delayed while a carriage return takes place.

The fifth control function is the supervision of the terminal from the network. In particular, the interface module monitors the terminal ready lead and controls the state of the carrier detect lead. Transitions on terminal ready indicate when the terminal wishes to place a new call or to terminate an existing one. Carrier detect indicates when a virtual circuit has been established. The states of these leads are monitored and controlled by the network control computer using single character messages that it exchanges with the terminal interface module.

The character asynchronous interface module has been used for interfacing directly to modems, to automatic calling units, and to the character asynchronous ports common on time-shared computers. In the interest of minimizing manufacturing cost, we have endeavored to make all of these applications compatible with one design of the interface module while the necessary differences in supervision procedure are reflected in the common control computer software.

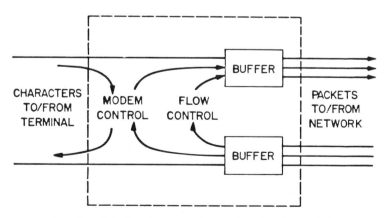

Fig. 11. Data flow in an asynchronous line interface module.

I. Data Format

The terminal interface module just described illustrates the need to transport three different types of information over a DATAKIT virtual circuit. In addition to user data bytes, there is information used for end-to-end protocols, such as flow control, and there is information transmitted between common control and the edge of the network for supervisory purposes. Rather than incur the cost and complexity of separate data paths for these three types of information, a DATAKIT packet switch employs a single information unit within which each of these three types can be encoded.

Within a DATAKIT node, on the back plane buses and through the switch, information is transmitted in 9 bit envelopes. Figure 12 shows the format. User data bytes are each 8 bits long and are prefixed with a 9th bit that is always a 1. End-to-end control characters are 7 bits long and are prefixed with two 0 bits. Supervisory characters, also 7 bits long, are prefixed by a 01 bit pattern. All three of these information types can be carried over every DATAKIT virtual circuit. All user data and network control information are encoded using these basic information units, and there are essentially no information paths within the network other than those that carry virtual circuits.

J. Supervision

In an earlier section we described the switching process for user data carried on a virtual circuit. The switch module operates in accordance with information stored in a control memory, and for ordinary user data that control memory specifies for each virtual circuit where the outgoing packets must be sent. In fact, there are two sets of routing information for each virtual circuit. The second set is used for packets that contain supervisory information. The switch hardware recognizes the 01 prefix on supervisory characters and switches them according to the second set of routing information.[4] Thus, by suitably initializing the switch control memories in a network it is possible to extract the supervisory information from a virtual circuit at any switching point. In that way supervisory information is extracted from a virtual circuit and routed to a control computer.

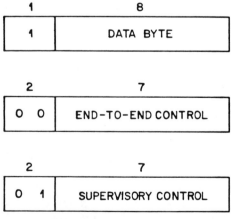

Fig. 12.   Envelope formats.

---

[4] Supervisory characters are constrained not to share a packet with user data so that the switch does not have to break packets apart when switching them.

The control computer of our experimental network is a PDP 11/23[5] running a special purpose multiprocessing system designed to handle many small and stereotyped processes. The design by L. E. McMahon [15] follows from earlier joint work by L. E. McMahon, J. H. Condon, and K. L. Thompson on an experimental software system for a voice PBX. The current PDP 11/23 system can handle about 300 active processes and it is hoped to increase this to about 1000 soon. There is a separate process for each active channel on each module of a DATAKIT node. Thus, a single asynchronous terminal is represented in the control computer by a single process, and it is to this process that the supervisory information from the terminal is sent. Other processes supervise the ends of channels from host computers and the ends of channels that pass over trunks. Unlike the processes in a time-sharing system, these processes have relatively simple contexts and can be created, destroyed, and switched with modest overhead. It takes about 3 ms on the PDP 11/23 for one process to send a message to another, relinquish the processor, have the other process scheduled, and then read the message.

The control computer is required when a new virtual circuit is established or when a virtual circuit is taken down. It is not required to handle any user data and, indeed, one can halt the control computer without impeding the flow of traffic on established virtual circuits. Che and Marshall [16] have made measurements of the response time seen by a host during circuit setup. They measured a response time of about 60 ms in a single node network under light load and with a PDP 11/23 control computer.

The control computer's supervisory process for a terminal implements the entire protocol required to supervise that one terminal, and the states that the terminal interface may go through are represented by the flow of control within the supervisory process. For example, the supervisory process for a dumb terminal keeps track of the changes in state of the terminal ready lead, sends and receives characters to and from the terminal while the terminal operator is placing a call, and effects the necessary call setup action by passing messages to other supervisory processes within the common control. In the case that a connection passes over a trunk to another DATAKIT node, the call administration messages are passed from the supervisory process at one end of a trunk to the corresponding process at the other end.

K. Host Interface

The earliest host interfaces to DATAKIT employed a parallel interface that terminated at a register on the host peripheral bus. All communication protocols had to be implemented by software in the host, and there was no hardware support for DMA. In order to increase performance and to allow a host to be located at a greater distance from the DATAKIT node, a more recent host interface design employs optical fiber transmission at the same speed as the DATAKIT back plane buses. By studying the actions required in a host front-end processor W. T. Marshall and H. Che have developed a more efficient host interface that uses a bipolar communications processor, the KMC11-B, for PDP 11 and VAX[6] computers.

Most of the computers attached to the network use the UNIX operating system, and Marshall and Che made measurements both of kernel-to-kernel and user-level-to-user-level information flow [16]. When all communication processing is done within the host, the

---

[5] PDP is a trademark of Digital Equipment Corporation.
[6] VAX is trademark of Digital Equipment Corporation.

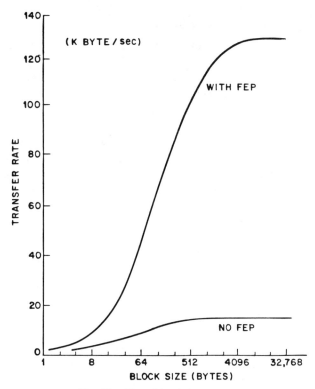

Fig. 13.   Kernel-level throughput.

maximum kernel-to-kernel throughput is about 20 000 bytes/s. Figure 13 shows that much higher speeds, up to about 120 000 bytes/s, are achieved with the aid of the communications processor. The computer used for these measurements was a PDP 11/45. When a user-level process on that machine does an internal file transfer to the local disk, we find that the peak data transfer rate is about 48 000 bytes/s, while the peak file transfer rate between user-level processes across the network is somewhat greater, as shown in Fig. 14. Thus, it appears that even with the 5 MHz front-end processor, host software and network interface are the limiting factors in obtaining high throughput.

IV. Conclusion

It is anticipated that the telecommunications network for data (and voice) will be hierarchically organized. At the toll level, high-speed transmission lines will interconnect toll switches that concentrate large volumes of traffic. Local access networks for the foreseeable future will be dominated by copper wire and usually be limited in speed to 56 kbits/s. Within a building there will be a higher-speed distribution system whose performance is dominated more by protocol handling and appliance interfacing requirements than by transmission bandwidth. End-to-end delay for short messages on the network can be expected to range between a few ms for short distances to about 60 ms for transcontinental terrestrial communications.

A study of this structure suggests a data transport service that implements switched virtual circuits with the following characteristics.

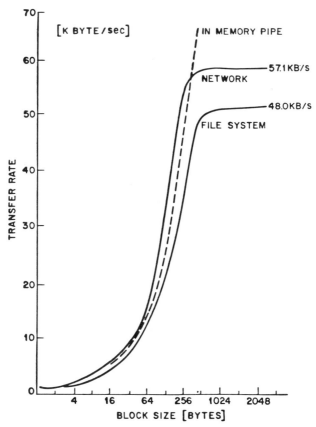

Fig. 14.   User-level throughput.

1) A virtual circuit provides asynchronous point-to-point communication.

2) The information bytes carried are of two types: control and user data.

3) A virtual circuit does not duplicate or rearrange transmitted data; sequence is preserved.

4) Information bytes corrupted in transmission are discarded within the network.

5) Data bytes lost in transmission are, when necessary, retransmitted end-to-end over the virtual circuit.

6) Each virtual circuit has a finite storage capacity defined at call setup time.

By experiment we have found that this type of data transport service can be implemented using simple hardware whose size and performance is more reminiscent of time-division equipment than of conventional packet switches. Yet we can obtain the transmission efficiency of a packet network by using asynchronous multiplexing techniques on long transmission lines. One indication of the implementation flexibility provided by the architecture is that a switch can itself be replaced by a network without violating the architecture. That suggests the possibility of building large switches from arrays of smaller switching devices (as is of course usual in time-division networks). This makes possible a switching machine that can grow gracefully in size and permits one to build the very high throughput switches that will in the future be required for toll switching.

The data communication service implemented by protocol levels A and B is the constant basis upon which different network users might build their particular communications arrangements and is the constant framework within which the network implementor is free to work. Additions to the DATAKIT implementation, perhaps using new technology, are made within the constraint that the service definition must remain constant. We have found this to be a quite liberal constraint.

Users are free to choose the communication functions and protocols that best suit their application. Telephony, for example, is not burdened with a packet structure that properly belongs to data communication. At one extreme, a user may choose to use the network as an intelligent "copper wire" that can tell the difference between valid data and idle transmission, and so employs statistical multiplexing for transmission efficiency. In this way, the network can efficiently support existing private networks with their own existing protocols. However, that is a short-term approach which does not enable effective communication between arbitrary pairs of terminals. The latter can only take place if users employ a common protocol. In due course, we expect users to migrate to a common standard but adoption of such a standard is not a precondition for using a DATAKIT network.

ACKNOWLEDGMENT

The author is indebted to the many people who have contributed their time and ingenuity to our work on the DATAKIT packet switch. The experimental hardware was constructed by J. R. Vollaro. Early versions of the control computer and host software were written by G. L. Chesson. More recently L. E. McMahon and W. T. Marshall have written the program used in the control computer, and W. T. Marshall, D. M. Ritchie, and H. Che have written the software used with the UNIX operating system. The 56 kbit/s trunk module software was written by G. G. Riddle, and S. P. Morgan has provided a study of trunk queueing delay. R. J. Elliott wrote the software for the network monitor, and J. P. Haggerty helped with diagnostic software. A. E. Kaplan designed the most recent fiber-based host interface. Through many discussions and through his work on circuit design aids software, J. H. Condon has provided the author with much support. The author is particularly grateful to J. R. Vollaro, E. J. Sitar, L. E. McMahon, and W. T. Marshall, who have all gone out of their way to bring our experimental network into successful operation.

REFERENCES

[1] K. E. Fultz and D. B. Penick, "The T1 carrier system," *Bell Syst. Tech. J.,* vol. 44, pp. 1405–1451, Sept. 1965.
[2] B. S. Bosik and S. V. Kartalopoulos, "A time compression multiplexing system for a circuit switched digital capability," *IEEE Trans. Commun.,* vol. COM-30, pp. 2046–2052, Sept. 1982.
[3] A. G. Fraser, "Spider—An experimental data communications system," in *Proc. IEEE Int. Conf. Commun.,* June 1974, pp. 21F1–21F10.
[4] A. Hopper and D. J. Wheeler, "Maintenance of ring communication systems," *IEEE Trans. Commun.,* vol. COM-27, pp. 760–761, Apr. 1979.
[5] J. H. Saltzer and K. T. Pogran, "A star-shaped ring network with high maintainability," *Comput. Network,* vol. 4, pp. 239–244, Oct./Nov. 1980.
[6] W. Bux, F. Closs, P. A. Janson, K. Kümmerle, H. R. Müller, and E. H. Rothauser, "A local-area communication network based on a reliable token-ring system," in *Local Computer Networks,* P. C. Ravasio, G. Hopkins, and N. Naffah, Eds., Amsterdam, The Netherlands: North-Holland, 1982, pp. 69–82.
[7] R. M. Metcalfe and D. R. Boggs, "Ethernet: Distributed packet switching for local computer networks," *Commun. ACM,* vol. 19, pp. 395–403, July 1976.

[8]   A. G. Fraser, "The architecture of a byte stream network," in *Proc. 6th Int. Conf. Comput. Commun.,* Sept. 1982, Amsterdam, The Netherlands: North-Holland, pp. 634–639.

[9]   H. Zimmermann, "OSI reference model—The ISO model of architecture for open systems interconnection," *IEEE Trans. Commun.,* vol. COM-28, pp. 425–432, Apr. 1980.

[10] M. Gerla and L. Kleinrock, "Flow control: A comparative survey," *IEEE Trans. Commun.,* vol. COM-28, pp. 553–574, Apr. 1980.

[11] A. S. Acampora, M. G. Hluchyj, and C. D. Taso, "A centralized-bus architecture for local area networks," in *Proc. Int. Conf. Commun.,* Boston, MA, June 1983.

[12] L. Tymes, "TYMNET—A terminal oriented communication network," in *Proc. Spring Joint Comput. Conf. AFIPS,* vol. 38, 1971, pp. 211–216.

[13] S. P. Morgan, private communication.

[14] D. Anick, D. Mitra, and M. M. Sondhi, "Stochastic theory of a data-handling system with multiple sources," *Bell Syst. Tech. J.,* vol. 61, pp. 1871–1894, Oct. 1982.

[15] L. E. McMahon, "An experimental software organization for a laboratory data switch," in *Proc. Int. Conf. Commun.,* Denver, CO, June 1981.

[16] G. W. R. Luderer, H. Che, and W. T. Marshall, "A virtual circuit switch as the basis for distributed systems," in *Proc. 7th IEEE Data Commun. Symp.,* Oct. 1981, pp. 164–179.

[17] A. G. Fraser, "A virtual channel network," *Datamation,* vol. 21, pp. 51–58, Feb. 1975.

[18] J. W. Mark, "Distributed scheduling conflict-free multiple access for local area communication networks," *IEEE Trans. Commun.,* vol. COM-28, pp. 1968–1976, Dec. 1980.

10

The Principles and Performance of Hubnet: A 50 Mbit/s Glass Fiber Local Area Network

E. STEWART LEE AND PETER I. P. BOULTON

Hubnet is a 50 Mbit/s local area network using glass fiber as a transmission medium. The performance of the network for different topologies and loads is analyzed. This analysis is supported by experience with prototype hardware. The network is shown to have excellent performance up to loads which are a large fraction of capacity.

I. INTRODUCTION

Hubnet is a packet-switching local area network using glass fiber as a transmission medium. It operates at a data rate of 50 Mbits/s. A simple rooted tree network structure is used. This new structure was developed because of the technical limitations of glass fiber as a communications medium. The purpose of this chapter is to describe the principles of operation of this structure and to obtain some performance results. A similar structure was reported by Closs and Lee [1], but their network does not operate in quite the same way (see Section II-C).

Most networks operating under very light load can perform extremely well. Since very light load is the normal operating mode of networks, in practice one rarely sees heavy loading. However, it is important to understand the effects of heavy loading. An impulse of load is a momentary heavy load. It could be caused, for instance, by a clock reaching a critical value, such as noon. The ability of a network to respond to any such impulse is important. In general, if a network handles a continuous heavy load well, it will also cope well with impulse loads. The performance of this network under both light and heavy loads is remarkably good. An analysis of the network to show this is included in this chapter. The results of the analysis agree in form with the observed properties of a full-scale prototype network which has been built.

II. PRINCIPLES OF THE ROOTED TREE STRUCTURE

Because of the properties of fiber-optic communications, it was evident that most conventional LAN topologies [2]–[4] were not well suited for that medium.

We looked for an unconventional structure for our network. It was clear that bidirectional transmission could be achieved at reasonable cost using a twin-fiber cable, one for each direction. Further, if these cables were packaged together forming a single unit, the cost remained competitive with that of copper coaxial cable capable of similar service. The costs and difficulties of using taps, and the capability of available transducers, implied point-to-point communications. The notion of using a bus structure, but with the bus of vanishingly short length, is consistent with these requirements. Taps are not required, and all communications can be point-to-point.

After due consideration of these points, a structure consisting of a pair of matching rooted trees has been adopted. Figure 1 shows these trees rooted at the *hub*. Intelligent devices called *network access controllers* (NAC's) are connected to the corresponding leaves of two matching trees sharing the same root hub. The internal nodes in each tree are technically similar to those at the hub. These nodes are called *subhubs*. The trees are known as the *selection tree* and the *broadcast tree*. Since the tree structures match exactly, the actual implementation of the network shown in Fig. 1 is closer to that shown in Fig. 2, in which the two trees are overlain. Significant hardware savings can be achieved by having selection nodes and broadcast nodes constructed together in this way, but they remain almost completely independent.

A packet being sent on the network is transmitted in a frame, which is arranged as shown in Fig. 3. This frame is different from the present practice of other networks largely to minimize the length of the shortest packet. The synchronizing pattern is 8 bit times in duration, and serves to warn the reception circuitry of the NAC that a new frame is arriving. The destination NAC address and the source NAC address are self-explanatory 16 bit fields. The destination network address and source network address are optional and are used only when packets are to be sent between interconnected networks.

One or more NAC addresses are permanently and uniquely associated with a NAC. The packet reception circuitry in each NAC is capable of recognizing every packet destined for it, from the appearance of any one of its NAC addresses in the destination field of the received packet. These packets are collected in a reception buffer for subsequent processing by higher levels of the protocol.

The reception circuitry in a NAC is also responsible for recognizing every packet sent by its corresponding transmission circuitry, from the appearance of its own address in the source address field of the packet. The receiver signals its corresponding transmitter when

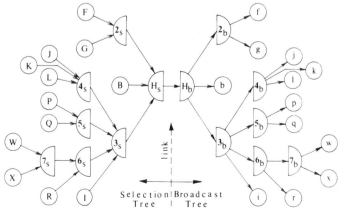

Fig. 1.   Hubnet showing the trees.

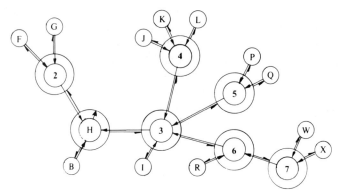

Fig. 2.   Hubnet with the trees overlain.

it detects a packet apparently originating from one of its NAC addresses. This detection of an *echo* of a packet is the only direct communication between the reception function of the NAC and its transmission function, below the transport layer of the protocol. The process of sending a packet depends in an important way upon this mechanism.

A. Transmitting a Packet

A packet to be transmitted is placed in a transmission buffer in the NAC by the host. The packet will remain in this buffer until it appears to have been successfully sent to its intended destination. When the packet being sent is the only one contending for service (Section II-B), the transmission process is particularly simple. When several NAC's are simultaneously attempting to send packets (Section II-C), the mechanisms required are somewhat more elaborate.

B. A Quiescent Network

A NAC which has a packet to transmit sends a frame containing the packet to the selection side of the hub to which it is connected. Since the network is quiescent, this hub

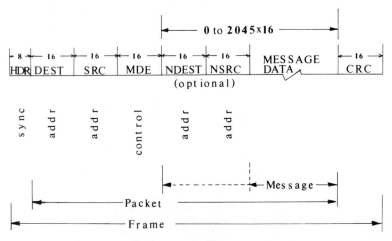

Fig. 3.   A frame containing a packet.

selects the frame and sends it to the yet-more-central hub to which its selection side is connected. Eventually, the frame will be selected by the selection side of the central hub. No other frame exists to interfere with this selection process. The frame will be sent from the root of the selection tree, across the link, to the root of the broadcast tree. Any frame entering the root of the broadcast tree will be sent up the entire tree. During this broadcasting, the reception circuitry in each NAC can inspect the packet. The packet will

a) be read into the reception buffer of the destination NAC,

b) cause an echo detection signal in the source NAC, and

c) be ignored by every other NAC.

For example, in Fig. 1, if NAC transmitter "W" sends a packet to NAC receiver "k," the frame will be selected along the path through nodes $7s$, $6s$, $3s$, to the selection side of the central hub, Hs. The frame will proceed across the link joining Hs and Hb. It will be broadcast to all NAC receivers by the broadcast tree. The path from Hb to NAC receiver "k" is through nodes $3b$ and $4b$.

The hubs do not make a copy of the frame they have selected. They pass the bits on in real time. In the prototype circuitry, the delay in the selection side of each hub is only about nine bit times. The broadcast side of the hub has no appreciable delay. Consequently, the time delay between a NAC starting transmission of a packet and the generation of the echo signal by its reception circuitry will be independent of the packet length, and will be bounded and predictable. It is mostly determined by the signal propagation time in the cables.

C. A Nonquiescent Network

If the network is not quiescent when a NAC starts transmitting the frame, a different situation may occur. As the frame is selected and sent to yet-more-central hubs, it may encounter a hub which has already selected a frame from some other NAC. The already committed hub will ignore the newly incoming frame. The NAC originating the unselected frame will never see an echo of the packet being sent. Since the echo signal is not detected within a specified time-out limit called the *retry time*, the NAC transmitter originating the transmission will assume that the packet will never be received by any NAC. Transmission of the unselected frame is immediately halted.[1] A few bit times after the expiry of the retry time, the transmission is attempted again. Transmission will be repeated until the frame has been selected all the way to the link joining the two trees, or a very large number of retries has been made (128 in the prototype). The exceptional cases where this series of retries does not eventually succeed, or where extra packets are introduced in the network due to hardware fault, are handled by higher level protocols.

This retry time is an important parameter of each NAC in the network. It must be at least long enough for the echo to be detected, if one occurs. It is set in practice by switches in the NAC. In many cases all NAC's will be set to the same retry time (see Section VII-C).

Referring to the example above, suppose that while the packet from NAC transmitter "W" to NAC receiver "k" is being sent, NAC transmitter "G" attempts to send a packet to NAC receiver "p." The new frame will be selected by node $2s$, but will be ignored by the already busy selection side of the central hub. NAC transmitter "G" will soon timeout because of the lack of an echo detection from its corresponding receiver "g." Transmitter "G" will halt transmission for a few bit times, and then retransmit the frame. Any other

---

[1] This action is unnecessary when the packet being transmitted is very short. The transmitter will have stopped already, and will be idle and awaiting the echo.

transmission attempts will also be retrying. The original frame from "W" to "k" must eventually end. The first of the retrying frames to be selected all the way to the link will be the next to be broadcast.

A NAC must not begin the transmission of a new packet until it has seen the echo signal for the previous packet. If a NAC is sufficiently far away from the link, then its timeout for the echo signal could be much larger than that for the other stations. Such a remote NAC will not be able to retry as often as other NAC's competing for selection. Under heavy load, this may result in larger than normal transmission delays at this remote NAC.

If a newly incoming frame is being ignored by a hub, it must continue to be ignored as long as it is being received at the hub. Only then does the hub become free for reselection of frames on that fiber path. This is so that all selected frames are seen in their entirety.

It is important that the hub distinguish which is first among several apparently coincident frames. This is the frame that should be selected. The prototype hardware which we have implemented determines a frame which is first in all cases. If the coincidence of frame arrivals is to within a small fraction of a bit time, one of them is deemed to have been first and is selected. The hardware has a fixed precedence ordering on the incoming fibers for this purpose. An important consequence of the selection of one of the apparently coincident frames as first is that useful work is done in all cases where there is any work to do. No network bandwidth is expended transmitting frames known to be defective. This determination of a packet to transmit in all cases is a significant distinction in principle between the lower layers of Hubnet and the work of Closs and Lee [1].

The retry time is different from the roundtrip time of CSMA/CD bus networks [3]. In the latter case, the packet duration must exceed the roundtrip time. Shorter messages must be padded to this length one way or another. In Hubnet, the retry time does not affect the packet length. It affects only the rate of generation of packets by an individual NAC. The packets themselves may be of any length up to some hardware limitation (4096 bytes in the prototype), provided that the appropriate address and mode fields are present.

III. THE NETWORK ACCESS CONTROLLER

A NAC contains an interface to the network including reception and transmission buffers, and an interface to the host device. The host interface design will be completely determined by the characteristics of each host. Host interfaces now exist for the Intel multibus, the DEC unibus, and the Q bus. Other host interfaces are under active development.

In detail, a NAC consists of:

- optical transceiver equipment with the required encoding, decoding, and serialization logic;
- transmit and receive buffers;
- a host bus interface and DMA control;
- address recognition and generation;
- the control logic for the NAC transmit and receive protocol;
- error checking.

IV. THE HUB

The central hub consists of a selection module and a broadcast module interconnected with a unidirectional link. The selection module of a hub monitors all the ingoing fibers connected to it, and if it detects an optical signal will either inject a copy of the optical signal into the link, or ignore the optical signal and inject nothing into the link. The broadcast module of a hub monitors the link for a signal, and in all cases copies this signal into all the outgoing fibers.

In the case of a subhub, this link does not exist. The selection side of a subhub is connected to a more central hub as if it were from the transmitter of a NAC. The corresponding broadcast side of the subhub is connected to the same more central hub as if it were the receiver in a NAC. Subhubs and central hubs differ materially only in this way.

V. EXPANDABILITY OF THE NETWORK

The network is designed so that a large configuration can be constructed from similar smaller components. In this way, growth of the network, and changing concentrations of hosts, can usually be accommodated without extensive restringing of cables or other expensive alterations.

Each hub can accommodate up to some limited number of NAC's, so that the simplest network consists of a few NAC's connected to a hub by pairs of fibers. In the prototype implementation, a total of 11 NAC's and subhubs may be connected to any hub. This limit of 11 was the result of the hardware packaging. The determination of the number of hubs and NAC's in a proposed network, and their interconnection, will in practice be determined more by installation and convenience issues than by network requirements.

The maximum number of NAC's which can be connected in this way is limited by two factors. First, the number of distinct addresses is 65 536. It is not considered likely that this limit will prove constrictive. Second, the interconnection of too many NAC's in the way specified is likely to result in an excessive number of packets with possible network overload, and resultant delays in transmission. This second limitation is much more likely to prove a problem.

VI. COMMUNICATIONS PROTOCOLS

The NAC protocol is an instance of the ISO physical, data-link, and network layer, to provide a connectionless-mode network service.

A. Frame and Packet Formats

All data passing through Hubnet are encapsulated in *frames* shown in Fig. 3. The data are encapsulated in a packet within the data fields of a frame, and consist of addressing and mode fields, and data fields.

NAC's are set up to recognize a particular address (or range of addresses) by the setting of internal ''address'' and ''don't care'' switches.

B. Frame Format

All the data fields in a frame are 16 bits long. The prototype network has a limit of 2048 such words in each frame. The minimum length packet contains no data fields.

The header (HDR) field is a synchronizing pattern 8 bits in length. Since a modified Miller ''single-zero-crossing-per-bit'' encoding is employed, the interval between frames is recognizable as containing no bits, hence the synchronizing pattern can be recognized uniquely. The CRC field contains a cyclic redundancy check value computed on all fields of the frame other than the header field. NAC's must discard as invalid frames which do not meet the CRC check when they are received. The higher level protocols will restart the transmission of packets over the virtual circuit in an orderly way. The CRC field is recognized by its position as the last 16 bit field in the frame.

C. Packet Format

The network layer packet is embedded in the data fields of a frame and has one of the following formats:

|DEST|SRCE|MDE|···data fields···|
|DEST|SRCE|MDE|NDEST|NSRCE|···data fields···|

The destination address (DEST) specifies a NAC within the local Hubnet, or reachable from the local Hubnet by one or more gateway hops. In the local case the destination address, DEST, uniquely identifies the destination NAC. In the nonlocal case additional information contained in the network destination address, NDEST, is needed to uniquely identify the destination NAC. NAC addresses may be specified (in the NAC hardware) as a range of addresses. The addressing action taken by any NAC with respect to packets it receives or transmits is determined by the values of mode bits as defined below.

The particular layout of a packet was chosen for efficiency reasons. A minimum length packet is sufficiently short (a 72 bit frame) that every datagram can be acknowledged without loss of two much bandwidth. In consequence, the details of the protocols were quite simple to design and implement.

The mode (MDE) field consists of 16 bits, only the first three of which are used. These are:

fd—This *foreign destination bit* is 0 to denote a packet addressed to a NAC on the local Hubnet, 1 otherwise.

fs—This *foreign source bit* is 0 to denote a packet from a NAC on the local Hubnet, 1 otherwise.

br—This *broadcast bit* is 1 to denote a packet that is to be received by all NAC's.

In the prototype network, each host contains an implementation of the TCP/IP protocols, such as is found in Berkeley 4.2 BSD UNIX. TCP/IP makes use of the connectionless-mode network service provided by Hubnet to supply all its usual services.

VII. PERFORMANCE ESTIMATES

Throughout the analysis, consistent basic notation and parameter values are used. It is assumed that the number of transmission errors is negligible. All acknowledgment frames are assumed to be 80 bits long, including allowance for 8 bit times extra length to represent the detection of the end of the frame. At 50 Mbits/s, an acknowledgment is $L_2 = 1.6\ \mu s$ long. A data frame is similar to an acknowledgment, except that it also includes data. All data frames in the network are assumed to be L_1 s long and to be independent. The retry time (r) of all NAC's is set to 5 μs, corresponding to a cable length of more than half a kilometer.

In order to send a packet or acknowledgment, the software in the host must intervene and activate most or all of its layers. This is an expensive procedure. The preparation of an acknowledgment in the host takes $T_{ap} = 2.5$ ms in the prototype, which is the value used here. A datagram takes this long, plus 10 ns packet preparation time per bit of data length (T_{mp}), to account for the time spent loading the buffers. These times are obviously the most significant factors in limiting the performance of NAC's.

The proportion of time that the link is transporting some frame is a very significant parameter in the performance of the network. It is called the *duty cycle* (*d*) of the link. The duty cycle cannot exceed one. The duty cycle is also the probability that an incoming frame will encounter an already selected hub, and be ignored.

A. Network Saturation

This analysis simplifies the network to a single hub with many NAC's, assumed identical, connected to it. The simplification to a single hub should not have a large effect upon the validity of the analysis, provided the results are confined to networks with a regular symmetrical structure. Clearly, if the offered load is low, the delivered load and the offered load will be identical. As the offered load approaches the capacity of the network, the probability of contention increases.

Suppose n NAC's are each attempting to transmit ∂ packets/s. When the packet which has just been selected finishes, some of these NAC's will attempt to have their packet selected within at most one retry time, and because of the way the hub operates the first frame to appear at the hub will be selected.

Let m frames be attempting to be selected at the hub. Since for selection purposes the frames are indistinguishable, the average time to select one of these m frames, from the time when the selection side of the hub becomes not busy, will be $r/(m + 1)$.

The proportion of capacity d being delivered on the link is $d = n\partial(L_1 + L_2)$. The packet rate ∂ can be expressed in terms of the time taken for the sequence of events involved in sending a packet. The packet first must be prepared (T_{mp}). Then there will be a delay of an average of T_s while the frame containing the packet is selected at the hub. After selection, the frame must be sent, taking L_1. The acknowledgment will go through a similar sequence, taking $T_{ap} + T_s + L_2$. The packet has now been sent and acknowledged, and a wait of T_w will occur until the next packet starts.

$$\partial = \frac{1}{T_{mp} + T_s + L_1 + T_{ap} + T_s + L_2 + T_w} .$$

The only term in this equation that presents any difficulty is T_s, the time to be selected. An average value for this time can be obtained. The time to be selected will be the time spent in a number of series of contentions. The first series of contentions, if it occurs, will start on average in the middle of the packet which has previously captured the network, and will average

$$T_f = \frac{L_1 + L_2}{4} + \frac{r}{dn + 1} .$$

Subsequent series of contentions, if they occur, will begin at the start of a packet which captures the network, and will be

$$T_a = \frac{L_1 + L_2}{2} + \frac{r}{dn + 1} .$$

These expressions are straightforward, except for the crude approximation that the number of frames attempting to be selected at any time is $m = dn$.

The probability of contention is d, and the probability that a specific frame has been selected from among the $m = dn$ equally probable frames is $1/m$. Hence,

$$T_s = d\frac{T_f}{m} + d \sum_{i=0}^{\infty} \left[T_f\left(1 - \frac{1}{m}\right) + T_a \left(1 - \frac{1}{m}\right)^i \frac{1}{m} \right]$$

$$= dT_f + dT_a$$

$$= \frac{3}{4} d (L_1 + L_2) + \frac{2dr}{dn + 1} .$$

These equations have three unknowns in them: ∂, d, and T_w. Within the constraints that $0 \leqslant d < 1$ and $T_w \geqslant 0$, $\partial = d/n(L_1 + L_2)$ may be evaluated for various duty cycles. These results are shown in Figs. 4–7.

In Fig. 4, the relationship between the packet rate and the duty cycle for a network with two NAC's attempting to transmit is shown for several message lengths. The effective limitation on performance is determined by the ability of the NAC to supply packets (shown as a dashed line in Fig. 4). This limit occurs when $T_w = 0$. On this line, both NAC's are supplying packets as rapidly as they can.

Figure 5 presents similar results for a more realistic network with ten NAC's transmitting. A network with 100 NAC's transmitting will perform as shown in Fig. 6. In this case, there are sufficient NAC's sending packets that at a message length above about 300 bytes the network may saturate.

In the hypothetical case of a network with 1000 NAC's transmitting, it is shown in Fig. 7

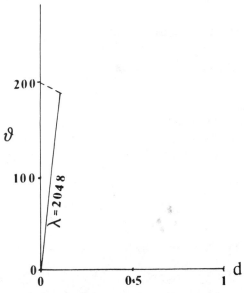

Fig. 4. Saturation of the packet transmission rate ∂ (packets/s/NAC) as a function of the link utilization d. Two NAC's.

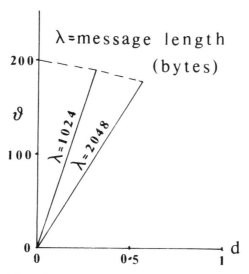

Fig. 5.   Saturation of the packet transmission rate ϑ (packets/s/NAC) as a function of the link utilization d. Ten NAC's.

that the network will be seriously overloaded unless the messages are very short, or the packet rate is very small.

Figure 8 shows the effect of a number of different packet preparation times for some packet lengths which are expected to be representative of those in actual use in the network. As mentioned in Section VII, these times are the most significant factor in determining the limits of the capacity of the network. Since they are dominant, an approximate value for the maximum message rate per NAC is $\vartheta_{max} = 1/2T_{ap}$. In the case where the message length is 512 bytes, 100 NAC's cannot simultaneously transmit frames at the maximum rate on a link operating at 50 Mbits/s.

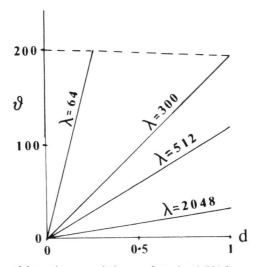

Fig. 6.   Saturation of the packet transmission rate ϑ (packets/s/NAC) as a function of the link utilization d. 100 NAC's.

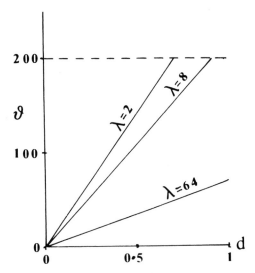

Fig. 7.   Saturation of the packet transmission rate ϑ (packets/s/NAC) as a function of the link utilization d. 1000 NAC's.

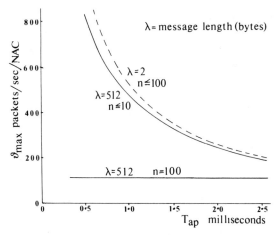

Fig. 8.   The maximum packet transmission rate ϑ_{max} as a function of packet preparation time T_{ap}.

B. Saturation with One NAC at a Different Rate

It is interesting to consider the case where n NAC's are each attempting to transmit ϑ_1 packets/s, and another particular NAC is operating at ϑ_2 packets/s. The analysis of Section VII-A easily adapts to this situation. The wait time of the n NAC's is T_{w1}, and that of the other is T_{w2}. With this notation, the following are easily obtained:

$$d = (n\vartheta_1 + \vartheta_2)(L_1 + L_2)$$

$$T_s = d\left(\frac{3}{4}(L_1 + L_2) + \frac{2r}{d(n+1)+1}\right)$$

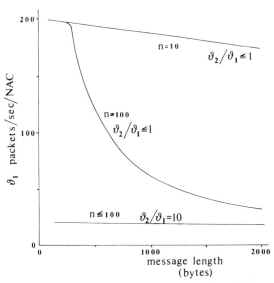

Fig. 9. Limits to the packet transmission rate ∂_2 when one other NAC is transmitting at ∂_2 packets/s.

$$T_{w1} = \frac{1}{\partial_1} - T_{mp} - T_s - L_1 - T_{ap} - T_s - L_2$$

$$T_{w2} = \frac{1}{\partial_2} - T_{mp} - T_s - L_1 - T_{ap} - T_s - L_2.$$

In Fig. 9, the case $n = 10$, $\partial_2/\partial_1 \leqslant 1$ shows that, up to the point where the capacity of the link is approached, the performance of the network is not a strong function of message length. For the case $n = 100$, $\partial_2/\partial_1 \leqslant 1$, the capacity of the link is approached at a message length of about 300 bytes. When $\partial_2/\partial_1 = 10$, the load is less than capacity because the n NAC's are supplying packets at a tenth of their maximum rate.

C. Effect of a Fast Retry Rate

If another NAC, with a retry time $\geqslant 1$ times smaller than the retry time of the n original NAC's, is added to the hub, it is interesting to determine the probability that a frame from this fast NAC will be preferred in the contention to be selected. This decrease in the retry time might be achieved by installing the faster NAC directly on the central hub.

For simplicity of analysis, time is measured in units of r s. Without the faster NAC, the time to the first request for selection will be uniform on $(0, 1)$. There are $m = dn$ frames contending for selection, and the distribution function is $F_m(t) = 1 - (1 - t)^m$. With the faster process, the probability chosen in the first selection interval is

$$P_f = \left(1 - \frac{1}{k}\right)^m + km \int_0^{1/k} t(1-t)^{m-1} \, dt$$

$$= \frac{k}{m+1} - \frac{k-1}{m+1} \left(1 - \frac{1}{k}\right)^m.$$

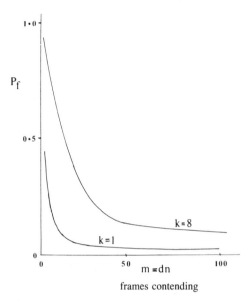

Fig. 10.   Probability P_f of a NAC with a faster retry being selected first, as a function of the average number of frames contending.

Numerical values of this probability are shown in Fig. 10. It is evident that, unless k is large compared to m, there is not much to be gained by reducing the retry time of heavily used NAC's. If $k \gg m$, in the limit $P_f = 1 - (m/2k) = 1 - (dn/2k)$ and the faster NAC can get very rapid service. This could be important, particularly for improving the rate at which sink-type services, such as a printer server, acknowledge packets.

D. Effect of a Subhub

Let n_1 NAC's be connected to a central hub, each operating at a packet rate of ∂_1. In addition, a subhub is connected to this central hub, and n_2 NAC's are connected to the subhub, each operating at a packet rate of ∂_2. The duty cycle of the link is d_1, and the duty cycle of the coupling from the subhub to the central hub is d_2. Assume that all NAC's are equally probable destinations for a packet.

A straightforward adaptation of the reasoning of Section VII-B will obtain the following results. $T_{s1}(T_{s2})$ is the selection time for frames originating in NAC's attached to the central (sub) hub.

$$d_1 = (n_1 \partial_1 + n_2 \partial_2)(L_1 + L_2)$$

$$d_2 = n_2 \partial_2 (L_1 + L_2)$$

$$T_{s1} = d_1 \left(\frac{3}{4}(L_1 + L_2) + \frac{2r}{d_1(n_1 + 1) + 1} \right) .$$

Let t_{s2} be the average time to select a frame at the subhub.

$$t_{s2} = d_2 \left(\frac{3}{4}(L_1 + L_2) + \frac{2r}{d_2 n_2 + 1} \right) .$$

The situation at the central hub is similar to that discussed in Section VII-B. On average, each frame at the central hub will experience a series of T_{s1}/r contentions before being selected. An approximate expression for the selection time for frames originating with the subhub's NAC's may be obtained in this way.

$$T_{s2} = \frac{T_{s1}}{r} t_{s2}.$$

Since all NAC's are equally probable destinations for a packet, the selection time T_{sa} for acknowledgments must reflect this.

$$T_{sa} = \frac{n_1}{n_1 + n_2} T_{s1} + \frac{n_2}{n_1 + n_2} T_{s2}$$

$$T_{w1} = \frac{1}{\partial_1} - T_{mp} - T_{s1} - L_1 - T_{ap} - T_{sa} - L_2$$

$$T_{w2} = \frac{1}{\partial_2} - T_{mp} - T_{s2} - L_1 - T_{ap} - T_{sa} - L_2.$$

Evaluation of these equations shows a situation in agreement with what might be expected. At packet rates and lengths which are practical with the hardware in use, the network performance is not very sensitive to the presence of the subhub. This is because the packet preparation time dominates the frame selection time. As long as this dominance prevails, the installation of a NAC on a subhub will not seriously degrade its performance.

VIII. CONCLUSIONS

A new local area network structure has been presented. Some of the implications of this structure are low delays in the network, rapid clearing of impulse loads, and practical and simple protocols.

The major drawback of structures like Hubnet is the reliability exposure caused by the hubs. Failure of the central hub will result in a complete breakdown. Failure of one of the other hubs will result in the loss of a section of the network.

A solution to this problem has been developed and is being studied. The results of this research will be reported elsewhere.

Simple modular networks of the Hubnet form can have superior performance. However, an extremely remote NAC, not involving relaying of the message through a gateway, may have poor performance if it is physically so far away that its retries at transmission are rare compared to the retries from other NAC's, and the load is high enough that contention is probable. Even then, the performance degradation applies only to the more remote NAC's, and then only when the load is sufficiently high. With the prototype hardware, such a remote NAC would be more than 10 km away from the central hub.

It is interesting that the structure was evolved by attempting to devise ways to cope with the properties of fiber optical communications systems, so that they can be effectively used in networks. Our first attempt was to consider an Ethernet-like scheme [3]. The inspiration for Hubnet followed directly from the adoption of the twin-fiber paths and from the intuitive observation that if one shrunk the Ethernet bus length to zero it was possible to avoid Ethernet collisions entirely.

ACKNOWLEDGMENT

The authors would like to acknowledge the contribution of G. Fedorkow, who did the early circuit design, and particularly the efforts of D. M. Lewis, who completed the hardware system. B. Thomson is responsible for most of the detailed design and the highly successful implementation of Hubnet as a working system.

REFERENCES

[1] F. Closs and R. P. Lee, "A multi-star broadcast network for local-area communication," in *Local Networks for Computer Communications*. Amsterdam, The Netherlands: North-Holland, 1981, pp. 61–80.
[2] A. S. Tanenbaum, *Computer Networks*. Englewood Cliffs, NJ: Prentice-Hall, 1981.
[3] R. M. Metcalfe and D. R. Boggs, "Ethernet: Distributed packet switching for local networks," *Commun. Ass. Comput. Mach.*, vol. 19, pp. 395–404, July 1976.
[4] A. Hopper, "Local area communications networks," Ph.D. dissertation, Cambridge Univ., Cambridge, England, 1978.

11
Expressnet: A High-Performance Integrated-Services Local Area Network

FOUAD A. TOBAGI, FLAMINIO BORGONOVO, AND
LUIGI FRATTA

Expressnet is a unidirectional broadcast bus local area network with a distributed access protocol which achieves a conflict-free round-robin scheduling. This protocol is based on an implicit token-passing mechanism. It is more efficient than existing bus access schemes such as CSMA/CD or the IEEE Standard 802.4 token-passing bus, as the time required to switch control from one active user to the next in a round is minimized (on the order of a carrier detection time), and is independent of the end-to-end network propagation delay. This improvement is particularly significant when the channel data rate is so high, or the end-to-end propagation delay is so large, or the packet size is so small as to render the end-to-end propagation delay a significant fraction of, or larger than, the transmission time of a packet. Moreover, some features of Expressnet make it particularly suitable for voice applications. In view of integrating voice and data, a simple access protocol is described which meets the bandwidth requirement and maximum packet delay constraint for voice communication at all times, while guaranteeing a minimum bandwidth requirement for data traffic. This voice/data access protocol constitutes a highly adaptive allocation scheme of channel bandwidth, which allows data users to recover the bandwidth unused by the voice application. It can be easily extended to accommodate any number of applications, each with its specific requirements.

I. INTRODUCTION

Local area communications networks can be broadly categorized into two basic types. These are broadcast buses and ring systems [1]–[3]. In ring systems the data flow is unidirectional, propagating around the ring from station to station. The interface between a station and the network is an active device which receives the signal from the incoming line and retransmits it on the outgoing line. Various techniques for accessing the channel exist which give rise to various types of ring networks such as token rings, slotted rings, and register insertion rings. Ring networks provide high channel utilization and bounded packet delay. However, reliable operation of the network relies on the integrity of explicit information such as a unique token, or slot boundaries and slot status, as well as on the proper operation of the active taps in relaying the packets and removing them at either the receiver or the sender.

In broadcast bus networks, random access methods such as carrier sense multiple access (CSMA) have been effectively employed. The Ethernet [4] is a common example. These schemes are simple to implement, robust, and are considered more reliable than ring networks since the taps and medium used are generally passive. However, due to random conflicts, a fraction of the bandwidth is wasted and packet delay is unbounded. Moreover, it has been shown that the performance of CSMA degrades significantly as the ratio $a \triangleq \tau W/B$ increases, where τ is the end-to-end propagation delay of the signal across the network, W is the channel bandwidth, and B is the number of bits per packet [5]. In Fig. 1 the channel utilization for CSMA/CD is plotted versus a for various values of N, the number of backlogged users. The utilization is rather insensitive to N and clearly decreases with increasing values of a. For present systems and applications, the parameter a does not exceed 1. Using estimates for the propagation delay in coaxial cables and for the various delays through interface components as given in [6], one finds that a good estimate for τ is 10 μs for each km of cable (assuming one repeater for each 500 m of cable). For 1 km cable, $W = 10$ Mbits/s and $B = 1000$, we get $a = 0.1$. For such a value, CSMA/CD provides adequate channel capacity, 0.65 or higher. If one increases the bandwidth to 100 Mbits/s, then a increases to 1. If, furthermore, $B = 100$ bits, then a becomes 10, etc. Thus, given the future needs in local communications (voice, graphics, video, etc.), one sees that a number of combinations for the values of the three parameters W, B, and τ may lead to larger values of a, such as 1, 10, or even 100, for which CSMA/CD performs very poorly.

More recently, a number of new demand assignment multiple access (DAMA) schemes has been proposed for broadcast bus networks. These schemes provide conflict-free transmission using distributed access protocols with *round-robin scheduling functions* which thus lead to bounded delay. The stations that are "alive" are ordered so as to form what is called a *logical ring*, according to which they are given their chance to transmit. In

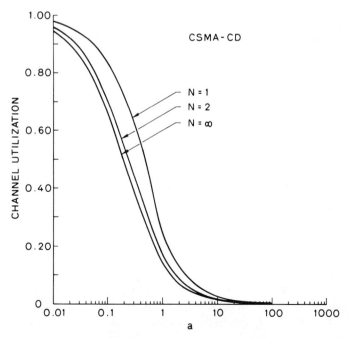

Fig. 1.   Channel utilization versus a for CSMA/CD.

some of these schemes, such as the IEEE Standard 802.4 Token-Passing Bus Access Method [7], an *explicit message* gets sent around the logical ring to provide the required scheduling; the station holding the token at any instant is the one that has access to the channel at that instant. It relinquishes its right to access the channel by transmitting the token to the next one in turn. Unfortunately, as in rings, the robustness of these networks depends on the integrity of the token and on the proper operation of the involved stations. As in random access networks, the performance degrades significantly with a [1].

In contrast to those schemes where a station transmits an explicit token to the next in turn, in Expressnet [8] the stations rely on various events due to activity on the channel to determine when to transmit. Since the token-passing operation is *implicit*, the overall robustness of the network is improved over token bus networks. Here too, packet delay is bounded; but in addition both throughput and delay can be made much less sensitive to a, thus rendering Expressnet particularly suitable for high bandwidth, small size packets (such as those arising from real-time applications), and long distances.

Expressnet is not the only implicit token-passing DAMA scheme. A number of such schemes has been proposed in recent years. These differ by the network topological configuration required, the method used to provide the conflict-free round-robin scheduling, and the resulting performance. In a recent survey written by Fine and Tobagi [9], these schemes are classified according to three basic access mechanisms. These are the *scheduling delay access mechanism*, the *reservation access mechanism*, and the *attempt and defer access mechanism*. The scheduling delay access mechanism is suitable to *bidirectional bus system* (BBS) configurations in which, as in Ethernet, the signal transmitted by a station propagates in both directions to reach all other stations on the bus; the means for coordinating the access of the various users is by staggering the potential starting time of these users following the end of each transmission. The reservation access mechanism is also mainly suitable for the BBS configuration; there, the stations use a control wire to place reservations and to reach a consensus on the next station to transmit, prior to the transmission on the bus. For examples and more detail on these DAMA schemes, the reader is referred to [9].

The attempt and defer access mechanism, which Expressnet employs, can only be implemented on a *unidirectional bus system* (UBS) configuration in which the transmitted signals propagate in only one direction. In this case, broadcast communication is achieved in various ways. One way is by means of two unidirectional buses in which signals propagate in opposite directions so as to provide each station with a direct path to every other station (see Fig. 2). This is referred to as the dual-bus configuration. Another way is to fold the cable onto itself (or use a separate frequency channel in the case of broadband signaling) so as to create two channels: an outbound channel onto which the users transmit packets, and an inbound channel from which users receive packets, and such that all signals transmitted on the outbound channel are repeated on the inbound channel (see Fig. 3); this is referred to as the folded-bus configuration. The attempt and defer access mechanism

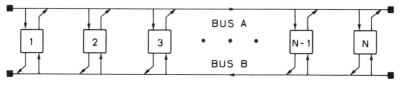

Fig. 2.   Dual bus configuration.

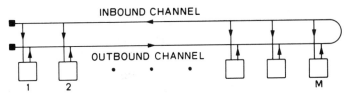

Fig. 3.   Folded-bus configuration.

rests on the fact that, in any UBS configuration, unidirectionality provides an implicit ordering of the stations. It operates basically as follows. A station wishing to transmit a packet on a bus waits until that bus is idle. It then begins to transmit, establishing its desire to acquire the bus. However, if another transmission from upstream is detected, the station aborts its transmission and defers to the one from upstream. The most upstream transmission is therefore allowed to continue conflict-free. This is precisely the idea behind Expressnet; it uses the folded-bus configuration, operates in asynchronous mode, accommodates variable packet size, and is entirely distributed. Another prominent example of a network that belongs to this class is Fasnet [10]. It employs the dual-bus configuration, and operates in a synchronous slotted mode. There a station wishing to transmit waits for the next slot to arrive, and subsequently asserts its desire to transmit in that slot by marking the slot as full. However, if the station finds that the slot has already been marked full, it defers and waits for the next slot. Fasnet is the subject of Chapter 12.

In Section II, we describe Expressnet. In Section III, we examine its performance, and in Section IV we address the issue of integrating voice and data.

II. EXPRESSNET

As already indicated in the Introduction, Expressnet is a unidirectional broadcast network which uses the folded-bus configuration. Thus, it comprises two channels: the outbound channel which all stations access in order to transmit, and the inbound channel which stations access in order to read the transmitted information. The transmission medium may be a twisted pair, a coaxial cable, or an optical fiber, as long as the transmit tap connected to the outbound channel is unidirectional. In addition to writing on the outbound channel, each station has the capability to sense activity on that channel due to stations on the upstream side of its transmit tap.

For clarity and rigor in presentation, we define the Boolean function $c(t, \text{OUT})$ as

$$c(t, \text{OUT}) = \begin{cases} 1 & \text{if carrier is detected present on the outbound channel at time } t \\ 0 & \text{otherwise.} \end{cases}$$

Note that $c(t, \text{OUT})$ signals the presence or absence of carrier with a delay of t_d seconds, where t_d is the time required for the detection operation. It is assumed here that the carrier detector is placed very close to the channel. (Other arrangements are also possible as set forth below.) The event EOC(OUT) is said to occur when $c(t, \text{OUT})$ undertakes a transition from 1 to 0. In a similar way $c(t, \text{IN})$ and EOC(IN) are defined.

Expressnet is considered to be operated in an asynchronous mode in which a transmission unit (TU) consists of a preamble followed by the information packet itself. Information packets may be of fixed or variable size. The preamble is for synchronization purposes at the receivers. It is sufficiently long for the receivers to detect presence of the unit, and then to synchronize with bit and packet boundaries.

A. Basic Access Mechanism

A station S_i, which senses the outbound channel busy, waits for EOC(OUT). Immediately following the detection of EOC(OUT), it starts transmission of its unit. Simultaneously, it senses carrier on the outbound channel (on the upstream side of its transmit tap). If carrier is detected [which may happen in the first t_d seconds of the transmission, and which means that some station S_j with a lower index has also started transmission following its detection of EOC(OUT)], then station S_i immediately aborts its current transmission. Otherwise, it completes the transmission of its unit. Note that all ready stations which detect EOC(OUT) act as described above. The only station to complete transmission is the one with the lowest index, among those ready stations which were able to detect EOC(OUT). Clearly, during and following the transmission of its TU, a station will sense the outbound channel idle, and therefore will encounter no EOC(OUT), and will not be able to transmit another TU in the current round.

Note that the possible overlap among several transmission units is limited to the first t_d seconds of these transmissions. It is expected that the loss of the first t_d seconds of the preamble of the nonaborted transmission will not jeopardize the synchronization process at the receivers. According to the above basic mechanism, two consecutive transmission units are separated by a gap of duration t_d seconds, the time necessary to detect EOC(OUT).

The succession of transmission units transmitted in the same round is called a *train*. A train can be seen by a station on the outbound channel only as long as the TU's in it are being transmitted by stations with lower indexes. A train generated on the outbound channel is entirely seen by all stations on the inbound channel. Since there is a gap of duration t_d seconds between consecutive TU's within a train, the detection of the presence of a train on the inbound channel can be best achieved by defining the new Boolean function TRAIN(t, IN) $= c(t - t_d, \text{IN}) + c(t, \text{IN})$. Clearly we have

$$\text{TRAIN}(t, \text{ IN}) = \begin{cases} 1 & \text{as long as a train is in progress} \\ 0 & \text{otherwise.} \end{cases}$$

The transition TRAIN(t, IN): $1 \rightarrow 0$ defines the end of a train (EOT(IN)), and the transition TRAIN(t, IN): $0 \rightarrow 1$ defines the beginning of a train (BOT(IN)).

B. Starting a New Round and the Topology of Expressnet

After the last TU in a train has completed transmission, a mechanism is needed to start a new train of transmission units. Clearly, it is essential that this mechanism gives access right to the ready station with the lowest index. A solution can be obtained by guaranteeing that the event EOT(IN) visits the receivers in the same order as the stations' indexes, which is also the order in which they can transmit. This is achieved if the inbound channel is such that signals on it propagate in the same direction as on the outbound channel.

Thus, we consider the network topology to comprise an outbound channel and an inbound channel which are parallel and on which signals propagate in the same direction (i.e., visiting stations in the same order), and a connection between the outbound channel and the inbound channel to allow the broadcast of all outbound signals on the inbound channel. The propagation delay along the connection τ_c is anywhere between 0 and τ seconds (where τ is again the end-to-end propagation delay on the outbound or inbound channel), depending on the geographical distribution of the users and the way the inbound and outbound channels are connected. The minimum of zero seconds is obtained, for example, if the inbound and outbound channels have a loop shape (or, more generally speaking, the stations with the lower and highest indexes are collocated), as illustrated in Fig. 4(a). The maximum of τ seconds is observed if the *connection* cable is made parallel to the inbound and outbound channels, as shown in Fig. 4(b). In all cases, the propagation delay between the outbound tap and inbound tap for all stations is fixed and equal to $\tau + \tau_c$.

The major feature of this topology rests on the fact that, when the inbound channel is made *exactly parallel* to the outbound channel, the event EOT(IN), used by *all* stations as the synchronizing event to start a new train, will reach any station exactly at the same time as the carrier on the outbound channel due to a possible transmission by a station with a lower index. This helps resolve the overlap of several transmissions at the beginning of a

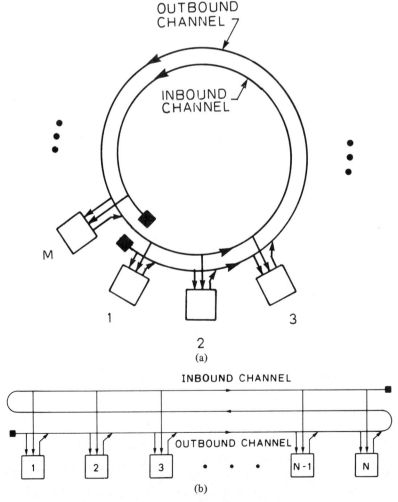

Fig. 4.   Examples of Expressnet topologies.

train in just the same manner as the resolution obtained in the basic mechanism for transmitting TU's. This mechanism again allows the ready station with the lowest index to be the first to complete transmission of its TU, and following that the new train will take its normal course. The time gap between two consecutive trains, defined as the time between the end of the last TU in a train and the beginning of the first TU in the subsequent train, is now $\tau + \tau_c + 2t_d$ seconds. (See Fig. 5.)

C. The Cold-Start Procedure and Keeping Expressnet "ALIVE"

The above algorithm and mechanisms are valid only if there are always events to which actions are synchronized, namely EOC(OUT) and EOT(IN). This assumes that at all times some station is ready, and therefore, trains contain at least one TU and are separated by gaps of fixed duration $\tau + \tau_c + 2t_d$. When this is not the case, the idle time on the inbound channel exceeds $\tau + \tau_c + 2t_d$ seconds. A station which becomes ready at time t_0 such that 1) TRAIN(t_0, OUT) = 0 (thus indicating that no EOC(OUT) will be encountered to synchronize action to) and 2) TRAIN(t, IN) = 0 during the entire period of time $[t_0, t_0 + \tau + \tau_c + t_d]$ (thus indicating that no EOT(IN) will be detected) has to undertake a *cold-start* procedure. This procedure must be designed such that if executed by several stations becoming ready under these conditions, it leads to a single synchronizing event to be used as a time reference, followed then by an orderly conflict-free operation of the network.

The simple one proposed here consists of the following. Once a station has determined that a cold-start procedure is needed, it transmits continuously an unmodulated carrier (called PILOT) until BOT(IN) is detected. At this time the station aborts transmission of the pilot. It then waits for EOT(IN) (consisting of the end of the pilot) and uses that event as the synchronizing event. (Of course, an alternative could be to use the BOT(IN) due to the pilot as the synchronizing event.) It is possible that pilots transmitted by several users overlap in time. This, however, will cause no problem. Note that as long as pilots are aborted as soon as BOT(IN) is *detected*, it is guaranteed that the resulting PILOT as observed on the *inbound channel* is continuous and of length $\tau + \tau_c + t_d$ seconds. Following its end, there will be the normal gap of size $\tau + \tau_c + 2t_d$ before a TU follows. (Of course, this gap is absent if BOT(IN) is used as the synchronizing event.)

Assume that no station is ready when EOT(IN) is detected. The network is then said to

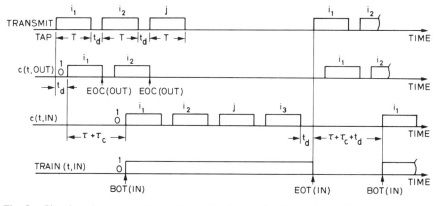

Fig. 5. Signals and events as observed by station j, assuming that stations with indexes $i_1 < i_2 < j < i_3$ are nonidle.

go *empty*. The *first* station to become ready when the network is empty spends $\tau + \tau_c + t_d$ seconds to determine the empty condition, by examining TRAIN(t, IN), after which it starts transmission of the pilot. Then it takes between $\tau_c + t_d$ and $\tau + \tau_c + t_d$ seconds before it detects BOT(IN). (The minimum $\tau_c + t_d$ is observed if the station in question is the lowest index station, and the highest index station happened to become ready exactly at the same time.) Regardless of which is the case, following BOT(IN) a pilot of length $\tau + \tau_c + t_d$ seconds is observed on the *inbound* channel, followed by the gap of $\tau + \tau_c + 2t_d$ seconds and then the transmission unit. Therefore, with the use of the PILOT, the time between the moment at which the *first* station becomes ready in an empty network and the moment at which the next EOT(IN) (due to the end of PILOT, and representing the synchronizing event) reaches the lowest index station is between $2\tau + 3\tau_c + 4t_d$ and $3(\tau + \tau_c) + 4t_d$ seconds. This is the time needed to start a new round and is to be compared to $\tau + \tau_c + 2t_d$ which is the time needed when the network does not become empty. Figure 6 shows the timing of the cold-start procedure when only one station becomes ready.

To avoid the cold-start operation each time the network goes empty, one needs to guarantee that, as long as some stations may still become ready in the future, synchronizing events [namely, EOT(IN)] are created artificially by all such stations. More precisely, we consider a station to be in one of two states: DEAD or ALIVE. A station which is in the ALIVE state has responsibility to perpetuate the existence of the synchronizing event EOT(IN) for as long as it remains in that state. To accomplish this, each time EOT(IN) is detected, the station transmits a short burst of unmodulated carrier, of duration sufficiently long to be very reliably detected (i.e., of a duration of at least t_d seconds). Such a burst is called LOCOMOTIVE. If the train were to be empty (i.e., no stations were to be ready when EOT(IN) is detected), now the LOCOMOTIVE constitutes the TRAIN, and EOT(IN) is guaranteed to take place. Clearly, if some station which is ALIVE is also ready, then immediately following the LOCOMOTIVE, it initiates transmission of its TU and follows the transmission mechanism giving access right to the lowest index. The network is said to be ALIVE if at least one station in the network is ALIVE; otherwise it is said to be DEAD. A station is said to be in the DEAD state if it is not engaging in keeping the network ALIVE and, therefore, is prohibited from transmitting any TU. To be able to transmit, a station has to become ALIVE. For a DEAD station to become ALIVE, it must first determine whether the network is ALIVE or not. Letting t denote the time at which a

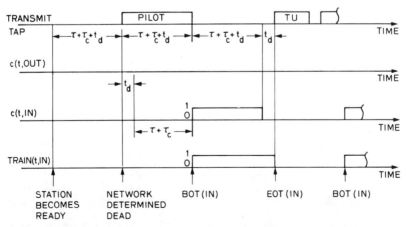

Fig. 6. Signals and events as observed at station j undertaking a cold start.

DEAD station wishes to become ALIVE, the network is determined ALIVE if a train is detected on the inbound channel anytime in the interval $[t, t + \tau + \tau_c + t_d]$. Otherwise, it is determined DEAD. If the network is determined ALIVE, then the station simply switches to the ALIVE state and acts accordingly. Otherwise, it executes the cold-start procedure following which it becomes ALIVE.

A station which is ALIVE can be either READY or NOT-READY at any moment. This is determined by the state of its transmit buffer, empty or nonempty. To that effect, we define for each station a function $TB(t)$ as

$$TB(t) = \begin{cases} 1 & \text{if its transmit buffer is nonempty} \\ 0 & \text{otherwise.} \end{cases}$$

An ALIVE station which becomes ready does not have to wait for EOT(IN) to undertake the attempts to transmit its packet. In fact, if an outbound train is observed, the station synchronizes transmissions with EOC(OUT). If, however, at the time it becomes ready, no train is observed on the outbound channel, then EOT(IN) is the synchronizing event.

D. The Expressnet Access Protocol

We now give a rigorous description of the entire algorithm. Define CTX as the event corresponding to the completion of transmission of the current TU, given that such a transmission has been initiated. We also define TIME-OUT (α) as the event corresponding to the completion of a period of time of duration α, starting the clock at the time when waiting for the event is initiated. From the above discussion, we may define PILOT as a continuous unmodulated carrier, and LOCOMOTIVE as an unmodulated carrier of duration t_d.

We consider that initially station X is in the DEAD state. Upon command (for bringing the station to the state ALIVE and eventually for transmission of data), the following basic algorithm is executed.

Step 1: [Check whether the Expressnet is ALIVE or not. If it is, then proceed with Step 2, otherwise undertake the "cold-start" procedure and then proceed with Step 2.] If TRAIN$(t, IN) = 1$ (i.e., the Expressnet is already ALIVE), go to Step 2. Otherwise, wait for the first of the following two events: BOT(IN) or TIME-OUT$(\tau + \tau_c + t_d)$. If BOT(IN) occurs first (then again it means that the Expressnet is ALIVE), go to Step 2. If on the contrary TIME-OUT $(\tau + \tau_c + t_d)$ occurs first (indicating that the Expressnet is not ALIVE), transmit PILOT immediately at the occurrence of TIME-OUT $(\tau + \tau_c + t_d)$, and maintain transmitting it until BOT(IN) is detected, at which time abort transmission of PILOT and proceed with Step 2.

Step 2: Wait for the first of the following two events: EOC(OUT) and EOT(IN). If EOC(OUT) occurs first then go to Step 4. Otherwise, go to Step 3.

Step 3: [A new train has to be stated.] Transmit a LOCOMOTIVE, and go to Step 4.

Step 4: [Determine the current state of the station. If it is ready, then attempt transmission of the TU packet.] If TB$(t) = 0$ go to Step 2. Otherwise, initiate transmission of the TU. If t_d seconds later $c(t, OUT) = 1$ (meaning it is not station X's turn), then abort transmission and go to Step 2. Otherwise, complete transmission of the packet and go to Step 2.

In Fig. 7 we present the flowchart of this basic algorithm. In Fig. 8 we give the diagram for the finite state machine which performs the algorithm. It contains seven states. The states labeled D_1, D_2, and D_3 are assumed when the station is DEAD and is in the process

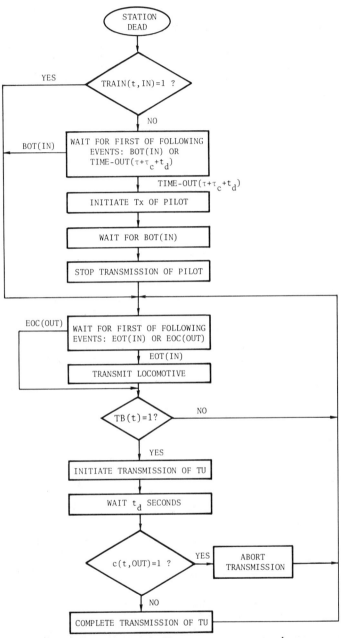

Fig. 7.   Flowchart for the Expressnet access protocol.

of becoming ALIVE; the states labeled $A_1 - A_4$ are assumed when the station is ALIVE. Each possible transition is labeled by the combination of events which causes the transition, followed by the action taken.

III. PERFORMANCE ANALYSIS

In this section we examine the performance of the Expressnet access protocol. The channel utilization is evaluated as the ratio of the average time in a train spent for data

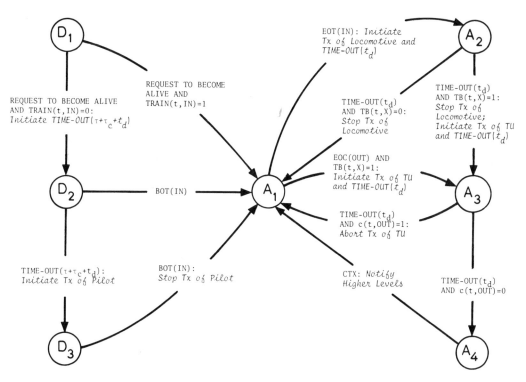

Fig. 8.   Finite state machine implementing the Expressnet access protocol.

transmission to the average time separating the start of two consecutive trains. Given that N stations are always busy, the channel utilization is independent of the total number of stations M and is given by

$$C=\frac{NT}{N(T+t_d)+\tau+\tau_c+2t_d} \tag{1}$$

where the additional t_d seconds in the intertrain gap is due to the existence of the LOCOMOTIVE. Neglecting t_d in comparison to T and τ, and taking $\tau_c = \tau$, (1) is rewritten in terms of $a = \tau/T$ as

$$C(M,\ N,\ a)=\frac{1}{1+\dfrac{2a}{N}}. \tag{2}$$

Clearly, the channel capacity attained under heavy traffic is given by (1) or (2) where $N = M$.

It has been assumed above that the carrier detector and transmit logic of a station are collocated with its taps on the channel. Accordingly, the time it takes for the station's logic to respond to any of the four events EOC(OUT), EOT(IN), BOC(IN), and BOC(OUT) is just the detection time t_d. This is how implementation is expected to be. However, when this is not the case then adjustments in the protocol and its performance analysis have to be made to take into account the propagation delay between a station and its tap. Let τ_s seconds denote the maximum such delay over all stations. By a simple argument it can be shown that it takes a station $t_d + 2\tau_s$ seconds to respond to the occurrence of any of the above-mentioned events on the channel. Note also that the possible overlap among several transmission units is now equal to $2\tau_s + t_d$ instead of just t_d, meaning that the preamble length has to be increased by $2\tau_s W$ bits, an additional overhead which needs to be taken into account in the performance analysis. Denoting by t_g the gap between two consecutive transmission units in a train, and by t_{ov} the maximum duration of overlap among several transmission units, the throughput with N stations always busy is then given by

$$C = \frac{NT}{N(T + t_g + t_{ov} - t_d) + \tau + \tau_c + t_g + t_d} \tag{3}$$

where $t_g = t_{ov} = 2\tau_s + t_d$. Neglecting t_d in comparison to T and τ, and letting $\tau_c = \tau$, (3) reduces to

$$C = \frac{1}{1 + \dfrac{2a}{N} + \dfrac{4\tau_s}{T} + \dfrac{2\tau_s}{NT}} . \tag{4}$$

As the introduction of τ_s causes degradation in channel throughput, one may conceive placing the critical functions of carrier detection and transmission abortion in the transceiver (close to the channel); then t_{ov} can be kept as small as t_d, and (4) now becomes

$$C = \frac{1}{1 + \dfrac{2a}{N} + \dfrac{2\tau_s}{T} + \dfrac{2\tau_s}{NT}} . \tag{5}$$

Note that the introduction of τ_s calls for slight modifications to the various parameters used in the above description of the algorithm.

In Fig. 9 we plot the channel utilization $C(M, N, a)$ versus a for various values of N. In this figure we neglect t_d and let $\tau_c = \tau$. Contrary to CSMA/CD, the channel utilization is not insensitive to N, and improves with increasing values of N. For large a, a high utilization is achieved only if N is large. However, even in the worst case $N = 1$, Expressnet performs at least as good as, if not better than, both CSMA/CD and the token-passing bus. We also plot in Fig. 9 the fraction of the bandwidth acquired per station versus a. This amount decreases with increasing values of N but slower than $1/N$ since the throughput improves with N.

In order to attain a tractable analysis of packet delay and to compare Expressnet to CSMA/CD, we consider a model consisting of M users each with a single packet buffer. A user is either idle or backlogged. An idle user generates a packet in a random time which is exponentially distributed with mean $1/\lambda$ seconds. A backlogged user does not generate any packet and becomes idle upon successful transmission of its buffer. A packet transmission time is considered to be fixed equal to T seconds (including the preamble). This model which corresponds to the case of interactive users and which has been referred to in the

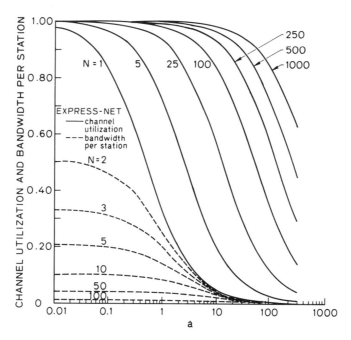

Fig. 9.   Channel utilization and bandwidth acquired per station versus a for Expressnet.

literature as the "*linear feedback model*" has been used previously to analyze ALOHA and CSMA/CD. It has also been recently used in [11] in a study on the performance of unidirectional broadcast systems (namely, Expressnet and Fasnet) and several round-robin service disciplines achievable in these systems. The analysis of Expressnet where users are serviced in a predescribed sequence is based on the work in [12], [13] as detailed in [11]. In this section we present the results which are most relevant to the understanding of the performance of Expressnet.

The throughput–delay tradeoff is displayed in Figs. 10 and 11 where the normalized average delay is plotted versus the throughput S for various values of M and a. Figure 10 corresponds to a small value of a, precisely 0.1, and compares Expressnet to CSMA/CD. (The CSMA/CD scheme considered is the slotted p-persistent version analyzed in [5].) Figure 11 corresponds to $a = 1$ and 10, and does not include CSMA/CD, as CSMA/CD achieves a very small network capacity. These figures clearly show the superiority of Expressnet for all values of a. In particular, note that, for a given throughput S, the delay in Expressnet is relatively insensitive to M. For each value of M, packet delay is bounded from above by the *finite* value attained at saturation, i.e., when $\lambda \to \infty$. This maximum delay is precisely $(M + 2a)T$ seconds. Finally, notes on the variance of delay can be found in [11].

IV. Integrating Voice and Data on Expressnet

A. Characteristics of Voice Traffic

It is assumed that vocoders digitize voice at some constant rate. Bits are grouped into packets which are then transmitted via the network to the destination vocoder. To achieve

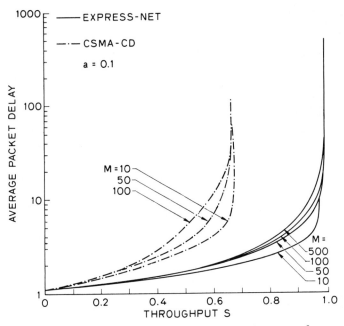

Fig. 10.   Throughput-delay performance of CSMA/CD and Expressnet for $a = 0.1$.

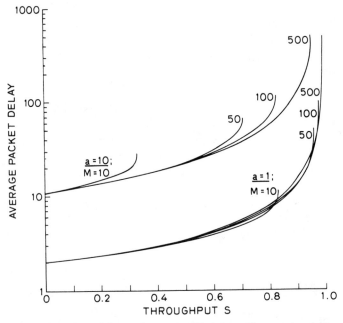

Fig. 11.   Throughput-delay performance of Expressnet for $a = 1$ and 10.

interactive speech and smooth playback operation, it is important to keep the end-to-end delay for each bit of information (from the time the bit is generated at the originating vocoder until it is received at the destination vocoder) within tight bounds. Two components of delay are identified: the packet formation delay and the network delay. The sum must not exceed the maximum allowed in order for all bits to satisfy the delay requirement of speech. An interesting property of round-robin schemes with finite number of stations is that the delay incurred in the transmission of a packet is always finite and bounded from above. This renders it particularly attractive for the packet voice application which we now examine in more detail.

Let W_v be the bandwidth required per voice user (i.e., the vocoder's rate in bits/s), and D_v the maximum delay allowed for any bit of digitized voice (not including the propagation delay). Let B_v denote the number of bits per voice packet. B_v is the sum of two components: $B_v^{(1)}$ which encompasses all overhead bits comprising the preamble, the packet header, and the checksum, and $B_v^{(2)}$, the information bits. Let T_f be the time required to form a packet; it is also the packet intergeneration time for a vocoder. Let T_v be the transmission time of a voice packet on a channel of bandwidth W. We clearly have

$$T_f = \frac{B_v^{(2)}}{W_v} \tag{6}$$

$$T_v = \frac{B_v}{W}. \tag{7}$$

Since packet generation is deterministic, occurring every T_f seconds, we can model each voice user by a $D/G/1$ queue. The packet service time D_n is the time from when the packet reaches the head of the queue until it is successfully received at its destination. Due to the bandwidth constraint we must have

$$T_f \geqslant D_n. \tag{8}$$

This is also the condition of stability for the $D/G/1$ queue.

Let N denote the number of *active* (off-the-hook) voice sources. (We consider again the case $\tau_s = 0$.) Assuming all queues are nonempty, a train is of length $N(T_v + t_d) + t_d$. The service time distribution of a packet can be bounded by a deterministic one, with the service time equal to a maximum cycle length (i.e., a train length plus the intertrain gap). That is, we now consider all queues to be (pessimistically) represented by $D/D/1$, where the interarrival time is T_f and the service time is $D_n = N(T_v + t_d) + \tau + \tau_c + 2t_d$. With these considerations, provided that the queue size is initially 0 and $T_f \geqslant D_n$, the waiting time of a packet is 0 and its total delay is D_n. The delay constraint for a voice bit is now written as

$$T_f + D_n \leqslant D_v. \tag{9}$$

The above two constraints lead to a maximum value for N when we choose $T_f = D_n = D_v/2$. Accordingly, we have the optimum packet size given by

$$B_v^{(2)} = \frac{D_v W_v}{2} \tag{10}$$

and the maximum number of voice users allowed at any one time given by

$$N_{\max} = \frac{D_v/2 - (\tau + \tau_c + 2t_d)}{B_v/W + t_d}. \tag{11}$$

We note that as long as $N \leqslant N_{\max}$, it is guaranteed that the length of a train never exceeds $N_{\max}$ transmission units, and the network packet service time never exceeds the maximum determined above: $N_{\max}(T_v + t_d) + \tau + \tau_c + 2t_d$; consequently, no queueing delay is incurred, the queue size at all users remains $\leqslant 1$, and the total delay constraint for all voice bits is *always* satisfied.

B. Integrating Voice and Data

The principal constraints we have to satisfy here are 1) the delay constraint for voice packets and 2) a minimum bandwidth requirement for data. Although we do not impose a delay constraint on data packets, it is important to provide the bandwidth "reserved" for data on as continuous a basis as possible, and to fairly allocate that bandwidth to data users. Furthermore, we require that the protocols be dynamic in allocating the bandwidth to voice and data applications, allowing data users (or background traffic) to gracefully steal the bandwidth which is unused by voice. To accomplish these objectives on Expressnet, we consider two types of trains, the voice train type and the data train type. Trains are always alternating between the two types, and stations transmit their packets on the train of the corresponding type. To satisfy the delay constraint for voice packets, it is important not only to limit the number of voice communications to a maximum, but also to limit the data trains to a certain maximum length.

Let W_d be the minimum data bandwidth required. Assuming that data trains are limited to a maximum length L, their effect on the calculation of the optimum value for $N_{\max}$ is to just increase the overhead between consecutive trains by the amount $L + \tau + \tau_c + 2t_d$. $N_{\max}$ is then given by

$$N_{\max} = \frac{D_v/2 - 2(\tau + \tau_c + 2t_d) - L}{B_v/W + t_d}. \tag{12}$$

Since the maximum period of time separating the beginning of two consecutive trains of the same type is $D_v/2$, L must satisfy

$$L = \frac{W_d D_v}{2W}. \tag{13}$$

It is important to limit data trains to the maximum length L at all times, even if the number of active voice users is smaller than $N_{\max}$. Otherwise, situations may arise where the packet delay for a voice packet will exceed D_v. This particularly will occur if, during a data train, a number of new voice users becomes ready, some of which might incur an initial delay longer than the maximum allowed.

Since a data train may not contain the TU's of all ready stations, it is important that the next data round resumes where the previous data train has ended. This is easily accomplished as follows. With respect to a given round, any user may be either ACTIVE if it has not yet transmitted in the current round or DORMANT if it has. A user who is idle or

DORMANT does not contend for the channel. To switch from the DORMANT to the ACTIVE state, data users have to monitor the length of data trains on the inbound channel: a dormant user switches to the ACTIVE state whenever the length of a data train has not reached its maximum limit L.

In order to alternate between the two types of trains, a station maintains a flag ϕ which gets complemented at each occurrence of EOT(IN). We use the convention $\phi = 0$ for a data train and $\phi = 1$ for a voice train. Now we face the problem of having a station properly initialize ϕ when it becomes ALIVE. The simplest way is as follows. If the network is found DEAD, then following the pilot the station initializes ϕ such that the first train is of the voice type. If the network is found ALIVE, then the station monitors the inbound channel until either a valid packet is observed or the network has gone dead. In the former case, the type of train is derived from the type of packet observed, and ϕ is initialized accordingly. In the second case, the station undertakes a cold start and the initialization of ϕ is independent of past history. Note that as long as the network is determined ALIVE, a station may not become ALIVE until it has observed a valid packet transmission; all empty trains are ignored. If it is highly likely that long successions of empty trains occur, the above mechanism may induce a high initial delay before the station becomes ALIVE. This can be overcome by including *explicit* information in the LOCOMOTIVE which indicates the type of train. That is, the LOCOMOTIVE now becomes a train-type indicator (TI) packet. The proper indicator packet must be transmitted following EOT(IN) (i.e., an attempt to do so is undertaken) by all ALIVE stations in the network, regardless of the type of packets they intend to transmit. Clearly, only one transmission of the train-type indicator packet is accomplished, by the station in the ALIVE state with the lowest index. With this mechanism, a station wishing to become ALIVE in a network determined ALIVE waits for BOT(IN) following which it receives and decodes the train-type indicator packet, and initializes the flag ϕ accordingly. The use of the train-type indicator packet increases the overhead caused by the LOCOMOTIVE from t_d to the transmission time of a (relatively short) TI packet. This extra overhead has a small impact on the performance which is still approximated by the equations given above.

We have indicated that in order to satisfy the delay constraint for voice packets it is necessary to limit the number of phone calls in progress at the same time. This requires that a mechanism exists to check whether a new phone call can be accepted or not. The decision is based on the number of calls already set up, and this can be obtained by simply measuring the length of the previous voice train. However, we note that if voice packets representing silence are not transmitted, this measure may not be accurate and one may have to collect data regarding the length of several voice trains before deciding on the acceptance of a new call. The savings on voice bandwidth obtained by silence suppression may be utilized to increase the average data bandwidth. If used to increase the maximum number of phone calls on the network, then a service degradation will have to be allowed as some packets may be delayed beyond the maximum delay D_v. This topic is not carried any further in the present chapter and the reader is referred to [14], [15] for comprehensive treatment.

In the above discussion, it was assumed that the integration of different types of traffic is obtained by using different types of trains and by requiring that a packet be transmitted only on a train of the corresponding type. Another possible approach is to allow mixing of the different types of packets on the same train. In this case there is no need to provide train indicators. However, each station is then required to measure not only the length of the current train but also the period of time in the train already utilized by each type of traffic so that the bandwidth utilized by each traffic does not exceed the maximum value allowed. In order to fulfill the delay requirements for voice traffic, it is easy to see that the global amount of data transmitted in a train has to be limited to $L/2$. Note, however, that this limitation does not affect the overall efficiency of the system nor the bandwidth assigned to each type of traffic.

For a more rigorous description, flowcharts, and finite state machine of the voice/data access algorithm, the reader is referred to [8].

V. Conclusions

In this chapter we have described Expressnet, a local area communication network, in which the access protocol used by all stations connected to the bus is a distributed algorithm which provides conflict-free transmission of messages. It is essentially a round-robin scheme in which the time to switch from one active user to the next in a round is kept very small, on the order of carrier detection time, thus achieving a performance which is relatively independent of the end-to-end network propagation delay. This feature represents the major improvement obtained with this protocol in comparison to other existing ones, such as CSMA/CD and token-passing bus. It makes it very suitable for local area networks in which, because of high channel speed, long end-to-end delay, and/or small packet size, the propagation delay constitutes a large fraction of or is even larger than the packet transmission time. Furthermore, we have shown that this protocol is particularly suitable for the transmission of packetized voice as it is able to guarantee an upper bound on the transmission delay for each packet. A possible way to integrate voice and data on the same network has been described in detail.

Additional work on Expressnet not reported upon here has been done. In particular, a complete evaluation of Expressnet when supporting voice and data applications has been performed [14], [15]. The issue of fiber-optics implementation of Expressnet has also been addressed in [16], [17]. Various topologies and components suitable to Expressnet have been examined. Recently, a two station prototype demonstration system has been successfully implemented at Stanford University, running at 10 Mbits/s. For details, the reader is referred to [17].

References

[1] W. Stallings, "Local network performance," *IEEE Commun. Mag.*, vol. 22, no. 2, Feb. 1984.

[2] D. D. Clark, K. T. Pogran, and D. P. Reed, "An introduction to local area networks," *Proc. IEEE,* vol. 66, no. 11, Nov. 1978.

[3] K. Kummerle and M. Reiser, "Local area communication networks—An overview," *J. Telecommun. Networks,* vol. 1, no. 4, Winter 1982.

[4] R. M. Metcalfe and D. R. Boggs, "Ethernet: Distributed packet switching for local computer networks," *Commun. Ass. Comput. Mach.*, vol. 19, no. 7, pp. 395–403, 1976.

[5] F. Tobagi and V. B. Hunt, "Performance analysis of carrier sense multiple access with collision detection," *Comput. Networks,* vol. 4, no. 5, Oct./Nov. 1980; see also this volume, ch. 20.

[6] "The ETHERNET: A local area network. Data link layer and physical layer specifications. Version 1.0," Xerox Corp., Sept. 1980.

[7] "Token-passing bus access method," ANSI/IEEE Standard 802.4-1985, 1985.

[8] F. Tobagi, F. Borgonovo, and L. Fratta, "Expressnet: A high-performance integrated-services local area network," *IEEE J. Select. Areas Commun.*, vol. SAC-1, no. 5, Nov. 1983.

[9] M. Fine and F. A. Tobagi, "Demand assignment multiple access schemes in broadcast bus local area networks," *IEEE Trans. Comput.*, vol. C-33, Dec. 1984.

[10] J. O. Limb and C. Flores, "Description of FASNET, a unidirectional local area communications network," *Bell Syst. Tech. J.*, vol. 71, Sept. 1982; see also this volume, ch. 12.

[11] F. A. Tobagi and M. Fine, "Performance of unidirectional broadcast local area networks: Expressnet and Fasnet," *IEEE Trans. Select. Areas Commun.,* vol. SAC-1, pp. 913–926, Nov. 1983.

[12] C. Mack, T. Murphy, and N. L. Webb, "The efficiency of N machines unidirectionally patrolled by one operative when walking time and repair times are constants," *J. Royal Statist. Soc.,* Ser. B., vol. 19, pp. 166–172, 1957.

[13] A. R. Kaye, "Analysis of a distributed control loop from data transmission," in *Proc. Symp. Comput. Commun. Networks Teletraffic,* Polytech. Inst. Brooklyn, Brooklyn, NY, Apr. 1972.

[14] M. Fine and F. A. Tobagi, "Packet voice on a local area network with round robin service," *IEEE Trans. Commun.,* vol. COM-34, Sept. 1986.

[15] T. A. Gonsalves, "Comparative performance of broadcast bus local area networks with voice and data traffic," Ph.D. dissertation, Dep. Elec. Eng., Stanford Univ., Stanford, CA, June 1986.

[16] M. M. Nassehi, F. A. Tobagi, and M. E. Marhic, "Fiber optic configurations for local area networks," *IEEE J. Select. Areas Commun.,* vol. SAC-3, Nov. 1985.

[17] M. E. Marhic and F. A. Tobagi, "Experimentation with a fiber optic implementation of Expressnet," in *Proc. EFOC/LAN,* Amsterdam, The Netherlands, June 25–27, 1986.

12

Description of Fasnet—A Unidirectional Local Area Communications Network

JOHN O. LIMB AND C. FLORES

Fasnet is an implicit token-passing, local area network aimed at supporting high data rates and carrying a wide mix of traffic (data, voice, video, and facsimile). Transmission is unidirectional with stations attaching to the medium passively via directional couplers. A link consists of two lines, one to carry traffic in each direction. Unidirectional transmission provides the potential for efficient operation at high data rates, while the passive medium provides the potential for high reliability. We describe the physical configuration and the protocol and give channel utilization for the condition of continuously queued sources. Mechanisms to control the access of various traffic types are described. Finally, the interconnection of multiple Fasnets is studied for one particular configuration, a ring.

I. INTRODUCTION

Local computer networks operating at 1–10 Mbits/s are being commercially offered and appear to adequately meet current demands for computer communications within the office environment. However, future needs stimulated by both a broader range of services than is now available and changes in system architecture (e.g., the trend towards distributed processing) could increase significantly the demand for digital capacity. For example, one would like to be able to handle video information, voice traffic, and facsimile, as well as computer traffic, in a single digital system. Thus, while today 10 Mbits/s may be regarded as an extremely generous bit rate for a local computer network, 200 Mbits/s may become limiting for an integrated communications network.

Fasnet is an implicit token-passing protocol developed to efficiently utilize the channel capacity when the ratio of packet duration to the maximum station-to-station propagation time is small (< 1). Information flows in only one direction on the medium, unlike the usual CSMA/CD configurations, but like CSMA/CD, the essential passivity of the medium is retained. The access method is closely related to a ring protocol (e.g., see [1]) and may be regarded as a variant of implicit token passing.

Reliability was an important consideration in the design of Fasnet. Consider both the transmission medium and the control electronics. Reliability of the transmission medium may be enhanced by keeping active electronics in the medium to a minimum. Bus architectures such as Ethernet have occasional repeaters, depending on the length of the signal path. Cable TV (CATV)-type architectures have periodic line amplifiers whose spacing is determined by the number of stations (taps), as well as by cable attenuation. Ring architectures usually have most electronics in the signal path; digital regeneration is usually provided at each station [1]. Turning to control, reliability considerations tend to favor distributed control. An alternative to a fully distributed system is to permit some stations to perform unique functions but have these functions assumable by any station on the network; however, this can result in a large cost penalty. A further alternative is to have the function performed on a server basis (two or more stations provide the service to all other stations). The Fasnet medium resembles that employed in CATV, and control is primarily distributed with some functions assumable by all stations.

The description of Fasnet starts in Section II with the physical loop; the access protocol is described in Section III. The performance of the basic system is given in Section IV, followed by a discussion of some of the system design issues (in particular, the synchronization and signaling procedures) in Section V. Section VI describes variations of the basic system, including methods for improving efficiency, particularly when the number of users is small. Section VII describes mechanisms to support the efficient management and control of mixtures of different traffic types. Section VIII describes the interconnection of Fasnets, with consideration of the impact of the topology on throughput and ability to handle localized sources of traffic. Section IX summarizes the chapter.

II. PHYSICAL CONFIGURATION

The basic link, as shown in Fig. 1, consists of two lines. One line passes all stations carrying traffic in one direction and the other line passes all stations carrying traffic in the other direction. For line A, station S_1 is referred to as the head station and S_n the end station. For line B the assignment is reversed. Together the two lines provide a connection between any pair of stations attached to the link. While the lines may be twisted pair, coaxial cable, or light fibers, we will be primarily concerned with a coaxial cable implementation. Each station makes two connections to each line. A read tap precedes a passive directional coupler used for writing. The nature of the directional coupler is such that very little energy travels in the reverse direction on the line so that the signal read virtually simultaneously from the read tap will be unaffected by the signal being written on the line via the directional coupler. A station writes on the line by adding energy to the signal already existing on the line. Except for specific fields of the header, the protocol ensures that only one station at a time writes on the line. Thus, once a signal is written on a

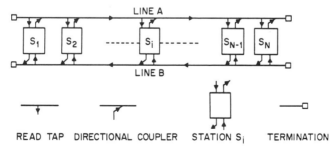

Fig. 1.   Physical configuration of a Fasnet link.

line, it is not removed or changed by any station. This has certain implications for the line code that is selected (Section V-B).

Depending on the length of the line, amplifiers are needed to boost and compensate the signal. The technology and design procedures used for CATV systems [2] are directly applicable here, although the noise margin required for a high-quality video signal is somewhat greater than that required for two- or three-level digital transmission.

Links may be joined together to form a network of links. Usually, links will be run in pairs of lines, but this is not always necessary. The advantage of using multiple links is that the traffic-carrying capacity of the network can be increased and reliability may be improved by the use of redundant paths.

An earlier version of Fasnet [3] differs primarily from the system described here in that a link consists of a single unidirectional line that passes each station twice—on the outbound or write side and on the inbound or read side. Each station makes three connections to the line: a read tap for control purposes, and a directional write tap on the write side, and a read tap for recovering data on the read side. The primary advantage of the scheme described here is that the link can carry approximately twice the traffic of the earlier version. A disadvantage is that a station must select the correct line on which to transmit, and this will depend on the relative physical location of the destination.

III. Protocol Description

The data link layer may be divided into two sublayers [4]. One sublayer, the logical link control with which we are less concerned here, provides functions like addressing, windowing, and acknowledgments. The other sublayer, the media access control with which we are more concerned, determines when and how to send information via the physical medium.

A. Access Control

Basic access control for Fasnet is as follows. The head station S_1 initiates a cycle on line A. After a cycle has been initiated, each active station on the line with packets destined in the right direction is allowed to access the line for one slot. To do this, each station monitors the line. When it senses the line idle, it seizes the line for one slot. It has to wait for a new cycle to be initiated before it attempts to access the line again. The exact manner in which this is done efficiently and fairly is described in the next paragraphs. If a station has priority, it is given permission to access the line for an integral number of slots. In this manner, the active stations can access the line for a specified duration in the order in which they are physically located on the line. The operation on line B is identical to that described above with S_N replacing S_1 as the head station.

To describe the operation in more detail, let $\{S_1, S_2, \cdots, S_N\}$ be the set of stations in the order of their physical locations as shown in Fig. 1. Let AQ_i and BQ_i be the number of packets queued at station S_i for access to lines A and B, respectively.

When the next packet arrives at S_i from the network layer interface:

if destination address $j > i$, then AQ_i is incremented by 1;

if destination address $j < i$, then BQ_i is incremented by 1.

The structure of the access control (AC) field is shown in Fig. 2. Let t_{fn} be the start of the nth frame. The AC field is from t_{fn} to t_{bn}. Station S_i gains access to line A in the following manner. Let S_i be permitted access for p_{max} packets each cycle. At t_{fn}, the start of the nth

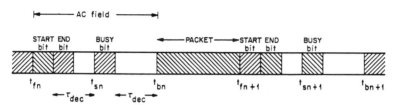

Fig. 2.   The frame structure of Fasnet. Each frame consists of i) an access control field containing START, END, and BUSY bits; and ii) the packet as provided by the logical link sublayer.

frame, the read tap reads the START bit of the AC field. The start of the cycle is indicated by START $= 1$. Because of gate delays in the decision circuitry and propagation delays in the tap cables, the outcome of the read operation is only known at t_{sn}. This additional time of duration τ_{dec}, shown in Fig. 3, is of the order of a few bit times for a 100 Mbit/s line and nanosecond logic. Next, the station simultaneously reads the BUSY bit via the read tap and writes BUSY $= 1$ via the directional coupler. Again, the outcome of the read operation is only known at t_{bn} after a delay of τ_{dec}.

At t_{bn}, if the read operation yields BUSY $= 1$, the station defers until the next frame. Note that the write operation does not alter the logical value of the busy bit. The nature of the signaling to achieve this is explained in Section V-B. If the read operation yields BUSY $= 0$, the station accesses the line for the remaining frame duration.

Station S_i is said to be in one of four states:

IDLE—if it has no packets to transmit, i.e., $AQ_i = 0$.

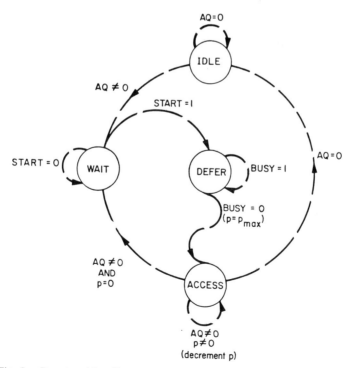

Fig. 3.   State transition diagram describing the operation of a Fasnet station.

WAIT—if it is waiting for the start of a cycle.

DEFER—if it is deferring to busy users who are upstream on the line.

ACCESS—if it is accessing the line.

The station makes transitions (denoted as $\rightarrow$) between states as follows (Fig. 3). While $AQ_i = 0$, S_i is in IDLE. Upon arrival of a packet for line A, $AQ_i > 0$ and $S_i \rightarrow$ WAIT. The station reads the START bit of every frame. When START $= 1$ $S_i \rightarrow$ DEFER, and the station simultaneously reads and writes the BUSY bit as described above for every frame. When BUSY $= 0$ $S_i \rightarrow$ ACCESS. Now it accesses the line for p_{max} frames and also writes BUSY $= 1$ for each. Then $S_i \rightarrow$ WAIT. The station may cease to access the line earlier if $AQ_i = 0$, whereby $S_i \rightarrow$ IDLE.

Station S_1 initiates cycles by START $= 1$ in the first frame of each cycle. There is an additional bit, END, in each frame to indicate the end of cycles. This bit can be conveniently located in the blank portion of the frame after the START bit. When station S_N reads BUSY $= 0$ on line A (indicating that all active stations have accessed the line), it sets END $= 1$ in the next frame on line B. On receipt of this frame on line B, S_1 then initiates a new cycle on line A. Thus, in the worst case, line A will be silent once every cycle for a time equal to twice the end-end propagation delay, plus twice the frame duration, as each end station has to wait until the next frame to set the START or END bits.

The operation on line B is identical, with the roles of S_1 and S_N reversed. Thus, the two lines cycle independently of each other with access being passed between the stations in the same order as their physical locations on each line.

In the protocol described above, the outcome of the read operation on the START bit needs to be known before the BUSY bit is written so that the first frame of a new cycle does not remain idle. Should the START and BUSY bits be adjacent to each other, a station will only learn that START $= 1$ after the BUSY bit has passed and the frame will not be used. However, for large cycle lengths and short packet lengths, the reduction of one decision interval, τ_{dec}, per frame would be greater than the addition of the extra idle frame.

A further alternative is to have the first frame of each cycle contain only an access field. However, unequal frame sizes complicate synchronization for a very small increase in efficiency.

B. Error Recovery

The protocol is controlled by the START, BUSY, and END bits. An error in a BUSY bit will have no lasting effect; it will result in a packet being overwritten if the busy bit is changed from a 1 to a 0. Alternatively, an empty slot will go unused if the busy bit is changed from 0 to 1. Of more significance is an error in the START and END fields. If a START bit is set to 1 in error, two START's or a START and an END would be simultaneously present on the loop.

It will now be shown that generation of additional START's and END's will not propagate and have little effect on the operation of the link. We will assume that end stations do not generate START's or END's that are closer together than the roundtrip delay time, τ_r; under normal operation this cannot occur. A false START $= 1$ will occur at the end station either in the active portion of a cycle (including the first empty slot) or in the empty slots occurring at the end of the cycle. If the former, a new cycle will start before, or as, the old one is finishing. Since the additional START $= 1$ will not generate an END $= 1$ on the return line (because no transition from busy slot to empty slot is detected), the condition will not propagate. If the false START $= 1$ occurs in the empty slots, other than the first, the new cycle will start prematurely (actually increasing utilization temporarily). One of two conditions results.

i) The busy part of the additional cycle terminates at least one slot before the next normally occurring START = 1, in which case the end station will detect an end condition. However, because the period since the last END = 1 is less than τ_r, a new END = 1 will not be generated.

ii) There is no empty slot before the next normally occurring START = 1. As a result, an additional end condition is not detected by the end station.

Thus, a START = 1 resulting from a fault condition will not produce additional END = 1 bits on the return line. On the other hand, END = 1 faults, unless they are closer together than τ_r, will produce additional START = 1 slots which, as just described, have a transient effect on the operation of the link.

Consider the condition where a START or END bit is changed from a 1 to a 0. A new cycle would fail to initiate. After a time-out greater than the longest permitted cycle time, the head station will issue a START = 1, and the link will continue to operate normally. Should a head or end station fail, the station next to the head or end station would assume the functions on detecting loss of timing or after timing out on the arrival of START = 1 or END = 1.

C. Fault Diagnosis

The independent lines of the Fasnet link provide the opportunity to localize and mitigate some types of faults. Consider first that a line is severed because of some catastrophic event or something trivial like a cable connector failing. The result will usually be either a short or open circuit leading to a gross impedance mismatch. The fault will most likely terminate all effective communication on the upstream side of the fault because of reflections from the mismatch traveling back into station interface units via the read tap. The downstream segment will be affected very little because the directional couplers will propagate little energy in the direction of the mismatch. Thus, a diagnostic program in the end station can determine between which stations the mismatch lies. This is done by having the end station send a query to each station via the intact line and determining which stations respond to the query.

A fiber-optic implementation [5], [6] differs from a coaxial implementation in that directional couplers are used for the read tap as well as the write tap. When a fiber breaks, 20 percent or more of the light energy may be reflected back along the upstream side of the line. A small fraction of this energy would be coupled into the write taps, and would be incident on the laser diode/light emitting diode light source. An even smaller fraction of this energy may be reflected from the source back into the line. Very little reflected energy would find its way into the directional read tap which is accepting energy from upstream, not downstream. While detailed analysis and testing needs to be done, it would appear that a fiber break would decrease the signal/noise ratio on a line by a small amount, and provided there was enough margin, the line could continue to operate on the upstream as well as the downstream side of the break.

A difficult type of station fault is to have a station continuously write garbage on a line. Diagnostic programs in the end stations can determine the faulty station as follows and remove it from service. The head station on the line with the fault, after being informed of the fault by the end station, via the other line, queries each station in turn. If the station fault is confined only to the write circuit, the faulty station will respond. The next station on the downstream side will not respond, since it will not be able to read the query sent by the head station because of the interference from the faulty station. If both read and write circuits in the faulty station are affected, the last correctly responding station will be the station on the upstream side of the faulty station. Thus, the fault is isolated to one of two stations. Both stations may then be disconnected by means of a control signal sent via the functioning line. The faulty station may then be uniquely determined by returning one of the stations to service. If the fault condition resumes, the returned station is faulty and is disconnected; otherwise, the other station is faulty.

IV. PERFORMANCE

A. Sample Operation

Typical operation of Fasnet for lines of 2.5 km individual length, 100 Mbits/s bandwidth, and 200-bit frame length is shown in Fig. 4. It shows the time-space relation of the frames on each line. The horizontal axis represents time divided into slots A_1, A_2, A_3, $\cdots$ for line A and B_1, B_2, B_3, $\cdots$ for line B. The vertical axis represents the physical locations of the active stations S_1, S_2, S_3, S_4, and S_5 with S_1 and S_5 serving, additionally, as end stations. The electrical line length is five frames. Station S_1 initiates the cycle in frame A_1, and access passes from S_1 to S_2 to S_3 to S_4. When the end station, S_5, senses BUSY = 0 in frame A_5, it sets END = 1 in frame B_9. Receipt of this frame by S_1 causes it to initiate a new cycle in A_{14}. Similarly, a cycle on line B starts at B_1. Assume that S_5 and S_4 are

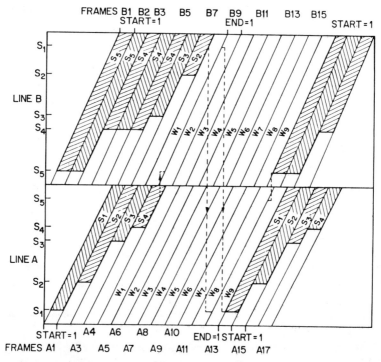

Fig. 4. A graph of activity on a Fasnet link (lines A and B) as a function of time. The dotted lines indicate the flow of information from one line to another.

permitted access for up to two and three packets, respectively. Station S_1 senses BUSY $= 0$ in frame B_8 and sets END $= 1$ in A_{13}. Receipt of this frame by S_5 causes it to start a new cycle in B_{17}.

B. Utilization

As there are no collisions, no capacity is lost through collision resolution. However, the utilization is not 100 percent as each line is idle at the end of each cycle. The idle period is nine frames, $W_1, W_2, \cdots, W_9$, on each line in Fig. 4. In the worst case, this is equal to twice the end-end propagation delay, plus twice the slot time (one slot time on average) as each end station has to wait until the start of the next slot to set the START or END bits. If

v = speed of propagation on the line (m/s)
W = line capacity (bits/s)
L = line length (m)
F = frame size (bits)
M = number of busy stations with downstream traffic,

then if each station is allowed access for only a single packet per cycle,

$$\text{cycle length} = \tau_c = M*(F/W) + 2*(L/v) + (F/W),$$

$$\text{duration of busy frames} = \tau_b = M*(F/W) \tag{1}$$

and

$$\text{utilization} = \eta = \frac{M*(F/W)}{M*(F/W) + 2*(L/v) + (F/W)}. \tag{2}$$

The effective utilization is lower since a fraction of each frame is devoted to access control. However, for large F, it results in only a small reduction in utilization. If $v = 2.5 \times 10^8$ m/s, $W = 100 \times 10^6$ bits/s, $L = 2.5 \times 10^3$ m,

$$\eta = \frac{M*F}{(M+1)*F + 2000}.$$

For $M = 100$,

$F = 50$	$\eta = 71$ percent
$F = 100$	$\eta = 83$ percent
$F = 200$	$\eta = 90$ percent
$F = 500$	$\eta = 95$ percent
$F = 1000$	$\eta = 97$ percent.

For the same values of v, W, and L, with $F = 500$ and assuming an Ethernet slot time T

$= 50 \times 10^{-6}$ s [7], we can compare the performance of Fasnet and Ethernet as the number of stations is varied. This is shown in Table I.

Unlike Ethernet, Fasnet has the desirable feature that as the load increases, the utilization also increases. The above figures do not reflect the fact that in practice the length of packets is variable and, consequently, the fixed frames of Fasnet frequently will be only partially filled. The effect on η depends on the distribution of packet size, and to some extent is determined by the system design. For example, in a system designed for large amounts of voice traffic, F could be set equal to the size of a voice packet.

V. IMPLEMENTATION CONSIDERATIONS

The design criteria previously stressed in the Introduction affect the implementation in important ways. In particular, the requirement to operate at high speeds and the unidirectional operation of the bus affect the design of the synchronization system; in turn, the type of synchronization and the use of directional couplers impact the choice of the line code that is used [8].

A. Synchronization

Bus systems in which signals travel in both directions on the line require the receiving stations to adapt to the signals transmitted by the sending station because the amplitude, dispersion, and phasing of the received signal vary depending upon the position of the transmitting station on the line. Synchronization· can be achieved very quickly when the signaling rate is low relative to the bandwidth of the transmission medium. At higher signaling rates, synchronization needs to be more accurate to achieve good error performance. Ethernet specifies a synchronization preamble of 64 bits and for higher transmission rates an even longer sequence may be required. Thus, for short messages efficiency would be significantly reduced.

Using a unidirectional bus, each station can be synchronized to a common clock issued from the head station. Thus, if all stations add signals to the cable in phase with the

TABLE I
FASNET VERSUS ETHERNET AS
A FUNCTION OF NUMBER OF
BUSY STATIONS

M	Fasnet	Ethernet[a]
	(in percent)	
5	50	4.1
10	67	3.9
50	91	3.7
100	95	3.7

[a] Note that since the minimum permissible packet length is 5000 bits, η is calculated as 0.1 of η with 5000-bit packets. Other CSMA protocols that do not require collision detection perform better.

transmitting clock, stations will receive the signals in correct phase. Similarly, fixed gain and frequency compensation can be employed. The problem of reliability can be overcome by giving each station the ability to supply clock. The clock drive would be inhibited by detection of, and locking to, an incoming clock.

Initial tests have shown that a simple, cost-effective method of synchronization is to synchronize to a continuously injected pilot tone placed at the high end of the signaling band. The synchronizing function then assumes a negligible fraction of the transmission capacity.

In addition to bit synchronization, frame synchronization is also required. This is achieved by sending a 4 bit framing word at the start of each slot [8]. With tight bit and frame synchronization, successive frames may be butted together without a gap.

B. Signaling

Because synchronization is achieved independently of the data signal, line codes with fewer transitions may be considered. It is particularly convenient if a code is chosen that couples no energy to the line when one of the logic states is continuously transmitted (assume logic 0). Each station at the end of transmission then simply returns to logic 0, and there is no need to "disconnect" the transmitter from the line. The two line codes we are investigating are a bipolar three-level code, Fig. 5(a), and a nonreturn to zero (NRZ) two-level code, Fig. 5(b). The two-level signal has a greater noise margin; however, one has to contend with the dc signal component [9].

There is one condition in which more than one station may add energy to the same bit in a frame—the BUSY bit of the AC field. As a result, the amplitude of this bit may far exceed the amplitude of the remaining signal. This may lead to errors in adjacent bits of the AC field. To prevent this, guard bands on either side of the BUSY bit should be used. Notice from Fig. 2 that the access field is configured so that the guard bands fall in the intervals τ_{dec} and, in practice, will have a comparable duration.

VI. IMPROVING UTILIZATION

As can be seen from (1), efficiency increases 1) as cycle length increases and 2) as the idle period at the end of each cycle (intercycle gap) decreases. At the expense of some increase in complexity, techniques may be devised to improve utilization by increasing cycle length or reducing intercycle gap.

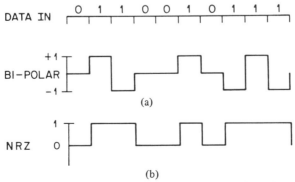

Fig. 5. (a) Bipolar three-level line code. (b) NRZ two-level line code.

A. Control of Cycle Length

Since START = 1 may be read by all stations, the length of the last cycle τ_c may be determined by any station. As previously described, each station may transmit up to p_{max} packets per access. Thus, by controlling p_{max}, stations may influence the value of τ_c. Station control of τ_c by manipulation of p_{max} is obviously limited. For example, let us assume that p_{max} is fixed at 1 and that we have stations each generating packets at a rate $< 1/\tau_c$. Increasing p_{max} will not change the cycle length since packets will be transmitted before a queue can form. On the other hand, increasing p_{max} for heavily loaded stations will lead to an increase of τ_c, provided τ_c is less than the accepted maximum.

B. Reducing Intercycle Gap

Three methods are available for reducing the intercycle gap, and hence increasing the line utilization. In the first, stations detecting the END = 1 bit seize empty slots on the other line; in the second, stations use the END field as a request field; in the third, the end station attempts to estimate the end of a cycle, setting END = 1 before BUSY = 0 is received. These methods are discussed in more detail in [10]. The improvement in utilization that these techniques provide has to be offset against the increase in complexity of the protocol and the difficulty of implementation at very high speeds. For applications requiring access times of less than a ms and spanning distances greater than 50 km, the improvement in utilization may indeed warrant the increased complexity.

VII. Serving Multiple Traffic Types

As previously explained, the function of the START bit is to signal to all stations that they should attempt transmission. If a multibit field is used to perform the start function rather than just a single bit, then the field may be used to enable one of a number of subsets of all stations to be served. For example, if three bits were used, then seven separate arbitrary classes of traffic could be addressed by the seven code combinations (the zero code is excluded). These classes could be priority classes, traffic-type classes, or some mixture. Further, a station may belong to more than one class. Figure 6 has been drawn to illustrate in concept how different types of traffic may be served on a single network. Four different types of traffic are assumed: 1) a private line type requirement, here typified by a

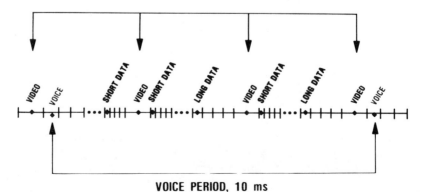

VOICE PERIOD, 10 ms

Fig. 6.   Example showing integration of four different traffic types.

high-speed video channel; 2) a number of voice stations; 3) a data channel for short data messages; and 4) a channel for long data messages (perhaps for file transfer purposes). The example of Fig. 6 starts with the periodic issue of a video START. After a predetermined number of video packets have been transmitted a voice START is issued and voice stations engaged in an ongoing speech spurt seize the first available packet. Ultimately, all voice stations requiring service will have transmitted a packet and an empty packet will propagate to the end of the line. This will cause an END bit to be written in the next slot returning to the other end of the line, thus permitting a new START to be initiated. In the example shown in Fig. 6 this would be a START for short data messages. Before all short data messages can be served, a video START is reissued, interrupting the transmission of short data messages. After the periodic video transmission the short data messages resume, to be followed by long data messages. This alternation of traffic type continues until it is time to issue a further voice START, here shown as 10 ms after the voice traffic was previously served.

In practice, serving mixed traffic is more complicated than the simplified example shown in Fig. 6. A detailed study of how voice and data may be combined is described in [11]. In that example a portion of the channel capacity is reserved for data. A procedure for blocking calls that arrive when the voice capacity of the channel is full is described together with a procedure for readmitting voice traffic that resumes after a silent interval (the elimination of silent intervals is assumed).

VIII. TOPOLOGY

A. Introduction

A population of stations may be connected together by either a single link, Fig. 7(a), or by several interconnected links, Fig. 7(b). The best topology will depend upon physical distribution, traffic patterns, and the particular performance measures that one seeks to optimize. We will not consider the general problem, but restrict ourselves to the linear interconnection of links forming closed loops. Fasnets may be connected as shown in Fig.

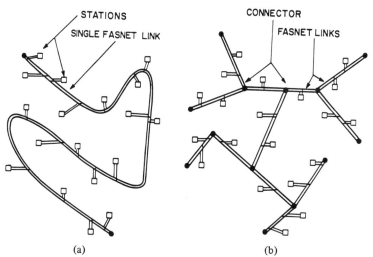

(a)   (b)

Fig. 7.   (a) A cluster of stations being served by a single Fasnet link. (b) The same station population being served by several interconnected links.

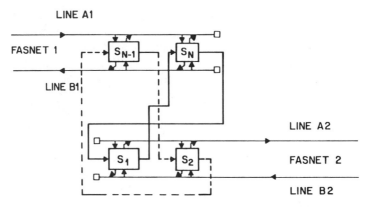

Fig. 8.   Structure of a connector used to interconnect two Fasnet links.

8. Packets in Fasnet 1 destined for Fasnet 2 would have an internetwork address recognized by station S_N. Station S_N transmits the packets to station S_1 which puts them on Fasnet 2. Similarly, for packets from Fasnet 2 destined for Fasnet 1. To provide reliability against single-station failures, interconnection stations would be provided in pairs. Thus, a similar connection would be provided between S_{N-1} and S_2. A detailed procedure may be specified whereby control of the interconnection passes from the $S_N - S_1$ connection to the $S_{N-1} - S_2$ connection in case of failure of the former. In principle, the secondary connection monitors both Fasnets and assumes the interconnection function after a suitable time-out period in event of failure. Provision can also be made for the primary connection to periodically check that the secondary connection is operational.

Interconnection of Fasnets as shown in Fig. 8 permits traffic to pass from one link to another with a minimum of delay. Since the connection is to the first station on the link, the incoming packet can utilize the next occurring slot. Because of differences in frame timing between two links, it may be necessary to buffer a maximum of one complete packet; this amount of buffering is normally provided in a station interface. In general, interconnection of more than two Fasnets will require larger buffers to be employed to handle the condition where traffic arrives simultaneously for one Fasnet from connecting Fasnets.

B. Traffic Localization

If stations on a Fasnet have traffic destined only for stations in the immediate vicinity, then total utilization can be significantly improved by dividing the single link into separate links that are connected. Only traffic that has not reached its destination link is allowed to cross the connector.

Consider K Fasnet links with K connectors connected to form a ring with an inner and outer loop, as shown in Fig. 9. Assume that each link is the same length with identical traffic sources and destinations uniformly distributed around the ring. Further assume that the traffic is routed by the path that traverses the fewest links. It can be shown that the gain G in capacity from using K links relative to one link with no connector is [10]

$$G = \frac{1}{0.25 + \dfrac{1}{K}}. \tag{3}$$

This is plotted in Fig. 10.

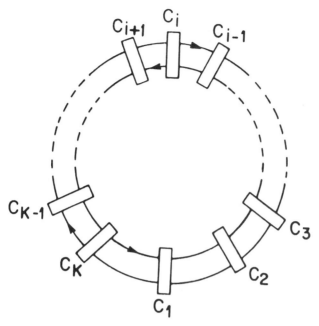

Fig. 9.   A Fasnet link with multiple connectors.

We can extend the same analysis to the case with K symmetric connectors C_1, C_2, $\cdots$, C_K, but with an arbitrary traffic distribution symmetric about the source station.

It can be shown that

$$G \approx \frac{1}{D + \dfrac{1}{K}} \tag{4}$$

where D is the expected value of $|d|$, the absolute value of the source-destination distance.

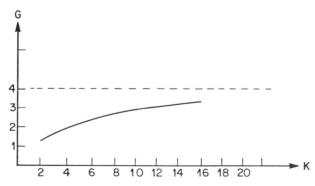

Fig. 10.   Plot of the gain in traffic handling capacity of interconnected links relative to a single link as a function of K, the number of connectors.

The approximation becomes exact if the distribution is uniform or if $K \rightarrow \infty$. Note that for the uniform distribution, $D = 1/4$ and (4) reduces to (3).

For a given traffic distribution, (3) is a good design formula for how capacity costs can be reduced at the cost of extra connectors. However, this tradeoff is useful only if accurate estimates of capacity and connector costs are available.

The above analysis highlights certain interesting features. For the uniform traffic distribution, it is seen that the gain G does not increase uniformly with K. This is fairly intuitive. Since the traffic is uniform, an extra connector, when K is large, removes the traffic over only a short link and results in only a marginal increase in the gain. On the other hand, as the traffic distribution becomes more localized (i.e., $D \rightarrow 0$) G increases uniformly with K. This is again fairly obvious, as with a high degree of localization the traffic on each link is almost independent of the traffic on the other links.

We have considered here some configurations of interconnected links. There are interesting graph theoretic questions relating to reliability. For example, given a graph like Fig. 7(b), what is the minimum number of additional links and their position so that full connectivity is still maintained if any link is cut at a single point? Development of realistic models of the physical traffic and cost structures of local environments still remains.

IX. CONCLUSION

The physical configuration of Fasnet consists of two communication lines passing each station. One line carries traffic in one direction, while the other line carries traffic in the opposite direction. Thus, this configuration carries twice the traffic of a previous system in which the two lines were connected at one end so that traffic was written on the outbound line and read from the inbound line. Each station makes two connections to each line: a nondirectional read tap and a directional write tap. Reliability of the physical medium is high because it contains no active electronics. The access protocol is partly centralized in that bit synchronization, framing, and start-of-cycle are provided by the end stations; however, these functions would be assumable by any station upon failure of an end station.

The access protocol is as follows: Upon reading a start-of-cycle, a station may transmit a prespecified number of packets in the first available empty slots. When all stations have transmitted their packets, a signal is sent on the return line to inform the head station to start a new cycle. The efficiency of Fasnet increases as the length of a cycle increases; cycle length depends upon the length of a packet, the number of active stations, and the number of packets, p_{max}, that each station is permitted to send in a cycle. By adaptively changing p_{max}, efficiency can be maintained at a high level even for a small number of active stations. A number of techniques for further improving efficiency are suggested. A tradeoff is necessary between increasing the complexity of the protocol, on one hand, and the resulting small improvements in efficiency on the other.

Bit synchronization of the stations is achieved through adding an out-of-band pilot tone, while framing is achieved through a periodically inserted code word. A three-level bipolar line code is preferred.

The potential of Fasnet for operation at high transmission rates makes it attractive as a conduit for the various types of traffic that may flow in a business environment. Mechanisms have been proposed to implement blocking, delaying, and request-for-service operations that are needed if mixed traffic is to be handled efficiently within a single medium. These operations can be implemented centrally or they can be distributed. The low-level access operations are best distributed while the more complex operations are best centralized.

Fasnets may be interconnected to increase the load that may be carried or to improve reliability. Investigation has been restricted to the connection of Fasnets to form a ring. As the number of segments in the ring increases, the throughput first increases rapidly (assuming uniformly distributed traffic). After about five segments, the increase is very small. Exploration of other topologies presents a challenge.

REFERENCES

[1] M. V. Wilkes and D. J. Wheeler, "The Cambridge digital communication ring," in *Proc. Local Area Commun. Network Symp.*, May 1979, pp. 47–61.
[2] W. A. Rheinfelder, *CATV System Engineering*, Third Ed., Blue Ridge Summit, PA: TAB Books, 1972.
[3] J. O. Limb, "Fasnet: Proposal for a high speed local network," in *Proc. OIS Workshop*, St. Maximin, France, Oct. 13–15, 1981; in *Office Information Systems*, N. Naffah, Ed. Amsterdam, The Netherlands: North-Holland, 1982.
[4] "IEEE standards for local area networks: Logical link control," ANSI/IEEE Standard 802.2-1985, 1985.
[5] C. W. Tseng and B. U. Chen, "D-net, a new scheme for high data rate optical local area networks," *IEEE J. Select. Areas Commun.*, vol. SAC-1, pp. 493–499, Apr. 1983.
[6] J. O. Limb and A. Albanese, "Passive unidirectional bus networks using optical communications," in *Proc. Globecom'85*, New Orleans, LA, Dec. 2–5, 1985.
[7] "The Ethernet, A local area network, data layer and physical layer specifications," DEC, Intel, Xerox, Version 1.0, Sept. 30, 1980.
[8] P. P. Giordano, J. O. Limb, and J. C. Swartzwelder, "Implementation of an experimental high-speed local area network transceiver," in *Proc. ICC'83,* Boston, MA, June 20–23, 1983, pp. F3.3.1–F3.3.5.
[9] F. D. Waldhauer, "A 2-level, 274 Mb/s regenerative repeater for T4M," in *Proc. ICC*, vol. 3, 1975, pp. 48.13–17.
[10] J. O. Limb and C. Flores, "Description of Fasnet, A unidirectional local area communications network," *Bell Syst. Tech. J.*, vol. 61, Part I, pp. 1413–1440, Sept. 1982.
[11] J. O. Limb and L. E. Flamm, "A distributed local area network packet protocol for combined voice and data transmission," *IEEE Trans. Commun.*, pp. 926–934, Nov. 1983; see also this volume, ch. 26.

13
The Zurich MAN

PETER L. HEINZMANN, FELIX KUGLER,
THOMAS H. BRUNNER, AND WILLI HUBER

The "Zurich MAN," the metropolitan area network of the Zurich Universities and its related institutions is one of the largest two-way broadband networks in the world. The broadband cable system, which today reaches approximately 6500 offices, uses more than 80 km coaxial cable and 111 broadband amplifiers. The implemented main-/subheadend configuration is an efficient solution for the broadband interconnection of the four main university centers. Currently, the most important service on the network, Sytek's LocalNet 20 for terminal-computer and computer-computer communication, gives direct access to sites which are located up to 40 km apart, using fiber optical cables, leased lines, and a 150 km microwave link. Thus, the "Zurich MAN" provides for direct access to more than 4200 RS-232C ports within one single address space. Measurements of the reverse channel frequency spectrum demonstrate that disturbances in large broadband networks with many users are mainly due to transmitted noise inserted by connected devices and to interference noise picked up from electrical apparatus in the system's vicinity. Traffic statistics for the LocalNet 20 service indicate similar load variations as they are known from telephony. The packet size distribution is bimodal and with the experienced loads of up to 70 percent, there are less than 0.05 collisions per packet.

I. INTRODUCTION

There are two academic institutions at the university level in Zurich, the University of Zurich (UNI) with more than 15 000 students and the Swiss Federal Institute of Technology (ETH) with approximately 10 000 students. Both universities have their main campuses near the center of Zurich and at several decentralized suburban sites (Fig. 1).

In 1981, the staff of the Computing Centers at the ETH and at the University of Zurich started a project aiming to realize a network that would satisfy all needs for computer communication over the next ten years. The network should permit data communication at higher speed than provided by the conventional solution with modems and the private telephone network (PABX). Future extension to multiple university sites within the metropolitan area of Zurich should be possible. Single cable broadband technology was chosen as the physical carrier system because at that time it was the only mature technology capable of feeding large areas and offering the required flexibility. Project management was with the Computing Center. Swiss CATV-companies have been contracted for the installation of the broadband system. As a major data communication facility, a packet communication service supporting standard EIA RS-232C electrical interfaces for terminals and host ports was installed.

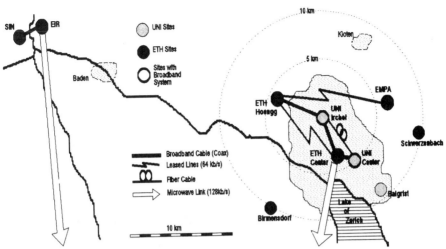

Fig. 1. The main areas of the Zurich Universities with the corresponding network interconnections.

This chapter gives a system overview of the "Zurich MAN" and describes the experiences gained since the beginning of the network installation in 1981. Some new results concerning the noise in the reverse frequency band of such large two-way broadband networks are presented. Finally, measured traffic characteristics for the main data service and problems concerning the network management and maintenance will be discussed.

II. ZURICH MAN SYSTEM OVERVIEW

Since the communication network of the Zurich Universities reaches various sites within a metropolitan area, it is called the "Zurich metropolitan area network" (Zurich MAN). It supports various data communication services as well as video and control services on a single broadband cable (Fig. 2) by means of frequency division multiplex (FDM). However, the "Zurich MAN" differs substantially in topology and technology from the proposal of the IEEE 802.6 MAN Committee for Standardization [1].

The most important service on the network is Sytek's LocalNet 20 [2] which is used for interactive terminal-computer communication. It is based on 15 parallel 128 kbit/s channels with 400 kHz bandwidth each. On each of these FDM channels multiple access is managed by carrier sense multiple access, with collision detection (CSMA/CD). Traffic between the channels and between similar networks on remote sites which cover the same address space is routed by five bridges. Today, LocalNet 20 handles more than 4200 RS-232C ports and supports the access at up to 19.2 kbits/s to over 50 multiuser computers (CDC Cyber, Data General, DEC 10, HP1000, IBM, ONIX, PDP, VAX), to many single user computers (PC, Workstations), to several dial-in and dial-out modems, to gateways to the public packet communication network, to file transfer controller, to libraries, and to a network information service. Apart from the sites near downtown Zurich, some research facilities sited farther away also belong to the system (Fig. 1). Two of them, which are located approximately 30 km from the ETH central area, are connected by a 128 kbit/s link. This connection utilizes an experimental microwave link of the army which passes a relay in the

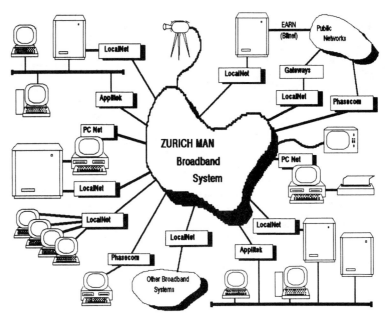

Fig. 2.   Services on the broadband network of the Zurich Universities.

Swiss Alps having a total length of 150 km. In the near future this link will be replaced by a 2 Mbit/s leased line, partially using fiber optics.

A 2 Mbit/s CSMA/CD data communication service for the interconnection of personal computers (IBM's PC-Net [3]) is used mainly for distributed printing services.

Finally, a 10 Mbit/s service (Applitek [4]) provides for the Ethernet interconnection of three VAX clusters. The employed access method adjusts automatically to the traffic on the network, providing the instant access of CSMA/CD as well as the guaranteed access of token passing.

Broadband modems for up to 102 simplex (51 duplex) connections within 6 MHz bandwidth allow special purpose point-to-point transmission at up to 19.2 kbits/s.

The video services, being of minor importance at the ETH, are used for educational programs at the UNI.

Since 1981, the network has grown continuously. After the positive experiences at the main campus area, it was extended to other sites in January 1985. Since the summer of 1986, the broadband cable service connects approximately 6500 offices using more than 80 km of coaxial cable and 111 broadband amplifiers. Today the broadband system is estimated to have reached 70 percent of its ultimate size. At the ETH, approximately 25 percent of the ports belong to multiuser computers (hosts). Although the number of RS-232C ports is higher today than ever expected, there is a constant demand for new LocalNet 20 access units.

III. SINGLE CABLE BROADBAND NETWORKS

A. System Overview

For a long time broadband systems have been widely used for Community Antenna Television (CATV), where coaxial cables in inverted tree-and-branch structure connect all

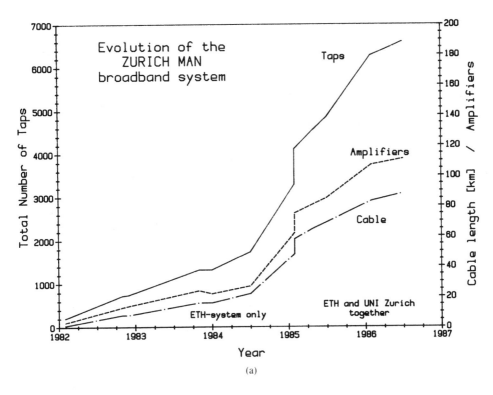

(a)

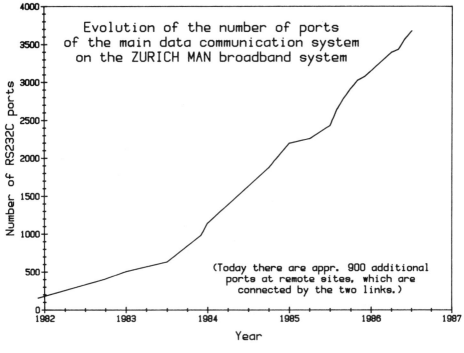

(b)

Fig. 3.   Evolution of the "Zurich MAN": broadband system and RS-232C-ports.

subscribers to the antenna site (headend). Almost all CATV systems use the network bandwidth of up to 450 MHz (i.e., up to 600 MHz with the most recent equipment) for unidirectional transmission (broadcasting only), although a small fraction (from 5 to 26 MHz) of the available spectrum is reserved for transmission from the subscriber towards the headend. CATV is installed in more than 60 percent of households because of generally difficult receiving conditions in Switzerland.

Broadband systems utilized for data communications use principally the same technology and network structure as CATV [5]–[7]. In order to achieve bidirectional transmission with more symmetrical capacity, the cable frequency spectrum is divided into two almost equal bands. The so-called midsplit technique uses a forward channel (downstream, downlink, outbound) which carries signals between 174 and 450 MHz from the headend at the tree's root to the devices on the distribution network. The reverse or return channel (upstream, uplink, inbound) carries signals in the opposite direction using the frequency band between 5 and 108 MHz. This allows bidirectional connectivity within a bandwidth of 103 MHz and permits the use of an additional bandwidth of 173 MHz for broadcasting systems.

The attached devices transmit signals only in the return frequency band. A frequency translator at the headend relocates and retransmits these incoming signals from the reverse channel to the higher frequencies of the forward channel. All passive (cable, taps) and active (amplifiers) components of the network are designed to support this bidirectional signal transmission, i.e., they provide a flat transfer function in the reverse and forward band for signals toward and away from the headend, respectively.

Broadband networks can carry data communication, video, and control services on the same cable by means of frequency division multiplex (FDM). Each service has its own frequency translation unit at the headend. With the changing needs of the network users, the supported communication services will also undergo certain modifications. Table I shows today's "Zurich MAN" services and their frequency allocations.

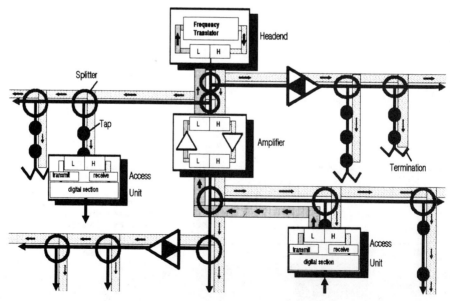

Fig. 4.   Basic layout of a broadband single cable system.

TABLE I
SERVICES AND FREQUENCY ALLOCATION

Application (Service Name)	Reverse Frequency	Offset	Forward Frequency
Data Communication:			
Terminal-computer communication			
(LocalNet 20)	70.00–76.00	156.25	226.25–232.25
(LocalNet 2000)	71.75–77.75	192.25	264.00–270.00
Personal computer interconnection			
(IBM PC-Net)	47.75–53.75	168.25	216.00–222.00
Ethernet interconnection (Applitek)	95.75–101.75	156.25	252.00–258.00
Point-to-point modems (Phasecom)	17.75–23.75	156.25	174.00–180.00
Video:			
Two-way	61.00–68.00	(281.00)	342.00–349.00
Broadcast Channel 1			181.00–188.00
Broadcast Channel 2			195.00–202.00
Broadcast Channel 3			293.00–300.00
Control:			
Amplifier gain and slope			
control pilot	7.00/93.00	—	182.25/343.25
Headend control pilots			
(TSwitch-pilots)	69.975/70.025	156.25	226.225/226.275
Amplifier remote monitoring			
and control (DSS)	29.5	—	288.00

B. Main-/Subheadend Configuration

A failure in the frequency translator at the headend would cause a dropout for the whole system. Therefore, standby translators automatically take over service in case of failures. The switching is controlled by a supervision unit, which continuously checks functionality by emitting and receiving pilot tones. In order to assure communication within the sites, even in case of an interruption on the trunk lines between the different campuses, a special network topology was chosen for the "Zurich MAN" (Fig. 5).

The main-/subheadend configuration has a headend at each site. Under normal conditions the whole network will be driven by the main headend and all other headends, i.e., the subheadends are in the standby mode. The main headend supervision unit checks the functionality of its own frequency translator. The supervision units of the subheadends continuously check the trunk lines by sending a pilot tone to the main headend, where its frequency is transposed and rebroadcasted. As soon as an interruption on a trunk line (or at the main headend) occurs, the appropriate subheadend does not receive its pilot tone and therefore takes over the service in its subnet. Site-to-site interconnection even in case of a trunk failure is assured by a 64 kbit/s backup link. At the price of higher cost and complexity, an even higher fault tolerance could be achieved by using more subheadends.

C. Installation

The Swiss PTT permitted the placement of the main trunk cable (Type: NKF bambus, 29.3 mm outer conductor diameter) between the sites in public cable ducts, side by side with the telephony cables. For the amplifiers (maximum spacing 1015 m) on these main

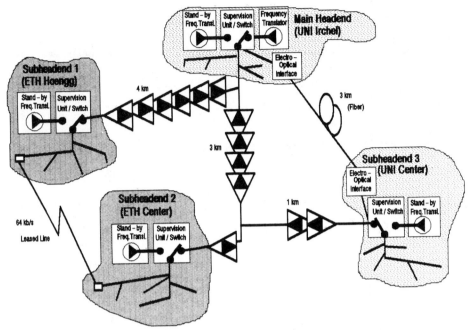

Fig. 5.   Main-/subheadend configuration.

trunk lines, special housings had to be constructed. Attenuation variations due to temperature changes on these long trunk lines are compensated by automatic amplifier gain and slope adjustment, using two pilot tones for each direction. One of the sites is connected to the main headend by a repeaterless 3 km fiber optical link (1300 nm, graded index fiber). This optical cable was installed inside a tunnel of the City of Zurich's remote heating system. It must withstand temperatures in the range of -20 to $+90°C$.

The cables between the buildings (Type: flooding compound, 12.9–22 mm outer conductor diameter) are laid mainly alongside the pipes of the ETH central heating system running underneath the buildings. Within the buildings the existing channels for energy, water, and gas distribution, which generally form a tree-like topology, were used for placement of the additional communication cabling.

Since CATV is installed in more than 60 percent of Swiss households, experienced companies could be contracted for the installation of the broadband system. It is recommended to take special care in the choice and installation of the connectors. Furthermore, it is advisable to use cables with good shielding (better than RG 59/RG 6) in the distribution network. Finally, proper termination is also very important in order to minimize the capture of FM- and TV-broadcasting signals.

IV. CHARACTERIZATION OF THE TWO-WAY BROADBAND CHANNEL

The wide experience of CATV industry in broadband network technology is mainly limited to the forward channel. The results being published on reverse channel experiences refer to subsplit networks with generally only small numbers of reverse direction subscribers [8]–[10]. With the goal of better understanding of two-way (midsplit) networks with many subscribers, extensive measurements using very sophisticated spectrum analyzer equipment (HP70000) were carried out on the "Zurich MAN" broadband system over the last two years. In order to also capture intermittent signals, the spectrum analyzer was generally in "peak hold" mode. For identification of constant signals or to characterize the intermittent signals, "minimum hold" and "video averaged" modes were used as well.

A. Amplitude Transfer Function

The amplitude transfer function for the reverse path (tap-to-headend) and for the total path including frequency translators at the headend (tap-headend-tap) was determined by inserting a sweeping generator signal at some far tap and measuring the spectrum at the headend and at some other far tap, respectively. The results indicate a flatness better than $+/-3$ dB for both paths. On long sections of the passive network, equalizers are installed to compensate for the slight slope in the transfer function, due to the increased cable attenuation at high frequencies.

B. Forward Channel Frequency Spectrum

Assuming the common "unity gain" design scheme [9], the white noise floor in the forward direction, i.e., the available noise power N_f within the bandwidth B at the final output terminal of a network with n identical cascaded amplifiers, is given by

$$N_f[\text{in dBm}] = 10 \log (kTB/1 \text{ mW}) + G + NF + 10 \log (n) \qquad (1)$$

where $k = 1.38 \, 10^{-23}$ J/K (Boltzmann's constant), $T =$ ambient temperature in K, $B =$ bandwidth in Hertz, $G =$ amplifier gain, $NF =$ amplifier noise figure, and $n =$ number of cascaded amplifiers.

Carrier-to-noise ratio in the forward direction thus decreases by 3 dB each time the number of amplifiers in cascade in the path from the headend to the individual subscribers is doubled. The longest cascade on the "Zurich MAN" is 12 amplifiers. The forward channel frequency spectrum measured at a user tap (Fig. 6) shows all signals which were inserted or transposed at the headend. As expected, the noise floor increases in the amplified band (174–450 MHz) and shows a slight frequency dependent slope due to the attenuation of the distribution net. In transposed bands without traffic, e.g., at 216–222 MHz, a significantly higher noise floor, resulting from the reverse band amplifiers, can be noticed. Furthermore, some interfering signals are present.

C. Reverse Channel Frequency Spectrum

In the reverse direction the inverted tree configuration accumulates the signals of all branches at the headend. One major concern of network planners was the collection of intrinsic noise (thermal noise, amplifier noise) produced in the active devices of the network [6], [8]–[10]. All amplifiers of the network contribute to the white noise addition and not just the amplifiers in cascade as it is the case for the forward direction. Therefore, calculating the reverse channel noise floor at the headend, the number of amplifiers n in (1) has to be taken equal to the total number of amplifiers in the network. The 111 amplifiers in the "Zurich MAN" cause an almost 10 dB higher noise level in the reverse path compared to a forward path with 11 amplifiers in cascade (see Fig. 6 at 216–222 MHz).

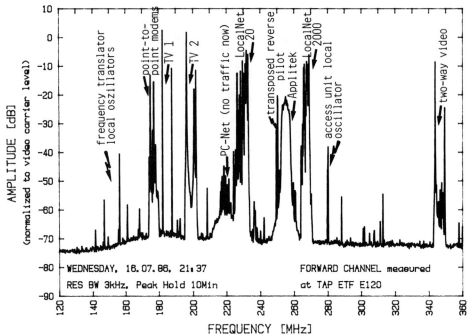

Fig. 6.   Forward channel frequency spectrum.

The subnet Hoengg (Fig. 7) illustrates this noise accumulation for the reverse channel frequency spectrum, as measured at the headend of the "pure" broadband system (before installation of access units). In addition to the intrinsic noise, ingress takes place from local TV and FM broadcasting, as well as intermittent disturbances due to shortwave signals around 6 MHz [8]. The increased noise level around 10 MHz which is caused by the emission of high frequency harmonics from switching power supplies could be eliminated by an improved amplifier design.

Repeated measurements of the broadband system after extension to the Department of Physics (Fig. 8) illustrate important ingress of intermittent noise, which is due to high-power apparatus (high-frequency ovens, lasers) in the near vicinity of the network.

The important disturbances caused by out-of-band signals occur (Fig. 9) after the installation of access units for the different network services. For one single unit such out-of-band signals are specified to be more than 65 dB below the data carrier level. However, due to the accumulation of out-of-band signals of all connected access units in the reverse direction, the data carrier to out-of-band signal ratio (COR) measured at the headend will decrease significantly. It might be only 35 dB, if there are 1000 access units connected. Again using the "unity gain" design scheme, the $COR_a(f)$ for a specific out-of-band signal can be approximated by

$$COR_a(f)[\text{in dB}] = COR(f) + 10 \, \log \, (k) \tag{2}$$

where $COR_a(f)$ and $COR(f)$ are the mean data carrier to out-of-band signal ratios at a specific frequency f (measured within 3 kHz bandwidth) for the sum of all access units and for a single access unit, respectively. The number k accounts for the total number of

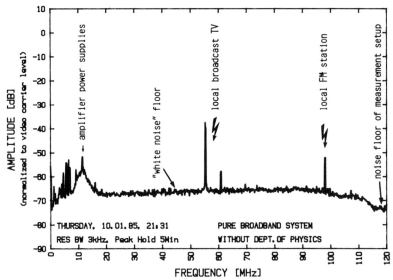

Fig. 7.   Reverse channel frequency spectrum of the "pure" broadband system (without the Department of Physics).

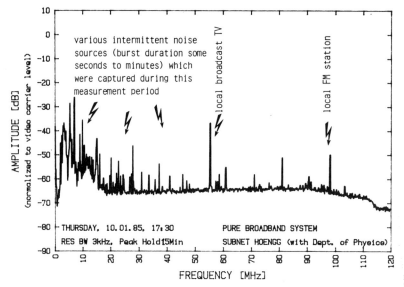

Fig. 8.   Reverse channel frequency spectrum of the "pure" broadband system (including the Department of Physics).

connected access unit modems. The out-of-band signals do not add up coherently because their frequencies differ slightly.

The measurements on the "Zurich MAN" show that with a large number of two-way subscribers transmitted noise, e.g., spurious signals (out-of-band signals) inserted by the connected devices, and interference noise which is picked up from outside, are more important than white noise power accumulation.

Sensitive points for picking up interference noise are loose connectors, opened

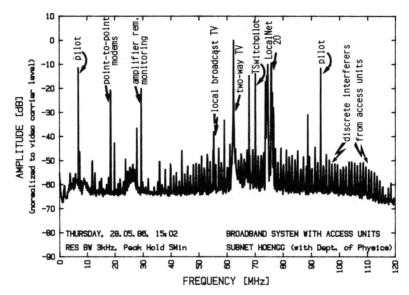

Fig. 9.   Reverse channel frequency spectrum of the broadband system with access units.

equipment housings, and unterminated cables. The distribution lines are the most sensitive network sections. The coaxial cable itself seems to provide an effective shielding. In a university environment there is always a wide spectrum of noise sources in the near vicinity of the highly distributed net. The most important interferers are high-power apparatus, local paging or radio communication systems, and computers. Localization and elimination of noise sources is very cumbersome and sometimes almost impossible without service interruptions.

Data transmission is generally not affected by the shown interferences. Video transmission, however, requires special precautions, e.g., a careful choice of the frequency bands for the video services. If disturbances become too severe, network segmentation in space [11], in time [12], or in frequency [13], [14] is recommended.

V. Traffic Flow Statistics for the Most Important Data Communication Service

Since there are not much data available on traffic in large data networks, extensive measurements on the ''Zurich MAN'' LocalNet 20 service are in process. In addition to the monitoring facilities offered by Sytek, a special purpose monitor box was developed at the Institute for Communication Technology.

Channel activity versus time (Fig. 10), for a regular working day, is very similar to that well known from telephony. There are distinct load peaks (busy hours) during the day around, dips at lunch time and during coffee break periods, and low loads at night. Generally, computer users tend to flatten out the activity curves, especially on channels with heavy loads.

Today, many channels show very high peak hour traffic loads (up to 70 percent and more). Fortunately, delays are less noticeable than expected and the collision rate increases intolerably at loads above 80 percent only (Fig. 11). It is planned to work around the high

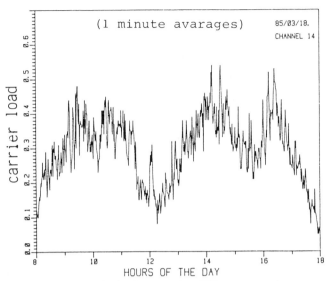

Fig. 10. Channel activity (carrier load) versus time (100 percent carrier corresponds to 128 kbit/s transmission rate on the channel).

load problems by installing more channels or subdividing the network. Furthermore, reorganizing channel allocation in order to minimize bridged traffic (i.e., connections which occupy more than one LocalNet 20 channel) should improve the performance.

The typical packet size distribution for interactive applications (Fig. 12) is bimodal [15] (in terms of data characters). There are many empty and one-character packets, for control

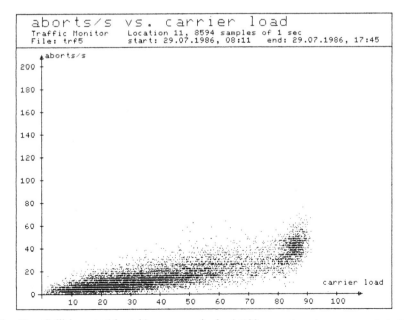

Fig. 11. Collision rate (aborts/s) versus carrier load (100 percent carrier corresponds to 128 kbit/s transmission rate on the channel).

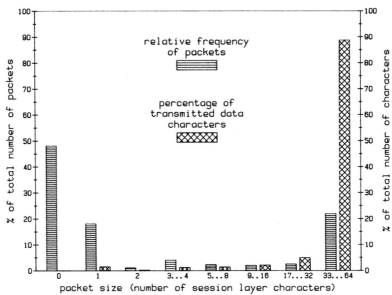

Fig. 12.   Relative frequency of packets and percentage of transmitted data characters versus packet length.

and terminal-to-computer traffic, respectively, and maximum size packets originating from computers (computer-to-terminal traffic and file transfer). The long packets account for approximately 20 percent of the total number of packets but carry more than 80 percent of the transmitted data characters. At high loads, generally more maximum size packets are present. Note that the packet size distribution is heavily dependent on the offered services, protocols, and user behavior, e.g., with increasing demand for file transfer it will change drastically. Furthermore, traffic is asymmetrical and inbalanced among the devices on the network.

VI. Experiences

A. System Reliability

The mean time between network failures (MTBF) is higher than the one of the computer systems. Furthermore, maintenance does not demand network interruptions. However, problems on the network generally affect more users than computer system failures. Up to now, there have been less than 10 failures of entire subnets with down time larger than 15 minutes. Almost all of them were caused by human error, e.g., switching off power at the headend, physical damage of cables, installation of uncalibrated equipment. Some early dropouts of new amplifiers were due to insufficient burn-in time. Finally, there was one problem with the headend supervision unit due to a fault in the power supply. Powering is by far the most critical problem of the broadband system.

In general, network extensions were possible without interruptions. The connection of UNI-Irchel to the net, and the corresponding change of network configuration and headends, required only two days of service interruption. Unfortunately, introduction of new services often leads to failures because of insufficient equipment testing or faulty installations.

Access units fail much more often than the broadband system, but generally these failures affect one single user and one single service of the network only. There were some modem problems with early LocalNet 20 versions, and recently many units with unreliable Z80-processor chips had to be replaced. Apart from these problems, approximately seven out of over 600 two-port access units have to be replaced every month, which leads to an estimate for the MTBF of seven years. More severe is the so-called "continuous carrier or streaming unit problem" where an access unit gets locked in the sending state. This blocks the channel for any traffic, and therefore generally affects more than 50 users. Fortunately, this has not happened very often (approximately once/year). During the first four years of service, localizing streaming units was very cumbersome and time consuming. Today, thanks to the amplifier remote control service, localization of a streaming unit or of any other unwanted carrier in a network section takes less than 15 min.

There were no problems at all with the reliability of the video services and the point-to-point modems, which both utilize standard technology. On the contrary, modern data communication devices generally cause a lot of problems (hardware and software) until a certain stability is reached.

B. Maintenance and Network Management

Up to now, no scheduled maintenance for the broadband system was performed. The broadband components have been checked or changed several times during the first five years of service because of the continuous network extensions and installation of new equipment (e.g., amplifiers, connectors). In the future, an annual preventive maintenance of the broadband system components is planned. There were some difficulties in maintenance because most measurement equipment (e.g., wobblers, sniffers) is designed for subsplit systems. Fortunately, more testing equipment is becoming available for midsplit systems now. Software updates for the main data communication service (changes of EPROM's in the access units), as well as a change of channel spacing from 600 to 400 kHz, were performed without network interruption. However, a downloading facility for new access unit software would provide an improvement.

For system management, maintenance, and service, six full-time employees are occupied at the ETH. This staff performs network planning, evaluation, testing, and introduction of new services and equipment, but also user support. Administrative, logistical and organizational tasks (e.g., contacts with installation companies, approvement of access unit orders) are at least as time consuming as user support, consulting, and trouble shooting.

With the growing size and complexity, improved network control and management functions are very important. There is no automatic diagnostic tool to detect and localize faults in the broadband system. In general, alarms are given by complaining users. A remotely operated amplifier control and monitoring service (digital system sentry, DSS [16]) is indispensable for such a large broadband system. It allows efficient fault detection and localization, when operated by skilled personnel.

Evaluation of the communication structure and of the traffic evolution is very important for network management, but difficult. A monitoring system for LocalNet traffic (Sytek's statistical monitor) gives information about the actual channel quality (e.g., collision rate), throughput, and packet size distribution. A special monitoring system has been developed at the ETH for determining the communication structure, i.e., the communication matrix. This system also identifies access units which are working in the privilege mode.

Furthermore, it gives information about session duration distribution and it helps to locate malfunctioning units.

VII. CONCLUSION

The experience with the "Zurich MAN," one of the largest multiple service broadband networks in the world, has proven high reliability and inherent flexibility. The broadband system allowed continuous extensions in size and permitted changes in the number and type of supported services. The chosen main-/subheadend structure is an efficient solution for network interconnection providing high connectivity and distributed redundancy. Investigations of the reverse channel frequency spectrum demonstrate that in large broadband networks with many users, disturbances are mainly due to transmitted noise, which is inserted by connected devices, and interference noise picked up from electrical apparatus in the systems vicinity. These disturbances usually do not affect data communication but demand special arrangements for video transmission. Network maintenance and management has to be supported by remote amplifier control capabilities and by data traffic monitoring systems. The traffic statistics of the most important data communication service on the network show the typical bimodal packet size distribution for interactive services and daily load variations similar to that known from telephony.

The main advantages of the homogeneous broadband solution are the flexibility and generality which support introduction of new data services with immediate access to all users. The parallel data services of the "Zurich MAN" provide the advantage of protocol optimization for each type of application, e.g., for interactive services (terminal access) CSMA/CD at 128 kbits/s, for streaming services point-to-point links, for Ethernet interconnections (mainly computer and workstation traffic) 10 Mbits/s with token passing possibility. The major disadvantages of such a structure are the difficult communication between the parallel data services, and the complicated administration and network management. A hierarchically organized clustered system, as it is widely used for business and industry applications, would be easier to manage.

Today, the most important data service, that for terminal access, is characterized by an inhomogeneous and unstructured behavior of the users, which is typical for the university environment. However, the unintelligent terminals grow more and more into workstations demanding much higher data rates, which is easier to implement with clustered solutions. Thus, cluster interconnection will become more important in the future.

REFERENCES

[1] D. T. W. Sze, "A metropolitan area network," *IEEE J. Select. Areas Commun.*, vol. SAC-3, Nov. 1985.
[2] G. Ennis and P. Filice, "Overview of a broad-band local area network protocol architecture," *IEEE J. Select. Areas Commun.*, vol. SAC-1, Nov. 1983.
[3] C. A. Sunshine and G. Ennis, "Broad-band personal computer LAN's," *IEEE J. Select. Areas Commun.*, vol. SAC-3, May 1985.
[4] A. M. Dahod, "An integrated data/voice local area network," *Telecomm., Mag.*, vol. 18, May 1984.
[5] E. Cooper, *Broadband Network Technology*, Sytek Press, 1984.
[6] R. Dunbar, "Design considerations for broadband coaxial cable systems," *IEEE Commun. Mag.*, vol. 24, June 1986.
[7] R. V. C. Dickinson, "Data transmission implementation on broad-band networks," *IEEE J. Select. Areas Commun.*, vol. SAC-3, Mar. 1985.
[8] R. Citta and D. Mutzabaugh, "Two-way cable plant characteristics," in *Proc. Nat. Cable Television Association (NCTA) 32nd Annual Convention*, Tech. Papers, 1983.

[9] A. S. Taylor, "Characterization of cable TV networks as the transmission media for data," *IEEE J. Select. Areas Commun.,* vol. SAC-3, Mar. 1985.

[10] H. J. Reichert, "CATV system return path interference," in *Proc. National Cable Television Association (NCTA) 32nd Annual Convention,* Tech. Papers, May 1982.

[11] G. Allora-Abbondi, "Interactive communications networks design concepts and operational experiences," presented at the 14th Int. TV-Symposium and Technical Exhibition, CATV-Session, Montreux, June 1985.

[12] R. Scholz and H. T. Hagmeyer, "A modular concept for return channels in CATV networks," presented at the 14th Int. TV-Symposium and Technical Exhibition, CATV-Session, Montreux, June 1985.

[13] N. F. Maxemchuk and A. N. Netravali, "Voice and data on a CATV network," *IEEE J. Select. Areas Commun.,* vol. SAC-3, Mar. 1985.

[14] T. G. Robinson, "Developing the right architecture—The first step to maximizing system reliability," presented at the 1st. Int. CATV-Congress, CATCOM, Luzern, Nov. 1984.

[15] J. F. Shoch and J. A. Hupp, "Measured performance of an Ethernet local network," *Commun. Ass. Comput. Mach.,* vol. 23, Dec. 1980.

[16] J. Staiger, "Status monitoring: For more efficient field technical service and less disconnects," presented at the 1st. Int. CATV-Congress, CATCOM, Luzern, Nov. 1984.

Part III
Fiber Optics Applied to
Local Area Networks

At first blush, optical fibers would appear to be an ideal medium for use in LAN's; they have low propagation loss and they are immune to electromagnetic interference, important for factory application. But optical fibers have some drawbacks too: they are difficult to connect and difficult to tap; optical components are expensive; the technology is new and still evolving. The cost of the medium (unless very large sites are contemplated) is not large enough relative to other costs to be a factor one way or another. Thus, today, very few fiber-optic LAN's are being installed; copper, in the form of twisted pair or coaxial cable is the medium of choice.

Perhaps the most likely area of application for the optical medium is in the area of high-speed LAN's, say above 100 Mbits/s, or for metropolitan area networks, use over distances greater than 5–10 km. In both these cases the higher attenuation of the most likely competitor, coaxial cable, increases as the square root of the frequency, so that typical large diameter cable has an attenuation of approximately 30 dB/km and smaller, more flexible cable may be three to five times that amount. By comparison, fiber might have an attenuation in the range 0.5–6.0 dB/km depending on the type of fiber and the wavelength of operation. Thus, it appears that for LAN's and MAN's operating at high speeds over long distances there is a strong incentive to look for fiber solutions.

In selecting papers for this section there was no attempt to "cover the field," but rather to concentrate on papers that speak directly to the specific issues raised by the application of fiber optics to LAN's. The one exception is the first paper which provides an introduction to optical LAN's and summarizes much of the work in the area in a very useful table (Table III).

The next three papers discuss attempts to do with fibers, things that are rather easily done with copper. The last paper describes a complete system, operating at 100 Mbits/s. Particular attention has been paid to the question of reliability of the system, a challenging problem for a ring configuration with active repeatered nodes.

It appears that we may soon have an international standard for a fiber LAN operating at 100 Mbits/s: FDDI (fiber distributed data interface). If you are overawed by standards documents you may care to peruse [1] and [2]. Other references that address interesting fiber LAN issues are [3]–[8].

REFERENCES

[1] F. E. Ross, "FDDI—A tutorial," *IEEE Commun. Mag.,* vol. 24, pp. 10–17, May 1986.
[2] W. E. Burr, "The FDDI optical data link," *IEEE Commun. Mag.,* vol. 24, pp. 18–23, May 1986.
[3] S. Matsushita, K. Kawai, and H. Uchida, "Fiber-optic devices for local area network applications," *J. Lightwave Technol.,* vol. LT-3, pp. 544–555, June 1985.
[4] T. H. Wood, "Increased power injection in multimode optical fiber buses through mode-selective coupling," *J. Lightwave Technol.,* vol. LT-3, pp. 537–543, June 1985.
[5] C. A. Villarruel, C. C. Wang, and W. K. Burns, "Single-mode data buses for local area network applications, *J. Lightwave Technol.,* vol. LT-3, pp. 472–478, June 1985.
[6] H. F. Taylor, "Technology and design considerations for a very-high-speed fiber-optic data bus," *J. Select. Areas Commun.,* vol. SAC-1, pp. 500–507, Apr. 1983.
[7] M. M. Nasshei, F. A. Tobagi, and M. E. Marhic, "Topological design of fiber optics local area networks with application to expressnet," *J. Select. Areas Commun.,* vol. SAC-3, pp. 941–949, Nov. 1986.
[8] S. Y. Suh, S. W. Granlund, and S. S. Hegde, "Fiber-optic local area network topology," *IEEE Commun. Mag.,* vol. 24, pp. 26–32, Aug. 1986.

14
Optical Fibers in Local Area Networks

MARION R. FINLEY, JR.

INTRODUCTION

In this chapter, we will examine the application of optical transmission technology to the local interconnection structures that we call local area networks (LAN's). These networks are a singular technological development with an application scope which may eventually overlap that of older conventional network structures, such as the local subscriber loop in telephone systems.

By the term LAN we understand a data communications system that allows a number of independent, nonhomogeneous devices to communicate with each other [1]. LAN's are usually distinguished from other types of data networks in that communication is confined to a modestly sized geographic area such as a single office building or a complex of buildings and laboratories such as a university campus. LAN application environments include the commercial, the industrial, and the institutional. Perhaps the major thrust of LAN's will be in office applications. LAN's must, therefore, support services such as file transfer, graphics applications, word processing, electronic mail, distributed data bases, interconnection to other LAN's, digital telephony, and, eventually, some kind of video service. Moreover, LAN's must support a wide variety of data devices: computers of all vintages (micro, mini, and maxi), video terminals, mass storage devices, printers, plotters, facsimile printers, and gateways to other networks.

As a transmission medium, optical fibers have proven to be extremely effective in CATV and telephone trunking applications [2]. However, when one restricts attention to LAN's, optical fibers have yet to be exploited to the limits of their enormous information-carrying capacity. Such things as optical tap losses, optical transmitter-receiver pair behavior, and complexity of the medium-access mechanisms needed limit their applicability at the present stage of technology.

OPTICAL-FIBER COMMUNICATIONS SYSTEMS

Optical fibers enjoy a number of charming properties that make them natural candidates for high-capacity transmission systems. The most important of these are:

- Large bandwidth × distance products supporting data attaining transmission at rates up to, say, 100 Gbits/s over 100 km [3]. Today's fibers typically offer bit rates of several hundred Mbits/s [4].

- Since glass is a dielectric medium, immune to electromagnetic interference and free from sparking, optical fibers are useful in EMI-rich and other hostile environments.
- Extremely small physical dimensions—the diameter of an uncabled optical fiber may vary from as little as 5–10 μm for the high-performance single-mode fibers to between 50 to several hundred μm for multimode fibers (see below for the definitions of these terms).
- Low attenuation, typically several decibels per kilometer, although values as low as 0.2 dB/km have been obtained [3].

The basic components of an optical-fiber communications system are [5], [6] optical transmitters, optical receivers, optical fibers connecting transmitter-receiver pairs, connectors and splices, and couplers. For further details regarding the nature of these components in an optical-fiber communications system, the interested reader might consult [7]. While in this chapter we shall deal primarily with systems using multimode fibers, that is, fibers permitting transmission of several modes of light injected from noncoherent sources, recent developments show a trend towards the use of single-mode fibers, that is, fibers allowing propagation of only one mode of the injected light. Single-mode fibers, sometimes also called monomode fibers, offer very large bandwidths and very low attenuation and as such are natural candidates for very high bit rate LAN's [7], [8]. Such LAN's with bit rates ranging from several hundred megabits/second to several gigabits/second might serve to interconnect LAN's having more modest bit rates. Single-mode fiber technology is, however, more demanding than multimode due, on the one hand, to the small physical dimensions of the monomode fibers and, on the other, to the transmission properties of monomodal light. In particular, fabrication of the single-mode version of the $n \times n$ passive couplers mentioned in the following paragraphs is problematical [7].

Let us now examine a simple link consisting of a transmitter-receiver pair interconnected by a single optical fiber (see Fig. 1): The optical transmitter consists of electronic circuitry that drives an optical source such as a light-emitting diode or a laser diode. The source output, a light beam in effect, is modulated according to the electrical input signals and launched into the fiber. At the opposite end of the fiber, light impinges on the surface of an optical detector such as a p-i-n or avalanche photodiode. The light energy is reconverted into an electrical signal and the electronic detecting circuitry of the optical receiver reconstructs the signal originally presented to the transmitter. Connectors serve to connect the fiber to the output fiber of the transmitter or the input fiber of the receiver, and to connect any two segments of fiber that must be joined. Connection may also be made by splicing, a procedure involving fusing together the ends of two fiber segments.

Several crucial system parameters determine whether the link just described works:

- the optical power of the signal received at the detector,
- the distortion of the signal transmitted through the fiber, and
- the system rise time.

Since the optical power of the received signal must exceed a certain threshold value, which is a function of the optical receiver, the optical power loss should satisfy a power budget for the link to function properly. This budget involves calculating all power losses incurred between the transmitter and the receiver. If these losses exceed the amount corresponding to the difference between the power injected into the fiber by the transmitter and the minimum power required by the receiver, then the link is not acceptable. In this event, one must either choose a more powerful transmitter, a more sensitive receiver, or a

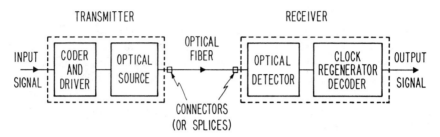

Fig. 1.   A simple optical-fiber communications link.

Optical Sources—LED's or laser diodes, transmission wavelengths in the 800–1300 (1550 on occasion) nm range.

Optical Detectors—p-i-n or APD photodiodes, similar wavelength windows as for source.

Optical Fiber—Glass fiber, perhaps plastic coated, pure plastic fibers for some applications. Wavelength windows as for sources.

Optical Connectors—Fiber-to-fiber interface, several types available. While great improvements have been made in these devices, the author finds them still a bit delicate for LAN applications in which frequent reconnections are made.

Optical Splices—Fiber-to-fiber permanent join, achieved through electric arc fusion or by other techniques. Perhaps better than connectors if no or very few disconnects/reconnects are foreseen.

The coding and driver circuits prepare the electrical signal modulated in the appropriate format, and present it to the LED or laser-diode source. The modulated light beam emitted by the source is coupled into a fiber ''pigtail'' which terminates in a connector. By the latter, the transmission fiber is connected to the source ''pigtail.'' The beam thus traverses the connector and the fiber to the ''pigtail'' that enters the receiver unit. This ''pigtail'' is then coupled to the detector, the light converted to electricity, and amplified. Clock recovery and decoding take place next, and the original input signal is reconstructed.

system rise time should also conform to a budget that is imposed by the desired bit rate. This budget involves two crucial fiber parameters—the material and the modal dispersions—both of which can cause pulse spreading, and hence intersymbol noise, as the light traverses the fiber. Material dispersion refers to the light impulse broadening due to the differential delay of the various wavelengths present in the beam, whereas modal dispersion refers to spreading caused by differential optical path lengths present in a multimodal fiber. For those interested in more details on these two budget calculations and the relevant parameters, [5] and [6] may be helpful.

Optical losses may occur at the transmitter-to-fiber coupling points, at all connectors and splices, and at the fiber-to-receiver coupling and throughout the fiber itself. Moreover, fiber cabling and environmental conditions may introduce additional optical losses and should be included in the power budget calculations.

A $1 \times n$ power coupler splits the light beam into n outgoing ports [Fig. 2(a)]. The amount of optical power coupled into each leg is a function of the coupler's construction and is determined by system requirements. In general, one has $m \times n$ couplers in which there are m input ports and n output ports [Fig. 2(b)]. Assuming equal distribution of power over each of the output ports of a $1 \times n$ coupler, power is reduced by at least a factor of $1/n$ while traversing the coupler, in logarithmic terms, decreased by $-10 \log n$ dB. Additional losses occur due to the coupler itself, and it is difficult to make the power division uniformly equal. It is clear that even when a transmitter-receiver pair conforms to power budget requirements, the careless use of power couplers may introduce extra optical power losses, resulting in link failure.

Another source of power loss is optical multiplexing and coupling, namely the

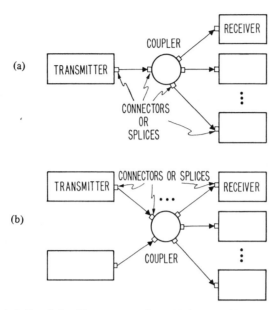

Fig. 2.   An optical-fiber link with power couplers. (a) $1 \times n$; (b) $m \times n$. Note: Optical transmitters and receivers as in Fig. 1.

multiplexing of several optical signals at different wavelengths onto the same fiber. This technique is called wavelength division or color multiplexing (WDM), where light signals from n sources, each one at different wavelengths, are combined by a wavelength division coupler or multiplexer into a composite light signal and injected into a single fiber (Fig. 3). An optical demultiplexer is used to separate signals from different sources. Thus, WDM permits several physical channels to coexist on the same fiber, and these channels may go in either direction.

The following network topologies appear most promising for optical-fiber-based LAN's [9] (see Fig. 4).

1) The bus, in which network interfaces are interconnected linearly; the connectivity requirement imposes bidirectionality.

2) The ring or loop, in which network interfaces are interconnected linearly, but with the last one connected back to the first one, thus forming a closed loop; unidirectional transmission is sufficient to guarantee total connectivity.

3) The star, in which every node is connected bidirectionally to a single central node, the "hub" of the star; connectivity is clearly obtained.

4) Hybrids of the above, for example, star-ring topologies in which a number of rings are interconnected through a centralized hub.

These topologies are listed without any consideration of the manner in which the network interfaces are coupled to the transmission medium, a crucial point for optical-fiber applications to LAN's. In the case of buses and rings, the network interfaces are coupled to the medium through a passive or active device. In the first case, the network interface receives a portion of the optical energy from the medium and it injects optical energy directly into the medium. The medium is not broken, so to speak. In the second case, all the optical signal energy enters the interface, an optoelectrical conversion and regeneration

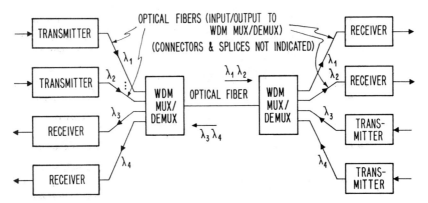

Fig. 3. Wavelength division multiplexing—Illustrated here is a hypothetical four-wavelength-channel optical-fiber transmission link using a single fiber. There are four transmission windows at λ_1, λ_2, λ_3, λ_4, respectively. λ_1 and λ_2 are transmitted in one, λ_3 and λ_4 in the other. The optical mixing takes place at the WDM MUX/DEMUX devices as indicated. The optical receivers and transmitters are as in Fig. 1, operating at their respective wavelengths.

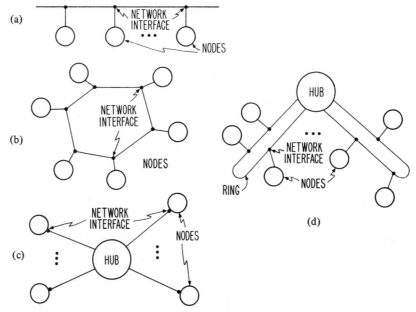

Fig. 4. Topologies for LAN's. Note: Recall that the nodes are concentrators/deconcentrators to which several devices may be connected. For example, one commercially available LAN permits up to 24 terminals, computers, etc., to be connected to a single node.

take place, the converted signal is presented to the node and perhaps modified by the latter, and then reconverted to optical energy and launched onto the outgoing fiber. An active network interface will have the general structure indicated in Fig. 5(a), whereas a passive network interface will follow that of Fig. 5(b).

Two remarks must be made at this point. First of all, optical repeaters, at the current state of the art, involve optoelectrical conversion, electrical regeneration, and electro-optical conversion, which is the case for active interfaces. True optical-to-optical repeaters not involving optoelectrical and electrooptical conversions are not yet available. Secondly,

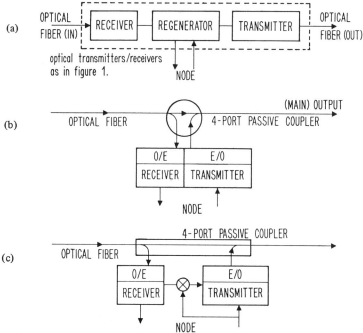

Fig. 5. Node interfaces. (a) Active. (b) Passive. (c) Fail-safe. Note: O/E and E/O refer, respectively, to the optoelectrical and electrooptical converters in the receiver and transmitter.

passive interfaces imply optical-to-optical coupling, hence, careful considerations for distortions and power losses have to be made to satisfy the system power budgets.

Finally, in Fig. 5(c) a hybrid network interface structure is indicated that combines the advantages of the active and passive structures of Fig. 5(a) and (b). This gives a "fail-safe" node—if the active regenerating portion goes down, the passive part remains intact.

Let us now examine the optical-fiber versions of the three principal topologies listed above.

BUSES

Active and passive configurations are shown in Fig. 6(a) and (b). Active buses entail the active couplers described above at each network interface, one for each direction, whereas passive buses have a complex passive coupler configuration. In the former case, the interface cost and electronic complexity are drawbacks for the implementation of active buses. In the second case, the lossy nature of couplers and transmitter-receiver pairs limits the number of network interfaces one may cascade in sequence to about 13 [10]. The optical equivalent of the high-impedance electrical tap has not yet been perfected.

An intriguing variant of the passive bus is the unidirectional bus, shown in Fig. 6(c), in which one end of the bus is closed, giving a "U" configuration. This configuration, proposed by the author and one of his assistants in 1977 [11] and considered recently by other researchers [10] offers the advantages of a linear bus coupled with the simplicity of ring topologies, especially when medium-access protocols are concerned. Once again, however, the number of network interfaces that one can introduce is limited by coupler losses, just as is the case for passive linear buses.

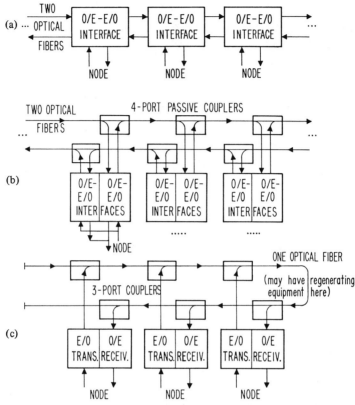

Fig. 6.   Linear fiber-optic buses. (a) Linear bidirectional bus. (b) Linear bidirectional passive bus. (c) Loop bus. Note: Connectors and splices not shown.

RINGS

Ring topologies, similar to linear bus topologies, allow two types of configurations, active or passive, as shown in Fig. 7(a) and (b), with fail-safe variants as suggested in Fig. 7(c) and (b). For an active ring, either node failure or a fiber break will cause a fatal crash; certain nodes will remain incommunicado. In the case of a passive ring, node failure need not bring down the whole network, but a fiber break certainly will.

One should note that the signal, once injected into the fiber, will circulate until it is completely attenuated. This may give rise to echoes, as there is no way to remove the signal from the ring, unless the fiber is physically discontinuous at, say, a master control station—in which case one does not have a true passive ring. The author has not yet seen an elegant solution to this problem, although the fail-safe version of such rings proposed by Albanese [12] has been reported to function properly [Fig. 7(b)].

Fail-safe variants for active rings include that of adding another loop going in the opposite direction, with the necessary switchover electronics to handle the case of a fiber break and an optical bypass switch, at each node, that is tripped if the node fails. Active rings are attractive for their structural simplicity and for the high-performance medium-access algorithms that have been developed. However, the cost and complexity of the interface electronics needed to implement these algorithms have been dampening factors in

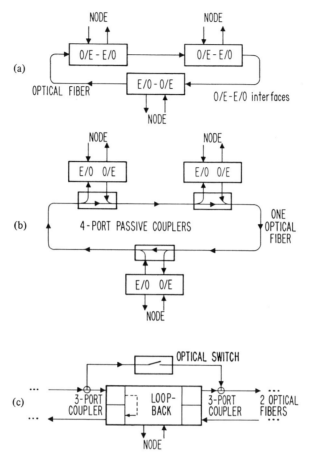

Fig. 7. Fiber-optic ring topologies. (a) Active ring: In this topology, regeneration takes place at every node. (b) Passive ring: This configuration introduces the problem of signal echo. Note: Passive ring with fail-safe mechanism: The topology is exactly the same as in (b), but the E/O-O/E mechanism is that of Fig. 5(c). If the active part of this mechanism fails, the ring may still continue to function [12]. (c) Active ring with fail-safe features (just one node interface is shown): If the interface fails, the optical switch is automatically tripped and the signals simply bypass it (note the need for couplers), and appropriate messages are sent to the maintenance modules of the network. If the principal fiber breaks, this is detected by software and the loop-back mechanism of the appropriate node is evoked. Again, maintenance procedures are set in motion.

their realization. Since this cost is steadily decreasing, active rings are now being introduced in the marketplace.

STARS

Centralized switched star network configurations have existed now for over a century in our telephone systems and represent perhaps the best-understood class of networks—at least, the one with which most people seem at ease. This is true for active stars in which the centralized hub exercises switching or medium-access functions. The PBX approach, collision detection for CSMA, "hub" accessing methods [9], [13], fast circuit switching,

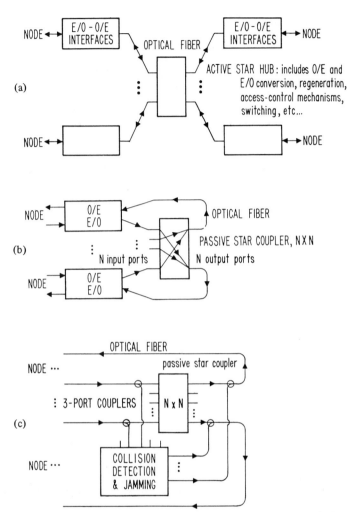

Fig. 8.   Fiber-optic star topologies. (a) Active star. (b) Passive star. (c) Passive star with centralized collision detection. (In (b) and (c) there are two fiber ends per node. In (a) there are one or two, depending upon use of WDM.)

and other approaches may be used. Optical-fiber technology may be used in these cases in its simplest and best-understood form, namely point-to-point [Fig. 8(a)].

What is surprising is that via an $n \times n$ passive star coupler, one can create an optical bus with properties similar to that of an Ethernet broadcast bus [Fig. 8(b)]. Thus, passive star buses may be used with the CSMA/CD protocols, giving one simple way to fiberize existing Ethernet-type networks. Several commercial examples are cited in the section "Some Contemporary Fiber-Optic LAN's." For the case of CSMA/CD, the collision event may create problems due to possible variations in optical power received by the different nodes of the network. To circumvent this difficulty and still retain a passively coupled network, a collision-detecting device may be passively coupled at the star coupler, as shown in Fig. 8(c). This, of course, influences the power budget, but does guarantee proper working of the collision-detection mechanism.

Some Design Considerations

In applying optical fibers to LAN's, the following points should be noted.

- Optical-fiber cable is frequently fabricated in 1 km segments. This means that for LAN applications, in which distances are usually less than 1 km between network interfaces, some splicing or connecting operations will be avoided.
- The relatively short distances between network interfaces involved in LAN's permit use of fibers with modest bandwidth × distance product values.
- The relatively modest bandwidth × distance product values required mean that the optical transmitter-receiver pairs needed are well within the reach of today's technology.
- The low bit error rates required by LAN's are virtually an industry standard.
- A point raised several times in this chapter: the connectability/reconnectability requirement implies the need for efficient, that is, low-loss, power couplers. This has motivated much research and development on passive and active "tee" and star couplers, and on innovative topologies designed to minimize optical power losses.
- While innovative, low-loss topologies are needed, particular attention must also be paid to the medium-access protocols used. Choice of topology and of such protocols goes hand-in-hand.

There are clearly tradeoffs to be made in the design process. For example, by choosing an active ring configuration, the problem of coupler or tap losses essentially disappears; one has the point-to-point link described earlier. However, one also has the problem of complexity with the medium-access method and the critical question of providing fault-tolerance mechanisms such as loop-back and bypass switching. Thus, one advantage may be outweighed by other considerations.

At this point, one may decide to throw out the active ring idea and try a passive star-coupled configuration instead. This approach is certainly interesting as it gives an optical equivalent of the Ethernet coaxial-cable bus. However, the efficiency of the CSMA/CD medium-access protocol hinges on the proper detection of the collision event. To guarantee this, it may be necessary to add special equipment at the star hub, as was mentioned in the previous section. Once again, an advantage may be countered by an inconvenience.

As one can see, the problem of determining an optimal configuration for a fiber-optic LAN is not trivial. The author and a colleague are currently exploring for the design of fiber-optic LAN techniques similar to the "silicon compiler" techniques that have been proposed for VLSI design. A simple design procedure led to the list of key parameters shown in Table I that characterize a fiber-optic LAN. The comparison table of the next section is based upon this list. Table II illustrates the list of Table I for the case of a bus network constructed by the MITRE Corporation for the NASA Goddard Space Flight Center.

Some Contemporary Fiber-Optic LAN's

In this section, some typical fiber-optic LAN activities are summarized and some more recent activities are characterized briefly in the following section. In some cases, the networks exist as finished products available in the marketplace. In others, the networks are in varying stages of development, ranging from theoretical studies, sometimes accompanied by experimental backup, to laboratory prototypes. The examples presented,

TABLE I
KEY PARAMETERS FOR FIBER-OPTIC LAN'S

1) Manufacturer
2) Network name
3) Operational status (experimental prototype, commercially available)
4) Date placed in service (if available)
5) Services offered
6) Span
7) Bit rate
8) Topology
9) Organization (centralized, partially distributed, distributed)
10) Multiaccess methods
11) BER
12) Number of nodes
13) Number of terminals
14) Fault tolerance
15) Coding scheme (NRZ, RZ, Manchester)
16) Fiber type
17) Fiber core diameter
18) Fiber outer diameter
19) Fiber windows
20) Source type (LED, LD)
    Source power
21) Source wavelength
22) Detector type
    Detector sensitivity
23) Detector wavelength
24) Coupler characteristics
25) Switches (optical)

sometimes incomplete due to lack of information, were selected in order to give readers an idea of what are, in the author's opinion, the major trends in this field.

The networks presented in this section permit the following general observations.

1) The multiaccess protocols are of critical importance to the designer in determining high throughput, low delay.

2) CSMA/CD-type protocols are used up to 32 Mbits/s, and ring token protocols may be used for higher bit rates.

3) Token rings dominate now for the high-speed commercially available networks (50–100 Mbits/s).

4) A variant of the token protocol method apparently works at 1 Gbit/s on a loop-bus architecture in a laboratory prototype [14].

CSMA/CD NETWORKS (ETHERNET COMPATIBLE)

Certainly one of the first LAN's to attract a great deal of attention is the Ethernet developed by the Xerox Corporation. This network has stimulated the creation of a number of look-alikes, as well as versions to be implemented on standard broadband coaxial-cable systems [1]. Therefore, it is natural that fiber-optic versions are developed. Two such versions are presented below, each one using slightly different approaches. The first is the Xerox Corporation's active-star-based Fibernet II; the second is Codenet, a passive-star-based system developed by the Codenoll Corporation. The Ungermann-Bass Corporation, together with the Siecor Corporation, has recently built a similar passive-star-coupled

TABLE II
VALUES OF KEY PARAMETERS FOR A SAMPLE CONFIGURATION

To illustrate the use of the parameters of Table I, the NASA Goddard Space Flight Center network, developed by the MITRE Corporation, is examined (CRES'82) [34]

1) NASA/MITRE
2) NASA GSFC fiber-optic local area network
3) Experimental, under development
4) Partially operational in 1982
5) Services: digital rates, 10 bits/s-10 Mbits/s per user,
   frames of 4800 bits
6) Span: 1.6 km (length of legs of bus)
7) Bit rate: aggregate bit rate estimated to be greater than 70 Mbits/s,
   100 Mbits/s for finished version, 50 Mbits/s for prototype
8) Topology: rooted tree using tee couplers in one version,
   star couplers in another version
9) Organization: centralized
10) Multiaccess: slotted TDMA
11) BER: less than 10^9
12) Number of nodes: in prototype 3, in finished version 100 (?)
13) Number of devices per node: 2–8
14) Fault tolerance: not specified
15) Coding scheme: NRZ (shown to be problematical with AC-coupled
    receiver; Manchester probably preferable)
16) Fiber type: GI (graded index, glass-on-glass)
17) Core diameter: 50 μm
18) Outer diameter (O.D.): 125 μm
19) Fiber window: not specified, 850 nm
20) Source type: Exxon OTX5100, LED @ 780–850 nm
    275 Mbits/s
    power greater than 100 μW
    rise time less than 1.5 ns
    price: $1100
21) Detector type: Exxon ORX5100, p-i-n, 850 nm
    0.1–150 Mbits/s
    BER: 10^9
    minimal detectable power: 5 μW @ 830 nm
22) Couplers: Version 1: biconically fused tapered 40/40, 60/20, 75/5
    insertion loss 20 percent
    Version 2: 6-legged transmissive star, -7.78 down per
    leg, -2 dB excess loss
Allowable optical power budget: 35 dB

configuration for their Ethernet-compatible Net/One. This version uses a centralized collision-detection mechanism that is passively coupled to the incoming fibers of the star coupler, as suggested in the previous section.

Besides the two efforts mentioned above, there are, of course, others. Apparently, Nippon Electric Corporation and Toshiba have developed Ethernet-compatible 10 Mbit/s CSMA/CD networks. The NEC network uses a tree architecture, whereas the Toshiba network (in prototype form) uses a passive-star-coupled bus [15]. These networks are summarized in Table III.

Fibernet II [16]: Fibernet II uses an active star repeater to create the equivalent of the baseband coaxial-cable "Ether" channel (Fig. 9). Collision detection is implemented electrically in the 25-port star repeater on a backplane which behaves like a small Ethernet and which is electrically compatible with the standard 10 Mbit/s Ethernet coaxial cable. The span of the network is about 2.5 km. Using 8-channel multiplexers, the network could

TABLE III
COMPARISON OF VARIOUS FIBER-OPTIC LAN'S

	Fibernet II	Codenet	Hubnet	Two-Way Bus	D-Net	Loop 6770 (NEC)	NASA/ITT	Hara's PBX
Topology	active star	passive star	star hub	loop-bus	several	active ring	passive star	active switched star
Organization	centralized	distributed	distributed	distributed centralized	distributed	distributed	centralized	centralized
Access	CSMA/CD	CSMA/CD	hub access	polled TDMA	"locomotive"	token	TDMA	circuit-switched TDMA
Bit Rate	10 Mbits/s	3.4 Mbits/s	50 Mbits/s	100 Mbits/s	100 Mbits/s	32 Mbits/s	100 Mbits/s	55.5 MHz, 10 Mbit/s sampling
Span (max loop length)	2.5 km	0.9–2.8 km	open	—	—	2.0 km	2.0 km	—
Max. # Nodes	200–1000	200–1000	65 536	13	—	126	16	—
Fault Tolerance	—	—	—	—	—	dual fiber, switchover, loop-back	—	—
Fiber Core	100 μm	100 μm	100 or 50 μm	—	—	50 μm	50 μm	—
Fiber O.D.	140 μm	140 μm	140 μm	—	—	125 μm	125 μm	—
Fiber Type	step-index	G.I.	G.I.	—	—	G.I.	G.I.	—
Fiber Window	—	850, 1300 nm	—	—	—	—	—	—
Source	LED	LED	LED	LED/LD	—	LED/850 nm	LD/820 nm	—
Detector	p-i-n	p-i-n	p-i-n	p-i-n/APD	—	p-i-n	APD	—
Coding	Manchester	Manchester	—	—	—	RZ	Manchester	—

	FACOM 2881 (Fujitsu)	FACOM 2883 (Fujitsu)	H-8644 (Hitachi)	Loop Network (Hitachi)	Loop 6530 (NEC)	Loop 6830 (NEC)	BRANCH 4800 (NEC)	(Prototype) (Toshiba)	SIGMA (Hitachi)	BILNET (Mitsubishi)
Topology	active ring	active ring	active ring	active ring	active ring	active ring	tree	passive star	active ring	passive ring
Organization	—	—	—	—	—	—	—	distributed	—	—
Access	TDMA	TDMA	token passing	TDMA	hybrid	hybrid	CSMA/CD	CSMA/CD	TDMA	TDMA
Bit Rate	4 Mbits/s	33 Mbits/s	32 Mbits/s	32 Mbits/s	32 Mbits/s	32 Mbits/s	10 Mbits/s	10 Mbits/s	32 Mbits/s	50 Mbits/s
Span (max)	3 km	9 km	2 km	2 km	7 km	12 km	1 km	1.5 km	2 km	—
loop length	96 km	576 km	100 km	—	—	—	—	—	—	—
Max. # Nodes	32 (?)	54 (?)	50 (?)	—	—	—	—	—	64	around 13
Fault Tolerance	(other details lacking at this writing)				(other details not available at this writing)				dual fibers, switchover, loop-back	—
Fiber Core									50 μm	
Fiber O.D.									125 μm	
Fiber Type										
Fiber Window									830 nm	
Source									LED/@830 nm	
Detector									p-i-n	
Coding										

Error Rate: Presumably less than 10^{-9} in all cases.

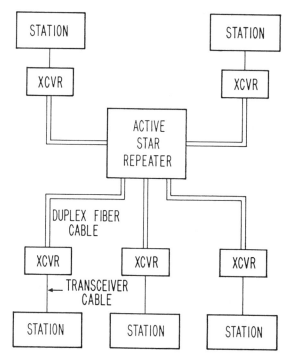

Fig. 9. Fibernet II topology. The XCVR units handle the optical transmitting and receiving units.

handle up to 200 stations, whereas by cascading the repeaters on their backplane Ethernets, over 1000 stations might be accommodated. Finally, the fiber star network might be used as a backbone to interconnect Ethernet segments.

Passive Star Configurations: Another Ethernet-compatible effort uses an 8-port passive star coupler to implement the "Ether" channel. The collision-detection mechanism is distributed, as opposed to the centralized version of Fibernet II, and is implemented in the station nodes. The latter are capable of supporting up to 24 serial RS-232 ports each, or various other combinations of serial and parallel ports. Thus, a 16-node configuration would support several hundred terminal devices. Extensions of the network might be achieved through making the star active, as in Fibernet II, or by the use of repeaters. As mentioned above, the Codenoll Corporation and Ungermann-Bass, jointly with Siecor, have produced such networks [17].

Nippon Telegraph and Telephone's Call for Bids: An interesting development is the call for bids put out by the Japanese Nippon Telegraph and Telephone Public Corporation (NTT) to U.S. firms, to develop medium-scale, passive-star-coupled CSMA/CD networks at 32 Mbits/s. The star is to be 32 or 100 ports, depending on the system specified. This reflects Japan's current interest in pushing office and factory automation [18].

Hub-Type Networks: A class of networks has recently evolved in an attempt to overcome some of the deficiencies of the Ethernet CSMA/CD-type networks. This class uses an ingenious centralized selection-broadcast mechanism, hence the term "hub."

Hubnet [13]: Hubnet is being developed by the University of Toronto's Computer Systems Research Group in collaboration with the CANSTAR Corporation. A prototype has been built and tested. Hubnet's designers set about to determine a network architecture that would overcome the following shortcomings of Ethernet: poor performance under heavy traffic conditions, low efficiency at high bandwidths, and (in the optical domain) coupler (tap) losses in linear bus configurations. As a consequence, an innovative architecture was derived in which these shortcomings would appear to have been eliminated. The key idea is to shrink the ''Ether'' channel to a point (the hub) at which an incoming signal is selected and broadcast to all outgoing lines (Fig. 10). While one incoming signal is being handled, signals arriving on other input lines are blocked, causing their transmitting units to time out and try again. There are, therefore, no collisions in the Ethernet sense. In the case of several signals arriving simultaneously when the hub is quiescent, one is chosen arbitrarily.

Hubnet may be expanded by the cascading of subhubs. A comparison of Hubnet's performance with that of Ethernet is given in Fig. 11.

Non-CSMA-CD Buses: A number of uni- and bidirectional buses have been developed recently. One example, using a passive-star-coupled topology as illustrated above but operating at much higher bit rates, was developed by ITT Electro-Optical Products Division as part of a NASA data base management system for archiving and retrieving satellite data [19]. This network uses a 16 × 16 fused biconical taper star coupler and operates at 100 Mbits/s (thus, far beyond the range of efficiency of CSMA/CD protocols). The maximum network span without repeaters is 2 km; the bit error rate is less than 10^{10}.

Another approach to bidirectional buses is that adopted by Albanese [10] illustrated in Fig. 12. This network, using a loop-bus topology, allows two functionally distinct networks to coexist on the same fiber. This is done by using 4-port couplers and transmission at different wavelengths for the two directions. Due to limitations of current coupler technology, the number of nodes is limited *in the best case* to about 13 for a 100

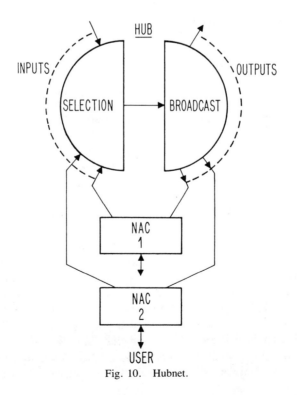

Fig. 10.   Hubnet.

PARAMETER	HUBNET	ETHERNET
data rate	50 Mbps	10 Mbps
span	open	2.5 km
max. # of stations	65,536	1024
medium	optical fibers	coaxial cable
topology	rooted tree, star	bus
message protocol	variable frame message size full acknowledgement delivery	variable frame message size best effort delivery
link control	multiple access echo detect of retry	CSMA/CD

Fig. 11.   Comparison of Hubnet with Ethernet.

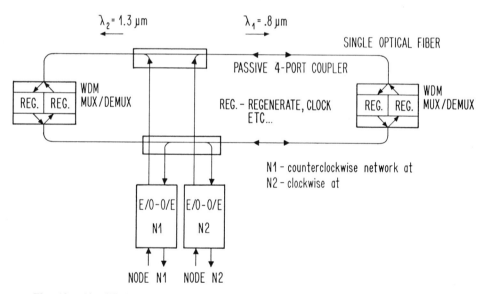

Fig. 12.   Simplified scheme for bidirectional loop bus using WDM on one fiber. Two networks may share the same fiber using WDM as shown.

Mbit/s system. Polling and TDMA are used for access. A unidirectional variant called XBN (for experimental broadband network) has been implemented by Hubbard and Albanese [20]. It uses dynamically assignable TDMA plus contention access methods simultaneously at a bit rate of 16.384 Mbits/s.

In Canada, work is underway on a joint project between the Communications Research Center of the Department of Communications, CANSTAR, and Sperry-Univac to develop a shipboard data bus with half-duplex connections at 10 Mbits/s [21]. Several topologies, including a hybrid linear and a hybrid star configuration, are being examined. Critical elements of these configurations are the hybrid star couplers and the asymmetric 4-port fused biconical tapered couplers.

Finally, an architecture has been proposed recently by Tseng and Chen at TRW [14], namely D-Net. D-Net may be realized using several topologies as illustrated in Fig. 13. In this network, a specialized node called the "locomotive generator" generates trains that define the access windows for the network interfaces. The result of this is an efficiency near one and, therefore, unlike Ethernet or Fibernet II, high bit rates, in the hundreds of Mbits/s, may be used. Network delay is tightly bounded so that packetized voice is feasible.

According to a recent paper [16], an experimental prototype of D-Net has been built with a transmission rate of 1 Gbit/s including 6 packet-switched television channels at 82 Mbits/s each. A variant of this type of network has been reported by Gerla *et al.* at the UCLA School of Engineering [22].

TDMA and Token-Passing Rings: Several examples of token ring networks are cited in Table III. For now, consider a typical example, the C&C-Net Loop 6770 built by the Nippon Electric Corporation, Ltd. [23]. This network operates at 32 Mbits/s and includes fault-tolerance mechanisms for ring interface bypassing in case of a ring interface failure, alternate path selection if a fiber is broken, and battery power backup. The ring consists of two optical-fiber loops transmitting in opposite directions. Under normal circumstances, one loop is idle and on standby, whereas the other is active. Since the ring interfaces are active, bypassing is achieved by electronic, as opposed to optomechanical, switching.

An interesting approach to passive ring configurations is that of the Communication Laboratory of the Mitsubishi Electric Company in Japan with their 50 Mbit/s BILNET (for bidirectional passive loop-structured network [24]). This network transmits bidirectionally on the same fiber using WDM, one wavelength for one direction, the other for the opposite

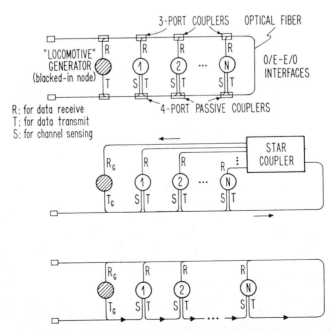

Fig. 13.   D-Net topologies. The first topology is a loop bus with the locomotive as shown. The second uses a star coupler for the inbound leg and the third is an "open" ring.

direction (840 and 900 nm, respectively). Normally the ring is "open," that is, the loop is broken at one point via an optical switch. This prevents signals from circulating more than once around the loop and thus creating echo interference. However, if the fiber cable is broken elsewhere, the switch closes, thus ensuring continuity of operation. Since the ring is passive, failure of a node as such should not bring down the network. Unfortunately, this network involves concatenating passive tee couplers, hence optical losses restrict the number of such tees to about 13, as mentioned earlier.

There are a number of ring networks that have been developed in Japan in addition to the ones mentioned above. These include the following:

- Facom 2881 and 2883 of Fujitsu;
- H-8644 Loop Network of Hitachi;
- SIGMA of Hitachi;
- Loops 6530 and 6830 of NEC.

These networks are included in Table III.

Fail-Safe Nodes: Networks with fail-safe nodes are of great interest to the designer who is considering active configurations in which failure of one node would interrupt the operation of the network, for example, a unidirectional active ring. Bypass mechanisms, such as that used in C&C-Net Loop 6770, are one way of handling this problem. However, there are other approaches, such as that suggested by Albanese at AT&T Bell Laboratories [12]. A 16 Mbit/s ring network was proposed whose nodes, based upon efficient 4-port couplers, allow automatic (that is, nonswitched) bypass if the active portion of the node goes down. If there is no problem with echo interference, then fail-safe nodes would permit implementation of large-scale ring networks using optical fibers similar to the C&C-Net Loop 6770 mentioned above.

PBX-Like Networks: Use of a centralized switcn for LAN's offers the simplicity of the circuit-switched telephone network, completely bypassing the multiaccess problems associated with rings and passive stars. The penalties to be paid are the need for expensive intelligence and duplication at the switch site and access mechanisms to the nodes. For now, the price seems still too high to pay, but with the effects of economies-of-scale, this might not remain a serious barrier. A major problem is that of constructing a broadband switch that is capable of switching very-high-bit-rate channels.

The recent development of a broadband optoelectronic switch by E. Hara [25] would permit 64 kbits/s and a video channel to be multiplexed on one fiber, allowing voice, video, and data on the same system. Hara's switch has been tested experimentally and is now under construction by Foundation Instruments in Ottawa. This switch uses optical-fiber methods internally to deliver signals to its crosspoints with acceptable crosstalk losses. Hara proposes this switch as the basis of a network for office communications systems and for high-rise building complexes.

The major characteristics of the configurations presented in the preceding sections are summarized in Table III.

Some Recent Activities: Activities involving fiber-optic LAN's over the last year or so have, if anything, increased in intensity as the advantages of using optical fiber become more widely appreciated on the one hand and as optical-fiber system components become more readily available on the other. For some applications, optical-fiber LAN's are the choice *par excellence*, for example, in military aircraft and ships and in EMI-rich environments. There is a significant trend towards high-bit-rate LAN's, thus inevitably, towards single-mode fiber LAN's. As far as network topologies are concerned, however, the networks cited in Table III remain typical. References [26]–[28] give a sample of current efforts.

Another current trend is towards the "intelligent building" [29] concept in which the internal communications system will offer video, voice, and data, and a rich set of integrated services such as energy management, electronic mail, security and alarms, word processing, videotext, and others. Once again, optical fibers are being proposed as the medium of choice [30].

CONCLUSIONS

Optical-fiber technology for LAN applications is maturing rapidly and there are now a number of commercial fiber-optic LAN's available. Active ring topologies using token-passing access methods and having a very high degree of fault tolerance are in the forefront, with several intriguing alternatives, such as Hubnet and D-Net, whose influences are yet to be seen. Passive- and active-star-coupled CSMA/CD bus configurations are also available; useful if compatibility with Ethernet-like components is desired. Several high-speed buses have been implemented.

There is the promise of greater exploitation of this technology: for example, recently a 100×100 passive star coupler was reported [31], made by a new process. Wavelength division technology is maturing as well. Commercial WDM multiplexers/demultiplexers permit only four or five wavelengths, yet a far larger number of wavelengths is feasible [32], for example, at the MITRE Corporation, experiments have been done using about 15 [33].

Thus, the potential of optical fibers is far from being exhausted. The intriguing point to note here is that a given optical-fiber network structure could coexist with many others on the same underlying optical-fiber support. The coexistence would be made possible precisely by the use of WDM, new low-loss power couplers, single-mode fibers, and the like.

Optical fibers thus hold out the promise of realizing powerful integrated-services local networks as key elements of the society of the twenty-first century.

ACKNOWLEDGMENT

The author would like to acknowledge the numerous contributions made by his colleagues in gathering data on fiber-optic LAN's. Special thanks are due to Dr. P. Polishuk, President, Information Gatekeepers, Inc., Boston, MA; to Dr. M. Kawahata, Managing Director, New Media Systems Development, Tokyo, Japan; to A. T. Szanto, President, Foundation Instruments, Ltd., Ottawa, Canada; to R. Pepper, Former President, Ungermann-Bass Canada, Ltd.; and to his colleague at Laval University, Dr. T. Vo-Dai, for his help in better understanding the role of medium-access protocols. The author also wishes to acknowledge the financial support received for his research in this area from the National Science and Engineering Research Council of Canada and the Department of Communications, Government of Canada. Finally, he wishes to thank the reviewers for their constructive remarks.

REFERENCES

[1] K. J. Thurber, Ed., *The LOCALNetter Designer's Handbook*. Minneapolis, MN: Architecture Technology Corporation, 1982.
[2] See, for example, the sections on telephone and CATV trunking applications in the Special Issue on Fiber Optic Systems of the *IEEE J. Select. Areas Commun.*, vol. SAC-1, no. 3, pp. 381–444, Apr. 1983.

[3] T. Li, "Advances in optical fiber communications: An historical perspective," *IEEE J. Select. Areas Commun.,* vol. SAC-1, no. 3, pp. 356–372, Apr. 1983.

[4] For detailed tables of currently available optical fibers and cables, see annual publications such as the *International Fiber Optics and Communications 1983–84 Handbook & Buyers Guide, Volume V.* Boston, MA: Information Gatekeepers, Inc.; or the similar volume published by *LASER FOCUS.*

[5] S. D. Personick, "Review of fundamentals of optical fiber systems," *J. Select. Areas Commun.,* vol. SAC-1, no. 3, pp. 373–380, Apr. 1983.

[6] W. Chou, *Computer Communications, Volume 1, Principles.* Englewood Cliffs, NJ: Prentice-Hall, 1983, pp. 299–300.

[7] M. Marhic, "Single-mode fiber optics for local area networks," presented at the LAN-84 Seminar, Information Gatekeepers, Inc., Arlington, VA, Mar. 29–30, 1984.

[8] V. J. Tekippe, "Single-mode fiber optic components," in *Proc. Ninth Int. Fiber Optics Commun. and Local Area Networks Exposition, FOC/LAN'85,* Sept. 1985, pp. 310–313.

[9] C. D. Tsao, "A local area network architecture overview," *IEEE Commun. Mag.,* vol. 22, pp. 7–11, Aug. 1984.

[10] A. Albanese, "Bidirectional light-wave bus," in *Proc. FOC/LAN'83,* Oct. 1983, pp. 214–215.

[11] M. R. Finley and P. Chartier, "Microprocessor optic fiber network-based information systems for the small enterprise," in *Proc. Canadian Inform. Process. Soc., CIPS'78,* May 1978, pp. 201–208.

[12] A. Albanese, "Fail-safe nodes for lightguide digital networks," *Bell Syst. Tech. J.,* vol. 16, no. 2, pp. 247–256, Feb. 1982; see also this volume, ch. 15.

[13] P. I. P. Boulton and E. S. Lee, "Hubnet: A 50-Mb/s glass fiber local area network," in *Proc. LAN'82,* Sept. 1982, pp. 15–17.

[14] C. W. Tseng and B.-U. Chen, "D-Net, a new scheme for high data rate optical local area networks," *IEEE J. Select. Areas Commun.,* vol. SAC-1, pp. 493–499, Apr. 1983.

[15] "Toshiba unveils fibre LAN," *Asian Computer Monthly,* p. 83, Feb. 1983; and "Local area network (LAN)," *EDP Japan Report,* pp. 57–58, Nov. 29, 1982.

[16] E. G. Rawson and R. V. Schmidt, "Fibernet II: An Ethernet-compatible fiber optic local area network," in *Proc. LAN'82,* Sept. 1982, pp. 15–17.

[17] J. R. Jones, J. S. Kennedy, and F. W. Scholl, "A prototype CSMA/CD local network using fiber optics," in *Proc. LAN'82,* Sept. 1982, pp. 86–90.

[18] Nippon Telegraph and Telephone Public Corporation, *Procurement Documentation—Medium Scale Local Area Optical Fiber System Equip.,* Engineering Bureau, Tokyo, Japan, 1983.

[19] D. R. Porter, P. R. Couch, and J. W. Schelin, "A high-speed fiber optic data bus for local data communications," *IEEE J. Select. Areas Commun.,* vol. SAC-1, pp. 479–488, Apr. 1983.

[20] W. M. Hubbard and A. Albanese, "The experimental broadband network," presented at GLOBE-COM'82, Nov. 29–Dec. 2, 1982.

[21] D. C. Johnson, P. W. Rivett, and W. W. Davis, "Designing a shipboard data bus with biconical taper couplers," in *Proc. Sixth Int. Fiber Optics and Commun. Expos., FOC'82,* Sept. 15–17, 1982, pp. 139–144.

[22] M. Gerla, C. Yeh, and P. Rodriguez, "Token protocol for high-speed fiber optic local networks," *Tech. Digest: Sixth Topical Meet. Optical Fiber Commun., OFC-83,* Feb. 28–Mar. 2, 1983, p. 88.

[23] M. Kiyono, M. Tada, K. Yasue, K. Takumi, and Y. Narita, "C&C net loop 6770—A reliable communication medium for distributed processing systems," in *Proc. LAN'82,* Sept. 1982, pp. 47–50.

[24] K. Ito et al., "Bidirectional fiber optic loop-structured network," *Electron. Lett.,* vol. 17, pp. 84–86, Jan. 1982.

[25] E. S. Hara, "A fiber optic LAN/OCS using a broadband switch," in *Proc. GLOBECOM'82,* Nov. 29–Dec. 2, 1982, pp. E1.4.1–1.4.5.

[26] N. Tokura, Y. Oikawa, and Y. Kimura, "High-reliability 100-Mbit/s optical accessing loop network system: OPALnet-II," *J. Lightwave Technol.,* vol. LT-3, pp. 479–489, June 1985.

[27] C. R. Husbands and B. D. Metcalf, "An expandable fiber optic LAN for tactical applications," in *Proc. FOC/LAN'85,* pp. 50–53, Sept. 1985.

[28] J-C. Roy, A. Luvison, and F. Toft, "An ESPRIT project: A local integrated optic network," in *Proc. FOC/LAN'85,* Sept. 1985, pp. 41–43.

[29] "The emergence of 'Smart Buildings'," *EDP Anal.,* vol. 23, pp. 1–16, Oct. 1985.

[30] E. S. Hara, "Integrated broadband services, the intelligent building strategy," Dep. Commun., Government of Canada, Ottawa, 1985.

[31] Y. Fujii et al., "A 100 input/output-port star coupler composed of low-loss slab waveguide," in *Proc. Fourth Int. Conf. Integrated Optics and Optical Fiber Commun., IOOC'83,* June 27–30, 1983, pp. 292–293.

[32] P. Polishuk, personal communication, Fall 1983.

[33] C. Husbands, personal communication, Spring 1983.

[34] R. Creswell and M. D. Drake, "Fiber-optic component test in high-speed data bus applications," presented at SPIE'82, Washington, DC, Apr. 1982.

15
Fail-Safe Nodes for Lightguide Digital Networks

A. ALBANESE

Fail-safe nodes in lightwave digital networks can be built by adding optical couplers to the optical regenerators at the nodes. A fail-safe node in the network can either regenerate or overwrite the information traveling in a ring or bus network, and keep the optical continuity at the failing node in the case of a power failure. A description of the components at a fail-safe node is presented together with an analysis of their design constraints.

I. INTRODUCTION

The use of regeneration at the nodes of a lightguide network introduces a reliability problem when the power at one node fails. Optical passive couplers solve this problem, but the number of passive couplers in a network is limited by the maximum insertion loss that can be tolerated between a transmitter and the receiver farthest away from it [1]–[3].

This chapter describes an arrangement for a lightguide digital network built with fail-safe nodes and with the characteristics that the number of stations is independent of the coupler insertion loss, and that the network keeps functioning when the power at one or more nodes fails. A fail-safe node consists of a lightguide receiver and a lightguide transmitter electrically connected by a regenerator and optically connected by a directional coupler. Figure 1 shows a configuration for a fail-safe node consisting of a lightwave receiver and transmitter pair connected by a regenerator and a directional coupler that provides optical continuity when the power at the node fails.

A node can regenerate, overwrite, or be off, depending on whether the regenerator is operating. In the regenerating configuration, the transmitter is controlled by the receiver, while in the overwriting state, the transmitter is independent of the receiver.

II. FAIL-SAFE NETWORKS

Fail-safe nodes can be connected together by a lightguide to form a ring-type network as shown in Fig. 2. Each node consists of a coupler C, a receiver R, a regenerator RG, and a transmitter T. The nodes are connected by lightguides L. The E input disables the regenerator. The ring architecture was selected as an example; fail-safe nodes may also be used in other optical subtype networks [1]. The nodes in the network are normally regenerating; that is, each node listens and regenerates the information flowing in the

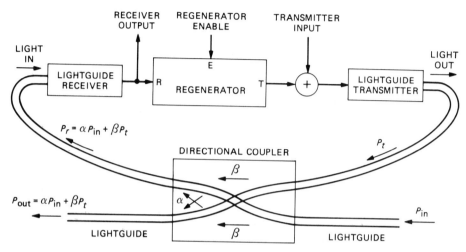

Fig. 1.   Fail-safe node.

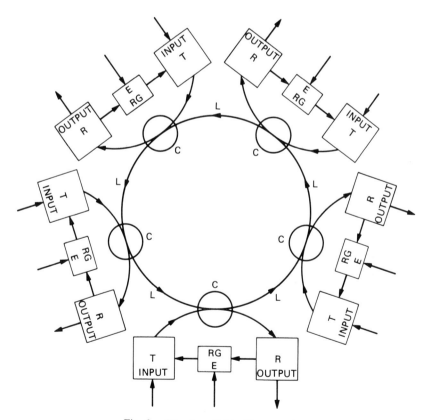

Fig. 2.   Ring-type lightguide network.

network. When a node wants to transmit, it turns its regenerator off and the information is inserted in the network by the lightguide transmitter. If the power at one node fails, or if the electronic components are removed for maintenance, the node is in the off state, and the optical coupler provides the continuity needed for the operation of the network. An additional advantage is that all the signals from different stations arrive with the same intensity at every receiver.

For proper operation of the fail-safe network, every node in the network must meet the three following constraints:

1) Sensitivity Constraint: The receiver of any node must be sensitive enough to receive the signal from a preceding transmitter when several nodes between the transmitter and the transmitter and the receiver are off.

2) Interference Constraint: When two nodes are transmitting simultaneously, a node down the line should receive the signal from the closer node. This discrimination between the two transmitters is achieved by the automatic gain control (AGC) of the receiver that adjusts the gain so the comparator circuit can detect only the stronger signal, while the less intense signal is below the threshold level.

3)Automatic Gain Control Response Time: In the case of a ring-type network, the sending node should be prevented from regenerating its own pulses to avoid having pulses traveling around the ring forever. This constraint is satisfied when the response time of the AGC in the lightguide receiver is longer than the time it takes a pulse to go around the ring once.

III. ANALYSIS

Each fail-safe node in the network may have one or two couplers, depending on whether the network uses return-to-zero or nonreturn-to-zero formats. Figure 1 shows the case where one coupler is used. The receiver has to be off during the time the transmitter is on to avoid saturation. This is achieved using a signal with a duty ratio less than 50 percent, and having the transmitter operating out of phase from the receiver [4]. Figure 3 shows the coupler arrangement when two couplers are used [5]. In this case, the receiver can always be on because it does not receive light from the transmitter.

The coupler used in both cases can be characterized by a four-port device with a

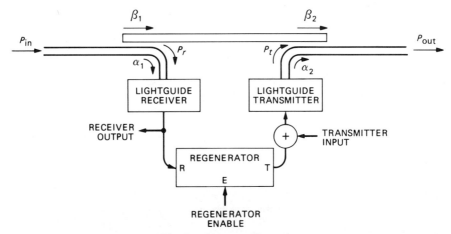

Fig. 3.   A two-coupler node.

transmission coefficient α, a coupling coefficient β, and an excess loss coefficient $\gamma = \alpha + \beta$. Couplers with γ better than -1 dB have been reported in the literature [6]. Single grin-lens directional couplers [7] and mode-selective couplers [8] have been suggested to improve the performance of fail-safe nodes in multimode lightguide networks. These multimode couplers can provide significant advantages at the expense of coupler complexity, but, we should analyze here, for simplicity, the case of single-mode couplers and lightguides.

In the case of Fig. 1, P_{in} is the light entering the coupler from the ring; P_t is the light entering the coupler from the transmitter; $\alpha P_{in} + \beta P_t$ is the amount of light entering the receiver P_r; $\alpha P_t + \beta P_{in}$ is the amount of light leaving the coupler and going into the ring P_{out}. In the case of Fig. 3, $P_r = \alpha_1 P_{in}$ and $P_{out} = \alpha_2 P_t + \beta_1 \beta_2 P_{in}$. These two node configurations will be analyzed next.

A. One-Coupler Nodes

Let us consider first the case of one-coupler nodes and analyze a hypothetical network where Q adjacent nodes have failed and they are off. The power received after Q failed nodes is $P_s + P_i$, P_s is the power received from the closest active transmitter:

$$P_s = P_t L^{Q+1} \beta^Q \alpha^2, \tag{1}$$

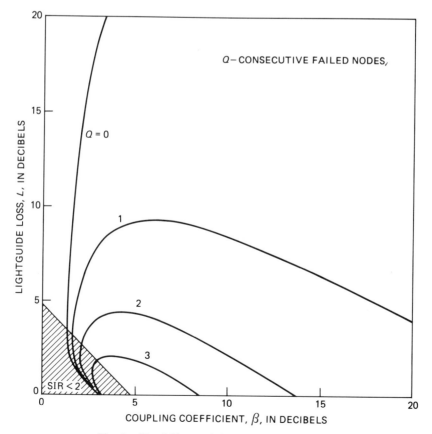

Fig. 4.   Feasibility graph for one-coupler nodes.

and P_i is the sum of all the powers received from all the other previous active transmitters that may cause interference:

$$P_i = \sum_{i=Q}^{i=\infty} P_t \alpha^2 L^{i+2} \beta^{i+1} = \frac{P_t L^{Q+2} \beta^{Q+1} \alpha^2}{1 - \beta L} . \tag{2}$$

In (1) and (2), L is the average lightguide attenuation between two adjacent nodes, and the infinite summation accounts for the worst case of interference.

The sensitivity and the interference constraints are satisfied when the effective received power $P_{re}(Q)$ is larger than the sensitivity of the receiver S

$$P_{re}(Q) = P_s - P_i \geq S; \tag{3}$$

the minus sign accounts for the reduction in the opening of the eye diagram caused by the interference.

Equations (1) and (2) and $\alpha = \gamma - \beta$ are used to rewrite (3) as

$$L^{Q+1} \beta^Q (\gamma - \beta)^2 \left| \frac{1 - 2\beta L}{1 - \beta L} \right| \geq \frac{S}{P_t} = M^{-1} \tag{4}$$

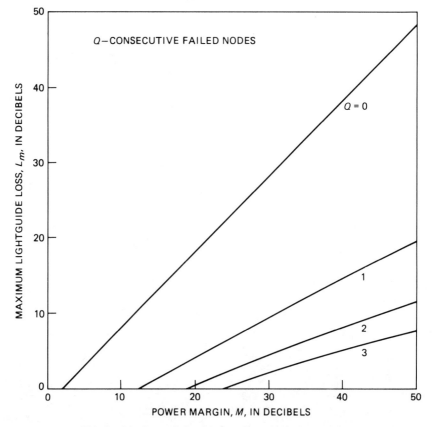

Fig. 5.   Maximum lightguide loss for one-coupler nodes.

which limits the values of β and L that satisfy the network constraints. In (4) M is the optical power margin between the transmitter and the receiver.

The interference is deterministic, and it will not be seen by the comparator in the receiver because the AGC circuit sets the threshold automatically to one-half of the peak amplitude which is precisely in the middle of the eye pattern. In addition to satisfying the sensitivity constraint expressed by (3), one should have a signal-to-interference ratio (SIR) greater than 2 to eliminate any possible error caused by variations in the pulse amplitude

$$\text{SIR} = \frac{P_s}{P_i} = \frac{1 - \beta L}{\beta L} \geq 2. \tag{5}$$

The SIR value of 2 was selected experimentally as the value where the error rate doubles. The power penalty due to the interference of the previous station has been computed for some specific cases [9].

Equations (4) and (5) are used to find the minimum value of L for a given β. This is done by defining a variable $V = \beta L$ that allows us to express L and β as a function of V:

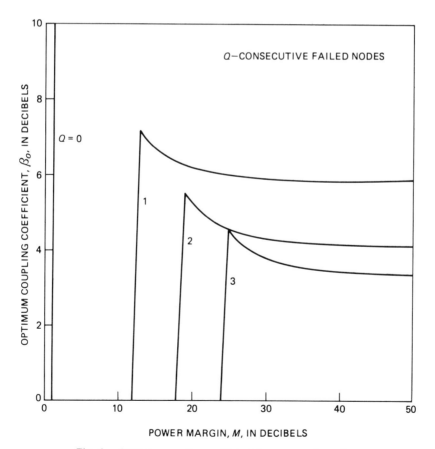

Fig. 6.   Optimum coupling coefficient for one-coupler nodes.

$$L = \frac{V}{\gamma} + F(V) + [F^2(V) + 2VF(V)/\gamma]^{1/2}$$

$$\beta = \frac{V}{L}, \tag{6}$$

where

$$F(V) = \frac{1 - V}{2M\gamma^2(1 - 2V)V^Q}.$$

Equation (5) restricts the possible values of V to be within the range from 0 to 0.33.

Figure 4 shows a relation between L and β as given by (6) for values $Q = 0, 1, 2,$ and $3, \gamma = -1$ dB, and $M = 30$ dB. Values L and β are generally expressed in decibels, and L is commonly called the lightguide loss.

We can define an optimum coupling, β_0, as the value of β that allows the maximum lightguide loss, L_m, for a given power margin M. Figures 5 and 6 show the values of the maximum L_m and β_0 as a function of M, and for a $\gamma = -1$ dB.

Figures 4 and 5 also show that the use of the fail-safe nodes in the network reduces the

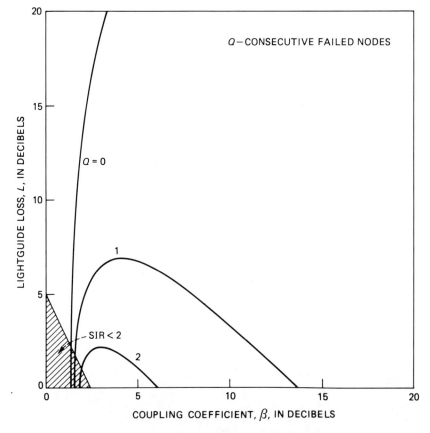

Fig. 7.   Feasibility graph for two-coupler nodes.

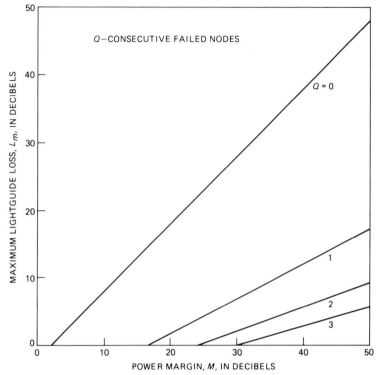

Fig. 8.   Maximum lightguide loss for two-coupler nodes.

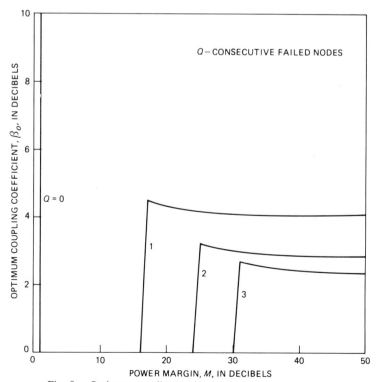

Fig. 9.   Optimum coupling coefficient for two-coupler nodes.

maximum lightguide loss between repeaters. This fact cannot be tolerated in transmission systems, but it may be possible in local area networks where the lightguide loss may not be a limiting factor.

Figure 4 shows that the maximum lightguide loss L_m is not sensitive to variations of β within ± 1 dB from the optimum value of β, β_0. From Fig. 6, one could establish that a coupler with β between 4 and 6 dB is adequate for different values of M and Q.

B. Two-Coupler Nodes

The analysis of a network with two-coupler nodes is similar to the case of one-coupler nodes substituting β by β^2 in (1), (2), and (5). Note that the expression of $\alpha = \gamma - \beta$ remains the same for both cases. In this case, β and L are related by the expression

$$L^{Q+1}\beta^{2Q}(\gamma - \beta)^2 \left| \frac{1 - 2\beta^2 L}{1 - \beta^2 L} \right| \geq \frac{S}{P_t} \tag{7}$$

for the sensitivity constraint, and

$$\text{SIR} = \frac{1 - \beta^2 L}{\beta^2 L} = 2 \tag{8}$$

for the interference constraint. Figure 7 shows a relation between L and β as given by (7) and (8) for values of $Q = 0, 1,$ and 2, $\gamma = -1$ dB, and $M = 30$ dB. Figures 8 and 9 show the values of L_m and β_0 as a function of M when $\gamma = -1$ dB.

A comparison of Figs. 7, 8, and 9 against Figs. 4, 5, and 6 indicates that there is a 3 dB penalty when using nodes made of two couplers instead of one.

IV. Conclusions

Two configurations of optical couplers were analyzed to provide continuity in an optical network in the case of a power failure at several consecutive nodes. The analysis determines the optimum coupling coefficient, and the maximum lightguide loss that a network can have. Optical networks with fail-safe nodes are of interest in local and metropolitan area networks where the lightguide transmission loss is substantially less than the optical power margin between the transmitter and the receiver.

References

[1] H. W. Giertz, V. Vucins, and L. Ingre, "Experimental fiber optic databus," in *Proc. Fourth European Conf. Opt. Commun.*, Genoa, Italy, Sept. 12–15, 1978, pp. 641–645.

[2] C. A. Villarruel, C. Wang, R. P. Moeller, and W. K. Burns, "Single-mode data buses for local area network applications," *J. Lightwave Technol.*, vol. LT-3, pp. 472–478, June 1985.

[3] J. O. Limb and A. Albanese, "Passive unidirectional bus networks using optical communications," presented at Globecom'85, New Orleans, LA, Dec. 2–5, 1985.

[4] N. Tokura, K. Oguchi, and K. Nosu, "An optically accessing loop system using pulse interlace technique," in *Tech. Dig. IOOC'83*, Tokyo, Japan, June 3, 1983, paper 29C1-2.

[5] M. Chown and J. G. Farrington, "Data transmission systems," U.S. Patent 4,166,946, Sept. 4, 1979.

[6] B. S. Kawasaki and K. O. Hill, "Low-loss access coupler for multimode optical fiber distribution networks," *Appl. Opt.,* vol. 16, pp. 1794–1795, July 1977.

[7] F. H. Levinson and S. W. Granlund, "Single grin-lens directional-couplers," *Bell Syst. Tech. J.,* vol. 63, pp. 431–439, 1984.

[8] T. H. Wood, "Increased power injection in multimode optical-fiber buses through mode-selective coupling," *J. Lightwave Technol.,* vol. 3, pp. 537–543, June 1985.

[9] N. Tokura, Y. Oikawa, and Y. Kimura, "High-reliability 100-Mbit/s optical accessing loop network system: OPALnet-II," *J. Lightwave Technol.,* vol. 3, pp. 479–489, June 1985; see also this volume, ch. 18.

16
Small Loss-Deviation Tapered-Fiber Star Coupler for LAN's

SHIGERU OHSHIMA, TAKAO ITO, KEN-ICHI DONUMA, HISAYOSHI SUGIYAMA, AND YOHJI FUJII

A biconical tapered-fiber star coupler with a mixer rod is proposed to achieve small loss-deviation and low excess loss. Design and fabrication techniques for this star coupler are discussed in detail, and a 100 × 100 star coupler was experimentally fabricated. The loss-deviation and average excess loss for this star coupler was 0.37 and 3.2 dB, respectively.

I. INTRODUCTION

An optical star network is one of the most promising approaches for optical local area networks. Some star network applications require 100-, or more- port optical star couplers [1]. The star coupler loss-deviation is required to be small so that the receiver dynamic range may be reduced [2]. Especially in the star network system based on the carrier sense multiple access with collision detection (CSMA/CD) access protocol, the loss-deviation is required to be fairly small (for example, within ± 1 dB [1]).

Two kinds of 100-port star couplers have been reported. One is the structure using a low-loss slab waveguide and fiber arrays [3]. The other is the biconical tapered-fiber star coupler [4]. The latter achieved low excess loss, but the loss-deviation was over 8 dB. The rotation-splice structure for the tapered-fiber star coupler [5] was developed in order to reduce the loss-deviation. However, this structure is not suitable for fabricating star couplers with more than 10-odd ports.

This chapter proposes a tapered-fiber star coupler with a mixer rod to achieve small loss-deviation. Design and fabrication techniques for the star coupler are described. Loss characteristics for the experimentally fabricated 100-port star coupler are also described.

II. STRUCTURE

Former biconical tapered-fiber star couplers have had large loss-deviation. This is because some modes of light in an input fiber are not converted into cladding modes of light in the contracting taper section, and they couple more strongly to a certain output fiber core [6]. Therefore, the loss-deviation is reduced if these nonconverted modes of light couple into the cladding at the input plane of the expanding taper.

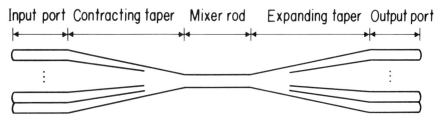

Fig. 1.   Structure of the star coupler.

The new star-coupler structure is schematically shown in Fig. 1. This star coupler is composed of contracting and expanding taper sections and a cylindrical mixer-rod section. The mixer rod is inserted between the tapers to couple the nonconverted modes of light into the cladding of the expanding taper.

The light incident on one of the input ports propagates through the contracting taper section, and some modes of light are converted into cladding modes of light. The other modes of light remain as core modes.

The converted modes of light are mixed effectively as they propagate through the contracting taper section and are mixed uniformly in the mixer rod. The light is reconverted into guided modes of light as it propagates through the expanding taper-fiber section and couple into every output fiber with equal power.

The nonconverted modes of light (remaining as core modes in the contracting taper) are spread in the mixer rod, and coupled into the expanding taper in two different ways. Some of the light couples into the cladding at the input plane of the expanding taper-fiber section. Then, the light is mixed uniformly and reconverted into core modes of light as it propagates through the expanding tapered-fiber section.

The remaining light couples directly into the cores of the expanding taper. The light may increase its loss-deviation when light mixing is not sufficient at the mixer-rod output face. However, the optical power of this kind of light is a very small portion of the total power (~0.2 percent) as discussed in Section III-A. Therefore, smaller loss-deviation is achieved.

III. DESIGN

A. Transmission Coefficient

The transmission coefficient C_{ij} from port i to port j is described as follows:

$$C_{ij} = \frac{1}{N} K_R K_T + \frac{1}{N}(1 - K_R)(1 - Ck^2)K_T + S_{(i,j)}(1 - K_R)Ck^2 \qquad (1)$$

where N is the number of ports, K_R is the power coefficient of the converting core modes into the cladding modes in the contracting taper, K_T is the power coefficient of the reconverting cladding modes into the core modes in the expanding taper, Ck^2 is the power coefficient of light coupled into the cores at the input of the expanding taper-fiber section, k is the ratio of the core diameter to the outer diameter, and C is the coupling constant. $S_{(i,j)}$ shows the power distribution at the mixer output face.

Now let us estimate $(1 - k_R)Ck^2$ because the deviation of C_{ij} is dependent on only the third term of (1). We assumed that a standard graded-index fiber (50 μm core diameter, 125 μm outer diameter, 0.21 numerical aperture) is used, and the modal power distribution in the input fiber is uniform. Under this condition, the parameters k and C are 0.4 and 2/3, respectively. K_R is calculated by the following equation:

$$K_R = 1 - 1/R^2 \tag{2}$$

where R is the taper ratio [7], [8].

When the taper ratio is 7, for example, $(1 - K_R)Ck^2$ is calculated to be 2×10^{-3}. This value is negligibly small. Therefore, small loss-deviation is achieved even if $S_{(i,j)}$ deviates from uniformity.

B. Taper Ratio

The taper ratio is an important parameter of the biconical taper-fiber star coupler. From (1) and (2), it is understood that a larger taper ratio gives smaller loss-deviation. However, excess losses are increased due to converting some cladding modes of light into radiation modes in the contracting taper section and mixer rod when the taper ratio exceeds a certain boundary value. The boundary taper ratio is discussed in this section.

The ray for the cladding modes of light must be traced to discuss the boundary taper ratio. Since the ray trajectories for cladding modes of light are very complicated, only the meridional ray incident on the center of the tapered-fiber core was traced by a numerical method. The core of a conical graded-index taper fiber was divided into multilayers. Each layer was considered to be a cone concentric with the z axis and its index was uniform. The propagation angle θ_1 at the input was made equal to the maximum propagation angle in the core modes. We defined the changing angle efficiency to be $\sin \theta_2/(R \sin \theta_1)$, where θ_1 and θ_2 are propagation angles at the input and output of the contracting tapered fiber. R is the taper ratio which is given by

$$R = a_1/a_2 \tag{3}$$

where a_1 and a_2 are the outer radii of the conical tapered fiber at the input and output, respectively (see Fig. 2). The ray behavior for the cladding modes of light approaches the ray behavior for core modes in a step-index fiber as the ray propagates through the contracting tapered fiber. For core modes in a step-index fiber, $\sin \theta_2/(R \sin \theta_1)$ is unity. Therefore, we defined the changing angle efficiency to be $\sin \theta_2/(R \sin \theta_1)$ and calculated this efficiency. Figure 3 shows the changing angle efficiency versus the taper ratio for $\tan \Omega = 0.01$, where Ω is the taper angle (see Fig. 2).

Almost the same calculated results as above were obtained when taper angles were 1° or less. The changing angle efficiency may be expressed by

$$\frac{\sin \theta_2}{R \sin \theta_1} \simeq k(1 - 0.2 \ k) \tag{4}$$

when the taper ratio is a large value, for example, more than 6. In comparison to that for a step-index tapered fiber [9], the changing angle efficiency was smaller by 0.2 k^2.

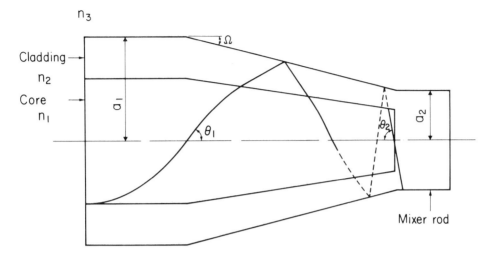

Fig. 2.   Ray trajectory in tapered fiber.

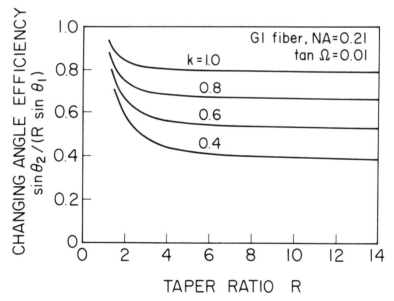

Fig. 3.   Changing angle efficiency sin $\theta_2/(R \sin \theta_1)$ versus taper ratio R.

The propagation angle θ_2 which does not lead to radiation modes is given as follows:

$$n_1 \sin \theta_2 < \sqrt{n_2^2 - n_3^2} \tag{5}$$

where n_1, n_2, and n_3 are, respectively, the refractive indexes of the core, cladding, and its surrounding media. The taper ratio R, which does not cause radiation loss, is obtained from (4) and (5).

$$R < \frac{\sqrt{n_2^2 - n_3^2}}{(NA)k(1 - 0.2 \ k)} \tag{6}$$

where (NA) is the numerical aperture of the fiber.

We considered the lossless requirement even for such a case when water was stuck around the tapered-fiber and mixer-rod section. We obtained $R < 7.8$ when the practical parameters of $k = 0.4$, $NA = 0.21$, $n_2 = 1.46$, and $n_3 = 1.33$ were applied. Therefore, the taper ratio was determined to be 7.

As for a tapered-fiber star coupler, the following relation holds:

$$R = \frac{a\sqrt{q}}{d} \tag{7}$$

where R is the taper ratio, a is the outer diameter of the fiber, q is the number of fibers, and d is the diameter of the mixer rod. The mixer-rod diameter d may be obtained from (7). For a 100-port star coupler, parameters of $a = 125 \ \mu$m, $R = 7$, and $q = 121$ (as discussed in Section III-C) yield $d = 200 \ \mu$m.

C. Redundancy Optimization of the Number of Ports

Redundancy of ports is very effective for reducing loss-deviation and increasing the yield rate, although it increases excess losses for the coupler. In this section, the effectiveness of the redundancy of ports for reducing loss-deviation is discussed under the following three assumptions.

i) When the jth input port is excited, the loss distribution at the output ports has a normal distribution with mean value m_j and standard deviation σ_j.

ii) Whether the loss for a certain output port is larger or smaller than another output port is independent of which input port is excited.

iii) The distribution of the mean values m_j is a normal distribution with standard deviation σ_m.

The standard deviation (s.d.) σ_q for the whole distribution of the $q \times q$ star coupler losses is expressed by

$$\sigma_q = \sqrt{\frac{\sum_{j=1}^{q} \sigma_j^2}{q} + \sigma_m^2}. \tag{8}$$

The s.d. σ_j is reduced to σ_j' by selecting the best p ports out of the q output ports. σ_j' is expressed by

$$\sigma_j' = \sigma_j \int_{-b}^{b} \frac{t^2}{\sqrt{2\pi}} e^{-t^2/2} \ dt \equiv \sigma_j F(b) \tag{9}$$

where b is given by the following equation:

$$\frac{p}{q} = \int_{-b}^{b} \frac{1}{\sqrt{2\pi}} e^{-t^2/2} \ dt. \tag{10}$$

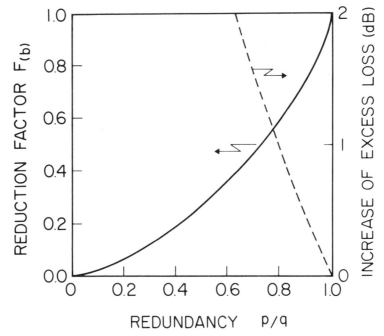

Fig. 4.   Reduction factor $F(b)$ as a function of redundancy p/q.

Similarly, the s.d. σ_m is reduced to σ'_m by selecting the best p ports out of the q input ports. Thus, the standard deviation σ_p of the best $p \times p$ star coupler loss-deviation distribution is $F(b)\sigma_q$. Figure 4 shows the reduction factor $F(b)$ as a function of p/q. When p/q is larger than 0.8, the s.d. σ_p is reduced effectively. Setting p/q to be less than 0.8 is not expected to further reduce the s.d. effectively but cause large optical loss. When p/q is equal to 0.8, for example, the s.d. σ_p is expected to become about half of the s.d. σ_q. For this case, the increase of excess loss is 1 dB.

IV. FABRICATION

The fabrication process of this star coupler is as follows. First, fibers are bundled together. The bundled fibers are heated with an oxyhydrogen flame and pulled into a biconical tapered shape. Next, the biconical taper is cut at the waist and a cylindrical mixer rod is inserted between the tapers by using the fusion-splice technique. The fibers must not be twisted throughout the taper fabrication to prevent increase of loss-deviation. This is because twisting the fibers puts the fiber arrangement out of order and causes microscopic bending of the fibers, and the bending leads to needless mode conversion increasing loss-deviation.

A 100×100 star coupler was experimentally fabricated using standard graded-index silica-glass fibers (50 μm core diameter, 125 μm outer diameter, 0.21 numerical aperture). The total number of fibers used in this star coupler was selected to be 121, based on the result discussed in Section III-C. The taper ratio R was selected to be 7 and the taper-waist diameter was nearly equal to 200 μm. The cross-sectional view of the fabricated tapered-

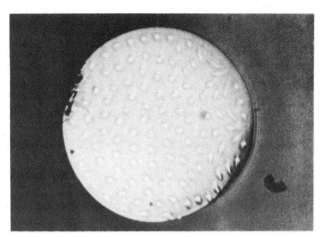

Fig. 5.   Cross-sectional view of the tapered-fiber waist.

fiber waist is shown in Fig. 5. The mixer-rod diameter was set equal to the taper-waist diameter. The mixer-rod length was set to be 50 times that of the diameter.

Figure 6 shows the exterior of the star coupler. It is possible to connect the transmission lines to the star coupler by an FC-type connector [10].

V. CHARACTERISTICS

The excess losses for the 121 $\times$ 121 matrix were measured automatically by computer-controlled equipment. A 0.85 μm wavelength light, radiated from an LED, was passed

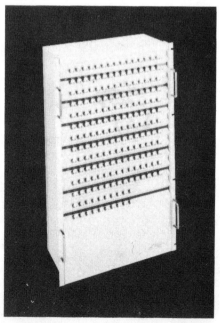

Fig. 6.   Exterior view of the star coupler.

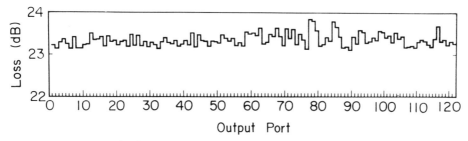

Fig. 7.   Examples of loss variations at output ports.

through a mode scrambler and coupled to the star coupler. An index matching liquid was used at both the input and output connections. Typical measured insertion losses for an input port are shown in Fig. 7. The insertion losses for the other input ports were almost the same as this figure. The best 100-port pairs were selected out of the 121-port pairs on the basis of the measured 121 × 121 matrix excess losses. Figure 8 shows a histogram for the 100 × 100 excess losses. The average excess loss was 3.2 dB. Maximum loss deviation was +0.37 dB.

Temperature dependence of excess loss is shown in Fig. 9. The maximum loss fluctuation was 0.3 dB within the temperature range of −40° ∼ 95°.

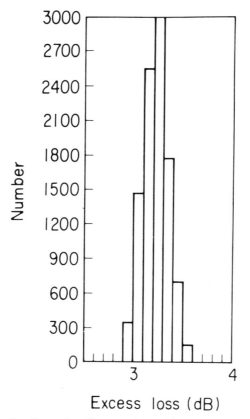

Fig. 8.   Excess loss histogram for a 100-port star coupler.

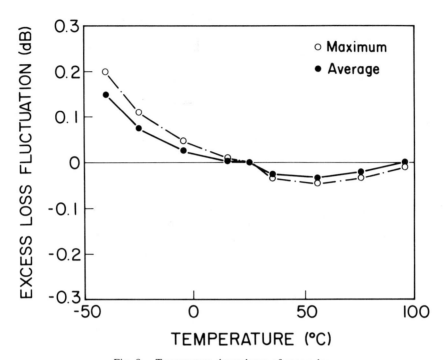

Fig. 9.   Temperature dependence of excess loss.

VI. Conclusion

A tapered-fiber star coupler with a mixer rod has been proposed. The transmission coefficient, the taper ratio, and redundancy optimization of the number of ports have been minutely discussed. A 100 × 100 star coupler was fabricated based on these discussions. The average excess loss for the coupler was 3.2 dB. The maximum excess loss was 3.6 dB and the loss-deviation was +0.37/−0.34 dB. The fluctuation of excess loss was only 0.3 dB for the −40° ~ 95° temperature change.

Acknowledgment

The authors wish to thank Dr. M. Koyama and Dr. J. Minowa of Yokosuka Electrical Communication Laboratory, NTT, Japan, for their helpful guidance and continuous encouragement, and A. Yoshinaga, Sakakibara, and other colleagues of Toshiba Corporation for their valuable discussions and measurements.

References

[1]   Y. Hakamada and K. Oguchi, "32 Mb/s star configured optical local area network design and performance," *J. Lightwave Technol.*, vol. LT-3, pp. 511–524, 1985.
[2]   J. C. Williams, S. E. Goodman, and R. L. Coon, "Fiber-optic subsystem considerations of multimode star coupler performance," in *Proc. Conf. Opt. Fiber Commun.*, New Orleans, LA, Jan. 23-25, 1984, paper WC6.
[3]   Y. Fujii, N. Suzuki, and J. Minowa, "A 100 input/output-port star coupler composed of low-loss slab-

waveguide," in *Tech. Dig. 4th Int. Conf. Integrated Opt. Fiber Commun.*, Tokyo, Japan, June 27–30, 1983, paper 29C2-4.

[4]   E. G. Rawson and M. D. Bailey, "Bitaper star couplers with up to 100 fiber channels," *Electron. Lett.*, vol. 15, pp. 432–433, 1979.

[5]   S. Ohshima and T. Ozeki, "Rotation-splice tapered fiber star coupler," in *Proc. Opt. Commun. Conf.*, Amsterdam, The Netherlands, Sept. 1979.

[6]   T. Ozeki and B. S. Kawasaki, "New star coupler compatible with single multimode-fiber data links," *Electron. Lett.*, vol. 12, pp. 151–152, 1976.

[7]   ——, "Mode behaviour in a tapered multimode fiber," *Electron. Lett.*, vol. 12, pp. 407–408, 1976.

[8]   T. Ito, M. Itoh, and T. Ozeki, "Bidirectional tapered fiber star couplers," in *Proc. 4th Eur. Conf. Opt. Commun.*, Geneva, Italy, Sept. 1978, pp. 318–322.

[9]   Y. Uematsu, T. Ozeki, and Y. Unno, "Efficient power coupling between an MH LED and a taper-ended multimode fiber," *IEEE J. Quantum Electron.*, vol. QE-15, pp. 86–92, 1979.

[10]   K. Nawata, "Multimode and single-mode fiber connectors technology," *IEEE J. Quantum Electron.*, vol. QE-16, pp. 618–627, 1980.

17
Methods of Collision Detection in Fiber-Optic CSMA/CD Networks

JEFFREY W. REEDY AND J. RICHARD JONES

Collision detection (CD) is easy to implement in baseband coaxial CSMA/CD networks, but is a formidable design challenge in optical fiber implementations. Seven different methods for detecting collisions in fiber-optic networks are described and analyzed. Attention is focused on CD accuracy, CD dynamic range, implementation considerations, and reliability issues.

INTRODUCTION

In many cases, unique system-level approaches are necessary when fiber-optic technology is applied to traditional local area network architectures which were originally developed for other transmission media. A prime example is the task of detecting collisions in fiber-optic CSMA/CD networks. Whereas collision detection is a routinely handled problem in baseband coax systems, several widely varying approaches to detecting collisions in fiber-optic systems have been proposed. These approaches are reviewed in this chapter, and compared in the context of typical applications requirements.

Collision detection in coax-bus CSMA/CD systems, such as the well-known Ethernet system, is handled in a straightforward manner. Each transmitter's Manchester encoded data stream contains d.c. voltage information. The transmitters monitor the media as they transmit, watching for a change in the d.c. voltage which indicates that another transmitter is also accessing the media. This scheme works because the d.c. attenuation of coaxial cable is negligible over a single-segment's span (less than 500 m), and because the output level of each transmitter is made uniform by design.

A general difficulty arises when an analogous method is implemented in optical fiber systems. In fiber systems, there may be large differences in the strength of transmitted signals seen at any given receiver. These differences are caused by variations in the cable attenuation, optical source outputs, and system topology. It is therefore possible for a strong signal to mask out a weaker signal in such a way that a receiving station cannot detect that a collision is occurring. In this chapter, we discuss the limitations of the collision-detection methods which are affected by this ''dynamic range'' problem, and look at other alternative methods which circumvent this situation.

An issue related to collision detection in fiber-optic CSMA/CD systems is the choice of network topology. A linear-bus structure can be supported with T-taps, but as shown in [1], the number of stations on the bus will be limited to about ten in a practical system. A linear bus also places a stringent dynamic-range requirement on the receiver design, since even in small node-count systems, signals from a nearby station can potentially be much stronger than that of a station further away. In practice, star-shaped topologies are usually preferred, with either a passive star coupler or an active star repeater providing the function of the broadcast bus, as shown in Fig. 1. In fiber-optic systems, a star topology generally allows the interconnection of more terminals, is less prone to catastrophic failure, and is relatively flexible and expandable. Therefore, for the purpose of our discussion, we will examine the different alternatives in the context of a star topology implementation, although in certain cases the application of a method to other topologies may be appropriate.

The following is a list and brief synopsis of the collision detection methods which we review.

1) *Average Power Sensing:* Detection of average power in excess of a station's own data signal.

2) *Code Violations Based on Pulse-Width Detection:* Detection of pulse width in excess of the acceptable coding patterns.

3) *Code Violations Based on Partial Response:* Improved detection of illegal code patterns using more sensitive methods.

4) *Time-Delay Violations:* Detection of another station's data packet before the expected echo of a station's transmitted packet is received.

5) *Directional Coupling:* Use of an interconnection system such that a station never hears its own transmission, thus making the detection of any packet while transmitting an indication of a collision.

6) *Hybrid Star Coupling:* Use of a passive star coupler monitor and centralized collision-detection electronics.

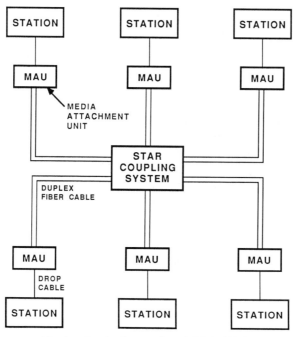

Fig. 1.   Star implementation of CSMA/CD bus.

7) *Active Star Coupling:* Use of active central electronics to perform both the interconnection and collision functions.

Note that the seven methods can be grouped in different ways. For instance, methods 1, 2, and 3 detect collisions in the amplitude domain at the station transceiver and are faced with the strong/weak signal problem mentioned above. Another way to group the methods is by special component requirements. As will be seen, methods 5, 6, and 7 require special interconnection components, whereas methods 1, 2, 3, and 4 can utilize a simple star coupling system.

REQUIREMENTS

Before discussing the collision-detection methods in detail, a look at system requirements is appropriate. Today the most important class of CSMA/CD networks is the IEEE 802.3 specification, based on the Ethernet LAN. This standard is specified for coaxial cable, but discussions have been held regarding fiber-optic transmission media, and the requirements generally cited [2] for such a system are cited below:

1) 100 percent collision-detection capability,
2) support system diameter of 2.5 km,
3) support up to 1000 stations,
4) bit-error rate less than 10^{-9},
5) AUI (auxiliary unit interface drop cable) compatibility, and
6) MAU (media attachment unit) functional compatibility (jabber control, CD, etc.).

Fulfillment of these requirements depends heavily on implementation. All of the methods under consideration can be used in implementations which in some form or another meet the requirements—the comparison of the alternatives then reduces to tradeoff analysis of complexity, reliability, and practicality.

Method 1: Average Power Sensing

The first method of detecting collisions that we discuss is perhaps the most straightforward to implement. In the average power-sensing method, a collision is declared when the received optical power at a transceiver exceeds the power of the transceiver's own data burst. The threshold of the collision-detection circuitry is adjusted to some level higher than the threshold of the data receiver. A key design issue is the CD dynamic range, i.e., the allowed signal-level difference which can be detected. In [3], an experimental transceiver detects signals up to 5 dB apart.

What is the required CD dynamic range in the IEEE 802.3 applications? The difference in signal attenuation at a given receiver comes from many sources, as listed below:

	Variability
LED Output	3 dB
Cable Loss/Length (1 km)	6 dB
Star Coupler Loss	1 dB
Margins	3 dB
TOTAL	13 dB

Thus, in this example, the 5 dB CD dynamic range would be insufficient. There are methods of reducing the signal variability, such as tuning the transmitters and using uniform-length cable leads. In [3], an experimental 32 node, 2 km system was achieved using such techniques.

Method 2: Pulse-Width Violations

This method takes advantage of the fact that in Ethernet systems, the data stream is Manchester encoded such that an information bit will always be encoded as either ''01'' or ''10.'' This places a limit on the pulse width of a collision-free data stream. In a 10 Mbit/s system operating at 20 Mbaud, a single pulse should nominally be no more than 100 ns in duration. Collision-detection circuitry, as shown in Fig. 2, can be used to detect signals which exceed the legal pulse width.

Like other amplitude domain techniques, this method is limited by a strong signal masking out another weaker signal. However, pulse-width violations can be used with the centralized collision-detection schemes [1], [4] described later as a means for detecting a ''jam'' signal at the transceiver. For instance, when a collision is detected by some centralized mechanism, a strong, oscillating jam signal (3 MHz, for example) is then broadcast to all transceivers, where the pulse-width violation is easily discerned. A jam signal can also be used to reinforce collisions in the distributed CD schemes, in which at least one station informs the other transmitting stations on the network that a collision has occurred.

A method analogous to the detection of pulse-width violations is the bit-by-bit comparison of a packet being received to the packet being transmitted. Implementation of this method results in a more complex MAU, since data and timing recovery circuits and data buffers must be employed. In fact, these circuits duplicate similar circuits in the attached station.

Method 3: Code Violations Using Partial Response

This method uses a technique to enhance the detection of code violations, based on ''partial response'' or ''duobinary'' encoding, which is used in telecommunications to increase the bit rate of a channel beyond the channel's available bandwidth. In general,

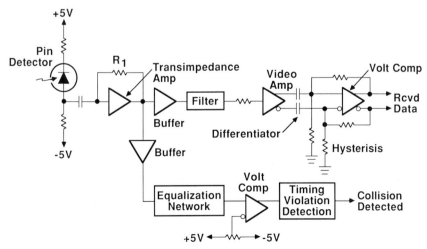

Fig. 2. Transceiver using pulse-width violation collision detection.

partial response signaling introduces intersymbol interference in a controlled way, allowing an original bit stream to be recovered from a received signal using correlation techniques. For the purposes of collision detection, errors caused by intersymbol interference, normally masked out by the correlation process, can be used to indicate that more than one station is transmitting.

A system based on these principles is described in [5], and illustrated in Fig. 3. Data are Manchester encoded and transmitted in the customary manner. At the receiver, the electrical signal is fed to a partial-response circuit, which produced one of three values ($-$, 0, $+$) based on the signal level over two symbol periods. An output signal is then derived from the partial-response signal via a threshold set slightly below the "0" level.

Note that the partial-response value for the second half of the Manchester encoded bit will be one of only two values ($-$, $+$), since there is always a transition in the middle of the bit cell. Data can be reconstructed from this half. On the other hand, the partial-response value for the first half of the Manchester encoded bit will be one of three values ($-$, 0, $+$), since there may be no transition between two adjacent bit cells. Therefore, when two colliding signals occupy the channel, decision "errors" can occur easily in this first half because the threshold is closely set to the "0" state. These decision errors can be used to indicate collisions, resulting in a more sensitive CD mechanism than normal amplitude domain techniques. The detection process can be further enhanced by grouping data bits into blocks to increase the number of illegal codes.

In [5], collisions were detected within 10 bit times for signals 8 dB apart, and within 100 bit times for signals 10 dB apart. In this method, the probability of decision errors (detecting collisions) is dependent on the relative phase of the colliding signals, with 90 degrees difference being the worst case.

Method 4: Time-Delay Violations

Collision detection based on time-delay violations [6], [7] circumvent the CD dynamic-range problem associated with amplitude domain techniques. The collisions are detected by transceivers connected to a passive star coupler, based on the transceiver's *a priori* knowledge of how long it takes the optical signal it transmits to loop through the star and return. If the transceiver detects data before the data sent out are due to return, it concludes that these data are from another transmitter, and a collision is declared. The other transceivers on the network are then notified of the collision via a special jam signal, as previously described. This is necessary because in certain scenarios a given transceiver, particularly if it is located near the star, will miss a collision because its own data packet will return in a relatively short time.

The main drawback of this approach is that the probability of detecting collisions is

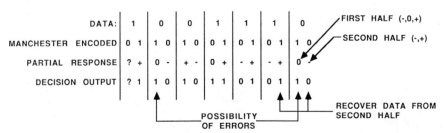

Fig. 3.   Partial-response decoding.

generally not 100 percent. Consider a system with uniform terminal-to-star spacings, and define the following parameters.

t_r Roundtrip propagation time of a data bit.
t_u Collision detection resolution time at the transceiver.
P_m Probability of missing a collision.

Suppose two stations begin to transmit about the same time. To be involved in a collision, the two stations would have had to start transmitting within t_r of each other. For the collision not to be detected, they would have had to begin transmitting within t_u of each other. Thus, the probability of missing a collision is simply

$$P_m = \frac{t_u}{t_r} .$$

For example, if $t_u = 100$ ns and $t_r = 5$ μs (corresponding to a 1 km system diameter) then the probability of missing a collision is 0.02. If more than two stations are trying to transmit, P_m is the probability that every possible pair combination fails to detect the collision

$$P_m = \left(\frac{t_u}{t_r}\right)^{n(n-1)/2} .$$

Several interesting conclusions can be drawn with regard to the above relationship. First, the probability of missing a collision decreases as network activity increases; this is consonant with the motivation for having collision detection on the CSMA network in the first place. Second, an artificial electronic delay could be added at each transceiver to increase the roundtrip delay (t_r) and improve CD performance. However, increasing the roundtrip delay decreases the overall network efficiency.

The above analysis assumes that the roundtrip delay can be "fine tuned" to a value which is insignificant compared to the resolution time. The roundtrip delay can be determined and manually set at installation time, although a more elaborate alternative would be for the transceiver to generate and transmit a special timing packet in order to self-determine the delay.

Method 5: Directional Coupling

This method uses special coupling, or interconnection techniques, which implement a system such that a transmitting station can listen to all stations but itself. Collision detection in these systems is straightforward. If a station senses data at its receiver while it is transmitting, it means that some other station is also transmitting, and thus a collision has occurred.

How is a directional coupling system constructed? A bidirectional two-fiber bus, shown in Fig. 4, is one example. In this case, each node transmits information to neighbors on the left over the bottom fiber, and transmits to neighbors on the right over the upper fiber. All but the transmitting station receive the data stream. Similarly, active repeaters arranged in an "open-ring" network would serve the same function.

Another possibility is a directional star coupler, as described in [8], in which optical power at each input port is evenly divided among all but one of the output ports. This type

Fig. 4.   Directional bus network.

of coupler is difficult to construct using conventional fused biconical taper or mixing-rod techniques. Therefore, a special construction is used based on splicing together smaller couplers. An M by M star coupler is made by splicing $2 * M$ by $(M - 1)$ couplers, which function as either optical splitters or optical combiners. The splitters and combiners are spliced in such a way that each input-port splitter is connected to all but one output-port combiner. In the four-port coupler shown in Fig. 5, each of the eight dots represent a three-port splitter or combiner.

An obvious drawback to the directional star coupler approach is the insertion loss of the star coupler. Even in the ideal case, assuming uniform splitting ratios and no splice loss, the insertion loss (port-to-port attenuation) is:

$$L \text{ (dB)} = 10 \ \log \ \frac{1}{(M-1)} 2$$

which is 9.5 dB in the 4 by 4 example. In [8], a "cascade star" system, as shown in Fig. 6, is proposed. This consists of a linear arrangement of bidirectional star couplers whose coupling ratios are optimized to minimize terminal-to-terminal attenuation. While this arrangement may in some aspects have merits, such as modularity and the use of less fiber, it results in more attenuation than the single star coupler described above. This is illustrated in the following example.

Consider the case when two $M/2$ by $M/2$ stars are cascaded to form an M by M system. There are three coupling ratios to be determined.

a Branch-to-branch coupling ratio.
b Trunk-to-trunk coupling ratio.
d Branch-to-branch coupling ratio.

In the ideal case, the attenuation between terminals connected on the same star should equal the attenuation between terminals on different stars

$$d^2 = a^2 * b^2.$$

There are also the constraints that the sum of coupling ratios for the splitters and combiners equal 1

$$(M/2 - 1) * d + a = 1$$

$$(M/2) * b = 1.$$

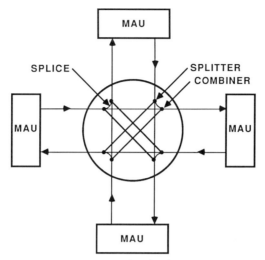

Fig. 5.   Directional star.

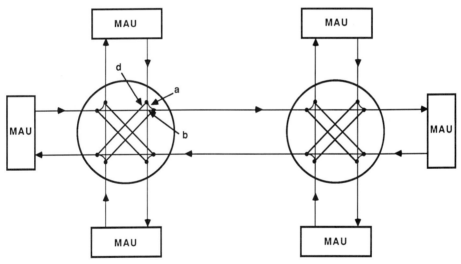

Fig. 6.   Cascaded directional stars.

Solving the three equations results in

$$a = M/2 * (M - 2),$$

$$b = 2/M,$$

$$d = 1/(M - 1).$$

In Table I, these coupling ratios are tabulated for various size systems, along with the terminal-to-terminal attenuation. Also shown for comparison are the terminal-to-terminal attenuation for a single directional star coupler and a standard star coupler. As can be seen,

TABLE I
COUPLING RATIOS FOR DIRECTIONAL STAR SYSTEMS

Number Of Stations (M)	Coupling Ratio			Terminal-To-Terminal Attenuation		
	a	b	d	Cascade Directional	Single Directional	Standard Star
4	.67	.50	.33	9.6 dB	9.5 dB	6 dB
8	.57	.25	.14	16.9 dB	14.4 dB	9 dB
16	.53	.12	.06	23.5 dB	20.0 dB	12 dB
32	.52	.06	.03	29.8 dB	25.2 dB	15 dB

the disparity between single and cascade star systems grows larger as the number of network nodes increases.

Method 6: Hybrid Star

The hybrid star approach [4] is based on a passive star coupler, but the inputs to the star are tapped and directed to centralized collision-detection electronics. The electronics detect when two or more stations are transmitting and, in turn, transmit an optical jam signal back into the star, where it is broadcast to all stations.

Figure 7 shows a block diagram of a hybrid star system. A passive three-port "star coupler monitor" is used in lieu of a traditional two-port star coupler. Functionally, 10 percent of the optical power at each input is tapped and made available to the corresponding monitor port pigtail. Each monitor pigtail connects to an optical receiver in the collision-detection electronics colocated with the star coupler monitor. Logic in the electronics detects when more than one station is transmitting, and enables an oscillating jam signal to be optically fed back into an untapped input of the star, where it broadcasts to all of the

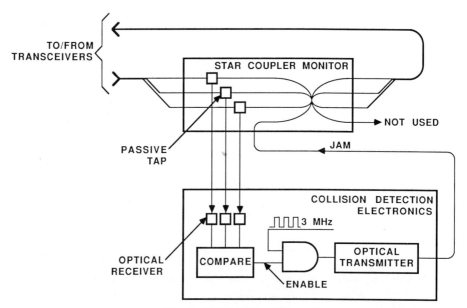

Fig. 7.   Hybrid star system.

transceivers on the network. At each transceiver, the jam signal is detected via the pulse-width violation method described earlier.

A primary benefit of the hybrid star approach is the elimination of the CD dynamic-range problem associated with amplitude domain techniques. This is because each signal accessing the channel is individually detected before it enters the star coupler, and the determination of a collision condition is based on the number of signals present, not their respective amplitudes. Furthermore, the actual implementation of the receivers in the CD electronics is simplified compared to the node transceivers, since distortion of data is of no concern. Also, the required receiver sensitivity in the CD electronics is usually less than the node transceiver, since the signal is tapped before being split. Moreover, the dynamic range can easily be designed to accommodate the entire range of node-to-star transceiver distances.

Like the directional star method, the hybrid star method requires a specially constructed unit—the three-port star coupler monitor. There are several alternatives to such a method, the most straightforward being simply to splice 1×2 taps to the inputs of a star coupler. A 14-node unit, for example, can be placed in a 3/4 in. by 6 in. by 12 in. housing, and add no more than 1.5 dB attenuation to the input–output path. More sophisticated star coupler monitors can be made using a mixing rod and beam splitters, or with reflective gratings and beam splitters [9]. These latter alternatives at present suffer from rather high (9 dB) excess loss, however.

Method 7: Active Star

The last method we look at differs from the previous methods in that a passive star coupler is not used to provide the bus interconnection. The active star network [1] consists of point-to-point fiber-optic links radiating outward from a centralized hub of electronics equipment, called the star repeater. In the star repeater the link terminations are electrically bused together, and collision detection takes place in the electrical domain.

Several tradeoffs are involved in the implementation of the star repeater. The most straightforward implementation of an M-node system consists of M pairs of receiver/transmitter modules connected via a "Little Ethernet" backplane bus. Each module converts optical signals received over its link to electrical signals, places the bit stream on the backplane bus, detects collisions, and optically transmits over the link either the bit stream, or an easily detected jam signal.

To lower implementation costs, collision-detection and transmitter circuits can be shared, at the expense of decreased reliability and power budgets. The following describes one implementation, shown in Fig. 8.

- There are three types of modules: receiver, transmitter, and control, and two unidirectional backplane buses, called the R (receive) and X (transmit) bus.
- The control module transfers data from the R bus to the X bus. It also performs the detection of collisions and will switch in a jam signal in place of the bit stream when a collision occurs. Thus, one collision-detection circuit serves the entire star repeater.
- In the transmitter, each LED circuit drives a group of three fibers which are bundled together with polished flat ends. Two transmitter modules fit on a board, and six receiver modules fit on a receiver board, so a basic six-node system consists of three boards. The system can be expanded in groups of six by adding transmitter and receiver boards.

A primary motivation for the active star network is that optical links are point-to-point,

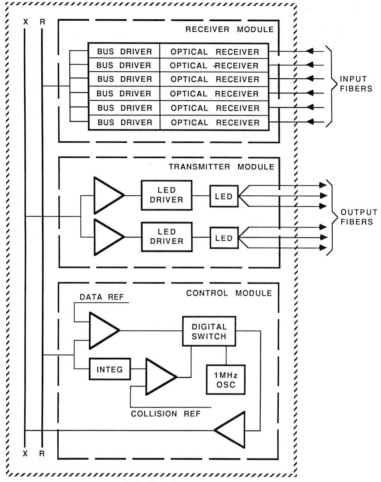

Fig. 8.   Active star repeater.

and thus power is not divided in a coupler. In a passive coupling system, terminal-to-terminal path length is a function of the number of nodes, but an active star network is topologically more flexible. High-performance transmitter/receiver pairs can be used for long links, and lower cost circuits for shorter runs. Ironically, however, there is a large dynamic-range requirement for the receivers in these systems, precisely because there is no coupler to split the optical power.

COMPARISON OF COLLISION-DETECTION METHODS

A summary of the collision-detection methods is given in Table II, in which CD accuracy, CD dynamic range, and required special components or circuits are noted. As discussed in the Introduction, a system based on any of the methods can be fitted or tuned to meet the requirements for a given application, but in the following discussion we note some of the important tradeoffs.

One area of comparison is the number of terminals a network can support. As shown in [1], a passive star network (methods 1, 2, 3, 4, and 6) spanning 500 m supports 13–80

TABLE II
COMPARISON OF COLLISION-DETECTION METHODS

Method	Interconnection	CD Accuracy	Reported CD Dynamic Range	Special Component Requirements
Average Power Sensing	Passive	100%	5 dB	Tuneable Source For Better Range
Pulse Width Violation	Passive	100%	4 dB	Pulse Width Detector
Partial Response Code Violation	Passive	100%	10 dB	Partial Response/Decoding Circuit At Receiver
Time Delay Violation	Passive	≤100%	Note 1	Timing Circuit At Transceiver
Directional Star	Passive	100%	Note 1	Directional Star Coupler
Hybrid Star	Passive With Central CD	100%	20 dB	Star Coupler Monitor, Collision Detection Electronics
Active Star	Passive With Central CD	100%	Note 1	Star Repeater

Note 1: CD Dynamic Range Is Same As Receiver Dynamic Range, Which Typically Ranges Between 10-20 dB.

nodes, depending on the sensitivity of the receiver. A directional star coupler network, (method 5) as presently implemented, would support considerably less, since the splitting ratio is essentially squared. On the other hand, an active star repeater is limited only by the number of circuit boards which can conveniently mount in a rack system. In all instances, repeaters and/or electrical Ethernet multiplexers can be used to increase system spans or terminal count.

It is important to understand, however, the applications in which fiber is used. Many times a fiber CSMA/CD network is used as a backbone segment to connect coax Ethernet systems, as shown in Fig. 9. These backbone segments are installed between buildings or between floors of a building to avoid grounding or EMI/RFI problems, to protect against lightning surges, or to comply with building codes. Another rationale often cited is potential migration to higher capacity fiber backbone networks in the future. In these applications, the actual node count on the fiber network may be relatively small, so the methods based on passive interconnection may be adequate.

Another area of comparison is the collision-detection dynamic range. Clearly, the amplitude domain methods are at a disadvantage, and the timing domain method, while solving the dynamic-range problem, requires precise tuning to achieve 100 percent collision detection. Methods 5–7 circumvent the dynamic-range problem, but at the expense of special components which add to the cost and complexity of the system.

The final area of comparison is system reliability. The amplitude domain and directional coupling methods have the advantage here, since they use passive interconnection and fully distributed collision-detection methods. Collision detection in the time domain is not quite fully distributed, since in some cases only certain nodes detect the time-delay violations and they must in turn notify the other nodes via a jam signal. The hybrid star utilizes passive interconnection but centralized collision detection; if the CD mechanism does fail, the jam detection circuit in the transceiver will provide a backup within the dynamic-range

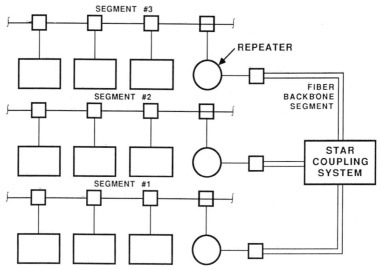

Fig. 9.   Fiber-optic backbone application.

constraints of the design. Moreover, the network will continue to operate in the less efficient pure CSMA mode. The active star system, on the other hand, introduces additional points of failure in each data path, since the optical signal is converted to electrical and back to optical. Failure of the repeater control board described would be catastrophic, although some means for switching in spares could be provided.

CONCLUSIONS

In this chapter we have described and analyzed seven different methods for detecting collisions in fiber-optic CSMA/CD networks. The method of choice depends on particular application considerations, but clearly there are practical systems at a reasonable cost which enable the use of fiber in these networks today.

REFERENCES

[1]   R. Schmidt *et al.,* "Fibernet II: A fiber optic Ethernet," *IEEE J. Select. Areas Commun.,* vol. SAC-1, no. 5, Nov. 1983.
[2]   Minutes, IEEE 802.8.3 Fiber Optic Technical Advisory Group CSMA/CD Task Force, Santa Clara, CA, Feb. 10, 1984.
[3]   T. Kitayama *et al.,* "Passive optical star network using 32-port star coupler," in *Proc. European Conf. Opt. Commun.,* Geneva, Switzerland, Oct. 1983.
[4]   R. Kelley, J. Jones, V. Bhatt, and P. Pate, "Transceiver design and implementation experience in an Ethernet compatible fiber optic local area network," in *Proc. 1984 IEEE INFOCOM,* San Francisco, CA, Apr. 1984.
[5]   Y. Fujii, Y. Hakamada, and K. Oguchi, "Highly sensitive CD method and small loss-deviation star coupler for CSMA/CD optical star transmission system," in *Proc. European Conf. Opt. Commun.,* Stuttgart, Germany, Sept. 1984.
[6]   S. Moustakas and H. H. Witte, "Novel collision detection technique for CSMA/CD-based fiber optic local area network," *Electron. Lett.,* vol. 19, July 1983.
[7]   V. J. Bhatt, "A time domain collision detection scheme for fiber optic local area networks," unpublished, Aug. 1982.
[8]   T. Tamura, M. Nakamura, S. Onshima, T. Ito, and T. Ozeki, "Optical cascade star network—A new configuration for a passive distribution system with optical collision detection capability," *J. Lightwave Technol.,* vol. LT-2, no. 1, Feb. 1984.
[9]   S. Barnes, N. Sandler, and F. Uterleitner, "Monolithic LANSTAR coupler monitor," in *Proc. FOC/ LAN 84,* Las Vegas, NV, Sept. 1984.

18

High-Reliability 100 Mbit/s Optical Accessing Loop Network System: OPALnet-II

NOBUYUKI TOKURA, YOSHINORI OIKAWA, AND
YUKIO KIMURA

A 100 Mbit/s optical loop network is described herein and several issues relevant to the construction of such a system are investigated.

The main features of the network are: its large capacity, which is capable of efficiently accommodating both circuit-switching and packet-switching services; high reliability due to its double-loop configuration and use of an optical accessor for bypassing; and quick recovery of the whole loop by means of the loop-back method when a line fails.

I. Introduction

The LAN's of tomorrow will need to accommodate many high-speed data and video terminals, as well as conventional terminals. To satisfy this demand, LAN's should provide both circuit-switching and packet-switching services.

The authors have been developing a 100 Mbit/s optical accessing loop network (OPALnet-II) [1] as an integrated high-speed optical network. The system inherits the basic concepts of the OPALnet [2]. The reliability of a single-loop network is low, but it can be improved by using a double-loop configuration [3], [4].

Design requirements for OPALnet-II include construction of: 1) a large-capacity (high-speed) network capable of accommodating both circuit-switching and packet-switching services; 2) a highly reliable network that uses an optical accessor for perpetual bypassing in a double-loop configuration; 3) a network applicable over a wide area; and 4) a network that can access other networks via a leased circuit.

Section II of this chapter describes the system configuration for OPALnet-II. Section III describes the design of a high-reliability optical loop using perpetual bypassing. Section IV describes loop access control for effective usage of the transmission line. Section V describes a method for quick recovery after a line fault. Section VI describes the field trial currently being conducted on OPALnet-II.

II. System Outline

The main system characteristics of OPALnet-II and the system configuration are shown in Table I and Fig. 1, respectively.

TABLE I
SYSTEM CHARACTERISTICS

Item	Properties	
Network Topology	Loop (bidirectional double-loop)	
Line Bit-Rate & Code	100 Mbits/s, 8B1C	
Optical Source/Detector	LD (= 850 nm), APD	
Optical Fiber	GI fiber (50/125 μm)	
Max. Station Separation	1 km	
Max. Number of Stations	100	
Optical D/I Element	Optical Accessor	
Action upon Failure	Optical Bypass & Loop-Back	
Gateway Connection	Leased Circuit	
Access Control	DA-TDMA (Circuit Switched)	Token Passing (Packet Switched)
Capacity[a]/Loop	< 64 kbits/s:480ch 1.5 Mbits/s: 20ch	90 Mbits/s
Max. Number of Terminals per Station	48(< 64 kbits/s) 2(1.5 Mbits/s)	48(64 kbits/s)
Terminal Interfaces	High-Speed Facsimile (1.5 Mbits/s) Digital Telephone (64 kbits/s) Data Terminal (Delimiter, Basic, X.20, X.21 bis, X.21, X.21 bis)	Data Terminal (HDLC, X.21)

[a] 0.2 erl/terminal

The center station (CS) and remote stations (RS's) are linked by optical fibers in a loop. Signals from such terminals as digital telephones (64 kbits/s), high-speed facsimiles (1.5 Mbits/s), and data terminals (less than 64 kbits/s) are collected by the stations and then conveyed on the loop through an optical accessor after electrical to optical conversion. The CS and other LAN's are linked through a gateway adapter by a leased circuit (1.5 Mbits/s).

The station configuration is shown in Fig. 2. The optical accessor at each station drops/ inserts an optical signal from/to the optical highway. The communication control block consists of a multiplexer (MUX), a circuit-switching block, and a packet-switching block. Referring back to Fig. 1, the circuit-switching block is used to communicate between the terminals affiliated with one station and between terminals of other stations, as well. The

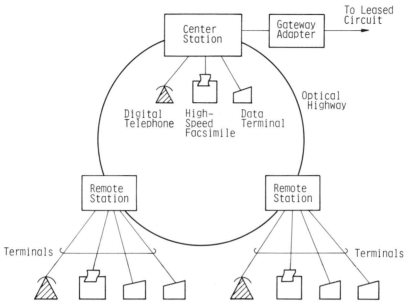

Fig. 1. Network configuration.

packet-switching block is used to communicate between affiliated packet terminals and between packet terminals of the other stations. It also handles packet assembling/disassembling under token-passing control. In addition the packet-switching block assembles/disassembles signaling packets for both circuit-switching and packet-switching terminals.

Four issues remain to be investigated for establishing this system:

1) reduction of interference between bypassing signals and an inserted signal;
2) construction of a high-reliability loop using the optical accessor;
3) simultaneous accommodation of both circuit-switching and packet-switching services; and
4) quick recovery from a line failure.

In the following, an optical-pulse interlace technique, reliability, access control, and recovery from a failure are discussed in detail. They supplement the system outline described above.

III. HIGH-RELIABILITY OPTICAL LOOP

Optical signals are dropped/inserted from/to the optical highway via an optical accessor that is able to bypass optical signals. This bypassing is used to avoid interruption of the whole network operation when a station breaks down.

A. Optical-Pulse Interlace Technique

The optical-pulse stream on the highway is illustrated in Fig. 3(a) and (b) for the station-active case and for a station-fault case, respectively. At each station, only the larger pulse stream in received optical pulses is regenerated by the peak-AGC function. Although the bypassed signal can travel through a fault station to the next active station in a station-fault

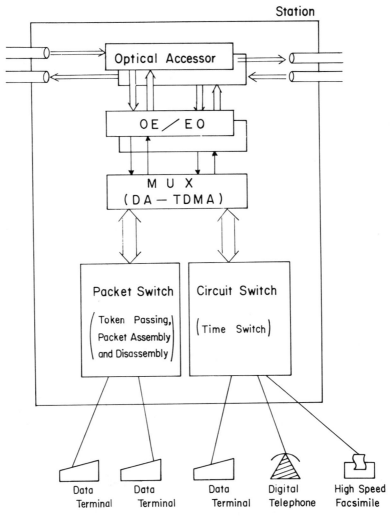

Fig. 2.   Station configuration.

case, it interferes with the inserted signals in the station-active case. Using the common-phase insertion method, the bypassed signals interfere with the inserted signals from the connected terminals. A pulse interlace technique [5], that is, a technique in which a pulse stream from a station is inserted in inverse phase to the bypassed pulse stream, reduces interference from the bypassed pulse stream.

The receiver sensitivity in this system was estimated from both the minimum received power when no bypassing signals exist and the power penalty (ΔP) caused by interference. The minimum received power was calculated at a bit error rate of 10^{-11} for a transmitted rectangular waveform passed through a Gaussian filter [6]. The relation between SNR degradation ΔSNR and interference $I = 1/(1 + A)$ is

$$\Delta\text{SNR} = -20 \log (1 - 2I) = -20 \log \frac{1-A}{1+A}. \tag{1}$$

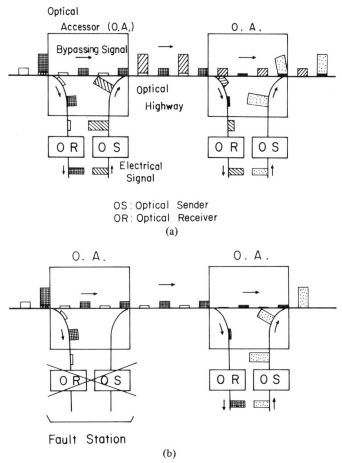

Fig. 3. Pulse interlace. (a) Active case. (b) Fault case.

Here, A is the ratio of bypassing signals to inserted signals. From [7], ΔP was calculated according to the following equation:

$$\Delta P(A) = \frac{2+X}{2+2X} \, \Delta\text{SNR}$$

$$= -\frac{10(2+X)}{1+X} \, \log \frac{1-A}{1+A}. \tag{2}$$

Here, X is the excess noise factor in an avalanche photodiode (APD).

Figure 4 shows the calculated result. A pulse duty ratio of 40 percent and a filter cutoff frequency (3 dB down) of $0.9 \, f_0$ (f_0: transmission bit rate) were chosen for the system parameters, considering the relation between the pulse duty ratio and the amount of interference.

Measured minimum received power was -38.9 dBm for 2 km transmission and -5 dB

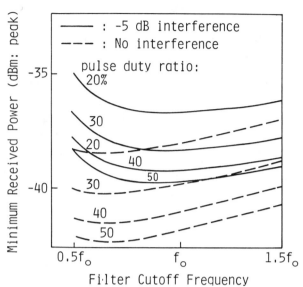

Fig. 4.   Minimum received power versus cutoff frequency.

interference. This value approaches the -39.3 dBm shown in Fig. 4. Figure 5 shows a received waveform containing interference from a pulse interlace signal.

B. Optical Accessor

Because the optical accessor is a passive device, we can expect high reliability from it. A buried-waveguide-type accessor made using the field-assisted ion-exchange method [8] is used for OPALnet-II. Its configuration is shown in Fig. 6. This waveguide has a refractive-index distribution of the graded index type, which is the same as the optical transmission fiber used in this system; therefore, it provides good coupling characteristics.

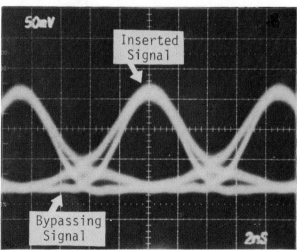

Fig. 5.   Received eye pattern. Equalizer output waveform for -7 dB interference and -36 dBm input.

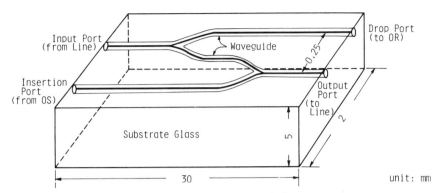

Fig. 6. Buried-waveguide-type optical accessor.

The coupling loss in the optical accessor must be designed to permit the setup of a multistation bypass. An accessor design that does not include a power penalty for interference is given in [9], [10]. Our exact design considers the power penalty due to interference from station-bypassing signals.

The accessor consists of two "Y" branch waveguides of the same characteristics. Loss in the "Y" branch waveguide is separated into drop/insertion loss: $\alpha + \delta_\alpha$ (dB), and bypass loss: $(\beta + \delta_\beta)/2$ (dB), where δ is the excess loss including loss in the two connectors. The relation between α and β is

$$\alpha = -10 \, \log \, (1 - 10^{-\beta/20}). \tag{3}$$

The total loss L_k between two active stations is

$$L_k = 2(\alpha + \delta_\alpha) + k(\beta + \delta_\beta) + l(k+1) \tag{4}$$

where k is the number of bypassed stations, l is the transmission line loss between the stations. A transmission line containing interference due to bypassing signals has power penalty $\Delta P(A)$ of (2). Accordingly, the equivalent transmission loss L is

$$L = L_k + \Delta P(A). \tag{5}$$

The coupling loss in the optical accessor is set to obtain minimum L.

When interference with bypassing signals takes place in a common phase, such interference can be described as follows:

$$A_0 = \frac{10^{-(\beta + \delta_\beta + l)/10}}{1 - 10^{-(\beta + \delta_\beta + l)/10}}. \tag{6}$$

In the case of pulse interlace (inverse phase interference), it becomes

$$A_\pi = \frac{10^{-(\beta + \delta_\beta + l)/5}}{1 - 10^{-(\beta + \delta_\beta + l)/5}} + \frac{10^{-(\beta + \delta_\beta + l + F)/10}}{1 - 10^{-(\beta + \delta_\beta + l + F)/5}}. \tag{7}$$

In (7), the first and second terms represent common-phase and inverse-phase interference, respectively. F is the interference-decreasing effect due to pulse interlacing. For example, with a pulse duty ratio of 40 percent and Gaussian filter bandwidth of 0.9 f_0, F has a value of 3.9 dB (41 percent) if the transmission line bandwidth is equal to f_0; and a value of 13 dB (5 percent) if the transmission bandwidth is infinitely larger.

The calculated values of equivalent transmission loss L are presented in Figs. 7 and 8. In these figures, excess losses in the optical accessor, including two optical connectors, are set empirically at 2 and 3 dB for drop/insertion loss and bypass loss, respectively.

Figure 7 shows such loss both with and without pulse interlace for 0 dB transmission line loss between the stations. The figure shows that better pulse interlace effects can be obtained when bypass loss in the optical accessor is reduced.

Figure 8 shows bypass loss versus equivalent transmission loss. Calculation was made under the following conditions: 1) Transmission line loss between the active station and neighboring active stations that produce interference is 0 dB. 2) The bandwidth of the transmission line between two active stations is equal to f_0. Figure 8 indicates that a value of 4 dB is the most suitable for bypass loss, if equivalent transmission loss is about 40 dB (Table II). This value allows more multiple-station bypasses.

Thus, the design value for optical accessor loss, including excess losses, is 7 dB and 6.3 dB for bypass loss and drop/insertion loss, respectively.

The measured values for the optical accessor are shown in Fig. 9, which clearly indicates

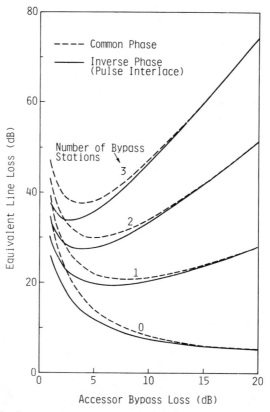

Fig. 7.   Equivalent line loss using pulse-interlace technique.

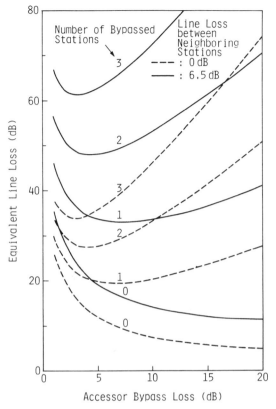

Fig. 8.   Equivalent line loss versus bypass loss in accessor.

that each loss satisfies the design value. The coupling-ratio variation of the accessor is about 1.2 dB. This variation is caused by the launching condition of the accessor.

As far as crosstalk is concerned, degradation of the receiver characteristics occurs because the optical sender (OS) output returns to the optical receiver (OR) of the same station. Since the phase of this crosstalk has been reversed, interference is reduced. For such crosstalk, 50 dB is specified as the value where the increase in maximum OS level can be neglected. From actual measurement, this value is more than 55 dB.

The optical levels for the system are shown in Table II. In that table, total line loss, including connector and splice losses, was evaluated for 2 km transmission, supposing one bypassed station. As shown in Table II, a margin of 4.4 dB was obtained.

C. Reliability

Using the availability of the transmission line between two stations, the reliability of the optical double-loop network can be evaluated. Two stations connected by the transmission line with minimum availability will be selected. Figure 10 shows a model of the optical double-loop network. The availability A between stations S_a and S_b can be given by

$$A = (1 - \bar{A}_1 \bar{A}_3)(1 - \bar{A}_2 \bar{A}_4) \qquad (8a)$$

TABLE II
OPTICAL LEVELS

Item	Value
Fiber Input Power	1 dBm (peak)

Optical Accessor Loss
  Drop
  Insertion
  Bypass
  Crosstalk
	
	6.3 dB
	6.3 dB
	7 dB
	50 dB

Fiber Loss	7 dB (at λ = 850 nm) (2 km for bypassing)
Connector Loss	3.6 dB (6 connectors for bypassing)
Splice Loss	2.4 dB (8 splices for bypassing)
Margin	4.4 dB
Optical Received Power	$-36 \sim -11$ dBm (peak)

with

$$\bar{A}_i = 1 - A_i, \qquad i = 1, \ 2, \ 3, \ 4 \tag{8b}$$

where A_i is the availability of each transmission line between S_a and S_b.

Figure 11 shows the optical transmission line scheme used to determine availability A_i. It is assumed that each station consists of an optical accessor having a station-bypass function, an optical sender, and an optical receiver. Availability for the model in Fig. 11 is given in [11]. This reference assumes that the number of consecutive bypass stations k is one.

In the present study, k is extended to more than 1; however, this availability is difficult to determine. Thus, instead of determining the actual availability, we shall calculate the lower limit A_L and upper limit A_U of such availability. A_L can be obtained by calculating the availability, conditional on the insertion of one active station after each kth bypass station. On the other hand, A_U can be obtained by calculating the availability without imposing any restriction on the position of bypass and active stations. We obtain the following formulas:

$$A_L = rr_a^n r_l^{n-1} \sum_{j=0}^{n-2-[(n-2)/(k+1)]} \left(n-2-\left[\frac{j-1}{k}\right] \atop j \right) \cdot (1-r)^j r^{n-2-j} \tag{9}$$

$$A_U = rr_a^n r_l^{n-1} \sum_{j=0}^{n-2-[(n-2)/(k+1)]} \binom{n-2}{j} (1-r)^j r^{n-2-j} \tag{10}$$

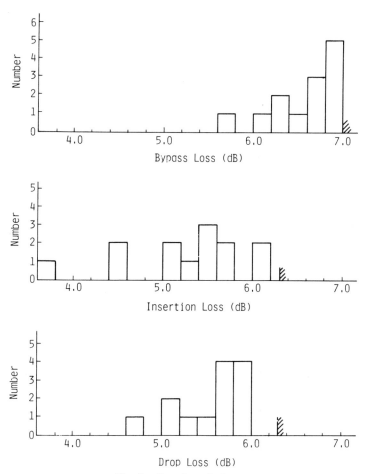

Fig. 9.   Loss in optical accessor.

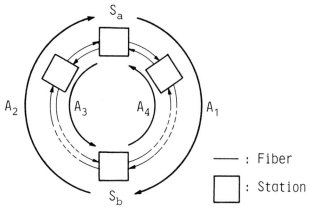

A_1, A_2, A_3, A_4: Transmission Line Availability

Fig. 10.   Double-loop configuration.

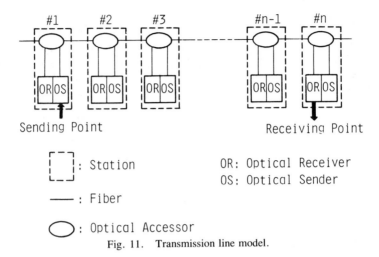

Fig. 11.   Transmission line model.

where r is the optical transceiver (OS and OR) availability, r_a is the optical accessor availability, r_l is the transmission line availability between stations, n is the number of stations, k is the maximum number of consecutive bypassed stations, and [ ] converts to the nearest integer of lesser or equal magnitude.

Using (9) and (10) and the conditions given in Table III, the calculated unavailability difference $(A_U - A_L)$ is 1 percent, or less. When k is 1, the value of (9) is the same as that given in [11]. We shall therefore use (9), which gives the optical transmission line availability on the conservative side.

Figure 12 shows the unavailability of the optical double-loop network calculated using (8) and (9). That figure indicates that the station-bypass function of the optical accessor provides a dramatic increase in network availability. However, it cannot be expected that increasing k to 2 or more improves availability. Therefore, OPALnet-II was designed to assure at least one station bypass. When the station-to-station distance is short, the number of stations that can be bypassed must be maximized since the same power supply may be

TABLE III
TRANSMISSION-LINE UNAVAILABILITY
PARAMETERS

Unavailability of Optical Accessor: $\bar{r}_a$	2×10^{-7}
Unavailability of Optical Transceiver (OS + OR): $\bar{r}$	3.2×10^{-5}
Unavailability of Station-Station Line (1 km): $\bar{r}_l$	10^{-6}
Number of Stations: n	$4 \sim 100$
Maximum Number of Consecutively Bypassed Stations: k	$1 \sim 5$

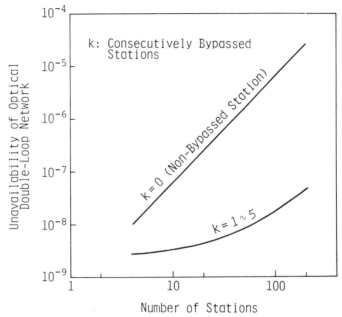

Fig. 12. Double-loop network unavailability.

used by more than one station, which may cause successive station failures if that power supply is faulty.

IV. ACCESS CONTROL

A. Multiplexing of the Circuit-Switching and Packet-Switching Signals

1) Frame Format: The system needs to implement both circuit-switching and packet-switching services in the loop network. Therefore, we decided to use the time-division multiple-access (TDMA) procedure for both circuit-switching and packet-switching signals. There are two types of assignment: the preassign (PA) method and the demand assign (DA) method. In PA, allocations for both services are decided beforehand. On the other hand, in DA, allocations are assigned dynamically according to the terminal traffic.

From the viewpoint of effective usage of the loop transmission line, we chose a DA method in which the unit attribute indicator is placed in the frame header. Here, a unit means a section in a using area. Figure 13 shows the frame format. The packet-switching signal is assigned to an area where no circuit-switching signal is being used.

2) Reliable Indication of the Assignment Area: The unit attribute indication (UAI) is the most important item of control information. Thus, it must be protected from transmission error. Therefore, an error detection (ED) function is set up in the frame header.

There are two typical error detection methods: parity checking and cyclic redundancy checking (CRC). The reliability of the two methods is discussed in the following. Figure 14 shows the UAI with ED structures of each method. M is the total number of bits including both UAI and ED.

a) Parity check method: Each byte consists of seven data bits and one parity check

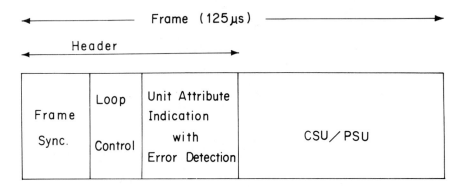

CSU : Circuit Switching Unit

PSU : Packet Switching Unit

Fig. 13. Frame format.

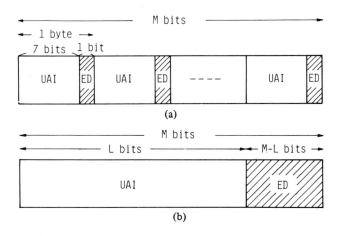

UAI: Unit Attribute Indication
ED: Error Detection

Fig. 14. Error detection methods. (a) Parity check method. (b) Cyclic redundancy check method.

bit, so the number of parity check bits is $M/8$ bits. An error condition is missed if it cannot be detected with parity bits. The error-free interval T_P is

$$T_P = \frac{8T}{n \cdot M \binom{8}{2} P^2}, \qquad (P \ll 1) \tag{11}$$

where n is the total number of stations, T is the frame period, and P is the bit-error rate for the transmission line.

  b) Double-error-detectable CRC method [13]: A double error can be detected using CRC if a generator polynomial $G(x)$ is employed. For a data length of L bits, $G(x)$ must be an N-degree polynomial that satisfies $L \leq 2^N - 1$. The error is missed if it cannot be detected with the CRC. The error-free interval (T_{C1}) can be described as

$$T_{C1} = \frac{T}{n \binom{M}{3} P^3}, \qquad (P \ll 1).$$
(12)

c) Triple-error-detectable CRC method [13]: A triple error can be detected using a CRC if the generator polynomial $G(x) \cdot (1 + x)$ is employed. Similar to b) above, the error-free interval T_{C2} is

$$T_{C2} = \frac{T}{n \binom{M}{4} P^4}, \qquad (P \ll 1).$$
(13)

For 64 kbit/s digital telephone transmission, one frame ($T = 125$ μs) is divided into 64 units (1.5 Mbits/s/unit). Therefore, the UAI requires 64 bits.

The calculated results for both the parity-checking and CRC methods are shown in Fig. 15. The parameters used for calculation are $n = 100$, $T = 125 \times 10^{-6}$ s, $M = 72$, and $L = 64$.

OPALnet-II utilizes a CRC that can detect a triple error under the following conditions.

- 100 stations are linked in the loop network.
- The bit-error rate for the transmission line is 10^{-5}.
- UAI error occurs less than once a year.

3) Assignment Control of the Circuit-Switching and Packet-Switching Signals: The circuit-switching and packet-switching signals are assigned to each unit individually. For a circuit-switching signal of 64 kbits/s, signals from 24 terminals are multiplexed into one unit. A UAI in the frame header shows the attributes of each unit that a circuit-switching or

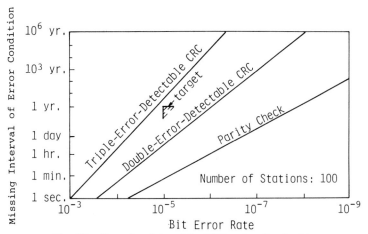

Fig. 15. Error-free interval for CRC and parity checking.

packet-switching signal uses. The procedures for assignment control by the CS are as follows.

a) At the beginning of operation, all loop transmission lines are assigned as packet-switching areas.

b) When a request for circuit switching arises, the CS changes one packet-switching unit area into a circuit-switching unit area using the DA-TDMA procedure. However, at least three units are reserved for signaling packets in a packet-switching area.

c) When a number of units in the circuit-switching area become vacant, the CS changes them into packet-switching areas.

For effective usage of the loop, the following grouping types are considered to be an efficient mixture of circuit-switching and packet-switching areas. Figure 16 illustrates the three grouping types discussed here:

1) 2-grouping: consisting of a circuit-switching group and a packet-switching group;
2) 3-grouping: consisting of a 64 kbit/s signal circuit-switching group, a 1.5 Mbit/s signal circuit-switching group, and a packet-switching group; and
3) ungrouped: no restriction on unit usage.

For comparison of groupings, time dependence of the size of the packet areas for two traffic variations was analyzed by computer simulation. Simulation parameters were as shown in Table IV. One of the traffic variations was a transition from no load to normal load (first condition), and the other was a transition from overload to normal load (second condition). Here, normal load means a well-balanced load among 64 kbits/s, 1.5 Mbits/s, and packet traffics.

The results are shown in Fig. 17(a) and (b) for the first and second conditions, respectively. For the first condition, the ungrouped method is superior, although the difference between each method is not very large. For the second condition, the ungrouped method is quite superior to the other methods. Recovery time to the steady state for 2-grouping and 3-grouping is several minutes longer than that for ungrouped. Packet area sizes of 2-grouping and 3-grouping in steady state are less than that of ungrouped.

The reason for this is described as follows. Even when 1.5 Mbit/s calls that use a unit far from the boundary of the circuit-switching area finish, no packet area can be assigned to the unit that becomes vacant in the 2- or 3-grouping methods. Because the amount of hardware

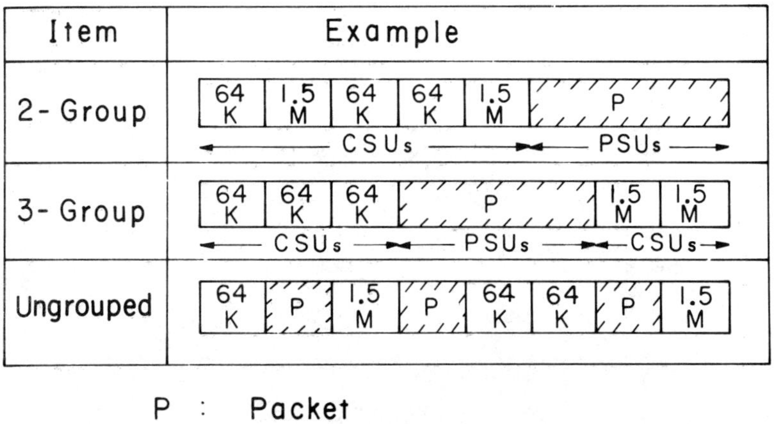

P : Packet

Fig. 16. Types of grouping.

TABLE IV
PARAMETERS USED FOR SIMULATION

Type of Terminal	Holding Time	Number of Terminals	Traffic Intensity	
			Normal load	Overload
Digital Telephone	180 s	1200	0.2 erl/Terminal	1.0 erl/Terminal
Data Terminal	360 s	1200		
High-Speed Facsimile	60 s	100		

Holding time: Exponential distribution
Originating rate: Poisson distribution

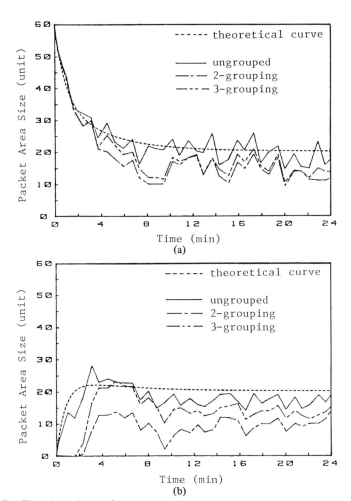

Fig. 17.   Time dependence of packet area utility. (a) First condition. (b) Second condition.

for each method does not differ, and due to the results obtained above, we adopted the ungrouped method. It has the following merits:

- wider packet area availability;
- higher efficiency of usage in the circuit-switching area;
- easier unit assignment for leased lines.

B. Token-Passing Control

Packet-switching signals access the loop network under token-passing control, which is suitable for a loop-type network. The management of packets and token is as follows. Source stations and the CS delete packets after one round. When the CS detects the loss of a token using the timer, the CS generates a new token.

Token-passing control permits two types [14] of token releasing:

1) Type 1—The token is released after waiting a roundtrip of its packet: IEEE 802.5 type [15].

2) Type 2—The token is released sequentially just after sending the packet: FDDI type [16].

The procedure for these types is shown in Fig. 18. Type 2 was chosen for this system, since it provides the superior transfer time characteristics shown in Fig. 19.

C. Switching Functions

The switching functions for the CS and RS are described in Table V. The CS manages the whole loop network using the DA-TDMA procedure, but the CS and each RS process their own intra-station calls. Signaling for both circuit-switching and packet-switching terminals is sent in packets under token-passing control. Three packet-switching units in the loop of OPALnet-II are reserved as signaling packet areas.

V. RECOVERY

For loop recovery from a line failure, a double-loop configuration, optical bypassing in each station, and loop-back are used in the system.

A. Optical Bypassing in a Station

In case of a station failure, signals from the preceding station can travel to the next station via the optical bypassing path in the optical accessor in the fault station. Therefore, the highly reliable bypass operation described in Section III-C is possible.

B. Loop-Back Operation

Many loop-back methods have been proposed. Most of them check individual stations sequentially to detect a failure. Therefore, the greater the number of stations, the longer the operating time required for loop-back to occur.

Concurrent loop back (CLB) is adopted in this system for quick recovery even when the number of stations increases. The principle behind CLB is shown in Figs. 20 and 21.

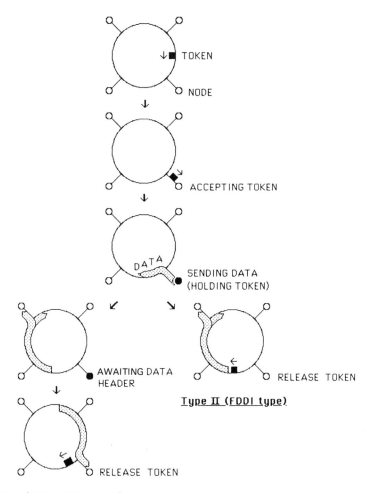

Fig. 18. Token-passing control.

Basically, it works as follows.

1) When the CS finds both loop line failure by optical-power-down-detection or frame-synchronization error detection, the loop-back command within the loop control region of the frame header (shown in Fig. 13) is broadcast to all RS's on both the R and L loops.

2) In each RS, a repeating operation is performed in the loop which first received the command, and loop-back operation is performed at the other loop.

3) RS's that can receive optical signals from both directions of the loop drop out of the loop-back state. Only the two RS's closest to the failure remain in the loop-back state. A new loop is now created.

VI. FIELD TRIAL

OPALnet-II has been undergoing a field trial at the Atsugi Laboratory since April 1984. The test route links three buildings and has a total loop length of 1.6 km. A center station

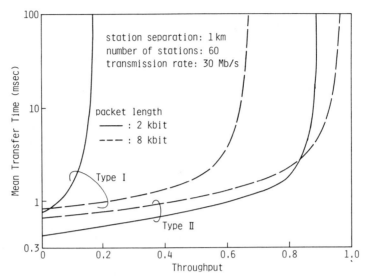

Fig. 19.   Performance of token-ring system.

TABLE V
STATION FUNCTIONS

	Circuit Switching	Packet Switching
Center Station	• Unit Assignment • CSU/PSU Area Assignment (DA-TDMA)	• Signaling • Packet Switching
Remote Station	• Intra-Station Exchange	(Token Passing)

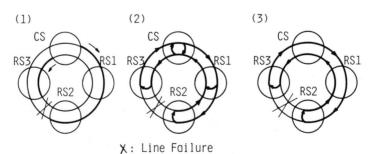

X : Line Failure

Fig. 20.   Loop-back control.

has been set up at the second basement level of the no. 1 laboratory building and a total of ten remote stations have been built, with one station located on each floor of the three buildings. Typical results obtained in the field trial so far are found within the following subsections.

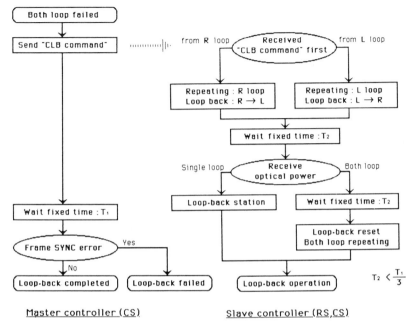

Master controller (CS)   Slave controller (RS,CS)

Fig. 21.   Flowchart of concurrent loop-back (CLB) control.

A. Component Test

The characteristics of the optical transceivers (OS and OR) used at each station are shown in Fig. 22. The OS and OR characteristics shown here satisfy the design values given in Table II.

B. Transmission Line

An optical-fiber cable containing 30 fibers is being used in the field trial, with two of the fibers used by OPALnet-II. The fiber is of the graded index type (50/125 μm). The fiber loss between stations has been measured at 2.3 ~ 4.1 dB. The fiber bandwidth is more than 500 MHz·km.

C. Loop Transmission Test

The bit-error rates measured in a transmission test of from one to ten repeating stations are given in Fig. 23. The results make it clear that repeating transmission causes virtually no increase in the bit-error rate. Error-free transmission has been achieved in a five-station-loop transmission test in which an optical bypass was constructed at every other station.

D. Loop Recovery Test

The time for switchover to the optical bypass state is less than 0.3 s. The loop-back time when both loop-transmission routes failed was also measured for up to ten remote stations. The results indicate that loop-back time is less than 0.8 s, and that it is not dependent on the number of stations.

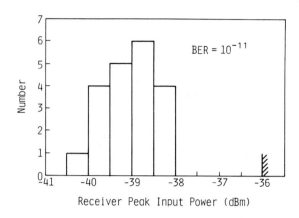

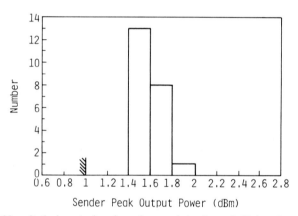

Fig. 22.   Optical sender/receiver characteristics for −7 dB interference.

E. Terminal-to-Terminal Communication Test

It has been clarified that simultaneous communication is possible between circuit-switching terminals (1.5 Mbit/s terminals, digital telephones, 9.6 kbit/s data terminals, 2.4 kbit/s data terminals) and between 9.6 kbit/s packet-switching terminals. It has also been confirmed that continuous communication is possible even if switchover to the loop-back state is made during communication.

Simultaneous communication between circuit-switching terminals (excluding the 1.5 Mbit/s ones) and between packet-switching terminals has been performed in communication between two OPALnet-II systems via gateway adapters. Furthermore, it has been demonstrated that communication between packet-switching terminals is possible by making a link with a SOLARnet [17] system via gateway adapters.

VII. Conclusion

The characteristics of a 100 Mbit/s optical accessing loop network (OPALnet-II) have been described. These characteristics include the following.

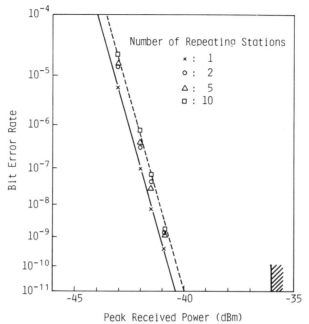

Fig. 23.   Transmission bit-error rate.

1) A highly efficient loop network capable of accommodating both circuit-switching and packet-switching services. High efficiency is derived by assignment of vacant circuit-switching areas for packet switching.

2) A highly reliable loop network using an optical accessor and an optical-pulse interlace technique. The technique permits both bypassing with little interference and easy recovery of the optical path when a station fails.

3) Quick recovery of the whole network using concurrent loop-back operation independent of the number of stations.

OPALnet-II is now operating with the above characteristics in a field test at our Atsugi Laboratory. It was used as the communication system covering the whole site of the International Exposition, Tsukuba, Japan, in 1985.

ACKNOWLEDGMENT

The authors wish to thank Dr. S. Simada and Dr. M. Koyama for their advice and encouragement, Dr. J. Minowa, Y. Hakamada, K. Oguchi, and Dr. K. Nosu for their advice and fruitful discussions. Thanks are also due to Matsushita Communication Industrial Co., Ltd., for the manufacturing of OPAL-net II equipment.

REFERENCES

[1] N. Tokura, K. Oguchi, Y. Kimura, and Y. Oikawa, "100 Mb/s optical fiber loop network for on-premises use," in *Proc. GLOBE COM'84*, Atlanta, GA, Nov. 1984, paper 2.6.
[2] M. Saruwatari, K. Nosu, and T. Miki, "Optically accessing loop (OPAL) network using wavelength-division-multiplexing technology," in *Conf. Rec. ICC '80*, Seattle, WA, June 1980, paper 28.6.

[3] P. Zafiropulo, "Performance evaluation of reliability improvement techniques for single loop communication systems," *IEEE Trans. Commun.*, vol. COM-22, pp. 742–751, June 1974.

[4] M. Akiyama and K. Sakaue, "Reliability of loop communication networks," *Trans. IECE Japan*, vol. J60-A, pp. 268–275, Mar. 1977.

[5] N. Tokura, K. Oguchi, and K. Nosu, "An optically accessing loop system using pulse interlace technique," in *Tech. Dig. IOOC '83*, Tokyo, Japan, June 1983, paper 29C1-2.

[6] K. Nakagawa, Y. Hakamada, K. Suto, and T. Ito, "400 Mb/s optical repeater design and performance," *Trans. IECE Japan*, vol. E65, pp. 657–664, Nov. 1982.

[7] Y. Okano and T. Miki, "SNR analysis for digital optical transmission," *Review ECL*, vol. 26, pp. 701–711, May–June 1986.

[8] E. Okuda, I. Tanaka, and T. Yamasaki, "Planer gradient-index glass waveguide and its applications to a 4-port branched circuit and star coupler," in *Tech. Dig. 4th Topical Meet. Gradient-Index Opt. Imag. Syst.*, Kobe, Japan, July 1983, paper F2.

[9] A. Albanese, "Fail-safe nodes for lightguide digital networks," *Bell Syst. Tech. J.*, vol. 61, no. 2, pp. 247–256, Feb. 1982; see also this volume, ch. 15.

[10] J. Limb, "On fiber optic taps for local area networks," in *Proc. ICC'84*, Amsterdam, The Netherlands, May 1984, pp. 1130–1136.

[11] K. Nosu, "The reliability of optical access fiber optic networks," *Trans. IECE Japan*, vol. E66, pp. 132–138, Feb. 1983.

[12] N. Tokura, Y. Oikawa, and Y. Kimura, "High-reliability 100 Mbit/s optical accessing loop network system: OPALnet-II," *J. Lightwave Technol.*, vol. LT-3, pp. 479–489, June 1985.

[13] W. W. Peterson and D. T. Brown, "Cyclic codes of error detection," *Proc. IRE*, vol. 49, pp. 228–335, Jan. 1961.

[14] W. Bux, "Local-area subnetworks: A performance comparison," *IEEE Trans. Commun.*, vol. COM-29, pp. 1465–1472, Oct. 1981; see also this volume, ch. 21.

[15] "Draft IEEE Standard 802.5 token ring access method and physical layer specifications," IEEE Project 802 LAN Standards, Working Draft, IEEE Computer Society, Feb. 1984.

[16] "Fiber distributed data interface token ring media access control," American National Standards Institute, proposed Draft-X3T9/83-X3T9.5/83-16 REV.5, June 1984.

[17] K. Hakamada and K. Oguchi, "32 Mb/s star configured optical local area network design and performance," *J. Lightwave Technol.*, vol. LT-3, pp. 511–524, June 1985.

Part IV
Performance

The performance of a network is given by two measures: throughput and message delay. Ultimately, it is these measures as seen by the users that count. But as we all know, a network is a complex system comprising several layers of protocols. Its performance is a function of the protocols in use and the way these protocols are implemented. A global and accurate performance analysis of the entire system giving the end-to-end user performance has proven very difficult, and little can be found which addresses this issue in its entirety. Instead, performance analysis has been done on specific areas of protocols. The single area that has been most extensively investigated is that of media access control, as it is believed to have a significant effect on performance, and since it is by such protocols that the various local area networks differ the most. This part deals precisely with this topic.

Computer traffic is known to be bursty in nature, and as a result it has been well recognized that it is more efficient to provide the available communication bandwidth as a single channel to be shared by the many contending users, thus attaining the benefits of the laws of large numbers. This clearly results in a multiaccess environment that calls for special schemes to control the access to the channel, known as media access control protocols. The first chapter in this part (Chapter 19) gives an overview of these protocols. The remaining chapters deal with the performance analysis of common standard protocols: namely carrier sense multiple access, the token ring, and the token-passing bus scheme. The fact that CSMA is contention-based and allows collisions has led to a greater difficulty in its analysis and to a wider set of papers in the literature on that subject. This explains the larger number of chapters in this part addressing this scheme. Furthermore, contrary to the token passing schemes which provide conflict-free operation based on a round robin scheduling, CSMA networks are prone to instability. A careful study and understanding of this issue is of primary importance. Two chapters (20 and 21) in this part are devoted to the mathematical analysis of CSMA/CD, followed by one chapter (22) that compares the performance of CSMA/CD with that of ring networks.

The mathematical analysis of complex schemes such as CSMA dictates the introduction of simplifying assumptions, thus the validation of analytical results can only be obtained by the means of measurements on a real network. Results of such measurements on Ethernets, supplemented by simulation where measurements proved impossible, are the subject of Chapter 23.

The newest of the three standards is the token-passing bus scheme. One of the main features of this scheme is that it defines different classes of services, and devises a mechanism for the allocation of the bandwidth to messages in the various classes. While the description of the mechanism is clear, the problem of selecting appropriate values for the underlying parameters in order to achieve the desired effect remains an open problem. Chapter 24 addresses some of the issues involved.

In general, a great deal of work has already been done in the area of performance evaluation of media access protocols. The results obtained so far have greatly helped in the understanding of the behavior of local area networks, their design, and operation. But a great deal of work remains to be done before the performance as seen by the user can be accurately assessed and understood.

19

Local Distribution in Computer Communications

JEREMIAH F. HAYES

INTRODUCTION

A significant part of the field of computer communications is concerned with providing transmission facilities for data sources which may be characterized as bursty, i.e., short spurts of activity interspersed with relatively long idle periods. It has been estimated, for example, that terminals in interactive data networks are active from 1 to 5 percent of the time [1], [2]. Because of this burstiness dedicating facilities to any one source is not economical; transmission facilities should be shared among a number of sources. In this chapter we shall consider a particular context in which transmission facilities must be provided--local distribution. In local distribution a number of sources dispersed in a geographical area in the order of a couple of square kilometers are to be connected to a central facility or to one another through a common transmission medium. The importance of the subject may be seen from the fact that local area networks (LAN), whose sole function is local distribution, are the most common class of computer communication networks. Furthermore, local distribution consumes a significant portion of the total cost of wide area networks (WAN). In this chapter we shall describe the basic approaches to local distribution.

There are several ways that local distribution systems can be classified. The transmission medium which is shared among the users may be twisted wire pairs, coaxial cable, or optical fiber. Although it is generally not used in local distribution systems, one could also list radio as a transmission medium. Generally speaking, local area networks using wire pairs operate up to the low Mbit/s range. The standard operating rate for coaxial cable is in the neighborhood of 10 Mbits/s. For optical fiber, a far wider range of line rates is possible. With LED transmitters over multimode fiber, rates up to 50 Mbits/s can be achieved. If lasers and single-mode fibers are deployed, the range of speeds is far higher— in the Gbit/s range.

Since local distribution systems extend over a limited area, line failure is much less of a problem than it is in wide area networks. Consequently, the topologies of local distribution systems that need not provide alternate routing and simpler configurations can be employed. At the present stage of development, four topologies are prevalent: the tree, the ring, the bus, and the star [see Fig. 1(a)–(d)]. In the tree [Fig. 1(a)], the terminals connected to bursty sources are at the end of the branches. A central processor broadcasts from the

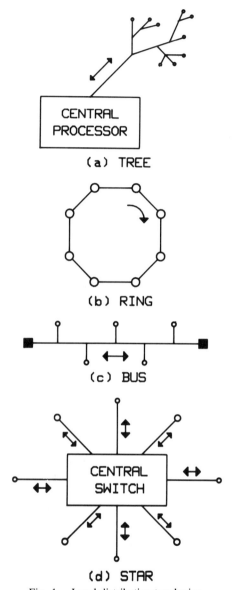

Fig. 1.   Local distribution topologies.

root of the tree. The ring[1] topology consists of a closed sequence of point-to-point links, in which the flow of traffic is in one direction [shown as clockwise in Fig. 1(b)]. Terminals arranged around the ring may communicate with one another in a distributed fashion using one of the several protocols explained in the sequel. The bus topology [Fig. 1(c)] is a sort of distributed tree in which all terminals may broadcast to one another. Finally, in the star [Fig. 1(d)] the sources are located at the end points. Traffic is switched by means of a central switch located at the hub of the star.

---

[1] In the early literature, the ring was referred to as the loop. We shall adhere to current practice which has discarded the term.

Since the data sources sharing the common medium are dispersed, coordinating the flow of traffic requires overhead. This overhead, which may be implicit or explicit, is embodied in access protocols. For each of the topologies considered in the preceding paragraph, one of several access protocols may be used. We may distinguish three main categories: polling, random access, and adaptive techniques. We also consider a fourth category: techniques that are suited to the ring topology. The discussion in the sequel is organized around these access protocols. The focus of our discussion is on fundamental principles without dwelling on details of implementation. As well as describing the techniques, we shall summarize the results of studies of performance. These results quantify the effect of various system parameters on performance.

POLLING SYSTEMS

The polling access protocol is most often used in systems with the tree topology [see Fig. 1(a)]. The most common implementation of the technique is roll-call polling. It is assumed that each terminal has a unique address. The central controller broadcasts each of these addresses in sequence over the common line. After broadcasting a terminal's address, the controller pauses for a message from the terminal. If a terminal has a message, the polling cycle is interrupted while the message is transmitted.

The ability to achieve economies by sharing transmission facilities is limited by performance requirements usually expressed in the delay experienced by a user in obtaining service. If there are too many terminals on the line, for example, the time required to cycle through all terminals is too large and user dissatisfaction ensues. The parameters of the mathematical models of performance are: the number of terminals, the volume of traffic generated by each terminal, the line speed in bits/s, and the line required by the polling protocol. As we shall see in connection with the analysis of polling models, a significant factor in performance is overhead, i.e., the time required to poll all terminals even when there are no messages. In the case of terminals equipped with voiceband modems, for example, this may involve equalizer training as well as the phase and timing recovery associated with the transmission of each polling message.

A close relative to roll-call polling is hub polling. In this case it is necessary that terminals communicate with one another as well as with the central processor. The controller begins a polling cycle by broadcasting the address of the most distant terminal, thereby granting to this terminal exclusive access to the line. After this terminal has transmitted any messages that it might have, it transmits an "end of message" symbol which acts to grant access to the next most distant terminal. Upon receiving this symbol, the next most distant terminal repeats the process, passing on access to the third most distant terminal when its messages have been transmitted. The process continues until all terminals have been given an opportunity to transmit messages whereupon the controller initiates a new cycle. This model contains the same parameters as roll-call polling. The salient difference between the two is the time required to grant access to a terminal. In roll-call polling, the time required to transmit a message and receive a reply is typically much longer than the time required to transmit a symbol from one terminal to another. However, hub polling requires that the line be such that terminals reliably receive transmissions from other terminals.

What was probably the first LAN was implemented in the ring topology with a form of hub polling as an access protocol [3]. In this case, control is distributed around the ring with only one terminal having access. Along with data messages, source and destination addresses are transmitted. The other terminals monitor transmission for messages addressed to them. As in the previous implementation of the hub-polling protocol, access is passed from a terminal to its nearest neighbor downstream. The passing of control is effected by appending an end of message character to the data from the controlling terminal. We have the same set of parameters as in the previous cases. The time required to pass access from one terminal to another is the time required to transmit the end of message character.

The hub-polling idea has recently been embodied in a technique called token passing [4]. As in the other polling systems, only one terminal has access to the line at any point in time. A terminal gives up access by transmitting a specific sequence of binary digits, the token. Terminals have a specified order in which they may gain access and the next terminal in the sequence seizes control of the line upon receipt of the token. In ring systems the logical order is position on the common line, however, the technique can also be implemented in systems employing other topologies. For example, in the bus topology depicted, terminals connected to a common medium can broadcast messages to one another. The token passing technique can be realized in this case by specifying in advance the order in which the token is passed.

Before going on to consider other local distribution techniques, we pause to consider the performance of polling systems as related to network parameters and to traffic. A useful measure of performance is the cycle time which is the time required to grant access to all terminals in the system at least once and to transmit messages from the terminals. We may view the cycle time as having two components, fixed and random. The overhead or fixed component is the time required to grant access to all terminals. In roll-call polling, for example, it is the time required to broadcast all of the terminal addresses and to listen for replies. In the hub-polling technique, overhead is the total time in a cycle that is required to pass access from one terminal to another.

The most studied model assumes Poisson arrival[2] at a terminal having storage facilities which may be regarded as being infinite, i.e., compared to the arrival rate of messages the terminal buffer is so large that the probability of overflow is negligible. Assuming that the arrival rates and message transmission times are the same for all terminals, it can be shown that T_c, the average duration of a cycle, is given by

$$T_c = W/(1 - S) \qquad (1)$$

where W is the total overhead in a cycle, $S = nm\lambda$, m is the average duration of a message, n is the number of terminals, and λ is the average arrival rate at each terminal. Equation (1) has a characteristic queueing theory form. The numerator represents overhead, the amount of time during a cycle for which a message is not being transmitted. All of the traffic dependency is contained in the quantity S in the denominator. This load S is the average work presented to the system normalized to the capacity of the channel. There is a point of instability when $S = 1$ since the average amount of work that is arriving is just equal to the capacity of the system and there is no allowance for overhead. We note that when $W = 0$, the average cycle time is zero. This is consistent if we consider that an infinite number of cycles occur in zero time when the terminals have no messages to transmit. Equation (1) indicates the effect of overhead on performance. Suppose, for example, that the total traffic load into the system is kept constant (i.e., S constant) while

---

[2] For an extensive and complete survey of the analysis of polling systems, see [5]. See also [6, ch. 7].

the number of terminals is doubled. If overhead is incurred on a per terminal basis, the cycle time is doubled with no increase in traffic.

A more tangible measure of performance for the user is message delay, which we define to be the time elapsing between the generation of a message and its transmission over the common line. This delay consists of several components. A message generated at a terminal must wait until it is the terminal's turn to be polled. If the terminal can store more than one message at a time, a queue is formed at each terminal which implies further delay. Finally, a certain amount of time is required simply to transmit the message. There have been a number of analyses of the performance of polling systems. In connection with cycle time, we considered the case of infinite buffers and Poisson message generation. Results on the average delay for this case with constant length messages are shown in Fig. 2 [7]. The average delay normalized to the time required to transmit a message is shown as a function of the total load into the system S. The parameters are n, the total number of terminals, and W/nm, the overhead per terminal normalized to the message transmission time. The curves show the characteristic rapid increase in delay as the load approaches one. A strong dependence on overhead is also evident. For loadings less than 0.5, which is the region

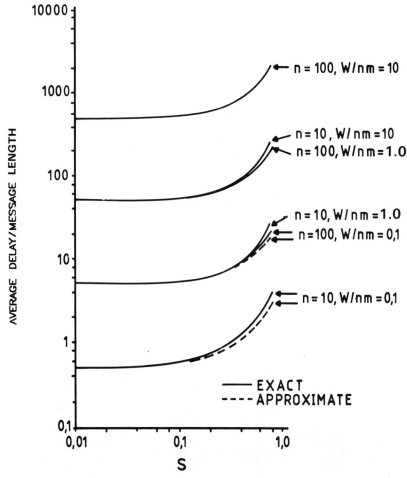

Fig. 2.   Delay infinite-buffer as a function of load.

where the system will be operated, overhead dominates. These points can be illustrated by an example. Suppose that ten terminals share a common 2400 bit/s line. Each terminal generates messages at an average rate of 288 messages per busy hour (0.08 messages/s). The messages are each 1200 bits long. Finally, assume that in order to poll each terminal and listen for a response, 50 ms are required. The load in the system is $S = 0.04$. From Fig. 2, the average delay is approximately 0.25 s. Now suppose that as a convenience to users the number of terminals sharing the line is doubled without increasing the load. We see from Fig. 2 that the average message delay doubles.

RING NETWORKS

The ring topology lends itself to particular accessing techniques which are appropriate to bursty sources.[3] The most obvious technique is a form of time division multiplexing which in this context is commonly called time division multiple access (TDMA). Assuming synchronous transmission, the flow on the line is partitioned into segments each of which is dedicated to a particular terminal. A terminal simply inserts messages into segments assigned to it. The shortcoming of this system in the case of many lightly loaded terminals is that very often terminals have nothing to send and segments are wasted. At the same time, empty segments may be passing by terminals which do have messages. The same drawback applies to frequency division multiple access (FDMA) in which each terminal is allocated a fixed bandwidth. We shall focus on TDMA since it has been shown that it is superior to FDMA in this context [9].

An alternate technique to TDMA in a ring network is demand assignment (DA) [10]. The flow is the same as in TDMA except that the blocks are not assigned to any terminal. When an empty block passes by a terminal which has a message to transmit, the block is seized by the terminal, and the message along with addressing information is inserted. There is an increase in the utilization of the line over TDMA at the cost of an increase in the complexity of the terminals. In Fig. 3, the average delay is shown as a function of the load with the number of terminals in the system as a parameter [11]. The results illustrate the inefficiency of TDMA for lightly loaded systems where the dominant factor is the time required to transmit a single message. At light loading, demand multiplexing is superior to TDMA by a factor equal to the number of terminals sharing the line. As the load increases, the difference between the two systems decreases, since in demand multiplexing, different terminals will tend to have messages at the same time. Once again, the lesson that we carry away from this study of ring systems is that in lightly loaded systems, a distributed control of access to the channel is more efficient.

RANDOM ACCESS (ALOHA)

The family of random access protocols is appropriate to media such as radio or coaxial cable where terminals may broadcast to one another [12], [13]. The origin of these methods is the ALOHA protocol which is the ultimate in distributed control. As soon as a terminal generates a message, it is transmitted on the common transmission medium. Along with the message, the terminal transmits address bits and parity check bits. If a message is correctly received by the central controller, a positive acknowledgment is returned to the terminal on the return channel. Since there is no coordination among the terminals, it may happen that

---

[3] For a survey of ring systems, see [8].

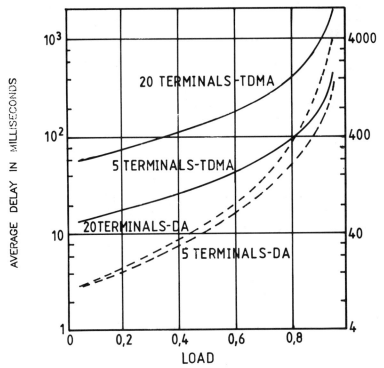

Fig. 3.   Average delay versus load in TDMA and DA [35].

messages from different terminals interfere with one another. If two or more messages collide, the resulting errors will be detected by the controller which returns a negative acknowledgment or no acknowledgment. An alternative implementation is to have the terminal itself detect collisions simply by listening to the channel. After a suitable timeout interval, a terminal involved in a collision retransmits the message. In order to avoid repeated collisions, the retransmission intervals are chosen randomly. The key element of the ALOHA protocol and its descendants is the retransmission traffic on the common line. If the rate of newly generated traffic is increased, the rate of conflicts among terminals increases to the point where retransmitted messages dominate and there is saturation. This effect is expressed succinctly in the formula

$$S = G \ \exp \ (-2G) \qquad\qquad (2)$$

where S is the normalized load into the system generated at all terminals and G is the total traffic on the line including all retransmissions. In the derivation of (2), it is assumed that all messages are the same length and that they are generated at a Poisson rate. The plot of (2) in Fig. 5 (see pure ALOHA) shows that the channel saturates at 18 percent of its capacity inasmuch as the input cannot be increased beyond this point. Thus, it appears that simplicity of control is achieved at the expense of channel capacity. We may view this as a form of implicit overhead.

The basic ALOHA technique can be improved by rudimentary coordination among the terminals [14]. Suppose that a sequence of synchronization pulses is broadcast to all terminals. Again, let us assume constant length messages or packets. A so-called slot or space between synch pulses is equal to the time required to transmit a message. Messages, either newly generated or retransmitted, can only be transmitted at a pulse time. This simple device reduces the rate of collisions by half since only messages generated in the same interval interfere with one another. In pure ALOHA, the "collision window" is two message intervals. The equation governing the behavior of slotted ALOHA is

$$S = G \exp(-G). \tag{3}$$

We see from the plot of (3) in Fig. 4 (see slotted ALOHA) that the channel saturates at approximately 36 percent of capacity.

For both pure and slotted ALOHA, we note that there are two values of total line flow for each value of input load. This is indicative of the basic instability of the protocol. In fact, it can be shown that if the number of terminals is increased while the load into the system remains constant, the line traffic is all retransmissions and the actual throughput is negligible [15], [16]. Instability can be avoided if the retransmission strategy is modified to take into account the number of backlogged terminals. It can be shown that, if the time between retransmissions in a slotted system is proportional to a reasonable estimate of the number of terminals with messages to transmit, the system is stable for input loads less than 36 percent of capacity [17].

An extension of the ALOHA technique that is particularly appropriate for local distribution is carrier sense multiple access (CSMA) [18]. Before transmitting a message, a terminal listens on the common channel for the carrier of another terminal which is in the process of transmitting. If the channel is free, the terminal transmits; if not, transmission is deferred. Variations on the basic technique involve the retransmission strategy. We illustrate retransmission strategies by means of the P-persistent CSMA strategy. If the channel is busy, then the terminal transmits at the end of the current transmission with probability P. With probability $1 - P$, transmission is delayed by τ seconds which is the maximum propagation time between any pair of terminals. Due to propagation delay, there

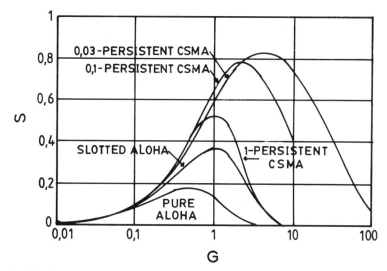

Fig. 4.   Input load as a function of channel traffic for several random access techniques [18].

may be more than one terminal transmitting at the same time, in which case messages are retransmitted after random timeout intervals. The value of P is chosen so as to balance the probability of retransmission with channel utilization. The characteristic equations for CSMA are plotted in Fig. 4. The form is similar to pure and slotted ALOHA. The ability to sense carrier from other terminals leads to considerable improvement in throughput. As indicated, decreasing P leads to improved throughput which is obtained at the expense of increased delay. The curves shown in Fig. 4 are for a propagation delay of 0.01 normalized to message transmission time. As this normalized delay is increased, the performance of CSMA degrades since the likelihood of terminals transmitting simultaneously increases.

There have been a number of analyses of random access protocols focusing on message delay as a function of throughput. In Fig. 5, we summarize the results of this work in the

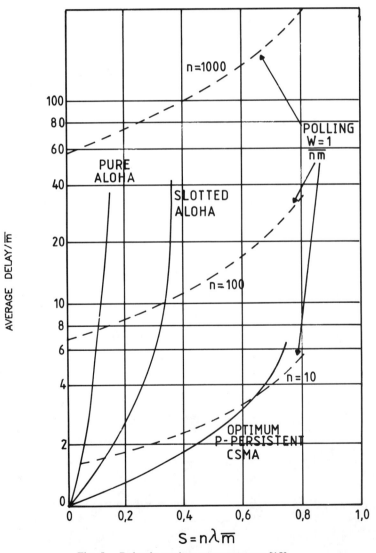

Fig. 5.   Delay in random access systems [18].

form of normalized message delay as a function of load. For lightly loaded systems, pure and slotted ALOHA perform well. However, as the load increases the increasing rate of retransmission rapidly degrades performance. Since the carrier sense protocol keeps the channel clear by avoiding retransmission, the degradation with increasing load is graceful. Also shown in Fig. 5 is delay for roll-call polling. As we have seen earlier, there is a severe penalty for overhead required when the number of terminals is increased. The curves also show that the performance of the polling protocol degrades more gracefully than that of the random access protocols. This is where the beneficial effect of the controller is seen. By scheduling transmission, the avalanche effect of retransmissions in the random access protocols is prevented.

Further improvement of the CSMA protocol is obtained by detecting collisions (CSMA/CD). As soon as a terminal detects a collision, it aborts its transmission and begins the collision resolution procedure. No time is lost on a transmission which must be repeated anyway. A form of the CSMA/CD approach is used in the Ethernet [19]. An analysis of the CSMA/CD protocol is given in [20].

A recent innovation for the carrier sense approach is virtual time CSMA [21]. The key to this protocol is that each terminal has two clocks, respectively, a virtue time clock and a real time clock. As its name implies, the real time clock runs continuously at the normal rate. The virtual time clock stops when the line is sensed busy and resumes running at a faster rate when sensed idle. A terminal may transmit a message when the virtual time clock catches up with the real time clock. The VTCSMA protocol ensures that messages are transmitted in their order of arrival. Messages collide only if they arrive within the propagation delay time of the system; in which event the usual collision resolution protocols are called into play. A second advantage of VTCSMA is that a station may be given priority over its fellows by allowing its virtual time clock to run at a faster rate.

ADAPTIVE TECHNIQUES

A great deal of recent activity has focused on adaptive techniques for resolving collisions.[4] In a sense we have come full circle inasmuch as the genesis of this approach may be seen in an improved polling protocol [23], [6]. As we have indicated earlier, the polling protocol is limited by overhead which increases linearly with the number of terminals in the system. This effect can be ameliorated if terminals are probed in groups instead of polling one at a time. In order to implement the technique, it is assumed that the central controller can broadcast to all terminals in a group simultaneously. If a member of a group of terminals being probed has a message to transmit, it responds in the affirmative by putting a noise signal on the common line. Upon receiving a positive response to a probe, the controller splits the group into two subgroups and probes each subgroup in turn. The process continues until individual terminals having messages are isolated whereupon messages are transmitted. The probing protocol is illustrated in Fig. 6 for a group of eight terminals of which terminal 6 has a message. The algorithm is essentially a tree search which the controller begins by asking, in effect, "Does anyone have a message?" Branches with affirmative responses are split into subbranches.

If only one terminal in a group of 2^k has a message, the probing process requires the controller to transmit at most $2k + 1$ inquiries rather than 2^k inquiries required by conventional polling. The comparison may not be so favorable when more than one

---

[4] For a survey of adaptive techniques, see [22].

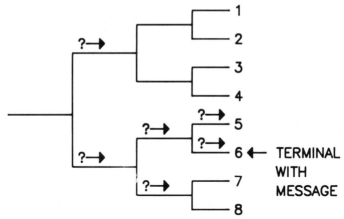

Fig. 6. Probing illustration.

terminal has a message. For example, if all terminals have messages, $2^{k+1} - 1$ inquiries are required for probing. This consideration leads to an adaptive tree search algorithm where the size of the initial group to be probed is chosen according to the probability of an individual terminal having a message. Thus, in Fig. 6, for example, one may begin a cycle by probing two groups of four rather than one group of eight. The criterion for choosing the sizes of the groups is the minimization of the time to transmit all of the messages in the system at the beginning of the cycle. It is assumed that messages that arrive during a cycle are held over until the next cycle. If the arrival of messages to terminals is Poisson, the probability of a terminal having a message can be calculated by the controller given the duration of the previous probing cycle.

The results of simulation for the adaptive technique are shown in Fig. 7 where the average time to probe all terminals in a 32 terminal network is shown as a function of message arrival rate. In Fig. 7, the cycle time and the message length are normalized to the amount of time required to make an inquiry. The comparison to conventional polling shows a considerable improvement in performance for light loading. Moreover, due to the adaptivity there is no penalty for heavy loading.

Although the probing concept was devised in connection with polling systems, it is also appropriate in a random access context [24]. Suppose that in response to a probe, a terminal transmits any messages that it might be harboring. Conflicts between terminals in the same group are detected by the controller and the group is divided in an effort to isolate individual terminals. Each subgroup is given access to the line in turn. Optimal initial group sizes can be chosen by means of very much the same criterion as in polling systems. Probing too large a group results in almost certain conflict. The opposite extreme gives too many probes of empty groups of terminals. Again, the optimum group size can be chosen adaptively as the process unfolds. The probability of a terminal having a message is a function of the previous cycle and the average message generation rate at a terminal. This probability determines optimum initial group size.

Control of the adaptive process need not be as centralized as in the foregoing [25], [26]. Suppose that as in slotted ALOHA, synchronizing pulses are broadcast to all terminals. Suppose further that the slots between synch pulses are subdivided into two equal subslots. In the tree search protocol, the first subslot is devoted to an upper branch and the second to a lower. Consider the example in Fig. 8(a) and (b) depicting an eight terminal system of

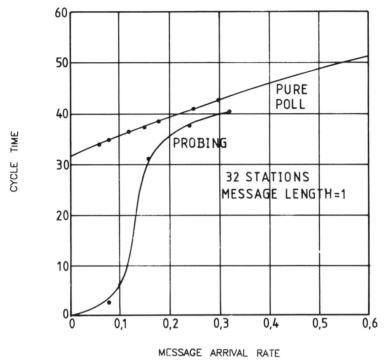

Fig. 7. Average cycle time versus message arrival probing technique [23].

which 5, 7, and 8 have messages. The first subslot is empty since it is dedicated to terminals 1–4. In the second subslot, terminals 5, 7, and 8 conflict. The conflict is resolved in subsequent slots. After this conflict resolution process has begun, any newly arrived messages are held over until the next cycle. Again, the algorithm can be made adaptive by adjusting the size of the initial groups to be given access to the channel according to the probability of a terminal having a message.

Upper and lower bounds on average delay as a function of the input load are shown in Fig. 9. Notice that the system saturates when the load is 43 percent of capacity, a figure which contrasts with 36 percent for slotted ALOHA. Moreover, there are no unstable states where the system is saturated by retransmissions and conflicts. If conflicts persist, each terminal is assigned an individual slot and the system reverts to TDMA. By eliminating redundant steps, the throughput can be increased to 46 percent of capacity.

A key idea in recent work on adaptive techniques was contained in much earlier work on group testing in which the problem is to find one or more defective members of a given population in a minimum number of steps.[5] Much of this earlier work bears a direct relationship to the polling model discussed above, in fact, the nested test plan algorithm of Sobel and Groll [28] can be applied directly. Again, we assume independent symmetric Poisson arrivals at each of the terminals and a gated strategy in conducting the search for terminals with messages. As in the tree search, the algorithm consists of probing groups of terminals. In carrying out this algorithm we distinguish three classes of subsets of terminals. Before a set is probed, the distribution of terminals with messages is binomial

[5] A summary of this work, together with applications to local distribution, is contained in [27].

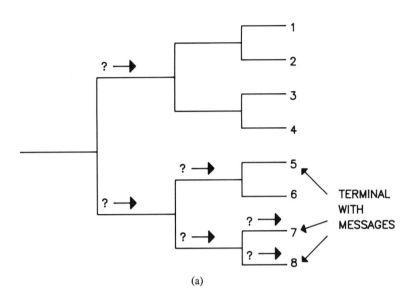

(a)

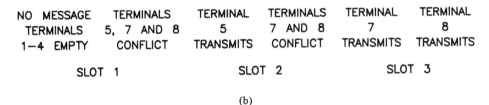

NO MESSAGE TERMINALS 1–4 EMPTY	TERMINALS 5, 7 AND 8 CONFLICT	TERMINAL 5 TRANSMITS	TERMINALS 7 AND 8 CONFLICT	TERMINAL 7 TRANSMITS	TERMINAL 8 TRANSMITS
SLOT 1		SLOT 2		SLOT 3	

(b)

Fig. 8.   (a) Tree search illustration. (b) Tree search illustration.

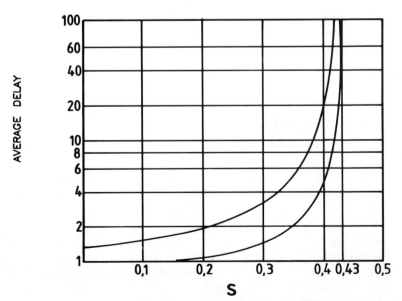

Fig. 9.   Average delay 1 versus load tree search [25].

which may be approximated by the Poisson distribution for a large number of terminals. If a probe is negative, i.e., no active terminals, the set is empty and can be eliminated from further consideration. A positive response to a probe yields the third class, sets with at least one active member. The nesting feature of the algorithm rests on the following observation. Let A be a set with at least one active terminal, suppose B a subset of A is probed with a positive response, then the subset $A - B$ has a binomial distribution of active terminals. In the course of the algorithm all binomially distributed sets are pooled to produce a single binomial set. Active sets are immediately split and probed so that there is only one of this class at any time. The algorithm consists of probing optimally chosen subsets of either active or binomial sets until active terminals are isolated. The initial condition is that all terminals belong to a binomial set.

It has been demonstrated that the application of optimal group testing yields improvement over the tree search algorithm in the polling context [29]. However, in contrast to the tree algorithm, practical implementation has not been considered. Which of the 2^N possible groups of N terminals are being probed must be conveyed to the terminals themselves in an efficient manner. Furthermore, the effect of transmission errors in the probe message or in the response has not been studied.

The same group testing ideas may be applied in the random access context [29]. In this case, the algorithm resolves conflicts among terminal transmitting messages simultaneously; algorithms which were developed independently of group testing but which embody the same basic principles in a distributed environment. In these algorithms, the key idea is that of pooling binomially distributed sets.

In the adaptive algorithms that we have considered thus far, messages may be considered to be segmented according to the terminal address. In the so-called Part and Try algorithm [30], messages are classified according to time of arrival. Again we may discern three sets: empty, active, and unknown (binomial). In this case the sets are segments of the time axis. The Part and Try algorithm is the current champion of the throughput sweepstakes, with a figure of 0.4878. The algorithm has the additional advantage of serving messages in the order of their arrival.

We may interpret the difference between the polling and the random access contexts as a difference between the amount of information that is fed back to the terminal. On the one hand we have "empty" and "not empty" and on the other "empty," "one message," and "collision." One can imagine situations where the amount of information fed back is augmented to include the number of terminals that are in conflict [31]. The salient result of studies of such systems [32] is that significant improvement can be gained by a relatively small increase in the feedback. For example, it is not necessary to know the total number in conflict but only if there are two or more than two.

In keeping with the information theoretic character of the work on adaptive techniques, the focus has been on the theoretical maximum throughput. Not a great deal of attention has been paid to the other important performance criterion, delay. Moreover, caution is necessary in interpreting the throughput results. For most of the models message arrival is assumed to be Poisson; consequently from basic by queueing theoretic considerations, the region near the boundary is one of instability where delay becomes unbounded. No such consideration applies to channel capacity in the information theoretic sense. Furthermore, delays due to propagation and processing have not been taken into account. Since the results are given for a large, indeed infinite number of terminals, this delay may have a serious effect on the theoretical maximum.

Related to random access multiplexing are a large number of reservation techniques in which sources, upon becoming active, reserve part of the channel. The reservation techniques are appropriate to sources which are active infrequently but transmit a steady stream while active. The traffic from such sources is not bursty. However, the request methods are and consequently may be treated by the techniques discussed in the foregoing. For example, reservations could be made using the ALOHA technique over a separate channel.

OPTICAL SYSTEMS

Optical fiber possesses a number of features that make it attractive as a transmission medium in local distribution. It has low transmission loss; a realizable standard is less than 4 dB/km. A second advantage of optical fiber is high bandwidth. Data rates over 20 Mbits/s seem to be easily attainable with LED's and multimode fiber. Much higher rates can be achieved with single-mode operation. In certain applications fiber also has the advantage of being immune to electromagnetic interference. Finally, optical fibers are small. A bundle of fibers with enormous capacity is about the same size as the standard coaxial cable with several orders of magnitude less capacity.

At the present state of development optical fiber has properties which heavily affect the topology for which it is appropriate. With current technology, fiber is inherently a point-to-point medium, since is is not possible to provide a large number of access points without unacceptable loss. This militates against the bus topology which requires a broadcast capability.

The ring and the star topologies have been used in optical-fiber systems.[6] The ring systems use the access protocols discussed above; for example, the protocol of [34] uses the demand assignment discussed above in the section on ring systems. Several systems with star topologies use a variation of the CSMA protocol; an example of such a system is Hubnet [35]. Terminals at the ends of the star transmit when they sense the line to be clear. The active hub rebroadcasts over all of the lines emanating from it. If a terminal sees its message on the line from the hub, it knows that it has been successful; otherwise, the message is retransmitted. In effect, the system is a bus of zero length.

REFERENCES

[1] P. Jackson and C. Stubbs, "A study of multiaccess computer communications," in *Proc. AFIPS Conf.,* vol. 34, p. 491.

[2] E. Fuchs and P. E. Jackson, "Estimates of distributions of random variables for certain computer communications traffic models," *CACM,* vol. 13, no. 12, pp. 752–757, 1970.

[3] W. D. Farmer and E. E. Newhall, "An experimental distributed switching system to handle bursty computer traffic," in *Proc. ACM Symp. Problems Optimiz. Data Commun. Syst.,* Pine Mountain, GA, Oct. 1969, pp. 1–34.

[4] W. Bux *et al.* "A reliable token system for local-area communications," presented at the National Telecommunications Conf., New Orleans, LA, Dec. 1981, A2.2.1–2.2.6.

[5] H. Takagi, *Analysis of Polling Systems.* Cambridge, MA: M.I.T. Press, 1986.

[6] J. F. Hayes, *Modeling and Analysis of Computer Communications Networks.* New York: Plenum, 1984.

[7] O. Hashida, "Analysis of multiqueue," *Rev. Elect. Commun. Lab.,* vol. 20, pp. 189–199, Mar. and Apr. 1972.

[8] B. K. Penney and A. A. Baghdadi, "Survey of computer communications loop network," *Comput. Commun.: Part 1,* vol. 2, no. 4, pp. 165–180; and *Part 2,* vol. 2, no. 5, pp. 224–241.

---

[6] In order to exploit the capabilities of the optical fiber medium, several new topologies have been proposed. We consider these to be beyond the scope of our chapter. The state of the art in optical fiber LAN's is given in [33].

[9] I. Rubin, "Message delays in FDMA and TDMA communications channels," *IEEE Trans. Commun.*, vol. COM-27, pp. 769–777, May 1979.

[10] J. R. Pierce, "A network for the block switching of data," *Bell Syst. Tech. J.*, vol. 51, pp. 1133–1145, July/Aug. 1972.

[11] J. F. Hayes, "Performance models of an experimental computer communications network," *Bell Syst. Tech. J.*, vol. 53, pp. 225–259, Feb. 1974.

[12] N. Abramson, "The ALOHA system—Another alternative for computer communications," in *Proc. 1970 Fall Joint Comput. Conf. AFIPS Conf.*, vol. 37, pp. 281–285.

[13] ——, "The ALOHA system," *Comput. Commun. Networks*, N. Abramson and F. Kuo, Eds. Englewood Cliffs, NJ: Prentice-Hall.

[14] L. G. Roberts, "ALOHA packet system with and without slots and capture," *Comput. Commun. Rev.*, vol. 5, pp. 28–42, Apr. 1975.

[15] A. B. Carleial and M. E. Hellman, "Bistable behavior of ALOHA-type systems," *IEEE Trans. Commun.*, vol. COM-23, pp. 401–410, Apr. 1975.

[16] S. S. Lam and L. Kleinrock, "Packet switching in a multiaccess broadcast channel: Performance evaluation," *IEEE Trans. Commun.*, vol. COM-23, pp. 410–423, Apr. 1975.

[17] B. Hajak, "Stochastic approximation methods for decentralized control of multiaccess communications," *IEEE Trans. Inform. Theory*, vol. IT-31, pp. 176–184, Mar. 1986.

[18] F. A. Tobagi and K. Kleinrock, "Packet switching in radio channels—Part I: Carrier sense multiple access modes and their throughput delay characteristics," *IEEE Trans. Commun.*, vol. COM-23, pp. 1400–1416, Dec. 1975; "Part III: Polling and (dynamic) split channel reservation multiple access," *IEEE Trans. Commun.*, vol. COM-24, pp. 832–845, Aug. 1976.

[19] R. M. Metcalfe and D. R. Boggs, "Ethernet: Distributed packet switching for local computer networks," *Commun. Ass. Comput. Mach.*, vol. 19, pp. 395–404, July 1976.

[20] F. A. Tobagi and V. B. Hunt, "Performance analysis of carrier sense multiple access with collision detection," *Comput. Networks*, vol. 4, pp. 245–259, Nov. 1980; see also this volume, ch. 20.

[21] M. Molle and L. Kleinrock, "Virtual time CSMA; Why two clocks are better than one," *IEEE Trans. Commun.*, vol. COM-33, Feb. 1985.

[22] R. G. Gallager, "A perspective of multiaccess channels," *IEEE Trans. Inform. Theory*, vol. IT-31, pp. 124–143, Mar. 1986.

[23] J. F. Hayes, "An adaptive technique for local distribution," *IEEE Trans. Commun.*, vol. COM-26, pp. 1178–1186, Aug. 1978.

[24] A. Grami, J. F. Hayes, and K. Sohraby, "Further results on probing," in *Proc. ICC '82*, Philadelphia, PA, June 1982.

[25] J. Capetanakis, "Tree algorithms for packet broadcast channels," *IEEE Trans. Inform. Theory*, vol. IT-25, pp. 505–515, Sept. 1979.

[26] B. S. Tsybakov and V. A. Mikailov, "Free synchronous access in a broadcast channel with feedback," *Problemy Peredachi Informaatsii*, vol. 14, pp. 32–59, Oct. 1978.

[27] J. K. Wolf, "Born again group testing: Multiaccess communications," *IEEE Trans. Inform. Theory*, vol. IT-31, pp. 185–192, Mar. 1986.

[28] M. Sobel and P. A. Groll, "Group testing to eliminate all defectives in a binomial sample," *Bell Syst. Tech. J.*, vol. 38, pp. 1178–1252, Sept. 1959.

[29] T. Berger *et al.*, "Random multiple access communication and group testing," *IEEE Trans. Commun.*, vol. COM-32, July 1984.

[30] R. G. Gallager, "Conflict resolution in random access broadcast networks," in *Proc. AFOSR Workshop Commun. Theory and Appl.*, Provincetown, MA, Sept. 1978, pp. 74–76.

[31] L. Kleinrock and Y. Yemini, "An optimal adaptive scheme for multiple access broadcast communication," presented at the ICC '78, Toronto, Ontario, Canada, June 1978.

[32] L. Geogiadis and T. Papantoni-Kazakos, "A collision resolution protocol for random access channels with energy detectors," *IEEE Trans. Commun.*, vol. COM-30, pp. 2413–2420, Nov. 1982.

[33] Special Issue on Fiber Optics for Local Communications, *IEEE J. Select. Areas Commun.*, vol. SAC-3, Nov. 1985.

[34] D. T. W. Sze, "A metropolitan area network," Special Issue on Fiber Optics for Local Communications, *IEEE J. Select. Areas Commun.*, vol. SAC-3, pp. 815–825, Nov. 1985.

[35] S. Lee and P. P. Boulton, "The principles and performance of Hubnet: A 50 Mbps glass fiber local area network," Special Issue on Local Area Networks, *IEEE J. Selected Areas Commun.*, vol. SAC-1, pp. 711–721, Nov. 1983.

20

Performance Analysis of Carrier Sense Multiple Access with Collision Detection

FOUAD A. TOBAGI AND V. BRUCE HUNT

   Among the various random access schemes known, carrier sense multiple access (CSMA) has been shown to be highly efficient for environments with relatively short propagation delay. In local area networks, the possibility of detecting collisions on the medium enhances the performance of CSMA by aborting conflicting transmissions, thus giving rise to the carrier sense multiple access schemes with collision detection (CSMA/CD). In this chapter we extend an analysis of CSMA to accommodate collision detection. The analysis provides the capacity as well as the throughput-delay performance of CSMA/CD and its dependence on such key system parameters as the average retransmission delay and the collision recovery time. The case of traffic with variable packet lengths is also considered.

I. INTRODUCTION

Given that computer communication traffic is bursty in nature, it has been well established that it is more efficient to provide the available communication bandwidth as a single high-speed channel to be shared by the many contending users, thus attaining the benefits of the strong law of large numbers. This results in a multiaccess environment that calls for schemes to control access to the channel referred to as random access schemes. The earliest and simplest such scheme is the so-called pure-ALOHA, first used in the ALOHA-system [1]; unfortunately, pure-ALOHA provides a maximum channel utilization which does not exceed 18 percent. Another such scheme, carrier sense multiple access (CSMA), has been shown to be highly efficient in environments with propagation delays which are short compared to the packet transmission time [2]. In essence, CSMA reduces the level of interference caused by overlapping packets in the random multiaccess channel by allowing devices to sense carrier due to other users' transmissions, and inhibit transmission when the channel is in use. Packets which are inhibited or suffer a collision are rescheduled for transmission at a later time according to some rescheduling policy.

Ethernet is a local communication network which uses CSMA on a tapped coaxial cable to which all the communicating devices are connected [3]. Given the physical characteristics of data transmission on the medium, in addition to sensing carrier, it is possible for Ethernet transceivers to detect interference among several transmissions (including their own) and abort transmission of their colliding packets. This produces a variation of CSMA which we refer to as carrier sense multiple access with collision detection (CSMA/CD).

CSMA in fully connected environments has been previously analyzed and its performance derived [2], [4]. We extend here the analysis of CSMA to accommodate collision detection. This analysis provides the throughput-delay performance of CSMA/CD and its dependence on such key system parameters as the average rescheduling delay and collision recovery time. We furthermore characterize the improvement gained by CSMA/CD over CSMA for fixed and variable size packets.

The CSMA/CD schemes are described in Section II, followed by the analysis in Section III. Numerical results are discussed in Section IV.

II. THE CSMA/CD SCHEMES

Carrier sense schemes require that each device with a packet ready for transmission senses the channel prior to transmission. A number of protocols exist which pertain to the action taken by the terminal after observing the state of the channel. In particular, a terminal never transmits when it senses that the channel is busy. Kleinrock and Tobagi described two such protocols in the context of ground radio channels [2]. They are the nonpersistent CSMA and the p-persistent CSMA protocols. These protocols are extended here to environments in which the collision detection capability is available.

In the nonpersistent CSMA/CD scheme, a terminal with a packet ready for transmission senses the channel and proceeds as follows.

1) If the channel is sensed idle, the terminal initiates transmission of the packet.

2) If the channel is sensed busy, then the terminal schedules the retransmission of the packet to some later time and repeats the algorithm.

3) If a collision is detected during transmission, the transmission is aborted and the packet is scheduled for retransmission at some later time. The terminal then repeats the algorithm.

In the 1-persistent CSMA/CD protocol (a special case of p-persistent CSMA), a terminal which finds the channel busy persists on transmitting as soon as the channel becomes free. Thus, a ready terminal senses the channel and proceeds as in nonpersistent CSMA/CD, except that, when the channel is sensed busy, it monitors the channel until it is sensed idle and then with probability one initiates transmission of the packet.

The p-persistent protocol is an enhancement of the 1-persistent protocol by allowing ready terminals to randomize the start of transmission following the instant at which the channel goes idle. Thus, a ready terminal senses the channel and proceeds as in the above schemes except that when the channel is sensed busy, the terminal persists until the channel is idle, and

i) with probability p it initiates transmission of the packet

ii) with probability $1 - p$ it delays transmission by τ seconds (the end-to-end propagation delay); if, at this new point in time, the channel is sensed idle, then the terminal repeats this process [steps i) and ii)], otherwise, it schedules retransmission of the packet to some later time.

Note that the p-persistent and nonpersistent protocols become identical if the rescheduling delays are chosen for both protocols as an integer number of τ delay units geometrically distributed, with parameter p (the parameter in the p-persistent protocol).

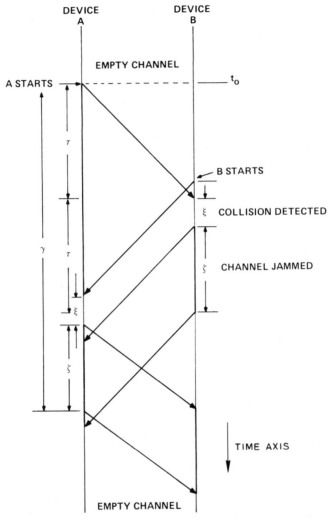

Fig. 1.   Collision detection and recovery time in CSMA/CD.

This follows because of the memoryless property of the geometric distribution. In this chapter we analyze only the nonpersistent and 1-persistent protocols.

In all CSMA/CD protocols, given that a transmission is initiated on an *empty* channel, it is clear that it takes at most one end-to-end propagation delay, τ, for the packet transmission to reach all devices, as depicted in Fig. 1; beyond this time the channel is guaranteed to be sensed busy for as long as data transmission is in process. [1] A collision can occur only if another transmission is initiated before the current one is sensed, and it will then take, at most, one additional end-to-end delay before interference reaches all devices. (See Fig. 1.) Let ξ denote the time it takes a device to detect interference once the latter has reached it. ξ depends on the implementation and can be as small as 1 bit transmission time, as is the case with Ethernet [3]. Furthermore, Ethernet has a collision consensus reenforcement mechanism by which a device, experiencing interference, jams the channel

---

[1] We assume that the sensing operation is instantaneous on this (high-bandwidth) channel.

to ensure that all other interfering devices detect the collision. We denote by ζ the period used for collision consensus reenforcement. Given that a collision occurs, the time until all devices stop transmission, γ, is thus given by[2]

$$\gamma = 2\tau + \xi + \zeta.$$

The time until the channel is again sensed idle by all devices is clearly $\gamma + \tau$.

III. ANALYSIS

We assume that the time axis is slotted where the slot size is the end-to-end propagation delay. For simplicity in analysis, we consider all devices to be synchronized and forced to start packet transmission only at the beginning of a slot. When a device becomes ready in some slot, it senses the channel during the slot and then operates according to the CSMA/ CD protocols described above.

A. Analysis of CSMA/CD with Fixed Size Packets

1) Channel Capacity: As in previous analysis of random access schemes, channel capacity is obtained by considering an infinite population model which assumes that all devices collectively form an independent Poisson source, and that the average retransmission delay is arbitrarily large [2].

Consider first the nonpersistent CSMA/CD protocol. We observe on the time axis an alternate sequence of transmission periods (successful or unsuccessful) and idle periods. A transmission period followed by an idle period is called a cycle (see Fig. 2). With the infinite population assumption, all cycles are statistically identical. Let g denote the rate of devices becoming ready during a slot. Let T denote the transmission time (in slots) of a packet. A successful transmission period is of length $T + 1$ slots. In case of a collision, the length of a transmission period is $\gamma + 1$ slots. Given that the source is Poisson, the probability that a transmission is successful is $P_s = ge^{-g}/(1 - e^{-g})$; the average idle period is $\bar{I} = 1/(1 - e^{-g})$; the average transmission period is $\overline{TP} = P_s T + (1 - P_s)\gamma + 1$; and the throughput is given by

$$S = \frac{P_s T}{\overline{TP} + \bar{I}}$$

$$= \frac{Tge^{-g}}{Tge^{-g} + (1 - e^{-g} - ge^{-g})\gamma + 2 - e^{-g}}. \tag{1}$$

The channel capacity is obtained by maximizing S with respect to g.

Ignoring ξ and ζ, we see that (1) can be rewritten as

$$S = \frac{1}{1 + H(g)a}$$

---

[2] This assumes that all interfering devices undertake the collision consensus reenforcement.

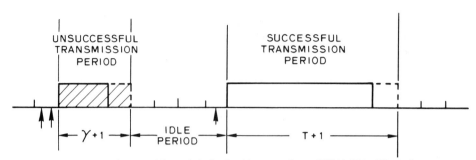

Fig. 2. Transmission and idle periods in slotted nonpersistent CSMA/CD. (Vertical arrows represent users becoming ready to transmit.)

where

$$H(g) = \frac{4e^g - 3}{g} - 2$$

and where $a \equiv 1/T$ represents the ratio of propagation delay to packet transmission time. Note that this result is valid only as long as $T \geqslant 2$; in order to always be in a position to perform the collision detection function even when $T < 2$, Ethernet specifies a minimum packet transmission time equal to 2, whether the entire packet carries useful information or not. Accordingly, for $T < 2$, the channel utilization is calculated as the fraction of time useful information is transmitted, and is given by $S/2a$. The channel capacity for the infinite population case is then given by the following simple expressions:

$$C(\infty, a) = \begin{cases} \dfrac{1}{1 + Ha} & a \leqslant 0.5 \\[2ex] \dfrac{1}{(2+H)a} & a > 0.5 \end{cases}$$

where H is a constant given by $\min_g\{H(g)\}$.

Consider now the 1-persistent CSMA/CD protocol. We observe on the time axis an alternate sequence of busy and idle periods, whereby a busy period is any collection of juxtaposed transmission periods surrounded by idle periods. A busy period followed by an idle period constitutes a cycle (see Fig. 3). Again, all cycles are statistically identical. Let B denote the average duration of a busy period, $\bar{I}$ the average duration of an idle period, and $\bar{U}$ the average time during a cycle that the channel is carrying successful transmissions. The throughput is given by $S = \bar{U}/(\bar{B} + \bar{I})$. In this infinite population model, the success or failure of a transmission period in the busy period is only dependent on the preceding transmission period (and thus, its length), except for the first transmission period of the busy period, which depends on arrivals in the preceding slot. Accordingly, given that a transmission period in the busy period is of length X ($X = T + 1$ or $\gamma + 1$), the length of the remainder of the busy period is a function of X, and we let $B(X)$ denote its average. In the same manner we define $U(X)$. Let $q_i(X)$ be the probability that there are i arrivals in X slots. Under the Poisson assumption, $q_i(X) = (gX)^i e^{-gX}/i!$. $B(X)$ is given by

$$B(X) = \frac{q_1(X)}{1 - q_0(X)} [T + 1 + (1 - q_0(T+1))B(T+1)] + \left[1 - \frac{q_1(X)}{1 - q_0(X)}\right]$$

$$\times [\gamma + 1 + (1 - q_0(\gamma + 1))B(\gamma + 1)]. \quad (2)$$

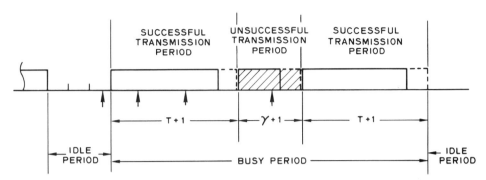

Fig. 3. Busy and idle periods in slotted 1-persistent CSMA/CD. (Vertical arrows represent users becoming ready to transmit.)

Writing (2) with $X = T + 1$ and $X = \gamma + 1$, we obtain two equations in the two unknowns, $B(T + 1)$ and $B(\gamma + 1)$. The average busy period $\bar{B}$ is then given by $B(1)$, expressed in terms of $B(T + 1)$ and $B(\gamma + 1)$.

Similarly, $U(X)$ is given by

$$U(X) = \frac{q_1(X)}{1 - q_0(X)} \left[T + (1 - q_0(T+1)) U(T+1) \right]$$

$$+ \left[1 - \frac{q_1(X)}{1 - q_0(X)} \right] \left[(1 - q_0(\gamma+1)) U(\gamma+1) \right]. \quad (3)$$

By taking $X = T + 1$ and $X = \gamma + 1$, we obtain two equations in the two unknowns $U(T + 1)$ and $U(\gamma + 1)$. As above, $\bar{U} = U(1)$ given in terms of $U(T + 1)$ and $U(\gamma + 1)$. $\bar{I}$ is simply equal to $1/(1 - e^{-g})$. Note that when $\gamma = T$, the expression for the throughput of 1-persistent CSMA/CD reduces to that of 1-persistent CSMA as given in [2].

2) Delay Analysis: We consider here the nonpersistent protocol. To analyze packet delay, we adopt the same "*linear feedback model*" used for the analysis of CSMA in [4]. The model consists of a finite population of M devices in which each device can be in one of two states: backlogged or thinking. In the thinking state, a device generates and transmits (provided that the channel is sensed idle) a new packet in a slot with probability σ. A device is said to be backlogged if its packet either had a channel collision or was blocked because of a busy channel. A backlogged device remains in that state until it completes successful transmission of the packet, at which time it switches to the thinking state. The rescheduling delay of a backlogged packet is assumed to be geometrically distributed with a mean of $1/\nu$ slots; this in effect is identical to considering that each backlogged user senses the channel in the current slot with a probability ν.

In this study, we assume M, σ, and ν to be time invariant. We consider τ (the slot size) to be the unit of time. We again denote by S the average stationary channel throughput defined as the fraction of channel time occupied by valid transmissions. We denote by C the channel capacity defined as the maximum achievable channel throughput. We finally denote by D the average packet delay defined as the time lapse from when the packet is first generated until it is successfully received by the destination device.

Let N^t be a random variable representing the number of backlogged devices at the beginning of slot t. We follow the approach used in [4], and consider the embedded Markov chain identified by the first slot of each idle period (see Fig. 4). We then use

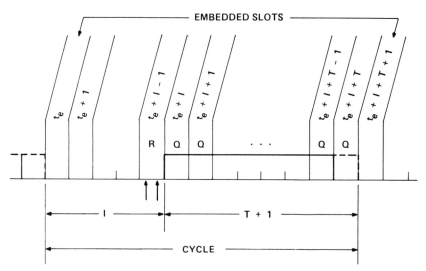

Fig. 4.   The embedded slots in nonpersistent CSMA schemes.

properties resulting from the theory of regenerative processes to derive the stationary channel performance under CSMA/CD, as outlined in [4].

We seek the transition probability matrix P between consecutive embedded points. P is the product of several single-slot transition matrices which we now define. N^t is invariant over the entire idle period except over slot $t_e + I - 1$. We denote by R the transition matrix for slot $t_e + I - 1$ and Q for all remaining slots of the busy period. Since the length of the busy period depends on the number of devices which become ready in slot $t_e + I - 1$, we write R as $R = S + F$, where the (i, k)th elements of S and F are defined as

$$s_{ik} = \mathrm{Pr}\ \{N^{t_e+I} = k \text{ and transmission is successful } |N^{t_e+I-1} = i\}, \tag{4}$$

$$f_{ik} = \mathrm{Pr}\ \{N^{t_e+I} = k \text{ and transmission is unsuccessful } |N^{t_e+I-1} = i\}. \tag{5}$$

For any slot t in the busy period, Q simply reflects the addition to the backlog from the $M - N^t$ thinking devices. If the transmission is successful, the transmission period has length $T + 1$; if it is unsuccessful, its length is $\gamma + 1$. The transition matrix P is therefore expressed as

$$P = SQ^{T+1}J + FQ^{\gamma+1} \tag{6}$$

where S, F, and Q are given by

$$s_{ik} = \begin{cases} 0, & k < i \\[2ex] \dfrac{(1-\sigma)^{M-i}[i\nu(1-\nu)^{i-1}]}{1-(1-\nu)^i(1-\sigma)^{M-i}}, & k = i \\[3ex] \dfrac{(M-i)\sigma(1-\sigma)^{M-i-1}[1-\nu]^i}{1-(1-\nu)^i(1-\sigma)^{M-i}}, & k = i+1 \\[3ex] 0, & k > i+1 \end{cases} \tag{7}$$

$$f_{ik} = \begin{cases} 0, & k < i \\[2mm] \dfrac{(1-\sigma)^{M-i}[1-(1-\nu)^i - i\nu(1-\nu)^{i-1}]}{1-(1-\nu)^i(1-\sigma)^{M-i}}, & k = i \\[4mm] \dfrac{(M-i)\sigma(1-\sigma)^{M-i-1}[1-(1-\nu)^i]}{1-(1-\nu)^i(1-\sigma)^{M-i}}, & k = i+1 \\[4mm] \dfrac{\dbinom{M-i}{k-i}(1-\sigma)^{M-k}\sigma^{k-i}}{1-(1-\nu)^i(1-\sigma)^{M-i}}, & k > i+1 \end{cases} \tag{8}$$

$$q_{ik} = \begin{cases} 0, & k < i \\[2mm] \dbinom{M-i}{k-i}(1-\sigma)^{M-k}\sigma^{k-i}, & k \geqslant i \end{cases} \tag{9}$$

and where J represents the fact that a successful transmission decreases the backlog by 1, its (i, k)th elements being defined as

$$j_{ik} = \begin{cases} 1, & k = i-1 \\ 0, & \text{otherwise.} \end{cases} \tag{10}$$

It is clear that with $\gamma = T$, the above expression for P then corresponds to CSMA without CD. Let $\Pi = [\pi_0, \pi_1, \cdots, \pi_M]$ denote the stationary probability distribution of N^t at the embedded points. Π is obtained by the recursive solution of $\Pi = \Pi P$.

Since N^{te} is a regenerative process, the average stationary channel throughput is computed as the ratio of time the channel is carrying successful transmission during a cycle (an idle period followed by a busy period) averaged over all cycles, to the average cycle length [4]. Therefore, we have

$$S = \frac{\displaystyle\sum_{i=0}^{M} \pi_i P_s(i) T}{\displaystyle\sum_{i=0}^{M} \pi_i \left\{ \dfrac{1}{1-\delta_i} + 1 + P_s(i)T + [1 - P_s(i)]\gamma \right\}}. \tag{11}$$

$P_s(i)$ is the probability of a successful transmission during a cycle with $N^{te} = i$, and is given by

$$P_s(i) = ((M-i)\sigma(1-\sigma)^{M-i-1}(1-\nu)^i + i\nu(1-\nu)^{i-1}(1-\sigma)^{M-i})/(1-(1-\nu)^i(1-\sigma)^{M-i}) \tag{12}$$

$(1 - \delta_i)^{-1}$, where $\delta_i = (1 - \nu)^i(1 - \sigma)^{M-i}$, is the average idle period given $N^{te} = i$.

Similarly, the average channel backlog is computed as the ratio of the expected sum of backlogs over all slots in a cycle (averaged over all cycles), to the average cycle length [4].

Therefore, we have

$$\bar{N}=\frac{\displaystyle\sum_{i=0}^{M} \pi_i \left[\frac{i}{1-\delta_i}+A(i)\right]}{\displaystyle\sum_{i=0}^{M} \pi_i \left\{\frac{1}{1-\delta_i}+1+P_s(i)T+[1-P_s(i)]\gamma\right\}} \tag{13}$$

where $A(i)$ is the expected sum of backlogs over all slots in the busy period with $N^{l_e} = i$, and is given by[3]

$$A(i)=\sum_{l=0}^{T} \sum_{j=i}^{M} j[SQ^l]_{ij}+\sum_{l=0}^{\gamma} \sum_{j=i}^{M} j[FQ^l]_{ij}$$

$$=\sum_{j=i}^{M} j \left[S\sum_{l=0}^{T} Q^l+F\sum_{l=0}^{\gamma} Q^l\right]_{ij}. \tag{14}$$

By Little's result [5], the average packet delay (normalized to T) is simply expressed as

$$D=\bar{N}/S. \tag{15}$$

The expressions obtained for throughput and delay become particularly simple when the condition of heavy traffic is considered, i.e., when $\sigma = 1$. In this case, $\pi_M = 1$, $\bar{N} = M$, and the throughput is given by

$$S=\begin{cases} \dfrac{1}{1+F(M, \nu)a} & a \leqslant 0.5 \\[3ex] \dfrac{1}{[2+F(M, \nu)]a} & a>0.5 \end{cases}$$

where

$$F(M, \nu)=\frac{4-3(1-\nu)^M}{M\nu(1-\nu)^{M-1}}-2.$$

To obtain the system capacity, $F(M, \nu)$ is minimized with respect to ν; ν must then satisfy

$$4(M\nu-1)+3(1-\nu)^M=0.$$

B. Analysis of CSMA/CD with Variable Size Packets

T is now a discrete random variable. Let

$$G_T(z) \triangleq \sum_{t=1}^{\infty} z^t \Pr \{T=t\} \tag{16}$$

---

[3] For an arbitrary matrix $\underline{B}$, we adopt the notation $[\underline{B}]_{ij}$ to represent the (i, j)th element of $\underline{B}$.

be the generating function of the distribution of T. In case of collision, regardless of the number of colliding packets and their lengths, the length of the busy period is $\gamma + 1$. In case of success, the length of the busy period is now random and has the same distribution as $T + 1$. The reason this is true, despite the fact that the length of a packet remains constant during its entire lifetime, is simply explained by the fact that the successful or unsuccessful outcome of a transmission period is solely dependent on the number of devices becoming ready at the beginning of that transmission period, and is independent of the lengths of the contending packets. Since the length of the busy period in case of a collision is constant (equal to $\gamma + 1$), the evolution of the channel over time is statistically identical to that in which the length of a packet is drawn from the packet length distribution only when its transmission is successful.

In the case of CSMA *without* collision detection, however, the collision period is a function of the lengths of the contending packets. Accordingly, the backlog at an embedded point is a function of not only the backlog at the previous embedded point but also on the length of packets in the backlog. Conversely, the packet length distribution for those packets in the backlog is correlated with the number of such packets. In order to compare the performance of CSMA/CD to that of CSMA in the presence of variable size packets, the authors considered in [8] an approximate analysis based on removing this correlation by continually redrawing the lengths of packets independently from the packet length distribution.[4]

The performance of nonpersistent CSMA/CD can thus be obtained from the previous analysis with the following simple modifications. The matrix P is now rewritten as

$$P = SG_T(Q)QJ + FQ^{\gamma+1} \tag{17}$$

and T is replaced by

$$\bar{T} \triangleq \sum_t t \ \text{Pr} \ \{T = t\} \tag{18}$$

the average packet size, in all of (1), (11), (13), and (14). In this case, the average packet delay given by (15) is normalized with respect to $\bar{T}$. For the same reason stated above, the average channel acquisition time (i.e., the time from when a packet is generated until it starts its successful transmission), denoted by W (in slots), is given by

$$W = D\bar{T} - \bar{T}. \tag{19}$$

Accordingly, the delay incurred by packets of length t is expressed as

$$D_t = W + t \ \text{(in slots)}. \tag{20}$$

It is interesting to note that for any throughput S, the difference in the delay incurred by packets of two different sizes is just the difference in transmission time of these packets. Smaller packets incur a smaller delay. The throughput contributed by packets of size t,

---

[4] This assumption was made by Ferguson in the analysis of pure-ALOHA which exhibits a similar correlation; the validity of the assumption in the context of pure-ALOHA was verified by simulation [8].

denoted by S_t, is expressed as

$$S_t = \frac{t \Pr \{T = t\} S}{\bar{T}} .$$

(21)

IV. Numerical Results and Discussion

A. Fixed Packet Size

The behavior of CSMA/CD for fixed γ is, as expected, similar to that of CSMA [4]; that is, its throughput-delay performance is sensitive to ν, and therefore to the average retransmission delay. Figures 5 and 6 display the throughput-delay curves for nonpersistent CSMA and CSMA/CD, respectively, with $M = 50$, $T = 100$, $\gamma = 2$, and various values of ν. For a fixed value of ν, the channel exhibits a maximum achievable throughput which

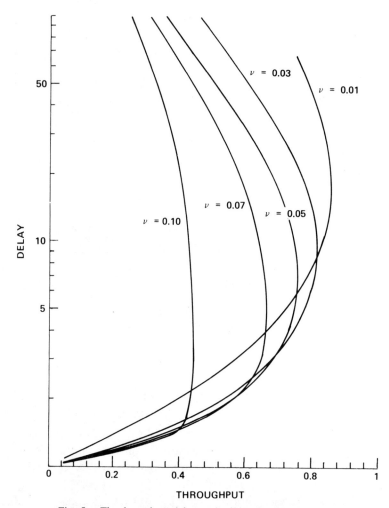

Fig. 5.   The throughput-delay tradeoff in CSMA at fixed ν.

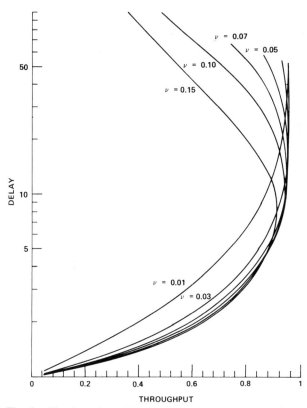

Fig. 6.   The throughput-delay tradeoff in CSMA/CD at fixed ν.

depends on that value, hereafter referred to as the ν-capacity. We observe that, for a given ν, CSMA/CD always achieves, again as expected, lower delay for a given throughput and a higher ν-capacity.[5] The optimum throughput-delay performance is obtained by taking the lower envelope of all fixed-ν curves. Overall, CSMA-CD provides an improvement both in terms of channel capacity and throughput-delay characteristics.

We discuss now the sensitivity of this improvement to the collision detect time γ and the packet length T. Just as with CSMA, the larger T is, the better is the CSMA/CD performance for fixed γ. In Fig. 7, we plot the channel capacity for the nonpersistent CSMA/CD versus γ for various packet lengths. The capacity at $\gamma = T$ is that of CSMA. The relative improvement in channel capacity obtained by CSMA/CD becomes more important as T decreases, that is, as the performance of CSMA degrades. We note for example that at best (i.e., when $\gamma = 2$) this relative improvement is about 16 percent (0.62 to 0.76) for $T = 10$ and about 11 percent (0.86 to 0.96) for $T = 100$. Clearly, for larger T ($T \geqslant 100$), nonpersistent CSMA provides relatively high channel capacity, and thus leaves little margin for improvement. With the 1-persistent protocol, however, the improvement can be more substantial. Channel capacity increases from about 0.53 for 1-persistent CSMA to about 0.93 for 1-persistent CSMA/CD with $\gamma = 2$.

---

[5] Note that for all values of ν used in plotting Figs. 5 and 6, the ν-capacity with CSMA/CD approached the channel capacity (maximized over ν); there are values of ν higher than $\nu = 0.15$) for which the ν-capacity is much lower than the CSMA/CD channel capacity similar to what is seen in Fig. 5 for CSMA and $\nu = 0.10$.

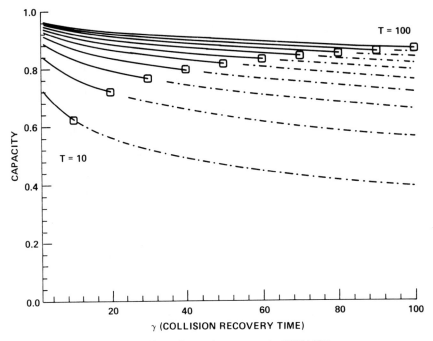

Fig. 7.   Channel capacity versus γ in CSMA/CD.

The effect of CD on the minimum delay (optimized with respect to ν) for a fixed channel throughput is seen in Fig. 8, where we plot this minimum delay versus γ for the nonpersistent case with $M = 50$ and $T = 100$. We note that the higher the throughput, the better the improvement. At low throughput (e.g., $S = 0.20$), the delay is insensitive to γ. With moderately high throughputs (e.g., $S = 0.68$), the delay with CSMA/CD (at $\gamma = 2$) is 70 percent that of CSMA. As the throughput approaches the CSMA channel capacity (e.g., $S = 0.84$) the ratio in delay can be as low as 1/3 in favor of collision detection ($\gamma = 2$). Of course, for even higher throughputs, CSMA/CD achieves a finite delay as long as γ is sufficiently small.

The (S, G) relationship for CSMA/CD is displayed in Fig. 9 along with the curves corresponding to the ALOHA and CSMA schemes. This figure exhibits again the improvement in channel capacity gained by CSMA/CD over all other schemes. For random access schemes in general, the fact that the throughput drops to zero as the offered channel traffic increases indefinitely is indicative of unstable behavior [4], [6]. With CSMA/CD the ability to maintain a throughput relatively high and near capacity over a very large range of the offered channel traffic (see Fig. 9) suggests that CSMA/CD may not be as unstable as the other schemes. That is, in the absence of dynamic control, CSMA/CD is capable of sustaining proper behavior when the channel load exceeds that for which the system has been tuned (i.e., optimized with respect to ν). (Note that, with respect to this stability argument, the nonpersistent CSMA/CD proves to be superior to 1-persistent CSMA/CD, in that if offers high throughput over a larger range of the offered traffic.) We further illustrate this important feature by plotting in Fig. 10, as a function of ν, the ν-capacity and the packet delay at various channel throughputs for both nonpersistent CSMA and CSMA/CD ($\gamma = 2$) with $T = 100$ and $M = 50$. As ν approaches zero, the delay at fixed throughput gets arbitrarily large (due to large retransmission delays), while as ν

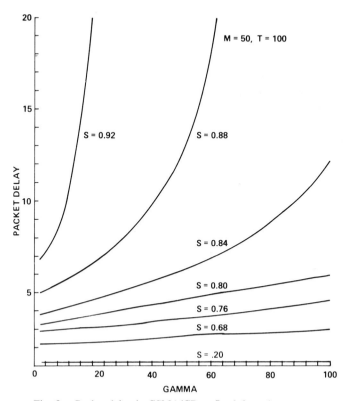

Fig. 8.   Packet delay in CSMA/CD at fixed throughput versus γ.

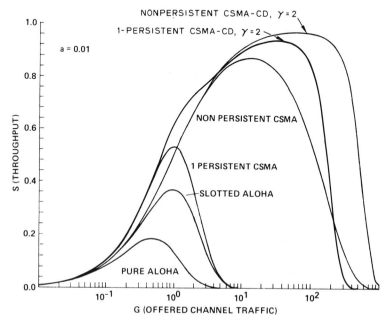

Fig. 9.   Throughput versus channel traffic (infinite population model).

approaches 1, the ν-capacity approaches zero (due to a higher level of interference among backlogged devices). Thus, there is a limited range for ν which is of practical interest. As we see in Fig. 10, for $T = 100$ this range is about $(0.005, 0.3)$. The ν-capacity curve for CSMA/CD is flat over a large portion of this range; with CSMA, the ν-capacity drops steadily as ν increases, and exhibits insensitivity only for smaller values of ν falling outside our range. Consider now CSMA. Given a channel throughput S, packet delay decreases as we increase ν (starting from relatively small values) and remains relatively constant, until, due to the decrease in ν-capacity, we reach a value of ν for which the ν-capacity approaches S, and thus the delay increases very sharply; this "practical" range of ν gets narrower as S increases, indicating that for high throughput, the system requires fine tuning. Let $S = 0.60$ be, for example, the (moderate) stationary channel throughput we expect the system to support. The channel is properly tuned (i.e., minimum delay is achieved) for ν in the range $(0.04, 0.08)$. Consider now that the offered load on the channel is time-varying and suppose that the desired throughput exceeds 0.60 reaching values close to channel capacity (e.g., $S = 0.84$). This actually happens for increasing values of σ (i.e., when devices generate packets at a faster rate). If the desired load remains at such a high value for a relatively long period of time, the channel saturates (i.e., the throughput drops to a low value, nearly all devices become backlogged and packet delay increases indefinitely). We

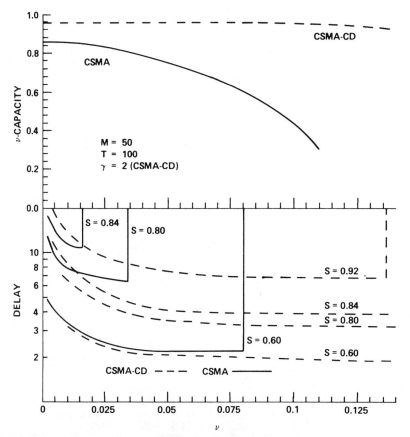

Fig. 10.   Channel capacity and packet delay at fixed throughput versus ν for CSMA and CSMA/CD.

can certainly support variations in offered load covering the entire range of achievable throughputs ($S \leqslant 0.84$) by setting ν at a value in the (now narrow) range corresponding to $S = 0.84$. This is achieved at the expense of increased average delay for $S = 0.60$ of 36 percent (from 2.2 to 3) unless, of course, dynamic control is exercised [4].

With CSMA/CD, on the contrary, there is a relatively wide range of ν for which the delay at fixed throughput is near optimum for all throughput levels up to 0.92.

Numerical results obtained for different values of the system parameters, namely $M = 50$ and 250, and $T = 10$ and 100 have shown that basically as T decreases or as M increases or both, then CSMA/CD starts exhibiting a behavior similar to that of CSMA, while always achieving improved performance.

In summary, the kind of improvement over slotted ALOHA we saw in [4] for CSMA due to carrier sensing is now seen in CSMA/CD over CSMA.

B. Variable Packet Size

It is clear from the above discussion that as the packet size decreases the improvement obtained with collision detection is more important. We inquire here about the performance of the channel with collision detection when packets are of variable length. Instead of examining the general message length distribution case, we present here numerical results for the simpler dual packet size case; that is, traffic consists of a mixture of short and long packets. This simple distribution represents accurately many real situations, among them the important instance of the mixture of short packets resulting from interactive traffic and long packets resulting from file transfers. In fact, measurements performed on Xerox's Ethernet have clearly exhibited such a distribution [7]. Moreover, results obtained here are expected to be representative of the performance of a channel in more general packet length distributions.

We let L_1 (L_2) denote the transmission time of short (long) packets. We let α denote the fraction of short packets generated. Figure 11 displays the nonpersistent CSMA channel capacity versus α for the case of short packets equal to 10 (slots) and three cases of long packets (100, 200, 400). The capacity of the channel decreases as α increases. With larger values of L_2 (e.g., $L_2 = 400$), this decrease is fairly slow until α is about 0.80; beyond 0.80 the capacity rapidly declines to reach the (lower) capacity of $T = L_1$. This shows that a relatively small fraction of long packets in the traffic mix can result in a channel utilization close to that obtained with only long packets. However, it is important to note that, as the fraction of long packets increases, the fraction of channel capacity due to long packets, denoted by C_2, increases extremely rapidly to the detriment of that due to short packets, denoted by C_1, which decreases dramatically. This is seen in Fig. 11 where we also plot C_1 and C_2 versus α. Recall that, by (21) which also holds for CSMA under the independence assumption, C_1 and C_2 are given by

$$C_1 = \frac{\alpha L_1}{\alpha L_1 + (1-\alpha)L_2}\, C, \tag{22}$$

$$C_2 = \frac{(1-\alpha)L_2}{\alpha L_1 + (1-\alpha)L_2}\, C, \tag{23}$$

where C is the channel capacity.

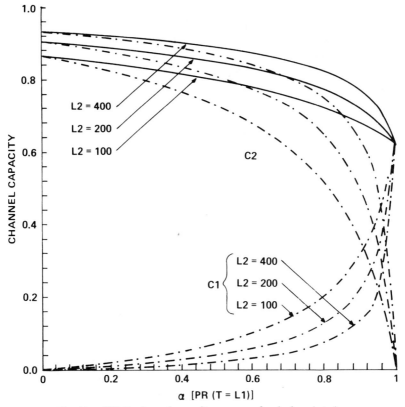

Fig. 11.   CSMA channel capacity versus α for dual packet size.

In Fig. 12 we plot the capacity versus α for CSMA/CD ($L_1 = 10$, $L_2 = 100$) at various values of γ, along with the corresponding CSMA capacity curve. The insensitivity of CSMA/CD capacity to variations of α over a large range of α is more apparent than with CSMA. However, the relative importance of C_1 and C_2 remains the same as in CSMA since the ratio of C_1 and C_2 is independent of the capacity.

In Fig. 13 we plot the packet delay (averaged over all packets and normalized to L_1) versus throughput for various values of α for both CSMA and CSMA/CD. Packet delay includes the (successful) transmission time of the packet; thus clearly as the fraction of long packets increases, so does the average packet delay. Figure 13 exhibits the clear tradeoff between average packet delay and attainable channel capacity as the mix α varies. The improvement due to collision detection is also apparent for all values of α.

Most commonly, short packets belong to interactive users who require small delay, while long packets result from file transfer which, when introduced, allow the recovery of an important fraction of the excess capacity. We inquire now as to the behavior and relative importance of the system performance measures with respect to each of the two packet sizes. Let $S_1(S_2)$ and $D_1(D_2)$ denote the throughput and packet delay for short (long) packets, respectively. In Fig. 14 we plot for CSMA/CD, D_1 and D_2 versus $S = S_1 + S_2$ for various values of α and $M = 50$; $L_1 = 10$; $L_2 = 100$; $\gamma = 2$. As pointed out in the previous section the difference between D_2 and D_1 for a given value of α is always $L_2 - L_1$. For a given globally achievable channel utilization S, D_1 and D_2 increase as the fraction

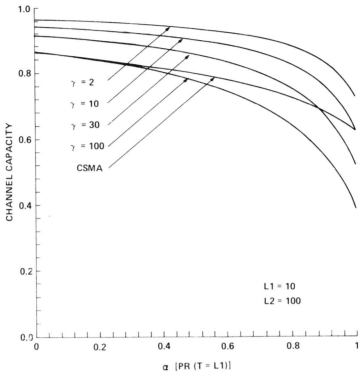

Fig. 12.   CSMA/CD channel capacity versus α for dual packet size.

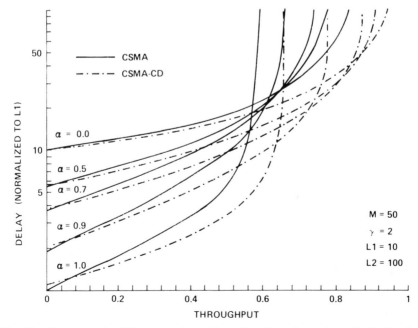

Fig. 13.   Average packet delay versus channel throughput for various values of α (dual packet size).

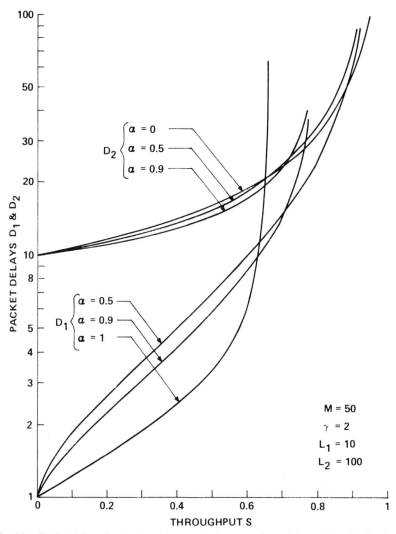

Fig. 14.   Packet delays for short and long packets versus channel throughput for fixed α.

of long packets increases in the mix; indeed the presence of long packets increases the waiting time W (the time to acquire the channel). In Fig. 15, we plot D_1 and D_2 versus S_1 and S_2, respectively, for various values of α, illustrating the degradation in throughput-delay tradeoff for short packets as the fraction of long packets, $1 - \alpha$, increases. The throughput-delay tradeoff for long packets, however, improves.

Consider now a channel required to support interactive traffic at some level S_1. Certainly, S_1 has to be lower than the channel capacity at $\alpha = 1$. Assume that S_1 is at some low level (e.g., 0.05 to 0.2). The introduction of long (file transfer) packets in view of achieving a higher channel utilization has the negative effect of significantly increasing the delay for the interactive traffic. This is illustrated in Fig. 16 where we plot D_1 versus $1 - \alpha$ for fixed values of S_1. Clearly the channel utilization increases with $1 - \alpha$ as shown in Fig. 17 where we plot S versus $1 - \alpha$ for fixed S_1. Thus, in summary, as the traffic mix includes

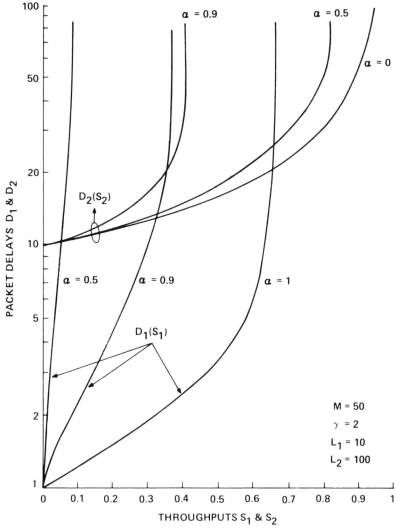

Fig. 15. Throughput-delay characteristics for short and long packets.

more and more long packets, the overall channel capacity is improved in favor of long packets and to the detriment of the throughput-delay performance of short packets, indicating the need for priority schemes to maintain good performance for interactive traffic.

V. CONCLUSION

We extended the models used in the analysis of CSMA to cover the cases of collision detection and variable size packets. It was shown that the throughput-delay characteristics of CSMA/CD are better than the already highly efficient CSMA scheme. We characterized the improvement in terms of the achievable channel capacity and of the packet delay at a

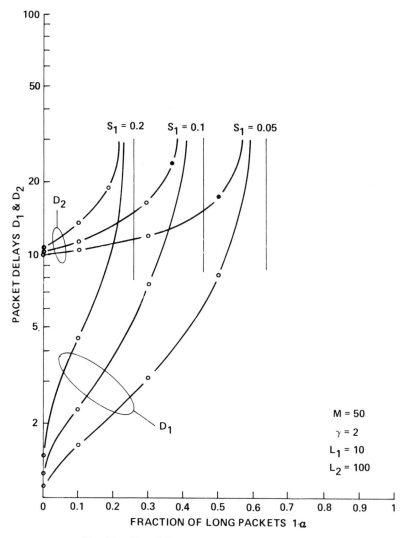

Fig. 16. D_1 and D_2 versus $1 - \alpha$ for constant S_1.

given channel utilization as a function of the collision detection time. Furthermore, we established the fact that in uncontrolled channels (i.e., with a fixed average retransmission delay) CSMA/CD is more stable than CSMA, in that with CSMA/CD both channel capacity and packet delay are less sensitive to variations in the average retransmission delay.

We then studied the performance of these schemes in the presence of variable size packets. Numerical results have been obtained for the interesting case of dual packet size. It was shown that a small fraction of long packets is sufficient to recover a channel capacity close to the (higher) capacity achieved with only long packets. However, the improvement experienced by the introduction of long packets is in favor of the latter and to the detriment of the throughput-delay performance of short packets, establishing the necessity to design and implement priority schemes.

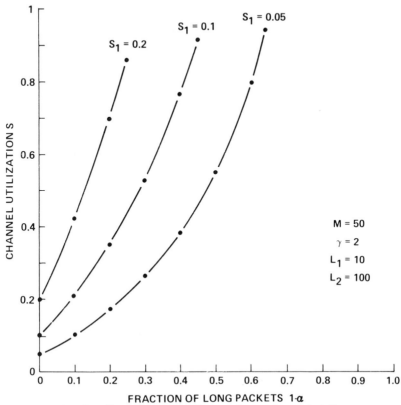

Fig. 17.   Channel throughput S versus $1 - \alpha$ for constant S_1.

REFERENCES

[1]   N. Abramson, "The ALOHA system—Another alternative for computer communications," in *Proc. 1970 Fall Joint Comput. Conf. AFIPS Conf.,* vol. 37, Montvale, NJ: AFIPS Press, 1970, pp. 281–285.

[2]   L. Kleinrock and F. A. Tobagi, "Packet switching in radio channels: Part I—Carrier sense multiple-access modes and their throughput-delay characteristics," *IEEE Trans. Commun.,* vol. COM-23, pp. 1400–1416, Dec. 1975.

[3]   R. M. Metcalfe and D. R. Boggs, "Ethernet: Distributed packet switching for local computer networks," *Commun. Ass. Comput. Mach.,* vol. 19, no. 7, pp. 395–403, 1976.

[4]   F. Tobagi and L. Kleinrock, "Packet switching in radio channels: Part IV—Stability considerations and dynamic control in carrier sense multiple access," *IEEE Trans. Commun.,* vol. COM-25, pp. 1103–1120, Oct. 1977.

[5]   J. Little, "A proof of the queueing formula $L = \lambda W$," *Operation Res.,* vol. 9, pp. 383–387, Mar.-Apr. 1961.

[6]   L. Kleinrock and S. S. Lam, "Packet switching in a multiaccess broadcast channel: Performance evaluation," *IEEE Trans. Commun.,* vol. COM-23, pp. 410–423, Apr. 1975.

[7]   J. F. Shoch and J. A. Hupp, "Measured performance of an Ethernet local network," *Commun. Ass. Comput. Mach.,* vol. 23, pp. 711–721, Dec. 1980.

[8]   F. A. Tobagi and V. B. Hunt, "Performance analysis of carrier sense multiple access with collision detection," *Comput. Networks,* vol. 4, Oct./Nov. 1980.

[9]   M. J. Ferguson, "An approximate analysis of delay for fixed and variable length packets in an unslotted ALOHA channel," *IEEE Trans. Commun.,* vol. COM-25, pp. 644–654, July 1977.

21

Stability and Optimization of the CSMA and CSMA/CD Channels

JAMES S. MEDITCH AND CHIN-TAU A. LEA

A study of the stability and optimization of the infinite population, slotted, nonpersistent CSMA and CSMA/CD channels is presented. The approach to both stability and performance optimization differs from previous work, and provides a number of new results including robustness in stability and performance in the presence of channel and control parameter variations. It is first shown that both channels are unstable under the usual assumption of random retransmission delay. Pake's lemma is then applied to study the properties of a type of distributed retransmission control which provides stable channels. Basic results are in the form of inequalities which define stability regions in the space of channel and control parameters, and further permit one to specify controls which maximize channel throughput as a function of packet length and CD time with stability guaranteed. The delay versus throughput characteristic for the stabilized channels is derived and used to demonstrate the performance achievable with these channels.

I. INTRODUCTION

It is generally recognized that certain random access packet broadcast channels are unstable in the absence of suitable channel control disciplines. This instability manifests itself in either of two ways. In the first, the instability is absolute and channel throughput becomes zero, even under light traffic conditions. The second type of instability is an oscillatory one in which the channel jumps at random times from one locally stable equilibrium point to another.

A number of studies of this phenomenon for the ALOHA channel have been presented in [1]–[6]. These include characterization of instability as a function of channel parameters, identification of stability-delay-throughput tradeoffs, and development and evaluation of dynamic control procedures for channel stabilization and performance optimization.

The dynamic behavior and stability of the slotted nonpersistent CSMA channel were studied in [7] using, in part, the stability theory from [2] for the slotted ALOHA channel. The finite population CSMA channel was considered and an adaptive retransmission control procedure, which stabilizes the channel and provides improved channel performance, was obtained via approximation techniques.

In this chapter, we provide a study of the stability and optimization of the infinite population, slotted, nonpersistent CSMA and CSMA/CD channels. We remark that a detailed performance analysis of the latter channel was presented in [8] for the finite population case. While the matter of stability was only touched upon there, it appears that the method in [7] could be extended to treat the finite population CSMA/CD channel as well. Our approach to both stability and performance differs from that in [7], [8] beyond the fact that we consider the infinite population channels. In particular, we address the stability issue first. The ensuing analysis not only leads to a set of sufficient conditions for stability in terms of the channel parameters, but also to expressions for channel capacity and throughput, the latter with stability guaranteed. Further, we find robustness in stability and performance in the presence of variations in channel and control parameters. By way of contrast, channel capacity was obtained first in [7], [8] via application of renewal theory to the infinite population channels. This was followed by a throughput-delay performance analysis for the finite population channels, pursuant to which stability and dynamic control were investigated in [7] for CSMA.

The contents of this chapter are as follows. In Section II, we formulate the imbedded Markov chain models for CSMA and CSMA/CD which provide the basis for our stability investigation. We then utilize these models to show that both channels are unstable under the usual assumption of random retransmission delay for blocked terminals, i.e., for a constant retransmission probability. This is in contrast to the finite population case where it is known [7] that the CSMA channel is stable for a sufficiently small retransmission probability. In this sense, the infinite population case imposes tighter stability constraints.

In Section III, we consider distributed retransmission control policies in which the retransmission probability is inversely proportional to the number of blocked terminals. Via Pake's lemma [4], we find that such control policies are sufficient to stabilize the channels. The basic results are in the form of stability inequalities which provide for a variety of tradeoff studies. We then show that these policies are robust in the sense mentioned above, and determine control parameter values which maximize channel throughput as a function of channel parameters.

We focus, in Section IV, on delay analysis for the stabilized CSMA and CSMA/CD channels. We find here for both channels that the values of the retransmission policy parameters which yielded maximum throughput also provide the best delay-throughput characteristics. Further, we see that delay is relatively insensitive to these parameters, especially in the case of CSMA/CD where the effect is quite dramatic.

We conclude, in Section V, with a discussion of our results and an indication of some related problems for future research.

II. CHANNEL MODELS AND STABILITY ANALYSIS

The development of the infinite population channel models in this section parallels that in [7], [8] for the finite population case. Hence, to avoid repetition, we assume that the reader is familiar with these references, and omit certain details. However, we note that our models are for the purpose of stability analysis, whereas the ones in [7], [8] were used to determine throughput and delay expressions.

For both CSMA and CSMA/CD, we assume that the time axis is partitioned into minislots of length τ s, the one-way propagation delay of the channel. We express time in units of minislots, assume that packets are of fixed length $T > 1$ minislots, and let $R < T$ denote the CD time in minislots. In CSMA, the transmission time of successful or collided packets is $T + 1$, whereas in CSMA/CD the values are $T + 1$ and $R + 1$, respectively.

The additional minislot is required in all cases for the transmission to clear the channel due to propagation delay.

Terminals which have been involved in a collision or found it necessary to defer transmission upon sensing the channel busy are said to be *blocked*. Otherwise, they are called *active*. A blocked terminal is assumed to schedule its resensing of the channel in the current minislot independently with probability $0 < f \le 1$, and the active terminals are assumed to generate new packets collectively in a Poisson stream with mean rate λ packets/ minislot.

To formulate an imbedded Markov chain for the infinite population CSMA channel, we proceed as in [7], [8] to consider a representative cycle which consists of an idle period I followed by a transmission period $T + 1$ as shown in Fig. 1. The first minislot of an idle period is taken as an "imbedded" minislot with t_i, $i \ge 0$, denoting that minislot for the ith cycle. We let N_i be the number of blocked terminals at the beginning of the ith cycle and take it to be the state variable for the imbedded Markov chain. We define $A = [a_{jk}]$ to be the one-step transition probability matrix between minislots $t_i + I - 1$ and $t_i + I$, conditioned on the number of blocked terminals in minislot $t_i + I - 1$, and let $Q = [q_{jk}]$ be the one-step transition probability matrix between successive minislots in the transmission period (see Fig. 1). Then, arguing as in [7], [8], it follows that the transition probability matrix $P = [p_{jk}]$ from the imbedded minislot i_t to the one at t_{i+1} is

$$P = AQ^{T+1}. \tag{1}$$

In order to evaluate A and Q, we need to introduce the following three probability functions. First, we let g_{kj} be the conditional probability that k blocked terminals will retransmit during a minislot given that there are j blocked terminals in the previous minislot, $j \ge k \ge 0$. From the definition of the transmission probability for blocked terminals, it follows that

$$g_{kj} = \binom{j}{k} f^k (1-f)^{j-k}. \tag{2}$$

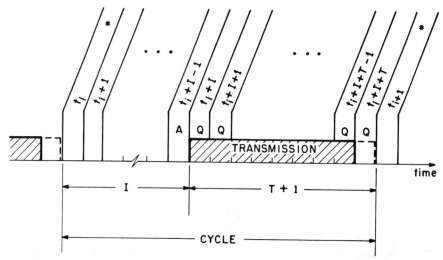

Fig. 1.   Representative cycle for slotted nonpersistent CSMA where * denotes imbedded minislots.

Second, we let c_n be the probability that the active terminals collectively generate $n \geq 0$ new packets during a minislot. Since the packet generation process for these terminals is Poisson with mean rate λ, we have

$$c_n = \frac{\lambda^n e^{-\lambda}}{n!}. \tag{3}$$

Third, we denote the probability that one or more terminals will transmit during a minislot given that the previous minislot was idle and there were $j \geq 0$ blocked terminals during that minislot by d_j. From (2) and (3), we see that

$$d_j = 1 - g_{0j} c_0. \tag{4}$$

With the aid of (2)–(4), it is a direct matter to verify that

$$a_{jk} = \begin{cases} 0 & k < j-1 \\ g_{1j} c_0 d_j^{-1} & k = j-1 \\ (1 - g_{1j} - g_{0j}) c_0 d_j^{-1} + g_{0j} c_1 d_j^{-1} & k = j \\ (1 - g_{0j}) c_1 d_j^{-1} & k = j+1 \\ c_{k-j} d_j^{-1} & k > j+1 \end{cases} \tag{5}$$

where $j = 1, 2, \cdots$.

The determination of Q is immediate, and we have

$$Q = \begin{bmatrix} c_0 & c_1 & c_2 & c_3 & c_4 & \cdots \\ 0 & c_0 & c_1 & c_2 & c_3 & \cdots \\ 0 & 0 & c_0 & c_1 & c_2 & \cdots \\ 0 & 0 & 0 & c_0 & c_1 & \cdots \\ 0 & 0 & 0 & 0 & c_0 & \cdots \\ \vdots & \vdots & \vdots & \vdots & \vdots & \vdots \end{bmatrix} \tag{6}$$

The model for the infinite population CSMA/CD channel now follows directly. In particular, we note that there are two types of cycles in CSMA/CD, viz., (idle, success) and (idle, collision/abort) with respective lengths $I + T + 1$ and $I + R + 1$ minislots. We let g_{kj}, c_n, d_j, A, and Q be as specified by (2)–(6) above, but rewrite A as

$$A = S + U \tag{7}$$

where

$$s_{jk} = \begin{cases} 0 & k < j-1 \\ g_{1j} c_0 d_j^{-1} & k = j-1 \\ g_{0j} c_1 d_j^{-1} & k = j \\ 0 & k \geq j+1 \end{cases} \tag{8}$$

and

$$u_{jk} = \begin{cases} 0 & k \leqslant j-1 \\ (1-g_{1j}-g_{0j})c_0 d_j^{-1} & k=j \\ (1-g_{0j})c_1 d_j^{-1} & k=j+1 \\ c_{k-j} d_j^{-1} & k>j+1. \end{cases} \tag{9}$$

We observe that S is the transition probability matrix from an idle period to a successful transmission period, while U is the transition probability matrix from an idle period to a collision/abort period. Since these two types of cycles are mutually exclusive and independent, it follows that the transition probability matrix for the CSMA/CD imbedded Markov chain is

$$P_c = SQ^{T+1} + UQ^{R+1}. \tag{10}$$

We thus have the two desired model formulations.

Our stability analysis is concerned with the behavior of the state variable N_i for both CSMA and CSMA/CD as $i \to \infty$. We thus begin with the following.

Definition: The infinite population, slotted, nonpersistent CSMA (CSMA/CD) channel is unstable if, as $i \to \infty$, the probability $P(N_i < j) \to 0$ for all finite $j \geqslant 1$. Otherwise, the channel is stable.

This definition follows that in [4] where the ALOHA channel was studied. It states that we have an unstable channel if the probability that the number of blocked terminals is less than any positive integer converges to zero for all such integers as time goes to infinity. This is equivalent to the imbedded Markov chains which are characterized by (1) and (10) being nonergodic.

As a consequence, we have the following result.

Theorem: The infinite population, slotted, nonpersistent CSMA and CSMA/CD channels are unstable for any constant $0 < f \leqslant 1$.

The proof is given in the Appendix.

III. STABLE RETRANSMISSION POLICIES AND MAXIMUM THROUGHPUT

We address the question of channel stabilization by considering retransmission policies in which $f = \alpha/n$ where $n \geqslant 1$ is the number of blocked stations and $\alpha > 0$ is a constant. We show that such control policies are sufficient to stabilize both channels. Utilizing the sufficient conditions which we obtain, we investigate a number of stability tradeoff cases involving the parameter sets (α, λ, T) and (α, λ, T, R) for the two channels, respectively, including throughput maximization.

Our approach to channel stabilization is based on the following.

Pake's Lemma [4]: Let $\{x_i\}^\infty$ be an irreducible aperiodic Markov chain whose state space is the set of nonnegative integers. The following conditions are sufficient for the chain to ergodic:

$$|E\{x_{i+1}-x_i|x_i=n\}| < \infty \tag{11a}$$

and

$$\limsup_{n \to \infty} E\{x_{i+1} - x_i | x_i = n\} < 0 \tag{11b}$$

where $E\{\cdot | \cdot\}$ denotes conditional expectation.

Since CSMA is a special case of CSMA/CD with $R = T$ in the latter, we begin with CSMA/CD. Letting i index the imbedded minislot times, we have from (10) that

$$E\{N_{i+1} - N_i | N_i = n\} = \left[\sum_{j=0}^{\infty} j(P_c)_{nj} \right] - n = \left[\sum_{j=0}^{\infty} \sum_{k=0}^{\infty} j s_{nk} (Q^{T+1})_{kj} \right.$$

$$\left. + \sum_{j=0}^{\infty} \sum_{k=0}^{\infty} j u_{nk} (Q^{R+1})_{kj} \right] - n = \left[\sum_{k=0}^{\infty} s_{nk} \sum_{j=0}^{\infty} j(Q^{T+1})_{kj} + \sum_{k=0}^{\infty} u_{nk} \sum_{j=0}^{\infty} j(Q^{R+1})_{kj} \right] - n \tag{12}$$

for $n = 0, 1, \cdots$, where $(\cdot)_{nj}$ and $(\cdot)_{kj}$ denote, respectively, the nj and kj elements of the indicated matrices. Via substitution into (12) from (3), (6), and (7), and evaluation of the result, we get

$$E\{N_{i+1} - N_i | N_i = n\} = \left[\sum_{k=0}^{\infty} k a_{nk} + \lambda(T+1) \sum_{k=0}^{\infty} s_{nk} + \lambda(R+1) \sum_{k=0}^{\infty} u_{nk} \right] - n \tag{13}$$

for $n = 0, 1, \cdots$.

Letting $P_s(n)$ denote the probability that a transmission is successful, given that a transmission has occurred and $N_i = n$, and recalling the definition of $S = [s_{nk}]$, we have with the aid of (8) that

$$P_s(n) = \sum_{k=0}^{\infty} s_{nk} = d_n^{-1}(g_{0n}c_1 + g_{1n}c_0) \tag{14}$$

for $n = 0, 1, \cdots$, where $g_{10} \triangleq 0$ when $n = 0$. From the definition of $U = [u_{nk}]$, we also have

$$\sum_{k=0}^{\infty} u_{nk} = 1 - P_s(n) \tag{15}$$

for $n = 0, 1, \cdots$. Finally, via substitution from (5) and evaluation of the result, we get

$$\sum_{k=0}^{\infty} k a_{nk} - n = d_n^{-1}(\lambda - g_{0n}c_1 - g_{1n}c_0) \tag{16}$$

also for $n = 0, 1, \cdots$. In view of (14)–(16), (13) becomes

$$E\{N_{i+1} - N_i | N_i = n\} = d_n^{-1}(\lambda - g_{0n}c_1 - g_{1n}c_0) + P_s(n)\lambda(T+1) + [1 - P_s(n)]\lambda(R+1)$$

$$= \lambda* \left\{ \frac{1}{d_n T} + P_s(n) \left(1 + \frac{1}{T} \right) + \frac{R+1}{T} [1 - P_s(n)] \right\} - P_s(n) \tag{17}$$

for $n = 0, 1, \cdots$, where $\lambda^* \triangleq \lambda T$. We remark that when the channel is stable, λ^* is its average throughput in packets/(full) slot, and is in the range $0 \leqslant \lambda^* \leqslant 1$.

For $f = \alpha/n$, $n \geqslant 1$, and f any value in $(0, 1]$ when $n = 0$, it is clear from (2), (4), and (14) that the right-hand side of (17) is finite for all finite n, α, λ, T, and R. Further, from (2), (4), and (14) for $f = \alpha/n$, we find that

$$\lim_{n \to \infty} P_s(n) = \frac{Ge^{-G}}{1 - e^{-G}} \tag{18}$$

where $G \triangleq \alpha + \lambda$ is the offered traffic in packets/minislot. We remark that (14) and (18) also follow from the results in [7], [8] for the finite population case via straightforward limiting arguments.

From (17), we now have

$$\lim_{n \to \infty} E\{N_{i+1} - N_i | N_i = n\} = \lambda^* \left[\frac{1}{T(1 - e^{-G})} + \left(1 + \frac{1}{T}\right)\left(\frac{Ge^{-G}}{1 - e^{-G}}\right) \right.$$

$$\left. + \left(\frac{R+1}{T}\right)\left(1 - \frac{Ge^{-G}}{1 - e^{-G}}\right)\right] - \frac{Ge^{-G}}{1 - e^{-G}} \tag{19}$$

whose right-hand side is finite for all finite G, λ^*, T, and R, equivalently (α, λ, T, R). Thus, (11a) of Pake's lemma is satisfied for all n. For (11b) to hold, we find from (19) that we must have

$$\lambda^*[1 + (T+1)Ge^{-G} + (R+1)(1 - e^{-G} - Ge^{-G})] < GTe^{-G}. \tag{20}$$

Setting $R = T$ in (20), we get

$$\lambda^*[1 + (T+1)(1 - e^{-G})] < GTe^{-G} \tag{21}$$

for CSMA.

Equations (21) and (20), respectively, define stability regions in the parameter spaces (G, λ^*, T), equivalently (α, λ, T), for CSMA, and (G, λ^*, T, R), equivalently (α, λ, T, R), for CSMA/CD. Hence, they can be used to conduct a variety of stability tradeoffs. We illustrate this below.

Example 1 (CSMA): a) Let $T = 20$ and $\lambda^* = 0.6$. Equation (21) holds if $0.10 \leqslant G \leqslant 0.70$. Since $\alpha = G - \lambda$, the channel is stable for all retransmission controls wherein $0.07 \leqslant \alpha \leqslant 0.67$ and provides constant throughput $\lambda^* = 0.6$ over this range. b) For $T = 100$ with $\alpha = 0.1$, (21) is satisfied for $0 \leqslant \lambda^* \leqslant 0.855$ or, equivalently, when $0 \leqslant \lambda \leqslant 0.00855$. c) Setting $\lambda^* = 0.8$ and $G = 0.1$, we find that $T > 61.04$ is required to satisfy (21). Since T must be an integer, we take $T \geqslant 62$.

Example 2 (CSMA/CD): a) Let $T = 20$, $R = 5$, and $\lambda^* = 0.6$. Equation (20) yields $0.091 \leqslant G \leqslant 1.638$, equivalently, $0.061 \leqslant \alpha \leqslant 1.608$, for stability. We observe here the increased ranges on G and α relative to part a) above. b) For $T = 100$, $R = 20$, and $\alpha = 0.1$, we get $0 \leqslant \lambda^* \leqslant 0.889$ for which $0 \leqslant \lambda \leqslant 0.00889$, about a 4 percent increase over that in part b) above. c) Taking $\lambda^* = 0.8$ and $G = 0.1$ with $R = 0.1T$, we find that $T \geqslant 50$ is required for stability in contrast to $T \geqslant 62$ above.

Comparison of the results in these two examples indicates some of the advantages which CSMA/CD offers over CSMA. In addition, the following points should be noted in connection with each part of the examples. Part a) shows the existence of a range of stabilizing retransmission controls for fixed packet length and throughput. This demonstrates robustness of stability in the presence of variations in the retransmission control parameter α. Part b) points to an allowable range on λ over which the channels are stable for a fixed α. This indicates robustness of stability in the presence of variations in λ over the range allowed by the given α. Finally, we note from part c) the presence of a lower bound on packet length for channel stability when the other parameters are fixed.

Since both (21) and (20) can be rewritten such that λ^* appears alone on the left-hand side, numerical search techniques can be employed to maximize the corresponding right-hand sides. The resulting right-hand side is then the channel capacity which we denote by λ^*_{max}. This is demonstrated in Fig. 2 where we show λ^*_{max} as a function of packet length with CD time as a parameter. Representative values are given in Tables I and II for CSMA and CSMA/CD, respectively.

Comparison of Tables I and II and examination of Fig. 2 show the improvement that CSMA/CD offers over CSMA in maximum achievable throughput. It is interesting to note that the range is about 4–5 percent for the longer packet lengths and up to about 17 percent for the shorter packets.

An alternate view is obtained from Fig. 3 where λ^*_{max} is depicted as a function of R with T as a parameter. For each curve, the right endpoint corresponds to CSMA and the left one to CSMA/CD with $R = 1$. For the longer packet lengths, we see a rather gradual improvement in λ^*_{max} for decreasing R, whereas the effect is more significant for the shorter packets as already noted from Tables I and II. In all cases, stability is guaranteed!

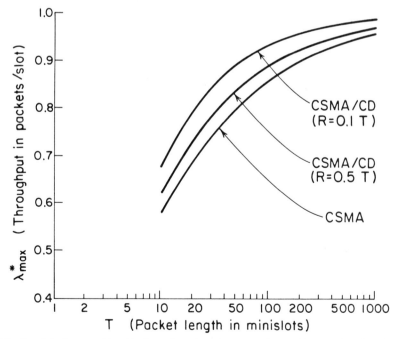

Fig. 2.   Maximum achievable throughput for CSMA and CSMA/CD as a function of packet length with CD time as a parameter.

TABLE I
MAXIMUM ACHIEVABLE THROUGHPUT AND RETRANSMISSION
PARAMETER FOR STABLE CSMA AS A FUNCTION OF PACKET LENGTH

T (minislots)	λ^*_{max} (packets/slot)	α
10	0.580	0.304
20	0.690	0.241
100	0.857	0.126
200	0.899	0.092
500	0.936	0.060
1000	0.955	0.043

TABLE II
MAXIMUM ACHIEVABLE THROUGHPUT FOR STABLE CSMA/CD AS A
FUNCTION OF PACKET LENGTH AND CD TIME

T (minislots)	λ^*_{max} (packets/slot)	
	R = 0.1 T	R = 0.5 T
10	0.677	0.623
20	0.795	0.735
100	0.933	0.889
200	0.957	0.923
500	0.976	0.953
1000	0.984	0.967

We now consider our stability results from the standpoint of renewal theory [9]. For $f = \alpha/n$, $\alpha > 0$, we know that, as $n \to \infty$, the traffic offered to the channel is a Poisson process with rate $G = \lambda + \alpha$. Letting I, B, and U denote the average duration of the idle period, the busy period, and the period within a cycle during which the channel is used without conflict, respectively, the average channel utilization is $S = U/(I + B)$. For our model, $I = 1/(1 - e^{-G})$, $B = (T + 1)P_s(\infty) + (R + 1)[1 - P_s(\infty)]$, and $U = TP_s(\infty)$. Substituting for $P_s(\infty)$ from (18), we find that

$$S = \frac{GTe^{-G}}{1 + (T+1)Ge^{-G} + (R+1)(1 - e^{-G} - Ge^{-G})} . \tag{22}$$

This result differs slightly from that in [8, eq. (1)], the difference being that instantaneous

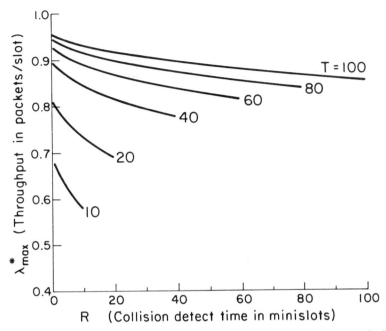

Fig. 3. Maximum achievable throughput for CSMA and CSMA/CD as a function of collision detect time with packet length as a parameter.

sensing at the end of a transmission period was assumed there, whereas we assume that a full minislot, viz., the first minislot of the idle period, is required for sensing. An important difference here, however, is that $G = \alpha + \lambda$ where α is explicitly the retransmission control parameter.

We observe that the right-hand side in (22) is identically the right-hand side in (20) when we rearrange the latter such that λ^* appears alone on the left. From Pake's lemma, the channels are stable if $\lambda^* < S$. Since this is a sufficient condition for stability, we can generate plots of S versus G for fixed T and R which are very useful for stability analysis. Three cases are shown in Fig. 4 for $T = 20$ with $R = 5$ and 10. For a specified value of λ^*, say at 0.6 as shown by the dotted line in the figure, we can determine the range of G for which the channel is stable from the two points at which the line $\lambda^* = 0.6$ intersects the throughput curve (recall part a) of Example 1). The widening stable range for G, and, therefore, for α, is clear as we proceed from CSMA to CSMA/CD with $R = 5$. This is the same as we found by comparing the results in part a) of Examples 1 and 2. Similarly, we observe the widening of the stable range which occurs if we are willing to settle for lower throughput λ^*.

We can also obtain from Fig. 4 the value of each channel's capacity λ^*_{max} and the corresponding $G = G_{max}$ at which this occurs. We observe, in this instance, the increasing flatness of the throughput characteristic in the vicinity of each λ^*_{max} which occurs as we consider CSMA/CD with decreasing CD time R. This, of course, implies a robustness in λ^*_{max} for variations in G about its optimal value, again with stability guaranteed.

Similar results are shown in Fig. 5 for two cases where R is significantly less than T. Here, however, the advantages of CSMA/CD over CSMA are more dramatic than for the case shown in Fig. 4. We note in particular that λ^*_{max} is essentially attainable for G (or α) over an extremely wide range in CSMA/CD with $T = 100$ and $R = 2$.

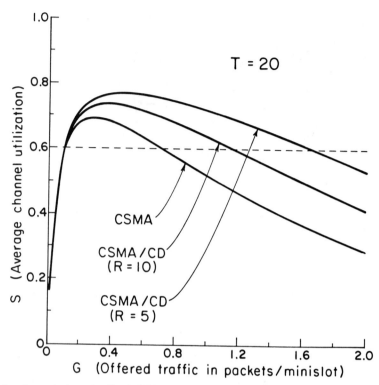

Fig. 4.   Average channel utilization for CSMA and CSMA/CD as a function of offered traffic
when $T = 20$ minislots.

Finally, we observe that for given values of T and R, and any $\lambda_1^* = \lambda_1 T$ arbitrarily close
to the channel capacity λ_{max}^*, the retransmission control defined by $\alpha_1 = G_{max} - \lambda_1$
provides a stable channel for all $0 \leq \lambda^* \leq \lambda_1^*$.

IV. Delay Analysis

In this section, we develop the delay versus throughput relation for the stabilized
channels. The imbedded Markov chain model used here differs from the one in Section II in
that we choose time at the end of a successful transmission as imbedded time. The reason
for this is that the average delay calculated from these imbedded times is the same as that
calculated over all points in time [10, p. 175].

The model is shown in Fig. 6 where RX denotes a packet collision with CD, I is the
length of an idle period between two successive transmissions, T indicates a successful
packet transmission, and t_i^*, $i \geq 0$ an integer, denotes imbedded time. We let $j = 0, 1,$
$\cdots, J$ index the number of collided packets in a cycle where J is a nonnegative integer-
valued random variable. For $j = 1, 2, \cdots, J, J \geq 1$, we define C_j to be the duration of
each such collided packet plus its ensuing idle period. Thus $C_j = (R + 1) + I$ for $j = 1,$
$2, \cdots, J$. For $j = 0$, we set $C_0 = 0$ which covers the case where there are no collisions
during the cycle. The duration of the period of collisions during a cycle is then $C = C_0 +$
$C_1 + \cdots + C_J$. Also, as is clear from the figure, y_{i+1} is the interval of time from the
beginning of the cycle to the beginning of the successful packet transmission within the

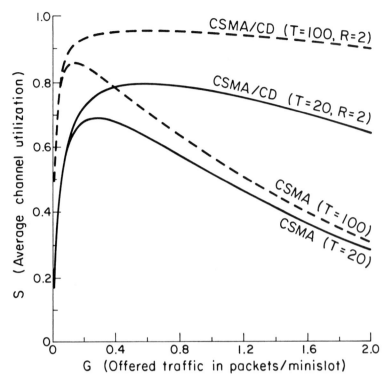

Fig. 5.   Average channel utilization for CSMA and CSMA/CD as a function of offered traffic when $T = 20$, $R = 2$, and $T = 100$, $R = 2$ minislots. ·

cycle. For each cycle, it is seen that $y_{i+1} = C + I$. Finally, the remaining variables which we shall need are u_{i+1} = the number of new arrivals during y_{i+1}, v_{i+1} = the number of new arrivals during the successful packet transmission in the cycle, and q_i = the number of blocked terminals left behind by the successful transmission at the end of the cycle. For these variables, it is obvious that

$$q_{i+1} = q_i + u_{i+1} + v_{i+1} - 1. \tag{23}$$

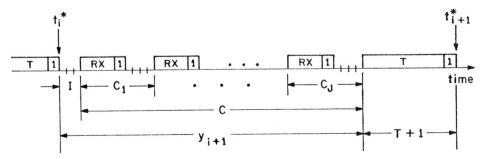

Fig. 6.   Representative cycle for slotted nonpersistent CSMA/CD model for packet delay analysis.

Letting $Q_i(z)$ denote the z-transform of the probability mass function of q_i, we have

$$Q_i(z) = \sum_{k=0}^{\infty} P[q_i = k] z^k.$$

Since the channels are stable, $Q(z) = \lim_{i \to \infty} Q_i(z)$ exists and is a well-behaved function of z.

From (23),

$$E[z^{q_{i+1}}] = E[z^{q_i + u_{i+1} + v_{i+1} - 1}] = E[z^{q_i + u_{i+1}}] \frac{V(z)}{z} \tag{24}$$

where $E[\cdot]$ denotes the expected value, and we have made use of the fact that v_{i+1} is independent of q_i and u_{i+1}, and that $E[z^{v_{i+1}}] = V_{i+1}(z) = V(z)$ since the probability mass function of v_i is independent of i.

We let $P_0(n)$ be the probability that no terminal transmits at the beginning of the next minislot given that there are $n \geq 0$ blocked terminals in the current minislot, and we recall $P_s(n)$ from (14). We thus have, respectively,

$$P_0(n) = (1 - f)^n e^{-\lambda}$$

and

$$P_s(n) = \frac{ne^{-\lambda} f (1 - f)^{n-1} + \lambda e^{-\lambda} (1 - f)^n}{1 - (1 - f)^n e^{-\lambda}}$$

for $n \geq 0$, the latter with the aid of (2)–(4). We next let f take on any value in $(0, 1)$ for $n = 0$ and set $f = \alpha/n$, $n \geq 1$. However, in order to proceed, it is necessary for analytical purposes to approximate both $P_0(n)$ and $P_s(n)$. Specifically, we use their exact values for $n = 0, 1$, and set $P_0 \triangleq P_0(n) \cong e^{-G}$ and $P_1 \triangleq P_s(n) = Ge^{-G}/(1 - e^{-G})$ for $n \geq 2$. A discussion of the errors so introduced and their impact on the interpretation of delay-throughput results is deferred to the end of this section.

From the definition of expectation,

$$E[z^{q_i + u_{i+1}}] = \sum_{k=0}^{\infty} P[q_i = k] E[z^{u_{i+1}} | q_i = k]. \tag{25}$$

In view of the approximation of $P_0(n)$ and $P_s(n)$ for $n \geq 2$, we have

$$E[z^{u_{i+1}} | q_i = k] \cong U(z) \tag{26}$$

for $k \geq 2$. Here, $U(z) = Y'(\lambda - \lambda z)$ [10, p. 184], where $Y'(s)$ is the Laplace transform of the pdf (probability density function) of $Y = \lim_{i \to \infty} y_{i+1}$, given that $q_i = k \geq 2$ as $i \to$

∞. Equation (25) may now be rewritten as

$$E[z^{q_i+u_{i+1}}] = P[q_i=0]E[z^{u_{i+1}}|q_i=0]$$

$$+ P[q_i=1]E[z^{u_{i+1}}|q_i=1]z + \left\{ \sum_{k=2}^{\infty} P[q_i=k]z^k \right\} U(z).$$

Substituting this result into (24) and letting $i \rightarrow \infty$, we get

$$Q(z) = \left\{ Q_0 U_0(z) + z Q_1 U_1(z) + \left[\sum_{k=2}^{\infty} Q_k z^k \right] U(z) \right\} \frac{V(z)}{z} \tag{27}$$

where

$$Q_k \triangleq \lim_{i \to \infty} P[q_i=k] \text{ for } k \geqslant 0,$$

$$U_0(z) \triangleq \lim_{i \to \infty} E[z^{u_{i+1}}|q_i=0],$$

and

$$U_1(z) \triangleq \lim_{i \to \infty} E[z^{u_{i+1}}|q_i=1].$$

Replacing the summation inside the brackets in (27) with $Q(z) - Q_0 - Q_1 z$, we find that

$$Q(z) = \frac{\{Q_0[U_0(z)-U(z)] + Q_1 z[U_1(z)-U(z)]\} V(z)}{z - V(z)U(z)}. \tag{28}$$

We need now to evaluate $U(z)$, $U_1(z)$, $U_0(z)$, $V(z)$, Q_0, and Q_1. For this purpose, we define the following Laplace transforms as $i \rightarrow \infty$ using $\mathcal{L}[\cdot]$ to denote the transform: $I'(s) \triangleq \mathcal{L}$ [pdf of I given that $q_i \geqslant 2$], $I_1(s) \triangleq \mathcal{L}$ [pdf of I given that $q_i = 1$], $Y_1(s) \triangleq$ [pdf of Y given that $q_i = 1$], $C_j'(s) \triangleq \mathcal{L}$ [pdf of C_j given that $q_i \geqslant 2$], $j = 0, 1, \cdots, J$, $C'(s) = \mathcal{L}$ [pdf of C given that $q_i \geqslant 2$], and $C_1(s) = \mathcal{L}$ [pdf of C given that $q_i = 1$]. The other Laplace transforms which we shall use are those of the pdf of the packet length which, since the packet length is fixed, is simply $B(s) = e^{-sT}$, and $Y(s)$ which has already been introduced.

The pdf of I is $p(x, n) = [1 - P_0(n)][P_0(n)]^{k-1}\delta(x - k)$, where $k = 1, 2, \cdots, n = 0, 1, \cdots$, and $\delta(\cdot)$ is the Dirac delta function. Since $I'(s)$ is defined for $n \geqslant 2$, we get

$$I'(s) = \frac{(1-P_0)e^{-s}}{1 - P_0 e^{-s}} \tag{29}$$

where

$$P_0 \cong e^{-G}.$$

Since the pdf for C_0 is $\delta(x)$ and $C_j' = (R + 1) + I'$ for $j \geqslant 1$, we have $C_0'(s) = 1$, and $C_j'(s) = I'(s) \exp[-(R + 1)s]$ for $j \geqslant 1$. Hence, from (29),

$$C_j'(s) = \frac{(1 - P_0)e^{-(R+2)s}}{1 - P_0 e^{-s}}. \tag{30}$$

Now let

$$C' \triangleq \sum_{j=0}^{J} C_j'$$

where C' is the random variable C given that $q_i \geqslant 2$ as $i \to \infty$.

Then,

$$C'(s) = E\left[e^s \left(\sum_{j=0}^{J} C_j'\right)\right] = E\{E[e^{s(C_0' + C_1' + \cdots + C_J')}|j=J]\}$$

$$= E\{[C_j'(s)]^J|j=J\} = \sum_{J=0}^{\infty} P[j=J][C_j'(s)]^J = F[C_j'(s)] \tag{31}$$

where $F[\cdot]$ is the z-transform of the probability mass function of J given that $q_i \geqslant 2$ as $i \to \infty$. Since $P[J = k] = (1 - P_1)^k P_1$, we have

$$F(z) = \frac{P_1}{1 - (1 - P_1)z} \tag{32}$$

where

$$P_1 \cong Ge^{-G}/(1 - e^{-G}).$$

In view of the fact that $Y = C + I$, we see that $Y'(s) = C'(s)I'(s)$, and it follows from (29)–(31) that

$$Y'(s) = \frac{(1 - P_0)e^{-s}}{1 - P_0 e^{-s}} \cdot F\left(\frac{(1 - P_0)e^{-(R+2)s}}{1 - P_0 e^{-s}}\right) \tag{33}$$

where $F(\cdot)$ is defined by (32) and $P_0 \cong e^{-G}$. From (33), it follows [10, p. 184] that $U(z) = Y'(\lambda - \lambda z)$.

For $q_i = 1$, we proceed in a similar way to arrive at

$$Y_1(s) = \frac{[1 - P_0(1)]e^{-s}}{1 - P_0(1)e^{-s}} \cdot F_1[C_1(s)] \tag{34}$$

where

$$C_1(s) = \frac{[1 - P_0(1)]e^{-s}}{1 - P_0(1)e^{-s}}$$

$$F_1(z) = \frac{P_s(1)}{1 - [1 - P_s(1)]z}$$

$P_0(1) = (1 - \alpha)e^{-\lambda}$, and $P_s(1) = [\alpha e^{-\lambda} + (1 - \alpha)\lambda e^{-\lambda}]/[1 - (1 - \alpha)e^{-\lambda}]$. However, recalling that λ is in packets/minislot, we typically have $\lambda \ll 1$[1] in which case $P_0(1) \cong (1 - \alpha)$ and $P_s(1) \cong 1$. In this case, (34) may be approximated by

$$Y_1(s) \cong \frac{\alpha e^{-s}}{1 - (1 - \alpha)e^{-s}}. \tag{35}$$

We then have $U_1(z) = Y_1(\lambda - \lambda z)$ from either (34) or (35).

We recall from (3) that $c_n = \lambda^n e^{-\lambda}/n!$ is the probability of $n \geq 0$ arrivals in a minislot. Given that $q_n = 0$, it is clear that

$$u_{i+1} = \begin{cases} 1 & \text{with probability } c_1/(1 - c_0) \\ j + \text{the number of arrivals during } (R+1) + Y' \\ & \text{with probability } c_j/(1 - c_0) \text{ for } j \geq 2 \end{cases}$$

where Y' is the random variable Y given that $j \geq 2$. Via an argument similar to the one which led to (34) and the evaluation of $U(z)$, we get

$$U_0(z) = \frac{c_1 z}{1 - c_0} + \frac{1}{1 - c_0} \{[e^{-(\lambda - \lambda z)} - c_0 - c_1 z] \cdot Y'(\lambda - \lambda z)e^{(R+1)(\lambda - \lambda z)}\} \tag{36}$$

with $c_0 = e^{-\lambda}$ and $c_1 = \lambda e^{-\lambda}$.

Determination of $V(z)$ is direct and we find that $V(z) = B(\lambda - \lambda z) = \exp[-(\lambda - \lambda z)T]$. To evaluate Q_0 and Q_1, we use the facts that $Q(1) = 1$ and $dQ(z)/dz = Q_1$ when $z = 0$. This leads to the pair of linearly independent equations

$$(u_0 - \lambda y')Q_0 + \lambda(y_1 - y') = 1 - \lambda(T + 1 + y')$$

and

$$Q_1 = \left[\frac{1}{B(\lambda)} - \frac{c_1}{1 - c_0}\right] \frac{1}{Y_1(0)} Q_0$$

where $u_0 = dU_0(z)/dz$ when $z = 0$, and $y' = -dY'(s)/ds$ and $y_1 = -dY_1/ds$, each when $s = 0$.

As a result, $Q(z)$ as given by (28) is now completely specified, and the average number

[1] In the calculations in the sequel, we have $\lambda < 0.04$.

of packets in the channel is $\bar{q} = dQ(z)/dz$ when $z = 1$. From Little's result [10], the average packet delay is then

$$D = \frac{\bar{q}}{\lambda*} \tag{37}$$

expressed here in full slots.

The results of calculations for CSMA with $T = 20$, and CSMA/CD with $T = 20$ and $R = 5$ are shown in Fig. 7, each for three different values of α in the stable range. In the case of CSMA, the value $\alpha = 0.241$ is the one determined in Section III which maximizes throughput, while $\alpha = 0.400$ is the one for CSMA/CD. The improved performance which CSMA/CD offers over CSMA is clear in this example.

In Fig. 8, we show delay-throughput behavior for the longer packet length $T = 100$ minislots for both CSMA and CSMA/CD, the latter for $R = 20$ and 2 minislots. Each curve represents the "best" possible behavior in the sense that the value of α used to generate each is the one that corresponds to λ^*_{max}. While the improvement in throughput for fixed delay, say $D = 10$ slots, is rather modest, it must be borne in mind that λ^*_{max} is much more sensitive to variations or uncertainty in α for CSMA than it is for CSMA/CD. Hence, there is an indicated robustness in the delay-throughput characteristics for CSMA/CD vis-à-vis α which is absent in CSMA. Further, it is to be noted that packet delay at the higher throughputs is much larger for CSMA than for CSMA/CD. From Fig. 8, we find, for

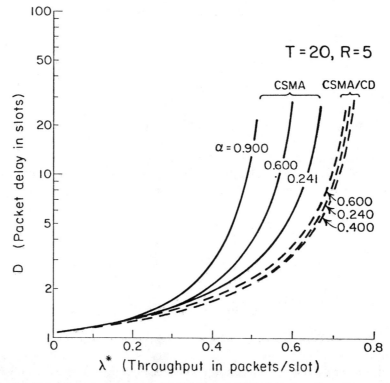

Fig. 7. Delay-throughput behavior for CSMA and CSMA/CD for $T = 20$ and $R = 5$ minislots as a function of the retransmission parameter α.

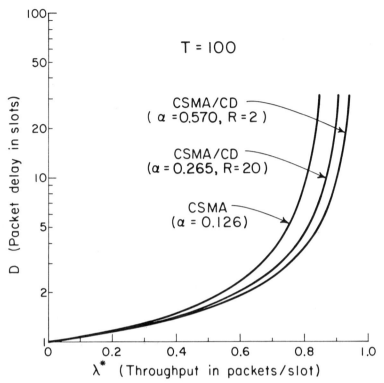

Fig. 8. Delay-throughput behavior for CSMA and CSMA/CD for $T = 100$, $R = 20$, and $R = 2$ minislots where the value of α used provides λ^*_{max} for each.

example when $\lambda^* = 0.8$, that $D \cong 10$ slots for CSMA compared to $D \cong 4$ slots for CSMA/CD with $R = 2$.

An alternative demonstration of delay-throughput behavior as a function of α is given in Fig. 9 for the case where $T = 20$ and the throughput is fixed at $\lambda^* = 0.6$. We observe, in particular, the small variation in D for CSMA/CD with $R = 5$ as α ranges from 0.30 to 0.60. The results here should be compared to those in Fig. 4 where the corresponding range on α for stability is evident when $\lambda^* = 0.6$.

The delay-throughput analysis in this section is an extension of the one given in [11]. In the earlier study, the existence of a stabilizing retransmission control was assumed, and it was further assumed that the probability of a successful transmission in the next minislot was a constant S independent of n, λ, and any control parameters. The value of S used there for calculations was e^{-1}, the optimum slotted ALOHA throughput. In our analysis, we have guaranteed a stable retransmission control in which the parameter α can be adjusted to optimize performance. Further, the two probabilities which we use, $P_0(n)$ and $P_s(n)$, are exact for $n = 0$ and 1, and depend on α and λ. For $n \geq 2$, we take $P_0(n)$ and $P_s(n)$ to be independent of n, but they continue to be functions of α and λ. It is clear from the exact and approximate expressions for $P_0(n)$ and $P_s(n)$ that the largest errors in approximation occur at $n = 2$. It is equally clear from the expressions that the difference between the exact and approximate values converges to zero rapidly for increasing n with α in the range 0.1–0.9 in our calculations. Of course, the approximations are better for the smaller values of α.

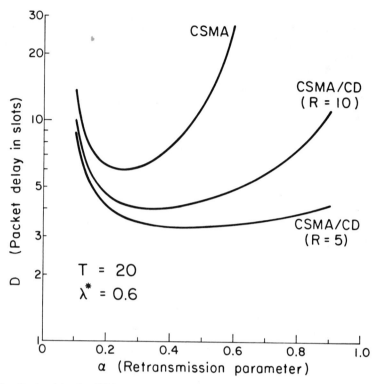

Fig. 9.   Packet delay for CSMA and CSMA/CD as a function of the retransmission parameter
α for $T = 20$ minislots and $\lambda^* = 0.6$ packets/slot.

While space limitations preclude a detailed error analysis, we can provide some insight via a worst case analysis. We consider first the ratio $\beta(n, \alpha) \triangleq P_0(n)/P_0$ for $n \geqslant 2$, noting that the ratio is independent of λ. From the above three figures, we see that $\alpha = 0.9$ and 0.6 are the largest values used in our calculations. For these α, the behavior of β is shown in Table III and applies to both CSMA and CSMA/CD. In the same way, we let $\theta(n, \alpha, \lambda) \triangleq P_s(n)/P_1$ for $n \geqslant 2$. The largest errors in approximation occur at the extreme right endpoints in Fig. 7 of the $\alpha = 0.9$ CSMA and the $\alpha = 0.6$ CSMA/CD curves where $\lambda = 0.025$ and 0.036, respectively. The corresponding behavior of θ is given in Table III.

TABLE III
WORST CASE ANALYSIS OF APPROXIMATION ERRORS

n	$\beta(n, 0.9)$	$\beta(n, 0.6)$	$\theta(n, 0.9, 0.025)$	$\theta(n, 0.6, 0.036)$
2	0.7440	0.8928	1.1439	1.1189
5	0.9119	0.9616	1.0461	1.0403
10	0.9578	0.9814	1.0217	1.0192
50	0.9918	0.9964	1.0041	1.0037

On this basis, the results in Figs. 7–9 are reasonable except for $\alpha = 0.9$ where they must be accordingly qualified even though $\beta(n, 0.9)$ rapidly converges toward one with n.

Our model reduces to that in [11] if we set $P_0(n) = P_0$ and $P_s(n) = P_1$ for all $n \geqslant 0$ with $G = 1$, and take $R = 1$ which is fixed in that model. For $T = 100$, the stability inequality (20) requires $\lambda < 0.0093$. If we choose to operate the channel at $\lambda^* = 0.90$, we must have $\alpha = 0.991$ for which the above approximations are not valid. This should be compared to our result in Fig. 8 where we achieve a $\lambda^* > 0.90$ for CSMA/CD with $T = 100, R = 2$, and $\alpha = 0.570$ for which the approximations are valid.

Finally, we remark that our model allows for improvement in the approximations of $P_0(n)$ and $P_s(n)$, but at the expense of additional computation. To illustrate this, we suppose that exact values are used for $n = 0, 1$, and 2, and that $P_0(n) = P_0$ and $P_s(n) = P_1$ for all $n \geqslant 3$. In this case, (27) assumes the form

$$Q(z) = \left\{ Q_0 U_0(z) + z Q_1 U_1(z) + z^2 Q_2 U_2(z) + \left[\sum_{k=3}^{\infty} Q_k z^k \right] U(z) \right\} \frac{V(z)}{z}$$

from which we see the introduction of Q_2 and $U_2(z)$ which must be evaluated.

V. CONCLUSION

In this chapter we have given a detailed study of the stability and optimization of the infinite population, slotted, nonpersistent CSMA and CSMA/CD channels. Our principal results on the stability question are the theorem and the two stability inequalities in Section II. These inequalities, which are sufficient conditions for stability, are new, and provide for a host of stability-throughput-channel parameter-control parameter tradeoffs. Of particular interest were 1) the robustness of stability in the presence of channel and control parameter variations and 2) the maximization of channel throughput as a function of packet length with stability guaranteed. In addition, we found that channel capacity followed directly from the stability condition (20).

The delay analysis in Section IV led to (37), and a number of performance analyses were conducted using this relation. Among them was a comparison of delay-throughput for CSMA versus CSMA/CD under identical traffic conditions. As expected, CSMA/CD is superior to CSMA in delay-throughput just as it was in the case of maximum achievable throughput. It was further found that the robustness in stability as a function of the retransmission parameter α which was also exhibited in Section III carried over to delay-throughput behavior.

While the stability analysis in Section III is exact, the delay-throughput investigation involved approximation of the two retransmission probabilities $P_0(n)$ and $P_s(n)$. The nature of these approximations was indicated and a worst case error analysis was provided. The latter served to qualify the numerical results presented in Section IV. The model formulated in Section IV was compared to an earlier one to point out differences in the two, particularly with respect to the basic assumptions and approximations employed by each.

In this study, we have not dealt with the issue of implementing the retransmission policy $f = \alpha/n$. Basically, the problem is that of each terminal estimating n by observing the channel. A study of this problem for the ALOHA channel has been given in [12], but the treatment is heuristic as is the one in [13] for our formulation here. It is known [14] that the estimation problem is infinite-dimensional, and, therefore, that approximation via "suboptimal" retransmission controls is indicated. In our case, the desired approximation would be $\hat{n}(i)$, an accurate estimate of $n(i)$, where i denotes imbedded time. Another avenue of research in this direction would be that where the extent to which the simplest of the fully decentralized retransmission controls, e.g., linear or binary exponential backoff, could approximate $\alpha/n(i)$.

Finally, in addition to the differences between our work and that in [8], which have already been indicated, it should be noted that [8] includes a performance analysis of the finite population channels for variable packet lengths.

APPENDIX

The proof of the theorem requires the following intermediate result.

Lemma: Let $\{x_n\}^\infty$ be an irreducible aperiodic Markov chain with transition probability matrix $P = [p_{ij}]$. If there exists a sequence $\{z_i, i = 0, 1, \cdots\}$ such that $z_0 \geq z_1 \geq z_2 \geq \cdots \geq 0$ with $z_0 > z_m$ for at least one $m \geq 1$ and $z_i \geq \Sigma_j p_{ij} z_j$ for all $i \geq N$ where $N \geq 0$ is an integer, then the chain is transient.

Proof: An irreducible aperiodic Markov chain is ergodic if and only if the probability of its state entering the set of states $C = \{x_0, x_1, \cdots, x_{N-1}; N \geq 1\}$ from any other state is one [15]. Consider a Markov chain having transition probability matrix $\tilde{P} = [\tilde{p}_{ij}]$ where $\tilde{p}_{ij} = \delta_{ij}$ for $i = 0, 1, \cdots, N - 1$, and $\tilde{p}_{ij} = p_{ij}$ for $i \geq N$ where δ_{ij} is the Kronecker delta and the p_{ij} are the same as those in the hypothesis. This is a chain having $C = \{x_0, x_1, \cdots, x_{N-1}\}$ as a recurrent class with all of its other states transient. Moreover, the first entrance time [15] from these other states into C is identical to that of the above chain. For this chain, $z_i > \Sigma_j \tilde{p}_{ij} z_j$ which implies that

$$z_i \geq \sum_j \tilde{p}_{ij} \left(\sum_k \tilde{p}_{jk} z_k \right) = \sum_j \tilde{p}_{ij}^{(2)} z_j$$

for all $i \geq 0$ where $\tilde{p}_{ij}^{(2)}$ is the ij element of $\tilde{P}^2 \triangleq \tilde{P} \cdot P$. Continuing in this manner, we have

$$z_i \geq \sum_j \tilde{p}_{ij}^{(n)} z_j \tag{A1}$$

for all $i \geq 0$ and $n \geq 1$.

Now let $\pi_{ij} = \lim_{n \to \infty} \tilde{p}_{ij}^{(n)}$. Since all states for which $j \geq N$ are transient, it follows that $\pi_{ij} = 0$ for all $j \geq N$. Hence, for all $i \geq N$, we have from (A1) and the definition of π_{ij} that $z_i \geq \pi_{i0} z_0 + \pi_{i1} z_1 + \cdots + \pi_{i,N-1} z_{N-1}$. By hypothesis, $z_0 \geq z_1 \geq \cdots \geq z_{N-1} \geq z_i$ for all $i \geq N$, and we can write

$$1 \geq \pi_{i0} \left(\frac{z_0}{z_1} \right) + \pi_{i1} \left(\frac{z_1}{z_i} \right) + \cdots + \pi_{i,N-1} \left(\frac{z_{N-1}}{z_i} \right). \tag{A2}$$

Then, from the assumption that $z_0 > z_m$ for at least one $m \geq 1$, there is at least one $i \geq N$ such that (A2) becomes $1 > \pi_{i0} + \pi_{i1} + \cdots + \pi_{i,N-1}$. This means that there exists at least one state x_i outside of C from which the probability of entering C is less than one. Hence, the original chain is transient.

Theorem: The infinite population, slotted, nonpersistent CSMA and CSMA/CD channels are unstable for any fixed $0 < f \leq 1$.

Proof: We consider CSMA first and recall that $P = AQ^{T+1}$. Referring to (2)–(6), we see that $\lim_{i\to\infty} a_{i,i-1} = 0$, $\lim_{i\to\infty} a_{ii} = c_0$, $\lim_{i\to\infty} a_{i,i+1} = c_1$, and $\lim_{i\to\infty} a_{i,i+j} = c_j$. For $\epsilon > 0$ sufficiently small this implies that there exists an N such that $a_{i,i-1} \leqslant \epsilon$, $a_{ii} \leqslant c_0 + \epsilon$, $a_{i,i+1} \leqslant c_1 + \epsilon$, and $a_{i,i+j} \leqslant c_j + \epsilon$ for all $i \geqslant N$.

For $0 < r < 1$, we observe that

$$a_{i,i-1} + a_{ii}r + a_{i,i+1}r^2 + \cdots \leqslant \epsilon + (c_0 + \epsilon)r + (c_1 + \epsilon)r^2 + \cdots = \frac{\epsilon}{1-r} + (c_0 r + c_1 r^2 + \cdots).$$

Now let r be chosen such that

$$r > \frac{\epsilon}{1-r} + c_0 r + c_1 r^2 + \cdots \tag{A3}$$

and note that

$$r - c_0 r - c_1 r^2 - \cdots = (r - r^2)c_1 + (r - r^3)c_2 + \cdots > (c_1 + c_2 + \cdots)(r - r^2) = (r - r^2)(1 - c_0).$$

Provided that $(r - r^2)(1 - c_0) > \epsilon/(1 - r)$ can be satisfied, then so can (A3). Since $\epsilon > 0$ can be made arbitrarily small, we can always find an $r \in (0, 1)$ such that the former holds. Hence,

$$a_{i,i-1} + a_{ii}r + a_{i,i+1}r^2 + \cdots < r \tag{A4}$$

for all $i \geqslant N$.

Define $\{z_i, i = 0, 1, \cdots\}$ to be the sequence specified by $z_i = 1$ for $i = 0, 1, \cdots, N - 2$, and $z_i = r^{i-N+1}$ for $i = N - 1, N, \cdots$. It follows from (5) and (A4) after some algebra that

$$z_i \geqslant \sum_{j=0}^{\infty} a_{ij} z_i \tag{A5}$$

for all $i \geqslant N$.

With $Q = [q_{ij}]$ from (6) and z_i defined above, we see that

$$\sum_{j=0}^{\infty} q_{ij} z_j = \sum_{k=0}^{\infty} c_k z_{i+k}$$

for all $i \geqslant 0$. However, using the fact that $1 - c_0 = c_1 + c_2 + \cdots$, we find that

$$z_i - \sum_{k=0}^{\infty} c_k z_{i+k} \geqslant 0.$$

Hence,

$$z_i \geqslant \sum_{j=0}^{\infty} q_{ij} z_j$$

for all $i \geqslant 0$. Via the steps in the proof of the lemma which led to (A1), we have

$$z_i \geqslant \sum_{j=0}^{\infty} q_{ij}^{(n)} z_j \tag{A6}$$

for $n \geqslant 1$.

Setting $n = T + 1$ in (A6) and substituting into (A5), we get

$$z_i \geqslant \sum_{j=0}^{\infty} a_{ij} \sum_{k=0}^{\infty} q_{jk}^{(T+1)} z_k = \sum_{k=0}^{\infty} (AQ^{T+1})_{ik} z_k$$

for all $i \geqslant N$ where $(AQ^{T+1})_{ik}$ is the ik element of AQ^{T+1}. From the lemma, the infinite population, slotted, nonpersistent CSMA channel is unstable.

The proof of the instability of the CSMA/CD channel follows in the same way by recalling from (7) and (10) that $A = S + U$ and $P_c = SQ^{T+1} + UQ^{R+1}$, respectively.

REFERENCES

[1] A. B. Carleial and M. E. Hellman, "Bistable behavior of ALOHA-type systems," *IEEE Trans. Commun.,* vol. COM-23, pp. 401–410, Apr. 1975.
[2] L. Kleinrock and S. S. Lam, "Packet switching in a multiaccess broadcast channel: Performance evaluation," *IEEE Trans. Commun.,* vol. COM-23, pp. 410–423, Apr. 1975.
[3] S. S. Lam and L. Kleinrock, "Packet switching in a multiaccess broadcast channel: Dynamic control procedures," *IEEE Trans. Commun.,* vol. COM-23, pp. 891–904, Sept. 1975.
[4] G. Fayolle, E. Gelenbe, and J. Labetoulle, "Stability and optimal control of the packet switching broadcast channel," *J. Ass. Comput. Mach.,* vol. 24, pp. 375–386, July 1977.
[5] J. I. Capetanakis, "Tree algorithms for packet broadcast channels," *IEEE Trans. Inform. Theory,* vol. IT-25, pp. 505–515, Sept. 1979.
[6] Y.-C. Jenq, "Optimal retransmission control of slotted ALOHA systems," *IEEE Trans. Commun.,* vol. COM-29, pp. 891–895, June 1981.
[7] F. A. Tobagi and L. Kleinrock, "Packet switching in radio channels: Part IV—Stability considerations and dynamic control in carrier sense multiple access," *IEEE Trans. Commun.,* vol. COM-25, pp. 1103–1119, Oct. 1977.
[8] F. A. Tobagi and V. B. Hunt, "Performance analysis of carrier sense multiple access with collision detection," *Comput. Networks,* vol. 4, pp. 245–249, Oct.–Nov. 1980; see also this volume, ch. 20.
[9] L. Kleinrock and F. A. Tobagi, "Packet switching in radio channels: Part I—Carrier sense multiple-access modes and their throughput-delay characteristics," *IEEE Trans. Commun.,* vol. COM-23, pp. 1400–1416, Dec. 1975.
[10] L. Kleinrock, *Queueing Systems, Vol. I: Theory.*   New York: Wiley-Interscience, 1975.
[11] S. S. Lam, "A carrier sense multiple access protocol for local networks," *Comput. Networks,* vol. 4, pp. 21–32, Feb. 1980.
[12] N. B. Meissner, J. L. Segal, and M. Y. Tanigawa, "An adaptive retransmission technique for use in a slotted-ALOHA channel," *IEEE Trans. Commun.,* vol. COM-28, pp. 1776–1778, Sept. 1980.
[13] C. T. A. Lea, "Channel access protocols for local area networks," Ph.D. dissertation, Dep. Elec. Eng., Univ. Washington, Seattle, Aug. 1982; also Tech. Rep. 224.
[14] A. Segall, "Recursive estimation for discrete-time point processes," *IEEE Trans. Inform. Theory,* vol. IT-22, pp. 422–431, July 1976.
[15] J. W. Cohen, *The Single Server Queue.*   Amsterdam, The Netherlands: North-Holland, 1969.

22

Local Area Subnetworks: A Performance Comparison

WERNER BUX

This chapter provides a comparative evaluation of the performance of ring and bus systems constituting subnetworks of local area networks. Performance is measured in terms of the delay-throughput characteristics. Systems investigated include token-controlled and slotted rings as well as random-access buses (CSMA with collision detection) and ordered-access buses. The investigation is based on analytic models which describe the various topologies and access mechanisms to a sufficient level of detail. This chapter includes a comprehensive discussion of how the performance of the different networks is affected by system parameters like transmission rate, cable length, packet lengths, and control overhead.

I. INTRODUCTION

The objective of this chapter is to shed some light onto the performance aspect of local area networks. We consider four important candidates for local area subnetworks: token ring; slotted ring (empty-slot technique); a random-access bus (carrier sense multiple access (CSMA) with collision detection); and an ordered-access bus (multilevel multiple access (MLMA) scheme).

The investigation is based on analytic models which describe the various topologies and access mechanisms to a sufficient level of detail.

Our performance measure of prime interest is the delay-throughput characteristic of the systems. Delay is measured as the mean transfer time t_f of the packets which we define as the time interval from the generation of a packet at the source station until its reception at the destination. This means the transfer time includes the queueing and access delay at the sender, the transmission time of the packet, and the propagation delay.

II. MODELING OF SUBNETWORKS

In this section, the four subnetworks studied are described to the extent necessary for understanding their performance models. Explicit analytic results for the mean transfer time of all systems are given. To allow for direct comparison of the results, consistent assumptions with respect to traffic properties are used for all models: 1) Packets are generated at the S stations according to Poisson processes with rates λ_1 through λ_S. (We denote by λ the aggregate arrival rate $\lambda_1 + \cdots + \lambda_S$ of all stations.) 2) The packet lengths L_p can be generally distributed. In the subnetwork, a header of length L_h containing control and addressing information is added to every packet.

Furthermore, we denote by v the transmission rate (speed) and by τ the maximum end-to-end propagation delay in case of a bus, or the roundtrip latency in case of a ring system (including possible delays of the signals caused within the stations). The propagation delay is assumed to be 5 μs/km cable length.

As pointed out above, the transfer time includes the propagation delay between source and destination of a packet. In what follows, we assume that the average distance between sender and receiver is half the maximum distance of the bus or ring. Finally, for this particular study, we exclude all effects related to transmission errors and their recovery.

A. Token Ring

In a token ring [1], [2], access to the transmission channel is controlled by passing a permission token around the ring. When the system is initialized, a designated station generates a free token which travels around the ring until a station ready to transmit changes it to busy and puts its packet onto the ring. The packet can, in principle, be of arbitrary length. The sending station is responsible for removing its own packet from the ring. At the end of its transmission, it passes the access permission to the next station by generating a new free token. Figure 1 illustrates this operation for a ring with four stations. It shows how stations 1 and 3 and again station 1 subsequently access the ring to transmit their packets.

This operation is described by the performance model shown in Fig. 2 which is a single-

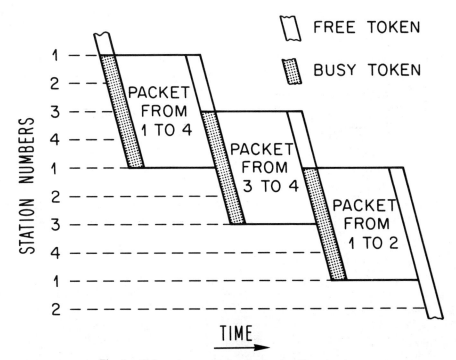

Fig. 1.   Token ring: example of operation (4 stations).

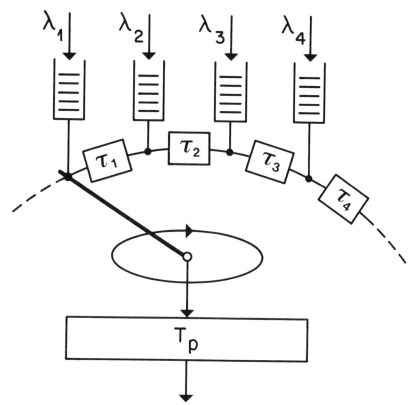

Fig. 2.   Token-ring model ($S = 4$ stations; λ_i: packet arrival rates; T_p: packet service time; τ_i: latency of station i plus propagation delay from station i to station $i + 1$).

server queueing model with as many queues as stations attached to the ring. The queues are serviced in a cyclical manner symbolized by the rotating switch which stands for the free token. The service time of a packet is given by $T_p = (L_h + L_p)/v$. The time needed for passing the free token from station i to station $i + 1$ (propagation delay plus additional latency within station i for token handling, etc.) is modeled by a constant switchover delay τ_i.

With respect to the order of service, several policies can be distinguished, e.g., that a queue is serviced until it is empty ("exhaustive service") or that only a limited number of packets (e.g., one) is serviced per access possibility ("nonexhaustive service"). Although, in principle, performance differences exist between these policies [3], it can be generally observed that for the parameters of interest in local networks, these differences are very small if the traffic is uniformly distributed among all stations. An intuitive explanation of this fact is that the total number of packets waiting simultaneously is distributed over a large number (e.g., 50 or more) of different queues, which means that the probability for more than one packet to be waiting within any queue is very low, unless the channel load is exceedingly high (e.g., > 90 percent). A comparison of the results given below for the model of Fig. 1 with exhaustive service and the model in [4] provides additional confirmation of the above statement.

Using a discrete-time approach, an explicit solution for the mean queueing delay of the model described has been derived by Konheim and Meister [5] under the assumption of equal arrival rates λ_i and equal switchover delays τ_i. In order to eliminate the impact of the discrete-time assumption for our comparison purposes, we subsequently consider the case of the discrete-time interval approaching zero. For this limiting case and Poisson arrival processes, we can deduce the following result for the mean transfer time t_f:

$$t_f = \frac{\rho E[T_p^2]}{2(1-\rho)E[T_p]} + E[T_p] + \frac{\tau\left(1 - \frac{\rho}{S}\right)}{2(1-\rho)} + \frac{\tau}{2} \tag{1}$$

with

$$\rho = \lambda E[T_p], \quad T_p = (L_h + L_p)/v.$$

Equation (1) is also in consonance with a result given by Sykes [6] for the special case of $S = 2$ queues.

A necessary assumption underlying (1) is that all stations generate the same amount of traffic. If the traffic offered is unbalanced among the stations, no explicit analytic result is known; however, the following consideration provides some insight into the nature of this case. Let us consider a newly arriving packet. Under our exhaustive-service discipline, the token-passing overhead associated with the transmission of this and subsequent packets is maximum if the probability that the packet joins an empty queue is as high as possible. The latter probability is maximum if the arrival rates of all stations are equal. Although this consideration is obviously not a rigorous proof, it suggests that, with respect to the transfer delay averaged over all stations, (1) is not only exact for the balanced-traffic case but, moreover, represents an upper bound on the overall mean transfer delay, irrespective of the station-specific arrival rates.

Since token rings differ in the way their stations issue a new token, we subsequently discuss how these different possibilities can be analyzed.

In the basic model developed so far, a new free token was generated immediately after the last bit of a packet had left the sending station. This implies that, depending on packet length and physical length of the ring at any given time, multiple tokens can exist on the ring; at most one of them, however, is in the free state ("multiple-token" operation).

From a reliability and recovery point of view, it may be desirable never to have more than one token at a time on the ring. This can be achieved in two ways: 1) The conservative approach is that the sender of a packet issues the new token when he has completely erased his entire packet ("single-packet" operation). In our performance model, this can simply be taken into account by prolonging the packet service time T_p by the total ring roundtrip delay τ. 2) A more efficient solution is that the sender of a packet does not issue a new token before he has received his own token ("single-token" operation). This rule becomes effective in cases when a packet is shorter than the ring latency. In our performance model, we can describe this mode by setting the service time T_p equal to the ring latency for all those packets shorter than the ring latency.

This means all three kinds of token-ring operation can be handled by the cyclical queueing model of Fig. 2 by appropriately adjusting the service-time distribution.

B. Slotted Ring

In the type of slotted rings [1], [2], [7] which we study, a constant number of fixed-length slots continuously circulates around the ring. A full/empty indicator within the slot header is used to signal the state of a slot. Any station ready to transmit occupies the first empty slot by setting the full/empty indicator to "full," and places its data into the slot. When the sender receives back the occupied slot, it changes the full/empty indicator to "empty." This operation prevents hogging of the ring and guarantees fair sharing of the bandwidth among all stations. Using a representation similar to the previous one, operation of the slotted ring is illustrated in Fig. 3. For simplicity, it is assumed that the ring carries a single slot only. Furthermore, it is assumed that both stations 1 and 2 have a packet ready to transmit. Usually, the slots in local rings are short, which means that a packet or message has to be transmitted within several slots. As the figure shows, both stations share the ring bandwidth in a fair way until they have completely transmitted their packets. Figure 3(b), in a different representation, shows when and by which station the slot is occupied. What can be clearly observed from this representation is that between two subsequent access possibilities of a certain station, the slot travels exactly once around the ring in empty state. To simplify the modeling, we slightly modify the sequence of Fig. 3(b) as shown in Fig. 3(c). All time periods of one cycle during which the slot is empty are lumped together in one contiguous empty-slot interval. The inaccuracy in the transfer time introduced by this simplification is on the order of the slot length, which is negligible since we subsequently study the case of short slots.

The operation illustrated in Fig. 3(c) is described by the queueing model shown in Fig. 4 with $S + 1$ queues, where S is the number of stations attached to the ring. Packets waiting

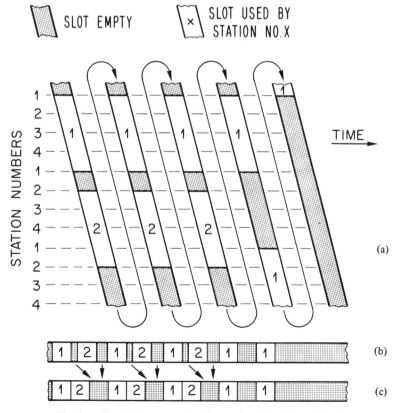

Fig. 3. Slotted ring: example of operation (4 stations, 1 slot).

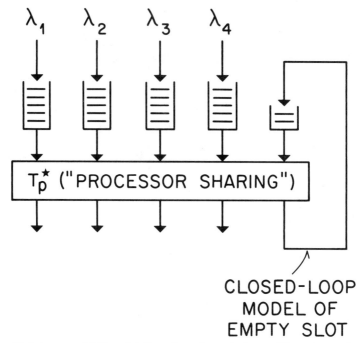

Fig. 4.   Slotted-ring model ($S = 4$ stations; λ_i: packet arrival rates; T_p^*: packet service time).

in one of the queues are served in sequence for a short time quantum Δt which corresponds to the slot length. Between two successive access possibilities of a station, the free slot has made exactly one complete cycle around the ring. Since the ring latency corresponds to one slot duration, it can be described exactly by the closed loop in Fig. 4 which constantly contains one fictitious customer.

For analytic convenience, we subsequently adopt the point of view that the service quantum Δt shrinks to zero. This concept was introduced by Kleinrock in the context of time-sharing systems [8]. It is well known that the resulting "processor-sharing" model yields very good approximations to the finite-quantum results if the quantum is sufficiently short compared to the mean service time [9]. Since in the local environment, on the average, packets are usually at least ten times longer than the slot, this condition is normally fulfilled.

If a ring operates with more than one slot, the exact description of the operation is less simple. However, if we again consider the limiting case of the slot size approaching zero, the processor-sharing model of Fig. 4 also applies for this case, as is subsequently explained. The concept for treating the case of $\sigma > 1$ slots is to fictitiously reorder the sequence of the slots such that always σ slots occupied by the same station can be conceived as lumped together forming one service quantum. The difference between the transfer time of the real scheme with the original slot sequence and the fictitious scheme with the reordered sequence is on the order of a slot, i.e., a service quantum. Hence, as the quanta shrink to zero, this reordering does not affect the transfer delay of the packets so that the processor-sharing model of Fig. 4 still applies.

In order to determine the mean transfer time, the model of Fig. 4 can be conceived as a simple mixed queueing network with $(S + 1)$ classes of customers [10]. If we denote by x_i the number of packets within queue Q_i, we can determine the steady-state probabilities of the model as

$$p(\vec{x}) = p(x_1, \cdots, x_S)$$

$$= (1-\rho)^2 \begin{pmatrix} x_1 + \cdots + x_S + 1 \\ x_1, \cdots, x_S \end{pmatrix} \rho_1^{x_1} \cdots \rho_S^{x_S} \tag{2}$$

with

$$\rho_i = \lambda_i E[T_p^*]; \quad \rho = \sum_{i=1}^{S} \rho_i.$$

With respect to the average packet service time $E[T_p^*]$, we must note that every slot consists of a data field of length L_d and a header field of length L_h. We take this into account by prolonging the mean packet service time according to

$$E[T_p^*] = \frac{L_h + L_d}{L_d} \cdot \frac{E[L_p]}{v} . \tag{3}$$

It should be noted that in this way the impact of the overhead for control and addressing is correctly taken into account and that this must not be confused with the concept of considering the limiting case of the service quanta approaching zero length.

From (2), the expectation of the total number of packets in the system is simply derived; application of Little's theorem [9] leads directly to the following simple expression for the mean transfer time:

$$t_f = \frac{2}{1-\rho} E[T_p^*] + \frac{\tau}{2} . \tag{4}$$

Depending on the number of attached stations, a gap between the slots exists in a real system if the buffering capacity of the ring is not an integral multiple of the slot size. For the examples in Section III, we assume that the length of this gap is always zero, in other words, that the ring bandwidth can be fully utilized. This means we assume for simplicity that the following relation holds among ring latency τ, transmission rate v, slot length $L_h + L_d$, and the number of slots σ:

$$\tau \cdot v = \sigma(L_h + L_d). \tag{5}$$

The above analysis of a local area slotted ring turns out to yield accurate results over a broad range of parameters as comparisons to simulation results show (see, e.g., Fig. 12).

C. CSMA Collision-Detection Bus

Among the numerous random-access schemes (see, for example, [9], [11]), carrier sense multiple access with collision detection (CSMA/CD) appears to be a very attractive solution for use on a bus system [2], [12]. Under a CSMA/CD protocol, every station wanting to transmit a packet must listen to the bus in order to find out whether any transmission is in progress. In this case, it defers its transmission until the end of the current transmission. In spite of carrier sensing, packet collisions cannot be completely avoided because of the nonzero propagation delay of the bus. Upon detection of a collision, transmission is aborted and the station reschedules its packet by selecting a random retransmission interval. Figure 5 illustrates this operation. To avoid accumulation of retransmissions, in other words, to achieve stability, the retransmission interval is dynamically adjusted to the actual traffic load.

Performance analyses of CSMA/CD systems have been performed by Lam [13] and Tobagi and Hunt [14]. For our comparison, we adopt the solution given in [13] which has been derived under the assumption that the system is stabilized by using a suitable adaptive algorithm. For reasons of analytical tractability, a slotted channel with slot length 2τ was assumed in [13]. A consequence of this assumption is that even if the utilization approaches zero, packets have to wait for the time τ on the average before they are transmitted. Since this access delay does not occur in a nonslotted system, it may be the source of possible misinterpretations of our comparative results. Therefore, we heuristically modify the delay formula in [13] by reducing the mean delay by τ. This is further motivated by the consideration that the mean queueing delay of a normal $M/G/1$ queue and that of an $M/G/1$ queue with clocked service differs by half the clock interval. With this slight modification of the delay formula in [13], the mean transfer time of the bus with CSMA and collision detection is given by

$$t_f = \frac{\lambda\{E[T_p^2] + (4e+2)\tau E[T_p] + 5\tau^2 + 4e(2e-1)\tau^2\}}{2\{1 - \lambda(E[T_p] + \tau + 2e\tau)\}} + E[T_p]$$

$$+ 2\tau e - \frac{(1 - e^{-2\lambda\tau})\left(\dfrac{2}{\lambda} + \dfrac{2\tau}{e} - 6\tau\right)}{2\left\{F_p^*(\lambda)e^{-\lambda\tau}\dfrac{1}{e} - 1 + e^{-2\lambda\tau}\right\}} + \frac{\tau}{2}. \tag{6}$$

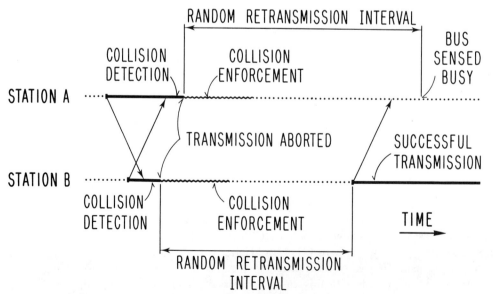

Fig. 5.   CSMA collision-detection bus: example of operation.

The term F_p^* in (6) stands for the Laplace transform of the probability density function of the packet service time $T_p = (L_h + L_p)/v$.

Two comments on the validity of this model are in order.

1) The model assumes that after a successful transmission, a time interval equal to the end-to-end signal propagation delay expires before stations sense end-of-carrier and start to transmit. This represents a slightly pessimistic view of the operation of a real CSMA/CD system [15].

2) The standardized CSMA/CD access protocol [15] requires to have a minimum frame length of twice the end-to-end propagation delay. This effect has not been taken into account in the above model.

Results from a modified model which accurately reflects the above effects as well as the parameters of the standard CSMA/CD protocol have been reported in [16].

D. Ordered-Access Bus

As an example of a bus system employing ordered access, we consider the reservation-type scheme MLMA (multilevel multiple access) proposed by Rothauser and Wild [17] which works as follows. Information transmission occurs in variable-length frames, the structure of which is shown in Fig. 6. A controller provides start flags at appropriate time intervals which signal the beginning of a frame. A frame is divided into two parts, a request slot and an arbitrary number of packets. In the version of MLMA considered here, every station attached to the bus owns one bit within the request slot. By setting its private bit, a station indicates that it wants to transmit a packet within this frame. At the end of the request cycle, all stations know which of the stations will make use of this frame. The transmission sequence is given by a priority assignment known to all stations.

The performance model to describe this kind of operation is shown in Fig. 7. The bus is modeled as a single-server facility. Packets from all stations, which have been newly generated and have not yet been scheduled, form the distributed queue Q_0. According to the above bus operation, these new packets cannot be transmitted within the current frame but have to wait until the new frame starts. At this point, all packets within Q_0 simultaneously

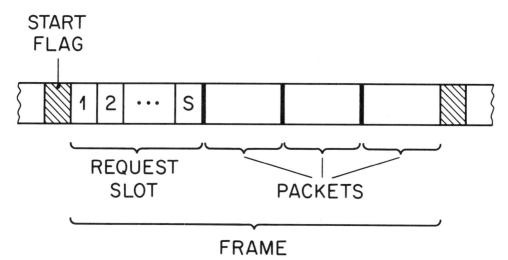

Fig. 6.   Frame structure of the ordered-access bus. From [18].

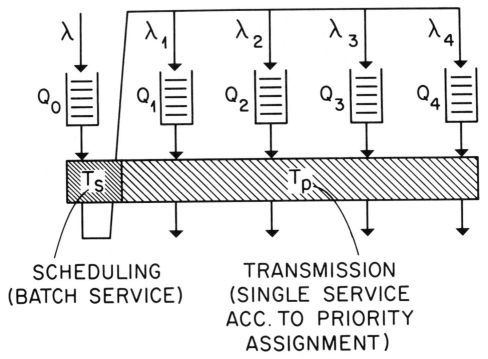

Fig. 7. Ordered-access bus model ($S = 4$ stations; λ_i: packet arrival rates; λ: total packet arrival rate; B: packet service time; T_S: scheduling time). From [18].

obtain a first service phase of length T_S which represents the time needed for scheduling. To ensure that all stations know the entries made in the request slot, the scheduling time T_S may have to be significantly longer than the pure transmission time of the request slot. In our examples, we set T_S equal to twice the time needed to transmit S bits plus twice the propagation delay τ. Following the batch service of length T_S, the packets are put into queues Q_1–Q_S, where Q_1 contains the scheduled packets of the station with highest priority and, accordingly, Q_S those with lowest priority. When all packets in queues Q_1–Q_S have been transmitted, a new frame is started.

The version of the MLMA method described above is similar in concept to a bus access method which has been described and approximately analyzed by Mark [19], and to a contention resolution method for computer-interrupt systems suggested by Taub [20].

In the Appendix, the mean transfer time of this ordered-access bus is derived as

$$t_f = \frac{\rho' \left\{ E[T_p^2] + \tau E[T_p] + \frac{\tau^2}{3} \right\}}{2(1-\rho') \left\{ E[T_p] + \frac{\tau}{2} \right\}} + E[T_p] + \frac{3-\rho'}{1-\rho'} \frac{T_S}{2} + \frac{\tau}{2} \tag{7}$$

with

$$\rho' = \lambda \left\{ E[T_p] + \frac{\tau}{2} \right\}, \qquad T_p = (L_h + L_p)/v.$$

The underlying assumption of (7) is that the distance between two stations transmitting in succession is uniformly distributed between zero and the maximum bus length.

III. Results

In this section, we present typical performance results for the four subnetworks. All subsequent figures show on the ordinate the mean transfer time t_f relative to the mean packet transmission time $E[L_p]/v$. (Note that packet transmission time is defined here as the time required to transmit a packet without header.) In Figs. 8–12, the abscissa represents the ratio of throughput rate $\lambda E[L_p]$ (bits/s) and transmission rate (speed) v.

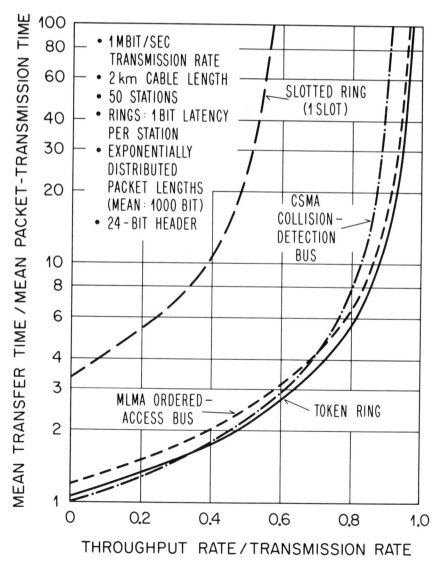

Fig. 8.   Transfer delay-throughput characteristics of the four subnetworks at 1 Mbit/s.

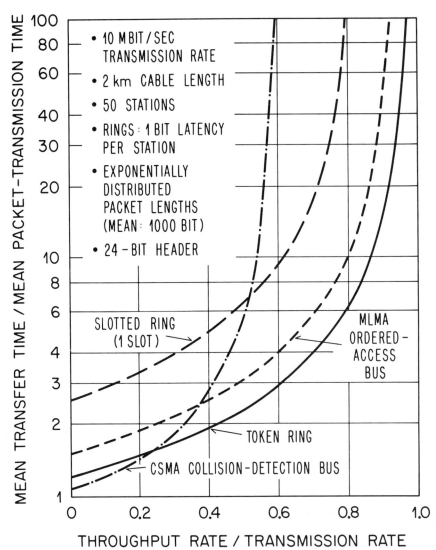

Fig. 9.   Transfer delay-throughput characteristics of the four subnetworks at 10 Mbits/s.

Figure 8 compares the delay-throughput characteristic of the four systems at a transmission rate of 1 Mbit/s. The figure shows that under these assumptions the token ring and the two buses perform almost equally well, because the overhead for the various access mechanisms is almost negligible. (Note that in this and the next two figures, the ''single-token'' kind of operation has been assumed for the token ring.) The slotted ring (one slot) exhibits considerably worse performance than the other systems because of the following two effects. 1) The buffering capability and, hence, slot length of the ring is small (60 bits in this example). This leads to an unfavorable ratio of the header length (24 bits assumed here) to the data field per slot. 2) The time needed for passing around access permission—in the form of an empty slot—is significant, as already discussed in the context of Fig. 3. An additional discussion of the delay behavior of slotted rings is provided in the context of Fig. 12.

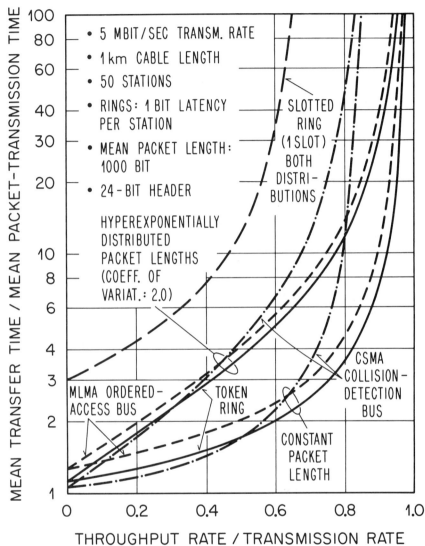

Fig. 10. Transfer delay-throughput characteristics of the four subnetworks for constant and hyperexponentially distributed packet lengths.

In Fig. 9, only one parameter has been changed as compared to the previous example, namely, the transmission rate, which is now 10 Mbits/s. The most remarkable difference is observed for the CSMA/CD bus: whereas for loads less than 0.2 it shows the best performance, the transfer delay increases rather rapidly for loads greater than 0.4 and has a vertical asymptote at about 0.6. The obvious reason for this behavior is that for higher throughput values, the frequency of transmission attempts during the vulnerable period of the propagation delay is such that a significant portion of transmission attempts ends in collision. Thus, the transfer delay increases due to the need for retransmissions.

Investigations of other policies indicate that the maximum achievable throughput can be slightly increased by using a different CSMA/CD protocol [14]. Nevertheless, the general conclusion drawn from this figure remains true, namely, that even a sophisticated random-

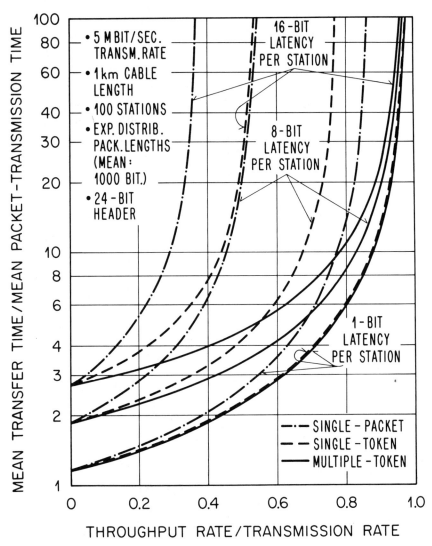

Fig. 11.   Transfer delay-throughput characteristic of token rings. Impact of station latency and operational mode.

access scheme like CSMA/CD leads to inefficient operation if the ratio of propagation delay to packet transmission time is too high. It should be noted that our assumption of only 5 μs propagation delay per km cable represents an optimistic view, since other delay components such as signal rise times or repeater delays may significantly increase the total end-to-end propagation delay. In contrast to the CSMA/CD bus, the token ring performs almost ideally for higher speeds. Its slightly higher delay for low throughput is due to the access delay of the ring until a free token arrives. The transfer time of the MLMA ordered-access bus is slightly longer than that of the token ring over the whole range of throughput values. This is mainly due to the bus-scheduling overhead. As can be seen from comparison of Figs. 8 and 9, performance of the slotted ring improves considerably if the transmission

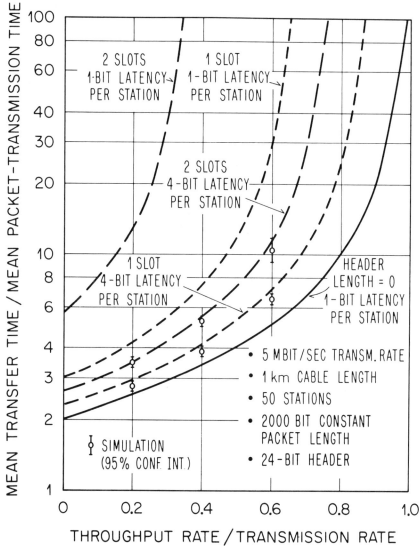

Fig. 12. Transfer delay-throughput characteristic of slotted rings. Impact of slot number and latency per station.

rate is increased: since the slots become longer, the relative overhead for control and addressing decreases.

The examples considered so far have been gained under the assumption of exponentially distributed packet lengths. Figure 10 shows the delay-throughput characteristics for two other types of packet-length distributions: constant length and hyperexponential distribution of order two with a coefficient of variation equal to two. According to (4), the mean transfer time of the slotted ring is independent of the type of packet-length distribution. This is a consequence of the processor-sharing type of operation. The other three subnetworks show growing transfer delay if the variance of the packet-length distribution increases. It can be seen, however, that the general relation among the transfer delay of the three systems is robust with respect to packet-length distribution.

The following figures show results for the individual subnetworks to demonstrate the impact of certain parameters especially critical for the different systems.

Figure 11 visualizes that in a token ring the latency caused within the stations by actions like token handling or altering of control information represents a critical quantity. It shows, in particular, how the three different operational modes of the token ring described in Section II-A, "multiple token," "single token," and "single packet," perform for different values of the station latency. Two conclusions can be drawn from this result: 1) In general, the station latency should be kept as low as possible, at least if a great number of stations is attached or short packets are used. 2) If the ring latency is low, no significant benefits can be drawn from allowing multiple concurrent tokens on the ring, whereas for greater latency, multiple-token operation appears necessary to achieve reasonable performance.

Figure 12 shows that, from an efficiency point of view, for a slotted ring in the local environment, the use of one slot is usually preferable to using two or more slots. This insight is in accordance with results gained from a simulation study of slotted rings [21]. The relation of header length to data per slot can be improved by inserting artificial latency in the ring. As shown in Fig. 12 for the case of four-bit latency per station as compared to one bit, this can actually result in shorter transfer times. However, as becomes clear from (4), the mean transfer time of the slotted ring is roughly twice that of an $M/M/1$ queue even if the header length is zero. One can consider this as the price paid for the advantages of the processor-sharing kind of operation. Also shown in Fig. 12 are results obtained with a simulation model in which the ring operation was modeled in full detail. This and other examples indicate the validity of the model developed in Section II-B over a broad range of slot numbers and sizes.

Figure 13 shows for a CSMA/CD bus the mean transfer time relative to the mean packet-transmission time as a function of the propagation delay relative to the packet-transmission time. For simplicity, the header length has been set to zero in this example. The figure indicates that the CSMA/CD bus behaves ideally as long as the ratio of propagation delay to mean packet-transmission time is sufficiently low. If for reasonable traffic loads this ratio exceeds 2–5 percent (as a rule of thumb), the increasing collision frequency causes significant performance degradation.

IV. SUMMARY

In this chapter, we considered the performance of four local area subnetworks: token ring, slotted ring, CSMA/CD bus, and an ordered-access bus. To guarantee a fair comparison, a prime objective was to study the systems based on consistent assumptions. Although the considered transfer delay-throughput behavior does not completely character-ize all performance aspects of local area networks, the analysis of this measure leads to basic insight into the performance properties of the different approaches.

APPENDIX

DERIVATION OF THE MEAN TRANSFER DELAY FOR THE ORDERED-ACCESS BUS

In this Appendix, we derive delay formula (7). We denote by $b(t)$ and $s(t)$ the probability density functions of the packet service time B and the scheduling interval T_S

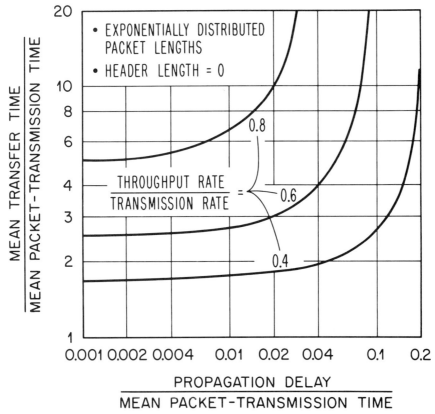

Fig. 13. Normalized mean transfer delay versus propagation delay relative to mean packet-transmission time for the CSMA/CD bus. From [18].

(assumed to be a random variable here). The service time B of a packet, i.e., the time it occupies the bus, has two components: 1) its transmission time, and 2) the propagation delay between subsequently transmitting stations. The assumption made for (7) is that the second component is uniformly distributed between zero and the maximum bus propagation delay.

We derive the mean transfer time $t_f(k)$ of the packets from queue Q_k by tracing a "tagged" packet of this queue on its way through the system. The transfer delay of the tagged packet consists of the following parts: 1) the time until the start of the next frame, subsequently denoted as residual frame length F_r; 2) the scheduling delay T_S; 3) the delay $D_1(k)$ due to packets in the higher priority queues $Q_1, \cdots, Q_{k-1}$; 4) the delay $D_2(k)$ due to those packets in queue Q_k which are transmitted before the tagged packet; and 5) its own service time B.

Taking expectations of these times, we obtain

$$t_f(k) = E[F_r] + E[T_S] + E[D_1(k)] + E[D_2(k)] + E[B]. \tag{A1}$$

We subsequently show how the unknown terms $E[F_r]$, $E[D_1(k)]$, and $E[D_2(k)]$ can be determined.

Residual Frame Length: If we denote by F the total random frame length, then the following relation is known from renewal theory (see, e.g., [9]):

$$E[F_r] = \frac{E[F^2]}{2E[F]} . \tag{A2}$$

We denote by $f_j(t)$ the probability density function of the length of the jth frame. Furthermore, let $F_j^*(p)$, $S^*(p)$, and $B^*(p)$ be the Laplace–Stieltjes transforms of $f_j(t)$, $s(t)$, and $b(t)$, respectively.

The length of the jth frame is given by the scheduling delay plus the sum of the transmission times of all packets which arrived during frame $(j - 1)$. Hence, the following recursive relation holds:

$$f_j(t) = \sum_{n=0}^{\infty} \{b^{(n)}(t)*s(t)\} \int_0^{\infty} e^{-\lambda t} \frac{(\lambda t)^n}{n!} f_{j-1}(t) \ dt \tag{A3}$$

where $b^{(n)}(t)$ denotes the nth convolution of $b(t)$.

Transforming (A3) yields

$$F_j^*(p) = \sum_{n=0}^{\infty} B^*(p)^n S^*(p) \int_0^{\infty} e^{-\lambda t} \frac{(\lambda t)^n}{n!} f_{j-1}(t) \ dt$$

$$= S^*(p)F_{j-1}^*(\lambda\{1 - B^*(p)\}). \tag{A4}$$

Under stationary assumptions, we obtain the following functional equation for the limit of F_j^* as j approaches infinity:

$$F^*(p) = S^*(p)F^*(\lambda\{1 - B^*(p)\}). \tag{A5}$$

By differentiating (A5) and taking values for $p = 0$, we finally obtain

$$E[F] = \frac{E[T_S]}{1 - \rho} \tag{A6}$$

$$E[F^2] = E[F]^2 + \frac{E[T_S^2] - E[T_S]^2 + \lambda E[F]E[B^2]}{1 - \rho^2} \tag{A7}$$

with $\rho = \lambda E[B]$.

We remark that an alternative, although less direct, way to derive (A6) and (A7) is to make use of a result for the number of customers served during one cycle of a multiqueue system [22].

Delay Component $D_1(k)$: The mean number of packets in queue Q_ν which are generated after the start of the last frame but before the tagged packet is given by

$$\psi_b(\nu) = \lambda_\nu E[F_e] \tag{A8}$$

where F_e is defined as the elapsed frame length until the arrival of the tagged customer.

Again, it is known from renewal theory that the distribution of the elapsed frame length is equal to the distribution of the residual frame length:

$$E[F_e] = E[F_r] = \frac{E[F^2]}{2E[F]} . \tag{A9}$$

The mean number of packets in queue Q_ν which are generated after the tagged packet but before the start of the next frame is given by

$$\psi_a(\nu) = \lambda_\nu E[F_r]. \tag{A10}$$

Therefore, the expectation of $D_1(k)$ is given by

$$E[D_1(k)] = \sum_{\nu=1}^{k=1} \{\psi_b(\nu) + \psi_a(\nu)\} E[B]$$

$$= \sum_{\nu=1}^{k-1} \rho_\nu \frac{E[F^2]}{E[F]} . \tag{A11}$$

Delay Component $D_2(k)$: Since we assume first-come/first-served within each queue, the delay $D_2(k)$ is due to packets in queue Q_k which arrived after the beginning of the last frame but before the tagged packet. Its expectation is therefore given by

$$E[D_2(k)] = \lambda_k E[F_e] E[B]$$

$$= \rho_k \frac{E[F^2]}{2E[F]} . \tag{A12}$$

Mean Transfer Time $t_f(k)$: We have now determined all components of the mean transfer time in (A1). By substituting (A2), (A6), (A7), (A11), and (A12) into (A1), we obtain

$$t_f(k) = \frac{1}{2}\left(1 + 2\sum_{\nu=1}^{k-1} \rho_\nu + \rho_k\right)\left\{\frac{E[T_S]}{1-\rho}\left(1 + C_s^2 \frac{1-\rho}{1+\rho}\right) + \frac{\rho E[B^2]}{(1-\rho^2)E[B]}\right\} + E[B] + E[T_S] \tag{A13}$$

with

$$C_s^2 = \frac{E[T_S^2] - E[T_S]^2}{E[T_S]^2} . \tag{A14}$$

For the case of a constant scheduling interval T_S and the particular definition of the packet service time given above, we finally obtain (7) from (A13) by averaging over all stations.

ACKNOWLEDGMENT

The author would like to thank K. Kümmerle for reviewing the manuscript, and H. L. Truong for his help in producing the simulation results.

REFERENCES

[1] B. K. Penney and A. A. Baghdadi, "Survey of computer communications loop networks: Parts 1 and 2," *Comput. Commun.*, vol. 2, pp. 165–180, 224–241, 1979.

[2] D. D. Clark, K. T. Pogran, and D. P. Reed, "An introduction to local area networks," *Proc. IEEE*, vol. 66, pp. 1497–1517, 1978.

[3] P. J. Kuehn, "Multiqueue systems with nonexhaustive cyclic service," *Bell Syst. Tech. J.*, vol. 58, pp. 671–698, 1979.

[4] A. R. Kaye, "Analysis of a distributed control loop for data transmission," in *Proc. Comput. Commun. Networks and Teletraffic Symp.*, Brooklyn, NY: Polytechnic, 1972, pp. 47–58.

[5] A. G. Konheim and B. Meister, "Waiting lines and times in a system with polling," *J. Ass. Comput. Mach.*, vol. 21, pp. 470–490, 1974.

[6] J. S. Sykes, "Simplified analysis of an alternating-priority queueing model with setup times," *Oper. Res.*, vol. 18, pp. 1182–1192, 1970.

[7] A. Hopper, "Data ring at computer laboratory, University of Cambridge," in *Computer Science and Technology: Local Area Networking*. Washington, DC: Nat. Bur. Stand., NBS Special Pub. 500-31, 1977, pp. 11–16.

[8] L. Kleinrock, "Time-shared systems: A theoretical treatment," *J. Ass. Comput. Mach.*, vol. 14, pp. 242–261, 1967.

[9] ——, *Queueing Systems,* Vols. I and II. New York: Wiley, 1975, 1976.

[10] F. Baskett, K. M. Chandy, R. R. Muntz, and F. G. Palacios, "Open, closed, and mixed networks of queues with different classes of customer," *J. Ass. Comput. Mach.*, vol. 22, pp. 248–260, 1975.

[11] L. Kleinrock and F. A. Tobagi, "Packet switching in radio channels: Part I—Carrier sense multiple-access modes and their throughput-delay characteristics," *IEEE Trans. Commun.*, vol. COM-23, pp. 1400–1416, 1975.

[12] R. M. Metcalfe and D. R. Boggs, "Ethernet: Distributed packet switching for local computer networks," *Commun. Ass. Comput. Mach.*, vol. 19, pp. 395–404, 1976.

[13] S. S. Lam, "A carrier sense multiple access protocol for local networks," *Comput. Networks,* vol. 4, pp. 21–32, 1980.

[14] F. A. Tobagi and V. B. Hunt, "Performance analysis of carrier sense multiple access with collision detection," *Comput. Networks,* vol. 4, pp. 245–259, 1980; see also this volume, ch. 20.

[15] "Carrier sense multiple access with collision detection (CSMA/CD), access method and physical layer specifications," ANSI/IEEE Standard 802.3, 1985.

[16] W. Bux, "Performance issues in local-area networks," *IBM Syst. J.*, vol. 23, pp. 351–374, 1984.

[17] E. H. Rothauser and D. Wild, "MLMA: A collision-free multi-access method," in *Proc. IFIP Congress 77,* Amsterdam, The Netherlands: North-Holland, 1977, pp. 431–436.

[18] W. Bux, "Local-area subnetworks: A performance comparison," in *Proc. IFIP Working Group 6.4, 80,* Amsterdam, The Netherlands: North-Holland, 1981, pp. 157–180.

[19] J. W. Mark, "Global scheduling approach to conflict-free multiaccess via a data bus," *IEEE Trans. Commun.*, vol. COM-26, pp. 1342–1352, 1978.

[20] D. M. Taub, "Contention-resolving circuits for computer interrupt systems," in *Proc. Inst. Elec. Eng.*, vol. 123, pp. 845–850, 1976.

[21] A. K. Agrawala, J. R. Agre, and K. D. Gordon, "The slotted vs. the token-controlled ring: A comparative evaluation," in *Proc. COMPSAC 1978,* Chicago, IL: IEEE, 1978, pp. 674–679.

[22] M. A. Leibowitz, "An approximate method for treating a class of multiqueue problems," *IBM J. Res. Develop.*, vol. 5, pp. 204–209, 1961.

23
Measured Performance of the Ethernet

TIMOTHY A. GONSALVES

Recently, local area networks have come into widespread use for computer communications. One protocol that has been widely implemented is the IEEE Standard 802.3 (Ethernet) version of carrier sense multiple access with collision detection (CSMA/CD). While prior analysis has shown that CSMA/CD achieves good performance with data traffic over a range of conditions, the Ethernet implementation has several aspects that are not easily amenable to mathematical analysis. These include the binary-exponential backoff algorithm and the physical distribution of stations. Performance measurements on operational 3 and 10 Mbit/s Ethernets are presented. These demonstrate that the protocol achieves high throughput with data traffic when packets are relatively long, as predicted by analysis. However, at 10 Mbits/s, with short packets on the order of 64 bytes, performance is poorer. These measurements span the range from the region of high performance of the CSMA/CD protocol to the upper limits of its utility where performance is degraded. In comparison to the predictions of existing analytical models, the correlation is found to range from good to poor, with more sophisticated models yielding better results than a simple one.

Simulation is then used to study two related aspects of the behavior of the Ethernet. First, the effects of different physical distributions of stations on the network are quantified. Stations at the center and in large clusters are shown to obtain a disproportionately large share of throughput. Next, it is shown that, with large numbers of stations, while the throughput of the standard Ethernet is poor, a simple modification to the retransmission algorithm enables near-optimal throughput to be achieved.

I. INTRODUCTION

Recently, the Ethernet has come into widespread use for local interconnection [1], [2] and has been accepted as the IEEE 802.3 standard [3]. With increasing usage of networks, high traffic loads and large numbers of stations on a single network are expected to become common, necessitating accurate performance evaluation. To this end, we use measurement on operational 3 and 10 Mbit/s Ethernet networks, conducted at the Xerox Palo Alto Research Centers in 1981–1982, to provide detailed, accurate characterization of performance under a wide range of conditions.[1] We show that the protocol achieves high performance in terms of both throughput and delay, as predicted by prior analysis [5], when the end-to-end propagation delay is small compared to the packet transmission time.

[1] We note that the 10 Mbit/s Ethernet is very similar to the IEEE 802.3 protocol. Thus, our measurements performed on the former are applicable to the latter.

This occurs, for instance, with packet lengths on the order of 1500 bytes on a 10 Mbit/s network. Under overload, throughput remains high at the expense of increase in mean delay and variance of delay. When the propagation delay is relatively large, for instance, with 64 byte packets on a 10 Mbit/s network, performance degrades.

Several analytical studies of various aspects of the *carrier sense multiple access with collision detection* (CSMA/CD) protocol have appeared in the literature [1], [4]–[8]. We compare the predictions of several of these models to our measurements. The correlation ranges from poor for a simple model to good over certain ranges of parameters for more sophisticated ones. We identify differences between the models and the Ethernet implementation that account for the discrepancies, and identify the regions of applicability of these models for prediction of Ethernet performance.

Due to the inflexibility of measurement on operational networks, we then resort to the use of detailed simulation, validated with our measurements, to address two related issues of CSMA/CD performance. First we consider the effects of several physical distributions of stations on performance. With stations uniformly distributed on a linear bus, stations at the center achieve higher performance compared to stations near the ends. While grouping stations into balanced equal-sized clusters has little effect, inequalities in cluster sizes result in stations in larger clusters achieving a disproportionately large share of throughput. Next we show that while the maximum throughput of the standard Ethernet drops with large numbers of stations, a simple modification to the retransmission algorithm enables high throughput to be maintained. Since the throughput of the modified algorithm is close to that predicted by prior analysis using optimum assumptions, we conjecture that this algorithm is near optimum.

A. Related Work

Few studies of the performance characteristics of actual networks have been reported. Throughput measurements on a 3 Mbit/s experimental Ethernet with artificially generated data traffic with fixed packet lengths showed that high throughput was achieved with packet lengths of 64 bytes or greater [9]. Throughput dropped with shorter packets. Extensive observations of traffic under normal operating conditions were also made in this study.[2] We extended these measurements to include delay characteristics and a bandwidth of 10 Mbits/s [10] and emulated voice traffic [11]. Toense described limited measurements on a 1 Mbit/s CSMA/CD network with six stations generating data traffic, reporting high utilizations owing to the low bandwidth [12].

II. EXPERIMENTAL ENVIRONMENT

The Ethernet architecture is described in [1]–[3]. In this section we present implementation details of the 3 Mbit/s *experimental* Ethernet and the 10 Mbit/s Ethernet used in our experiments. We also describe the experimental procedures used.

A. The 3 Mbit/s Experimental Ethernet

The channel length is 550 m with baseband transmission at 2.94 Mbits/s. The propagation delay in the interface circuitry is estimated to be about 0.25 μs [13] yielding an

---

[2] The network used in this study is the 3 Mbit/s experimental Ethernet on which our measurements were performed.

end-to-end propagation delay τ_p of 3 μs. On collision, a *truncated binary exponential backoff* algorithm is used. The mean retransmission delay is doubled after each of the first eight successive collisions of a packet, with a time unit of 38.08 μs. Thereafter, the mean is kept constant and the packet is discarded after 16 successive collisions. Hence, the maximum retransmission delay is 255 × 38.08 μs = 9.7 ms.

B. The 10 Mbit/s Ethernet

The 10 Mbit/s Ethernet is similar to the network described in the previous section with the following exceptions. The channel consists of three 500 m segments connected in series by two repeaters. τ_p is estimated to be about 30 μs, including circuit delays (see [2, p. 52]). The backoff algorithm uses a time unit of 52.2 μs, with the mean being doubled after the first ten collisions. Thus, the maximum retransmission delay is about 53.4 ms. Again, a maximum of 16 attempts is made for each packet.

C. Experimental Procedures

To set up and run an experiment, a test program is loaded into each of N idle stations. A control station is then used to set parameters describing the traffic patterns to be generated by the test programs. Next, the test programs are started simultaneously to generate traffic and record statistics for the duration of the run. At the end, statistics are collected from the participating hosts by the control station. In the 3 Mbit/s Ethernet experiments, the design of the operating system of the stations, Alto minicomputers [14], allowed us to run the entire experiment from a single control station [9]. On the 10 Mbit/s Ethernet, however, loading of the test programs was done manually in each station. The duration of each run was 60–120 s. Our tests show that there is no significant variation in statistics for run times from 10 to 600 s.

Measurements on the 3 Mbit/s Ethernet [9] and our informal observations of traffic on the 10 Mbit/s Ethernet indicate that at night the normal load rarely exceeds a small fraction of 1 percent of the network capacity. Thus, it is possible to conduct controlled experiments with specific traffic patterns and loads on the networks during the late night hours.

Each of the N stations is assumed to have one packet buffer. After completion of transmission of a packet, the station waits for a random period, with mean θ, before the next packet is queued for transmission in its buffer. Note that this corresponds to a central server model, with the network being represented by the central server. The *offered load* of station i, G_i, is defined to be the throughput of station i if the network had infinite capacity, i.e.,

$$G_i = T_p / \theta_i$$

where $T_p = P/C$. The *total offered load* G is given by $\Sigma_{i=1}^{N} G_i$.[3] The idle period is uniformly distributed and packet length P is fixed for all stations for the duration of each run, i.e., we assume a homogenous population.

We assume that if a packet is successfully transmitted it is also successfully received since it has been shown that packet loss due to collisions that the transmitter cannot detect

---

[3] This usage of G differs from the conventional usage to denote the channel offered traffic in infinite population analyses [15]. In the latter, G denotes the rate at which packets, new or previously collided, are scheduled for transmission on the channel.

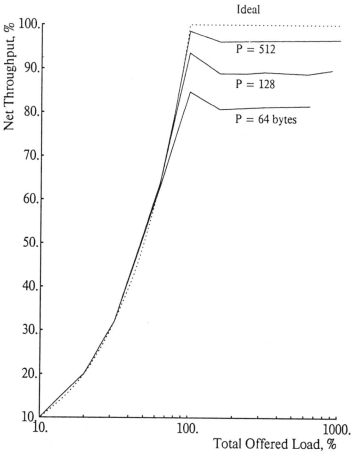

Fig. 1.   3 Mbit/s Ethernet: Throughput versus offered load. Measurements. 32 stations. Parameter, *P*.

[16, p. 72] and due to noise are very infrequent [9]. In computing throughput η, we assume that the entire packet, except for a 6 byte header and checksum,[4] is useful data. Thus, our results represent upper bounds on performance since many actual applications include additional protocol information in each packet. Packets whose transmission is abandoned due to too many collisions are not included in the mean delay computations.

III. MEASURED PERFORMANCE

We now present the measured performance of a 3 and a 10 Mbit/s Ethernet. First we discuss the performance of the networks separately and then make some comparisons.

A. 3 Mbit/s Experimental Ethernet

In this section we describe the measured performance characteristics of a 550 m, 3 Mbit/ s Ethernet. In all the experiments reported, the number of stations *N* was 32.

Throughput: Figure 1 shows the variation of total throughput η with total offered load *G*

[4] We assume 4 bytes of overhead in the case of the 10 Mbit/s Ethernet.

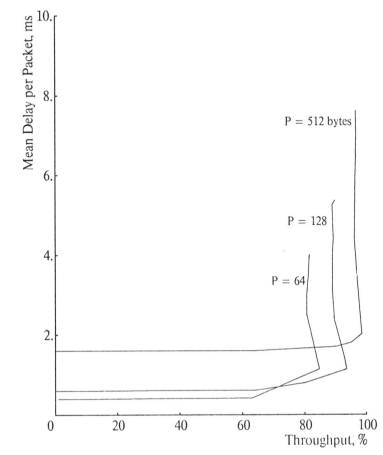

Fig. 2.   3 Mbit/s Ethernet: Delay versus throughput. Measurements. 32 stations. Parameter, *P*.

for $P = 64$, 128, and 512 bytes. For G less than 80–90 percent, virtually no collisions occur and η is equal to G. Thereafter, packets begin to experience collisions and η levels off to some value directly related to P after reaching a peak, η_{max}. For short packets, $P = 64$, this maximum is about 80 percent; for longer packets, $P = 512$, it is above 95 percent. Even under conditions of heavy overload, the load-regulation of the backoff algorithm maintains stability, i.e., throughput η under overload tends to a saturation value that is equal to or marginally lower than η_{max}.[5]

Delay: Figure 2 shows the delay-throughput performance for the same set of packet lengths. In each case, for η less than η_{max}, the delay is approximately equal to the packet transmission time, i.e., there is almost no contention delay for access to the network. As the throughput approaches the maximum, the delay rises rapidly to several times the packet transmission time owing to collisions and the associated backoffs. While a station is incurring a backoff delay, it is not contending for network access. Thus, large delays effectively reduce the instantaneous offered load and help maintain stability.

Figure 3 shows the histograms of the cumulative delay distributions for low, medium,

---

[5] These curves are similar to the ones obtained by Shoch and Hupp [9].

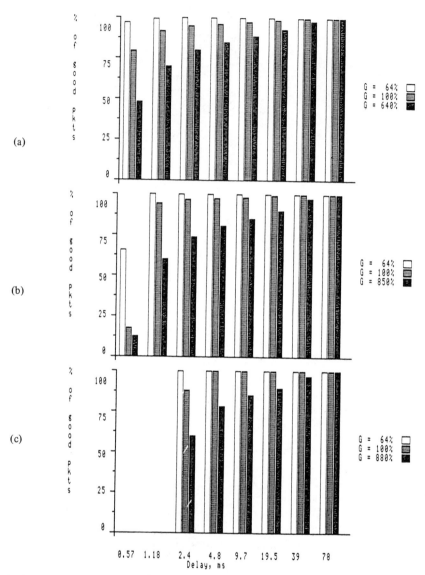

Fig. 3. 3 Mbit/s Ethernet: Cumulative delay distribution. Measurements. 32 stations. (a) P = 64 bytes. (b) P = 128 bytes. (c) P = 512 bytes.

and high offered loads for P = 64, 128, 512 bytes. The delay bins are logarithmic. The labels on the X-axis indicate the upper limit of each bin. The leftmost bin includes packets with delay $\leq$ 0.57 ms, the next bin, packets with delay $\leq$ 1.18 ms, and so on. The ordinate is the number of packets expressed as a percentage of all successfully transmitted packets. Table I gives the fraction of the total packets generated that were successfully transmitted.

We see that for G = 64 percent, the delay of all packets is minimal, i.e., there is little queueing for network access. Even with G = 100 percent most packets suffer delays of less than 5 ms. Under heavy load conditions, however, only about 75 percent of the packets have delays of less than 5 ms, with the remainder suffering delays of up to 80 ms.

TABLE I
3 Mbit/s ETHERNET: SUCCESSFULLY TRANSMITTED
PACKETS AS A PERCENTAGE OF TOTAL PACKETS

$P,$ bytes	$G,$ percent	$\dfrac{\text{Successful Packets}}{\text{Total Packets}}$, percent
64	64	100.0
	100	99.8
	640	96.1
128	64	100.0
	100	99.7
	850	88.3
512	64	100.0
	100	99.9
	880	58.2

Fairness: To investigate the fairness of the protocol to contending stations, we examine variations in performance metrics measured by individual stations with increase in G. In Fig. 4 we plot the normalized mean of the individual throughputs versus G for $P = 64$ and 512 bytes. The vertical bars indicate the normalized standard deviation, i.e., the coefficient of variation. Also shown are the maximum and minimum individual throughputs. For low G, there is little variation in individual throughput. Under overload, the variation increases but remains less than ± 10 percent.

Figure 5 contains similar plots for the mean delay per packet measured by each station. The variations with G are seen to be similar to those in Fig. 4. Thus, the protocol appears to be fair to all contenders. (This has been noted in other experiments [9].) In Section V-A we show that the variations seen in station metrics are not purely random but are dependent in part on the physical location of the stations on the network. Further, the bias due to location is greater with larger a, where a is the ratio of end-to-end propagation delay τ_p to the packet transmission time T_p.

The metrics show slightly higher variation for $P = 512$ than for $P = 64$ bytes. During the successful transmission of a 512 byte packet, a larger number of stations is likely to queue for access to the network. At the end of the transmission all these stations will attempt to transmit and will collide. The time for resolution of the collision is dependent on the number of colliding stations, and hence may be expected to be longer for $P = 512$ than for $P = 64$.

B. 10 Mbit/s Ethernet

We now consider the performance of a 10 Mbit/s Ethernet network. The results presented were obtained using 30–38 transmitting stations.[6]

Throughput: Figure 6 shows the throughput as a function of total offered load G for P ranging from 64 to 5000 bytes. The shape of the curves is similar to the corresponding curves for the 3 Mbit/s Ethernet. However, maximum throughput varies from 25 percent for $P = 64$ bytes (the minimum allowed by the Ethernet specifications [2]), to 80 percent for $P = 1500$ bytes (the maximum allowed), to 94 percent for very long packets of 5000

---

[6] The number of stations for a given set of experiments, i.e., for a single packet length, was constant.

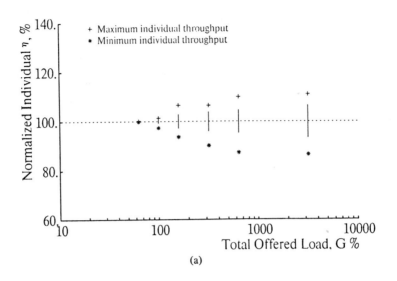

(a)

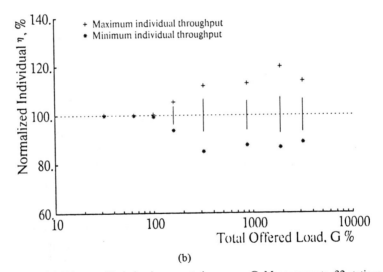

(b)

Fig. 4.   3 Mbit/s Ethernet: Variation in η per station versus G. Measurements. 32 stations. (a) $P = 64$ bytes. (b) $P = 512$ bytes.

bytes. We note that for each curve, for G below the knee point, the throughput is approximately equal to G. Even under conditions of heavy overload, the network remains stable.

Delay: Figure 7 shows the delay-throughput performance for the same set of packet lengths. Again, the curves are similar in shape to those for the 3 Mbit/s network. For G below the knee points, the delay is minimal, while above the knee points, it rises sharply. The knees in this case are less pronounced, especially for larger P.

Figure 8 shows the histograms of the cumulative delay distributions for low, medium, and high offered loads for $P = 64$, 512, and 1500 bytes. Table II gives the fraction of the total packets generated that were successfully transmitted. For low loads, delay is minimal for $P = 512$ and 1500 bytes. For $P = 64$, however, even at $G = 19$ percent, delays range

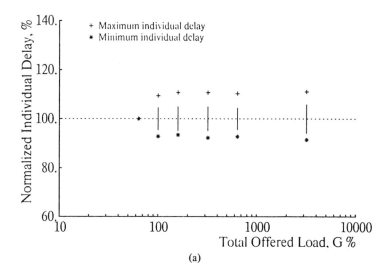

(a)

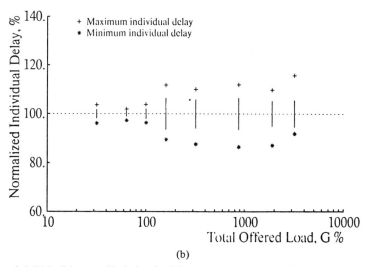

(b)

Fig. 5. 3 Mbit/s Ethernet: Variation in delay per station versus G. Measurements. 32 stations. (a) $P = 64$ bytes. (b) $P = 512$ bytes.

up to $10T_p$. At high loads, for all packet lengths, the majority of packets suffer moderately increased delays, while a fraction suffer very high delays, up to 0.5 s. For $P = 512$ and 1500, about 75 percent of all packets suffer delays $\leq 10T_p$. For $P = 64$, 75 percent of packets suffer delays $\leq 15T_p$.

Fairness: To examine fairness, we plot in Figs. 9 and 10 the normalized means of the individual throughputs and delays, respectively, versus G for $P = 64$ and 512 bytes. The vertical bars indicate the normalized standard deviation, i.e., the coefficient of variation. Also shown are the maximum and minimum individual throughputs.

The metrics show higher variation than in the 3 Mbit/s case, in the range ± 35 percent. This may be attributed to the larger retransmission delays in the 10 Mbit/s Ethernet backoff algorithm. Also, the dependence on G is less marked. Contrary to the 3 Mbit/s case, the

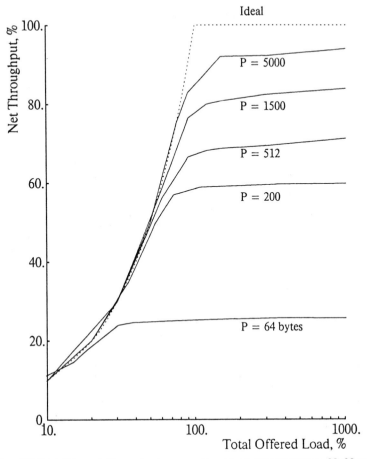

Fig. 6.   10 Mbit/s Ethernet: Throughput versus offered load. Measurements. 30–38 stations. Parameter, P.

variation is slightly lower here for the larger packet size. The issue of fairness is considered further in Section V-A.

C. Comparison of the 3 and 10 Mbit/s Ethernets

In this section we examine the effect of the difference in bandwidth between the two Ethernets on performance. The differences in some important parameters, such as network length, in the two cases should be borne in mind.

Throughput: Figure 11 shows the throughput η as a function of total offered load G for several packet lengths for the two networks. For $P = 64$ bytes, the throughputs of the two networks are almost equal. For longer packets, the 10 Mbit/s network exhibits substantially higher throughput. The throughput increases less than linearly with increases in bandwidth. This is shown in Table III in which the ratio of the absolute throughput at 10 Mbits/s to that at 3 Mbits/s is given for several values of P.

Delay: Figure 12 shows mean packet delay as a function of total offered load, in Mbits/s,

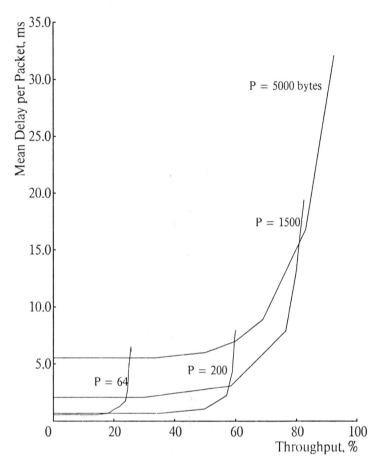

Fig. 7. 10 Mbit/s Ethernet: Delay versus throughput. Measurements. 30–38 stations. Parameter, *P*.

for the two networks and several values of *P*. The shapes of all the curves are similar: there is a region of minimal delay at low *G*, then there is a rapid increase in delay to some saturation value at high *G*. For low *G*, the delay is lower in the 10 Mbit/s network than in the 3 Mbit/s one for a given *P*. However, in the region of overload, the 3 Mbit/s network exhibits lower delay. This is due to the more severe backoff algorithm of the 10 Mbit/s network (Sections II-A and B).

IV. COMPARISON WITH ANALYSIS

Since analytic models of the Ethernet are not available, we are interested to see whether models of CSMA/CD from the literature may be used to predict Ethernet performance. This investigation allows us to use the insights gained from such models for the improvement of the Ethernet protocol. First, the models are briefly described, with the differences from the Ethernet implementation being emphasized. Next, we present a comparison of the analytical predictions to our measured results. This indicates several

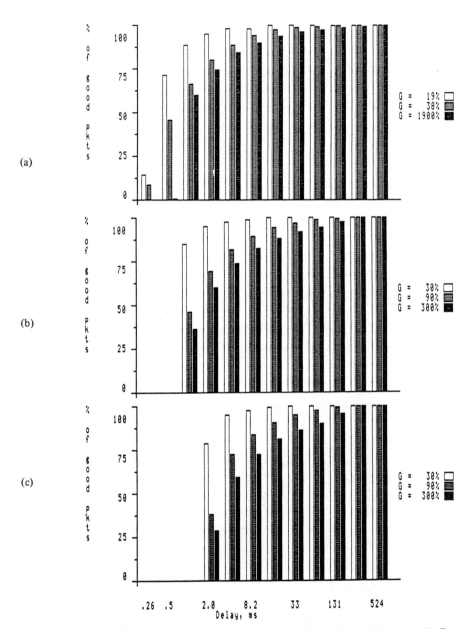

Fig. 8.   10 Mbit/s Ethernet: Cumulative delay distribution. Measurements. 38 stations. (a) P = 64 bytes. (b) P = 512 bytes. (c) P = 1500 bytes.

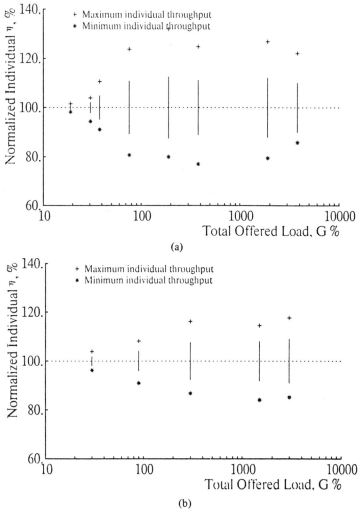

Fig. 9. 10 Mbit/s Ethernet: Variation in η per station versus G. Measurements. 30–38 stations. (a) $P = 64$ bytes. (b) $P = 512$ bytes.

TABLE II
10 Mbit/s ETHERNET: SUCCESSFULLY TRANSMITTED
PACKETS AS A FRACTION OF TOTAL PACKETS

P, bytes	G, percent	$\dfrac{\text{Successful Packets}}{\text{Total Packets}}$, percent
64	19	100.0
	38	100.0
	1900	99.9
512	30	100.0
	90	99.9
	300	98.7
1500	30	100.0
	90	99.7
	300	93.3

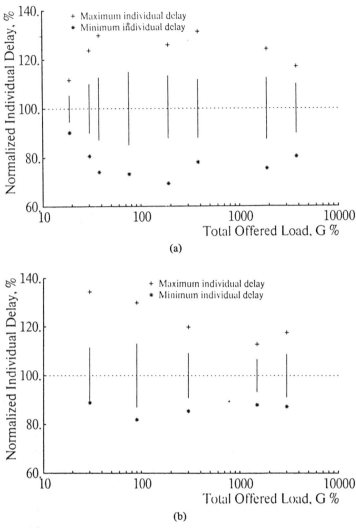

Fig. 10.   10 Mbit/s Ethernet: Variation in delay per station versus *G*. Measurements. 30–38 stations. (a) *P* = 64 bytes. (b) *P* = 512 bytes.

differences, especially in the region where performance begins to degrade, i.e., when $a = \tau_p/T_p$ is large and/or the number of stations is large.

A. The Analytical Models

We choose three analyses for further study here. Metcalfe and Boggs derived a simple formula for prediction of the capacity of finite-population Ethernets [1]. This is of interest because of its simplicity and because it was presented along with the first published description of the Ethernet implementation. Later, more sophisticated stochastic analyses of delay and throughput appeared. Lam used a single-server queueing model to obtain fairly simple expressions for delay and throughput [4]. Tobagi and Hunt applied the method

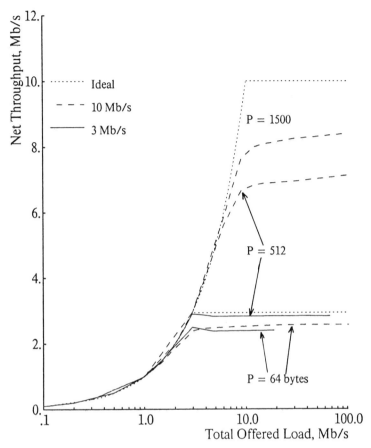

Fig. 11. 3 and 10 Mbit/s Ethernets: Throughput versus G. Measurements. 30–38 stations. Parameter, P.

TABLE III
INCREASE IN η WITH INCREASE IN C
FROM 3 TO 10 Mbits/s

P, bytes	Ratio of throughputs η_{10}/η_3
64	1.05
512	2.45
1500	2.90

of embedded Markov chains [17] to more accurately model CSMA/CD [5]. This study obtained delay characteristics even for the finite population case but involves greater computational complexity. These models differ from the Ethernet primarily in the retransmission strategy used upon a collision. Other differences include the assumption of slotted operation and the topology as noted below. For complete details of the analyses, the reader is referred to the papers cited above.

Metcalfe and Boggs [1]: Metcalfe and Boggs derive a simple formula for η_{max} with a finite population of stations N and fixed packet length P. The topology is assumed to be a

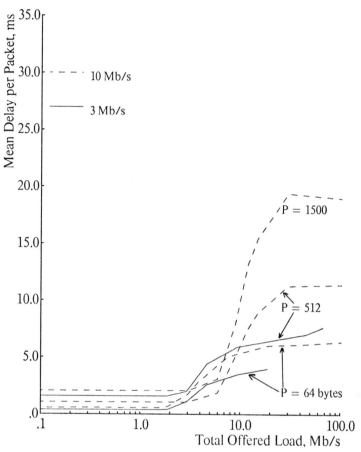

Fig. 12. 3 and 10 Mbit/s Ethernets: Delay versus G. Measurements. 30–38 stations. Parameter, P.

balanced star, i.e., the propagation delay between every pair of stations is assumed to be τ_p. The channel is assumed to be slotted in time. Packets arriving during a slot wait until the start of the next slot at which time all ready stations simultaneously begin transmission. The slot duration is chosen to at least $2\tau_p$ so that any collision can be detected and transmission aborted within one slot. This slotting lumps together two independent parameters τ_p and the jam time t_{jam}. This is especially poor if $t_{jam} \gg \tau_p$. Packet arrivals at each station, both new and retransmissions, are assumed to be such that each station attempts to transmit with the optimum probability of $1/N$ in each slot. The Ethernet implementation attempts to approximate this behavior. With N stations attempting to transmit, the probability of a success is the probability that exactly one chooses to transmit in the slot, i.e., $A = (1 - 1/N)^{N-1}$. Thus, the mean number of slots until a success is $W = (1 - A)/A$. Thus, we have the efficiency

$$\eta = \frac{P/C}{P/C + W \cdot 2\tau_p} = \frac{1}{1 + 2aW}$$

where C is the channel bandwidth, T_p the packet transmission time, and $a = \tau_p/T_p$.

Tobagi and Hunt [5]: Tobagi and Hunt first present a model for estimating the maximum throughput of a CSMA/CD network under the assumption of an infinite population. The topology is assumed to be the balanced star. The channel is assumed to be slotted in time, with slot duration τ_p, to permit the formulation of a discrete-time model. In contrast to Metcalfe and Boggs, t_{jam} is not included in the slot time but, more accurately, is assumed to be independent. Retransmission delays are assumed to be arbitrarily large since the aim is to obtain the maximum throughput. Hence, the arrival of new and retransmitted packets can be assumed to be independent and to form a Poisson process.

Next, a delay-throughput analysis is presented for a finite population system.[7] It is shown that for sufficiently large populations, e.g., 50 stations at $a = 0.01$, the maximum throughput predictions of the finite and infinite population analyses converge, relatively insensitive to N, and so we use the computationally simpler infinite population analysis to obtain η_{max} for our comparisons.

Lam [4]: Lam uses a single-server queueing model to approximate the distributed protocol of the Ethernet [4]. As such it is unable to capture many of the details of the protocol although it is attractive as the expressions obtained are computationally simpler than those of the more exact analysis described above. New packets are assumed to arrive from an infinite population of users in a Poisson process. The balanced star topology is assumed. As in the Metcalfe and Boggs model, the channel is assumed to be slotted with a slot duration of $t_{jam} + 2\tau_p$, leading to inaccuracy when $t_{jam} \gg \tau_p$. Unlike the Ethernet, the retransmission algorithm is assumed to be such that the probability of a successful transmission in each slot is $1/e$. The mean number of slots from the end of the first collision until the next successful transmission is geometrically distributed with mean $(e - 1)$. This optimal retransmission algorithm requires that full knowledge of the state of the system be instantaneously available at all stations. Owing to the constant probability of a success, the system is stable, with throughput tending to an asymptote as load increases. The asymptotic throughput η_{max} is the value we use in the comparison.

B. Measurement and Analysis: Comparison

We now compare the predictions of the models described in the previous section to our measurements. From the formula of Metcalfe and Boggs, we compute η with $N = 32$ to correspond to our measurements (the predicted η does not vary much with N). We use the infinite population analysis of Tobagi and Hunt to obtain η_{max} from the formula for η as a function of G. Table IV shows measured and computed values of maximum throughput for various values of P for the 3 Mbit/s Ethernet. τ_p is estimated to be 3 μs (see Section II-A). Tables V and VI show corresponding sets of values for the 10 Mbit/s Ethernet. The measured values in Table V were obtained on a configuration consisting of 750 m of cable with one repeater while those in Table VI were obtained on the configuration described in Section II-B. τ_p is estimated at 11.75 and 15 μs, respectively.[8]

It is seen that the simple formula of Metcalfe and Boggs overestimates η_{max}, with the error being small for $a < 0.01$ but as high as $+ 100$ percent at large values of a. This may be attributed to the assumption of an optimum retransmission policy. The assumption of slotted operation is also expected to lead to higher predicted capacity. On the other hand, the assumption that every pair of hosts is separated by τ_p would lower the predicted

---

[7] The analysis for the 0-persistent case is presented in [5]. This is extended to the 1-persistent case in [18].
[8] a is computed using the total packet length, including overhead. Throughputs shown are net, excluding overhead.

TABLE IV

3 Mbit/s ETHERNET: MAXIMUM THROUGHPUT, PERCENT.

$\tau_p = 3 \ \mu s \ (550 \ m)$

P, bytes	a	Measured	Metcalfe and Boggs, 76	Tobagi and Hunt, 80	Lam, 80
64	0.016	82	87	80	80
128	0.008	89	93	89	89
512	0.002	97	98	97	97

TABLE V

10 Mbit/s ETHERNET: MAXIMUM THROUGHPUT, PERCENT.

$\tau_p = 11.75 \ \mu s \ (750 \ m \ + \ 1 \ repeater)$

P, bytes	a	Measured	Metcalfe and Boggs, 76	Tobagi and Hunt, 80	Lam, 80
64	0.22	26	55	40	28
200	0.072	62	79	60	54
512	0.028	72	91	77	75
1500	0.0098	86	97	91	90
5000	0.0029	95	99	97	97

TABLE VI

10 Mbit/s ETHERNET: MAXIMUM THROUGHPUT, PERCENT.

$\tau_p = 15 \ \mu s \ (1500 \ m \ + \ 2 \ repeaters)$

P, bytes	a	Measured	Metcalfe and Boggs, 76	Tobagi and Hunt, 80	Lam, 80
64	0.28	26	49	37	25
200	0.092	60	75	58	51
512	0.036	72	88	74	72
1500	0.012	85	96	89	89
5000	0.0037	94	99	96	96
10000	0.0019	97	99	98	98

throughput, but appears to be less significant than the other assumptions. Note that with larger t_{jam}, the value of a at which the error becomes large would be lower because t_{jam} is lumped into the slot duration.

The model of Tobagi and Hunt provides better estimates of η for $a < 0.1$. However, the correspondence is inconsistent, especially at large a. The primary difference between the model and the Ethernet is the nature of the retransmission algorithm. The inconsistency may be due to the accuracy of the estimation of τ_p and to the opposing effects of two assumptions: the optimistic slotted assumption and the pessimistic balanced star topology assumption. Finally, the comparison of infinite population analysis to finite population measurements may be misleading. These issues are addressed in Section V-B.

Considering Lam's model, it is seen to provide fairly good estimates of throughput. However, the correspondence is strongly dependent on the particular parameters under which the measurements were conducted. As we will see in Section V-B the correspondence is poor for other sets of parameters yielding the same value of a. This is due to the approximations introduced in modeling CSMA/CD by a simple single-server queueing model. We note that as in Metcalfe and Boggs' model the validity of Lam's model is further limited by the lumping of t_{jam} and τ_p.

V. FURTHER EXPLORATION VIA SIMULATION[9]

We now study two issues raised by the work discussed hitherto. First, we examine the effects of various physical distributions of stations on performance and on fairness. Next, based on the theoretical predictions that for a given N stable behavior can be achieved by using a fixed retransmission delay, dependent on N, we propose and study a modification to the Ethernet algorithm [20], [5]. This enables high throughput to be maintained even with large numbers of stations. Owing to the inflexibility of measurement on operational networks, especially for the first issue, we use a detailed simulator validated with our measurements [21, Appendix B.2]

The simulation parameters are chosen to resemble the 10 Mbit/s Ethernet and IEEE Standard 802.3 networks. The end-to-end propagation delay τ_p is assumed to be 10 μs, corresponding to a channel length d of 2000 m with a single cable segment, or to a lower value with repeaters. The balanced star topology is assumed, except where otherwise noted, to facilitate comparison with analysis. There are N identical stations.

For each simulation, to allow transients to die down, no statistics are collected for the initial 1 s. Thereafter, the simulation is run for 10 consecutive subruns, each of duration 1 s. This yields 95 percent confidence intervals on the order of 0.5 percent for aggregate statistics. In cases with large delays, longer run times are used.

We have seen that Ethernet performance is dependent on the parameter $a = \tau_p/T_p$. Performance is high at low a and degrades as a increases. We use fixed length packets of $P = 40$ bytes, resulting in $a = 0.313$, to stress the network to its limits. Smaller values of a, corresponding to normal operating conditions, are also studied. To simplify calculations, packet overhead is included in net throughput. Each station has one packet buffer. Interpacket arrival times are exponentially distributed with mean θ. Packets arriving when the buffer is full are discarded. Network interface unit parameters are: carrier and collision detection time, $t_{cd} = 1$ μs; interframe gap (minimum time between the end of one transmission and the start of the next), $t_{gap} = 1$ μs; length of the jam signal, $t_{jam} = 5$ μs.

A. Clustering

We have seen from measurement that there is variation in performance obtained by different stations on a linear bus. We now consider the effect of various distributions of stations on these differences.

We consider $N = 40$ stations, identical except for location. For ease of notation and description we assume, without loss of generality, that the stations are numbered from 1 to N, the numbers increasing monotonically from one end of the network, referred to as the left end, to the other or right end. The stations are distributed along the network in the following configurations.

---

[9] This section contains excerpts from a report published in full elsewhere in collaboration with F. A. Tobagi [19].

- *Uniform:* Stations are spaced uniformly along the length of the network, with every pair of adjacent stations being d/N m apart.
- *Clustered:* The stations are divided into n_c clusters. The stations within each cluster are uniformly spaced 1 m apart. The number of stations in each cluster is not necessarily the same (Fig. 13).

It is useful to define the *vulnerable* period of station i, the period during which another station would have to start transmission in order to cause a collision with i's transmission. Assume that the propagation time from station i to the farthest end of the network is τ and that station i starts transmission at time t. A packet from station j situated at the farthest end of the network will collide with i's transmission only if j starts transmission in the interval $[t - \tau, t + \tau]$. This interval is the vulnerable period of i. The probability that j causes a collision with i's packet is simply the probability that j starts transmission during i's vulnerable period. Note that a station closer to i than the farthest end of the network has a shorter interval about t during which it could cause a collision with i's packet.

To bring out performance differences, we consider moderately heavy loads of $G = 400$ percent. The performance effects to be discussed were noted in simulations with G ranging from 100 to 2000 percent, although with differing magnitudes.

Uniform: With stations uniformly distributed on the network, Fig. 14(a) shows the throughput measured by each station plotted against the station number. (Note that the abscissa is not distance.) The average throughput per station, 1.36 percent, is shown by a dotted line. Likewise, individual delays are plotted in Fig. 14(b), with the average being 1.69 ms. The stations at the center of the network obtain the highest throughput with the lowest delay, while the stations at the ends obtain a lower share of the total throughput. This occurs because the vulnerable period ranges from τ_p for a station at the center to $2\tau_p$ for a station at the end. Thus, centrally located stations suffer fewer collisions per packet, and hence obtain higher throughput, while stations at the ends suffer more collisions, and hence experience higher delays due to retransmissions and longer backoffs.

Clustered: We now consider asymmetrical distributions of stations. We start with three

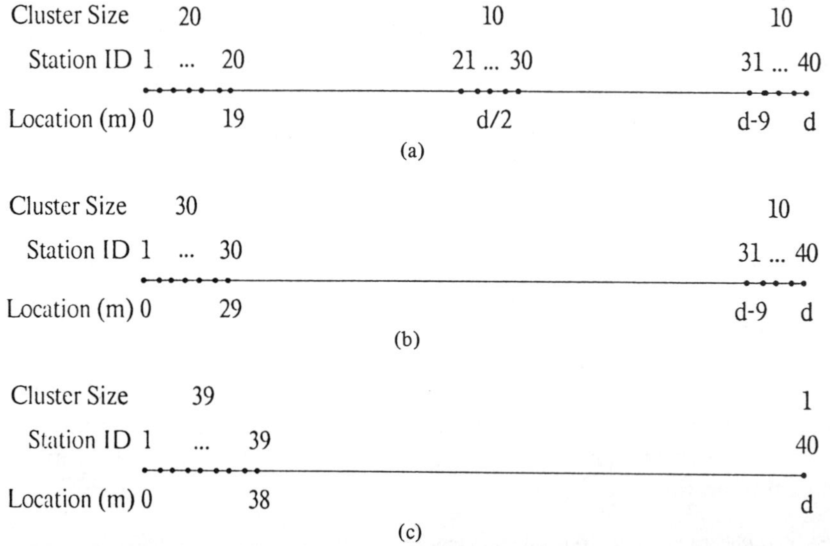

Cluster Size	20		10	10
Station ID 1	...	20	21 ... 30	31 ... 40
Location (m) 0	19		d/2	d-9 d

(a)

Cluster Size	30		10
Station ID 1	...	30	31 ... 40
Location (m) 0	29		d-9 d

(b)

Cluster Size	39		1
Station ID 1	...	39	40
Location (m) 0	38		d

(c)

Fig. 13. Station distribution: clustered. Sizes: (a) 20 + 10 + 10. (b) 30 + 10. (c) 39 + 1.

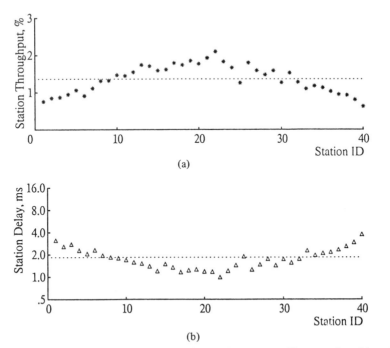

Fig. 14.   10 Mbit/s Ethernet: Individual station performance, uniform spacing. $N = 40$ stations, $G = 400$ percent. (a) Throughput. (b) Delay.

equally spaced clusters of equal sizes and then progressively move stations from the right to the left of the network resulting in the distributions shown in Fig. 13. In the most asymmetrical configuration considered, we have all 40 stations in the leftmost 39 m of the network (effectively, a 39 m network with uniformly spaced stations).

The distributions of individual throughput and delay are plotted in Figs. 15 and 16, respectively. As the asymmetry increases, the net throughput increases markedly from 52 percent in the fully symmetrical case to 68 percent in the case when all the stations are at one end. Considering the performance distributions, stations in the larger clusters obtain a disproportionately large share of the net throughput. When a station in a cluster starts to transmit, the signal propagates in a short period to the ends of that cluster. Hence, the vulnerable period of the station to collision from other stations in the same cluster is small. The packet is vulnerable to collision from stations in other clusters for a relatively much longer time. Thus, a station in a large cluster is less vulnerable than one in a small cluster. In the 20 + 10 + 10 case, the two 10-station clusters obtain significantly different performance, with the one in the center obtaining higher performance due both to being in the center and to being closer to the large 20-station cluster.

C. The Backoff Algorithm

The Ethernet backoff algorithm attempts to dynamically estimate the number of contending stations. For each packet, the estimate starts with 1 and is doubled with each successive collision. If the number of stations is fixed, theoretical studies show that stable and high performance is achieved for some fixed value of retransmission delay. This suggests that an improvement on this algorithm is to use a higher initial estimate which can

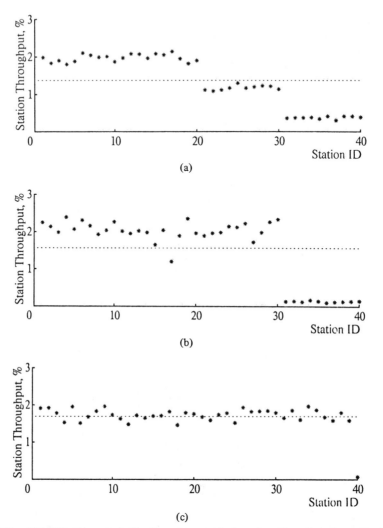

Fig. 15.   10 Mbit/s Ethernet: Station throughputs with clustering. N = 40 stations, G = 400 percent. Cluster sizes: (a) 20 + 10 + 10 stations. (b) 30 + 10 stations. (c) 39 + 1 stations.

be derived from the collision history of previous packets. We assume that some such algorithm exists such that the initial estimate is 2^m, $m > 0$. After the nth collision, the backoff is $\chi \times 51.2$ μs, where χ is a uniformly distributed random variable in the range [0, M) such that:

$$M = \begin{cases} 2^{\min[\max\,(n,m),10]} & \text{if } m < 10 \\ 2^m & \text{if } m \geq 10. \end{cases}$$

For $m \geq 10$, we use M greater than the maximum of 2^{10} specified in the standard Ethernet because the latter value is found to be too small for our purposes as will be shown below. [10]

---

[10] We note that the Intel 82586 Ethernet controller chip allows M to be specified as $2^{\min(n+m,10)}$, for $m > 0$. For $m \leq 10$, this uses the same initial value of χ as our algorithm. With multiple collisions, χ increases more rapidly but reaches the same maximum of 2^{10}.

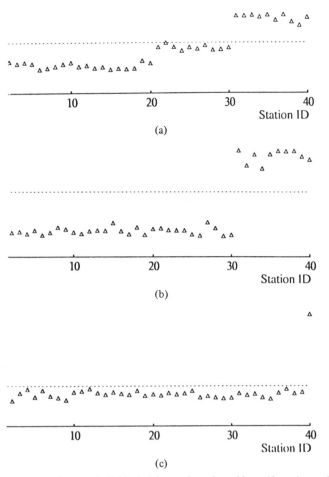

Fig. 16. 10 Mbit/s Ethernet: Individual delays, clustering. $N = 40$ stations, $G = 400$ percent. Cluster sizes: (a) 20 + 10 + 10 stations. (b) 30 + 10 stations. (c) 39 + 1 stations.

To describe the behavior of throughput as offered load varies, we note that at any time a station is in one of three states: the *idle* state, while awaiting the arrival of a new packet; the *active* state, while contending for the channel; and the *backlogged* state, while incurring a retransmission delay after a collision. Note that the active state includes time spent in carrier sensing as well as in transmission.

In Fig. 17 throughput is plotted as a function of χ_{av} for $a = 0.313$ and $N = 400$. Throughput is seen to increase with χ_{av} initially and then to decrease. For a given set of parameters, with the system in equilibrium there is some combined mean arrival rate of new and collided packets. This determines the probability that an arrival will occur during the vulnerable period of a packet, causing a collision. As χ_{av} increases, stations spend longer periods in the backlogged state. Thus, the combined arrival rate decreases leading to a lower probability of collision and hence an increase in η. For sufficiently large values of χ_{av}, for some fraction of time all stations are backlogged and the network is idle resulting in a decrease in η. The optimum value of the mean initial backoff increases with N, being 194, 394, and 1024 for $N = 200$, 400, and 1000, respectively, for the parameters in Fig. 17. Note that these optimum values depend on parameters such as a and G.

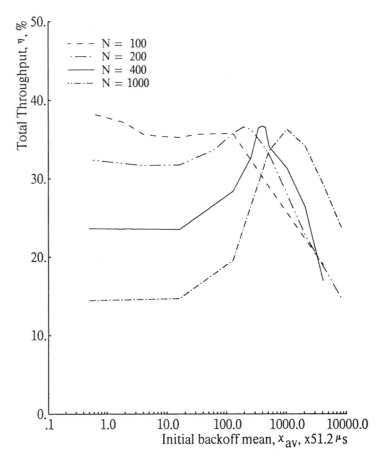

Fig. 17.   10 Mbit/s Ethernet: Throughput versus initial backoff mean. $a = 0.313$. $N = 400$.

Throughput at high loads in the standard Ethernet is a function of N. This dependence is shown in Fig. 18. Throughput at saturation ($G = 3600$ percent) is plotted as a function of N for the standard Ethernet and with the modified backoff algorithm. For the latter the optimum value of m is chosen for each N. By using the optimum backoff throughput remains approximately constant for N ranging from 200 to 1000. For small N, less than about 100, the standard Ethernet algorithm is optimal. For smaller values of a we expect that similar behavior will be observed except that the value of N at which the standard Ethernet algorithm becomes suboptimal will increase due to the relatively shorter vulnerable periods.

If a system is to support a large number of simultaneously active stations each generating a small load, for optimum throughput, a large initial value of x_{av} should be chosen. For example, with $N = 1000$, the optimum is 1024. This yields a total throughput of 36 percent for $a = 0.313$ (Fig. 17) and throughput per station, $\eta_{av} = 0.036$ percent. If at some time fewer stations are active, the total throughput decreases but the throughput per station increases. In our example, with $N = 1000$, 400, and 200, $\eta_{av} = 0.036$, 0.078, and 0.14 percent, respectively, with average delays of 87, 40, and 25 ms, respectively. Thus, individual stations are not adversely affected by the modified algorithm at light loads.

Comparison Revisited: The packet arrival processes used in the simulation and in the

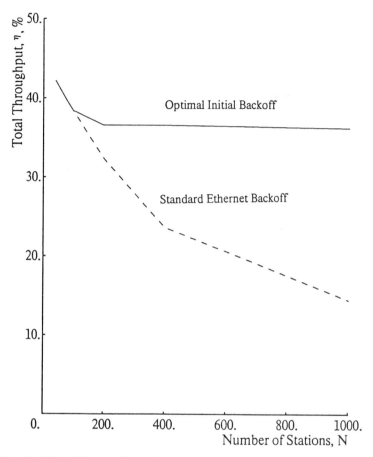

Fig. 18.   10 Mbit/s Ethernet: Throughput versus N. $a = 0.313$. Standard and modified backoff.

two analytical models are similar in that Poisson assumptions are made. However, retransmissions are handled differently as noted above. Hence, it is not meaningful to compare performance at any specific offered load. Rather, we compare the maximum throughput predictions. The simulations were run with $G = 2000$ percent, well within the saturation region. Table VII shows throughput for the balanced star with $d = 2000$ m and 39 m. These correspond to $a = 0.313$ to 0.006, respectively. t_{jam} is constant at 5.0 μs. For the simulations, for $N = 400$, maximum throughput is shown for the standard and modified backoff algorithms described in the previous section.

At small a, the analysis of Tobagi and Hunt corresponds well with the simulation. The analysis should be compared to the simulation of the modified algorithm at large N. The analytical prediction of 43.3 percent is higher than η_{max} of 36.6 percent with $N = 400$. The difference is due primarily to the assumption of slotted operation in the analysis. [11] If we consider the standard Ethernet, the analysis is seen to greatly overestimate η_{max} at $N = 400$. As N is decreased, the η_{max} increases and at $N = 40$ approximately matches that of the

[11] Considering an analysis of slotted and unslotted 1-persistent CSMA [17], at $a = 0.006$, the slotted model leads to a 0.1 percent overestimation of η_{max} compared to the unslotted model; at $a = 0.1$, the difference increases to 4 percent, and at $a = 0.3$, to 15 percent.

TABLE VII
10 Mbit/s ETHERNET: SIMULATION AND ANALYSIS, η_{max}.
BALANCED STAR TOPOLOGY. $P = 40$ bytes

a	Simulation ($N = 400$)		Analysis ($N = \infty$)	
	Standard backoff	Modified backoff	Tobagi and Hunt	Lam
0.313	23.7	36.6	43.3	28.2
0.006	61.9	73.9	70.0	63.3

analysis. As N is further decreased, the analysis underestimates the standard Ethernet performance.

Considering Lam's analysis, we compare its prediction to η_{max} of the optimized algorithm with $N = 400$, as above. For $a = 0.313$ and 0.006, η_{max} is consistently underestimated by 14 and 23 percent, respectively. This is due in part to the pessimistic assumption that the slot duration is $t_{jam} + 2\tau_p$. The use of a large slot size also leads to lower predictions than the model of Tobagi and Hunt. Considering the standard Ethernet, at large N, the analytical prediction is optimistic, at small N, pessimistic. The crossover point occurs at about 300 for $a = 0.006$ and 0.313.

VI. SUMMARY AND CONCLUSIONS

We have used actual measurements on 3 and 10 Mbit/s Ethernets with artificially generated traffic loads to characterize the performance of the protocol under a range of conditions. These include various packet lengths and offered loads ranging from a small fraction of network bandwidth to heavy overload. These experiments span the range from the region of high performance of CSMA/CD networks to the limits at which performance begins to degrade seriously.

The 3 Mbit/s Ethernet is found to achieve utilizations of 80–95 percent for the range of packet lengths considered, 64–512 bytes. In the 10 Mbit/s Ethernet, with short packets, e.g., 64 bytes, T_p becomes comparable to τ_p and hence the maximum throughput is low, about 25 percent. With long packets, greater than 500 bytes in length, high throughputs are achieved. Thus, packet lengths on the order of 64 bytes on a 10 Mbit/s network approach the limit of utility of the Ethernet protocol. This does not imply that such short packets should not be used. Traffic on a local computer network typically exhibits a bimodal packet length distribution with short packets comprising approximately 20 percent of the total traffic and the remainder of 80 percent consisting of long packets [9]. The 10 Mbit/s Ethernet studied could support a high throughput with such a traffic mix.

For $G < 100$ percent, i.e., most practical situations, the delay is within a small multiple of the packet transmission time T_p. Under such conditions, the network could provide satisfactory service to real time traffic with delay constraints. However, at heavy load, delays are as high as 80 ms and 500 ms in the 3 and 10 Mbit/s networks, respectively. The majority of packets still suffer relatively minimal delays.

Individual stations were found to achieve similar although not identical performance. We used simulation to further examine the sensitivity of the Ethernet to various distributions of stations on the network. With stations uniformly distributed along a linear bus, stations at the center obtain better performance than stations at the ends. Asymmetrical clusterings of stations increase total throughput, with the stations in the larger clusters obtaining a greater than proportionate share. An implication of these findings is that a configuration such as a cluster of workstations at one end of an Ethernet simultaneously accessing a server at the remote end may lead to unexpected congestion as the server experiences higher than normal collision rates. In such a situation it may be advantageous to alter the backoff strategy of the server's network interface unit to mitigate the effects of collisions.

Comparison of our measurements with analytical models from the literature indicate that a simple model [1] matches the Ethernet implementation for $a < 0.01$. More sophisticated models [4], [5] provide correspondence for $a < 0.1$. Note that this is dependent on other parameters such as t_{jam}. If accuracy of prediction for a specific implementation is a concern, recourse must be had to the more expensive options of simulation or experimental measurement. At large a, the performance of the Ethernet is poor due to the nonoptimum rescheduling algorithm which always begins, independently for each packet, with a low value for the average rescheduling delay. A modified algorithm was presented, which results in significantly improved throughput. With these modifications, close correspondence is obtained between simulations of the Ethernet with large N and the predictions of two infinite population analytical models of CSMA/CD performance [4], [5]. This leads us to conjecture that the modified algorithm is near optimal.

Thus, the Ethernet protocol is seen to be very suitable for local interconnection when the packet length can be made sufficiently large and occasionally highly variable delays can be tolerated. This matches the nature and requirements of most computer communication traffic. The range of utility of the protocol can be extended by a simple modification to the retransmission algorithm.

ACKNOWLEDGMENT

Thanks are due to several people for their contributions to this work. J. Shoch made available the measurement tools which he and J. Hupp developed for the 3 Mbit/s Ethernet. A. Freier and H. Murray provided assistance in the development of measurement tools for the 10 Mbit/s Ethernet. F. Baskett, Y. Dalal, and L. Garlick provided advice at various stages of the experiments. F. Tobagi's guidance and suggestions during the simulation study were invaluable.

This work was supported by the Xerox Palo Alto Research Centers and by an IBM Graduate Fellowship. The experimental facilities were provided by Xerox PARC. Additional support was provided by the Defense Advanced Research Projects Agency under Contract MDA 903-84-K-0249.

REFERENCES

[1] R. M. Metcalfe and D. R. Boggs, "Ethernet: Distributed packet switching for local computer networks," *Commun. Ass. Comput. Mach.,* vol. 19, pp. 395–404, July 1976.
[2] DEC, Intel, & Xerox Corps., *The Ethernet, A Local Area Network: Data Link Layer and Physical Layer Specifications,* Version 1 ed., 1980.
[3] "Carrier sense multiple access method and physical layer specifications," ANSI/IEEE Standard 802.3-1985, 1985.
[4] S. S. Lam, "A carrier sense multiple access protocol for local networks," *Comput. Networks,* vol. 4, pp. 21–32, Feb. 1980.
[5] F. A. Tobagi and V. B. Hunt, "Performance analysis of carrier sense multiple access with collision detection," *Comput. Networks,* vol. 4, pp. 245–259, Oct./Nov. 1980; also in this volume, ch. 20.
[6] E. J. Coyle and B. Liu, "Finite population CSMA/CD networks," *IEEE Trans. Commun.,* vol. COM-31, pp. 1247–1251, Nov. 1983.

[7] J. S. Meditch and C.-T. A. Lea, "Stability and optimization of the CSMA and CSMA/CD channels," *IEEE Trans. Commun.*, vol. COM-31, pp. 763–774, Nov. 1983; also in this volume, ch. 21.

[8] K. Sohraby, M. L. Molle, and A. N. Venetsanopoulos, "Why analytical models of Ethernet-like local networks are so pessimistic," *IEEE Global Telecommun. Conf.*, Atlanta, GA, pp. 19.4.1–19.4.6, Nov. 1984.

[9] J. F. Shoch and J. Hupp, "Measured performance of an Ethernet local network," *Comm. Ass. Comput. Mach.*, vol. 23, pp. 711–721, Dec. 1980.

[10] T. A. Gonsalves, "Performance characteristics of 2 Ethernets: An experimental study," in *Proc. ACM SIGMETRICS Conf. on Measurement and Modeling of Comput. Syst.*, Austin, TX, Aug. 1985, pp. 78–86.

[11] T. A. Gonsalves, "Packet-voice communication on an Ethernet local network: An experimental study," *ACM SIGCOMM Symp. on Commun. Architectures and Protocols*, Austin, TX, Mar. 1983, pp. 178–185.

[12] R. E. Toense, "Performance Analysis of NBSNET," *J. Telecommun. Networks*, vol. 2, no. 2, pp. 177–186, Spring 1983.

[13] D. R. Boggs, Private communication, Xerox PARC, 1982.

[14] C. P. Thacker, E. M. McCreight, B. W. Lampson, and D. R. Boggs, "Alto: A personal computer," in *Computer Structures: Principles and Examples,* D. P. Siewiorek, C. G. Bell, and A. Newell, Eds. New York: McGraw-Hill, pp. 549–572, 1982.

[15] L. Kleinrock, *Queueing Systems, Volume 2: Computer Applications.* New York: Wiley, 1976.

[16] J. F. Shoch, "Design and performance of local computer networks," Ph.D. dissertation, Dep. Comput. Sci., Stanford Univ., Stanford, CA, Aug. 1979.

[17] L. Kleinrock and F. A. Tobagi, "Packet switching in radio channels: Part I—Carrier sense multiple-access modes and their throughput-delay characteristics," *IEEE Trans. Commun.*, vol. COM-23, pp. 1400–1416, Dec. 1975.

[18] N. Shacham and V. B. Hunt, "Performance evaluation of the CSMA/CD (1-persistent) channel-access protocol in common-channel local networks," in *Proc. IFIP TC 6 Int. In-Depth Symp. on Local Computer Networks,* Florence, Italy, Apr. 1982, pp. 401–412.

[19] T. A. Gonsalves and F. A. Tobagi, "On the performance effects of station locations and access protocol parameters in Ethernet networks," Comput. Syst. Lab., Stanford Univ., Stanford, CA, Tech. Rep. 86-292, Jan. 1986.

[20] F. A. Tobagi and L. Kleinrock, "Packet switching in radio channels: Part IV—Stability considerations and dynamic control in carrier sense multiple access," *IEEE Trans. Commun.*, vol. COM-25, pp. 1103–1119, Oct. 1977.

[21] T. A. Gonsalves, "Comparative performance of broadcast bus local computer networks with voice and data traffic," Ph.D. dissertation, Dep. Elect. Eng., Stanford Univ., Stanford, CA, June 1986.

24
Performance Evaluation of the MAP Token Bus in Real Time Applications

DITTMAR JANETZKY AND KYM S. WATSON

Now that the token bus local area network IEEE Standard 802.4 is part of the MAP (manufacturing automation protocol) profile and has been adopted for IEC's process data highway (PROWAY), its performance characteristics are of widespread interest. We present a detailed performance analysis of token bus which reveals its performance behavior and shows what performance can be achieved by suitably tuning the token bus parameters. The investigation is based on three benchmark load patterns which describe the frames to be sent over the bus. The performance in terms of throughputs and waiting times is measured for each benchmark load pattern. Several performance requirements, including a stringent real time requirement, are defined and the token bus parameters are set to meet these requirements.

I. INTRODUCTION AND SCOPE

Complex industrial automation systems for large manufacturing plants are being designed with the application of new communication standards for efficient networking between computers, machine controllers, and operating systems. Local area networks are the key for interoperation of this equipment.

Local area networks based on proprietary protocols for industrial control applications have had proven reliable operation for about one decade. Network performance has been designed to meet the special requirements of the system functionality. Newly designed communications standards developed by ISO and IEC have very broad applicability.

A selection of ISO protocol standards for manufacturing automation is being specified by General Motors and is known as MAP specification (manufacturing automation protocol specification) [6]. For automation systems in the industrial control area, a process data highway PROWAY [4] is being developed by IEC. Both specifications use the IEEE 802.4 token bus standard as a kernel. From the view of this performance evaluation the difference in their specification is that PROWAY specifies 1 Mbit/s and MAP specifies 5 Mbits/s and 10 Mbits/s at the physical layer. The 1 Mbit/s PROWAY is specified for applications in process control industry to interface sensors, actuators, and process controllers under real time requirements. The 10 Mbit/s MAP network is intended to be applied as a backbone at the factory level and the 5 Mbit/s network is expected to provide sufficient performance for data communication under real time requirements within the automation cell at the station or process level.

In process and manufacturing control, the critical factor of system performance has to ensure that messages are transmitted on time. Guaranteed access to the transmission medium within 20 ms as defined by PROWAY becomes the most important feature of real time applications in industry and generally in the presence of high mean data loads of 50–70 percent of transmission capacity [3]. The availability of prioritized access in the media access control (MAC) protocol facilitates network design and tuning of network performance. Performance studies of token bus have been carried out in [7].

The IEEE 802.4 token bus standard uses timers to control priority classes which may be assigned to specific message types to guarantee bounded waiting times as required by the application. In this performance evaluation we develop a method for setting these control parameters and discuss bounds on the attainable throughput.

A simulation of the essential media access control functions validates the method and yields fundamental information on the performance behavior under specific benchmark load patterns envisaged in the field of application. The benchmark load pattern essentially defines the length distribution of frames of each priority class, their service request process, and their proportion of load. Various parameter configurations in conjunction with the benchmark load patterns give insight into the sensitivity of the network to changes of system parameters.

II. THE PERFORMANCE MODEL

A. The Service Model

This section describes those features of the MAC sublayer which are important from a performance point of view. We consider only stable configurations under fault-free operation. This means, in particular, that the system's reaction to lost or duplicated tokens as well as to various other fault situations is irrelevant in the simulation model.

The access to the medium in token bus is controlled by token passing. The token is passed cyclically from station to station in a logical ring. We will denote the stations by $S(i)$, $i = 1, \cdots, N$, where N is the number of stations throughout this work. The token is passed from $S(i)$ to $S(i - 1)$ $(i = 1, \cdots, N, (S(0) = S(N)))$ (cf. Fig. 1).

Token bus provides for four frame priorities, called access classes, within the MAC sublayer of each station. The access classes are numbered 6, 4, 2, and 0, and are intended to be in decreasing order of importance. As we will see, the quality of service offered to each access class depends on certain parameters. Every station $S(i)$ $(i = 1, \cdots, N)$ has a queue $Q(i, j)$ for MAC frames of access class j $(j = 6, 4, 2, 0)$. The queues $Q(i, j)$ behave

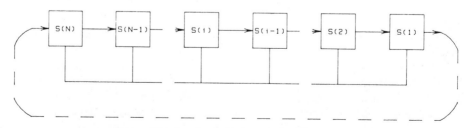

Fig. 1.   Logical token passing ring.

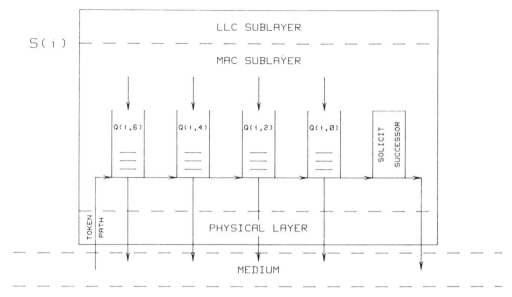

Fig. 2. Logical path of token within station $S(i)$.

as virtual substations in the logical token passing ring (cf. Fig. 2). The token is passed within $S(i)$ from $Q(i, 6)$ to $Q(1, 4)$, from $Q(i, 4)$ to $Q(i, 2)$, from $Q(i, 2)$ to $Q(i, 0)$, and from $Q(i, 0)$ to $S(i - 1)$ via the logical maintenance block "solicit successor." We assume that its parameters have been set such that it has a negligible influence on performance and do not consider it further (but for details, see [1]).

Only the queue possessing the token may send frames. We assume that only MAC data frames of the confirmation class RQ (request with no response) are sent from the queues $Q(i, j)$. All frames sent (or received) by the MAC sublayer have the format shown in Fig. 3. The function of the frame fields PREAMBLE, SD (start delimiter), FC (frame control), DA (destination address), SA (source address), FCS (frame check sequence), and ED (end delimiter) is not relevant for this performance study—only their respective lengths are of interest. We assume that the destination and source address fields are 2 octets long, and do not consider the other option of 6 octets. We will let Cap denote the transmission capacity (nominal bit rate) in Mbits/s. The PREAMBLE length PL is taken to be 1, 2, and 3 octets for Cap = 1, 5, and 10 Mbits/s, respectively. This ensures that the transmission time for the PREAMBLE is at least 2 μs as required in [1]. The length L of the DATA UNIT must be no more than 1014 octets.

Moreover, we assume that an additional *thinking time* of 0.01 ms is needed every time a frame is sent. The token, when passed from $S(i)$ to $S(i - 1)$, is itself a MAC frame with no DATA UNIT. The service order in every queue is first come, first served and all queues are assumed to be of infinite capacity. The length of time $Q(i, j)$ may keep the token and use it to send frames is determined by the token hold timer THT (cf. Fig. 4). As soon as

Fig. 3. MAC frame format with respective octet lengths.

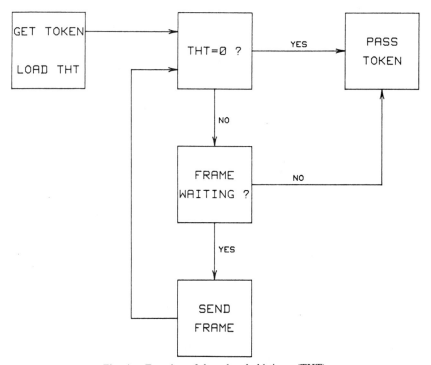

Fig. 4.   Function of the token hold timer (THT).

$Q(i, j)$ receives the token, THT is loaded with a certain start value and immediately starts to run down. All timers have a nonnegative start value and run down until they expire at 0. $Q(i, j)$ may start servicing a new frame as long as THT has not expired, whereby the service of a frame is not interrupted.

The value with which THT is loaded depends on the access class j. For queues of the access class 6, THT is loaded with a constant start value t_6. This guarantees the access class 6 use of the token, and hence transmission time. The timer start value t_6 is called the *high-priority token hold time*. For queues of the lower access classes 4, 2, and 0, THT is loaded with a value dependent on the time taken by the token to complete its last rotation of the logical ring. Every queue $Q(i, j)$ of the lower access classes ($j = 4, 2, 0$) has a token rotation timer $TRT(i, j)$ which allows $Q(i, j)$ to assess the time taken for the last token rotation as seen by $Q(i, j)$. Upon receipt of the token in $Q(i, j)$, the residual value of $TRT(i, j)$ is loaded into THT and $TRT(i, j)$ is restarted. Thus, the transmission time available to $Q(i, j)$ (i.e., the start value of THT) is a decreasing function of the time taken for the token to complete its last rotation as observed by $Q(i, j)$. The start value of $TRT(i, j)$ is a constant denoted by t_j ($j = 4, 2, 0$). This mechanism is displayed in Fig. 5. At station initialization $TRT(i, j)$ is loaded with 0, meaning that $Q(i, j)$ cannot send any frames when it receives the token for the first time. After that, $Q(i, j)$ has always observed a ''proper'' token rotation when it receives the token and THT is loaded with max ($t_j - r$, 0), where r is the last token rotation time as seen by $Q(i, j)$.

The timer parameters t_4, t_2, and t_0 are called *target rotation times* for access classes 4, 2, and 0, respectively. t_6, t_4, t_2, and t_0 are all user-defined parameters with which the quality of service offered to each access class may be tuned.

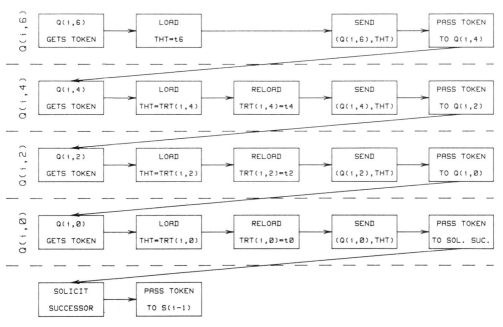

Fig. 5.   Timer mechanism within station $S(i)$.

B. The Benchmark Load Patterns

The benchmark load patterns BM 1 (Fig. 6), BM 2, and BM 3 (Fig. 7) were chosen for the performance investigations. They describe the proportion of frames of each access class, the lengths of their respective DATA UNIT's, and how they are generated.

Although BM 2 and 3 are artificial patterns, they are intended to reflect the typical load and priority assignments in process control: class 6 is for urgent messages such as alarms, class 4 is for normal control and ring maintenance actions, class 2 is for routine data gathering and display and data base updates, and class 0 is for file and program transfer.

ACCESS CLASS	FRAME TYPE	SERVICE REQUEST PROCESS	DATA LENGTH	COMMUNI- CATION	PROPOR- TION OF FRAMES
6	RQ	M	D,80	U	25 %
4	RQ	M	D,80	U	25 %
2	RQ	M	D,80	U	25 %
0	RQ	M	D,80	U	25 %

Fig. 6.   Benchmark load pattern BM 1.

ACCESS CLASS	FRAME TYPE	SERVICE REQUEST PROCESS	DATA LENGTH	COMMUNI- CATION	PROPOR- TION OF FRAMES
6	RQ	M	D, 60	U	5 %
4	RQ	SD	D, 80	U	10 %
2	RQ	M	D, 80	U	83 %
0	RQ	M	D, 1000	U	2 %

Fig. 7. Benchmark load pattern BM 2. For BM 3 data loads up to 0.5 are composed as for BM 2, while data loads over 0.5 are composed of a base data load of 0.5 distributed as in BM 2 and an additional load in access class 2.

The following performance requirements were considered in conjunction with BM 2 and 3.

PR_6:
a) The access delay for an arbitrary class 6 queue does not exceed 50 ms.
b) The waiting time for an arbitrary access class 6 frame exceeds 50 ms with probability 10^{-4} at most.

PR_4: The mean waiting time in class 4 does not exceed 100 ms.

PR_2: The mean waiting time in class 2 does not exceed 500 ms.

PR_0: The mean waiting time in class 0 does not exceed 5 s.

The access delay for a queue is the time from a given point until the token may be used to serve requests from that queue. The waiting time (or queueing delay) does not include the service time. The two parts of PR_6 are real time performance requirements, which, at least for BM 2 and 3, play a much more important role than the weaker performance requirements for the lower access classes.

PROWAY requires an access delay in class 6 of no more than 20 ms, but places no requirement on the waiting time which includes frame queueing. The PROWAY requirement is fulfilled when the maximum token rotation time is no more than 20 ms. The waiting time, on the other hand, is dependent on the statistical arrival process and consequently PR_6b) is a better definition of real time requirements in an implemented system with frame queueing.

BM 1 has been included as a simple benchmark to help explain the affect of the timer parameters on waiting times and attainable throughputs in each access class.

Benchmark load patterns coupled with performance requirements are a useful aid in gaining insight into what performance behavior in terms of waiting times and throughputs is to be expected from token bus. They can form the basis of a comparison between systems and are necessary when actual load patterns are unknown. For background information on benchmarks as well as on their use in performance evaluation, the reader is referred to [2], [5].

The attribute *RQ* in the column "frame type" means that all frames are of type request with no response. The attribute *M* for Markov in the column "service request process" means that frames of this access class form a Poisson stream of arrivals. The attribute *SD* stands for a synchronized discrete arrival process. This means that there are synchronized, periodic arrivals at every station: at times $n * d$, $n = 0, 1, 2, \cdots$, a class 4 frame arrives at every station. This arrival process was chosen in preference to asynchronous periodic arrivals as the former was expected to be a harder performance test than the latter. This was confirmed in a few experiments. The attribute pair D, L in the column "data length" means that all frames of this access class have a constant (D = discrete) number L of octets in their DATA UNIT.

The attribute U for uniform communication means that the source/destination addresses of frames of this access class are uniformly distributed. The proportion of frames of a given access class which are to be sent from $S(i)$ is $1/N$. This is automatic for the access class with service request process *SD*. For access classes with service request process M we assume that the service request process in this access class is of type M (Poisson) at each individual station. It is important to note that both service request processes M and *SD* are completely determined by their respective rates.

The last column of the benchmark, proportion of frames, simply describes how the frames are divided up among the four access classes. The total data load is not specified by the benchmark—it is a variable throughout. Before we quantitize this explicitly, we make the following definition.

Definition: The total data load is the rate at which bits belonging to the DATA UNIT field of frames enter the queueing system relative to the nominal bit rate. The total data load will be denoted by δ.

Notation and Load Calculations: For $j = 6, 4, 2,$ and 0:

DL_j length in octets of the DATA UNIT of access class j frames
λ_j total arrival rate of access class j frames/ms
b_j service time of access class j frames in ms
δ_j total data load due to access class j frames
p_j proportion of frames of access class j in BM 1, 2.

DL_j and p_j are given explicitly in the respective benchmark. From Section II-A we have

$$b_j = (PL + 11 + DL_j)/(125 * \text{Cap}) + 0.01 \text{ ms.}$$

The total data load δ is the control variable which determines the arrival rates $\lambda_6, \lambda_4, \lambda_2, \lambda_0$ in accordance with the benchmark.

For BM 1 and BM 2 we have for $j = 6, 4, 2, 0$:

$$\lambda_j = p_j * \delta * 125 * \text{Cap}/\Sigma(p_n * DL_n : n = 6, 4, 2, 0).$$

The benchmark load pattern BM 3 is a modification of BM 2. BM 2 spreads the load over the four access classes in constant proportions, independent of the total load. The motivation for BM 3 was provided by the fact that in practical situations it is more likely that higher loads have higher proportions of particular classes (corresponding to the system functions carried out with increased frequency).

For a given total data load δ BM 3 works as follows.

Case 1: $\delta \le 0.5$: Proceed as for BM 2. The arrival rate of access class j in frames/ms is

$$\lambda_j = p_j * \delta * 125 * \text{Cap}/\Sigma(p_n * DL_n : n = 6, 4, 2, 0) \ (j = 6, 4, 2, 0).$$

Case 2: $\delta \geq 0.5$: The data load is composed of a base data load of 0.5 distributed according to BM 2 and an additional data load of $\delta - 0.5$ in access class 2 alone.

The arrival rates corresponding to the base data load are

$$\nu_j = p_j * 0.5 * 125 * \mathrm{Cap}/\Sigma(p_n * DL_n : n = 6, 4, 2, 0) \text{ frames/ms } (j = 6, 4, 2, 0).$$

The arrival rate in access class 2 corresponding to the additional load of $\delta - 0.5$ in this class is

$$\eta_2 = (\delta - 0.5) * 125 * \mathrm{Cap}/DL_2 \text{ frames/ms.}$$

Hence, the arrival rates yielding a BM 3 data load of δ are

$$\lambda_j = \nu_j \qquad \text{for } j = 6, 4, 0$$

$$\lambda_2 = \nu_2 + \eta_2.$$

III. PARAMETER CONFIGURATIONS AND THE SIMULATION METHOD

The results of the simulation runs are displayed in Figs. 8 and 10–15. The captions show the parameter configurations chosen for the performance evaluation. The timer parameters t_6, t_4, t_2, and t_0 are all multiples of one octet time (the time required to send 8 bits at the nominal bit rate). The motivation for the choice of timer parameters will be indicated below. The plotted curves labeled 6, 4, 2, and 0 show the mean waiting time (excluding the service time) of access class 6, 4, 2, and 0 frames as a function of the offered data load, respectively. The plotted curve labeled T is the mean token rotation time.

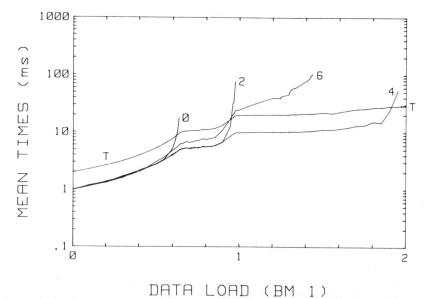

Fig. 8. Mean waiting times and mean token rotation time for parameter configuration $N = 64$, Cap $= 5$ Mbits/s, $t_6 = 0.0784$ ms, $t_4 = 30$ ms, $t_2 = 20$ ms, $t_0 = 10$ ms. $R_{max} = 40.1632$ ms.

The mean values recorded in the simulations were plotted and the successive points were joined by a straight line. No regression analysis was performed. The number of frames generated during a simulation run depended on the time required for the measured mean values to stabilize. Approximately 10 000–15 000 frames were generated for the lower data loads up to 0.5, whereas 35 000–40 000 frames were generated for the high data loads.

IV. PERFORMANCE RESULTS WITH BM 1

Figure 8 shows the basic performance characteristics of token bus with BM 1. The high priority token hold time t_6 is small enough such that at most one class 6 frame can be sent per station per token rotation. Up to data loads of about 0.55 very little queueing is taking place and the timers are playing no significant role. The mean wait in all classes is simply the mean residual token time—the queues just have to wait until the token returns before sending any frames, and there is usually at most one frame to send. The mean waiting time in each class is therefore approximately $R_{av}/2$, where R_{av} is the mean token rotation time.

As the data load increases from 0.55 to 0.65 the average token rotation time increases to 10 ms, the target token rotation time for class 0. There are insufficient token rotations shorter than t_0 to allow all class 0 frames to be served completely and this class becomes unstable.

In the data load interval [0.65, 0.8] the mean token rotation time stays almost constant as the throughput in class 0 is being suppressed by that in the higher classes. During this data load interval the mean waits in classes 6, 4, and 2 increase only gradually.

By data load 0.99 the average token rotation time has reached 20 ms, the target token rotation time for class 2, and class 2 becomes unstable.

The performance behavior during the data load interval [1, 1.4] is as for the interval [0.65, 0.8] discussed above. The mean token rotation time stays almost constant. By the time the data load has reached 1.45 we have paid the price for having allowed only one class 6 frame to be served per station per token rotation: class 6 has become unstable. In contrast to the lower classes though, every station can continue to serve one class 6 frame per token rotation, independent of the total offered load. That is, class 6 has a guaranteed throughput.

By data load 2 the average token rotation time has risen to nearly 30 ms, the target token rotation time for class 4, and class 4 has become unstable. The mean token rotation time stays constant thereafter. The timer parameter settings ensure that the token rotation time is always less than 41 ms.

V. PERFORMANCE RESULTS WITH BM 2

The performance evaluation aimed to show that the performance requirements PR_6–PR_0 can be fulfilled for BM 2 by suitably choosing the timer parameters.

If we let R_{max} and R_{min} be the maximum and minimum token rotation time, respectively, which can be observed by a class 6 queue, then

$$R_{min} = N * ((PL + 11)/(125 * \text{Cap}) + 0.01) \text{ ms}$$

$$R_{max} = (N - 1) * M * b_6 + \text{MAX (MAX } (t_j + b_j : j = 4, 2, 0), M * b_6 + R_{min})$$

where M is the maximum number of class 6 frames which can be served per station per token rotation. The formula for R_{min} is obvious. The derivation of that for R_{max} is straightforward, once one has realized that if a class j queue ($j = 4, 2, 0$) sends a frame in a token rotation, then the rotation time observed up until the end of its sending can be no more than $t_j + b_j$. The interested reader may compare [5]. Both formulas are valid for all benchmarks with constant frame lengths within each access class. The performance requirement PR_6a) can be expressed as $R_{max} \leq 50$ ms. It partly dictates the choice of the timer parameters t_6, t_4, t_2, and t_0. Figure 9 shows the maximum attainable data throughput relative to the channel capacity under the assumption that the load is distributed as in BM 2 and $R_{max} \leq 50$ ms is guaranteed by appropriate choice of the timer parameters. We see that bit rates of 5 Mbits/s or more are to be recommended.

An analytical Markov model, called the walking server model, was used to verify the fulfillment of the real time requirement PR_6b) even under worst case conditions (every token rotation of maximum duration). In addition, a number of robust (i.e., largely benchmark independent) bounds on the attainable data throughput were obtained as functions of the timer parameters. Details on the walking server model and the throughput bounds will appear elsewhere. Both guided the selection of the four timer parameters. Finally,

$$\text{Rule A: make } t_4 \geq t_2 \geq t_0$$

$$\text{Rule B: make } t_4 + b_4 \geq t_2 + b_2 \geq t_0 + b_0$$

were applied.

These two rules aim to guarantee truly differentiated service qualities for the lower three access classes, even if the load pattern should change. If the load increases, resulting in increasing token rotation times, then frames of a given access class will be precluded from

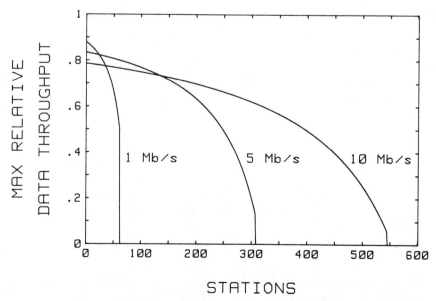

Fig. 9. The maximum attainable relative data throughput for BM 2 and $R_{max} \leq 50$ ms as a function of the number of stations for Cap = 1, 5, 10 Mbits/s.

service when the token rotation time reaches the target rotation time belonging to this access class. As the token rotation time increases, the access classes will be precluded from service in the order determined by their target rotation times. This order should be 0, 2, 4. That is, Rule A is desirable and will be a necessary safety condition in many applications. Rule B ensures that lower access classes are inconspicuous for higher access classes. Due to $t_2 + b_2 \geq t_0 + b_0$, for example, a queue of access class 0 cannot cause the token rotation time to climb (by servicing frames) any more than a queue of access class 2.

The purpose of the simulation was to verify the fulfillment of the performance requirements PR_4, PR_2, and PR_0. A cross section of the results is shown in Figs. 10–14.

The vertical dashed line on each graph marks the upper bound on the attainable relative data throughput (data throughput relative to the nominal bit rate) given by the theory referred to above. We remark that frame overheads alone mean that the attainable relative data throughput is no higher than 0.84 and 0.79 for Cap = 5 and 10 Mbits/s, respectively. We see that this loss in data throughput is much higher than the additional loss which has to be accepted in order to meet the performance requirements. In order to meet PR_6b) the timer parameters often had to be set such that R_{max} was less than 50 ms.

For light data loads the mean wait in the classes 6, 2, and 0, which have Poisson arrival processes, is approximately $R_{av}/2$ as explained above for BM 1. Frames of access class 4 with its synchronized discrete arrival process may have to wait for more than one token rotation before being served, even for very light data loads.

How the mean waits are affected by varying t_0 is shown in Figs. 10 and 11 for $N = 16$, Cap = 5 Mbits/s, and in Figs. 12 and 13 for $N = 64$, Cap = 5 Mbits/s.

A lower value of t_0 leads to access class 2 being noticeably favored over access class 0 for high data loads. A higher value of t_0 ensures that even access class 0 gets a reasonable quality of service for higher data loads, but this is at the expense of a diminished service quality for access class 2.

As is to be expected, the performance for $N = 64$, Cap = 10 Mbits/s is better (Fig. 14).

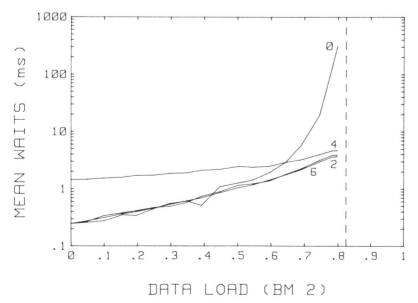

Fig. 10.   Mean waiting times for parameter configuration $N = 16$, Cap = 5 Mbits/s, $t_6 = 0.696$ ms, $t_4 = 38.4288$ ms, $t_2 = 35.2208$ ms, $t_0 = 5.8656$ ms. $R_{max} = 49.9996$ ms.

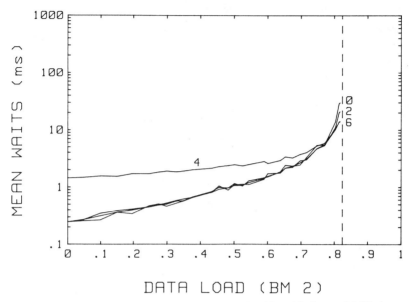

Fig. 11.   Mean waiting times for parameter configuration $N = 16$, Cap = 5 Mbits/s, $t_6 = 0.696$ ms, $t_4 = 38.4288$ ms, $t_2 = 35.2208$ ms, $t_0 = 33.7488$ ms. $R_{max} = 49.9996$ ms.

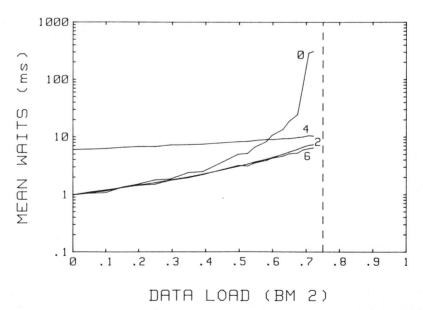

Fig. 12.   Mean waiting times for parameter configuration $N = 64$, Cap = 5 Mbits/s, $t_6 = 0.3168$ ms, $t_4 = 18.8752$ ms, $t_2 = 17.3904$ ms, $t_0 = 10$ ms. $R_{max} = 42.9992$ ms.

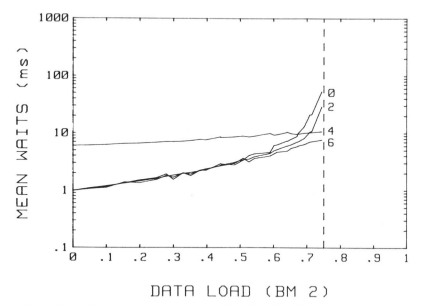

Fig. 13. Mean waiting times for parameter configuration $N = 64$, Cap $= 5$ Mbits/s, $t_6 = 0.3168$ ms, $t_4 = 18.8752$ ms, $t_2 = 17.3904$ ms, $t_0 = 15.9184$ ms. $R_{max} = 42.9992$ ms.

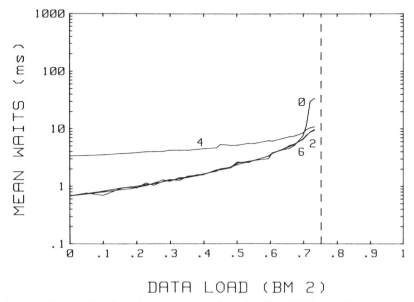

Fig. 14. Mean waiting times for parameter configuration $N = 64$, Cap $= 10$ Mbits/s, $t_6 = 0.2416$ ms, $t_4 = 30.476$ ms, $t_2 = 27.9048$, $t_0 = 20$ ms. $R_{max} = 47.9996$ ms.

VI. Performance Results with BM 3

The performance with the most promising set of timer parameters for $N = 64$, Cap = 5 Mbits/s and BM 2 (cf. Fig. 13) was looked at in more detail with BM 3. The results are shown in Fig. 15. The vertical dashed line at δ (data load) = 0.5 is the point after which the data load in classes 6, 4, and 0 is held constant and the increase in total data load is due entirely to class 2. The second vertical dashed line at $\delta \simeq 0.738$ is the upper bound on the data load under which all classes are stable. The third vertical dashed line at $\delta \simeq 0.822$ is the upper bound on the data load under which all classes except class 0 are stable. For data loads up to about 0.55 there is little queueing taking place and the mean waiting times observed can be explained as before.

The data load interval [0, 0.55] (or even [0, 0.6]) is the region of excellent system performance in all access classes. The next data load interval of interest is [0.55, 0.73], which ends at the upper bound on the data load under which all classes are stable. The mean token rotation time climbs from 6 to 16 ms in this interval.

Although class 0 is unstable for a data load of 0.74 and cannot be completely served, it receives a good quality of service even for a data load of 0.73 just under the saturation point. There are just enough token rotations less than t_0 for class 0 to be satisfactorily served, even though $R_{av} > t_0$ at $\delta = 0.73$. This behavior was to be expected as we selected t_0 to be as high as allowed by the timer selection rules. Since, however,

$$t_0 + b_0 = t_2 + b_2 > t_2$$

class 2 has to "struggle" to suppress class 0 in the region of saturation about 0.738. This is especially true as the increase in data load is coming completely from class 2. Still, the timers t_2 and t_0 such that $t_2 > t_0$ ensure that class 0 will be suppressed.

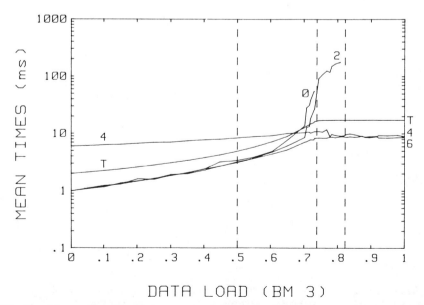

Fig. 15.   Mean waiting times and mean token rotation time for parameter configuration $N =$ 64, Cap = 5 Mbits/s, $t_6 = 0.3168$ ms, $t_4 = 18.8752$ ms, $t_2 = 17.3904$ ms, $t_0 = 15.9184$ ms. $R_{max} = 42.9992$ ms.

We now look at the data load interval [0.74, 0.82] in which classes 6 and 4 are stable, class 0 is unstable, and class 2 stays stable until about 0.815. The class 0 data throughput is suppressed linearly by the increasing class 2 data throughput and the mean token time stays constant at about 17 ms. For data loads $\delta \geq 0.82$ the data throughputs in all classes and the mean token time stay constant. The data throughput in class 2 is less than the offered data bit rate (class 2 is unstable). Only classes 6 and 4 are stable. The data throughput in class 0 is negligible.

VII. CONCLUSIONS

The parameters high priority token hold time t_6 and the target token rotation times t_4, t_2, and t_0 have to be set appropriately to meet given performance requirements (waiting times, throughputs) for a given load pattern. At least the maximum frame length in each priority class should be known to set the parameters, as then they may be selected to guarantee a given maximum token rotation time.

In general, the parameters should be kept as high as possible, but separated according to Rules A and B. This strategy maximizes the attainable throughput in each priority class, ensures that lower priorities are suppressed at high loads, and leads to acceptable waiting times in all classes over a wide range of loads. Although all the results are dependent on the benchmark load patterns chosen, it can be claimed that token bus can fulfill real time performance requirements in the highest priority as well as offering sufficient capacity to the lower priorities. Moreover, the use of benchmarks revealed important performance characteristics of token bus.

REFERENCES

[1] "Token-passing bus access method and physical layer specifications," ANSI/IEEE Standard 802.4-1985, ISO Draft International Standard 8802/4, 1985.
[2] D. Heger and K. Watson, "Modeling of load patterns and benchmarks for performance evaluation of local area networks," *Informatik-Fachberichte*, vol. 61, pp. 93–106, 1983.
[3] M. Kaminski, "Protocols for communicating in the factory," *IEEE Spectrum*, pp. 56–62, Apr. 1986.
[4] IEC Process Data Highway (PROWAY C), IEC Publication 955, SC65C (Central Office) 17-I, Jan. 1986.
[5] IITB, Ed., "Final Report for COST 11 bis: Performance analysis of LAN's for real time environments," *Fraunhofer-Institut für Informations- und Datenverarbeitung* (IITB), Karlsruhe, Rep. 9797, 1984.
[6] MAP: General Motors' Manufacturing Automation Protocol. Version 2.1. GM Technical Center, Warren, MI, 1985.
[7] R. Rosenthal, Ed., "Workshop on analytic and simulation modeling of IEEE 802.4 token bus local area networks," NBS Special Publication 500-127, June 1985.

Part V
Integrated Traffic

Today computer traffic is mostly carried by LAN's and voice traffic is carried by private branch exchanges (PBX's). Traditionally, voice communication has been provided by analog or digital circuits and not transmitted in packet form. So too for other types of traffic (such as video), where dedicated channels have been employed. Perhaps the first example of a commercial packet speech LAN was the SILK system (Chapter 7).

Techniques for integrating traffic on a single medium range between two extremes. One extreme is to divide the available capacity into a number of separate channels and have a central controller allocate channels to users as required. The request for a channel is made via a special channel (sometimes a packet channel) dedicated for this purpose. The channels are usually allocated in units of a basic rate (e.g., 64 kbits/s) and permit synchronous communication over the channel using some well-established PTT protocol. The drawbacks of this approach are that: 1) constant capacity synchronous channels are ill-suited for most types of traffic in that information comes in bursts rather than at a constant rate; and 2) a separate control channel usually with a different protocol, is required. The other extreme is to transmit all types of traffic via packets. The drawback of this approach is that there is no orderly access to the medium. Consequently, a particular user or a particular type of traffic could hog the channel.

Schemes designed to handle a mix of traffic on a LAN usually fall between the above two extremes. Perhaps the most common approach is to divide the channel into 125 μs frames. Each frame is further divided into blocks which are allocated for packet or circuit use by a central server. The blocks for circuit use may be further subdivided into individual synchronous 64 kbits/s channels, allocated by a central server. An example of such a system is OPAL-net II, described in Chapter 18 and [1].

An alternative common approach is to packetize all traffic. The channel is then cycled between periods when only data users are served and periods which only voice (or some other traffic type) is served. The capacity reverts to serving data traffic when all voice traffic has been served. Thus, data traffic is able to exploit any unused voice capacity. The allocation to voice generally has an upper limit so as to guarantee a residual capacity to data traffic; such an algorithm can be largely distributed and thus executed in the individual stations. However, there is frequently some centralized component which controls the boundary between voice and data. Chapters 26 and 27 describe schemes of this type.

We would have liked to include more material in this section on the use of LAN's for communicating other types of traffic besides data and voice. Coded videophone images with bit-rates in the range 0.25–2 Mbits/s and large single-frame image files of perhaps 1–8 Mbits are applications that are not well supported by existing data protocols. Unfortunately, little appropriate work could be found in this area. There is a need for more work on these topics. For example, coding speech and video for packet communication where we are not so concerned with variations in the instantaneous rate of the coder presents opportunities for further reducing channel requirements compared to the usual technique of coding for a fixed capacity channel.

REFERENCES

[1] T. Kohashi, A. Kitamura, M. Murai, T. Usukura, Y. Watanabe, and N. Horii, "Integrated circuit and packet-switching applications to a loop system for local area networks," *J. Select. Areas Commun.,* vol. SAC-3, pp. 574–583, July 1985.

25
A Simulation-Based Comparison of Voice Transmission on CSMA/CD Networks and on Token Buses

JOHN D. DeTREVILLE

Digitized speech can be transmitted over a variety of digital media. An interesting choice is the use of a local area network (LAN), for which digitized speech is packetized at the transmitter and depacketized at the receiver. Many local area networks exhibit good throughput but poor delay characteristics; variable or excessive transmission delay can become noticeable and objectionable to the users of such a voice system. A number of simulations were performed to assess the delay characteristics of a carrier sense multiple access/collision detection (CSMA/CD) LAN and of a similar token bus LAN. A comparison of the results shows that the token bus performs somewhat better. The CSMA/CD LAN's performance was characterized by carrying voice well until a point of collapse is reached; the token bus's performance degraded more continuously. In either case, throughput close to the theoretical capacity of the LAN was found achievable with appropriate techniques.

I. CHARACTERISTICS OF DIGITAL VOICE

Human speech of telephone quality can be easily encoded into a 64 kbit/s bit stream containing 8000 8 bit speech samples per second; although much more efficient encodings are possible, this synchronous 64 kbit/s speech encoding is assumed throughout this chapter.[1] Speech consists of *talk spurts* separated by *silences:* a speaker in a typical conversation talks about 40 percent of the time and is silent for the remainder, and an approach that transmits speech only during talk spurts can therefore be desirable. Silences, of course, are relative. Ideally, no speech should be lost by being considered silence, and no extraneous background sounds should intrude during silences. This ideal can be approached through the use of cutoff levels with memory.

---

[1] As a simple improvement, the use of delta modulation to transmit only the differences between successive samples could produce savings of approximately 2:1. More extensive processing could result in more extensive savings by taking further advantage of the regular properties of human speech. Improvements in the encoding bit rate will result in improvements in the performance figures presented in this chapter, but these performance improvements will typically not be linear, since a reduction in the bit rate will make other factors relatively more important. Similarly, although variable bit-rate encodings can produce further savings over fixed bit-rate encodings, they can lose many of the advantages shown for fixed bit rates in this chapter, and will again have less of a total impact than might otherwise be expected.

Transmitting digital speech over a shared packet network entails packetizing the digital signal at the transmitter, transporting it over the network, and depacketizing it at the receiver; these operations can introduce delay. Table I gives a high-level breakdown of the delay in the transmission. The delay includes a fixed component and a variable component. Because of the variable component, if the receiving station begins playing a packet as soon as it is received, this can introduce artificial silences at some points (when a packet is delayed more than the one before it) and lost speech at others (when a packet is delayed less than the one before it), ultimately producing effects audible to the users. This variability of performance can be partially overcome by artificially delaying packets at the receiver, such that only those packets whose variable delay is greater than some threshold will cause anomalies; since speech is inherently real time, arbitrary queueing of packets at the transmitter or receiver is not possible.

The user-level model of speech used in this chapter is that of a typical two-way conversation, in which real time constraints exist at both ends. If either side of the voice conversation were to be a computer or similar device, knowledge of this fact could be used to ease the constraints somewhat, although this optimization is not considered in this chapter. If both ends were known to be computers, speech could then be transmitted as a nonreal time data transfer.

If packets are artificially delayed, the one-way voice sample delay from the transmitter to the receiver during successful transmission will roughly equal the packet size plus the threshold delay. Increasing the packet size will increase the effective bandwidth of the system (by reducing per-packet overhead); increasing the artificial delay will reduce the incidence of anomalies (by reducing the probability that a packet will have been delayed for longer than the threshold). Reducing the traffic speeds access to the shared network; reducing anomalies postpones the onset of overload. On the other hand, increasing these values increases the delay through the system, which will eventually become perceptible to the user; this suggests a compromise between the extremes. For example, the one-way delay on a single-hop synchronous-orbit satellite voice circuit is 270 ms, which many users view as disruptive; the double-hop delay of 540 ms is considered much worse. Considering

TABLE I
SPEECH SAMPLE DELAY BREAKDOWN

Type of Delay		Consisting of
Fixed	The (nominal) temporal length of the packet: the packet size measured by its acquisition time	The delay after the packet is acquired until the packet is completed and transmitted (the temporal length of the portion of the packet following this sample)
		Plus the delay after the packet is received until the sample is played back (the temporal length of the portion of the packet preceding this sample)
	Plus much smaller fixed delays	(e.g., the transmission time)
Variable	The delay in transmitting the packet	The delay in obtaining the transmission medium
	Plus (typically) smaller variable delays	

that a system built on one LAN may frequently communicate with another system on another LAN (thereby at least doubling the end-to-end delay), this suggests that the one-way delay on a given LAN should be kept well below 270/2 = 135 ms. An alternative might be to treat inter-LAN connections differently from intra-LAN connections; this possibility is not considered here. In any case, the delay cannot be allowed to grow without bound. It should be noted that echo is perceived as being much more disruptive than simple delay, with the audible threshold occurring much earlier, but echos, where they might occur, can be controlled through the use of echo cancelers. The exact nature of this compromise depends upon the precise psychoacoustic characteristics of the importance of this delay compared to, say, the effect of the anomalies caused by variable delay; this tradeoff is not well understood.

II. A TYPICAL CSMA/CD LAN

Ethernet® is a typical carrier sense multiple access/collision detection (CSMA/CD) LAN [1]. Data packets are transmitted bidirectionally over a coaxial cable with an acyclic branching topology. Access to the net is distributed ("multiple access") and statistical. A station wishing to transmit first listens to determine whether the net is in use ("carrier sense"); if it is, the station defers until the current user has finished transmitting its packet. If the net is not in use, the station begins to transmit. Due to race conditions, two stations could begin to transmit simultaneously; when one station notices another transmitting ("collision detection"), it aborts its transmission, jams the net to ensure that other stations also notice the collision and abort their transmissions, and retries after a random amount of time, thereby statistically avoiding recollision.

An *Ethernet* CSMA/CD network is bit serial and runs at 10 Mbits/s; a bit time is thus 0.1 μs. Assuming 64 kbit/s speech, complete utilization of the bandwidth would result in carrying up to 195.3 two-person conversations (in which each person spoke 40 percent of the time). Such efficiency, however, can never be achieved in practice.

One reason is simple per-packet overhead. A transmission on an *Ethernet* CSMA/CD network begins with 64 sync bits, followed by the packet. A packet contains 112 bits of header, a 368 to 12 000 bit data field (thus between 5.75 and 187.5 ms of 64 kbit/s speech) and a 32 bit CRC field. A station may begin to transmit when it has seen the net idle for 96 bit times. Assuming (arbitrarily) that voice stations are uniformly distributed along a maximum-length linear CSMA/CD network, computations based on the *Ethernet* propagation delay budget give a worst-case mean one-way propagation time of about 10.06 μs; we can expect an arbitrary station to see the net go idle 100.6 bit times after the arbitrary preceding station actually ceased to transmit. A linear CSMA/CD network is in ways a "best case," since the mean distance between stations will be less than in a more general topology. However, the limiting case in complex topologies is extremely unlikely. Similarly, uniform distribution is a "best case," but a more accurate characterization seems difficult to achieve.

Taking per-packet overhead into account, we see that, at the smallest packet size, the speech samples can occupy only 47.6 percent of the bandwidth, allowing a maximum of 93.0 conversations; at the largest packet size, 96.7 percent of the bandwidth can be speech samples, allowing 188.9 conversations.

Studies of the *Ethernet* specifications under varying load conditions have typically

---

® *Ethernet* is a trademark of Xerox Corporation.

shown *Ethernet* CSMA/CD networks to have very desirable throughput characteristics (e.g., see [2]). Throughput tends to rise linearly with offered load until saturation is approached, and then levels off, with an asymptotic throughput within a few percent of maximum for large packets and within several percent for small packets. (For an experimental *Ethernet* CSMA/CD network described in [2], whose numerical parameters differed significantly from those of the specifications discussed here, measured throughput reached 96 percent for maximum-size packets, and 83 percent for minimum-size packets. The traffic in this study, as in the case considered here, was produced by a number of stations each offering a fraction of the total load.) Throughput may decrease under certain cases of extreme overload (for example, two stations each attempting to offer 100 percent load to the net would ultimately transmit less data together than either would individually, due to their contention), although this decrease evidently does not become pathological.

On the other hand, individual packets may experience significantly greater delays under heavy loads than under light loads. The nature of this increase in the delay has not been well characterized in past studies of data traffic, which is not as badly affected by variable delays as is real time voice. Although we can be reasonably certain that the voice samples will make the journey from the transmitter to the receiver, almost up to the physical transport limits of the network, this might be inadequate if they require excessive time to do so.

III. A SIMULATION STUDY

To determine the performance characteristics of voice traffic on a CSMA/CD network, a computer simulation was prepared based on *Ethernet* specifications. The stations were assumed to be uniformly distributed over a maximum-length network. Both voice and data traffic were modeled.

The voice stations modeled typical two-person conversations. The stations were therefore paired, with an appropriate distribution and correlation of talk spurts and silences (adapted from Brady, as discussed in [3]). Brady's study included filtering out very short silences and very short talk spurts, thereby increasing the mean length of silences and talk spurts and otherwise modifying their distribution. The exact type of voice filtering best suited for transmission over a LAN is still uncertain. Voice packets were not transmitted during silences. The simulations began with one conversation, after which an additional conversation was added every 0.5 s of simulated time, until the system had passed saturation. This staged introduction of conversations helps to eliminate anomalies associated with the startup of several conversations at once. Although it is possible that the monotonically increasing number of conversations could produce history artifacts in the simulation results, none were observed in the CSMA/CD simulations; these did occur in the token bus studies outlined in Section IX.

Figure 1 shows the actual number of speakers over time, as a function of the number of conversations, for one particular voice traffic pattern; this pattern and another like it were used throughout the simulations to control the effect of differing traffic patterns in separate simulations. (As it turned out, the effect of a particular voice traffic pattern on observed behavior was less than anticipated, and is easily compensated for. Thus, the use of the same voice traffic patterns throughout the simulations seems to have been unnecessary.)

The data stations presented a bimodal distribution of packet lengths, typical of data traffic on real nets, with 80 percent minimum-size packets and 20 percent maximum-size packets (giving approximately the opposite distribution when weighted by length). The

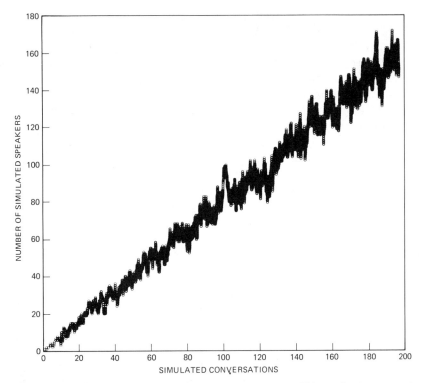

Fig. 1.   Number of simulated speakers in a voice traffic pattern. This graph presents a voice traffic pattern used in most of the simulations presented in this chapter, plotting the number of instantaneous speakers as a function of the number of conversations. One simulated two-person conversation is added every 0.5 s of simulated time; there are 0.8 expected instantaneous speakers per conversation. Speakers divide their time between talk spurts and silences. This simulation uses an empirically derived distribution of the lengths of talk spurts and silences and of the correlation between the states of the two potential speakers in a conversation.

packet arrivals were modeled by a Poisson process: the traffic generated by a Poisson process is not as bursty as real data traffic, but the difference was expected to be relatively unimportant in determining the effect of the data traffic upon the voice traffic. The simulations included between 0 and 10 percent steady data loading of the system, the latter value being well beyond the measured steady loadings of current *Ethernet* CSMA/CD networks.

IV. VOICE TRANSPORT ALGORITHMS

The simplest algorithm for transmitting voice would be to packetize the digital speech, dropping packets containing only silences, and to send them to an autonomous network interface to be transmitted asynchronously. The simplest algorithm for receiving voice would be to receive packets asynchronously from an autonomous network interface, and to begin to play back the first packet of a talk spurt after some artificial delay, with subsequent packets of the talk spurt each immediately following its predecessor.

An important improvement on the transmission algorithm at the source deals with the case when packet transmission must be delayed until the net can be acquired. If, while the packet is waiting to be transmitted, more speech samples are being buffered, these can be appended to the old packet before it is transmitted instead of being used to start a new packet. This approach has the following three advantages.

1) It tends to transmit fewer packets under a heavy load, thereby applying a degree of negative feedback.

2) The varying length of a packet serves as a sort of time stamp. Since the last speech sample in the packet was collected just before the packet was successfully transmitted, this allows the receiver to determine the exact age of the first speech sample, allowing more precise control over packet playback.

3) It produces an adaptive effect. In the simplest case, each station will begin to attempt to transmit a new packet one packet time after beginning to attempt to transmit the previous packet; here, though, this will occur one packet time after the last packet was successfully transmitted. In the first case, if two stations happen to collide with each other once, they will then collide with each other every packet time afterwards until one of them begins a silence; in the second case, a collision once resolved creates a phase shift that persists thereafter.

At the receiver, we buffer packets to cope with their variable delay. If the speech samples are implicitly time stamped by the variable packet size, it is possible to correct for the delay that the first packet of a talk spurt has already experienced in transmission.

The receiver implementation can be quite simple. The voice path is implemented as a first in first out (FIFO) buffer: packets are inserted as they are received while samples are extracted synchronously. The first packet of a talk spurt is preceded in the FIFO by the appropriate amount of artificial silence; the beginning of a talk spurt can be detected by the FIFO being empty. This scheme is easily extended to the case of connections with more than one other speaker, with multiple independent speech sources being merged together; each speaker is assigned a separate FIFO and summing is performed on the outputs of the FIFO's. The FIFO's can be implemented in hardware or software.

Samples that are too late are discarded; they will have been preceded by an artificial silence. Excessive delays can result in packets that are longer than the FIFO, in which case part of the packet can be discarded. For every amount of artificial silence we accidentally introduce, we lose an equivalent amount of speech, except when the last samples of a talk spurt are delayed excessively, in which case the artificial silence before playing them back is matched by losing part of the real silence elsewhere. With proper matching between transmitter and receiver, it is possible for the transmitter to predict which samples the receiver would discard, and simply not transmit these in the first place, thereby reducing net traffic under heavy load and avoiding a potential instability.

V. BASIC CSMA/CD PERFORMANCE

Simulations were performed to measure the voice capacity and related characteristics of CSMA/CD LAN's. For a simulation in which voice stations used (nominally) minimum-size voice packets (5.75 ms), and in which there was no data traffic, Fig. 2 shows the transmission delays that voice packets experienced. Note that the delay is essentially zero (i.e., less than the quantizing sample time of 125 μs) until the equivalent of approximately 60 conversations is reached, at which point the delay rises roughly linearly. (While the expected number of speakers at an arbitrary point in the simulation is 0.8 times the number of conversations, the actual number of speakers will vary from this, depending on the details of the traffic pattern. We define the *effective* number of conversations at a point in

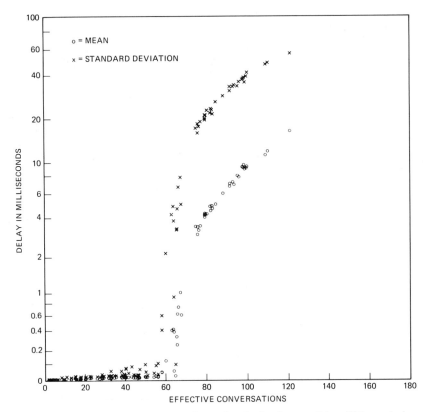

Fig. 2.   CSMA/CD delay for 5.75 ms voice packets in the absence of data. This graph shows
the mean and standard deviation of the delay experienced in the transmission of (nominally)
5.75 ms (i.e., minimum-size) voice packets in the absence of data traffic, as a function of the
number of effective conversations. Note that both the mean and the standard deviation are
essentially zero (i.e., less than the quantizing sample time, 125 μs) until about 60 effective
conversations are reached, at which point they grow roughly linearly (distorted here by the
logarithmic vertical scale) and become quite large; the standard deviation far exceeds the mean.

time as the actual number of speakers divided by 0.8 (the expected value of the effective
number of conversations is the actual number of conversations). It was found that much
smoother graphs were obtained by plotting transmission performance using the effective
number of conversations rather than the actual number, and that the curves were thereby
made much more similar across different traffic patterns. Most of the graphs in this chapter
are based on effective conversations rather than actual conversations; they may be
converted to actual conversations by the addition of appropriate axial randomness.) Note
that the standard deviation is several times the mean, due to the long tail of the distribution
of delays; this is illustrated in Fig. 3, which shows the distribution of delays at a 50-
conversations loading.

  If we set a threshold of an additional 5.75 ms artificial delay of voice samples, we can
bring the total delay through the system to 11.5 ms. (Given a desired total delay of 11.5 ms,
it would be possible to allocate less of the total to variable delay and more to packet size;
the reverse would also be possible. An extreme position in either direction can be
counterproductive, so an equal division is not totally unreasonable. However, as will be

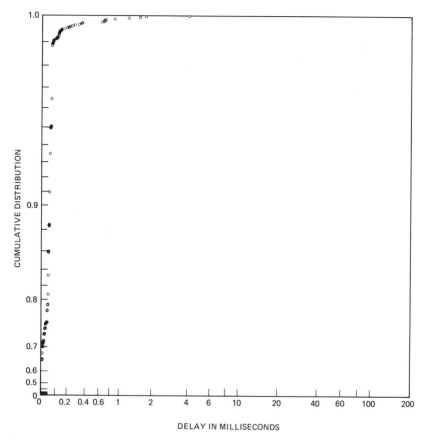

Fig. 3. CSMA/CD cumulative distribution of voice packet transmission delays for a loading of 50 conversations and 5.75 ms packets. This graph shows the cumulative distribution of the variable transmission delays experienced over a period of 0.5 s when the simulated CSMA/CD network was loaded with 50 conversations and no data traffic. The vertical axis is exponential; the horizontal axis is logarithmic. We see that about 65 percent of the packets experienced no delay, that over 99 percent were transmitted in less than 125 μs (the quantum phase shift possible using the adaptive algorithm), and one took over 4 ms. The shape of this curve causes the standard deviation to exceed the mean, as shown in Fig. 2.

shown later in this chapter, it seems more optimal, for CSMA/CD networks, to allocate significantly more delay to packet size than to variable delay.) At this delay we can expect to transmit up to about 60 conversations well, and to lose some speech samples past that point, as shown in Fig. 4. Here, the vertical axis measures the percentage of speech samples lost, which roughly models the degradation of the channel. Further study is needed to determine the effect of other parameters of the artificial silences and loss of speech upon human users: for example, the number and length of these anomalies are probably important.

As a test of validity, the results of these simulations (as well as the ones following) were compared to a previous study of voice transmission on CSMA/CD networks [4]; the results were found to correspond closely.

As an example of the importance of the adaptive nature of the variable packet-size

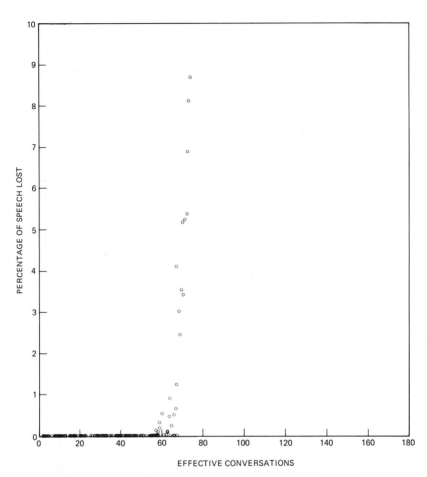

Fig. 4. CSMA/CD voice channel degradation with increasing load with 5.75 ms packets and 5.75 ms artificial delay. This graph shows the voice signal degradation experienced on a simulated CSMA/CD network with 5.75 ms packets and an additional 5.75 ms artificial delay at the receiver. Two simulations with different voice traffic patterns were performed and their results superimposed. Degradation is measured as the percentage of voice samples that are discarded (here at the transmitter). There is no degradation until about 58 effective conversations, soon after which the degradation rises roughly vertically; the network is saturated and each new conversation causes a conversation's worth of speech samples to be lost.

algorithm, Fig. 5 shows the effect of using fixed packet sizes; we see that the channel degrades much sooner.

VI. EFFECT OF DATA TRAFFIC ON CSMA/CD CAPACITY

As we have seen, the natural synchronous nature of voice traffic in conjunction with an adaptive algorithm enables the transmitters, in effect, to slot themselves and thereby interfere only minimally with each other. As the traffic increases, though, talk spurts begin to arrive faster than they can settle in and this structure begins to disintegrate. It is therefore to be expected that the addition of data traffic, with its inherent asynchronous nature, will

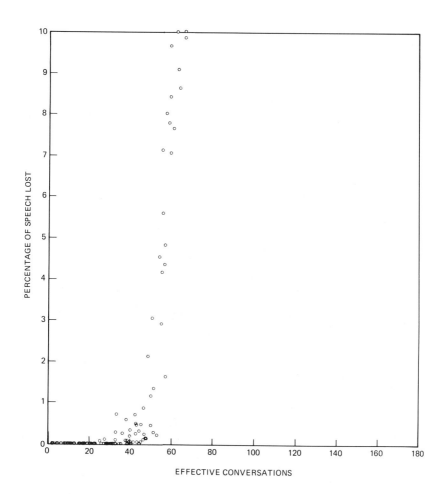

Fig. 5. CSMA/CD voice channel degradation with increasing load with 5.75 ms packets and 5.75 ms artificial delay, with a nonadaptive algorithm. This graph shows the same relation between simulated network load and voice channel degradation as does Fig. 4, except that it uses a simple nonadaptive transmission algorithm. As we see, the expected performance of such a system is significantly poorer than one with the adaptive algorithm, in regard both to the point at which degradation begins and the point at which the curve becomes essentially vertical.

interfere with the voice traffic more than its share, so that the addition of some amount of data traffic will eliminate more than an equivalent amount of voice traffic capacity.

This phenomenon does in fact occur. Figure 6 shows the delay experienced by voice packets on an CSMA/CD system with 5 percent data loading. Note that there is no longer any region of essentially zero delay, as in Fig. 2 without data loading, and that the knees of the curves, although significantly less well-defined here, certainly occur more than 5 percent sooner than earlier. Figure 7 shows the channel degradation allowing 5.75 ms buffering at the receiver.

Additional simulation results, not shown here, were obtained for 10 percent data loading; they basically extend this trend.

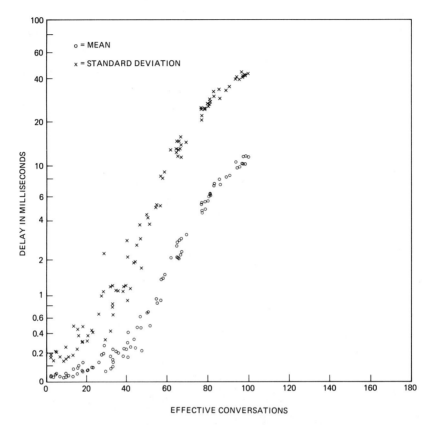

Fig. 6.   CSMA/CD delay for 5.75 ms voice packets with 5 percent data loading. This graph shows the effect of a 5 percent data traffic loading on the mean and the standard deviation of the voice packet delay on the simulated CSMA/CD network; it should be compared to Fig. 2, where no data loading was assumed. Notice that there is no longer any large region of essentially zero delay, and that the 5 percent data loading has shifted the curves to the left far more than 5 percent.

VII. Increasing the Delay in a CSMA/CD System

We can increase the effective bandwidth of the system by increasing the packet size at the transmitter or by increasing the variable delay threshold at the receiver. If we choose a relatively large value of 50 ms for each, resulting in a 100 ms total delay through the system, we find that, as shown in Fig. 8, about 150 effective conversations can take place on the *Ethernet* CSMA/CD network in the absence of data. Assuming 5 percent data loading reduces this number to about 125 effective conversations, as shown in Fig. 9.

It seems likely that the point of diminishing returns has been reached at the 50 ms level; further increases in the packet size or receiver delay cannot produce any great increase in the capacity of the network, but they could subjectively degrade the channel by increasing its delay.

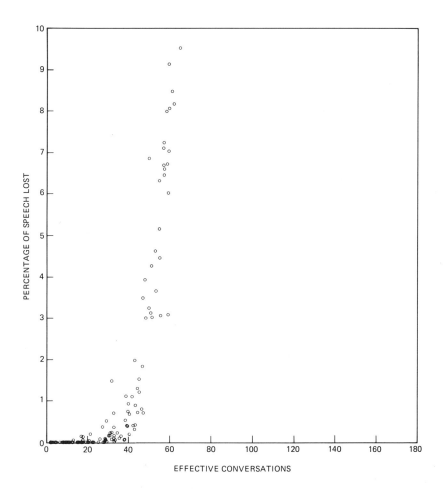

EFFECTIVE CONVERSATIONS

Fig. 7.   CSMA/CD voice channel degradation with increasing load with 5.75 ms packets and 5.75 ms artificial delay, with 5 percent data loading. This graph shows the signal degradation on simulated voice channels over a CSMA/CD network in the presence of 5 percent data loading; it should be compared to Fig. 4, in which there was no data loading. Again, two simulations were performed. Degradation rises significantly earlier than with no data loading; there is more than a 5 percent degradation in the effective bandwidth. The effect of a 5 percent data loading on a system with a nonadaptive fixed packet size (not shown here) is comparatively less, since it does not take advantage of the synchronous nature of the voice packets.

VIII. A TOKEN BUS

An additional simulation study was performed to determine the suitability of a *token-passing* LAN for carrying voice. In a token-passing LAN, contention is resolved through use of a conceptual circulating token. A station may transmit only if it has possession of the token, and must then pass the token to the next station in logical sequence. A *token ring* is a token-passing LAN with a physical ring topology; the logical sequence is typically the same as the physical sequence of stations on the ring. A *token bus* is a token-passing LAN

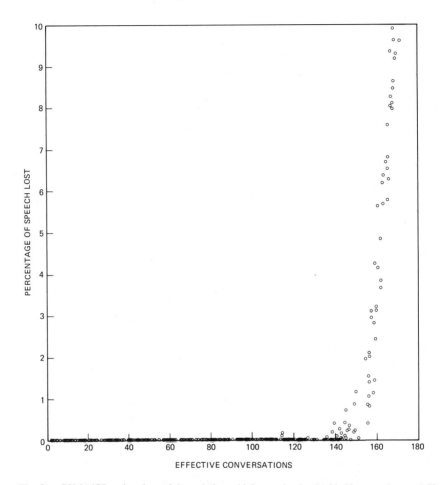

Fig. 8.   CSMA/CD voice channel degradation with increasing load with 50 ms packets and 50 ms artificial delay. This graph shows the signal degradation experienced on simulated voice channels over a CSMA/CD network with 50 ms packets and an additional 50 ms artificial packet delay at the receiving station; it should be compared to Fig. 4, which assumes smaller numerical values. As in Fig. 4, two simulations were performed and their results superimposed. We see that a large increase in the delay through the system can produce a significant increase in its effective bandwith.

with a physical bus topology (linear or acyclic branching); the logical sequence can often be arbitrary but is most efficient if it corresponds to the physical sequence.

A token bus was chosen as the token-passing LAN most directly comparable to a CSMA/ CD LAN, and the numerical parameters of the token bus were chosen to be as similar as possible to those of the *Ethernet* specifications and the choices of the above CSMA/CD simulations. These choices are quite possibly far from optimal for a token-passing LAN, but they allow for a simple comparison with the CSMA/CD results; there is no typical design for token-passing systems that corresponds to *Ethernet* among CSMA/CD systems.

The simulated token bus LAN has a single token circulating; when a station receives the token, it either transmits a packet, which implicitly passes the token to the next station in logical sequence, or it transmits an abbreviated packet, containing only a header, to

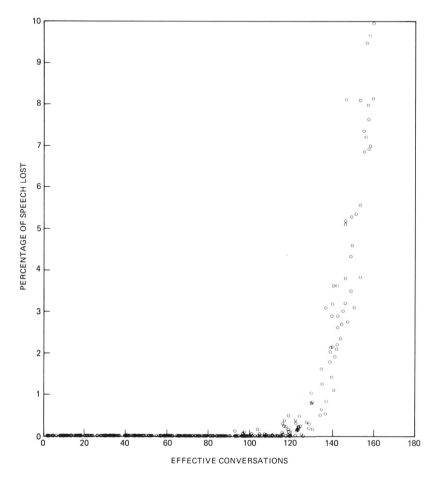

Fig. 9.   CSMA/CD voice channel degradation with increasing load with 50 ms packets and 50 ms artificial delay, with 5 percent data loading. This graph shows the signal degradation experienced on simulated voice channels over a CSMA/CD network with a long delay through the system, in the presence of 5 percent data loading; it should be compared to Fig. 8, in which there was no data loading. Again, two simulations were performed and their results superimposed. Note that the proportionate drop in effective bandwidth caused by the data traffic is much less than when small delays were considered, as in the difference between Figs. 4 and 7.

explicitly pass the token. The bus is linear, of maximum *Ethernet* length, with stations uniformly distributed. No attempt is made to match the token-passing sequence to the physical sequence of stations on the bus, or to model the (small) control traffic needed to expand the sequence when new conversations, and their associated stations, are added.

The voice packet delays in the token bus simulation are shown in Fig. 10. (To understand the strange shape of the curves in Fig. 10, consider a simplified case. We transmit (nominally) 5 ms packets. There are enough stations in the ring for the token to require 2 ms to circulate in the absence of any transmissions. Assume that for each active station (one associated with an active speaker) to transmit its 5 ms packet each time around would require an additional 4 ms total. An active station will be ready to transmit 5 ms after it has last transmitted, but if every station transmits every time around, the token will take (over)

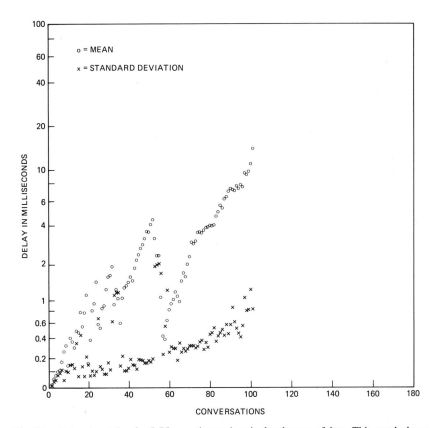

Fig. 10.   Token bus delay for 5.75 ms voice packets in the absence of data. This graph shows the mean and standard deviation of the transmission delay on a simulated token bus with no data; it should be compared to Fig. 2, which shows the corresponding delay for a CSMA/CD network. The mean delay is never less than for the CSMA/CD case; the standard deviation under heavy load is much less than for the CSMA/CD case but greater under light load. The sawtooth shape of the curves show that these figures are nonunique and depend on the transmission history. The horizontal axis measures actual conversations instead of effective conversations since even silent stations take part in token circulation.

6 ms to circulate, and so every station will experience the same (over) 1 ms delay; this can remain as constant as the load on the net. On the other hand, if the token were circulating faster, so that it needed only 4 ms for its transit, then a station would transmit only every other time around and experience a delay of 3 (4 + 4 − 5) ms. If stations transmitted only every other time around, the time needed under the original assumptions for a token cycle will be 2 + 4/2 = 4 ms, as assumed; this shows that the performance of a token-passing system can be nonuniquely determinable from the load, and can therefore depend upon history.) We note that the mean delay is never less than the mean delay for the corresponding CSMA/CD case shown in Fig. 2. However, the standard deviation for a token ring under sufficient load is much smaller than for the CSMA/CD network: all packets experience very similar delays, as shown in Fig. 11.

Adding 5 percent data loading to a token bus increases the delays to those shown in Fig. 12. Again, the mean is never less than the mean for the CSMA/CD case shown in Fig. 6, but the standard deviation is much smaller under heavy load.

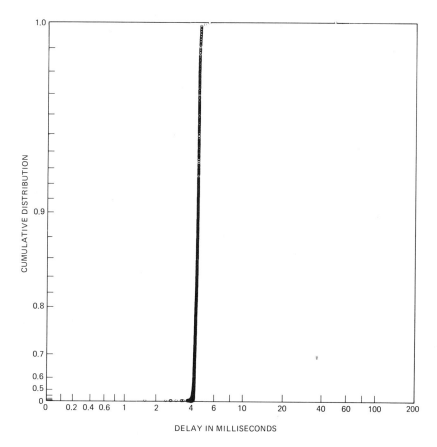

Fig. 11. Token bus cumulative distribution of voice packet transmission delays for a loading of 50 conversations and 5.75 ms packets. This graph shows the cumulative distribution of the variable transmission delays experienced on a simulated token bus loaded with 50 conversations and no data traffic; it should be compared to Fig. 3, which shows the equivalent case for a simulated CSMA/CD network. We note that almost all packets are delayed essentially the same amount of time, which reflects an essentially constant token circulation rate during this period.

To allow a more direct comparison, Fig. 13 shows the capacity of a CSMA/CD network as a function of the amount of buffering at the receiver, with 5.75 ms packets and no data loading, and allowing 1 percent speech sample loss. No compensation at the transmitter for the buffering at the receiver, in the form of locally discarding samples that would otherwise simply be discarded remotely, was performed in these simulations. Figure 14 shows CSMA/CD capacity with 5 percent data loading. By contrast, Figs. 15 and 16 show the corresponding relations for the token bus with no data loading and with 5 percent data loading, respectively. Figures 13 through 16 show the token bus to offer significantly more capacity than the CSMA/CD network, suggesting that a token-passing network is superior to a CSMA/CD network for voice transmission. We can see that the CSMA/CD LAN's performance is much less dependent on the receiver delay than is that of the token ring, suggesting that the increase in the overall delay caused by increasing the receiver buffering would be better spent in increasing the packet length while keeping the receiver delay

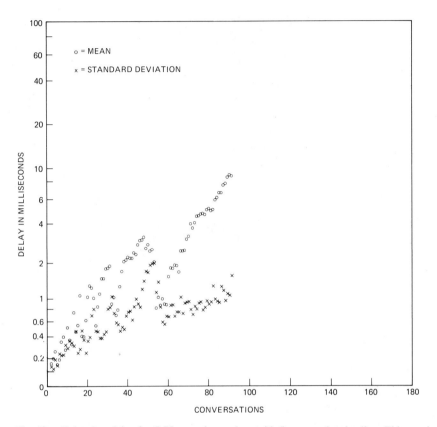

Fig. 12.   Token bus delay for 5.75 ms voice packets with 5 percent data loading. This graph shows the mean and the standard deviation of the delay experienced in the transmission of voice packets on a simulated token bus with 5 percent data loading; it should be compared to Fig. 6, which shows the corresponding delay for a CSMA/CD network. Note that the mean delay is never less than for the CSMA/CD case; the standard deviations for a token bus are significantly less than for CSMA/CD under heavy load, although they are greater under light load.

relatively small. On the other hand, a token bus can efficiently keep a relatively small nominal packet size and benefit directly from an increase in receiver buffering, as shown.

IX. CONCLUSIONS

It is possible to transmit a large number of voice conversations on either a CSMA/CD LAN or a token-passing LAN in the presence of reasonable data loading. The performance of token passing seems superior to that of CSMA/CD.

There are even better mechanisms for transmitting digital voice: time-division multiplexing schemes, for example, can do an excellent job for voice, but are not exceptional for carrying data because of their inherently synchronous nature. Similarly, CSMA/CD LAN's can be superior to token passing for many data applications. It is still a research problem to find a LAN that can carry both voice and data ''optimally,'' or to identify more exactly the appropriate tradeoffs.

One significant unanswered question is the potential of such a system for serving large

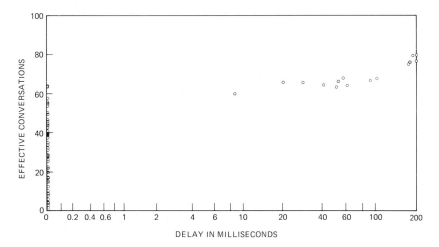

Fig. 13. CSMA/CD capacity as a function of receiver buffering delay, with 5.75 ms packets, 1 percent sample loss, and no data loading. This graph shows the capacity, measured in effective conversations, of a simulated CSMA/CD network as a function of the buffering delay at the receiving station, with (nominally) 5.75 ms packets and allowing up to 1 percent of the speech samples to be lost (at the receiver), in the absence of data. We note that the capacity depends very little on the buffering at the receiver; this suggests that, of some total allowable delay through the system, more delay should be allocated to packet length than to receiver buffering.

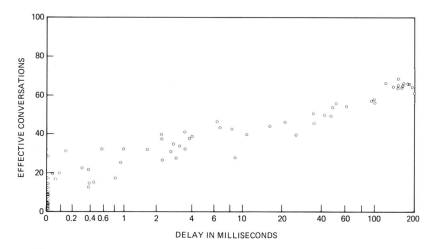

Fig. 14. CSMA/CD capacity as a function of receiver buffering delay, with 5.75 ms packets, 1 percent sample loss, and 5 percent data loading. This graph shows the capacity, measured in effective conversations, of a simulated CSMA/CD network as a function of the buffering delay at the receiving station, with (nominally) 5.75 ms packets and allowing up to 1 percent of the speech samples to be lost (at the receiver), with 5 percent data loading. As in Fig. 13, which considered the corresponding case with no data loading, the capacity depends fairly little on the amount of buffering at the receiver, again suggesting that receiver buffering should be kept fairly small and its share of the overall delay used in allowing the packet size to grow.

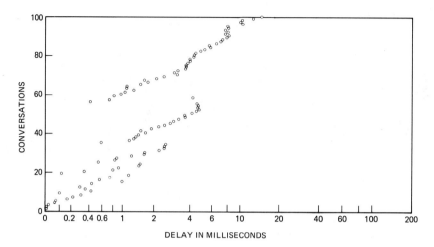

Fig. 15. Token bus capacity as a function of receiver buffering delay, with 5.75 ms packets, 1 percent sample loss, and no data loading. This graph shows the capacity, measured in actual conversations, of a simulated token bus as a function of the buffering delay at the receiving station, with (nominally) 5.75 ms packets and allowing up to 1 percent of the speech samples to be lost (at the receiver), in the absence of data. The significant increase in capacity with increased receiver buffering, plus some reasoning on the nature of token passing, suggest that the total delay through a token bus system should be allocated predominantly to receiver buffering, with relatively small nominal packet sizes.

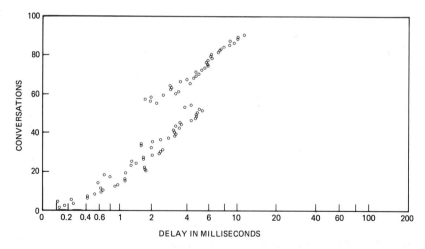

Fig. 16. Token bus capacity as a function of receiver buffering delay, with 5.75 ms packets, 1 percent sample loss, and 5 percent data loading. This graph shows the capacity, measured in actual conversations, of a simulated token bus as a function of the buffering delay at the receiving station, with (nominally) 5.75 ms packets and allowing up to 1 percent of the speech samples to be lost (at the receiver), with 5 percent data loading. As in Fig. 15, which considered the corresponding case with no data loading, the capacity depends significantly on the amount of buffering at the receiver, again suggesting that receiver buffering in a token bus system should be kept fairly large and the nominal packet size fairly small.

numbers of users; there is an inherent limit of the number of users on one LAN. It is uncertain to what extent internetworking can help, since internetworking would increase the mean and standard deviation of the delays.

REFERENCES

[1] *The Ethernet/A Local Area Network/Data Link Layer and Physical Layer Specifications,* Digital Equipment Corporation, Intel Corporation, and Xerox Corporation, Version 1.0, Sept. 30, 1980.
[2] J. F. Shoch and J. A. Hupp, "Measured performance of an Ethernet local network," *Commun. Ass. Comput. Mach.* vol. 23, pp. 711–721, Dec. 1980.
[3] P. T. Brady, "A statistical analysis of on-off patterns in 16 conversations," *Bell Syst. Tech. J.,* vol. 47, pp. 73–91, Jan. 1968.
[4] G. J. Nutt and D. L. Bayer, "Performance of CSMA/CD networks under combined voice and data loads," *IEEE Trans. Commun.,* vol. COM-30, pp. 6–11, Jan. 1982.

26
A Distributed Local Area Network Packet Protocol for Combined Voice and Data Transmission

JOHN O. LIMB AND LOIS E. FLAMM

Local area networks designed to carry a variety of traffic such as data, voice, facsimile, and video should be able to implement low latency virtual circuits to meet the demands of periodic traffic. We have designed a partially distributed algorithm to efficiently schedule voice traffic on a unidirectional bus system called Fasnet. Virtual channels are allocated for the duration of a talk spurt and relinquished during the intervening silent intervals. Conversations already in progress, but without an assigned circuit, take precedence over newly arriving calls. Unused voice capacity may be utilized by data stations when required.

Simulations of the system indicate that performance is close to that obtained by an ideal TASI multiplexer. While the algorithm is unfair, this is not a significant factor unless the network is loaded very heavily. Further, except for a "sojourn" time unused voice capacity is utilized by the data stations.

I. INTRODUCTION

The initial, and still dominant, application of local area networks is for interconnection of computers and computer terminals. There is a good match between the capabilities of these networks and the bursty nature of the traffic. The extension of these networks to carry other types of traffic (e.g., voice, video, and facsimile) is now receiving increasing attention [1], [2]. In particular, combining voice traffic and computer traffic on a single network has the potential for reducing overall communications costs and facilitating the design and implementation of services that depend integrally on voice and data communication (e.g., electronic voice mail).

High-speed local area networks have been designed and constructed for the transmission of mixtures of traffic types. A recently described local area network [3], [4] which operates at 200 Mbits/s could be used for carrying approximately 2000 simultaneous voice conversations by straightforward coding of the voice signal. If data and other traffic were also to be transmitted, however, the number of conversations that could be accommodated would be reduced significantly. Techniques are needed to permit different types of traffic to be efficiently combined on the one system.

Different types of traffic have different transmission requirements. For example, voice packets are generated at a constant rate while a person is talking and, for the integrity of the

448

conversation, these packets must be delivered with a maximum delay comparable to the period between generation of consecutive voice packets. From 1 to 2 percent of all packets can be lost without seriously degrading the voice signal [5]. Further, it is acceptable to occasionally prevent a telephone call from completing (i.e., blocking the call). Once a call is established, however, it should be possible to continue uninterrupted. Data, on the other hand, must be transmitted with a very low error rate, but in many applications a delay of as much as 100 or 200 ms does not present a problem.

Telephone traffic has both a coarse and a fine structure. The coarse structure is associated with the origination and termination of individual calls which typically last for about 3 min. The fine structure is associated with the talk spurts and silent intervals between talk spurts that punctuate a conversation. An average talk spurt lasts for 1.5 s and depends to some extent on the setting of the speech detector used to "define" the talk spurts [6]. Since a telephone user tends to talk for only 40 percent of the time that a call is in progress, the efficieny of a system can be more than doubled by not transmitting a signal during the silent intervals [7]. For a network transmitting a large enough number of simultaneous voice conversations (say 100), talk spurts begin and end with sufficient frequency that intuitively one would expect to be able to utilize the statistical fluctuations in the number of talk spurts for the transmission of data without incurring large delays in the data path. Entire conversations, on the other hand, are more than 100 times longer than talk spurts. In most cases, attempts to exploit short-term changes in the number of calls lead to unacceptably large delays of the data traffic [8].

In this chapter we describe protocols that efficiently utilize the Fasnet local area network to transmit mixtures of data and voice traffic in such a way that the specific characteristics of the two types of traffic are accommodated [4]. In our simulations of the protocols we assume a fixed number of active conversations so as to focus on the dynamics within conversations rather than call origination and duration effects. We show that the proposed protocol performs almost as well as an ideal multiplexer. Further, unused voice slots are utilized by data except for a "sojourn" time that occurs between the voice and data subcycles.

II. OVERVIEW OF FASNET OPERATION WITH MIXED TRAFFIC

Figure 1 illustrates the physical configuration of a Fasnet link [4]. The basic link consists of two unidirectional transmission lines with stations making attachments to both the upper

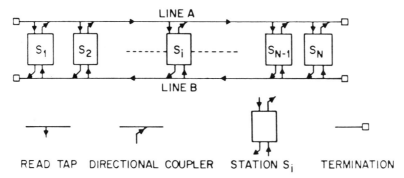

Fig. 1.   Physical configuration of Fasnet.

and lower lines. The upper line is used to communicate with stations to the right of the transmitting station, and the lower is for stations to the left. A station wishing to transmit a packet will first sense the line by means of the nondirectional read tap to determine when to transmit, and then write signals using the directional write connection. The receiving station reads the signal by means of the nondirectional tap.

The first and last stations control access to the link. By means of timing provided by the end stations, a station is able to read any bit or group of bits from a passing slot. This is facilitated by requiring slots to be of a fixed length. A station wishing to transmit inspects a busy bit associated with each slot to see whether the slot has already been used. If the slot is free (BUSY = 0), the station sets the busy bit (BUSY = 1) and writes its packet into that slot. If the slot has already been used, a station must wait for the next free slot to arrive.

To promote fairness, the link is operated in cycles. By this we mean that all stations are permitted to transmit a given number of fixed-length packets after the start of a cycle. Only when all stations have been given the opportunity to transmit will a new cycle begin, permitting active stations to transmit again. The cycling operation is achieved by centralized control located, in the present example, in the end stations [3]; alternatively it may be achieved by distributing control among all stations [9]. Experience suggests that some centralization of control yields simpler protocols [4] and the descriptions herein are only partially distributed.

It is possible to have more than one type of cycle. In Fig. 2, we give an example of a mixture of voice and data cycles. Shown is a temporal representation of the activity on a single line with each small square denoting one slot. An expanded view of one of these slots is shown. The first few bits on the front of the slot constitute what is called the access control field. Bits within the access control field describe, among other things, if the packet is the first packet in a cycle and the type of cycle. Each slot starts with all bits set to zero except for the 4 bit synchronizing word. By way of example we assume that each line of the link shown in Fig. 1 transmits at a rate of 10 Mbits/s (20 Mbit/s system) and further that speech is transmitted in 10 ms packets. If the speech is PCM coded at 64 kbits/s, then each 10 ms packet will contain 640 data bits. We will assume that each packet contains an additional 60 bits for the previously mentioned access field, and for addressing and error control functions. Since the line operates at 10 Mbits/s and slots are 700 bits long, there will be 142 slots between each start of a voice cycle.

Cycles are initiated by the head station (first station on a line) writing a "start of voice" code (START = V) or a "start of data" code (START = D) in the START subfield of the access control field (Fig. 2). Since speech samples must be sent periodically at 10 ms intervals, a START = V is written every 10 ms to initiate a voice cycle. The cycle may be divided between voice and data as desired. Let us assume that we allow a maximum of 50 voice slots in the cycle. This would allow a minimum of 92 packets to be used by data stations. Thus, after 50 voice slots, at most, the head station would issue a START = D, which would prohibit further voice stations from accessing the line (until the next START = V) and at the same time allow the data stations to start accessing the line. Thus, the start signals (V and D) may be viewed as a method for switching stations on and off depending on the traffic type. In this way the interval between two START = V's can be divided in whatever proportion is required between voice traffic and data traffic.

While only two types of traffic are of concern here, data and voice, the concept may be generalized to handle many different types of traffic with different characteristics. For example, dedicated packets for a "private line" of a specific capacity could be incorporated by using an additional code in the start field that would periodically permit

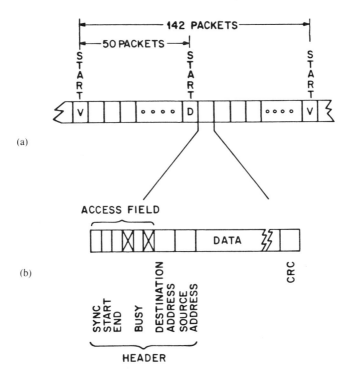

Fig. 2. (a) Sequence of packets occurring during a 10 ms period. It is assumed that speech is coded at 64 kbits/s giving 640 bits of data per packet with a total packet size of 700 bits. This results in 142 packets per speech sample interval assuming 10 Mbit/s Fasnet line. (b) Details of the fields within a slot showing the access field, packet header, and data.

access to the private line by the station or stations enabled by that start code. A control station anywhere on the system could determine the required combination of start fields and their timing appropriate for the specific mix of traffic and transmit this information to the end stations.

Our protocol addresses two important problems associated with implementing a working system. Firstly, when all voice slots are full, new calls should be fairly allocated to the channel as old calls drop off. Secondly, in a TASI environment where advantage is taken of the silent intervals between talk spurts, calls that return from silent to talking should be rescheduled without introducing excessive clipping of the talk spurt. In this chapter we describe techniques that efficiently permit the scheduling of new voice calls and the elimination of the silent intervals in ongoing voice conversations. This is done in a way that allows unused voice capacity to be made available to any data traffic that may wish to exploit the link. Other work combining voice and data on a single channel is described by Bially *et al.* [8].

The algorithm presented here was designed to be robust and simple. In the case of the station protocol, information is not required from the reverse line to control access to the forward line; the station protocol can be implemented via a simple state table with no arithmetic. Counting is performed only in the first station. The last station protocol also requires only a simple state table.

III. Description of Protocol

A. Telephone Conversation Dynamics

We assume that a three-state Markov model [Fig. 3(a)] characterizes the dynamics of the telephone conversation [10]. When a conversation commences, the source changes from state idle to state talk. The state of the source will then switch rapidly between talk and silent states until the end of the conversation. A transition will then be made back to the idle state from either talk or silent states. Accordingly, a conversation is defined as being either idle or nonidle. If the station is idle, no conversation is taking place. If the station is nonidle, however, a talk spurt could be in progress (the station is active) or the station may be silent and not generating traffic.

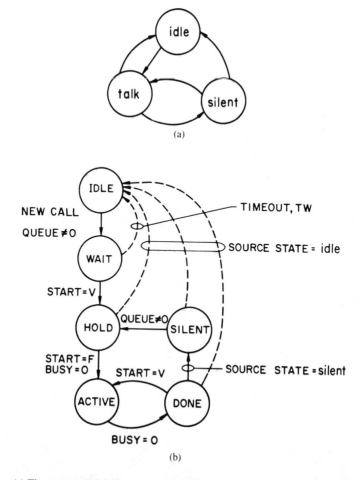

Fig. 3.   (a) Three-state model of speech source. (b) State diagram of speech station. Queue ≠ 0 denotes voice packets ready to be transmitted.

TABLE I
DESCRIPTION OF START FIELD
CODES

D	Start of data subcycle.
F	"Free" slot available for use by voice station in state HOLD.
V	Start of voice subcycle in which the preceding voice subcycle contains unused F slots.
W	Start of voice subcycle in which all F slots in the preceding voice subcycle were used.
0	No change of condition.

B. Voice Station Protocol

A voice station has six states[1] [Fig. 3(b)] and moves between them in response to the state of the source and the information in the start and busy fields read from the access field of passing slots.

The start field of each packet may contain START $= V, W, F, D$, or zero; a zero indicates none of the other conditions (see the summary in Table I). Upon initiation of a call (customer goes off-hook), the station state will change from IDLE to WAIT [Fig. 3(b)]. Upon reading START $= V$, the station will transit to HOLD.

The first station is aware of the number of active stations that transmitted voice packets in the previous cycle, denoted by AC (for "active channels"). After AC voice slots have occurred, the first station will start marking slots as "free" using the code START $= F$. Stations in the HOLD state may now compete for these free slots. Priority is given to ongoing calls, in that a call going from silent to talk can always transit from the SILENT state to the HOLD state. On the other hand, new calls can only move from the WAIT state to the HOLD state when all waiting calls in the HOLD state have been served. This preferential treatment for calls in progress is achieved by means of the start codes issued by the first station. A START $= W$ is written if any stations remained in the HOLD state at the end of the previous cycle (i.e., there were insufficient free slots in the previous cycle for all calls in HOLD to be served); otherwise, the cycle beings with START $= V$. Under heavy traffic conditions a transition from WAIT to HOLD may be delayed for a number of cycles. Eventually, if the station is not served, a timeout TW will occur and the station state will change back to IDLE, with the user being returned a busy tone.

After switching to state HOLD, the station seizes the first slot with START $= F$ and BUSY $= 0$ and, after acquiring a slot, is guaranteed access to a slot in all subsequent voice cycles until the end of the talk spurt. While the conversation remains in the talk state, the station will transit between the ACTIVE and DONE states. At the start of each cycle,

---

[1] Note that the state names "IDLE" and "SILENT" are used in both the source model and the station model, and do not denote the same state. Source states are indicated in lower case, and other states in upper case.

stations in state DONE move to state ACTIVE. When they have transmitted their packet they move back to DONE. At the end of the talk spurt, voice samples will cease to be generated and as a result of having no samples to transmit (QUEUE = 0) the station state will move from DONE to SILENT. The start of a new talk spurt is signaled by having speech samples to transmit (QUEUE $\neq$ 0), and the station state moves directly from SILENT to HOLD and competes for free slots along with any other calls in state HOLD. At some point, when in DONE or SILENT, the conversation ends (QUEUE = 0 and state = idle) and the state will switch to IDLE.

C. First Station Protocol

The first and last stations together interact to control the voice and data station access to the medium. We will start by describing the action of the first station, whose state diagram is shown in Fig. 4(a). A cycle is initiated periodically at the rate of 100/s in the example previously discussed where each voice sample was assumed to be 10 ms long. The station switches to the VOICE state at the initiation of a voice subcycle, and at the same time, writes the START = V or W in the access field of the next occurring packet. By means of signals transmitted by the last station, the first station counts the number of active voice channels in a cycle (which must always be less than or equal to 50 in the above example) and stores the value in a variable AC. The station stays in the VOICE state and performs no other action until the number of slots issued equals AC. Each subsequent slot has START

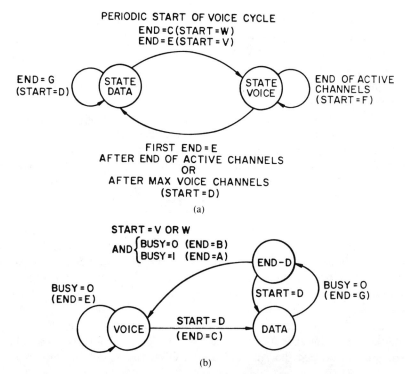

(a)

(b)

Fig. 4. (a) State diagram of the first station where EVENT (ACTION) indicates the event that triggers the state transition and the action that occurs as a result of the transition. (b) State diagram of the last station.

$= F$ (see Table I), signaling to all voice stations that the slot is free and may be taken by a station waiting for service in the HOLD state.

To describe how the station switches from state VOICE to state DATA, bear in mind that the last station writes a slot with END $= A$ for "acknowledgment" see (Table II), upon detecting the start of a voice cycle, and thereafter writes END $= E$ in every slot on the reverse line for which the immediately preceding slot on the forward line is empty. Thus, by observing the state of the end field on the reverse line, the first station can recognize the first empty slot after AC number of slots have been received. As indicated in Fig. 4(a), this condition is used to make the transition from state VOICE to state DATA. Alternatively, a transition from VOICE to DATA will take place after the maximum number of voice slots has been issued on the forward line. The first of the above two conditions to occur will cause the transfer from VOICE to DATA. Upon transition to state DATA, START $= D$ is written in the start field on the forward line. Further START $= D$'s will be written on the forward line in response to receiving END $= G$ in the end field on the reverse line. Data subcycles will continue on the forward line until the start of the next cycle.

The first station also inspects the end field of the last packet in the voice subcycle to determine whether a START $= V$ or W should be used on the forward line. If END $= E$, one or more F slots were unused in the previous voice cycle. If, on the other hand, END $= C$, all F slots were used and START $= W$ is written.

D. Last Station Protocol

The role of the last station is to sense the condition at the end of the forward line and to relay that condition back to the first station via an appropriate code. Thus, the last station's role is nothing more than a repeater for the first station. The codes written in the end field

TABLE II
DESCRIPTION OF END FIELD CODES

A	Written in response to receiving START $= V$ or W on the forward line (start of voice subcycle).
B	Written instead of an A when there is no voice traffic.
C	Written in response to receiving START $= D$ on the forward line when in a voice subcycle (i.e., start of first data subcycle in the cycle).
E	Written in response to receiving an empty slot in the voice subcycle, except when it is the first slot in the voice subcycle.
G	Written in response to receiving an empty slot in the data subcycle.
0	Written when none of the above conditions hold.

by the last station are A, B, C, E, G, and zero, with the meanings denoted in Table II. As seen in Fig. 4(b), the last station has three different states. Assume that a START = V has just been detected. As a result, the end station will go to state VOICE and write an "A" for acknowledgment in the end field of the next packet on the reverse line. If there were no calls in progress, the first slot on the forward line (with START = V) would be empty. Should this occur, the last station echoes an END = B rather than A, enabling the first station to immediately start a data subcycle rather than wait for the next packet which would contain END = E. Thereafter, the station writes an END = E in the end field of all packets on the reverse line that are preceded by an empty packet on the forward line (BUSY = 0). Upon receiving a packet on the forward line with START = D, the station transits to state DATA. A transition to state END-D occurs when the last station detects an empty slot on the forward line, as shown in Fig. 4(b), and END = G is written in the next slot on the reverse line. The station remains in this state until either a START = V is received, in which case a transition is made to state VOICE, or START = D is received, in which case a transition is made to state DATA.

IV. SUMMARY OF INTERACTION

Figure 5 is meant to illustrate a typical sequence of events occurring on the lines of a Fasnet system. The previous example is used, where we assume a 2×10 Mbit/s system with 700 bit packets and a cycle time of 142 slots, with up to a maximum of 50 slots dedicated to voice traffic. We assume that the roundtrip delay of the system is just less than the duration of two slots. Further, assume that at this instant of time $AC = 35$, that is, on the previous cycle there were 35 active voice channels. The first station writes START = V in slot 0. We assume that during the last cycle, three conversations were discontinued so that now slots 32–34 are empty and, as a result, the end station writes END = E in the corresponding slots on the reverse line. The first station writes START = F in slots after 34 to indicate that these slots may be used by calls waiting in state HOLD. From Fig. 5, we see that two new voice slots have been seized. We conclude that there are now no unserved calls in HOLD. Upon seeing the first empty slot at 37, the end station will write END = E in the end field of the next slot on the reverse line. It will continue to write END = E until the first station reads an END = E and determines that the voice subcycle should now be

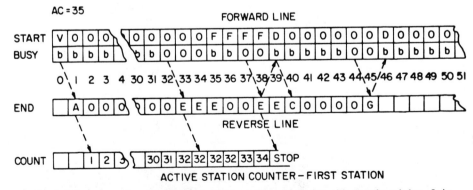

Fig. 5. Sequence of packets demonstrating operation of Fasnet with speech and data. It is assumed that speech is coded at 64 kbits/s giving 640 bits of data per packet with a total packet size of 700 bits. This results in 142 packets per speech sample interval assuming 10 Mbit/s Fasnet lines.

discontinued. As shown, we assume this takes two slots to occur so that a START $= D$ is written in slot 39, enabling the data stations to seize subsequent slots. When the last station detects an empty slot while in the DATA state, it writes an END $= G$ in the first occurring slot on the reverse line. Two slots later, the first station detects this END $= G$ and, as a result, issues a START $= D$, at slot 46, beginning another data subcycle. Data subcycles continue until slot 142 is reached, at which point the first station writes a START $= V$ which initiates a new cycle. Notice that by counting the number of packets in which END $\neq E$, the first station is able to determine that the number of active voice channels AC has decreased from 35 to 34 corresponding to the termination of three old voice calls and the initiation of two new voice calls.

V. SIMULATION

While simulation has been used to help design and verify the protocol, it can also be used to answer a number of performance questions. One concerns the efficient use of the voice channels by voice stations; another is the extent to which data stations can exploit unused voice capacity [8], [14].

We now summarize the conditions under which the simulations were run. A fixed number of ongoing conversations were assumed. The telephone call is modeled as a three-state Markov process with states idle (on-hook), talk (active), and silent (pauses between talk spurts). We assume that voice stations are in the nonidle state 40 percent of the time with an average talk duration of 1.5 s and an average silent duration of 2.25 s. All data stations generate traffic at the same mean rate, and each station may transmit a maximum of three packets from its queue during one cycle. Packets arrive at each station according to a Poisson distribution.

The length of the line was 2 km, resulting in a normalized propagation delay of 0.143 slots. An additional delay of 0.039 slots for the electronics gives a total of 0.182 slots for a single line. Data and voice stations were randomly positioned along the line. While the number of voice stations was varied between 100 and 130, there were always 30 data stations. Simulation runs were equivalent to 10 and 20 s speech segments.

It is important that the simulation has reached "steady state" before data are recorded. In order to shorten the time taken to reach steady state, voice stations were assigned probabilistically to either talk or silent states according to the steady-state probability that they would be in those states. Data queues are generally very short (certainly for a traffic intensity below 0.9) and stabilized relatively quickly. Data were gathered only after 11 599 packets (or 1.0 s had elapsed).

A. Utilization of Voice Channels

For a specific voice traffic intensity, we wish to know the probability that a talk spurt will be clipped. This will happen if a station switches from silent state to talk state while no free voice slots are available. We will assume that each station can store five voice packets at most. If five or fewer packets are queued before a slot is seized, the packets are transmitted in turn and the talk spurt is not clipped but delayed by up to five sample periods (5 × 10 ms). If the length of the queue exceeds the five packets, all packets are discarded except the most recent one and the talk spurt becomes clipped.

A centralized algorithm would be able to assign silent traffic that has become newly active to the first free channel on a first-come-first-served basis (an ideal multiplexer). The multiplexer would perform better than the partially distributed algorithm presented here. The reason is that in the distributed algorithm empty packets occur as stations become inactive. These empty packets implicitly signal from the voice stations to the last station that, in fact, voice stations have become silent or idle. We can compare the multiplexer and the distributed algorithm in the fraction of speech that is clipped or delayed as a function of the traffic intensity. Using the analytical result of Weinstein [11], we plot the freeze-out fraction (the fraction of speech lost before a channel assignment is made) of the ideal multiplexer as a function of the loading on the channel as the full curve in Fig. 6. The experimental points of Fig. 6 correspond to Fasnet simulations of between 10 and 20 s segments of simulated speech. If we assume an acceptable freeze-out fraction of 0.5 percent, then approximately 100 stations could be multiplexed onto 50 voice channels. This is consistent with TASI experience [12]. As expected, the distributed algorithm produces more freeze-out, but marginally so, indicating that the algorithm efficiently allocates the voice channels. The combination of delay and clipping (rather than clipping alone) will also affect the results relative to the pure loss system. In effect, the delay process prevents clipping when it occurs and produces extra packets to transmit at the end of the talk spurt when there will be less probability of clipping (since it is a low probability event in a practical channel).

Of more interest than the freeze-out fraction is the fraction of talk spurts with freeze-out

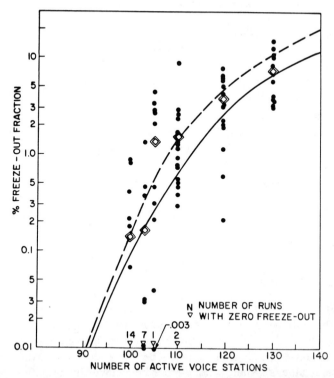

Fig. 6. Plot of freeze-out fraction as a function of the number of active voice stations assuming 50 speech channels and a speech activity of 40 percent. Full curve, ideal multiplexer [8]; diamonds give the average freeze-out fraction over all runs. The dashed curve was fitted to the diamonds by eye. The variance of the freeze-out fraction is suggested by the filled circles which are the average freeze out for individual 20 s runs.

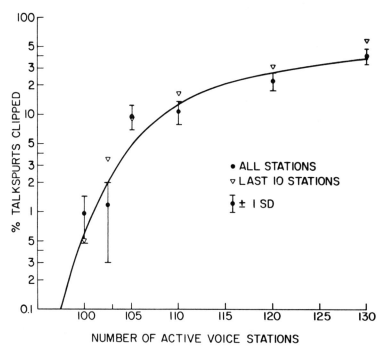

Fig. 7. Fraction of talk spurts clipped by more than 50 ms as a function of number of stations.

large enough to be perceptible to the user. The threshold for detection of clipping at the start of a talk spurt is around 50 ms [13]. Therefore, we have counted the number of talk spurts in which more than five packets (= 50 ms) are clipped. In Fig. 7 we show the percentage of talk spurts that are clipped by more than 50 ms as a function of the number of active stations. As a criterion for acceptable speech quality, Campanella [13] has suggested that no more than 2 percent of talk spurts be clipped. By that criterion also approximately 100 stations may be served.

The allocation of slots to traffic waiting in the HOLD state is unfair; that is, a station transiting from SILENT to HOLD will have precedence over a station already in HOLD waiting for a slot if it is "upstream" (i.e, closer to the first station) from the other station. It is important to ascertain the extent of this unfairness. Also shown in Fig. 7 is the percent of talk spurts clipped for just the last 10 stations on the line. While the clipping is greater for these stations, it is only marginally so. Another view of the extent of unfairness is obtained by plotting the distribution of the length of clipped or delayed speech segments. The average distribution of the first 60 stations is compared to the average distribution of the last 60 stations in Fig. 8. As may be expected, when there is little or moderate clipping, the algorithm is reasonably equitable. It only becomes objectionably unfair at unacceptable levels of clipping.

The results presented here assume that voice traffic is transmitted in packets containing 10 ms (or 640 bits) of digitized speech, and that the packet overhead is 60 bits. The performance of the system could be improved by going to larger packet sizes, but the improvement would be small (4.3 percent if the packet size were doubled) unless the overhead were larger than the 60 bits assumed here.

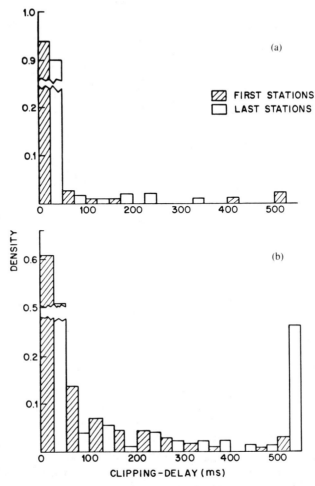

Fig. 8.   Distribution of clipping and delay assuming 120 voice stations, 50 channels, and speech activity of 40 percent. (a) Sample with freeze-out fraction of 1.1 percent. (b) Sample with freeze-out fraction of 8.9 percent.

B. Use of Voice Slots by Data

Ideally, any unused voice slots would be used by data traffic if the demand required it. In order to explore the ability of data traffic to capitalize on unused voice slots we ran 10 s speech segment simulations with the same voice traffic characteristics as in the previous simulations.

We first examine the case where data may not utilize unused voice slots, and compare the result to a data-only Fasnet system. We see from Fig. 9 that the data-voice system gives increased average delay for a given traffic intensity although the increase is relatively insignificant at higher intensities and, hence, higher average delays. The increased delay is due largely to the fact that data generated during the last data subcycles of a cycle are delayed by an additional amount up to the duration of the voice subcycle. Notice that the absolute delays would be unimportant for most applications, even for traffic intensities approaching one (e.g., a delay of 15 slots corresponds to 1.0 ms).

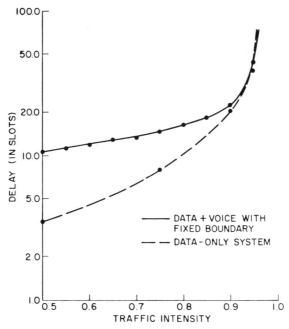

Fig. 9. Comparison of a mixed data-voice system to no sharing of the unused voice capacity by the data stations with a data-only system. Delay, measured in slot durations, is shown as a function of traffic intensity.

Results are shown in Fig. 10 for a variable boundary between the voice and data subcycles. The left-most curve, repeated from Fig. 9, is the "fixed boundary" case. The other sets of points give the delay versus traffic intensity for the variable-boundary case for different amounts of voice traffic.

One could approximate the performance of the variable boundary case by the fixed boundary case having the same data capacity as the *average* capacity of the variable boundary case. This is done in the following manner.

Assume there are 80 active voice stations. If we ignore the small probability that more than 50 stations are active simultaneously, then on the average, $80 \times 0.4 = 32$ of the 50 available voice slots are being used for voice conversations. Two slots will be "wasted" to inform the first station that the voice subcycle has finished, leaving an additional 16 slots per cycle for use by the data stations. Thus, the average capacity available to the data stations increases from 92 to 108. We now calculate the delay performance of a *fixed* boundary scheme with 34 voice slots and 108 data slots. This estimate is shown plotted as X's in Fig. 10; note that they have been scaled in the horizontal direction by the ratio 108/92 for plotting in this figure. We see that this estimate of the delay utilization function is close to the simulation results. The following factors are not accounted for in the estimate. 1) Truncation of the number of voice calls by a hard limit means that the average number of voice calls is less than the mean of the underlying binomial distribution as mentioned above. 2) When all voice slots are full, a data subcycle will start without an intercycle gap, increasing by two the number of slots available to the data subcycle. 3) The effective duration of a talk spurt will be lengthened by up to three slot durations due to transmission of partially filled slots at the beginning and end of a talk spurt and due to the additional empty slot required by the protocol to indicate the end of a talk spurt.

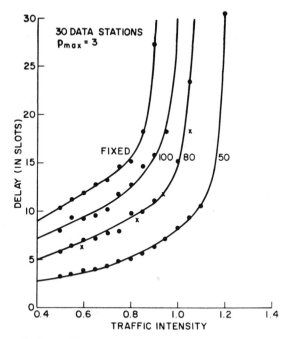

Fig. 10.   Increase in data traffic capacity as unused voice slots are utilized by data. Traffic intensity is measured relative to 100 percent utilization of the dedicated data channel. Curves are shown for no sharing (fixed boundary), and sharing with 100, 80, and 50 nonidle voice stations. Smooth curves have been drawn through the results of the simulation (dots). The X's are estimates of the curve for 80 voice stations.

Of course, even larger exploitation of unused voice capacity would occur if the maximum capacity allocated to voice traffic were a larger percentage of the total channel capacity than the 35 percent assumed here.

VI. COMPARISON

Other studies have considered the combined transmission of voice and data [1], [15], [16], [9]. Nutt and Bayer simulated voice and data on 10 Mbit/s Ethernet [1]. With 5 ms packets of 64 kbit/s voice, a maximum of 93 conversations could be supported if packets were ideally scheduled.[2] Their simulation showed that with a voice load of 50 conversations and a data load of less than 5 percent, less than 0.5 percent of voice packets were delayed by more than 5 ms. Note, however, that a slot time of 10 μs, was used rather than the Ethernet standard of 51.2 μs.

In a recent more detailed simulation of voice and data traffic on Ethernet, DeTreville [15] demonstrated that approximately 60 conversations could be supported on standard Ethernet, assuming 64 kbit/s digitization, an activity factor of 0.4, 5.75 ms speech packets,[3] and a 5.75 ms packet assembly time at the receiver (less than 1 percent of speech packets lost). Under the same conditions but with an additional data loading of 5 percent, the number of conversations that can be supported drops to approximately 35. Of course,

---

[2] Based on "half-duplex conversations." We assume this is tantamount to assuming that each speaker utilizes the channel half of the time.

[3] With this size of packet the voice data just fill the smallest permitted Ethernet packet.

with larger packets the number of conversations that can be accommodated increases significantly [15].

In order to reduce the penalty caused by collisions, Maxemchuk [16] proposed movable-slot time-division multiplexing (MSTDM). Voice packets are given priority over data packets by means of a preempt header attached to the start of each voice slot. As voice traffic builds to a maximum, the random access of Ethernet converges to pure time-division multiplexing. The penalty paid in this scheme is in the preempt header which must be greater than or equal to a slot time. For short packets of 5.75 ms, with the standard Ethernet slot time of 51.2 μs, this overhead can be significant, permitting 61 conversations for 64 kbit/s voice with an activity factor of 0.4. By comparison, assuming the same packet structure but with an additional 16 bit access field, Fasnet would permit as many as 272 conversations for the link or 136 per line.

None of the above schemes considers either limiting access to some number of voice conversations or scheduling new conversations as space becomes available. Presumably, algorithms could be invented to achieve this; they would probably be more complex than those described here for Fasnet since the communication channel provided by the start and end subfields of the access field are not inherent in Ethernet.

The Expressnet network of Fratta, Borgonovo, and Tobagi [9] most closely resembles the work reported in this chapter. They describe how voice and data may be combined on Expressnet. The system alternates between voice subcycles (trains) and data subcycles. Calls are bocked by letting no more than a maximum number of calls join the voice subcycle. The length of the data subcycle is limited in order to permit the maximum number of voice conversations to join the voice subcycle at all times and preserve the constraint on voice packet delay. The algorithms as described could presumably permit the generation of two or more voice subcycles within the voice packet generation interval. As with the previous studies, the problem of rescheduling conversations returning from silent to active is not considered. Because of the similarity between Fasnet and Expressnet, an algorithm such as the one presented in this chapter could easily be applied to Expressnet. It might well be argued, however, that the partially centralized control described here is not in the fully distributed spirit of Expressnet.

The work described here has been extended in [17] in that the strict limit placed on the maximum number of active voice stations that may be admitted to the system is relaxed in the following way. Once a voice conversation is admitted, a station can always make the transition from SILENT to ACTIVE and consequently speech is never clipped. The capacity available to data now varies randomly about a target value depending on the fraction of conversations that are active. The number of voice conversations is maintained close to the target by means of a distributed strategy for admitting new calls.

VII. CONCLUSION

An algorithm for multiplexing voice and data conversations onto a local area network of the unidirectional bus type (Fasnet) has been described. While talking is occurring, a virtual channel is assigned to each conversation; it is relinquished during silent intervals. Unused voice slots are available for use by data stations. The algorithm is partially distributed in each voice and data station and partially centralized in stations located at each end of the bus. Decisions that need to be made fast (whether to seize a packet or not) are made in the individual stations while slower decisions about when to change from virtual circuits to packets is made in the end stations.

A field (called the START field) in the header of each packet is used by the two end stations to communicate both with each other and with the other voice and data stations on the bus. Each station reads the START field of every passing packet and uses the value of the field together with the value of a BUSY field to determine when to transmit. By means of these signals the interval between speech samples, called a cycle, is divided into one part for virtual circuits and one part for data packets.

Simulation of the algorithm shows that the scheme is close to the efficiency of an ideal multiplexer. Thus, approximately 100 voice stations with an activity level of 40 percent may comfortably share 50 virtual circuits with fewer than 2 percent of the talk spurts clipped by more than 50 ms. The algorithm as studied here is unfair in that upstream stations are scheduled before downstream stations. An embellishment of the algorithm would make it more equitable but this seems unwarranted since the extent of the unfairness is small at practical levels of circuit loading.

The algorithm permits efficient exploitation of unused voice slots by data stations. A "sojourn" time or roundtrip delay time is required to switch from the voice subcycle to the data subcycle but otherwise all unused voice slots are utilized.

REFERENCES

[1] G. J. Nutt and D. L. Bayer, "Performance of CSMA/CD networks under combined voice and data loads," *IEEE Trans. Commun.*, vol. COM-30, pp. 1–11, Jan. 1982.

[2] K. Kümmerle, "Multiplexer performance for integrated line and packet switched traffic," in *Proc. 2nd Int. Conf. Comput. Commun.*, 1974.

[3] J. O. Limb, "Fasnet: Proposal for a high speed local network," presented at the Office Inform. Syst. Workshop, St. Maximum, France, Oct. 1981.

[4] J. O. Limb and C. Flores, "Description of Fasnet—A unidirectional local-area communications network," *Bell Syst. Tech. J.,* vol. 61, pp. 1413–1440, Sept. 1982, see also this volume, ch. 12.

[5] N. S. Jayant, "Effects of packet losses in waveform-coded speech," in *Conv. Rec., Int. Conf. Commun.*, 1980, pp. 275–280.

[6] J. G. Gruber, "Delay related issues in integrated voice and data networks," *IEEE Trans. Commun.*, vol. COM-29, pp. 786–800, June 1981.

[7] P. T. Brady, "A statistical analysis of on-off patterns in 16 conversations," *Bell Syst. Tech. J.*, vol. 47, pp. 73–91, Jan. 1968.

[8] T. Bially, A. J. McLaughlin, and C. J. Weinstein, "Voice communication in integrated digital voice and data networks," *IEEE Trans. Commun.*, vol. COM-28, pp. 1478–1490, Sept. 1980.

[9] L. Fratta, F. Borgonovo, and F. A. Tobagi, "The Express-net: A local area communication network integrating voice and data," in *Performance of Data Communication Systems,* G. Pujolla, Ed. Amsterdam, The Netherlands: North-Holland, 1981, pp. 77–88.

[10] H. B. Kekre and C. L. Saxena, "Three-state Markov model of speech on telephone lines," *Comput. Elect. Eng.*, vol. 4, no. 3, pp. 235–250, 1977.

[11] C. J. Weinstein, "Fractional speech loss and talker activity model for TASI and for packet-switched speech," *IEEE Trans. Commun.*, vol. COM-26, pp. 1253–1257, Aug. 1978.

[12] K. Bullington and J. M. Fraser, "Engineering aspects of TASI," *Bell Syst. Tech. J.*, vol. 38, pp. 353–364, Mar. 1959.

[13] S. J. Campanella, "Digital speech interpolation," *COMSAT Tech. Rev.*, vol. 6, pp. 127–158, Spring 1976.

[14] A. Leon-Garcia, R. H. Kwong, and G. F. Williams, "Performance evaluation methods for an integrated voice/data link," *IEEE Trans. Commun.*, vol. COM-30, pp. 1848–1858, Aug. 1982.

[15] J. DeTreville, "A simulation-based comparison of voice transmission on CSMA/CD networks and on token buses," *Bell Syst. Tech. J.*, vol. 63, pp. 33–55, Jan. 1984; see also this volume, ch. 25.

[16] N. F. Maxemchuk, "A variation on CSMA/CD that yields movable TDM slots in integrated voice data local networks," *Bell Syst. Tech. J.*, vol. 61, pp. 1527–1549, Sept. 1982.

[17] J. W. Mark and J. O. Limb, "Integrated voice data services on Fasnet," *AT&T Bell Laboratories Tech. J.*, vol. 63, pp. 307–336, Feb. 1984.

27
Orwell: A Protocol for an Integrated Services Local Network

R. M. FALCONER AND J. L. ADAMS

Advances in optical-fiber links offer the prospect of a new generation of higher speed local area network with the capability to switch speech as well as data traffic. The limitations of established LAN protocols for such a purpose are briefly outlined, and a new protocol, known as Orwell, is introduced and described in detail. The Orwell protocol is based on the slotted ring principle with slots released at the destination node. A novel load control mechanism is used to bound ring access delays to a maximum of 2 ms or less, and simulation results are used to show that a 140 Mbit/s Orwell ring can carry over 170 Mbits/s of speech while containing these delays to under 200 μs. No central control is provided for slot allocation; all control functions are fully distributed.

I. INTRODUCTION

Today's local area network (LAN) products have been designed to meet the burgeoning need for local data communications facilities. They ease the sharing of computing resources and provide a common access point for wide area networks. For LAN's using digital technology, typical operating speeds are fairly low and the capacity available for data seldom exceeds 5 Mbits/s.

With the reducing cost of optical-fiber links [1] has come the potential for another generation of LAN, with much larger bandwidths and an increase in the maximum distance between nodes. This introduces the possibility of transporting and switching not only data, but all the communications traffic of the office, factory, or campus (including voice and perhaps, in the future, compressed video). In the UK such a concept, illustrated in Fig. 1, has been called the integrated services local network (or ISLN) [2]. The ISLN, it is claimed, offers several advantages over independent speech and data networks:

- the economies from resource sharing
- a rationalization of communications wiring
- easier communications between different services and facilities
- a reduced dependence on accurate traffic forecasts for each service type.

Supporting studies [3] have shown that networks which share the available capacity between different services have an increased tolerance to the inevitable uncertainties in the forecasts of traffic mix.

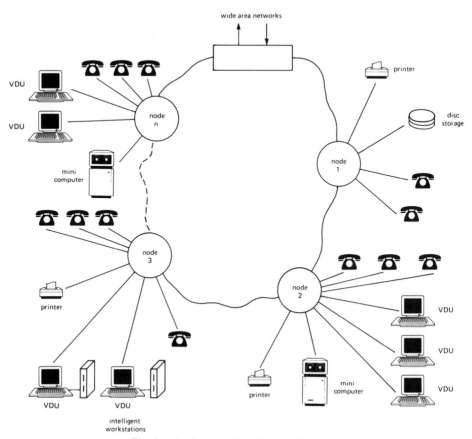

Fig. 1.   An integrated services local network.

Unfortunately, the concept of sharing capacity between such diverse services as data and voice does introduce some significant technical difficulties. The topology of the network (e.g., bus, ring, or star), and the protocols used to access the bandwidth, both affect its delay and throughput characteristics. Previous work [4], [5] has suggested that the unidirectional traffic flows in a ring structure are more suited to delay-sensitive services, such as voice. However, the established LAN protocols for accessing a ring, such as token-passing or the Cambridge slotted ring [6], were not developed for mixed traffic. An initial appraisal had suggested that the Cambridge ring could perhaps form the basis of an ISLN, but a detailed simulation study [5] revealed significant limitations at high speeds with speech traffic.

In summary, performance studies have shown that existing LAN access protocols (with their associated topologies) would suffer from one or more of the following limitations if used as the basis for an ISLN:

- inability to offer guaranteed bandwidth for the duration of a call
- the risk of excessive or unbounded delays to transmissions
- no inherent means for recognizing the onset of overload
- a reduction in relative throughput with increasing speed and/or network size
- inability to handle unbalanced loads efficiently
- inefficient use of the available bandwidth.

One, relatively straightforward, way around these difficulties is to separate the voice and data services in a hybrid structure (Fig. 2). The simplicity of this approach is gaining popularity, and a hybrid of time division multiplexed (TDM) speech and token controlled data is currently being considered for a future standard by the American National Standards Institute (ANSI).

Unless the boundary can be arranged to move dynamically with the traffic, many of the advantages outlined earlier for complete sharing are sacrificed in a hybrid structure. Unfortunately, dynamic boundaries can introduce practical difficulties, such as having to rearrange the time slots of calls in progress.

Overall, it was felt that the slotted ring architecture offered the most potential for high-speed operation in a fully integrated local network. The capability for several nodes to be transmitting simultaneously into different slots should, in principle, lead to lower delays than polling techniques such as token-passing.

The Orwell protocol described in this chapter (so called because of the proximity of the British Telecom Research Laboratories of the River Orwell) was developed from a simulation model of the Cambridge slotted ring. Despite this, it now has little in common with its predecessor. Slots are released at the destination (rather than the source) node, and operation is no longer dependent on the number of slots on the ring. A novel, fully distributed, technique for load control has been developed to keep delays within acceptable bounds.

The operation of the protocol is described in detail, and simulation results are used to show how a 140 Mbit/s Orwell ring can transport over 170 Mbits/s of speech and data, while containing ring access delays for speech to below 200 μs.

II. SLOTTED RINGS AND OPEN SYSTEMS

The Orwell protocol is only part of a hierarchy of protocols necessary for reliable data communications. It is important at the outset to bring the role of Orwell in this hierarchy into focus. The International Standards Organization's (ISO) reference model for open systems interconnection provides a suitable basis for doing this.

A. The Physical Layer

A signal injected into a digital communications loop will take a finite time to return to the sender. This delay has two sources:

- the finite velocity of electromagnetic radiation in the transmission medium (approximately constant)

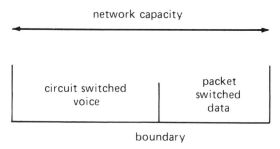

Fig. 2. A voice/data hybrid.

- the delay introduced by the nodes on the loop (usually a fixed number of bits, and therefore inversely proportional to operating speed).

As an example, a 5 km, 100 Mbit/s ring with 25 nodes, each introducing a serial register of 16 bits, would have a roundtrip delay of

$(5 \times 4 \times 10^{-8}) + (25 \times 16 \times 10^{-8})$ (assuming a propagation delay of 4 μs/km)

$$= 24 \ \mu s, \text{ (containing 2400 bits, or 300 octets).}$$

In a slotted ring, this delay is used to contain a fixed number of circulating slots with self-contained node addressing. These form the basic transport mechanism (Fig. 3). As each slot can contain a block of either data or speech, its actual size is important; too large and there will be delays to speech in accumulating sufficient samples to fill it, too small and the fixed slot header overheads become excessive. Currently, a reasonable compromise is seen as 20 octets, resulting in 15 slots in the above example. This system of circulating slots forms the physical layer (layer 1) of the ISO reference model.

B. The Data Link Layer

Access to the physical layer is via layer 2, the data link layer. This has been further subdivided by the IEEE in its LAN standards activities (Committee 802) into the logical link control (LLC) and the media access control (MAC) (Fig. 4). Orwell forms the part of the MAC which controls access to the slots. The MAC as a whole provides a basic datagram service to the LLC, which in turn provides error recovery, framing, and, where appropriate, flow control.

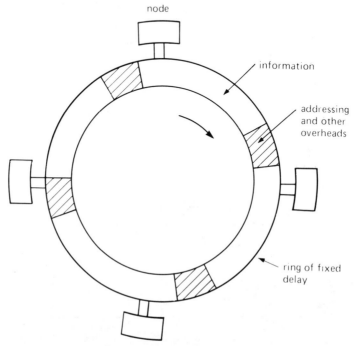

Fig. 3.   The slotted ring concept.

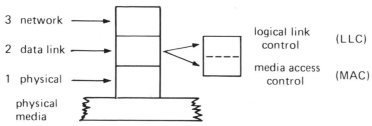

Fig. 4. Subdivision of the data link layer.

In general, Orwell supports two classes of service: class 1 for delay-sensitive services, such as voice, that require a guaranteed bandwidth with a bounded delay; and class 2 for delay-tolerant asynchronous data. The facilities offered by the LLC are inappropriate for class 1 transmissions, and a suitable MAC for an ISLN must also provide such services with a direct interface. In general, the class 1 services will emanate from a constant bit rate source (e.g., 64 kbits/s), and the link from source MAC, to physical layer, to the destination MAC must therefore provide a transparent constant bit rate path.

One, apparently obvious, way of doing this would be to provide dedicated slots for class 1 transmissions. Unfortunately, this is not as straightforward as it might first appear. A slot on a 14 slot, 140 Mbits/s, ring has a roundtrip capacity of around 10 Mbits/s (after allowing for reasonable slot overheads). This is clearly not suitable for, say, two or three 64 kbit/s transmissions from a node. To try and arrange for the correct rate of empty slots to arrive at the appropriate nodes, in synchronism with the arriving traffic would require a complex central controller for slot allocation. The logical extension of this argument is a hybrid TDM/slotted ring with the loss of the advantages outlined earlier for full integration.

For an Orwell based switch to carry both class 1 and class 2 services in a common MAC and physical layer, the delays in accessing empty slots from the MAC must be bounded to an acceptable level; at least for the class 1 services. This allows the constant bit rate stream to be resurrected at the destination MAC by appropriate buffering. To bound the access delay implies a feedback mechanism from the MAC to the node control; enabling it to reject new calls if their acceptance would risk a breach of the maximum tolerable access delay.

III. THE ORWELL PROTOCOL

Part of the philosophy of the Orwell ring is that nodes make autonomous decisions on the guaranteed bandwidth. When a new class 1 call is generated at a node, the current ring load is checked before the call is accepted. If sufficient capacity remains, the node reserves an appropriate extra share.

This agreed bandwidth is, however, only the minimum guaranteed to the node. In practice, the nodes are (at least initially) allowed completely free access to passing empty slots. These slots are released at the destination and made available for reuse. As the ring load increases, so the extra bandwidth available at the nodes is correspondingly reduced, until, in the limit, all nodes are constrained to their minimum allocation of empty slots per unit time and all new requests are rejected.

This policy of destination release, and random access at light to medium loads, is conducive to very small delays and high bandwidth utilization, but the need for load control poses some interesting problems. Unlike source release rings, the available capacity is not constant, but a function of the distribution of node hops from source to destination, and the phasing of block arrivals in the MAC buffer. Without control, the positioning of a node on the ring could affect its access to bandwidth and possibly lead to hogging (Fig. 5).

A. Principle

Nodes on the ring that are ACTIVE (i.e., are permitted to transmit and have an information block ready), are at first given unrestricted access to arriving empty slots, but for every block transmitted a local block counter is incremented by 1 (Fig. 6). If the block counter reaches a locally agreed maximum for the node (Di) the node enters what is known as the PAUSED state and further transmissions are temporarily inhibited. This releases capacity on the ring for downstream nodes, thereby helping to relieve any congestion. The extra bandwidth increases the serving rate, and downstream nodes soon exhaust their queues, or also reach the PAUSED state.

The ring therefore accelerates towards all nodes being either PAUSED or momentarily IDLE (i.e., the block counter is still less than Di but the queue is now exhausted). Ring activity has now ceased, at least temporarily, and an opportunity has been given to redress any positional advantages that some nodes may have had, i.e., any hogging on the ring has now been controlled (e.g., node B in Fig. 5). The block counters at all nodes can now be reset (the Di allocations refreshed) and activity restarted. The process ensures that the nodes which use their Di allocations relatively quickly are forced periodically to ensure that other nodes have the opportunity to access their share of the bandwidth, without incurring excessive delays.

It is worth stopping to consider what has been gained from this. In Fig. 6 all nodes have a different Di, corresponding to their individual bandwidth requirements. The nodes are all

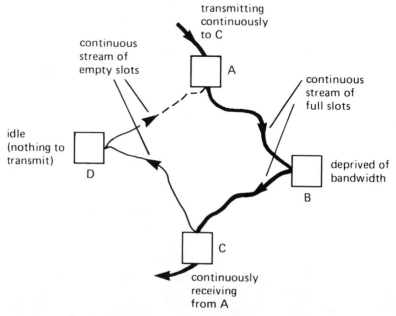

Fig. 5.   Hogging on a destination release slotted ring.

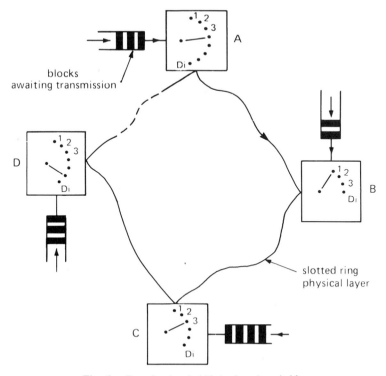

Fig. 6. Ensuring bandwidth is shared equitably.

flooded with traffic, so that empty slots are seized as soon as they become free. The nodes will increase their counters until the PAUSED state is reached. Some will do this before others, depending on the source to destination pattern (cf. Fig. 5). If, when all nodes are PAUSED, the counters are reset, the pattern will repeat (i.e., each node can send its Di allocation of blocks per counter reset).

If, in practice, one of the nodes in Fig. 6 is not fully flooded, say C, the remaining nodes could potentially wait indefinitely on all nodes being PAUSED. By resetting the counters when nodes are either IDLE or PAUSED this is avoided. Node C can recover its share of the bandwidth as soon as its load increases, but in the meantime the extra capacity is available, but not guaranteed, to the other nodes.

This share of Di blocks per counter reset can be translated into guaranteed bandwidth if the reset interval (RI) is known, and controlled to an upper bound. First, what remains to be described, is a fully distributed mechanism for resetting the block counters when all nodes have reached either the PAUSED or IDLE states.

This is achieved as follows. When a slot is emptied, the node converts it into a TRIAL slot by loading its own address into the slot destination address field and by marking the TRIAL bit in the slot control field ($T = 1$). However, the slot is still empty and available for use by downstream nodes. If this happens the trial is terminated. Most TRIAL slots will meet this fate. If, however, all nodes are in the IDLE or PAUSED state, a TRIAL slot will succeed in circumnavigating the ring, thereby informing the originating node of the current inactivity.

A successful TRIAL slot is converted to a RESET slot by the originating node. This is achieved by simply changing the full/empty (F/E) bit on the successful TRIAL to full and leaving the TRIAL bit set ($F/E = 1$, $T = 1$) and then allowing the slot to circulate once more. Being a full slot, its passage cannot now be interrupted. The RESET slot is recognized by all nodes as a broadcast message of ring inactivity, however brief, and is used to reset the block counters at every node; irrespective of whether they have reached their Di allocation or not. Note that any node can perform a trial and therefore issue a RESET, and the process is fully distributed; no recourse is made to a central control.

So far we have a mechanism that gives all nodes the opportunity to transmit Di blocks prior to a RESET. Thus providing the reset interval (RI) can be contained within T ms (where T is the maximum tolerable block queueing delay), the delay-critical services at a node can be supported with a guaranteed bandwidth of at least Di blocks/T ms. On a lightly loaded ring there will be spare capacity, frequent successful TRIALS, and therefore, frequent RESET slots; perhaps one every two or three ring revolutions. The block counters at the nodes will invariably be reset before reaching Di and, from the point of view of the nodes, access will appear unrestricted. As the total load approaches the maximum capacity of the ring, more nodes will be forced into the PAUSED state prior to a RESET, and the RESETS themselves will become less frequent.

These characteristics are reflected in the simulation results of Fig. 7. As the load rises the RESET rate decreases, while the probability of a PAUSED node generating the reset increases. These properties of the RESET rate are exploited in the Orwell ring to provide a novel, fully distributed, load control.

Upon receipt of a request for guaranteed transmission capacity on the ring (e.g., a call arrival), the node control first examines the current RESET rate. By using a simple relationship derived from Fig. 7 the node control can then assess the worst-case increase in the RESET interval (RI) that the new service would engender. If this is acceptable (i.e., the RI would still be $< T$ ms and established connections would not be prejudiced), the request is granted and the local Di ceiling is incremented appropriately to cater for the increased

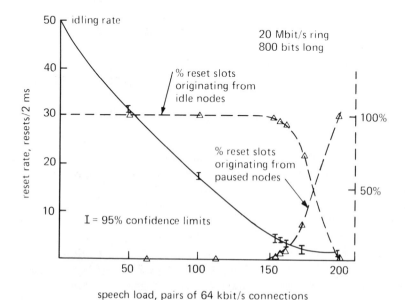

speech load, pairs of 64 kbit/s connections

Fig. 7.   Effect of load on resets.

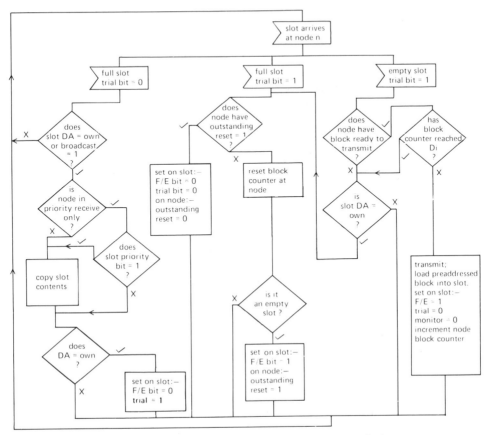

Fig. 8.   Decision algorithm for an Orwell node (nonmonitor).

demand. At the end of the session the Di ceiling is similarly decremented. A ring with a maximum RI of 2 ms would have a Di allocation of 1 for every 64 kbit/s connection (for a 16 octet block information field).

Thus, each node monitors the current short-term RESET rate, assesses whether the granting of a new request would take the interval between RESETS beyond T ms and accepts or rejects accordingly; adjusting the total Di blocks/T ms ceiling to match the new requirement. Every node therefore has a guaranteed bandwidth matched to its needs and, because the RESET interval is contained to less than T ms, so too is the maximum delay.

The decision processes at a nonmonitor node are more formally described in the outline flowchart format of Fig. 8. The detailed logic has been designed to cope with potential problem areas, such as multiple simultaneous RESETS and possible deadlock states.

B. Handling Data

So far the discussion has concentrated on handling synchronous services, primarily because they introduce new problems for LAN technologies. By definition it is, of course, also necessary for an ISLN to support traditional LAN data traffic, preferably on demand and without any recourse to a node control.

One way to do this is to allocate a small minimum value of Di (D min, e.g., 1) to all nodes. This provides some guaranteed bandwidth for signaling and allows access for delay-tolerant class 2 data services. Such services do not request bandwidth from the node control and do not affect its Di allocation. On a ring that is lightly loaded with class 1 traffic, the reset rate is much higher than the minimum tolerable. Class 2 services can take advantage of this as the D min allocation comes much more frequently. As the class 1 traffic load increases, the class 2 bandwidth is reduced until, in the limit, each node is constrained to D min blocks per T ms.

This is demonstrated in the simulation results of Fig. 9. With no class 1 traffic the class 2 capacity available is 100 Mbits/s for a D min of 1 and 144 Mbits/s for a D min of 5 (the difference is due to the much higher overheads of the PAUSE and RESET controls when D min is small). Increasing the class 1 traffic (and therefore the Di allocations) reduces the reset rate, and with it the class 2 capacity which, at full load, is constrained to 8 Mbits/s and 1.6 Mbits/s for D min = 5 and 1, respectively.

An alternative method for controlling the data allocation, when high data bandwidths are required, is to adjust Di using feedback from a block counter on each node counting the number of data block arrivals in consecutive 2 ms periods. The method takes advantage of each node being able to monitor the reset rate, so that a decision on whether to increase Di

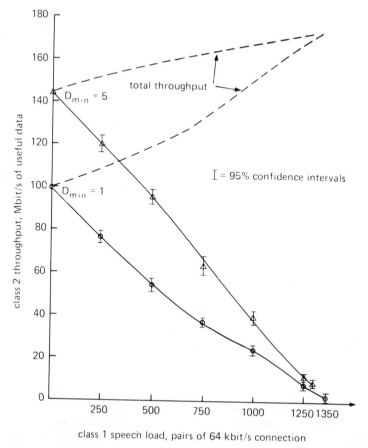

Fig. 9.   Bandwidth capacity sharing between class 1 and class 2 services.

can be made quickly. *Di* would be increased whenever a higher arrival rate occurs on any node provided the ring reset rate is above 1 reset every *T* ms. By restricting the size of the permissible increase in *Di* (e.g., *Di* can be increased by 1) the allocation is increased slowly over successive 2 ms periods and no sudden large increase in load occurs from several nodes simultaneously operating in this way.

Orwell is a fully integrated system, with priority for class 1 services over class 2. Before gaining access to the ring, class 1 services must first communicate with the local node control, which in turn checks the RESET rate and raises the *Di* threshold (if sufficient capacity is available). On the other hand, class 2 services can occupy any spare capacity on the ring, but the bandwidth is subject to preemption by class 1 services (up to a predefined limit defined by the minimum *D* setting at the node). The Orwell ring, therefore, behaves like a conventional data LAN for class 2 services and a flexible digital switch for class 1.

C. Parallel Rings

In principle the protocol can also be extended to cover several synchronous rings in parallel with the slots spaced in phase. In such a system the nodes would have access to all rings, and from the point of view of the protocol the only change is an increase in the slot arrival rate. A RESET slot could be created on any ring and would be recognized by all nodes.

This configuration, known as the Orwell Torus, has the potential for capacities in excess of 1 Gbit/s. It is also resilient to the failure of one of the rings, as this merely reduces the size of the pool of circulating slots.

IV. Slot Structure

The actual size and format of the slots are fundamental to the operation of the protocol. To contain speech delay, the number of samples that can be accumulated before transmission must be kept as low as possible, commensurate with minimizing the proportion of overheads. A reasonable compromise is seen as 16 octets for the voice information field. This would take 2 ms to fill at 64 kbits/s.

Voice and data share the common slot structure shown in Fig. 10. The destination address (DA) is simply used to route slots between nodes, with the first bit being used to indicate a broadcast. For speech, a further 2 octets of local addressing are carried in the slot information field. Note that no frame check sequence, nor source address, is supplied for speech connections (the latter is provided during the signaling phase at call setup).

Primarily because of the speech constraints, the data block structure is small in comparison to the size of frames likely to arrive at the MAC from the LLC (see Section II-B). There are two ways of tackling this problem. One approach would be to constrain the length of the LLC frame to match the slot size. This would result in incompatibility with the LLC as defined by IEEE Standard 802.2 and necessitate a frame check sequence on the contents of each slot (as shown in Fig. 10). Alternatively, full length LLC frames could be carried in the information fields of several slots and rebuilt at the destination MAC. In this case the frame check sequence would be checked by the MAC on a frame by frame basis. For error logging, a simple parity check on the slot contents may be desirable. The destination address need only be big enough to identify the destination node as full addressing is in the LLC frame which is carried in the slot information field.

The control field comprises 4 bits. The full/empty (*F/E*) bit indicates whether or not the

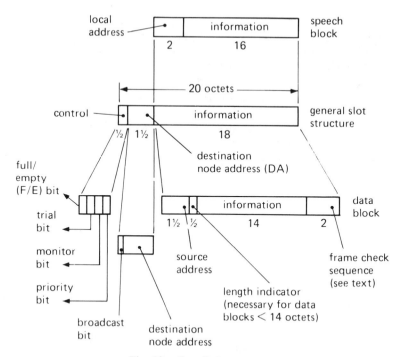

Fig. 10.   Orwell slot structure.

slot is occupied; it is also used in conjunction with the TRIAL bit to indicate a RESET slot. A monitor node, perhaps chosen by an initial polling process, sets the monitor bit on all passing full slots. This bit is reset when the slot is filled so that any full slot returning to the designated monitor node with the monitor bit set is assumed to be in error and cleared (in much the same way as in the Cambridge ring [6]). The priority bit is used to indicate the status of the information field contents, and can be used by the node control during peak loads.

V. NODE DESIGN

The effect of increasing ring delay on performance is insignificant until it is of the same order as the maximum RI of T ms. At high bit rates, with LAN length rings, this insensitivity allows scope for inserting more buffering in the ring path at the node interface. This eases considerably the timing constraints which pose difficulties for most ring protocols.

Figure 11 shows, in outline, one possible node implementation. Class 1 services are terminated at a line interface and the signaling is directed to the node control (which in turn communicates with the load monitor). Accepted class 1 transmissions are directed to the block assembler to be partitioned into 16 octet blocks, prefixed by an appropriate DA. Class 2 services need not access the node control, but have direct access to the ring, as in a conventional LAN. The capacity available, however, is constrained by the load monitor to D_{min} blocks per reset.

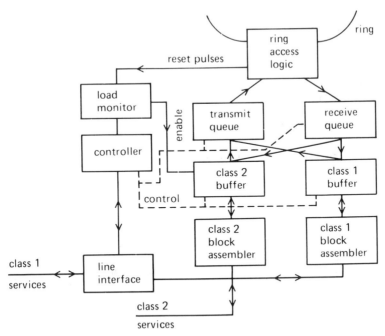

Fig. 11. Possible structure of Orwell ring node.

VI. PERFORMANCE

The information carrying capacity of the Orwell ring is a function of several factors; for example, the ring speed, the range of services (and their relative mix), the acceptable blocking probabilities, and the maximum tolerable delays.

In Fig. 12, the delay characteristic is shown for a ring carrying a near maximum speech load of 1350 pairs of simultaneous speech calls. At this load 97 percent of blocks were transported within 100 μs and all blocks within 200 μs. The reset rate was one per millisecond.

It is interesting to compare the mean delay versus load profile with that of a broadly equivalent token-passing ring (Fig. 13). For a token-passing ring, the mean access delay equals approximately half the token rotation time (the time taken to serve all the nodes and return).

$$\text{The token rotation time} = \frac{\text{ring delay}}{1 - \dfrac{\text{input load}}{\text{ring capacity}}}.$$

To conform to the speech delay constraints, packets on the token ring are assumed to be the same size, with the same overheads, as those on the Orwell ring. Multiple packets may be transmitted, and the token is placed at the end of the last packet transmitted from a node.

The main points to be drawn from this comparison are:

- the increased capacity of Orwell due to the destination release of slots

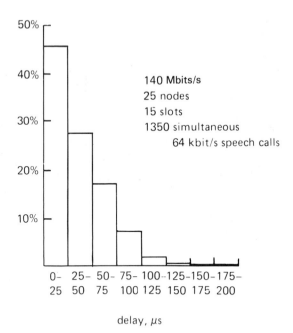

Fig. 12.   Speech block delay histogram (simulation result).

• the much lower mean delays resulting from the slotted structure, i.e., all nodes can be transmitting more or less continuously.

These characteristics make the Orwell protocol particularly attractive for transporting delay-sensitive speech.

VII. Conclusions

There is an increasing interest in the possibility of using high speed LAN's to integrate a wider range of information types, including speech and potentially low bit rate video. Such a network would offer several advantages over the conventional approach, the more important being increased flexibility and relative freedom from accurate traffic forecasting.

Established LAN protocols are limited in their ability to meet the delay and guaranteed bandwidth requirements necessary for an integrated services local network. Such a network must have the capability for low, preferably bounded, delays with a load control mechanism that allows synchronous services in progress to continue until their natural cessation.

The Orwell slotted ring protocol was designed specifically for this purpose. By allowing multiple simultaneous access to the bandwidth, and releasing slots at the destination, the delay and throughput performance offers a significant improvement over conventional LAN protocols. The performance is relatively insensitive to ring length and this permits extra buffering of the ring highway at the nodes; significantly easing timing constraints for the node/ring interface logic.

Simulation results have shown a 140 Mbit/s ring to be capable of transporting over 170

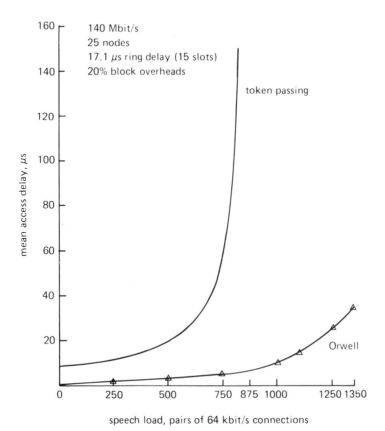

Fig. 13. Comparison of the mean delay of Orwell and an equivalent token-passing ring.

Mbits/s of mixed services, while the fully distributed load control mechanism can contain delays to an absolute maximum of 2 ms. The actual delays incurred, however, are an order of magnitude less, even at full load.

REFERENCES

[1] D. W. Faulkner and R. C. Turner, "Integrated subsystems for high data rate LAN's" in *Proc. EFOC/ LAN,* Montreux, Switzerland, June 1985, pp. 156–162.
[2] I. Watson, "The integrated services local network," *J. British Telecom. Technol.,* vol. 2, Sept. 1984.
[3] S. A. Johnson, "A performance analysis of integrated communications system," *J. British Telecom. Technol.,* vol. 3, Oct. 1985.
[4] J. O. Limb, "Performance of local area networks at high speed," *IEEE Commun. Mag.,* vol. 22, Aug. 1984.
[5] R. M. Falconer, J. L. Adams, and G. W. Walley, "A simulation study of the Cambridge ring with voice traffic," *J. British Telecom. Technol.,* vol. 3, Apr. 1985.
[6] M. W. Wilkes and D. J. Wheeler, "The Cambridge digital communications ring," in *Proc. Local Area Commun. Network Symp.,* Boston, MA, 1979.

Part VI
Bridges and Gateways

Local area networks must be capable of interconnecting a large number of stations over distances of several kilometers. Whenever the requirements are such that they exceed the limitations of a single bus or ring pertaining to a variety of design parameters, e.g., maximum number of stations, physical extent, or performance, means to interconnect subnetworks become necessary. In addition, facilities are required to obtain access to both PBX's and wide area networks.

The terms bridge and gateway have not been clearly defined yet and are sometimes used synonymously. Usually, an interconnection element is called a gateway either when it provides a common internetwork layer or protocol translation. In contrast, bridges provide interconnection at the data link layer with two different possibilities: 1) logical link control is executed hop-by-hop, i.e., between source station and bridge and between bridge and destination station with a thin relay function on top of logical link control in the bridge; or 2) logical link control is performed end-to-end with only a single routing function and frame buffering in the bridge. Intuitively, the latter seems to have the best potential for high performance. The underlying assumption for the last two examples was that logical link control represents a connection-oriented protocol, e.g., IEEE Standard 802.2 Type 2. In case of a connection-less logical link control protocol, i.e., IEEE Standard 802.2 Type 1, the protocol corresponding to the connection-oriented logical link control is the transport protocol.

Relatively little quantitative insight is available pertaining to the relative merits of the architectural concepts outlined above. In addition, investigations such as the chapter by Bux and Grillo in this section on the interconnection of LAN's of the same architecture suggest that protocols which are well understood in a teleprocessing environment show a significantly different behavior when used in the high-speed LAN environment. Much additional work is required before all aspects of LAN interconnection will be understood sufficiently.

28
Transparent Interconnection of Local Networks with Bridges

BILL HAWE, ALAN KIRBY, AND BOB STEWART

A class of devices known as bridges can be used to provide a protocol-transparent interconnection of similar or dissimilar local area networks (LAN's). The motivation for building such devices is briefly described followed by a discussion of their desirable characteristics. We describe the architecture, operating principles, and services provided by a bridge which may utilize a flat address space and is self-configuring. This is followed by a simple resource model of the bridge. The performance of individual LAN's is contrasted with the performance of a hybrid network composed of dissimilar LAN's connected with bridges.

INTRODUCTION

As a LAN installation grows, it may exceed the design parameters of an individual LAN. Restrictions such as physical extent, number of stations, performance, and media may be alleviated by the interconnection of multiple LAN's. Further, as new LAN architectures are introduced, a simple method of connecting these to existing LAN's would be valuable. The traditional method of providing this interconnection borrows techniques from wide area network technology, requiring the use of a common internetwork protocol or protocol translation gateways. We will discuss a class of devices which address these problems in an alternative manner suited to the LAN environment.

A. Bridges

A *bridge* (also referred to as a media access control (MAC) bridge or data link relay [3]) is a device which interconnects LAN's and allows stations connected to different LAN's to communicate as if both stations were on the same LAN (Fig. 1). For example, node *A* could send frames to nodes *Q*, *X*, or *P* in the same manner in which it sends frames to node *B*. The collection of LAN's and bridges will be referred to as an *extended* LAN. Any local network (or collection of local networks) that carries traffic between two other local networks operates as a *backbone* with respect to those networks. In its simplest form, a backbone is an interconnecting local network where all of its stations are bridges.

The extended LAN's proposed here require no routing or internet information to be supplied by the sending stations. Bridges differ from devices such as amplifiers and repeaters in that they are intelligent filtering devices which store-and-forward frames.

Bridges therefore are used to interconnect LAN's. Repeaters, on the other hand, are used to interconnect cable segments within a LAN. Bridges also differ from internet routers, which are explicitly addressed by source nodes and which make their forwarding decisions based upon a network layer address supplied by the sending node. In terms of the ISO model, a bridge functions within the data link layer (Fig. 2). Conceptually, a bridge is an n-port device (where $n \geq 2$). However, for simplicity, in the remainder of this chapter we will refer to two port bridges.

Bridges make use of data link layer addresses to make forwarding decisions. They have no knowledge of any other address space, such as a network or internet address space. Because of this characteristic, bridges are relatively insensitive to the higher layer protocols used by the communicating stations. As will be seen later, the bridge is a useful component in the construction of networks which contain more traditional devices such as routers and gateways which operate above the data link layer.

B. Useful Properties

Bridges connecting LAN's have several useful properties.
- *Traffic Filtering:* Bridges isolate LAN's from traffic which does not need to traverse that LAN. For example, in Fig. 1, traffic between nodes A and B is not sent on the LAN's to which P and Q are connected. Because of this filtering the load on a given LAN can be reduced, thus improving the delays experienced by all users on the extended LAN.
- *Increased Physical Extent:* LAN's are limited in physical extent (at least in a practical sense) by either propagation delay or signal attenuation and distortion. Since the bridge is a store-and-forward device, it forwards frames after having gained access to the appropriate LAN via the normal access method. In this way, the extended LAN can cover a larger extent than an individual LAN. The penalty for this is a small store-and-forward delay.
- *Increased Maximum Number of Stations:* Because of physical layer limitations or stability and delay considerations, most LAN architectures have a practical limit on

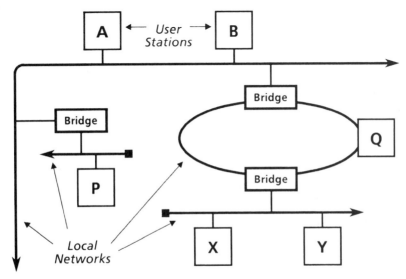

Fig. 1. Bridged network configuration.

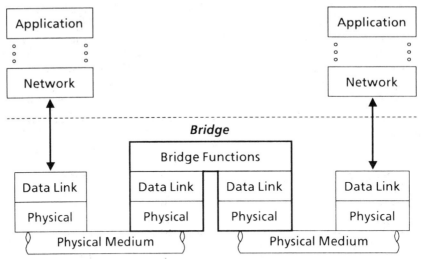

Fig. 2. Bridges and data links.

the number of stations on a single LAN. Since the bridge contends for access to the LAN as a single station, one bridge may "represent" many nodes on another LAN or extended LAN.

- *Use of Different Physical Layers:* Some LAN architectures support a variety of physical media (baseband coax, broadband coax, or optical fiber) which cannot be directly connected at the physical layer. Bridges allow these media to coexist in the same extended LAN.
- *Interconnection of Dissimilar LAN's:* LAN's of different architecture are typically interconnected with routers or gateways. Often, these devices are complex with only moderate throughput. This may be inappropriate for a LAN environment. It is possible to build a bridge in which its LAN's are dissimilar (within constraints to be discussed later). For example, such a bridge would allow stations on an IEEE Standard 802.3 (CSMA/CD) LAN to send frames to stations on 802.4 (token bus) or 802.5 (token ring) [7]–[9].

C. Desirable Characteristics

There are a number of characteristics which an ideal extended LAN should possess. These are as follows.

- *Minimize Traffic:* Only traffic generated by user stations should exist on the individual LAN's (i.e., no traffic due to complex routing algorithms). Further, this traffic should traverse only those LAN's necessary to best reach its destination.
- *No Duplicates:* The bridges should not cause duplicate frames to be delivered to the destination(s).
- *Sequentiality:* The combination of LAN's and bridges should not permute the frame ordering as transmitted by the source station.
- *High Performance:* In the LAN environment, users expect high throughput and low delay. The extended LAN should preserve these characteristics. In practice, this means that the bridges should be able to process frames at the maximum rate at which

they can be received. Since many LAN's operate in the multimegabit per second range, this requires a fast switching operation.

- *Frame Lifetime Limit:* Frames should not be allowed to exist in the extended LAN for an unbounded time. Some higher layer protocols may operate poorly if frames are unduly delayed. This is especially true for protocols designed to depend on the low delay characteristics of a LAN.
- *Low Error Rate:* LAN's typically have a low effective bit error rate. Higher layer protocols are often designed with this in mind. This allows the protocols to operate more efficiently since they can assume that errors are infrequent. Extended LAN's should not increase this error rate substantially.
- *Low Congestion Loss:* Individual LAN's minimize congestion by employing access control schemes which prevent excessive traffic from entering the LAN. Extended LAN's are more vulnerable to congestion loss since the bridges may be forced to drop frames when the frames queued to be transmitted match the available buffers. This phenomenon should be minimized by proper design (placement/sizing) of the extended LAN.
- *Generalized Topology:* For purposes of traffic splitting and reliability, it would be useful to allow arbitrary interconnection of LAN's via bridges.

D. Bridge Types

There are two categories of bridges which are transparent at the data link layer. These are distinguished by the method used to make the forwarding decision.

The best known technique for forwarding is based upon the use of a hierarchically organized address space in which the data link address of a station is dependent upon its physical location in the extended LAN [18]. With this approach often the address space is partitioned into fields describing on which LAN in the hierarchy of LAN's the station resides. Such a scheme permits the use of a very simple forwarding process in the bridge.

However, there are several problems associated with such a scheme. First, the topology is restricted to a rooted tree (where the LAN's are edges and the bridges are nodes). Second, the end nodes must be told their own addresses. This might be accomplished manually or perhaps with a dynamic binding. However, a dynamic binding scheme would require the existence of a protocol to accomplish the binding. In any case, when a station physically moves, its address must change. The difficulty of joining previously disjoint LAN's may be significant if manual address administration is used. Third, the depth of the physical hierarchy is predefined by the number of fields in the address space.

For the remainder of this chapter, we will concentrate on a different type of bridge which uses a flat address space and an adaptive learning algorithm to locate stations [6]. Such a bridge requires no relationship between the address of a node and its location in the extended network. Further, nonrooted tree topologies may be supported. This type of bridge can also operate on a mixed hierarchical/flat address space, giving it significant flexibility in both operation and configuration. Also, such bridges are particularly well suited to use with IEEE Standard 802 LAN's which exhibit consistent global address space administration.

ROUTING ALGORITHMS

The bridge uses *backward learning* [1], with flooding as its backup strategy. Backward learning depends only on local information; inherently available by observing the traffic. Loops are prevented by dynamically restricting the logical topology to a branching tree.

The bridge routing algorithm is thus isolated and adaptive. This results in bridges that are simple to install and use.

The bridge routing algorithms depend on a unique address for every station within the extended network. These source and destination addresses are part of the data link header. Bridges must receive *all* frames on each local network to which it is connected, *regardless* of a frame's destination address. Also, the bridge must be able to forward a frame with the frame's original source address, not the bridge's source address. These assumptions are the basis for the following descriptions.

Each bridge independently constructs and maintains its own routing data base. The routing data base contains one entry for each station address the bridge knows. Each entry provides an association between a station address and the bridge's local identification of the channel leading to that station. Each entry also contains an age field, used to delete obsolete entries.

Forwarding a frame requires looking up the destination in the routing data base. If the bridge finds the destination, it forwards the frame on the indicated channel, unless that channel was the source for the frame, in which case it discards the frame. If the bridge does not find the destination, it floods the frame on all channels except the one on which it was received. To avoid excessive flooding at startup, a restarted bridge does not forward frames for several seconds, allowing the update process to establish an initial routing data base. Finally, whenever the forwarding process uses an entry, it resets the entry's age.

The bridge updates the routing data base by recording the source address of each received frame, along with the source channel identification and initialized age. The bridge does not know or care if a channel represents a single LAN or an extended LAN. In order to avoid obsolete entries in the routing data base, and to ensure correctness when stations move, the bridge removes entries that have not been used for several minutes. The timing of this process is not critical. The event occurs infrequently and is therefore low overhead.

In order to avoid frame congestion (and thus frame loss) waiting for a forwarding decision, the forwarding process must be very fast and of high priority. In particular, if there is a requirement to handle worst case traffic loads, the forwarding process must make a forwarding decision within the minimum frame interarrival time from all channels. This avoids instability in the queue for the forwarding process. The update process may be of lower priority, but must make progress so that a bridge does not continue to flood indefinitely. Although the forwarding and update functions are presented here as separate processes, in practice they are somewhat interwoven, being closely allied in the processing of an incoming data link protocol header.

Although any arbitrary physical topology of LAN's and bridges is allowed, the topology is dynamically pruned to a spanning tree to avoid loops [16]. This is done by placing the appropriate bridge or bridges into a nonforwarding mode. The algorithm that accomplishes this runs only in the bridges. It is dynamic and automatic. Thus, the extended LAN will autoconfigure. In addition to precluding looping frames due to configuration errors, this same algorithm also provides a mechanism for increasing the availability of the extended LAN by allowing redundant bridges and LAN's. A redundant bridge or LAN will automatically be used when needed to recover from a failure which would have partitioned the extended LAN.

SERVICES ACROSS BRIDGES

Bridge routing algorithms should allow accurate and efficient forwarding of data. A bridge only relays data frames. It does not forward data link specific control information such as a token. The transparent forwarding of data can take two forms: *pass through* and *translation*.

Pass through is the simplest form of forwarding. It is possible only when the incoming and outgoing LAN's have identical frame formats. In this case, the bridge forwards frames unchanged.

Translation is necessary when the LAN's have different frame formats. Translation is only possible, however, if the formats are sufficiently similar. In this case the bridge forwards a frame that appears to have originated within the outgoing LAN, but is actually a transformation of the frame from the incoming LAN.

At best, translation involves simple transformations such as different framing, transposing fields, or directly mapping control values. At worst, it requires invention or loss of fields representing unmatched services. For example, in forwarding from a LAN that supports priority to one that does not, the translation process loses the priority information. When forwarding in the opposite direction the bridge must insert some default priority.

Another potential incompatibility is in frame sizes. One LAN may require minimum size where another does not, or one LAN may support larger frame sizes than another. In the minimum size case, translation requires adding or removing padding. This works best where padding mechanisms are part of the data link protocol; otherwise, some bridge-dependent convention must be chosen or translation becomes impossible. Frames that are too large, on the other hand, must be either segmented and reassembled, or simply discarded. Although the former is possible, it is best to accept a maximum extended network frame size and discard oversized frames. This keeps bridge operation simple and fast.

Translation implies the need for address space size compatibility. It also may introduce issues when mapping one space into another. All stations must therefore have a unique representation in the address space of any LAN within the extended LAN. A globally administered address space in the extended LAN alleviates this problem.

Certain data link specific operations can affect bridge operation in an undesirable manner. For example, if the operation of accepting a frame removed it from the medium (as it could in a ring), a bridge may have difficulty operating in a receive-all manner. Any bridge will change the semantics of a data link layer acknowledgment. From the sender's point of view, a data link layer acknowledgment will have a different meaning depending on whether the destination was reached on the same LAN or through a bridge. In the former case, the acknowledgment means the frame arrived at the destination. In the latter case, it merely means it arrived at the bridge.

A. Higher Level Protocols

Higher level protocols have no direct cognizance of the existence of bridges. The protocols may make assumptions about delay, error rate, etc. However, bridges could affect the validity of these assumptions thus removing some transparency. This may adversely affect the operation of the protocols.

By their nature as store-and-forward devices, bridges necessarily introduce delay. It is important that this delay be kept to a minimum. This topic, along with the related topic of congestion control, is treated more fully later in the performance discussion.

Bridges must also avoid introducing frame corruption. A bridge must not subvert the protection of the data link's frame check sequence. The most straightforward way for a bridge to preserve the protection is to pass along the frame check as received. This is possible with pass-through forwarding, as long as hardware controller implementations allow it. Passing the frame check through is not possible for translating bridges. In this case, the bridge should take measures such as error detection on the memory and buses to avoid introducing undetectable corruption.

B. Incompatible LAN's

Bridges can interconnect incompatible LAN's, but not as effectively as similar LAN's. When LAN addressing, services, or formats are so different that translation is impossible or impractical, the bridge has another option. Bridges can use a simple interbridge protocol to encapsulate incompatible frames. These frames can then be carried through a LAN (or extended LAN) to another bridge for decapsulation and forwarding back into their native environment. This service remains transparent to the source and destination LAN's, making them a closed group that "tunnels" through another network. The stations in one closed group cannot communicate with stations in a different closed group, but at least physical coverage can be extended.

Encapsulation has the interesting benefit of preserving all original information, including frame check. On the other hand, it increases bridge complexity and does not attain the degree of compatibility in pass-through or translation forwarding.

RESOURCE MODELS

In order to characterize performance in extended LAN's one must have a model for the resources that can be consumed. Additionally, one must understand the processes which generate work for those resources. In an extended LAN the resources that affect performance are the data links, the buffering capacity, and processing capabilities in the bridges. Figure 3 depicts these resources.

There are also resources in the end stations which affect performance. These are buffer pool sizes, internal bus bandwidths, CPU and disk speeds, etc. However, for the purposes of this analysis we ignore those resources since we will focus on the LAN channels themselves. We assume that those other resources are not bottlenecks. In doing so, we imply they do not affect the performance of the LAN channels. This allows the channels to be modeled as "open" queueing systems. Therefore, the traffic sources operate independently of the state of the channel.

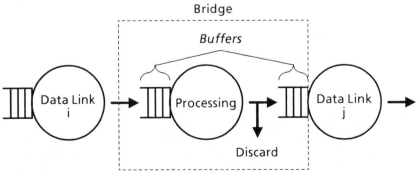

Fig. 3.   Bridge (2 port) resource model.

In reality, a LAN (or any other network) operates as a "closed" queueing system. This means that the load carried by the LAN at any instant cannot be separated from the performance of the other resources. For example, limited buffering capacity in a low cost end station may result in a large amount of frame loss when receiving traffic from a high performance server. The resultant retransmissions increase the effective load on the LAN channels and any bridges that might be present (not to mention the CPU's). To account for these effects all resources must be modeled. To avoid this complexity though, we assume the LAN's will be the bottlenecks. In the analysis, the system is configured with enough end stations to support the modeled throughput.

A. Special Considerations at Bridges

Bridges contend for the resources of a given LAN along with other stations. In some cases, a backbone may contain only bridges. A *subnet* contains end stations and one or more bridges to connect it to a backbone or other subnets. The policies used for the allocation of resources on a subnet or backbone will affect the fairness as perceived by the stations.

In an extended LAN a bridge acts essentially as a concentrator for N stations. That is, the traffic that actually flows through the bridge is due to N stations. However, it may only be allocated bandwidth on a given LAN as if it were a single station. It may require allocation of resources as if it were N stations since it likely generates more traffic than any one station. One may therefore wish to operate bridges at a higher priority than user stations. This can be done in several ways. On token access LAN's, the token holding times, token priorities, etc., can be adjusted to give bridges more of the LAN resources. On CSMA/CD LAN's, the collision resolution or backoff algorithms could similarly be adjusted to favor bridges when necessary. On the other hand, under a static allocation of priorities, a bridge with only one station's traffic flowing through it will essentially give that station more than its fair share of resources. The ideal scheme then would be for the allocation to adjust to the demand based on the nature of the stations generating it.

PERFORMANCE CONSIDERATIONS

The performance of an extended LAN is determined by a number of design parameters, including the expected capacity of the backbone and subnets, the overall system capacity, the applied load, frame loss rates, etc. The designer must not only be concerned with providing adequate performance for current usage but must also allow for growth.

Ideally, the system is designed to be sufficiently robust to changes in the user population as well as their characteristics. As an example, [10] contains workload information from measurements of users in a program development environment. This can be used directly to estimate the applied load due to N of those users. To do so however, requires that one also model *all* layers of protocol involved in transferring this information across the extended LAN.

In order to achieve the highest level of performance while at the same time maintaining the desired flexibility in the configuration, low cost to interface, etc., the network designer must understand the tradeoffs in using different LAN technologies in different parts of the extended LAN. Here we consider the differences in the performance of a few popular LAN technologies. In doing so, we consider the parameters which are most important in affecting performance.

Backbone services may require that a large physical extent be covered. Additionally, the backbone may carry several classes of traffic (voice, data, video, etc.), perhaps on separate logical networks. These are reasons that often lead designers to use broadband media as a backbone. Here we are concerned primarily with services supporting high-speed frame distribution.

Subnet services usually require high performance as well as ease of configuration, wiring, etc. Subnet operation should not be compromised by stations (such as personal computers) coming up or going down frequently. The entire extended network or subnet should not need to be manually reconfigured to respond to these frequent events.

Another consideration is congestion loss. This can occur in an extended LAN when buffering resources are exhausted in a bridge. This typically is due to transient traffic overloads. There are two reasons: one is when the forwarding process fails to keep up with the incoming traffic; the other is when the effective capacity of an outbound LAN is less than the rate of traffic being forwarded on that LAN. In general, it is desirable that frame loss be due to congestion on the outbound LAN's, not because of inability to process frames. This simply defines which server will be the bottleneck. It also implies that the forwarding process should operate at a rate at least as great as the total arrival rate on the inbound LAN's.

A. Effect of Bridges on CSMA/CD Channels

The performance of CSMA/CD channels is determined by several factors. (See [4], [7], and [14] for examples of CSMA/CD systems.) These factors include the number of stations, their locations, the applied load, the propagation delay between stations, and the signaling rate of the channel.

Bridges have several effects on the performance of CSMA/CD channels. One is due to the filtering function which prevents traffic from entering a subnet which it need not traverse. This reduces the applied load on the channel thus improving performance for the local users of that channel.

Another effect is more subtle. Consider a CSMA/CD system of a given extent (D meters) with N stations distributed uniformly over the extent. Without the use of bridges, all N stations share the resources of that one channel extended over D meters. The delay and capacity are determined then by the applied load as described in the references. Consider adding a bridge in the center of the system, thus partitioning the system into two channels each with $N/2$ stations. The collision windows on each of the partitions have been cut in half. This reduces α. The net effect then is not only to reduce the load applied to a given channel (through filtering), but also to improve the overall efficiency or capacity of that channel since the extent it must cover is smaller. In other words, the channel gets more efficient while at the same time the load applied to it is reduced. Given these factors along with performance information characterizing the behavior of the channels under load, one can investigate the performance of bridged networks using these channels. (See [17], [19], [13], and [5] for examples of single channel performance.)

B. Token Access Channels

Two key parameters of token access channels are the token passing delay and the number of nodes. Increasing either parameter will adversely affect the mean time to access the channel [2]. The token passing delay is a function of the effective size of the token, the signaling rate, the propagation delay between stations, and the delay per station.

The number of nodes has other effects on system performance. One is that the reliability of the system will decrease as more nodes are added. This is because it is more likely that a given interface, link, etc., may fail. The wiring strategies mentioned above attempt to address this, and other, configuration problems [15].

Token access protocols typically perform well at heavy load and are often used for real-time systems where a worst case delay (in the absence of bit errors) is to be calculated. Unfortunately, they are not suited for large numbers of nodes for the reasons mentioned above.

As one of many possible examples of how a system could be configured, consider the use of token access protocols for backbone services. The number of stations need not be large since most would be bridges connecting subnets to the backbone. Large populations of user stations could then be partitioned across subnets using CSMA/CD since it is more flexible to the changing environment at the user stations. Presumably, the backbone would offer good performance at heavy load as long as the number of bridges is not too large [2]. Figure 6 depicts the performance of a 10 Mbits/s broadband token bus using an exhaustive service policy. L is the network extent in kilometers and N is the number of nodes. This uses the model found in [2] which is based on the work in [12].

Performance degradation due to network configuration could be a problem with these protocols. When used as a backbone this may not be serious since the bridges are not expected to go on/off line very often.

PERFORMANCE OF EXTENDED LAN's

It is important to size the capacity of an extended LAN. Given the characterization of user demands, this is expressed in the number of users that it can "support." The difficulty with using the number of users as the independent variable is that one must account for the resource consumption from all layers of protocol. This is difficult to do in general.

Another problem is that the performance requirements may vary for different higher level protocols. Some may be delay-sensitive. For example, terminal access protocols which return echoes end-to-end are quite sensitive to the delay. Other terminal access protocols which allow local editing and echoing are not as delay-sensitive. File transfer protocols are not sensitive to the delay but require high throughput. Therefore, to determine the capacity of an extended LAN one must investigate both delay and throughput as applied to the requirements of a particular protocol and application which uses it.

Certain LAN's place constraints on the configuration that are due to either physical layer limitations (such as the distance over which the line drivers can operate) or the interaction between the data link layer access method and the propagation delay. For example, the Ethernet places a limit on the maximum number of repeaters between any two communicating stations [4]. This constraint assures that the propagation delay budget (which is assumed by the access method protocol) will not be exceeded in any configuration. In an extended LAN, one may also wish to place constraints on the configuration based on the performance expectations of higher layer protocols. For example, a constraint may be that there be no more than N bridges between two stations that use a delay-sensitive protocol. In general though, the rules may need to be more complex when an extended LAN is configured with dissimilar LAN's. This is because the individual LAN's may provide different delay/throughput characteristics.

Another problem when attempting to determine capacity is estimating the amount of traffic that remains local to a given subnet and the amount that leaves a subnet. The worst case occurs when all of the traffic must be forwarded off a subnet through one or more levels of backbones. This creates the largest demand on the resources of the backbone(s). One way to handle this is to assume that all of the locally generated traffic must also be carried by the backbone. Increasing the load will then define the system's saturation point. At that point, the resources of the subnets will likely be underutilized. The additional capacity of the subnet can be used for local-only traffic. This defines the limits for the system with respect to the ratio of local to transit traffic that is possible.

A. An Example

To illustrate one of the many ways extended LAN concepts can be applied, consider a hypothetical configuration. The purpose of the example is to demonstrate the concepts of the architecture, not to represent a real application. A 10 Mbit/s broadband token bus extending 16 km is used as a backbone for N 10 Mbits/s baseband CSMA/CD subnets, each extending 2.8 km. This forms a two level extended LAN. Figure 4 depicts this configuration.

The processing delay (for the forwarding process only) in the bridges can be neglected if it is a small part of the store-and-forward delay. This assumption is made here. We assume that there are two main classes of traffic to be carried by this extended LAN. One class is terminal/host traffic. (For examples see [5] and [10].) The other traffic class is comprised of remote file access and transfer.

File traffic on a LAN may have greatly varying characteristics depending on the system architecture. For example, in a client/server system where there is sufficient memory in the file server, there can be a good deal of caching done at the server. This means that accesses done to the file server may return data for a brief period at a rate limited only by the I/O speeds of the server. Less memory at the server, more file transfers than file accesses, or more users sharing the server will result in arrival rates limited by head contention on the disks at the server.

Terminal traffic can also have greatly varying characteristics. This depends on the nature of the user behavior as well as the terminal communications model. For example, the

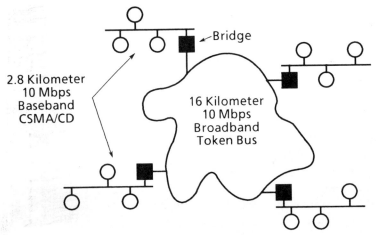

Fig. 4.   Example of extended LAN.

terminal access protocols may perform echoing over the channel or it may be done locally at the point the terminal interfaces to the extended LAN. In the case of echoes carried over the channel, the responsiveness of the channel is very important since it may be visible on almost every user keystroke.

We select two of the several possibilities for file and terminal traffic outlined above. We assume that disk traffic is characterized as a Poisson process with a mean arrival rate of λ_d frames/s. We assume that frames associated with these sources have a mean size of x_d bytes. The arrival rate and frame sizes include all protocol overheads. We also assume that traffic due to terminal access is a Poisson process with a mean of λ_t frames/s and a mean size of x_t bytes. This also includes all protocol overheads. We use a hybrid model that uses simulation and analytical methods to estimate performance. The CSMA/CD portions of the system are simulated in detail [5] and the token bus performance is computed analytically [2]. Since we also apply the independence assumption [11], and are interested in merely illustrating the example, this hybrid is adequate. However, a more detailed overall model is ultimately required to fully understand performance. This is because we are unable to investigate effects such as congestion loss at bridges with this approach. The amount of loss will depend on traffic patterns, bridge processing speeds, bridge and end station buffering capabilities, higher layer protocol parameters (window sizes, timers, etc.), and higher layer congestion avoidance algorithms (such as dynamic window sizing).

As mentioned previously, it is important to consider both delay and throughput when sizing the capacity of a LAN or an extended LAN. In doing so here, we increase the number of users while observing the delay and utilization of the components of the extended LAN. When the utilization of any resource in the extended LAN reaches 0.9 the user population is no longer increased. (Note that this is utilization not offered load. The offered load is less than 0.9 when this occurs because of the overheads described earlier.) Similarly, if the *mean* delay across the extended LAN exceeds a threshold (T seconds), the user population is no longer increased. We assume that there are sufficient resources (computers, etc.) added to the extended LAN to support the user population while maintaining the I/O rates for each user class (λ_d and λ_t). This allows the system to be viewed as an open queueing network.

Figure 5 shows several aspects of extended LAN performance. For this figure, $\lambda_d = 25$ frames/s, $\lambda_t = 5$ frames/s, $x_d = 600$ bytes, $x_t = 100$ bytes, and $T = 10$ ms. We show three different partitionings of the user population. This includes 10, 20, and 30 percent of the user stations generating file traffic as defined. The remainder generates terminal traffic also as defined. Plotted in Fig. 8 are the utilizations of a given CMSA/CD subnet and the token bus backbone. (Note that the utilization will include overhead such as collisions or token passing.) We make the worst case assumption here that the user population is divided evenly across the subnets and (as another worse case assumption) that all the subnet traffic must also enter the backbone. This places a lower bound on the supported user population.

Figure 8 demonstrates that there are two regions of performance. One region is where the bandwidth of the backbone is not sufficient to allow for more users. This occurs for small numbers of bridges. The other region is where the token passing delay on the backbone is too large to allow the extended LAN to meet the mean delay goal (T seconds). This occurs when the number of bridges is large.

CONCLUSION

We have shown the usefulness of flat address space, learning bridges in extending LAN's. These extended LAN's can make use of desirable characteristics of the LAN's

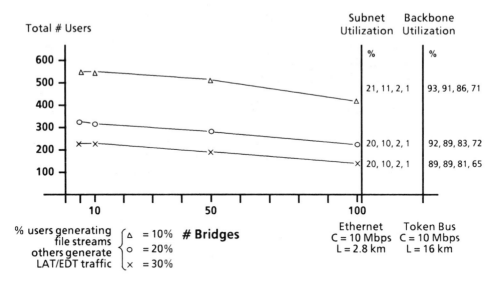

Fig. 5.   Example of extended LAN capacity with mixed traffic.

from which they are formed providing overall characteristics which an individual LAN cannot provide. For this architectural approach, we have stated the requirements placed on the bridges including their LAN interface operation, the routing algorithms, etc. We have also described topological constraints and mentioned issues regarding the number of bridges in the extended LAN. Finally, we have discussed the performance aspects of several LAN's as well as those issues relating specifically to extended LAN's. We have also provided an example of a hypothetical extended LAN and discussed its performance.

ACKNOWLEDGMENT

The authors wish to acknowledge the major technical contributions of M. Kempf and G. Koshy to the concepts in this chapter.

REFERENCES

[1]   P. Baran, "On distributed communication networks," *IEEE Trans. Commun. Syst.*, vol. CS-12, pp. 1–9, Mar. 1964.

[2]   W. Bux, "Local-area subnetworks: A performance comparison," *IEEE Trans. Commun.*, Oct. 1981.

[3]   R. Callon, "Internetwork protocol," in *Proc. IEEE* (Special Issue on Open Systems Interconnection), Dec. 1983.

[4]   Digital, Intel, and Xerox, *The Ethernet: A Local Area Network, Data Link Layer and Physical Layer Specifications,* version 2.0, Nov. 1982.

[5]   B. Hawe and M. Marathe, "Predicting Ethernet capacity—A case study," in *Proc. Comput. Perform. Evaluation Users Group Conf.,* Washington, DC, Oct. 1982.

[6]   B. Hawe, A. Kirby, and A. Lauck, "An architecture for transparently interconnecting IEEE 802 local area networks," submitted to IEEE 802, Document IEEE-802.85*1.96, Oct. 31, 1984.

[7]   IEEE Project 802 Local Area Network Standards, "IEEE Standard 802.3 CSMA/CD access method and physical layer specifications," Approved IEEE Standard 802.3-1985 (ISO/DIS 8802/3), July 1983.

[8]   IEEE Project 802 Local Area Network Standards, "IEEE Standard 802.4 token passing bus access method and physical layer specifications," Approved IEEE Standard 802.4-1985 (ISO/DIS 8802/4), Dec. 1985.

[9]   IEEE Project 802 Local Area Network Standards, "IEEE Standard 802.5 token ring access method and physical layer specifications," Approved IEEE Standard 802.5-1985 (ISO/DIS 8802/5), Dec. 1985.

[10] R. Jain and R. Turner, "Workload characterization using image accounting," in *Proc. Comput. Performance Evaluation Users Group Conf.,* Washington, DC, Oct. 1982.

[11] L. Kleinrock, *Queueing Systems, Volume II.* New York: Wiley, 1976.

[12] A. G. Konheim and B. Meister, "Waiting lines and times in a system with polling," *J. Ass. Comput. Mach.,* vol. 21, pp. 470–490, 1974.

[13] M. Marathe, "Design analysis of a local area network," presented at the Comput. Networking Symp., Washington, DC, Oct. 1980.

[14] R. M. Metcalf and D. R. Boggs, "Ethernet: Distributed packet switching for local computer networks," *Commun. Ass. Comput. Mach.,* July 1976.

[15] J. Saltzer, "Why a ring?," in *Proc. 7th Data Commun. Symp.,* Mexico City, Mexico, Nov. 1981.

[16] R. Perlman, "An algorithm for distributed computation of a spanning tree in an extended LAN," in *Proc. 9th Data Commun.,* Vancouver, Canada, Sept. 1985 (also submitted to IEEE Standard 802, Document IEEE-802-85* 1.97, Oct. 31, 1984).

[17] J. F. Shoch and J. A. Hupp, "Measured performance of an Ethernet local area network," *Commun. Ass. Comput. Mach.,* vol. 23, Dec. 1980.

[18] N. C. Strole, "A local communications network based on interconnected token-access rings: A tutorial," *IBM J. Res. Develop.,* vol. 27, Sept. 1983.

[19] F. A. Tobagi and V. B. Hunt, "Performance analysis of carrier sense multiple access with collision detection," *Comput. Networks,* vol. 4, Oct./Nov. 1980; see also this volume, ch. 20.

29
Flow Control in Local Area Networks of Interconnected Token Rings

WERNER BUX AND DAVIDE GRILLO

We investigate flow-control issues in local area networks consisting of multiple token rings interconnected through bridges. To achieve high throughput, bridges perform only a very simple routing and store-and-forward function, but are not involved in error- or flow-control. In case of congestion, bridges discard arriving frames, which will be recovered through an appropriate end-to-end protocol between the communicating stations. The end-to-end protocol considered is the IEEE 802.2 type-2 logical-link-control (LLC) protocol. Extensive simulations show that performance can be severely degraded if, in such a network, the LLC protocol is employed as defined today. Therefore, we suggest an enhancement to this protocol in the form of a dynamic flow-control algorithm. As our results demonstrate, this enhancement guarantees close-to-optimal network performance under both normal traffic load and overload conditions.

I. INTRODUCTION

Local area networks must be capable of interconnecting a large number of stations over distances of several kilometers. Whenever the limitations of a single ring or bus subnetwork are reached with respect to the maximum number of attachments or maximum distance, means to interconnect subnetworks become necessary.

In this chapter, we consider a network of interconnected token rings. Rings operate as specified in the ECMA and IEEE standards [1], [2]. Ring interconnection is provided by nodes called bridges [3]. To meet the high throughput requirements for interconnecting high-speed rings at reasonable costs, the bridge functions have to be simple, which excludes their performing any complex flow or error control. In case of congestion, bridges simply discard frames they cannot handle momentarily. Discarded frames will be recovered through the end-to-end protocol between the communicating stations. We consider a network architecture in which type 2 of the IEEE 802.2 logical-link-control (LLC) standard [4] is employed as end-to-end protocol.

A potential problem in such a network is that recovery of frames lost in congested bridges may worsen congestion, but, without a detailed analysis, it is very difficult to predict how severe this problem will be. Therefore, we developed a detailed model of a multiring network including all the relevant medium-access-control and logical-link-

496

control functions. Since the complexity of such a model is far beyond the one of queueing models that can be analytically treated today, we employed simulation. Specifically, we used the RESQ2 simulation tool [5] which, for our modeling purposes, turned out to be a very flexible and powerful instrument. Our simulations show that network performance can be severely degraded in case of congestion. To overcome this problem, we suggest providing a dynamic flow-control mechanism in the LLC protocol which, in case of congestion, throttles the input traffic to the network.

In the next section, the elements of the multiring network are described. Section III shows how this network performs when the IEEE 802.2 type-2 LLC protocol as defined today is employed. In Section IV, we introduce a new flow-control mechanism in this protocol, and show the improvement attained. Section V summarizes our findings.

II. ELEMENTS OF THE MULTIRING NETWORK

The network topology underlying our study is depicted in Fig. 1. Several token rings are interconnected through bridges and a "backbone" token ring, the latter serving to interconnect bridges.

A. Token Rings

The token-ring standards [1], [2] define a priority mechanism by which eight levels of priorities can be provided. We study two different kinds of ring operation. The so-called "nonpriority mode" assumes that all stations and the bridges operate at the same ring-access priority level and are only allowed to transmit a single frame per token. In "priority mode," bridges operate at a higher ring-access priority level than normal stations. Whenever a bridge has a frame ready for transmission on a local ring, it will either seize the low-priority token, if available, or make a reservation for high-priority access. This forces the currently transmitting station to issue a priority token which will then be used by the bridge. After the bridge has completed transmission, circulation of the low-priority token is resumed at the next station downstream from the one which last transmitted. In priority

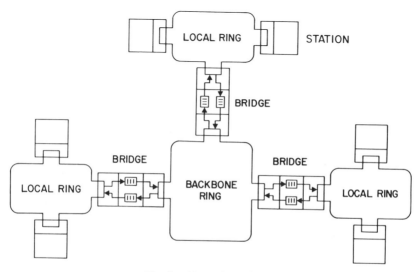

Fig. 1. Network topology.

mode, bridges are allowed to transmit continuously until their transmit buffer has been emptied, i.e., we assume a very long token-holding timeout. Stations transmit only one frame per token. On the backbone, priority access is not employed and each bridge transmits a single frame per token. For simplicity, we assume that both token-passing overhead and transmission errors can be neglected.

B. Bridges

Bridges provide a basic routing and store-and-forward function [3]. Frames are buffered in a bridge until they can be transmitted on the local or backbone ring. We assume that the bridge memory space is partitioned into two separate buffer pools, one for each data-flow direction; see Fig. 2. The buffer pools are structured in segments of a fixed size. Frames which do not find a sufficient number of free segments upon their arrival at a bridge are lost.

A bridge is controlled by two processors, each of which handles one direction of data flow. These processors are modeled by two independent single servers which process all frames on a first-come first-served basis.

C. Stations

A conceptual representation of a user station is shown in Fig. 3.

Application and Higher Layers: An application is represented by a traffic source in the sending station, which generates messages with given length and interarrival-time distributions, and a corresponding sink at the receiving station. The following two functions pertaining to the "higher layers," i.e., layers above LLC, are modeled in detail: 1) segmentation/reassembly of messages when the maximum frame length specified for LLC is exceeded, and 2) the "higher layer interface" on top of LLC, which works as follows. Data units provided by users of the LLC service are transmitted by LLC in the form of information (I-) frames. If LLC cannot transmit I-frames at the rate data units are supplied, it will apply backpressure on the higher layers. Specifically, a data unit supplied by a higher layer entity is not accepted by LLC when the total number of I-frames and data units being currently handled by the LLC entity has reached a threshold value B. This number encompasses 1) the number of I-frames already transmitted but not yet acknowledged, 2) the number of I-frames waiting to be transmitted, and 3) the number of

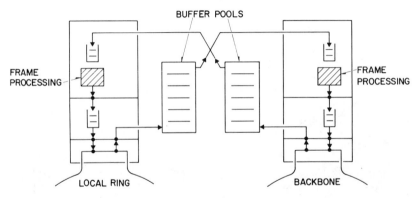

Fig. 2.   Bridge.

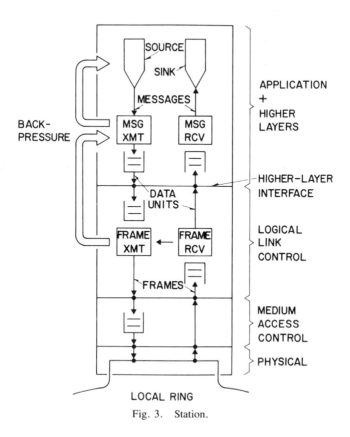

Fig. 3. Station.

accepted data units not yet processed, i.e., formatted as *I*-frames. An unaccepted data unit together with all subsequent data units pertaining to the same message are queued by the higher layer entity. At the same time, the generation of further messages is halted. When LLC service again becomes available, queued data units, if any, are handled first and the application resumes generation of new messages.

Logical Link Control: Particular emphasis was placed on a complete and detailed representation of all LLC functions. We subsequently give a brief outline of these functions; for a detailed specification, the reader is referred to [4].

Flow Control: Flow control is realized by a window mechanism, i.e., a sender is permitted to transmit up to a fixed number W (the window size) *I*-frames without having to wait for an acknowledgment. In our LLC implementation, for each *I*-frame successfully received, one receive-ready (RR) frame is transmitted back carrying the acknowledgment. We do not make use of the receive-not-ready (RNR) function provided in [4].

Error Recovery: If the send sequence number of a received *I*-frame is not equal to the one expected, the receiver will return a reject (REJ-) frame. It then discards all *I*-frames until the expected one has been correctly received. The sender, upon receiving a REJ-frame, retransmits *I*-frames starting with the sequence number received within the REJ-frame.

In addition to reject recovery, a timeout mechanism is provided. At the instant of transmission of an *I*-frame, a timer is started when not already running. When the sender receives an acknowledgment, it restarts the timer when there are still unacknowledged *I*-

frames outstanding. When the timer expires, the station performs a "checkpointing" function by transmitting an RR-frame with a dedicated bit (the "*P*-bit") set to 1. The receiver, upon receiving this frame, returns an RR-frame with the "*F*-bit" set to 1. When this RR-frame is received by the sender, it either proceeds with transmitting new *I*-frames or retransmits previous *I*-frames, depending on the sequence number contained in the RR-frame received. The checkpointing function itself is protected by timeout. The timer is started upon transmission of the *P*-bit, and stopped when the *F*-bit is received. When the timer expires, transmission of an RR-frame with the *P*-bit set is repeated.

Medium-Access Control: User systems are attached to the rings through ring adapters which implement the medium-access control functions described in Section II-A. We assume that ring adapters do not cause any noticeable increase in delay or decrease in throughput.

III. Network Performance for IEEE 802.2 Type-2 LLC

In this section, we first define the performance measures and list the assumptions underlying our examples. We then discuss simulation results pertaining to a network in which the IEEE 802.2 type-2 LLC as defined in [4] is employed.

A. Performance Measures

We shall restrict the discussion to two basic performance measures, throughput and end-to-end delay, both measured at the higher layer interface, because data units are delivered there without errors and in the proper sequence.

Throughput of a connection is defined as the mean number of bits received at both ends across the higher layer interface per unit time. In the subsequent examples, we shall usually show the total throughput of all connections in the network.

End-to-end delay is defined as the time elapsed between supplying a data unit to LLC at the higher layer interface in the source node until receiving it across this interface at the sink node.

For the subsequent discussion, we need to specify a further quantity called "offered data rate." This is defined as the mean number of bits generated by an application for transmission per unit time under the condition that the application is not halted because of backpressure (cf. Section II-C).

B. Assumptions

The choice of values for the simulation parameters given below is based on the parameters specified in [1], [2], and [4], and on experience gained in experimental implementations [6].

The transmission rates investigated are 4 Mbits/s for the local rings and 4 or 16 Mbits/s for the backbone. Bridges are assumed to need 300 μs to process one frame, unless otherwise specified. The default size of each of the two bridge buffer pools is assumed to be 4 kbytes. The maximum *I*-field length is 0.5 kbyte; the framing overhead of *I*-frames and the length of *S*-frames is 24 bytes. The time intervals between generation of messages are assumed to be exponentially distributed. The mean message length is 1 kbyte; the coefficient of variation 1.5. This message length distribution, together with the effect of message segmentation and the superposition of *S*-frames, results in an overall frame-length distribution that resembles the bimodal distribution observed in measurements [7] with a mean of about 250 bytes.

Execution of the LLC protocol is assumed to require the following processing times: a) transmit I-frame (first time): 2 ms; b) receive in-sequence I-frame and transmit RR-frame: 2.5 ms; c) receive RR-frame and delete I-frame(s): 0.75 ms; d) receive out-of-sequence I-frame and transmit REJ-frame: 1 ms; e) receive REJ- or RR-frame with F-bit and retransmit I-frame(s): 1 ms; f) receive out-of-sequence I-frame and transmit nothing: 0.5 ms; g) handle timer interrupt and transmit RR-frame: 1 ms; h) receive RR-frame with P-bit and transmit RR-frame with F-bit: 1 ms.

The LLC timeout value chosen is 250 ms. The backpressure threshold value B defined in Section II-C is set to the window size plus 4. This gives a source node sufficient flexibility to prepare I-frames for later transmission also during times when the LLC window is closed.

C. Results

Figure 4 shows the total throughput as a function of the total offered data rate. Each of the 12 stations attached to a ring is assumed to generate the same amount of traffic and to have a logical link set up to a station on a different ring. I-frame transmission on each logical link is two-way. The backbone transmission speed is 4 Mbits/s. Bridges operate in nonpriority mode.

When the offered data rate is increased from zero, throughput initially follows linearly. As the backbone becomes noticeably loaded, queues of frames waiting to enter the backbone build up in the bridges, and eventually buffer overflow occurs. Loss of an I-frame leads to the retransmission of one or more I-frames, depending on the number of I-

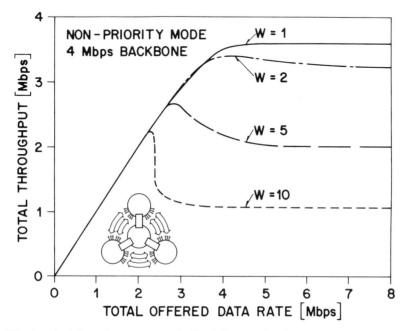

Fig. 4.   Total throughput versus total offered data rate for different window sizes W.

frames a station has outstanding when it receives an REJ or has performed checkpointing. Since the window size sets an upper limit to the number of frames to be retransmitted per lost frame, the additional traffic created by retransmissions decreases with smaller window sizes. This explains the significant differences between the throughput values pertaining to different window sizes.

For the same example, Fig. 5 shows the mean end-to-end delay as a function of the total throughput. At small throughput values, the message delay is higher for small window sizes. This is caused by the time periods during which stations cannot transmit pending I-frames because the window is closed. As throughput increases, delay also increases, owing to contention at the various network resources. When the throughput approaches the maximum value attainable, delays increase very steeply. Further increase of the offered data rate leads to both a decrease in throughput and an increase in delays. In the traffic-load range beyond the maximum throughput, delays grow to unacceptably high values. Taking into account possible fluctuations in the traffic, it is advisable to configure the network such that the offered data rate is sufficiently smaller than the maximum throughput. However, given the peakedness of data traffic, it is an open question whether this can always be guaranteed in a real installation.

We next consider the network performance under the same assumptions as above, except for a significantly faster backbone, i.e., 16 Mbits/s; see Fig. 6. In contrast to the previous example, here the system bottleneck is not the backbone but the local rings. At higher ring utilizations, queues of frames waiting to enter the local rings build up in the bridges, and eventually overflow of the buffer pools in the direction backbone to local rings occurs.

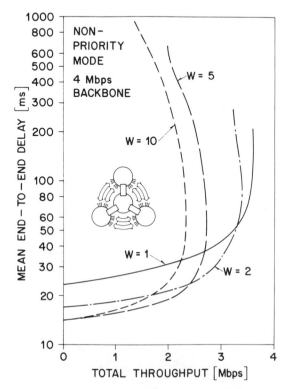

Fig. 5.   Mean end-to-end delay versus total throughput for different window sizes W.

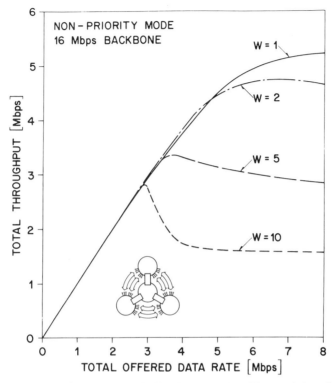

Fig. 6.   Total throughput versus total offered data rate for different window sizes W.

Frame losses have the same effect as described in the context of Fig. 4; hence, we obtain a similar throughput characteristic.

Figure 7 shows the delay-throughput characteristic for the same scenario. Except for smaller absolute delay values, we observe the same tendencies as for the lower backbone speed.

In both of the above examples, bridges do not make use of priority access to the local rings. In Fig. 8, we consider the same scenario as in the previous example; however, bridges employ priority access to the local rings. We observe substantial improvement compared to nonpriority mode (Fig. 6). In fact, for all the window sizes investigated, no or negligibly few frame losses were observed. The explanation of this remarkable effect is as follows. When priority access for bridges is employed, access of stations to their local ring is delayed, slowing down both the injection of new I-frames into the network and the returning of acknowledgments. Delayed acknowledgments, in turn, further throttle the transmission of I-frames because of the LLC window flow-control mechanism. The overall effect is similar to that of flow-control schemes suggested for wide-area packet-switching networks, in which packets are handled with higher priority the closer they are to their destination [8]–[10].

Figure 9 shows the corresponding delay-throughput characteristic. It should be pointed out that [as will become clear from a subsequent example (Fig. 13)] the effectiveness of the priority-mode operation is due to a great extent to the symmetry of the traffic pattern assumed in this example.

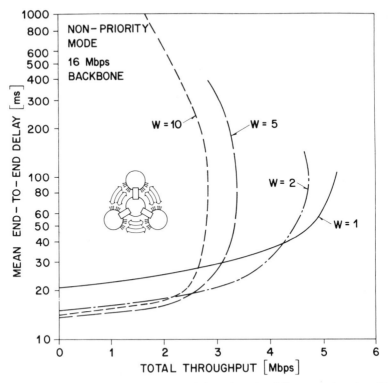

Fig. 7.   Mean end-to-end delay versus total throughput for different window sizes W.

A discussion of priorities for bridges would be incomplete without considering their impact on how fair local-ring bandwidth is shared between intra-ring and inter-ring connections. Figure 10 addresses this question for the following scenario: 24 stations are attached to each ring; 12 of them communicate with 12 stations attached to two other rings; each of the other 12 stations has a logical link set up with a station on the same ring. I-frame flow is two-way on each connection. All stations generate the same amount of traffic. The figure shows the throughput of all inter-ring and all intra-ring connections as the offered data rate is varied. When priority mode is employed, we observe a fair sharing of the bandwidth between the two connection types in the sense that the total throughput of both is equal, almost completely independent of the traffic load and the LLC window size. In nonpriority mode, throughput becomes very unbalanced when the local rings are heavily utilized: high throughput for intra-ring connections, low throughput for inter-ring connections. The explanation for this effect is as follows. In nonpriority mode, the intra-ring connections as a whole obtain much better service than the inter-ring connections, because the latter have to share the single-access points of the bridges to the local rings. Furthermore, at larger window sizes, a significant portion of the bandwidth available for inter-ring traffic is lost due to retransmissions; therefore, unfairness between inter- and intra-ring connections is even more pronounced.

Figures 11 and 12 present further results for a network carrying both inter- and intra-ring traffic. The situation considered here is that 12 stations attached to two rings transmit information frames to 12 stations on the third ring. Further connections are set up among

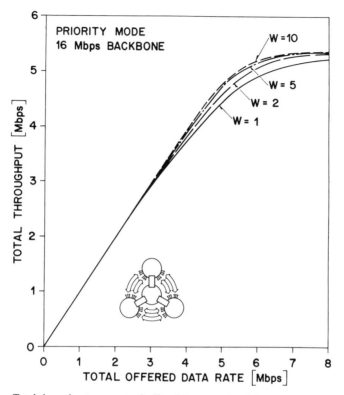

Fig. 8.   Total throughput versus total offered data rate for different window sizes W.

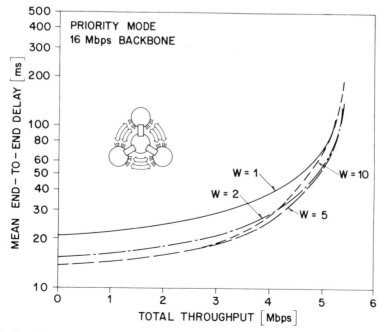

Fig. 9.   Mean end-to-end delay versus total throughput for different window sizes W.

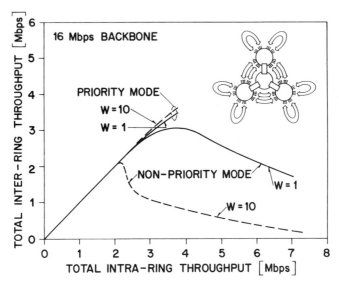

Fig. 10.   Total inter-ring versus total intra-ring throughput for different window sizes W.

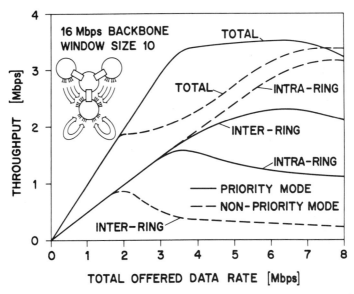

Fig. 11.   Inter-ring, intra-ring, and total network throughput versus total offered data rate.

12 additional stations on the third ring. We consider both priority and nonpriority modes for a window size of 10. Figure 11 shows the throughput on the inter- and intra-ring connections and the total network throughput as a function of the total offered data rate; Figure 12 gives the corresponding end-to-end delay results. In nonpriority mode, we again observe unfair sharing of the ring bandwidth between intra- and inter-ring connections. It is interesting that this unfairness already exists at relatively small offered data rates and becomes very pronounced at high loads. In priority mode, fair ring bandwidth sharing is

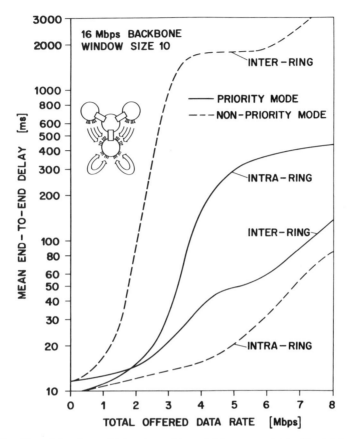

Fig. 12.   Mean inter-ring and intra-ring end-to-end delay versus total offered data rate.

achieved up to rather high offered data rates. At very high traffic loads, priority mode tends to favor the inter-ring connections, and then delays on both connection types deviate distinctly. However, this unfairness effect is by far less severe than the one in nonpriority mode. Furthermore, Fig. 11 reveals that also from a total network throughput point of view, priority mode is superior to nonpriority mode.

The conclusion from the examples shown so far is that use of priority ring access for bridges has two distinct advantages. It yields better overall efficiency and fairer sharing of the ring bandwidth.

It is important, however, to understand that priority mode does not avoid congestion problems under all circumstances, as the following two examples demonstrate.

1) When, in the scenario of Figs. 4 and 5, priority mode is employed, we observe basically the same throughput and delay characteristics as for nonpriority mode. This is not surprising, since the network bottleneck is the backbone, and hence, providing bridges with priority access to their local rings cannot change performance significantly.

2) Even the combination of a fast backbone with ring-access priority for bridges is not always sufficient to avoid congestion problems, as our next sample in Fig. 13 demonstrates. Six stations attached to one ring and the same number of stations attached to a second ring transmit *I*-frames to 12 stations on the third ring. For larger window sizes, we observe the typical throughput characteristic, indicating congestion in the bridge

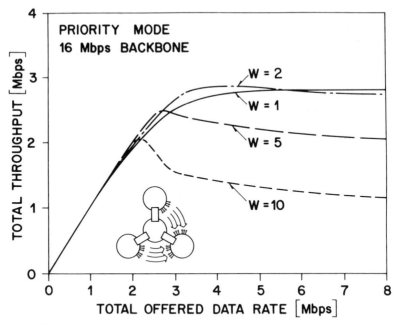

Fig. 13.   Total throughput versus total offered data rate for different window sizes W. 2 × 4 kbyte bridge buffer.

connecting the backbone with the third ring when the offered data rate exceeds a certain value.

A further important question is to what extent the bridge-buffer size affects performance. Figure 14 shows the throughput characteristic for the same scenario as in Fig. 13, except that bridges now have twice as much buffer space as before. Comparison of Figs. 13 and 14 indicates that there is some gain in throughput by enlarging the bridge-buffer size from two

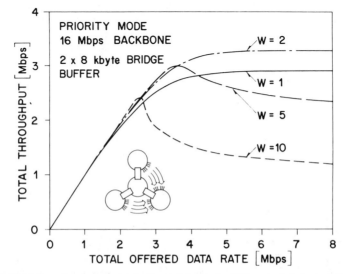

Fig. 14.   Total throughput versus total offered data rate for different window sizes W. 2 × 8 kbyte bridge buffer.

times 4 kbytes to two times 8 kbytes. However, the gain is modest, especially in an overload situation, for the following reason. When the input traffic to a bridge approaches its output capabilities, its buffers tend to fill up completely, irrespective of the absolute buffer size, and therefore, frame losses cannot be reduced by increasing the bridge-buffering capacity.

All the results shown so far have indicated that a small window size is an effective means of minimizing congestion. However, a small window size can also be a disadvantage, e.g., when only a small number of stations is simultaneously active. In Fig. 15, we show the throughput characteristic of a network in which only two stations on each ring communicate with two stations attached to a different ring. We observe that the total throughput can be substantially improved by increasing the window size. This indicates that at small window sizes, a small number of stations are not able to make full use of the available bandwidth, because acknowledgments do not return sufficiently quickly.

IV. DYNAMIC FLOW CONTROL

A. Concept

The results shown in the previous section demonstrate that in case of congested bridges, network performance can be severely degraded. This suggests that the architecture should be enhanced by providing an effective flow-control mechanism to ensure efficient operation under both normal traffic load and overload.

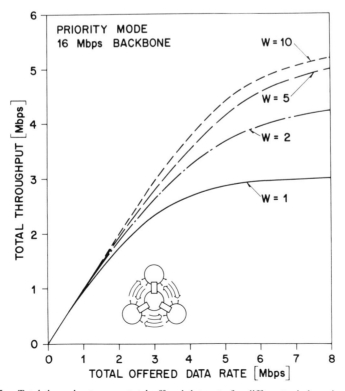

Fig. 15.   Total throughput versus total offered data rate for different window sizes W.

Our specific proposal is to introduce the following dynamic flow-control algorithm into the IEEE 802.2 type-2 protocol. Initially, stations use the window size as defined during the setup of the logical link. Whenever a station needs to retransmit an *I*-frame (either because of a received reject frame or after checkpointing), it sets its window size to 1. Afterwards, the window size is increased by 1 (up to the initial value) for every *n*th successfully transmitted (i.e., acknowledged) *I*-frame.

The rationale behind this algorithm is as follows. Under normal conditions, i.e., no congestion, the actual window size used is the one initially chosen by the communicating stations. By reducing the window size to 1 whenever there is an indication of a possible congestion, we achieve a high responsiveness of the flow-control mechanism in the sense that an immediate and very effective throttling of the network input traffic is performed. Subsequent to reduction, stations again attempt to increase their window sizes. This process is tightly coupled to the reception of acknowledgments. Hereby, we achieve control of the speed by which the window size is increased, by the momentary ability of the network to transport frames successfully.

We subsequently show how the multiring network performs when this enhanced LLC protocol is employed.

B. Results

We first address the question of selecting an appropriate value for the parameter *n* in the dynamic window-size algorithm. The value of *n* specifies how many *I*-frames a station needs to transmit successfully (following a window-size reduction) before it increases its window size by 1.

For the scenario previously studied in Figs. 4 and 5, in Fig. 16 we show the total network throughput as a function of the total offered data rate for different values of *n*. The initial

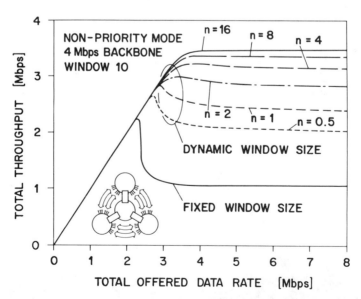

Fig. 16. Total throughput versus total offered data rate for dynamic window-size LLC with initial window size 10. (Note: *n* = 0.5 means that the window size is increased by 2 per acknowledgment.)

window size is 10. We observe substantial improvement in throughput when the window size is dynamically adjusted; the gain is higher for larger n. The incremental gain in throughput decreases, however, as n increases; see, for example, the small difference between $n = 8$ and $n = 16$. For small values of n, the window is opened too rapidly, i.e., the throttling effect does not last long enough.

For the same example, Fig. 17 shows the end-to-end delay as a function of the total throughput. It can be seen that the delay characteristic is better for larger parameter n; in particular, for $n = 8$ or greater, the behavior is almost ideal.

For the scenario previously considered in the context of Fig. 13 where the entire I-frame traffic is flowing to one ring, Fig. 18 shows the improvement attained through the dynamic window algorithm. Again, a value of $n = 8$ already yields excellent performance. A general observation from numerous simulations has been that, even under extreme overload, the frame-loss frequency in bridges is never substantially greater than 1 percent, when the dynamic window-size algorithm with $n \geq 8$ is employed. Under this condition, only a very small fraction of the bandwidth is lost for retransmissions, and hence, performance is excellent. For this reason, we chose to use $n = 8$ in the subsequent examples, intended to show further interesting aspects of the dynamic flow-control algorithm.

The first question we address is whether the dynamic window-size algorithm has an

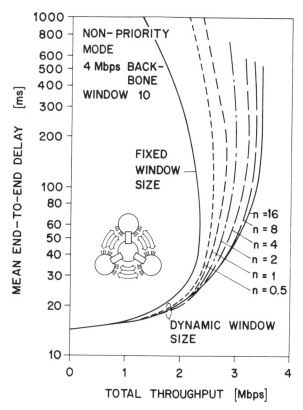

Fig. 17.   Mean end-to-end delay versus total throughput for dynamic window-size LLC with initial window size 10. (Note: $n = 0.5$ means that the window size is increased by 2 per acknowledgment.)

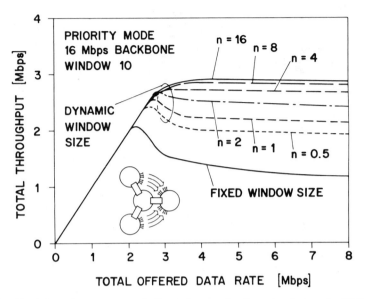

Fig. 18. Total throughput versus total offered data rate for dynamic window-size LLC with initial window size 10. (Note: $n = 0.5$ means that the window size is increased by 2 per acknowledgment.)

impact on fairness. We consider the same example as in Fig. 11. For the dynamic window-size algorithm with an initial window of 10 and $n = 8$, Fig. 19 shows the throughput of the inter- and intra-ring connections and the total network throughput for both priority and nonpriority modes. The figure demonstrates that the overall efficiency in terms of the total throughput is excellent for both modes when the dynamic window-size algorithm is employed. In the case of nonpriority mode, throughput of the inter-ring connections is significantly improved compared to the fixed-window LLC; at medium and high traffic

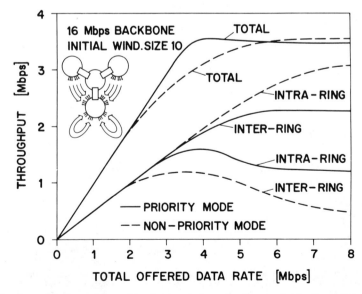

Fig. 19. Inter-ring, intra-ring, and total network throughput versus total offered data rate.

loads, however, there still exists a distinct unfairness between the two connection types in nonpriority mode. In priority mode, fairness is good for offered data rates up to the ring transmission rate of 4 Mbits/s. At high overload, priority mode tends to favor the inter-ring connections.

For the scenario underlying Figs. 13, 14, and 18, we compare in Fig. 20 the throughput characteristics of the dynamic window-size LLC and the fixed window-size LLC for three different bridge-buffer sizes. We have already observed (see Figs. 13 and 14) that for larger fixed-window sizes, the overload behavior is not improved through bigger bridge buffers. On the other hand, the dynamic window-size algorithm yields a stable throughput behavior even for relatively small bridge-buffer sizes, in the sense that throughput never decreases with increasing offered data rate. With the dynamic window, throughput is improved by bigger bridge buffers, but increasing the buffer size beyond the two times 8 kbytes shown in the figure does not yield any noticeable further improvement.

For both fixed and dynamic window-size LLC, Fig. 21 shows the total throughput of the network with a 16 Mbit/s backbone ring and priority ring access for bridges. For the case of 0.3 ms mean bridge-processing time per frame, we have already seen from Fig. 8 that performance is excellent even with the fixed window-size LLC. Consequently, the dynamic window-size algorithm yields equally good results in this case. If the frame-processing times in the bridges are substantially longer, i.e., 1.2 ms on the average, the bridge processors become the system bottlenecks at larger values of the offered data rate; hence, we again observe the negative effects of frame losses and retransmissions. The dynamic window also helps to improve performance in this case. The algorithm works in such a way that the bridge processors are very highly utilized, but at the same time, the frame-loss frequency remains small, typically on the order of 1 percent.

In our last example, we reconsider the scenario of a 4 Mbit/s backbone ring and

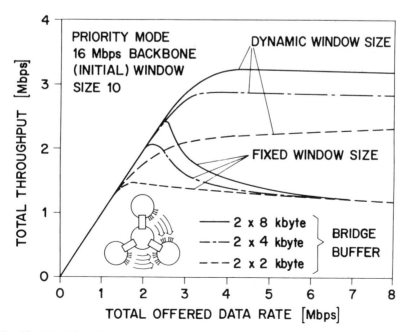

Fig. 20. Total throughput versus total offered data rate for different bridge-buffer sizes.

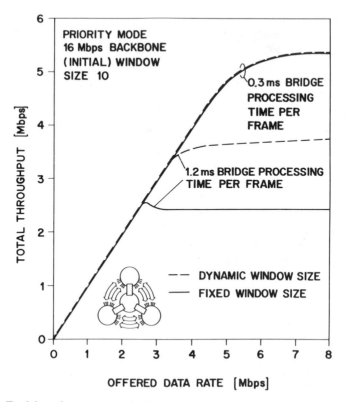

Fig. 21.   Total throughput versus total offered data rate for different bridge-processing times.

completely symmetrical traffic; however, the number of active stations is varied. For the fixed-window protocol, we observe from Fig. 22 that congestion generally becomes worse when the number of stations increases. In contrast, network performance is no longer sensitive to the number of stations, when the dynamic window-size algorithm is employed. These observations shed additional light onto the necessity of a dynamic flow-control scheme in multiring networks. We conclude the discussion of the dynamic flow-control scheme with two final remarks.

1) In all cases where the fixed window-size protocol works without congestion problems, the dynamic flow-control algorithm yields equally good performance since the window size is never, or only very rarely, reduced. A typical example is the one of Fig. 15, for which the throughput characteristic of the dynamic-window LLC with an initial window size of 10 is identical to the result for the fixed window of 10, namely, almost ideal.

2) If I-frames are lost owing to transmission errors and not congestion, the window will be unnecessarily reduced. However, for normally functioning rings with bit error rates of, e.g., 10^{-9} or less, this will not cause any noticeable performance degradation. On the other hand, in failure situations, e.g., transient periods with high error rates or short ring interruptions, our flow-control method may be very helpful. After a failure, heavy overload can occur owing to backlogged traffic and increased recovery activity. Initial experiments suggest that this overload can be very effectively controlled by the dynamic window mechanism. This is the subject of an ongoing study.

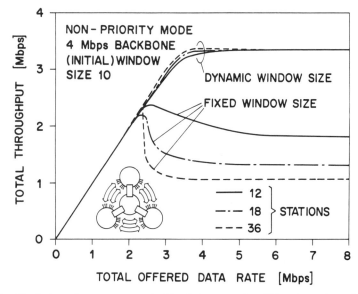

Fig. 22.   Total throughput versus total offered data rate for different number of active stations.

V. Conclusion

In this chapter, we have investigated the performance of local networks consisting of interconnected token rings. We first considered networks in which the IEEE 802.2 type-2 LLC protocol as defined today is employed end-to-end. The key observations of this part of the study are as follows.

1) In a congested network, large fixed window sizes can lead to severe performance degradation. On the other hand, small windows are unnecessarily restrictive and can lead to poor performance if the network is not congested.

2) If bridges are provided with priority to access the local rings, significant improvements both with respect to overall efficiency and fair sharing of bandwidth can be achieved.

3) To a limited extent, performance can be improved by providing larger buffers in bridges. However, large bridge buffers are not sufficient to overcome congestion problems in general.

4) Generally, the congestion problem becomes more severe for larger numbers of active stations in the network.

From these observations, we concluded that the architecture should be enhanced by a suitable flow-control mechanism. Our proposed solution is to add a dynamic window-size algorithm to the LLC protocol. Simulations demonstrate that the algorithm suggested yields close-to-optimal network performance under both normal traffic load and overload conditions, different traffic patterns, different number of stations, and even relatively small bridge-buffer sizes. Besides its effectiveness in minimizing congestion, the new flow-control method has the following attractive properties: 1) it is simple to implement; 2) it is local to the station sending information frames, and hence, no additional information exchange is required; 3) it is compatible with the fixed window-size protocol; 4) bridges need not be involved in flow control; and 5) the medium-access control protocol is not affected.

ACKNOWLEDGMENT

The authors would like to thank D. W. Andrews, N. A. Bouroudjian, K. Kümmerle, D. A. Pitt, and K. K. Sy for many helpful discussions.

REFERENCES

[1] "Local area networks token ring technique," Standard ECMA-89.
[2] "Token ring access method and physical layer specifications," ANSI/IEEE Standard 802.5-1985.
[3] K. K. Sy and D. A. Pitt, "An architecture for interconnected token rings," Proposal to IEEE 802.5 Comm., Feb. 1984.
[4] "Logical link control," ANSI/IEEE Standard 8.02.2-1985.
[5] C. H. Sauer and E. A. MacNair, *Simulation of Computer Communication Systems.* Englewood Cliffs, NJ: Prentice-Hall, 1983.
[6] W. Bux, F. Closs, K. Kümmerle, H. Keller, and H. R. Mueller, "A reliable token ring for local communications," *IEEE J. Select. Areas Commun.,* vol. SAC-1, pp. 756–765, Nov. 1983.
[7] J. F. Shoch and J. A. Hupp, "Measured performance of an Ethernet local network," *Commun. Ass. Comput. Mach.,* vol. 23, pp. 711–721, 1980.
[8] M. Gerla and L. Kleinrock, "Flow control: A comparative survey," *IEEE Trans. Commun.,* vol. COM-28, pp. 553–574, 1980.
[9] A. Giessler, A. Jaegemann, E. Maeser, and J. O. Haenle, "Flow control based on buffer classes," *IEEE Trans. Commun.,* vol. COM-29, pp. 436–443, 1981.
[10] S. S. Lam and M. Reiser, "Congestion control of store-and-forward networks by input buffer limits—An analysis," *IEEE Trans. Commun.,* vol. COM-27, pp. 127–134, 1979.

30
Source Routing for Bridged Local Area Networks

DANIEL AVERY PITT, KIAN-BON K. SY, AND
ROBERT A. DONNAN

Large local area networks in a single establishment can consist of more than one individual local area network interconnected in some fashion. Bridges that interconnect the individual local area networks, using protocols below the network layer, route frames from one local area network to another when the communicating stations are on different local area networks. Source routing is a method in which the source of a frame explicitly identifies the route that a frame is to follow. This chapter discusses the bridging of local area networks and an application of source routing to bridged networks. Participation by the stations and by the bridges that interconnect pairs of local area networks is described. Possible frame formats are shown as enhancements to the standard frame formats of the IEEE Standard 802 local area networks.

INTRODUCTION

Although local area networks have been standardized in the United States [1], Europe [2], and internationally [3], the three medium access control (MAC) standards apply to stations on a single CSMA/CD bus, token bus, or token ring. They contain no architecture for the interconnection of individual local area networks in the same facility or establishment into what we call a *bridged local area network*. The bridging of local area networks, called *segments* of the bridged local area network, may be desirable for a variety of reasons, including improved performance (since each local area network segment contributes its own bandwidth), signal quality (compared to attaching all stations in the establishment to the same local area network segment), and availability (since the breakdown of one segment does not cause all stations on all segments to lose service), as well as simple connectivity when individual local area networks already exist.

In this chapter we explore the subject of local area network interconnection within an architectural framework and describe a particular means of providing interconnection called source routing. Succeeding sections describe the notions of bridge and gateway, the routing problem, the source routing solution, and frame formats to support source routing within an IEEE Standard 802 context.

BRIDGES AND GATEWAYS

Devices that interconnect local area networks may operate at any one of several architectural layers; those that operate within the data link layer are called *bridges*. For local area networks, this layer is subdivided into two sublayers. The *medium access control* sublayer governs the sharing of a common medium by multiple stations, using, for example, token passing, polling, or contention methods, and also the delimiting of frames, the recognition of addresses, and the detection of frame errors. The *logical link control* sublayer governs the exchange of frames between user entities in the end stations, and the standard protocols include provisions for reliable data transfer, using HDLC's asynchronous balanced mode of operation, as well as datagram operation. Bridges, according to our definition, are not involved in these logical link control protocols and so are said to operate within medium access control. A *gateway*, on the other hand, operates at the network layer, thereby terminating both logical link control and network layer protocols and becoming a protocol partner with the end stations at these layers. Figures 1 and 2 show the flows between architectural layers when two *end stations* attached to two different local area networks communicate across the bridged local area network through a bridge and gateway, respectively. Interconnection devices that terminate the logical link control protocols but not the network layer protocols, thereby concatenating logical links, have been proposed but we do not discuss them here.

In both Figs. 1 and 2 each segment retains its own independent medium access control, such as token passing or contention. Since the access controls are asynchronous, the interconnecting devices must buffer complete frames and are not simply bit-stream repeaters.

When local area network segments are connected by bridges, the bridged local area network retains the single local area network properties of short, bounded delay (to allow logical link control timers to operate properly) and uniform address space. Local area network standards [1]–[3] define 16 and 48 bit address formats and require each station on a given local area network to have a unique individual address. The frame formats described in the medium access control standards include both destination and source address fields. The source address must always be the unique individual address of the transmitting station but the destination address can be either an individual or a group address. (Group addresses carry an explicit designation in their first transmitted bit.)

In a bridged local area network, individual station addresses must still be unique, not just

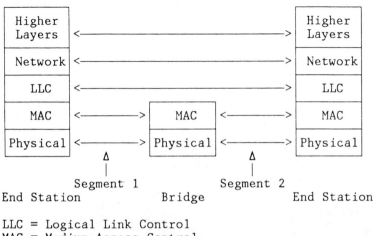

Fig. 1. Protocol flows with a bridge.

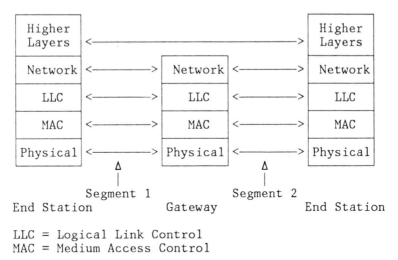

LLC = Logical Link Control
MAC = Medium Access Control

Fig. 2. Protocol flows with a gateway.

unique on one segment. While each of the two stations on a bridge has its own individual station address, the end station does not use this address in the destination address fields of its frame. Rather, it uses the address of the end station it is communicating with. When gateways are used, only network layer addresses must be unique, and local area network station addresses need be unique only on a given segment. When end stations communicate through a gateway, they use the gateway's station address in the destination address field.

Unlike gateways, bridges possess no capabilities for flow control, at either the logical link control sublayer or the network layer, and so, with finite buffer space and no guarantee of timely access to an adjacent segment, are subject to congestion. When congested, a bridge discards frames it cannot store. Recovery of lost frames is the responsibility of the end stations, which can combine error recovery with flow control in a manner that reduces congestion in the bridges [4].

By not being involved in the logical link control or network layer protocols, a bridge obtains several advantages over a gateway. First, performance should be superior to a gateway because fewer layers of protocol must be processed by the bridge. Second, the bridge can avoid mediating incompatibilities between types of link control service employed by the end stations. ANSI/IEEE Standard 802.2-1985 for logical link control defines both connectionless and connection-oriented services, and one or the other should prevail in a sequence of one or more links between end systems.

Finally, the services of a bridge are available to all stations on the bridged local area network regardless of their higher layer protocols. Since local area networks will be populated by stations employing a variety of public and private network architectures, whose differences appear at the network layer and above, only a bridge can act as a service facility available to all. Layers above medium access control can be implemented in a bridge, but only if communication to the bridge as an end station is desired; network management is an example of such communication.

The forwarding of a frame by a bridge involves receiving or *copying* a frame from one local area network segment, processing it internally to the bridge, and transmitting it on an adjacent segment. When a bridge copies a frame, ostensibly because the bridge has determined that the frame should be forwarded, it examines the frame check sequence so that only error-free frames are accepted. A bridge adds or deletes fields that are present in the frame format of only one of the local area networks and, for source routing, might modify existing fields in the frame. If one of the local area networks transmits the most significant bit first (such as an IEEE 802.5 token ring) and the other transmits the least significant bit first (such as an IEEE 802.3 CSMA/CD bus or IEEE 802.4 token bus), the bridge reverses the transmission order of the bits in each byte of the information field (compared to the order of reception). Finally, the bridge calculates a new frame check sequence if the two local area networks have different fields in their frame formats or different orders of bit transmission; such is the case for any dissimilar pair of IEEE Standard 802 networks.

The source and destination addresses are *not* modified by the bridge, and so the bridge transmits frames containing the source address of the originating end station, not its own address. As a corollary, the destination address of a frame is that of the target end station, not that of the bridge. The transmission by the bridge of a frame with a foreign source address requires the bridge to recognize the foreign address in order to properly remove the frame from a token ring. A complete discussion of all aspects of forwarding and frame treatment can be found in [5] for all combinations of IEEE Standard 802 networks.

If the bridge applies a new frame check sequence, the receiver cannot detect errors introduced into the frame by the bridge. Thus, the probability of undetected error in a frame delivered by the data link layer to its user can be increased if the bridges are not extremely reliable. Gateways can introduce undetectable errors as well.

THE ROUTING PROBLEM

Communication between two stations anywhere in the bridged local area network requires the existence of a route between the individual local area network segments on which the two stations reside and also a means for a frame to follow that route. A route constitutes an ordered sequence of local area network segments on which the frame must be transmitted. Bridges are responsible for assuring that a frame follows an appropriate route to its destination, and must therefore decide which frames to forward. However, the determination of which route a frame is intended to follow can be the responsibility of the end stations, the bridges, or a central management facility. (Indeed, certain topologies (spanning trees) allow no choice of routes in a bridged network.) *Source routing* [6]–[9] is an example of the involvement of the end stations in the determination of a route.

While routing in a bridged local area network is similar in many ways to the classical routing problems for networks in general, it does maintain some important differences. Frames on a local area network pass a bridge at high speed and, with no flow control, the bridge must make routing decisions before the next frame arrives. The most common routing criterion in traditional telecommunication networks, cost, is of no importance in the bridged local area network because traffic on a local area network is not subject to tariffs. Instead, a bridge's main criterion is simply whether or not the destination of the frame is on the other side of the bridge. Source routing allows additional criteria, path length and largest supported frame size, to be employed in the selection of a route, but by the end stations, not the bridges.

How a bridge determines whether or not to forward a frame is the most fundamental issue in bridging. Source routing allows bridges to examine a specific routing information field, distinct from the destination address. Other schemes use addresses. Routing on addresses has several disadvantages. Primarily, bridges must maintain routing tables and must be able to execute a table lookup in the time it takes to receive a minimum length frame. Thus, their feasibility is speed-dependent. The tables must also represent up-to-date topology or station-location information. The routing tables can be programmed into the bridge or transmitted to the bridge by a human or program responsible for management of the network, or they can be learned by the bridges by observing frames on the network [10].

Different address structures in the routing tables yield different properties as well. Flat addresses (those with no structure to them) require routing tables of a size that can be on the order of half the number of stations in the network [11] and constrain the interconnection topology so that only spanning trees and individual bridges (no loops, multiple paths, or parallel bridges) are allowed [11], [12]. Hierarchical addresses, in which subfields of the address correspond to segments or regions in the bridged network, allow the routing tables to be smaller but constrain the interconnection topology further [11], require a station to obtain a new address when it moves, and prevent the use of universally administered addresses because addresses are location-dependent. Group-addressed frames must always be forwarded, or broadcast, to all segments in the bridged network unless the bridge somehow knows where all members of each group are located. Frames addressed to stations whose addresses are not in the tables, because of aging of the tables or other causes, are also broadcast.

The routing information for source routing consists of a series of identifiers of the local area network segments that a frame transmitted from one station to another must traverse. Arbitrary binary numbers, unique within the bridged network, suffice for the identifiers in the routing information field.

Consider the example of a bridged network in Fig. 3. In this example, the bridged network consists of two buses (CSMA/CD or token), two rings, and five bridges. Each segment has a unique identifier (a number between 1 and 4) and the bridges are labeled $B0$ through $B4$. Segments 1, 2, and 3 themselves form a loop, and bridges $B0$ and $B1$ connect

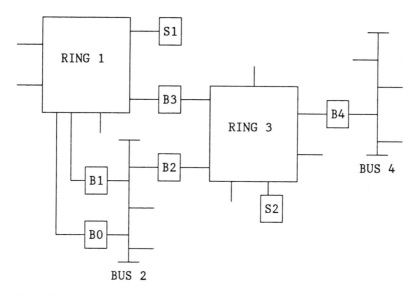

S = End Station   B = Bridge

Fig. 3.   Bridged network example.

ring 1 and bus 2 in parallel. Either route (1, 3) or route (1, 2, 3) allows communication between station $S1$ on ring 1 and station $S2$ on ring 3. The same route followed in the opposite direction allows communication between station $S2$ and station $S1$. The distinction between the parallel bridges between ring 1 and bus 2 is discussed later.

SOURCE ROUTING: THE END STATIONS' VIEW

The term source routing stems from the specification by the transmitter, or source, of a frame of the route the frame is to follow. The concept applies to any type of network, not just local area networks [6]–[9]. The source associates the route with the destination station and includes the route in the frame header. Although the route consists of a sequence of segments, identified by their numbers, over which the frame travels, the end stations need not understand or interpret this information. Their involvement is limited to the understanding of only some control information and to some manipulation of the field containing the route. This field, the routing information field, is described later in the chapter.

Route Determination

For any but the smallest of networks, the only practical method of route determination is the dynamic discovery of the route. A station that has no route to a designated target station follows a procedure for learning the route. Once the station knows the route, it merely includes it in each frame to the target station.

A key element of dynamic discovery is the broadcasting of frames throughout the network to explore all possible paths to the target. (With the absence of tariffs, broadcasting in a bridged local area network is more feasible than in a wide area network.) A path is found when one or more of these frames reaches the target station. Since broadcasting uses bandwidth on all segments, it is important to broadcast only when necessary. Thus, source routing includes an explicit distinction between broadcast and nonbroadcast frames. Broadcast frames are forwarded by bridges so that they travel all possible routes to all segments. They are identified by an indicator in the (two-octet) control subfield of the routing information field and for route discovery carry the individual address of the target station in the destination address field. They are sometimes called *all-routes broadcast* frames to distinguish them from *all-stations broadcast* frames, which, as defined in [1]–[3], carry the all-stations broadcast group address (all ones) in the destination address field.

Considerable choice exists in the combination of individual, group, or all-stations broadcast addressing (in the destination address field) and nonbroadcast or all-routes broadcast routing (in the routing information field). The routing information field determines if a frame stays on the originator's segment only, traverses a specific sequence of segments, or reaches every segment. The destination address, independently and orthogonally, determines which stations *on segments determined by the routing information field* receive the frame.

For route discovery, the first step is the transmission of a frame, addressed to the target's individual address, containing a broadcast indication. Any frame type can be used, but with caution. When there are multiple routes to the target, the target will receive multiple copies. Therefore, only those frames that can be safely received multiple times should be used. Alternatively, a *single-route broadcast* can be used to avoid multiple copies of a given frame from reaching a station even when multiple routes exist. A single-route broadcast capability requires certain bridges, configured in a spanning tree, to be specially designated to forward frames carrying the single-route broadcast indication. Note that even though a broadcast frame appears on all segments, no station other than the desired target will receive the frame because of the uniqueness of individual station addresses in the bridged network. Since the source's desire is to have the target return the frame, which has acquired routing information (as the next major section describes), a frame that stimulates an immediate response is also desirable.

Consider again the example of Fig. 3 and suppose station $S1$ needs to establish a route to station $S2$. Station $S1$ transmits a frame carrying station $S2$'s individual address in the destination address field and an all-routes broadcast indication in the routing control field. Bridges $B0$ and $B1$ forward the frame onto bus 2 (resulting in two frames on bus 2) and bridge $B3$ forwards the frame onto ring 3. Bridge $B2$ forwards both frames from bus 2 onto ring 3. Station $S2$ receives all three frames that have reached ring 3 since all carry its address. Each carries a different route: (1, 3) directly, (1, 2, 3) via bridge $B0$, and (1, 2, 3) via bridge $B1$. At the same time, all three frames reach bus 4 since bridge $B4$ forwards them because of their broadcast designation. This apparently unnecessary broadcasting to bus 4 is the price paid for the freedom of allowing a station to reside anywhere in the bridged network without the bridges having to know its location.

Route Association Between Stations

When a station, in this case the target, receives a broadcast frame, the frame contains routing information, so the station returns the frame without the broadcast designation. The frame follows the route contained in the routing information field, thereby traversing only a specific sequence of segments, not all segments. The data or information field of the response depends only on the information field of the broadcast frame and is unrelated to route discovery.

An alternative method of exploring all possible routes is the transmission by the source of a single-route broadcast frame and the return, by the target, of a response broadcast to all routes. This method relieves the target of the burden of multiple responses, and makes sense for popular targets such as servers. With either method, the source receives a response for each possible route.

When multiple responses to the broadcast frame (one for each possible route) return to the source, the source chooses which one to use. The decision can be based on which returns first (indicating perhaps the path with least delay), which contains the fewest segment numbers (indicating perhaps the path with the least likelihood of failure), or the path allowing the largest frame size (a feature discussed later). If the source possesses more information about the intervening segments, it could discriminate according to security or other considerations. Routes not chosen can be stored for future use in case the chosen route subsequently fails.

The chosen route is then associated with the target and included in all subsequent frames sent to it. Similarly, the target associates the route with the source, allowing more straightforward problem determination should the route fail. The association can be solely with the destination address or with the combination of destination address and destination and source link service access points. The former case restricts all communication between two stations to the same route. The latter case allows different link connections or conversations to use different routes.

The duration over which the routing information is associated with a destination station depends on the type of link control employed. If connection-oriented service is used, the routing information can be maintained for the duration of the link connection. If connectionless service is used, an aging timer can be implemented, the station can wait for indications that the link has failed or that the destination station has moved, or the routing information can be correlated with a transport connection.

SOURCE ROUTING: THE BRIDGES' VIEW

The actions of bridges in forwarding frames can be partitioned into two classes, corresponding to the treatment of broadcast and nonbroadcast frames.

Broadcast Frames

A bridge distinguishes a broadcast frame by the broadcast indicator in the routing control field. Note that source routing bridges make routing decisions based on the routing information field, not on the destination address. A bridge that receives a broadcast frame assists in assuring that it reach all segments and accumulate routing information as it does so. Bridges provide that information by *inserting into the frame* the segment numbers that describe the route. To accommodate routes of different length, the routing information field is of variable length. In addition to the two octets of routing control, there are two octets for every segment number. A length field in the routing control field describes the length of the routing information field, including routing control.

The first bridge in the route receives a broadcast frame with only the two octets of routing control and no segment numbers. It inserts into the frame two segment numbers, that of the segment from which it received the frame and that of the segment on which it is about to transmit the frame. Successive bridges insert only the number of the adjacent segment on which the frame is about to be transmitted. Before transmitting the frame, the bridge modifies the length field to include the two (or four for the first bridge) additional octets and recalculates the frame check sequence since the frame has been modified.

When a broadcast frame reaches the target, which recognizes its own address in the destination address field, the frame contains a route describing exactly the sequence of segments from the source to the target. Frames that wander to other parts of the bridged network, accumulating irrelevant routing information, never reach the target and so never get received by any station.

In the network of Fig. 3 station $S1$ transmits a broadcast frame with only the two octets of routing control in the routing information field. Bridges $B0$ and $B1$ each add the segment numbers 1 and 2 to the frame (with no indication of whether the segment is a ring or a bus) and transmit the frame on bus 2. Bridge $B3$ inserts the numbers 1 and 3 to the frame with no segment numbers and transmits it onto ring 3. Bridge $B2$ adds segment number 3 to the two frames containing segment numbers 1 and 2. Thus, three frames appear on ring 3 with routing information (1, 3), (1, 2, 3), and (1, 2, 3), respectively. Bridge $B4$ forwards each of these to bus 4 and adds segment number 4 to each route. Since station $S2$ resides on ring 3, only the frames with routes ending in 3 are saved and responded to.

Bridges employ two techniques to prevent broadcast frames from circulating indefinitely around the network. Each bridge maintains a limit on the number of hops a frame it transmits can cover. If the frame has already reached that limit, indicated by the length of the routing information field, the bridge does not forward the frame. The bridge also scans the routing information field for the number of the segment on which it is about to transmit the frame. If that number is already present in the routing information field, the bridge does not forward the frame. This check allows the user to configure a network topology containing loops, for multiple routes, short path lengths, or redundancy, without allowing frames to circulate around them.

Hence, in the example network, bridge $B1$ does not forward back to ring 1 the frame forwarded from ring 1 to bus 2 by bridge $B0$, and similarly for bridge $B0$. Bridge $B3$ forwards neither frame forwarded from bus 2 to ring 3 since the frames already carry segment number 1. But bridge $B2$ *does* forward the frame on ring 3 that bridge $B3$ forwarded from ring 1, since that frame had not yet been on bus 2. It goes no further, however, because bridges $B0$ and $B1$ recognize that the frame has been on ring 1 already.

Nonbroadcast Frames

A bridge distinguishes a nonbroadcast frame, too, by the indicator in the routing control field. Such a frame is assumed to contain routing information and the bridge needs only to determine if it should forward the frame. If the bridge is in the route, it will find in the routing information field the sequence of two segment numbers corresponding to the segments it joins and can then forward the frame. If the two segment numbers are not present, or are present but not adjacent, the bridge does not forward the frame. Again, to avoid indefinite circulation, the bridge also checks to make sure that the number of the next segment does not appear more than once in the routing information field.

For the example network, suppose that station $S1$ chooses the shortest route, (1, 3), to station $S2$ and transmits a nonbroadcast frame to it. Both bridges $B0$ and $B1$ scan the routing information field for the sequence (...1, 2...) and not finding it do not forward the frame. Bridge $B3$ does find the sequence (...1, 3...) that it scans for and so forwards the frame to ring 3. Bridge $B2$ does not see its characteristic sequence (...3, 2...) nor does bridge $B4$ see its sequence (...3, 4...). Notice that the two sides of a bridge scan for the same sequence of segment numbers but in the opposite order.

Parallel Bridges

Parallel bridges between adjacent segments serve two purposes. One purpose is to provide multiple routes between two adjacent local area networks, for the reasons of reliability, backup, or different route characteristics. The other purpose is to provide greater throughput than a single bridge can maintain. Additional bridges can be added in parallel with no disruption of existing traffic, as traffic needs increase. The new bridge will accumulate traffic as routes are established, especially if the old bridges are congested and impose greater delays on the discovery frames they forward. In general, the random nature of new route requests distributes the routes that are established over the set of possible routes, whether through parallel bridges or parallel segments [13].

When parallel bridges are employed, special provisions are required to partition the traffic between them; otherwise multiple copies of nonbroadcast frames will be generated. A straightforward solution is the subdivision of the segment number field into a portion shared by the parallel bridges and a portion distinct for each. For example, the 16 bit segment numbers can be divided into 12 bits for the common segment portion and 4 bits for the individual bridge portion, allowing up to 16 parallel bridges between a given pair of adjacent local area networks. This subdivision prevails for all bridges in the bridged network. Thus, bridges examine only the common segment portion when checking for looping broadcast frames but test the whole segment number when checking for a route match in nonbroadcast frames.

For example, bridges $B0$ and $B1$ in Fig. 3 receive the frame broadcast by station $S1$ on ring 1. Bridge $B0$ inserts the common segment portion for segment 1 and its own individual bridge portion, plus the common segment portion for segment 2. (What it inserts for an individual bridge portion for segment 2 is immaterial as any succeeding bridges will overwrite it.) The routing information can then be described by the notation $(1|0, 2| -)$ for "segment 1; bridge 0; segment 2; don't care." Similarly, bridge $B1$ inserts the routing information $(1|1, 2| -)$ in the frame it forwards. When bridge $B1$ scans bridge $B0$'s broadcast frame, it checks only for $(...1|...)$; because it finds it, bridge $B1$ does not forward the frame back to ring 1. After bridge $B2$ forwards both frames onto ring 3, they appear as $(1|0, 2|2, 3| -)$ and $(1|1, 2|2, 3| -)$. Bridge $B3$ sees $(...1|...)$ in both frames and correctly forwards neither back to ring 1.

Suppose finally that station $S1$ chooses the route $(1|0, 2|2, 3| -)$ to station $S2$. Bridge $B0$ always scans nonbroadcast frames on ring 1 for the sequence $(...1|0, 2| - ...)$, which is present in station $S1$'s frames to station $S2$. Bridge $B1$ scans for $(...1|1, 2| - ...)$, which it does not find, and bridge $B3$ scans for $(...1|3, 3| - ...)$, which it does not find.

In this example we have suggested that the individual bridge portions are unique in the bridged network but this is not necessary. We have allowed the individual bridge portions, which are part of the format, to match the labels in Fig. 3, which are not part of the format, only for clarity. Individual bridge portions need to be unique only among the bridges in parallel between the same two segments. Thus, bridges $B0$, $B2$, $B3$, and $B4$ could all use the individual bridge portion zero $(- |0)$.

FRAME FORMATS FOR SOURCE ROUTING

A possible frame format to support source routing is based on the format defined by IEEE Standard 802, with the addition of a routing information field between the source address and information fields. Figure 4 illustrates the new field along with the fields that are common to all three frame formats defined for CSMA/CD bus, token bus, and token ring. Additional fields that are present in only one or two of the standards are not shown. Since the routing information field, as illustrated below in Figs. 5 and 6, contains its own length field, the length field present in a CSMA/CD frame could appear either before or after the

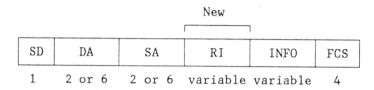

Fig. 4. Frame format for source routing.

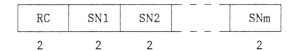

Numbers Indicate Field Length in Octets

RC = Routing Control   SN = Segment Number

Fig. 5. Routing information field.

routing information field. If it appears before the routing information field, it needs to be updated after a bridge has added segment numbers, but the calculation of the length field is a normal part of the transmission of a CSMA/CD frame and in most implementations is performed automatically.

Since the presence of the routing information field is not always mandatory, as when the two stations are on the same segment, an indication of its presence has been added to the source address field. By having the choice of allowing a frame to leave its own local area network segment or not, a station can look first for a target on its own segment, avoiding the additional overhead of broadcast traffic on the other local area networks. This is particularly useful when looking for servers, sharing a group address, that may be present on a number of the interconnected local area network segments.

The first bit of the source address and destination address fields that is transmitted on the physical medium has been defined as the individual/group bit. A source address must always be an individual address, however, so this bit has always been set to 0. This bit is therefore used to indicate the presence of a routing information field. When the indicator is set to 1 by the transmitter of a frame, a routing information field is included in the frame. A transmitter can optionally set the bit to 0 and omit the field in frames that do not leave its own segment.

The routing information field, when present, consists of a two-octet routing control field and up to m two-octet segment number fields, as illustrated in Fig. 5.

The segment number fields, not present when a frame that is broadcast to all local area networks is first transmitted, are added as the frame passes through a sequence of bridges. The number m is limited by the length of one of the subfields within the routing control field. The ordered sequence of segment numbers represents the sequence of segments from the source segment to the target segment.

The routing control field, shown in Fig. 6, is two octets in length. The first octet contains

First Octet   Second Octet

B	LTH	D	LF	r
3	5	1	3	4

Numbers Indicate Field Length in Bits

B   = Broadcast   D = Direction   r = Reserved
LTH = Length   LF = Largest Frame

Fig. 6. Routing control field.

three bits to indicate broadcast (nonbroadcast, all-routes broadcast, or single-route broadcast) and a length (*LTH*) field. The second octet contains a direction indicator (*D*) and three bits for a largest frame code (*LF*).

The unreserved bits in the routing control field are defined as follows.

• *Broadcast (B):* These bits are encoded as shown with the symbol X indicating "don't care."

$$0XX = \text{Nonbroadcast}$$

$$10X = \text{All-routes broadcast}$$

$$11X = \text{Single-route broadcast.}$$

• *Length (LTH):* This five-bit field is used to indicate the length of the routing information field, including the routing control field, in octets. Since the routing information field is of variable length, while all other fields in the frame header are of fixed length, a length indicator is needed so that the rest of the frame can be parsed.

For broadcast frames, the length field indicates to a bridge where to insert the next segment number. Thus, for a broadcast frame, this field is initialized to 2 by the transmitting station. It is incremented by 4 by the first bridge that forwards the frame because the first bridge places both the first and second segment numbers in the frame. Successive bridges insert only one segment number and therefore increment the length by 2. The length field also indicates how many networks have been traversed.

For a nonbroadcast frame already carrying routing information, the field indicates the length of the routing information field, and remains unchanged as the frame traverses the network. Allotting five bits to the length field allows the number of segments in a route m to be as high as 14. The number of segments in a bridged network, of course, can be enormous, depending on the configuration of the network, the desired mean path length, and the number of bridges [11], [12].

• *Direction (D):* This bit indicates to a bridge whether a frame is traveling from the originating station to the target or the other way around. Its use allows the list of segment numbers in the routing information field to appear in the same order for frames traveling in both directions along the route.

For broadcast frames, the transmitting station sets $D = 0$, and receivers can uniformly complement the received D bit when they glean routing information from frames with routing information fields. For nonbroadcast frames, the originator normally sets $D = 0$ in all frames transmitted to the target, while the target sets $D = 1$ in all frames to the originator.

• *Largest Frame (LF):* These bits specify, through an encoding, the largest size of the information field (at the medium access control level) that may be transmitted between two end stations on a specific route. Proposed encodings are shown below with their origins.

000: ≤516 octets (ISO subnetwork including LLC header)

001 : ≤1500 octets (IEEE Standard 802.3)

010: ≤2052 octets (80×24 character screen with control)

011 : ≤ 4472 octets (FDDI, or IEEE Standard 802.5 with 9 ms THT)

100 : ≤ 8191 octets (IEEE Standard 802.4)

101 : Reserved

110 : Reserved

111 : Initial value on broadcast frames.

A station originating a broadcast frame sets the LF bits to $B'111'$, the largest possible encoding. Bridges that relay a broadcast frame examine the LF bits. If the designated size of the LF is greater than the bridge can handle or than its adjoining segments allow, the bridge reduces the largest frame encoding accordingly. The LF value returned in the responses to the broadcast indicates the largest possible frame each specified route can handle.

CONCLUSION

An application of source routing to the interconnection of local area networks has been introduced. This interconnection enables large networks to be comprised of multiple local area network segments, for improved connectivity, signal quality, performance, and availability. Devices called bridges, which connect individual local area networks into a bridged local area network, operate below the logical link control sublayer. Source routing is effected by a routing information field in the frame and a previously unused bit in the source address field to indicate its presence. The routing information is discovered by the communicating stations and provided by the bridges, which then use the information to make routing decisions. The routing information field also provides end stations with a means of determining the largest frame size a route can accommodate, since certain local area networks allow smaller maximum frame sizes than others.

This routing technique is efficient in its use of transmission resources on each local area network, requiring the broadcasting of frames only when locating the target station. Medium access control protocols on each local area network are not affected by the interconnection of local area networks, and only the physical and medium access control layers in a bridge are involved in forwarding frames. The only routing data stored in a bridge are the numbers of the two local area networks it attaches. Neither maintenance of routing tables nor management determination of routes is required.

Source routing allows freedom of station movement and local area network reconfiguration with minimum management intervention and without diminishing the any-to-any connectivity of stations that single local area networks provide. Multiple routes and parallel bridges are supported, both for active redundancy and for incremental additions of capacity. Any addressing scheme is allowed, as are any logical link control and network layer protocols in the end stations. The end stations also learn the maximum frame size supported by a path so that the interconnection of segments supporting different maximum frame sizes does not result in the end stations unknowingly transmitting frames that will be discarded somewhere in the path because of excessive length. This capability allows source routing to be applied to any of the three local area network types standardized by the IEEE, ECMA, and ISO, in any combination.

REFERENCES

[1]   ANSI/IEEE Standards 802.2-1985, 802.3-1985, 802.4-1985, and 802.5-1985, Institute of Electrical and Electronics Engineers, Inc.

[2]   Standards ECMA-80, -81, -82, -89, and -90, European Computer Manufacturers Association.

[3]   Standards ISO 8802/2, 8802/3, 8802/4, 8802/5, International Organization for Standardization.

[4]   W. Bux and D. Grillo, "Flow control in local area networks of interconnected token rings," *IEEE Trans. Commun.*, vol. COM-33, Oct. 1985.

[5]   J. A. Berntsen, J. R. Davin, D. A. Pitt, and N. G. Sullivan, "MAC layer interconnection of IEEE 802 local area networks," *Comput. Networks and ISDN Syst.*, vol. 10, no. 5, 1985.

[6]   D. J. Farber and J. J. Vittal, "Extendibility considerations in the design of the distributed computer system (DCS)," in *Proc. Nat. Telecommun. Conf.*, Nov. 1973.

[7]   C. A. Sunshine, "Source routing in computer networks," *ACM Comput. Commun. Rev.*, vol. 7, Jan. 1977.

[8]   B. Forss, E. Hafner, and M. Tschanz, "Distribution of logical processes in telephone systems," in *Proc. Nat. Telecommun. Conf.*, Nov. 1977.

[9]   J. H. Saltzer, D. P. Reed, and D. D. Clark, "Source routing for campus-wide internet transport," in *Local Networks for Computer Communications*, A. West and P. Janson, Eds. Amsterdam, The Netherlands: North Holland, 1981.

[10] W. Hawe, A. Kirby, and R. Stewart, "Transparent interconnection of local area networks with bridges," *J. Telecommun. Networks*, vol. 3, pp. 116–130, Summer 1984.

[11] D. A. Pitt and K. K. Sy, "Address-based and non-address-based routing schemes for interconnected local area networks," in *Local Area and Multiple Access Networks*, R. L. Pickholtz, Ed. Rockville, MD: Computer Science Press, 1986.

[12] D. A. Pitt and F. Farzaneh, "Topologies and routing for bridged local area networks," in *Proc. IEEE Infocom*, Miami, FL, Apr. 1986.

[13] B. R. Smith, "Routing in interconnected local area networks," Dep. Comput. Sci., Univ. Waterloo, Waterloo, Ontario, Comput. Commun. Networks Group Rep. T-144, May 1986.

Part VII
Software and Applications

Local area networks offer high-speed communication between distributed system components such as intelligent workstations and shared resource controllers. However, a fast physical communication medium is only the first step towards high-speed internode and interprocess communication: the overhead of protocols above medium access control, the way these protocols are implemented, and operating system features can significantly reduce the communication bandwidth that can be utilized by applications. On the other hand, there are very few applications which can efficiently use a data-transfer rate in the Mbit/s range since applications are also limited by the hardware and software context in which they execute. For example, for a file transfer, the ultimate limitation is the speed with which file blocks can be fetched from and stored on disks. Thus, a reasonable goal is to develop communication software that will not limit applications beyond their own intrinsic constraints.

One of the issues which received and still receives a lot of attention is the question of whether to use connectionless or connection-oriented protocols, e.g., to use a connectionless logical link control protocol (IEEE Standard 802.2 Type 1) combined either with the OSI transport protocol class 4 for end-to-end error recovery or with special nonstandard protocols where end-to-end error recovery is left to the application; or to use a connection-oriented logical link control protocol (IEEE Standard 802.2 Type 2) where end-to-end error recovery is not needed at higher protocol layers. Clearly, performance plays a prominent role in determining which protocols or protocol combinations should be used to achieve a desired performance level, e.g., throughput for a file transfer application. On the other hand, it should be noted that criteria like compatibility with communication software which already exists for wide-area communication might represent important economic factors which could outweigh performance considerations. Associated with protocol issues are implementation questions such as buffer passing and context switching. A variety of investigations and implementations showed that copying data to and from buffers between protocol layers is one of the major sources of overhead and that it is preferable to pass buffers between layers by reference. In addition, there are applications like file transfers which involve many levels of software and many I/O operations with associated interrupts and frequent switching between system and user codes. It is intuitively clear that operating systems with inefficient context switching can cause significant performance degradation.

From an application point of view, it can be said that local area networks are a prerequisite for distributed processing. Three different models of distributed processing are conceivable and used in real systems. First, the client/server model where separate server machines support work performed on workstations. The key characteristic of this model is a high degree of autonomy for the individual workstations. This autonomy is achieved by managing the shared resources by highly available machines, usually called servers rather than controlling them by the workstations. The benefit for the user is to be able to insert and remove workstations from the network without affecting other users. An alternative model, sometimes called integrated distributed computing, assumes that each node or processor controls some resources, which can be used from any other node in the system. The basic difference between this scenario and the previous one is that there is no distinction between a server machine and a client machine, i.e., each machine is both a server and a client. Finally, there exists a scenario which is based on a general purpose host machine. Such systems represent a natural evolution from a central time-shared facility towards a distributed system. Intelligent workstations make it possible to off-load many tasks, particularly those dealing with the user interface, while the host continues to provide access to data bases and services developed in the past.

31
A Distributed Experimental Communications System

JOHN D. DeTREVILLE AND W. DAVID SINCOSKIE

The packet experimental communications system (packet XCS) is a new experimental voice and data switch. It uses a local area network (LAN) for digital voice transmission, with local intelligence for switching. The packet XCS also has highly distributed control. The individual sites cooperate to provide user services as well as internal data management.

We have learned that several local networks, including CSMA/CD networks, can be made to work well for voice transmission and that highly distributed control is practical in such a system. A system has been constructed which is used as a testbed for distributed voice and data communications experiments.

I. INTRODUCTION

We have recently designed and implemented a new voice and data switch for experimental use. Our switch, the packet experimental communications system (packet XCS), uses a local area network (LAN) for transmission of packetized digital voice among the voice sites. We have thereby eliminated the central switch. The sites have individual controllers to access the LAN and local intelligence to support switching. We have also eliminated centralized control and data management. The packet XCS distributes these functions to the individual sites, which transmit and receive control and data messages over the LAN. In short, the packet XCS uses a shared transmission facility but has distributed switching, distributed control, and distributed data. Figure 1 shows the XCS system architecture.

While transmission and switching of data have historically been provided on top of voice-oriented mechanisms, recent innovations and cost reductions in digital networks make it possible to implement voice on top of data. The most rapidly evolving field in data communications is LAN technology [1]; high bandwidths can give reasonable voice capacity, recent VLSI support has made LAN's less expensive, and emerging standards promise to aid in planning. The design of the packet XCS is relatively independent of the LAN used (which need only support point-to-point and broadcast packet transmission) although performance is affected by the choice of LAN.

The packet XCS is an experimental system, and this has heavily influenced its design. It has served as a testbed for distributed systems research. Our goal of a highly distributed packet XCS has led us to many interesting theoretical issues. We have had an opportunity

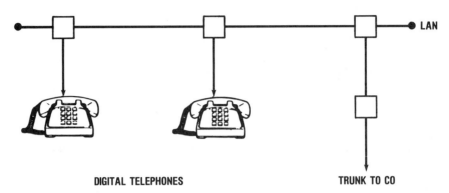

DIGITAL TELEPHONES   TRUNK TO CO

Fig. 1.   XCS system architecture.

to consider the effect of alternative architectures. For example, we achieve reliability by the packet XCS's lack of central failure points rather than by their duplication. Now that an early implementation exists, the packet XCS seems natural for supporting ongoing research in integrated voice and data services. In the end, the packet XCS may point the way to a useful design in its own right, with essentially zero initial cost and consistent incremental cost per site.

II. Transmission and Switching

The packet XCS incorporates shared transmission and distributed switching. Voice packets are transmitted over the network by the voice sites; local switching functions at the sites implement voice paths and other switching abstractions.

A. Transmission

The selection of a LAN for the packet XCS can greatly affect the performance, cost, and reliability of the system. The only constraint we place on the LAN is that it be capable of broadcasting a message to all sites on the network. This is required by several of the switching algorithms presented in the next section. We looked for a number of qualities in a LAN. Since the failure of the LAN would disrupt an entire XCS, the chance of such a failure should be small. The network should be able to carry enough voice traffic to make construction of a medium size packet XCS possible. In addition, a moderate amount of data capacity should be available.

There are several LAN technologies that meet our constraints. Many types of ring networks would be suitable, since they broadcast efficiently [4], [7], [14], [16]. Some of these networks, however, have "head-end" hardware which arbitrates access to the network. This is less desirable than a distributed contention mechanism, since a failure in the head-end could bring down the whole network. Other ring-like networks such as Fasnet and the Zurich ring have distributed contention which lessens this problem [7], [11]. Another interesting class of LAN's is the CSMA/CD network [2], [10], [13]. Since CSMA/CD networks are based on a shared broadcast media, they meet our prime constraint. Our experience indicates that they are very reliable.

For our experimental packet XCS, we chose the CSMA/CD network defined in [10]. This network has broadcast capability, is reliable, appears to have enough capacity to meet our needs, and has commercially available implementations. This network has also been standardized by the IEEE [2].

Several questions about carrying voice traffic on a CSMA/CD network need to be answered. For example, how many voice circuits can be provided? What is the effect of packet size on capacity and delay? How much data will be lost due to excessive delays? And, finally, are there transmission strategies or slight modifications to the contention mechanism that will improve transmission? The next few paragraphs will address these questions.

As a starting point, we assume that speech is digitized using a $\mu 255$ PCM coder at 64 000 bits/s. To better utilize available bandwidth, we assume that speech detection will be implemented in the site, and that each site will transmit an average of 40 percent of the time [5]. If the channel capacity is 10 Mbits/s, complete utilization of the bandwidth would result in a capacity of 195 conversations. This is an ideal, since efficiency is decreased by per-packet overhead and contention overhead.

Transmission on the network is bit-serial, beginning with 64 sync bits, followed by the packet. A packet contains 112 bits of header, a data field of between 368 and 12 000 bits, and a 32 bit CRC field. Assuming 64 kbits/s speech, a packet can hold from 5.75 ms to 187.5 ms of speech. A site may begin to transmit when it has seen the network idle for 9.6 μs. If voice sites are uniformly distributed along a maximum-length network, computations based on the network propagation delay budget give a worst-case mean one-way propagation time of 10.06 μs. We can expect an arbitrary site to see the network go idle 100.6 bit-times after the preceding site actually ceased to transmit. Taking this overhead into account, the capacity of the network is reduced to between 93 conversations (at the minimum packet size) and 188 conversations (at the maximum packet size).

Transmission strategy can have a significant effect on the network capacity. Since speech packets are periodic, if two sites' transmissions collide once, they will collide again on the next packet (ideally). This will continue until one of them ceases talking. To avoid this effect, an adaptive packet size is used. A site that experiences a collision will delay and then attempt retransmission. Instead of retransmitting the same packet, any speech samples acquired during the delay will be added to the packet. Since the delays of the colliding sites will be different, their packet sizes will differ, the next transmission times of the sites will differ, and successive collisions will be avoided. An adaptive packet size strategy can increase the throughput of the network by 25 percent or more by reducing the number of excessively delayed packets. The throughputs given in this chapter assume the use of an adaptive packet size strategy.

Contention overhead is more difficult to determine. When two or more sites attempt to transmit nearly simultaneously, a collision will result. The rate of collisions and their duration are affected by such factors as the number of sites and their spacing on the network. Since these effects are difficult to describe analytically, a simulation was performed [9]. The result is that 50 conversations can be transmitted if a packet contains 5.75 ms of speech, and 150 conversations can be transmitted if packets contain 50 ms of speech (larger packets introduce unacceptable delay into the system). At these loads, a very small ($\ll 1$ percent) number of packets will be delayed so long that they will not arrive at their destination in time to avoid a gap in the conversation. These results are consistent with earlier work [16] but with greater detail.

A CSMA/CD network carrying periodic traffic has a steady-state traffic pattern much like a TDM network. There are few collisions, since each site finds a slot in which it does not collide with other sites. When a new site is added to the network (such as when a talk spurt begins), it may experience a few collisions, which may in turn cause other sites to experience collisions. However, the cascade effect is heavily damped, and steady state is achieved rapidly. This arrangement falls apart in the presence of aperiodic traffic such as data. When a 5 percent data load is added to the simulation, the voice capacity of the network drops by as much as 25 percent. Extra collisions between the periodic and aperiodic traffic cause the drop in voice capacity. However, 5 percent average data is a large load, corresponding to hundreds of medium speed sites, or a few large computers.

Even though simulations show that a CSMA/CD network can carry voice, the stochastic nature of the contention mechanism will cause a very small number of packets to be excessively delayed, even under low loads. Thus, no guarantee can be made that a given packet will make a timely arrival at its destination. In practice, the authors do not believe this will cause significant degradation of a voice channel, unless the network is overloaded. Overloading can be avoided by engineering the packet XCS for slightly less than capacity traffic.

CSMA/CD networks give all sites equal access to the network, and do not favor any given sites. Unfortunately, this is not the optimal strategy in a mixed data-voice environment. In the presence of data, voice should have priority, so that it can meet its real-time constraints. Most data can be delayed with no serious effects. A particularly interesting variation of CSMA/CD, called movable-slot TDM (MSTDM), offers a solution to these problems [12].

The idea behind MSTDM is to allow voice packets to preempt data packets on the network. This is done by having voice packets ignore collisions with data packets. When a voice and data packet collide, the data packet transmission is stopped, and retried later. The voice packet continues and acquires the channel. Voice packets have a ''preempt header'' that can be garbled by collisions with no ill effects. Collisions between voice packets are impossible, due to the nature of the access mechanism. The important thing about MSTDM is that it places an upper bound on the delay of a voice packet transmitted through the network. Thus, no voice packets will be lost due to excessive delays.

In his paper, Maxemchuk [12] considers a CSMA/CD network that has different parameters from the one we have been considering. It operates at 3 Mbits/s, and has much lower per-packet overhead. In addition, the voice is encoded at 32 000 bits/s. These parameters are picked to increase the efficiency of the network. If one applies the MSTDM technique to the 10 Mbit/s CSMA/CD network we have been considering in this chapter, a considerable reduction in efficiency might be expected. However, preliminary calculations show that MSTDM operating on our network permits a voice capacity almost identical to pure CSMA/CD. In pure CSMA/CD, channel capacity is lost to collisions. In MSTDM, no voice collisions are possible, but voice packets have an additional preempt header one slot time (512 bits) long, which approximately negates the advantage gained by collision reduction.

In summary, it is possible to transmit reasonable numbers of voice channels on a standard CSMA/CD network, with very low losses. If the MSTDM technique is applied, no voice packets will be lost due to the contention mechanism.

B. Switching

Switching is performed at each site. There is no crucial centralized switching hardware. As shown in Fig. 2, peripheral control software implements a voice protocol layered above the underlying LAN protocol. Peripheral control also includes local primitives for

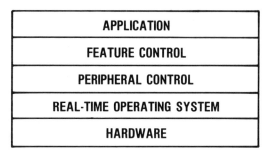

Fig. 2.   XCS software architecture (per station).

providing station or trunk tones and receiving station or trunk inputs (switchhook and keypad, supervision and tones). These operations are supported by local hardware.

Real time constraints keep us from using a complex protocol in the voice paths. By the time the loss of a voice packet could be noticed, it would already be too late to retransmit it, and modifying timing constraints to allow retransmission would do more harm than good. Our voice protocol is unidirectional and simply time stamps voice packets; we depend on known network transmission characteristics to achieve good results.

Switching voice paths involves buffering and transmitting speech samples from the mouthpiece and receiving, uniformly delaying, and playing back speech samples into the earpiece. Peripheral control implements abstract operations on voice connections. For a two-site connection, peripheral control would transmit voice packets point-to-point. For a multisite connection, peripheral control might transmit the voice packets point-to-point or to a multicast address. Each site involved in a multisite connection receives the other's packets and reconstructs them into a single stream for playback; although the processing power required is potentially unbounded as the size of a connection grows large, intuition tells us that the instantaneous number of speakers will probably be small and that extreme cases can be allowed to result in some lost speech.

III. CONTROL

Given the underlying approach to transmission and switching in the packet XCS, there were many possible approaches to the design of the system's higher-level feature control functions, with each choice having a major effect on the resulting system. Accordingly, we first chose a set of guiding principles which then directed our further design. Our decisions were often arbitrary but were ultimately interdependent; together, they helped to narrow our options and contributed significantly to the conceptual cohesiveness of the packet XCS.

Many control features of the packet XCS could have been centralized or distributed. In each case, we chose the distributed approach as an opportunity to study distributed processing. The distributed approach was also considered a challenge, since voice switching features have evolved in a centralized control environment and it was not obvious whether they could be implemented well, or at all, in a distributed environment. We also chose to distribute all data functions in the packet XCS.

We assumed that the underlying network would be extremely reliable. This reliability, useful in transmission, is also useful at higher levels. Instead of building protocol layers to eliminate lost messages, we decided to live with them. Since a switching system can tolerate some number of failed call attempts, we chose to design our system so that lost messages could result in call failures or degraded service, but in which only the associated call would be affected. This decision requires that messages be associated with only a single call, since losing a global message could have unbounded effects. We also decided to take advantage of the broadcast nature of the LAN for certain data operations.

Sites may fail or come up at arbitrary times. Again, we chose that such downtime and such transitions should affect only calls to and from those sites; this again eliminates having sites with global responsibilities.

We decided that the programming for each site would be specialized. A site supporting a station would contain the code only for that type of station; a site supporting a trunk would contain the code only for that type of trunk. Another consequence of this principle is that trunk selection on an outgoing call should be performed at the trunk sites themselves instead of at the station sites, since the knowledge of the selection criteria should be specific to the trunks.

We decided to rely heavily on automated techniques in the design and implementation of the system. For example, we want lost messages to cause only transient errors; a given design of feature control will have some messages where this is naturally the case but others that must be "reinforced" by extending the protocol. We found that it was possible to distinguish such cases mechanically and to automate the reinforcement.

Some of our philosophical guidelines had to be stretched when special problems arose (in areas as diverse as billing and unassigned numbers), but overall they were extremely useful in helping us focus our design effort.

Feature control for the packet XCS adopts the popular architecture of one process per site. This process executes on a processor at the site, possibly shared with peripheral control. The feature control process contains an extended finite-state control component and a data-management component.

A. Extended Finite-State Control

The extended finite-state control is a finite-state machine whose inputs are site inputs and control messages from other sites, and whose outputs are site outputs and control messages to other sites. Site inputs and outputs go through peripheral control while control messages are transmitted over the LAN. Each state of the machine accepts some set of possible inputs, each resulting in some list of outputs and a transfer to a new state. For example, from the initial state, the input "off-hook" produces the output "start dial tone" and transfers to a state where the input "digit" produces the outputs "stop dial tone" and "remember digit" and so forth. The extension to the finite-state control is the ability to manage small amounts of data local to the extended machine, such as the digits dialed.

The extended finite-state control is generated mechanically using program synthesis. A specification language allows a nonprocedural listing of facts concerning voice sites (e.g., stations cannot give a dial tone when they are on-hook) as well as the features to be provided (e.g., stations should give a dial tone when they go off-hook). Our specification language is very close to extended propositional temporal logic [17]. While ultimately equal in power to finite-state machine specification, our specification language seems much easier to use. Independent facts or features can be specified with fewer interdependencies arising as artifacts of the specification. Specifications are mechanically translated to finite-state machine form, with the translator detecting inconsistencies and underspecifications, eliminating some automatically while interacting with the user to resolve the others.

Each site's protocol for interaction with other sites is explicit in the specification. Messages are treated as additional inputs and outputs. Progress has been made toward protocol synthesis, where the specification might describe only the cumulative behavior of a set of interacting sites and the necessary protocol could be derived mechanically. Our initial protocols have been constructed manually, with semiautomated checking for protocol bugs. (As with programs, not all protocol bugs can be found automatically, although protocol synthesis can guarantee their absence.)

B. Data Management

Just as switching and control are distributed in the packet XCS, so is data management. For example, translation data (giving the mapping from dialed numbers to hardware site addresses) are not stored centrally; they are distributed among the sites involved. To use the translation data, a site broadcasts a query to all of the sites and the site(s) with the appropriate dialed number responds with its network address. This approach requires only $O(1)$ (i.e., constant) space per site as a function of the number of sites but requires $O(n)$ (linear) time per site, with some small constant factor, as the number of sites and, thus, of queries grows.

In general, each site holds those data that pertain directly to it (thus there are no purely ''system'' data); the data form data relations and each relation can span many or all sites. When the contents of a relation are desired, the requesting site can broadcast a request for the contents. Each site replies with its tuple(s), and the requesting site performs some operation on these tuples. If a tuple is to be modified, it is first located by broadcasting and then modified using a point-to-point message.

Often, the operation following the query can also be performed in a distributed manner. In the translation data example, the operation is selection of the tuple(s) whose key is the dialed number. The individual sites can perform this selection, with only the site(s) matching the dialed number replying: this reduces the number of replies from $O(n)$ to $O(1)$.

Many such optimizations are possible. A typical operation is to maximize or minimize the value of a key. This is useful in least-cost routing, where we must find the trunk that minimizes some cost; another use is the maintenance of a queue of sites, where finding the head of the queue becomes finding the site with the greatest time in the queue. Here, the first operation is selection of appropriate trunk sites or of sites in the queue; the sites can perform this selection themselves. Next, since the keys are stored only implicitly, they must be recomputed on each access; computing them at the target sites instead of the requesting site is another transformation. Another is having the target sites desiring to reply first listen for other replies and drop out if they see one better than theirs. Yet another is to have the sites' initial periods of listening inversely related to their perceived goodness of their results. Together, these transformations can produce a family of efficient protocols for accessing distributed data [8].

This data distribution technique is only approximate. It can fail if a queried site is down or misses the query or its reply is lost. In the packet XCS this can affect at most the associated call. At best, the resulting behavior can be desirable; if a site in a queue goes down, it will no longer be considered to be in the queue. We rely on the underlying LAN and the relative infrequency of queries to keep the number of lost queries or replies small.

IV. PROTOTYPE DESIGN AND IMPLEMENTATION

In order to further understand the distributed packet XCS concept, a prototype packet XCS was implemented. It currently consists of about 60 phone stations, installed across three different sites. A small number of these stations have been slightly modified to function as trunk interfaces, providing connection to the public switched telephone network. A number of features have been implemented, including plain old telephone service (POTS), three-way calling, and digital voice storage. The Department of Defense standard TCP/IP protocols have also been implemented, and are used to provide a TTY switching service, and the voice storage service. This section will discuss our experiences and the insights we have gained from this implementation.

The current hardware implementation is shown in Fig. 3. It is based on a 68000 CPU, and consists of 46 integrated circuit chips mounted on a single 6 × 9 inch board. Each station consists of a CPU, 1 Mbyte of random access memory, 128 kbytes of read-only memory, a LANCE based Ethernet-controller, a codec and DMA controller for voice digitization, a dual UART for TTY interface, and a keypad and switch hook interface. The board was custom designed for this application, but no custom VLSI design has been performed. The board, power supply, keypad, and handset are mounted in a 9 × 9 × 4 inch standard desktop telephone case.

Both peripheral and feature control run on top of a real-time operating system which allows the rest of the software to be structured as a set of cooperating processes. A message-passing IPC mechanism is also provided. The interface between the peripheral control and the feature control is defined by a set of 19 messages divided into four groups: tone generation, user input, switching, and transmission. Tone generation is used to start and stop dial tone, busy signal, audible ringing, and ringing. The peripheral control software generates these tones from tables. User input messages are sent from peripheral control to the feature control when the user dials a digit or takes the handset on-hook or off-hook. Switching messages are messages between the feature control layers of the phones involved in a conversation. They are transmitted but not interpreted by the peripheral control. For POTS there are only two transmission messages: talk and stop talk, which cause the peripheral control to set up and tear down a simplex path between the local mouthpiece and the remote earphone.

A conversation consists of two independent, identical, simplex voice paths. The algorithms to implement a basic voice path are simple. The transmitter collects samples until a packet is filled, and transmits it over the LAN. The receiver catches packets addressed to it, and plays them out to the phone. This simple algorithm must then be augmented to handle variable packet spacing and speech detection.

There are two unavoidable causes of variable packet spacing: transmission delay and clock drift. Transmission delay is to be expected in a CSMA/CD network. The simulations

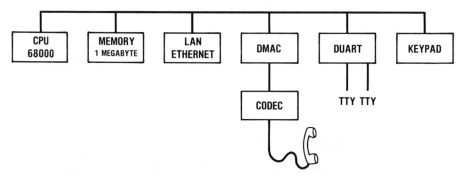

Fig. 3.   Experimental communications system hardware.

discussed previously predict that in a pure CSMA/CD network, with 5.75 ms voice packets, 5 percent data loading, and 40 conversations in progress, the mean packet delay will be 0.2 ms, and the standard deviation will be 1.0 ms. If one provides 5.75 ms of artificial delay at the receiver, approximately 1 percent of the voice samples will be lost. With no data loading, the mean and standard deviation of the delay drop to less than one sample (125 μs). If MSTDM is added to the network, the maximum delay for a voice packet is less than 350 μs under any data load. With at least 350 μs of buffering at the receiver, no voice will be lost.

Clock drift is a less obvious cause of lost voice samples. Since the packet XCS is completely distributed, the two codecs involved in a conversation are sampling at a different rate. Over a period of time, the receiver will see either too few or too many samples. This will eventually cause a break in the conversation. In our implementation, the tolerances of the crystal clocks is ± 0.1 percent. This means that the receiver can overflow or underflow by as much as 1.6 samples per second. We currently use 16 ms voice packets, with a total of 32 ms of buffering available in the receiver. If the extra 16 ms of buffering is divided in half to give equal protection against underflow and overflow, a voice sample can be lost in a minimum of 40 s. Our experience indicates that this is a more common cause of lost voice packets than the variable transmission delay caused by CSMA/CD. Only when voice and data loading on the network approach saturation does the transmission delay become predominant. Fortunately, the small amounts of speech lost due to clock drift are easily compensated for. When speech detection is implemented, the receiver can readjust its buffer between talk spurts. Since the average talk spurt is very much less than 40 s, voice samples will rarely be lost.

In order to increase the network capacity to reasonable levels, speech detection is necessary. As each packet is copied from the transmitter's voice FIFO to the LAN buffers, the maximum amplitude sample is noted. If the maximum amplitude sample in a packet does not exceed a threshold, the packet is deemed ''quiet.'' When the transmitter notices a number of quiet packets in a row, it stops transmitting. When it again notices a nonquiet packet, transmission is resumed. The amplitude threshold and number of quiet packets to transmit are fixed. This speech detection algorithm works nicely in an office environment with one exception. When a speaker stops talking, there is a noticeable delay before the transmitter stops transmitting. During this time, all of the background noises in the speaker's environment can be heard. These then abruptly cease when the transmitter stops. The traditional solution to this problem is to have the receiver play white noise into the earphone when the transmitter stops. We chose to implement an alternate strategy, however. The human ear is very sensitive to abrupt changes in amplitude but much less sensitive to subtle changes. So, our transmitter applies negative gain to quiet packets. The nth packet of a sequence of quiet packets has a gain of $-6n$ dB. The gain is implemented by table lookup in the transmitter. The result of this is to make the speech detection effect unnoticeable in a office environment. In noisier environments, or with trunks, an adaptive threshold would probably have to be used.

V. CONCLUSIONS

The packet XCS represents an innovative new design of an experimental switching system. It uses a LAN as a shared transmission facility; it distributes switching, control, and data. A prototype implementation has been constructed and is currently in use.

We have learned that, with proper care, a CSMA/CD LAN can be used as a voice transmission facility. With MSTDM, voice transmission is deterministic while data transmission retains the desirable CSMA/CD performance. We have also learned that distributed control is possible for such a system, and that various aspects of system design can be profitably automated.

ACKNOWLEDGMENT

The authors wish to thank D. Weller, N. Jackson Jr., E. Donofrio, and C. Connolly, who were responsible for the design and implementation of the XCS hardware; J. Lacy, who was responsible for the nonautomatic part of the POTS and three-way calling software; P. Karn, who supplied the software to implement the TCP/IP protocols; K. Minnich, who implemented the voice storage software; J. Kaiser for the invention of the speech detection algorithm; N. Maxemchuk for his MSTDM protocol; P. Wolper for discussions on temporal logic; and D. Bergland for his continuing support.

REFERENCES

[1] A. S. Acampora, M. G. Hluchjy, and C. D. Tsao, "A centralized-bus architecture for local area networks," in *Conf. Rec. IEEE ICC,* June 1983, vol. 2, pp. 932–938.
[2] "Carrier sense multiple access with collision detection (CSMA/CD) access method and physical layer specifications," ANSI/IEEE Standard 802.3-1985, IEEE, New York, 1985.
[3] "Token passing bus access method and physical layer specifications," ANSI/IEEE Standard 802.4-1985, IEEE, New York, 1985.
[4] "Token ring access method and physical layer specifications," ANSI/IEEE Standard 802.5-1985, New York, 1985.
[5] P. T. Brady, "A statistical analysis of on-off patterns in 16 conversations," *Bell. Syst. Tech. J.,* vol. 47, Jan. 1968.
[6] F. Braun and E. Hafner, "SILK—Concept and general system design," *Hasler Rev.,* vol. 15, Jan. 1981.
[7] W. Bux, *et al.,* "A local area communication network based on a reliable token-ring system," in *Proc. Int. Symp. Local Comput. Networks,* Florence, Italy, Apr. 1982.
[8] J. DeTreville and W. D. Sincoskie, "Program transformations for data access in a local distributed environment," *Bell. Syst. Tech. J.,* vol. 63, July–Aug. 1984.
[9] J. D. DeTreville, "A simulation-based comparison of voice transmission on CSMA/CD networks and on token buses," *Bell. Syst. Tech. J.,* vol. 63, Jan. 1984.
[10] Digital Equipment Corporation, Intel Corporation, and Xerox Corporation, "The Ethernet—A local area network, data link layer and physical layer specifications," Version 1.0, Sept. 1980.
[11] J. O. Limb and C. Flores, "Description of Fasnet—A unidirectional local-area communications network," *Bell. Syst. Tech. J.,* vol. 61, Sept. 1982; see also this volume, ch. 12.
[12] N. F. Maxemchuk, "A variation on CSMA/CD that yields movable TDM slots in integrated voice/data local networks," *Bell. Syst. Tech. J.,* vol. 61, Sept. 1982.
[13] R. M. Metcalfe and D. R. Boggs, "Ethernet: distributed packet switching for local computer networks," *Commun. Ass. Comput. Mach.,* vol. 19, July 1976.
[14] P. V. Mockapetris, M. R. Lyle, and D. J. Farber, "On the design of local network interfaces," in *Proc. Inform. Processing '77, IFIP Congress,* 1977.
[15] G. J. Nutt and D. L. Bayer, "Performance of CSMA/CD networks under combined voice and data loads," *IEEE Trans. Commun.,* vol. COM-30, pp. 6–11, Jan. 1982.
[16] M. V. Wilkes and D. J. Wheeler, "The Cambridge digital communications ring," in *Proc. Local Area Commun. Network Symp.,* 1979, pp. 47–61.
[17] P. Wolper, "Temporal logic can be more expressive," in *Proc. 22nd Symp. Foundations Comput. Sci.,* Nashville, TN, Oct. 1981, pp. 340–348.

32

A Distributed UNIX System Based on a Virtual Circuit Switch

G. W. R. LUDERER, H. CHE, J. P. HAGGERTY, P. A. KIRSLIS, AND W. T. MARSHALL

The popular UNIX® operating system provides time-sharing service on a single computer. This chapter reports on the design and implementation of a distributed UNIX system. The new operating system consists of two components: the S-UNIX subsystem provides a complete UNIX process environment enhanced by access to remote files; the F-UNIX subsystem is specialized to offer remote file service. A system can be configured out of many computers which operate either under the S-UNIX or the F-UNIX operating subsystem. The file servers together present the view of a single global file system. A single-service view is presented to any user terminal connected to one of the S-UNIX subsystems.

Computers communicate with each other through a high-bandwidth virtual circuit switch. Small front-end processors handle the data and control protocol for error and flow-controlled virtual circuits. Terminals may be connected directly to the computers or through the switch.

Operational since early 1980, the system has served as a vehicle to explore virtual circuit switching as the basis for distributed system design. The performance of the communication software has been a focus of our work. Performance measurement results are presented for user process level and operating system driver level data transfer rates, message exchange times, and system capacity benchmarks. The architecture offers reliability and modularly growable configurations. The communication service offered can serve as the foundation for different distributed architectures.

I. INTRODUCTION

The UNIX® time-sharing system is widely known and used [22]. The virtues of distributed systems have been extolled in many places (for a comprehensive treatment, see [3], [6], and [26]). Thus, the idea of a distributed UNIX system has appealed to many.

In the spring of 1979, when we began to study possible designs, we saw several major short-term goals for a multicomputer UNIX system arrangement:

1) increased capacity, i.e., being able to give better service to more simultaneous users,
2) modular growth, i.e., being able to add computers as the load increases,
3) increased availability, i.e., computer failure should not cause system failure,
4) faster recovery, in particular, file system checking and repair.

Figure 1 shows our first configuration. Connected through a high-bandwidth switch are two kinds of computers. The processors in the top row run the user processes, while those

---

® UNIX is a trademark of AT&T Bell Laboratories.

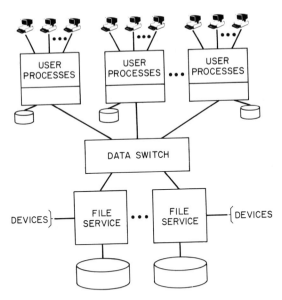

Fig. 1.   System with terminals on computers.

in the bottom row implement a global file system. All the user files are handled by the file server computers.

Since the disks in the top row hold only local files, such as temporaries or the boot image, whose identities are of no interest to the user, the user processes can run on any of these computers. All files and devices that need to be shared are on the bottom row computers. Here, the terminals are connected to the top row computers in an interleaved hunt sequence, which enables some primitive load balancing.[1] For growth, computers can be added in both the top and the bottom rows. For reliability, spares in both rows can prevent total service outage, and operator intervention can allow recovery from a degraded state.

Figure 2 shows a variation of our configuration with the terminals connected through the switch. It is more flexible and provides potential cost savings.

The above two configurations model a computer center and not the geographically distributed system that many envision for the future. We feel, however, that our design takes a step in that direction, as shown in Fig. 3. The same file servers appear at the bottom, but the top row consists of remote personal computers each serving a single user.

The operating subsystems in the two types of computers are different and specialized, i.e., we have a heterogeneous network. We hope this results in a very important long-term benefit: reduced software complexity.[2] Not having to handle disparate tasks reduces component complexity; being able to replace functional components as user needs change and technology advances helps with the management of system complexity. Of course, the decomposition has to be "right," and the interfaces must be long-lived (like the system bus of a computer family).

S-UNIX is the name we have given to the specialized operating subsystem that runs user

[1] This configuration does not allow direct communication between two terminals on different computers as offered by the *write* command.

[2] The emphasis here is on "long-term"; a substantiation follows later under "Potential Extensions."

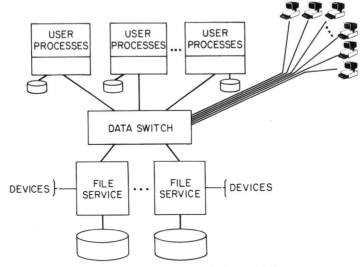

Fig. 2.   System with terminals on switch.

processes; it is "stripped" of most files, and models the later-to-be-achieved "single-user" UNIX system. The subsystem running on the file server is called F-UNIX. The remainder of the chapter has the following structure. Section II presents some general design considerations. We have separated the UNIX operating system related discussion from a discussion of the communication service subsystem. These topics are treated in Sections III and IV, respectively. Section V discusses performance, and Section VI gives some ideas about possible future extensions. Finally, in Section VII we compare our system with related efforts of others.

II. General Design Considerations

We gave ourselves the strict requirement of preserving the UNIX process environment and file system behavior, i.e., full compatibility with an existing version. We made as few

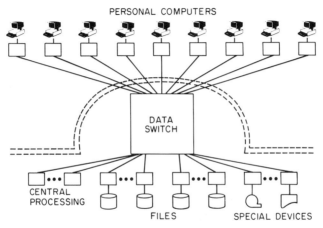

Fig. 3.   System with personal computers.

changes to the UNIX code as possible, but we did make radical changes when they became necessary. The division between the file system and the rest of UNIX is not across a well-defined interface and required major redesign. It was also clear at the outset that the success of this project hinged upon efficient interprocessor communication software and hardware, and about half of our effort was applied towards this goal.

The obvious choice for the computer hardware was the high end of Digital Equipment Corporation's PDP-11 line. More unusual is our choice of the interconnection medium. Most contemporary designs of distributed systems use a packet switch and a message or datagram discipline for intercomputer communication. We wanted to explore the suitability of virtual circuits as the underlying communication architecture. One frequently encounters two objections to the use of circuit switches for distributed computer systems. First, fixed bandwidth allocation is particularly wasteful for the bursty kind of traffic common to data communication. Second, there seems to be more algorithmic complexity in programs that have to keep track of circuit states. (As one reviewer observed, "virtual circuits are always necessary, for reliability; the question often asked is at what level of the protocol hierarchy." We decided to push them to as low a level as possible, under the assumption 1) that they are generally useful; 2) that they require a lot of host resources to manage which can be more easily off-loaded to a peripheral if the circuit protocol is a low-level basic service.) One might say that there is intrinsic atomicity in pure message disciplines. We took the second argument as a challenge: if we could develop a workable and efficient communication architecture based on virtual circuits, we expected to see potential advantages in the areas of system management and extension to other services than data communication, e.g., voice, facsimile, etc. The first objection we could easily overcome. We found a switch that combines the desirable properties of both packet and virtual circuit switching: the Datakit switch [12]. It offers the functionality of a virtual circuit switch with dynamic bandwidth allocation, since it uses packet switching (demand multiplexing) in its internal implementation.

As to the second objection, we must leave it to the reader to judge whether the modest amount of added complexity is worth the advantages gained.

III. THE S-UNIX AND F-UNIX SUBSYSTEMS

The UNIX file system name space is a singly rooted tree, and intermediate nodes representing directories and with leaves representing files or devices.

Our initial intent was to remove all files from the S-UNIX side and put them on the F-UNIX side. We ended up keeping local files for the following four reasons.

1) An S-UNIX subsystem should be able to access more than one file server. To preserve a singly rooted name space tree with no name recognition in S-UNIX would require a file server hierarchy, which is undesirable because of reliability and performance.

2) It is impractical, at least for exploratory development, if one cannot bootstrap an S-UNIX subsystem from a local file.

3) There are potential efficiency gains if some frequently used files like load modules are kept locally.

4) The down-stream model of a personal UNIX system should have the option of local files.

Point 1) actually calls for a local name space, not local file space. For example, one could add a small name space management facility in the operating system. However, we decided to keep the root of the global file system tree on the S-UNIX side.

In the current UNIX system, the file space is extended by "mounting" a properly formatted disk volume on top of an existing directory. We have expanded this concept by allowing the S-UNIX user to "mount a file server" in an analogous way. Whereas the existing mount procedure requires a special file representing a properly structured block device (e.g., a formatted disk volume), our new procedure substitutes a device communicating with a file server, i.e., a circuit to the switch. Multiple mounts of both kinds can be active simultaneously.

Figure 4 shows the file name space of a configuration of two S-UNIX systems which have mounted F-UNIX file servers F-UNIX$_1$ and F-UNIX$_2$ on mount points F1 and F2, respectively, in their local name space.

Processes on the S-UNIX side see no difference between local and remote files, except for performance. All system calls of the S-UNIX subsystem apply to both local and remote files. This includes special files, i.e., devices, on the F-UNIX subsystem. No F-UNIX system can access files of another F-UNIX nor can it get to local S-UNIX files.

Growth and recovery from failure can thus be handled by adding or removing S-UNIX and F-UNIX computers from in-service configurations, subject to appropriate operating procedures. Failure of an F-UNIX system can be handled by moving the disk volumes (or back-up versions) to a spare computer and mounting that new file server on the failed F-UNIX machine's mount point in each S-UNIX. Failure of an S-UNIX machine disrupts all user sessions on that system, but the other systems remain unaffected.

File access control in the UNIX system depends on the user *id* and group *id*. For philosophical and pragmatic reasons, we have chosen to have a single password file on our systems; thus, the *id* numbers denoting file ownership are global to all S-UNIX and F-UNIX machines.

By taking the position that the operating subsystems and the communication mechanism are trustworthy, we avoid having to deal with problems of authentication beyond those present in the current UNIX system. We realize that, once we allow remote "personal" computers, the local operating system cannot be trusted anymore. We shall return to this problem under "Potential Extensions."

A. S/F-UNIX Implementation

The following description requires an understanding of UNIX internals [25]. The reader unfamiliar with or uninterested in UNIX internals may skip Section III.

B. The Cut Between S-UNIX and F-UNIX

Accessing files from multiple computers and preserving local files turned out to be conflicting objectives. There are two obvious ways of introducing remote files. The first is to have the remote file server look like a block-addressable device [13]. Because blocks contain housekeeping information and we wanted to preserve the shared file access properties of the UNIX system, we would have to introduce an inordinate amount of extra messages for locking and unlocking. The second way is to translate all remote-file-related system calls into appropriate messages. This is complicated because the operating system itself makes file system references, e.g., for core dumps, for writing the accounting file, and for loading programs. Our implementation followed this second choice closely. We introduced changes wherever the name-to-disk-address converter (*namei*) is invoked, to handle remoteness.

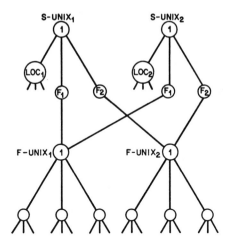

Fig. 4.   File name space of a 2/2 configuration.

C. Remote Inodes

In the UNIX system, each file on a volume is described by a data structure called an *inode,* which is read into memory when the file is opened. The *inode* contains almost all the information about a file, e.g., its type (directory, ordinary file, device, etc.), owner, access permissions, length, and physical address. We introduce an *inode* of 'type *remote* that is created in memory when a remote file is opened. It contains just enough information for the S-UNIX subsystem to talk about the file:

- a pointer to a data structure identifying the F-UNIX machine holding the file,
- a unique number assigned by that F-UNIX machine.

All other information about a remote file, e.g., its access permission and length, is maintained only by the remote file server. This allows all S-UNIX machines to see a consistent description of the file. The introduction of the remote inode enables us to restrict the number of messages exchanged to one request and one reply per call. The basic algorithm is: if a path name crosses the mount point of a remote file server, stop interpreting the path name and send a message with the remaining path name. If a remote file is being opened or created, the F-UNIX subsystem returns a tag of its choosing to be used in future references. Tags are also returned in response to *chroot* or *chdir* system calls. All absolute path names carry the root tag, and all relative path names carry the current directory tag. Thus, the file server always sees the equivalent of an absolute path name and does not have to remember the current directory; yet the tag (really an inode number) serves to speed up the search process.

In order to allow several S-UNIX machines to update the same remote file concurrently, the cache of disk blocks in S-UNIX memory had to be restricted to local files only. The F-UNIX subsystem, on the other hand, can use a large part of its memory as a cache, since it does not run user processes.

D. Special Files

Devices are treated like special files in the UNIX system. Peripherals on the F-UNIX subsystem can thus be easily accessed in the usual manner. For example, an S-UNIX machine can write to a tape drive on an F-UNIX machine. Special peripherals like printers or phototypesetters could be handled by F-UNIX subsystems running on small dedicated computers with or without local secondary storage.

A new special UNIX interprocess communication mechanism is the *fifo,* which provides communication between unrelated processes by associating a new special file type with a file name. Since *remote fifos* are legal, they can be used for interprocessor communication between S-UNIX machines or between an S-UNIX machine and an F-UNIX machine.

E. File Server Details

The file server computers are running under the F-UNIX operating subsystem. There is one file server process for each circuit connected to an S-UNIX machine. These processes execute in the kernel mode. When started, they are connected to the circuit and obey the S-UNIX controlled file service protocol starting with a ''mount file server'' request. Each S-UNIX machine is then handled by at least one server process on each F-UNIX. F-UNIX multitasking is simply implemented by starting several server processes per S-UNIX, each on a different circuit. The degree of multiplexing is thus chosen on the S-UNIX side, where as many requests can be outstanding as there are circuits to F-UNIX systems.

One design decision concerns the amount of S-UNIX state information to be kept in the F-UNIX subsystem. The file server does not keep a count of all open-operations against a file. Rather it keeps track of which S-UNIX machine has the file opened (at least once). Disappearing S-UNIX systems that do not properly close their files are discovered, and the files are closed.

F. File Service Protocol

Interaction between both subsystems at the functional level is handled by the file service protocol, which is strictly a sequential message exchange over one virtual circuit. Error and flow control are supported by the circuit mechanism.

Out of 27 system call types related to files, 18 result in message traffic if remote files are involved. Of these, 10 contain a path name as an argument, and the remaining 8 refer to already opened files. Path names or the data read or written can be up to 64 kbytes long. The structure of each message is a type code followed by type-dependent data.

IV. COMMUNICATION SUBSYSTEM

The communication subsystem is built on the concept of a virtual circuit service. It is thus independent of the S/F-UNIX architecture and can be used as the foundation for different distributed system designs [18]. In the following, we shall introduce the Datakit switch, then explain how we use it, and finally give details about the protocols and the switch interface.

A. The Datakit Switch

Datakit is functionally a virtual circuit switch [12]. Computers and terminals are connected in a star topology to interface modules interconnected by a backplane. Packet switching occurs on the up-link and down-link of a folded bus on the backplane. The switch module at the pivot replaces packet source addresses with destination addresses (Fig. 5).

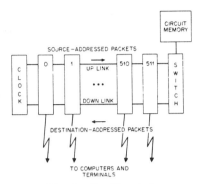

Fig. 5.   Datakit switch.

The aggregate data rate is 7 Mbits/s which corresponds to a payload of 42 000 16-data-byte packets per second. Due to asynchronous time-division multiplexing, it effectively provides dynamic bandwidth allocation on virtual circuits. The subscriber link interface is that of a Digital Equipment Corporation (DEC) DR11-C program-controlled, word-parallel communication device. We converted this interface to direct memory access with the help of a very fast (200 ns instruction time) communication front-end processor, the DEC KMC11-B, which also handles our link protocol [9]. The Datakit switch, in its largest configuration, can address a quarter million distinct subscriber circuits, which are usually partitioned into 511 physical subscriber links each multiplexed into a maximum of 511 full-duplex virtual circuits.

B. Connection Procedure

The switch contains a table that defines the end points of each circuit, i.e., the subscriber's interface module address and one of its virtual circuits. Circuit set-up and take-downs are managed by a subscriber computer designated as Common Control. We have implemented a control program that resides in a DEC LSI-11 computer. This computer also holds a monitor program that in addition to other functions periodically receives status information from each subscriber interface module, e.g., a count of packets lost due to errors.

The switch is initialized such that the control program is connected to each bootstrapped subscriber's circuit 1, which is the signaling circuit for all circuit set-ups and take-down. By convention, the subscriber manages only its odd-numbered circuits, starting with 3; Common Control owns and manages the subscriber's even-numbered circuits.

Common Control contains a simple name server that will establish circuits between any two subscribers. For example, when an F-UNIX computer is restarted, it announces to the name server that it is willing to accept file service requests on a specified service circuit. Likewise, when an S-UNIX computer is restarted, it selects an odd-numbered circuit and asks Common Control to connect it to the file server. Common Control will then allocate and set up an even-numbered circuit on the F-UNIX machine being called, which will be informed of the request and in turn acknowledged it to the requestor.

The same mechanism is used to request other kinds of service. For example, small computers with no local secondary storage (e.g., PDP-11/23's) have a program in ROM that requests a circuit to a preestablished boot server, and a higher level protocol used on that circuit down-loads the image of the operating subsystem.

C. Circuit Protocol

A great deal of attention has been paid to the design of a simple and efficient circuit mechanism (we actually implemented four different designs). Major guidelines were to take advantage of the switch's hardware properties and to design a protocol that would fit into the front-end processor (4 kbytes data, 8 kbytes of code). The error behavior of the switch is characterized by very high reliability (we observed one faulty packet in six months) and the fact that the only possible error is loss of a packet (16 bytes). We call our protocol the NK protocol (network kernel). It is unusual in that it places the burden of error control solely on the transmitter site. This greatly simplifies the logic of the receiver, which has only one state and two local counters.

The NK protocol provides an error-free stream of bytes on a virtual circuit. The Datakit interface hardware expects and delivers 17-byte packets. The first byte identifies the virtual circuit. The format of the remaining 16 bytes is dictated by the NK protocol. The first byte is always a control byte followed by 0–15 data bytes. The control byte consists of a 3-bit command and a 5-bit argument. We will sketch the protocol by explaining the receiver action for the four commands it recognizes.

1) Initialization: The transmitter bids for a window size (i.e, number of buffers). The receiver accepts it or reduces it to its liking, and returns its decision.

2) Data Packet with Sequence Number: If the number is expected, the packet is accepted and the local count is incremented (modulo window size). Otherwise, the packet is flushed. No response is sent.

3) Data Packet with Sequence Number and Request for Response: Same action as above, except that, in case of success, the sequence number is returned.

4) Enquiry Request: A reply command with the last accepted sequence number is returned.

The above protocol has been working to our full satisfaction for data transfer on virtual circuits. However, it had to be modified to serve reliably for communicating with Common Control in the circuit set-up process. Here we operate with short messages only (one packet). The problem was survival of the system in case of failure of Common Control. A workable solution was found by letting Common Control delay the packet acknowledgment (case 3 above) until an acknowledgment of the reply was received. This causes a circuit set-up message to be resent repeatedly, even across crashes, until the required action is complete.

We have investigated the properties of this protocol to determine the choice of window size and acknowledge frequency as a function of the delay parameters of the network. Results will be reported elsewhere.

D. The Switch Interface

The driver on the host computer copies the data to be transmitted into a system buffer and gives a write command with a buffer pointer and the circuit number to the front-end processor, which empties the buffer and implements the above circuit protocol. Since buffer allocation is on a per-circuit basis on both ends, multiple circuit transmission is interleaved. For receiving, blocks are assembled in the front-end from packets and then copied into the waiting system buffer.

In order to further improve performance, we have built a peripheral to the front-end

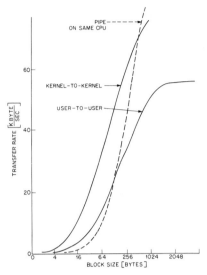

Fig. 6.   Data transfer rates between PDP11-45's.

processor that eliminates the DR11-C and connects directly (i.e., not over the UNIBUS®)
to the Datakit switch.

V. Performance Measurements

We distinguish three major dimensions when characterizing the performance of a
computing system:

1) Capacity: What is the rate at which useful work can be performed?

2) Responsiveness: What is the delay before a desired action takes place?

3) Overhead: How many system resources are used to perform a specified activity?

For distributed systems, we characterize interprocessor communication by three
measurements along these dimensions:

1) the achievable data transfer rate,

2) the time to exchange a null message,

3) the CPU time needed to perform communication.

The measurements given below refer to a configuration of two DEC PDP-11/45
computers[3] connected through the Datakit switch. Unless otherwise stated, the interface is
a KMC11-B controlled special line card.

A. Data Transfer

Figure 6 shows data transfer rates between two processors as a function of the block size.
The two solid curves show user level data transfer, i.e., process to process, and kernel
level transfer, i.e., between specially instrumented drivers on each computer, respectively.
The latter is more typical of the file server which runs in kernel mode. For comparison, the
intracomputer pipe rate between user processes is shown as a dotted line. The data were

---

® UNIBUS is a trademark of Digital Equipment Corporation.

[3] Neither computer had a cache memory. The core memory on the file server computer slowed it down by
about 10 percent compared to the other computer, which had MOS memory.

generated within one computer and thrown away after arrival at the receiver. Figure 7 shows the CPU utilization of the host computer for the three experiments of Fig. 6. As with many communication media used for local area networking, the Datakit switch is supposed to be operated in an area of light loading. Notice that, as the load increases, so does the throughput since there are no losses due to collision.

B. Responsiveness

A test script that invokes commands which use all of the remote file system functions was executed in two modes, and the total elapsed time and CPU resources used were measured. Figure 8 shows the results. Notice that all programs had to be loaded from the remote file server. In both cases, CPU time contains 2 s of user CPU time.

Another measure of responsiveness is the elapsed time in which a short message can be sent and acknowledgment received. We measured 11 ms for an exchange between user processes on different processors.

However, at the kernel-to-kernel level we successfully sent a message in 870 μs. We believe this result bodes well for new computer architectures with low context switch overhead and segment switching instead of copying.

C. Capacity

A multithread benchmark script was executed to determine system capacity. The set of application processes in the script is assumed to be a crude approximation of some realistic work load. A series of experiments was performed, increasing the number of scripts beyond saturation. As the script is executed many times, one can determine the maximum numbers of processes that terminate per hour as a relative measure of capacity.

1) Virtual Circuit Set-Up: We have measured the time for setting up a virtual circuit between two processes in different computers, i.e., the elapsed time for a process issuing a dial request until the called process has opened the new circuit. About half of this time is

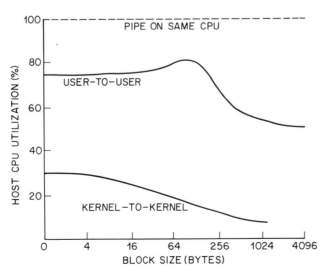

Fig. 7. CPU overhead for communication.

Experiment: Script Run With	Elasped Time	CPU Time (S-UNIX)
Local files only	39 s	12 s
Remote files only	51 s	16 s

Fig. 8.   Response time test.

Measurement	Local Files	Remote Files
s/Run	1699	1988
Scripts completed	20	15
Scripts/h	43	28
s/Script		
Real Time	419 + −22	651 + −46
User	28 + −0.4	30 + −1
System	42 + −1	69 + −1
CPU Utilization		
Local	84 percent	79 percent
Remote	0 percent	43 percent

Fig. 9.   Throughput test.

due to UNIX file system activity. Figure 10 shows the measurements for different computers serving as Common Control.

2) Performance Discussion: Many researchers have found the actually achieved data transfer rates across unloaded high-bandwidth communication media to be disappointingly low due to the complexity of the communication software. At the outset, using DR11-C hardware, we observed user level transfer rates in the 10–15 kbyte/s range with practically 100 percent host CPU utilization. Similar results have been reported by others using a variety of communication media. For example, going through several levels of protocol (some unnecessary), UNIX systems connected over the 6.25 Mbyte/s Hyperchannel® from Network Systems Corporation achieve an effective rate of 18 kbytes/s [14]. Likewise, user level data transfer on a 370 kbyte/s (2.94 Mbit/s) Ethernet® has been observed as 10 kbytes/s [23], and as 50 kbytes/s on the 10 Mbit/s Ethernet between the much faster Dorado computers [7]. Even the highly optimized Tandem system with two 13 Mbyte/s Dynabus connections yields only a rate of 65 kbytes/s at a buffer size of 512 bytes [27].

In light of these reported results, we consider the performance of our current interface to be an advance in the design of efficient communication interfaces:

1) a user level transfer rate of 48–55 kbytes/s at a host CPU utilization of 45 to 80 percent with a relatively slow CPU (11/45),[4]

2) a kernel level transfer rate of 125 kbytes/s,

3) a kernel level message transfer time of 870 μs across the switching system.

® Hyperchannel is a trademark of Network Systems Corporation.

® Ethernet is a trademark of Xerox Corporation.

[4] The variation is due to different driver designs which allow some tradeoff of transfer rate against CPU intensity.

Common Control Computer	Elasped Time
LSI-11	100 ms
PDP-11/23	62 ms
PDP-11/45	50 ms

Fig. 10.   Circuit set-up time.

With the same interface hardware (a 1 Mbit/s DEC DMC-11), and the DDCMP network protocol, used as a machine-to-machine link, the network in use at Purdue has been able to achieve 31.25 kbytes/s between 2 PDP-11/70's.

System performance observations indicate that command execution times are increased by an average of 55 percent if remote files are accessed, showing a range of 37–75 percent. Throughput measurements show a decrease of about 35 percent. Distributing the load of one computer across two specialized computers does not double the capacity; at best, we may achieve that two computers carry the load of one in our current architecture. (We have optimized only the lower communication protocol; the file service protocol carries, among other things, the overhead of accommodating computers with different data representations.) An explanation for this phenomenon is that the transmission delays can be overlapped with local processing (hence, no losses), but the off-loaded file service is compensated for by the communication load (hence, no gains). A very promising result is the short circuit set-up time. Once switch interfaces supporting a larger number of virtual circuits become available, a more dynamic use of circuits can be made; e.g., one will be able to afford setting up circuits for a brief message interchange.

We have conducted extensive communication performance measurements using both software and hardware monitoring techniques. Our results indicate that in order to achieve high transfer rates a fast front-end processor is essential. In our case, the speeds of the host and the front-end are 0.3 and 5 MIPS, respectively. Conversely, the degree of responsiveness is dominated by the speed of the host processor.

VI. POTENTIAL EXTENSIONS

A. Computer Pool

UNIX protocol creation uses the "fork" system call. A process calling *fork* is duplicated: the child process shares the code and all the outside connections (open files) with the parent process. Both continue execution following the *fork* call, but each knows about its identity, and, of course, the parent recognizes the *fork* operation's success or failure. We propose to extend this mechanism by supplying an argument to *fork,* the name of the computer on which the child process is to start. The name could be a generic name asking for any free member of a pool of computers. The *fork* call would then result in a service request to Common Control which would forward it to an available server, an operation similar to a hunt sequence on a telephone switch. The servers in this pool are assumed to have announced their availability.

The computer pool could be used in a variety of ways. First, one could assign each user logging on from a terminal a "personal" computer for the duration of the session. The obvious advantages are: no sharing with other users and no dependence on one specific computer. Second, one could assign additional computers to a user as the need arises. For example, the UNIX command interpreter recognizes "&" at the end of a command as a request for background execution, which is implemented via *fork*. In our model, the background work could be executed on another computer. Further, heavily used commands currently resulting in a pipeline of so-called filter processes could run on several processors. However, there are several problems yet to be solved with this approach. First, one would need communication between S-UNIX subsystems, e.g., through pipes. Second, one would have to bequeath the user's identity to the forked-to pool processor. Third, a particular problem occurs due to the UNIX feature of "set-user-id," which allows processes to assume the privilege of acting on behalf of a user different from the invoker ("effective user" as opposed to "real user"). This set of problems would be greatly simplified if the S-UNIX subsystem were not allowed to have local files.

In a nutshell, the access control problem boils down to the following choice: In a multiuser S-UNIX architecture (our current implementation) the file server trusts the S-UNIX side, which is supplying a (presumably unforgeable) user id with each file open request, assuming that the authentication (login, password) has been valid. Privileged processes (set-user-id) supply the changed "effective user id" with each open request and can thus run on the S-UNIX subsystem. On the other hand, with a remote single-user S-UNIX, the file server has to remember the established "real-user-id" for each subsystem, and a privileged process could not run on the remote system, since there is no way to guarantee that its open requests do not come from an impostor process. One way out would be to restrict privileged processes to run on the file server, which is only possible if it does not require access to files on other S-UNIX or F-UNIX systems.

In summary, the extended *fork* mechanism in connection with a computer pool could be used to exploit obvious parallelism to give users the power of one or more dedicated computers.

B. Further Specialization of Subsystems

Redesign of the component subsystems would preserve the protocols but move towards more specialization. For example, the file server could be redesigned to achieve the following:
1) greater reliability,
2) higher performance,
3) faster recovery from failure,
4) less component complexity.

Specifically, we would redesign the housekeeping algorithms according to the concept of a "stable storage system." This would reduce the damage caused by file server crashes and shorten the recovery time. The latter would be a much welcome improvement, since significant time is currently spent in checking and repairing crashed file systems. The fact that the F-UNIX subsystem offers a full UNIX process environment is an advantage; all that is needed is a special message from the S-UNIX side to start a check and repair process. (Currently, the F-UNIX local operator console has to be used for this activity.)

For extreme reliability requirements, mirrored writing or incremental back-up could be implemented. There are several obvious avenues for performance improvement: a large disk buffer cache, improved in-memory and on-disk search techniques, lower overhead for task switching, contiguous storage and read-ahead for executable files, etc. Reduced complexity would result from restricting the file server to be a computer that handles one disk drive (including name management) and nothing else.

We see significant potential gains in performance and simplicity if the virtual circuit interface we are using could be further exploited by supporting a large number of virtual circuits on each computer; by offering short circuit set-up times; and by implementing the protocol up to the user process level in the hardware (front-end processor). Given these opportunities, we would map each open file into a circuit, which would let all the (de)multiplexing work be done in the front-end.

An architectural revision towards economy of mechanisms and less algorithmic complexity is to merge our concept of "mounting a file server" by extending the UNIX concept of mounting a file system to encompass remote file systems implemented as file servers.

VII. RELATED WORK BY OTHERS

The literature on distributed systems is extensive and surveyed elsewhere [3]. Issues of remote file service have been thoroughly discussed in [24]. We shall, therefore, restrict ourselves here to the UNIX-related efforts.

The idea of interconnecting several UNIX systems has been explored by several people. The most widely used file transfer utility is known as *uucp* (UNIX-to-UNIX Copy). It uses the dial-up network and spools explicitly named remote/local file transfer requests for asynchronous execution [20].

The above scheme is the least transparent of a number of heterogeneous approaches, which all deal with a network of autonomous and more or less equal UNIX systems. To access remote files in addition to local ones, they have been augmented to also recognize remote file names. The remote files are either identified explicitly with a system prefix [4], [17], [1], or the names are integrated into a global name space [13]. The latter, however, provides only read access to remote files and uses user-level daemon processes for intercomputer communication.

Another approach is heterogeneous: computers are specialized to handle only a subset of the operating system functions. At the two ends of the scale are the satellite processor systems [19], [2], which off-load all system calls including file service to a mother system, and the file server in the Spider Network [10], which is a full-fledged UNIX system restricted to and modified for safe keeping of valuable files.

Virtual circuits on multiplexed direct links have been used in the Purdue network [8]. Virtual circuits and the Datakit switch have been used to connect autonomous UNIX systems [11], [4]. The use of pipes and I/O redirection for connection to remote resources was proposed by [15], who has master and slave processes on each computer manage the interaction.

In the light of this prior work, our architecture combines the following attributes: a heterogeneous system with specialized computers, a global file system view with complete read/write transparency, full integration into the operating system kernel with no communication daemon processes, use of virtual circuits within the operating system, and an emphasis on performance that makes operation without local files feasible, since remote files can be accessed almost as fast as local ones.

VIII. CONCLUSION

We have built a distributed system with functionally specialized computers connected by a high-bandwidth virtual circuit switch. The two operating system components allow us to construct configurations with differing degrees of file system access and terminal-to-terminal communication. All configurations share the attribute of presenting a single global file system implemented by a varying number of file server computers. Local files accessible only from the home computer are optimal. Terminals can be connected in several ways: to local hosts, through the switch, or through a front-end. Communication between users on different hosts is more restricted than in uniprocessor UNIX systems: terminal-to-terminal communication and interprocessor pipes are not implemented, but a new mechanism ("fifos") can to some degree replace the latter.

Besides preserving as much of the UNIX capabilities as possible, we concentrated on performance issues. The performance degradation due to the separation of file service from user process handling has been made tolerable by an efficiently designed communication service with novel hardware and software. We have shown that communication based on virtual circuits can achieve high transfer rates, fast response, and low local overhead.

The resulting configurations offer modular growth and potentially more reliability. In spite of advances made in the efficiency of communication, the cost per user of such systems cannot yet compete with a multiplicity of smaller systems each serving smaller communities. A rough and safe estimate is that the CPU and memory resources ought to be doubled to achieve comparable capacity and responsiveness in an aggregate configuration.

However, we believe that with the cost of hardware steadily decreasing and with the efficiency of communication interfaces increasing, the extra costs of such architectures will become affordable when weighted against the additional advantages:

1) the ability to provide a single service to a larger community;
2) the opportunity for modular growth with increasing load;
3) less variability in the level of service;
4) increased service availability;
5) faster recovery from failures;
6) the potential to react faster to changes in user needs;
7) the potential to introduce new technology in a less disruptive manner than in the past.

ACKNOWLEDGMENT

A. G. Fraser and G. L. Chesson gave the authors access to their Datakit hardware and software [5]. E. Sirota from Brown University built the KMC/Datakit interface under the direction of R. C. Haight during a summer assignment. M. J. Bach converted the S-UNIX operating system to a more recent release. M. D. Beck conducted several of the measurements reported here, using facilities developed by J. Feder and D. A. De Graff.

D. L. Bayer, R. H. Canaday, C. F. Simone, E. N. Pinson, J. M. Scanlon, and B. A. Tague deserve the authors' thanks for encouraging and furthering this work.

Finally, this work would not have been possible without K. Thompson and D. Ritchie having supplied the authors with a foundation to build upon: an efficient and understandable operating system, the UNIX system.

REEFERENCES

[1] C. J. Antonelli, L. S. Hamilton, P. M. Lu, J.J. Wallace, and K. Yueh, "SDS/NET-An interactive distributed operating system," in *Proc. COMPCON Fall '80, 21st IEEE Comp. Soc. Conf.,* 1980, pp. 487–493.

[2]   A. B. Barak and A. Shapir, "UNIX with satellite processors," *Software Practice and Experience,* vol. 10, pp. 383–392, May 1980.

[3]   G. von Bochmann, *Architecture of Distributed Computer Systems.* (Lecture Notes in Computer Science #77). New York: Springer-Verlag, 1979.

[4]   G. L. Chesson, "The network UNIX system," *Operating Syst. Rev.,* vol. 9, no. 5, pp. 60–66, 1975; also in *Proc. 5th Symp. Operating Syst. Principles.*

[5]   G. L. Chesson, "Datakit software architecture," *Proc. ICC 79,* Boston, MA, pp. 20.2.1–20.2.5.

[6]   D. Clark, "An introduction to local area networks," in *Proc. IEEE,* vol. 66, pp. 1497–1517, Nov. 1978.

[7]   R. C. Crane and E. A. Taft, "Practical considerations in Ethernet local network design," presented at the Hawaii Int. Conf. Syst. Sci., Jan. 1980.

[8]   W. J. Croft, "UNIX networking at Purdue," presented at the UNIX Usenix Conference, University of Delaware, June 1980.

[9]   Digital Equipment Corporation, Maynard, MA, *pdp11 Peripherals Handbook,* 1978, pp. 331–339, *KMC11-B Unibus Microprocessor,* YM-C093C-00, Jan. 1979, *COMM IOP-DUP Programming Manual,* No. AA-5670A-TC, *Terminals and Communications Handbook,* 1979.

[10] A. G. Fraser, "Spider—An Experimental data communication system," in *Proc. IEEE Conf. on Commun.,* June 1974, pp. 21–30; IEEE Cat. No. 74CH0859-9-CSCB.

[11] A. G. Fraser, "A virtual channel network," *Datamation,* vol. 21, pp. 51–58, Feb. 1975.

[12] A. G. Fraser, "Datakit—A modular network for synchronous and asynchronous traffic," in *Proc. ICC 1979,* Boston, MA, June 1979, pp. 20.1.1–20.1.3.

[13] A. Glasser and D. M. Ungar, "A distributed UNIX system," in *Proc. 5th Berkeley Workshop on Distributed Data Management and Comput. Networks,* Feb. 3–5, 1980, p. 241.

[14] S. Goldsmith, private communication, measurement at Bell Labs Murray Hill Comp. Center.

[15] S. F. Holmgren, "Resource sharing UNIX," presented at the 17th IEEE Comput. Society Int. Conf., Washington, DC, Sept. 5–8, 1978; New York: IEEE, 1978, pp. 302–305.

[16] J. C. Kaufeld and D. Russell, "Distributed UNIX system," *Workshop on Fundamental Issues in Distributed Computing, ACM SIGOPS and SIGPLAN,* Fallbrook, CA, Dec. 15–17, 1980.

[17] P. M. Lu, "A system for resources sharing in a distributed environment—RIDE," in *Proc. IEEE Comput. Society's 3rd Int. COMPSAC,* 1979.

[18] G. W. R. Luderer, H. Che, and W. T. Marshall, "A virtual circuit switch as the basis for a distributed system," presented at the Seventh Data Commun. Symp. 1981, ACM, IEEE Computer Society, IEEE Communications Society, Oct. 27–29, 1981.

[19] H. Lycklama and C. Christensen, "A minicomputer satellite processor system," *Bell Syst. Tech. J.,* vol. 57, July–Aug. 1978.

[20] D. A. Nowitz and M. E. Lesk, "Implementation of a dial-up network of UNIX systems," in *Proc. COMPCON Fall '80, 21st IEEE Comp. Soc. Conf.,* 1980, pp. 483–486.

[21] J. L. Peterson, "Notes on a workshop on distributed computing," *ACM Operating Syst. Rev.,* vol. 13, pp. 18–30, July 1979.

[22] D. M. Ritchie and K. L. Thompson, "The UNIX time-sharing system," *Commun. Ass. Comput. Mach.,* vol. 17, pp. 365–375, July 1974.

[23] A. L. Spector, Stanford University and Xerox Corporation, private communication.

[24] H. Sturgis, J. Mitchell, and J. Israel, "Issues in thre design and use of a distributed file system," *ACM Operating Syst. Rev.,* vol. 14, p. 55–69, July 1980.

[25] K. Thompson, "UNIX implementation," *Bell Syst. Tech. J.,* vol. 57, pp. 1931–1946, July–Aug. 1978.

[26] K. J. Thurber and G. M. Masson, *Distributed Processor Communication Architecture,* Lexington, MA: Heath, 1979.

[27] A. M. Usas, private communication of measurements done under Tandem's Guardian operating system at Bell Laboratories.

33
Protocols for Large Data Transfers Over Local Networks

WILLY ZWAENEPOEL

In this chapter we analyze protocols for reliably transmitting large amounts of data over a local area network. The data transfers analyzed in this chapter are different from most other forms of large-scale data transfer protocols for three reasons: 1) the definition of the protocol requires the recipient to have sufficient buffers available to receive the data before the transfer takes place; 2) we assume that the source and the destination machines are more or less matched in speed; 3) the protocol is implemented at the network interrupt level and therefore not slowed down by process scheduling delays.

We consider three classes of protocols: stop-and-wait, sliding window, and blast protocols. We show that the expected time of blast and sliding window protocols is significantly lower than the expected time for the stop-and-wait protocol, with blast outperforming sliding window by some small amount. Although the network error rate is sufficiently low for blast with full retransmission on error to be acceptable, the frequency of errors in the network interfaces makes it desirable to use a more sophisticated retransmission protocol.

Our results are based on measurements collected on SUN workstations connected to a 10 Mbit Ethernet network using 3-Com interfaces. The derivation of the elapsed time in terms of the network packet error rate is based on the assumption of statistically independent errors.

I. INTRODUCTION

Recent studies have shown the importance of using large page sizes in order to achieve high performance file access, both locally as well as over a network [10], [12], [15]. This is due to economies in accessing the disk in large quantities as well as to economies in accessing the network in large quantities. In this chapter we study the latter phenomenon. In particular, we study the performance of protocols for transmitting large amounts of data across a local network characterized by a low error rate, low propagation delay, and high bandwidth.

By large amounts of data, we denote amounts that are one or two orders of magnitude larger than the maximum network packet size. We show how our analysis can be extended to larger sizes such as those involved, for instance, in remote file system dumps. We study three classes of protocols: stop-and-wait, sliding window, and blast protocols (see Fig. 1). With stop-and-wait protocols, the source refrains from sending a packet until it has received an acknowledgment for the previous packet. With a blast protocol all data packets are transmitted in sequence, with only a single acknowledgment for the entire packet sequence. Different protocols within the category of blast protocols are distinguished by

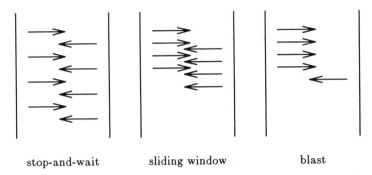

stop-and-wait   sliding window   blast

Fig. 1.   Stop-and-wait, sliding window, and blast protocols.

their retransmission strategies (e.g., all packets can be retransmitted, or some form of selective retransmission can be used). With sliding window protocols every packet is individually acknowledged but the sender continues to transmit data without waiting for an acknowledgment. In typical sliding window protocols, the sender is silenced when the window "closes." Here we assume that the window is large enough so that it never gets closed.

For error-free transmissions, stop-and-wait protocols do not perform as well as sliding window or blast protocols because of delays in waiting for the acknowledgment for every packet. Given the low latency and the high bandwidth of local networks, one would expect the difference in performance to be rather small. However, experimental evidence shows that the penalty for using a stop-and-wait protocol on a local network is substantially higher than expected because of significant extra delays in generating and receiving packets. Sliding window protocols are slightly inferior to blast protocols because of the overhead involved in handling the extra acknowledgments.

We then consider the performance of the protocols in the presence of transmission errors on the network. Given typical error rates on a local network, the expected elapsed time of a given transmission is almost identical to the error-free transmission time. As a result, under normal local network operating conditions, blast and sliding window protocols outperform stop-and-wait protocols. In fact, network error rates are sufficiently rare to make it possible to use full retransmission on error in conjunction with a blast protocol without significant degradation in the expected elapsed times. However, frequent interface errors force a more sophisticated retransmission strategy in order to maintain a near-optimal expected time and a small standard deviation.

Our results are based on measurements of transmissions between SUN-2 workstations connected to a 10 Mbit Ethernet network using a 3-COM Multibus interface, and on a probabilistic analysis of the performance in the presence of errors. Since our measurements are done in the absence of any substantial network load, contention delays are all but absent from the results. Our conclusions are therefore valid only under low load conditions. Fortunately, such conditions are typical of most local network based systems. We also use delay under low load as a measure of performance, rather than throughput under high load, because low load conditions are so prevalent. In the error analysis, we assume that packet transmissions are statistically independent events with a constant failure probability. In practice, this assumption is a reasonable approximation of reality, although burst errors occasionally occur.

The outline of the rest of this chapter is as follows. Section II describes measurements of error-free transmissions using each of the three protocols considered. In Section III, we compare the performance of these three protocols in function of the error rate of the network. In Section IV we study different retransmission strategies that can be used in conjunction with blast protocols. Related work is covered in Section V and conclusions are drawn in Section VI.

II. Error-Free Data Transmissions

The large data transfers discussed in this chapter occur as part of the interprocess communication functions provided by the V kernel [3], [6], [20]. The V kernel is a distributed operating systems kernel, currently implemented on a variety of SUN workstation models and on DEC MicroVaxen. The results reported here were gathered on a 68010-based SUN-2 workstation connected to a 10 Mbit Ethernet [8] by a 3-Com interface [1]. As part of its interprocess communication facilities, the V kernel provides two operations, MoveTo and MoveFrom, which allow one process to move an arbitrary amount of data from its address space into the address space of another process, or vice versa. Both operations are network transparent: the destination process may or may not be on the same machine as the source process. By definition of the V interprocess communication primitives (see [3], [6], [20]), the recipient must allocate sufficient buffers to receive the data prior to the transfer. In the remote case, prior allocation of buffers by the recipient allows the kernel(s) to move data from the source address into the network interface of the sending machine, and from the network interface of the receiving machine into the destination address space without an intermediate copy.[1]

The total time necessary to execute a MoveTo or a MoveFrom is the sum of the cost of network communication and the cost of kernel overhead. In Section II-A, we describe a set of experiments to quantify the cost of network communication. Measurements with the V kernel implementation of MoveTo and MoveFrom, including both network communication and kernel overhead, are discussed in Section II-B.

A. Network Communication Overhead

1) Experimental Method and Results: In order to quantify the cost of network communication, two standalone programs are run on two different machines connected to the network. One program acts as the source of data and the other as the destination. Data are transmitted from the source in 1 kbyte packets, and 64 byte acknowledgments are returned from the destination as appropriate, according to which protocol is used. For statistical accuracy, the experiment is repeated a number of times and the results are averaged. In all measurements, the network is essentially idle, so no significant contention delay is experienced. The transfers are implemented at the data link layer and device level so that no protocol or process switching overhead appears in the results. In particular, no header (other than the Ethernet data link header) is added to the data, and no provisions are made for demultiplexing packets, or for retransmission. If a transmission error occurs, the experiment halts and is restarted. Also, both programs simply busy-wait on the completion of their current operation, thereby avoiding interrupt handling overhead. The experiment therefore provides an accurate approximation of the "raw" communication cost involved in the data transfer. Measurement results for the elapsed time of multipacket transfers in stop-and-wait (SAW), sliding window (SW), and blast (B) mode are reported in Table I.

[1] At least with suitable network interfaces.

TABLE I
STANDALONE MEASUREMENTS OF ERROR-FREE TRANSMISSIONS

Size	SAW	SW	B
1 kbyte	4.1 ms	4.1 ms	4.1 ms
8 kbyte	32.7 ms	21.7 ms	19.8 ms
64 kbyte	261.6 ms	161.5 ms	141.1 ms
512 kbyte	2 093.0 ms	1 284.0 ms	1 149.0 ms

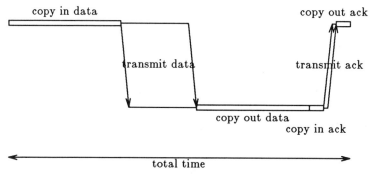

Fig. 2. Network packet transmission.

2) Interpretation: Let us first consider data transfers that fit within a single network packet, for instance a 1 kbyte transfer.[2] The reliable transfer of 1 kbyte of data, using a 64 byte acknowledgment, takes 4.1 ms (see Table I). This is significantly more than the transmission time of the data and the acknowledgment packet, which would be 0.87 ms when computed at the 10 Mbit data rate of the network. The difference between the network time, computed at the network data rate, and the measured elapsed time is accounted for almost exclusively by the time necessary for the processors to copy the packets into and out of the interface (see Fig. 2).

Table II shows a breakdown of the total elapsed time over its various components. As can be seen, of the 4.1 ms total elapsed time, only 21 percent is network transmission time, while 75 percent is copying overhead, the rest (presumably) being network and device latency.

Let us now consider the case where the data transfer requires N packets to be sent from the source to the destination. The reason for the superior performance of the blast and sliding window protocols is explained in Fig. 3. Figure 3(a) corresponds to the transmission in stop-and-wait mode, (b) corresponds to the blast transmission, and (c) depicts the sliding window protocol. The time axis runs horizontally from left to right and the example is for the case of $N = 3$.

Consider first the sequence of events in the case of a stop-and-wait protocol. The sending processor copies a packet from main memory to its interface and then the interface puts the packet on the network. After a time period equal to the network propagation delay, the packet arrives at the receiver's interface and then it is copied from the receiver's interface into the receiver's memory by the receiving processor. This process repeats itself in the

[2] The maximum packet size on the 10 Mbit Ethernet is 1536 bytes.

TABLE II
BREAKDOWN OF TRANSMISSION COST OVER ITS
VARIOUS COMPONENTS

Operation	Time
Copy data into sender's interface	1.35 ms
Transmit data	0.82 ms
Copy data out of receiver's interface	1.35 ms
Copy ack into receiver's interface	0.17 ms
Transmit ack	0.05 ms
Copy ack out of sender's interface	0.17 ms
Total	3.91 ms
Observed elapsed time	4.08 ms

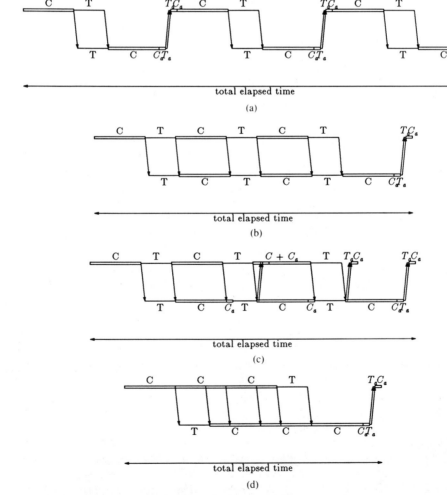

Fig. 3. (a) Stop-and-wait. (b) Blast protocol. (c) Sliding window protocol. (d) Double buffered interface with blast protocol.

reverse direction for the acknowledgment packet, and then again for the next packet, and so forth. Note that the two processors are never active in parallel. This is not the case when the transfer is done in blast mode, as shown in Fig. 3(b). Due to the very low propagation delay of a local network, the packet is received in the receiver's interface almost completely concurrently with the sender's interface transferring it over the network.[3] Therefore, the processor on the sending machine can start copying the next packet from memory to its interface in parallel with the processor on the receiving machine copying the previous packet out of its interface into its memory. Due to the fact that these copies happen in parallel, and, as we saw before, the copy times contribute significantly towards the overall elapsed time, blast transfer results in elapsed times that are substantially lower than those obtained for stop-and-wait transfers.

Finally, consider the operation of the sliding window protocol [Fig. 3(c)]. Again, the copy operations in and out of the interface happen in parallel on the sender and on the receiver. The reason for the slightly inferior performance of the sliding window protocol versus a blast protocol is that for each packet an acknowledgment has to be copied in and out of the interfaces, while for the blast protocol, there is only an acknowledgment for the last packet.

3) Formulas for Error-Free Transmissions: From Fig. 3 we can derive formulas for the elapsed times of multipacket data transfers in the absence of errors. Let C be the time necessary to copy a data packet into or out of the interface and let C_a be the time necessary for a copy of the acknowledgment packets. Similarly, let T be the network transmission time for a data packet, and T_a the network transmission time for an acknowledgment packet. Ignoring latency, the elapsed times for stop-and-wait, blast, and sliding window are, respectively,

$$T_{SAW} = N \times (2C + T + 2C_a + T_a)$$

$$T_B = N \times (C + T) + C + 2C_a + T_a$$

$$T_{SW} = N \times (C + C_a + T) + C + T_a.$$

Note that the utilization of the network U_n, even when using a blast protocol, is still significantly below 100 percent:

$$U_n = \frac{N \times T + T_a}{N \times T + T_a + N \times C + C + 2C_a}.$$

For instance, for the 64 kbyte transfer shown in Table I, the network utilization is only 38 percent. Better elapsed times and better network utilization can be obtained if a double buffered interface is used. In that case, the processor can start copying a packet into the second buffer in the interface while the interface is transmitting the previous packet over the network, and similarly on the receiving machine. Note that having a third transmission buffer does not provide any further improvement over double buffering, since we assume that both C and T are constant. The value of T is constant as long as there is no significant contention delay. The value of C is also constant since we assume the network transfer is

---

[3] In fact, the propagation delay is far exaggerated in Figs. 2 and 3 to make it visible at all: typical propagation delays on a local network are on the order of 10 μs while the copy and transmission times considered are on the order of 1 ms.

the only activity occupying the processor, and therefore there is no delay in performing the copy operation. The elapsed time $T_{d/b}$ becomes [see Fig. 3(d)]

$$T_{d/b} = N \times C + T + C + 2C_a + T_a \qquad (T \leq C)$$

$$T_{d/b} = N \times T + 2C + 2C_a + T_a \qquad (T \geq C).$$

Figure 4 compares the performance of the different protocols in terms of N for values of C, C_a, T, and T_a as on the SUN-2 workstation with a 10 Mbit Ethernet (see Table II).

One might wonder whether it is possible to get rid of the copy into the interface altogether, by simply moving the data from main memory onto the network. An interesting design that allows network access without an intermediate copy appears in the Xerox Alto personal computer, where network access is incorporated as an independent task in the processor's microengine [19]. The copy can also be avoided by virtual memory techniques (if the origin and the destination of the data are aligned on a page boundary). The Apollo Domain architecture supports this feature [11]. For more conventional architectures, one would like a DMA interface to copy the data from main memory directly onto the network. Note that many currently available DMA interfaces do not allow such a direct copy and require the data to be copied first from main memory to private memory buffers on the DMA device. In this case, the formulas derived above for the elapsed time therefore remain valid, provided that C and C_a are no longer the time required for the host processor to make the copies, but rather the time required for the DMA processor to do so. Our experience to date suggests that using such devices does not improve elapsed times significantly, although it reduces host processor overhead related to network access. We are currently experimenting with the LANCE DMA Ethernet controller which allows a direct copy, but measurements are not available to date. As a final comment on the design of "intelligent" network interfaces, the relative importance of the copy operation indicates that memory and bus bandwidth are the critical factors. Therefore, it seems likely that a processor with a fast block move operation, accompanied by very high-speed device

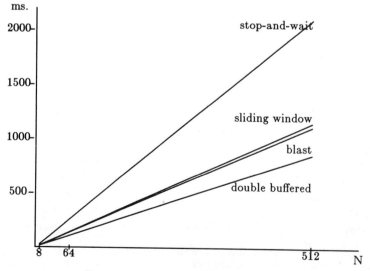

Fig. 4.   Comparison of different protocols.

TABLE III
V KERNEL MOVETO MEASUREMENTS

Size	SAW	B
1 kbyte	5.9 ms	5.9 ms
8 kbyte	43.1 ms	24.8 ms
64 kbyte	340.2 ms	173.0 ms
512 kbyte	2 719.0 ms	1 370.0 ms

memory is more promising than any kind of special purpose packet handling hardware on the interface (see also [9]).

B. Large Data Transfers at the Kernel Level

The protocol used for the set of measurements in the previous section is impractical in many ways. A realistic protocol must contend with transmission errors by means of a retransmission strategy. Incoming packets have to be demultiplexed, the access rights of the sender have to be checked, and the processor has to be shared with other activities by handling the network in an interrupt-driven rather than a busy-wait fashion. Performing these functions typically requires extra headers to be sent with the data, increasing the transmission time, and introduces additional packet handling overhead on the hosts.

All of these functions have been implemented as part of the *V* kernel's network interprocess communication. Table III gives the results of our measurements of the *V* kernel's MoveTo operation.[4] The results only confirm the measurements of Section II-A. The formulas derived for the elapsed times under various combinations of transmission protocols and network interfaces remain valid, if the extra overhead is added to C and C_a. For instance, for the blast protocol, the modified values of C and C_a are 1.83 and 0.67 ms versus 1.35 and 0.17 ms in the standalone experiments. The relative increase of C and C_a, compared to T and T_a, makes the blast protocol even more advantageous than in the case of a standalone program. In fact, in the case of the *V* kernel, the extra overhead is relatively minimal compared to other protocols and protocol implementations, which suggests that the use of a blast protocol would be even more advantageous under those circumstances.

III. EFFECT OF TRANSMISSION ERRORS

We first compare stop-and-wait with retransmission of a single packet on timeout to blast with retransmission of the full sequence of packets after a certain retransmission interval. For typical local network error rates, we show that the expected time of the blast transmission is significantly better than the expected time of the stop-and-wait transmission. We then consider various retransmission strategies that can be used in conjunction with a blast protocol. The sliding window protocol is not discussed in any detail in this section: its error characteristics are similar to those of the blast protocol with selective retransmission.

In this analysis, we assume that packet transmissions are statistically independent events with constant failure probability p_n. This is a reasonable first-order approximation of the

---

[4] Measurements for the sliding window protocol are not available at the time of writing. We would expect the elapsed times for sliding window to be slightly higher than those for blast, as suggested by the standalone measurements in Table I.

behavior of the network. Analysis of the performance under other error distributions is beyond the scope of this chapter.

A. Expected Time

Let $T_0(1)$ be the elapsed time for an error-free 1-packet exchange in stop-and-wait mode, let T_r be the retransmission interval, and assume D packets have to be transmitted. Then it can easily be shown that the expected time μ_{SAW} for transmitting D packets by means of a stop-and-wait protocol is[5]

$$\mu_{SAW} = D \times \left[T_0(1) + (T_0(1) + T_r) \times \left(\frac{p_{e,\,SAW}}{1 - p_{e,\,SAW}} \right) \right]$$

with

$$p_{e,\,SAW} = 1 - (1 - p_n)^2.$$

Similarly, let $T_0(D)$ be the elapsed time for an error-free D-packet exchange in blast mode, then the expected time μ_B for a D-packet exchange in blast mode is

$$\mu_B = T_0(D) + (T_0(D) + T_r) \times \left(\frac{p_{e,B}}{1 - p_{e,B}} \right)$$

with

$$p_{e,B} = 1 - (1 - p_n)^{D+1}.$$

Figure 5 compares the two strategies for different values of T_r. (The other parameters in the figure are $D = 64$, $T_0(1) = 5.9$ ms and $T_0(D) = 173$ ms, from Table III.) In addition to these curves we need some idea about the error rate on a 10 Mbit Ethernet. Surprisingly enough, very little empirical data are available about the error rates on local networks. Shoch and Hupp report an observed error rate of 1 in 200 000 packets on the experimental Xerox PARC 3 Mbit Ethernet [16]. Measurements on our local 10 Mbit Ethernet indicate an error rate of approximately 1 in 100 000 under normal circumstances. However, when one workstation transmits at full speed to another workstation, the error rates rise an order of magnitude, to approximately 1 in 10 000. We assume that most of the additional errors are due to failures and buffer overruns in the Ethernet interface. (See also [5], [13] for additional evidence of large packet losses in interfaces.) We, therefore, operate somewhere in the region between 10^{-4} and 10^{-5} in Fig. 5. Consequently, the expected time of the blast protocol is notably better than that of the stop-and-wait protocol. With improved network interfaces the difference between the two protocols would be even more outspoken.

These results also allow us to make a stronger conclusion: since the expected time for a blast protocol with the crudest retransmission strategy, full retransmission on error and no negative acknowledgment, results in a nearly optimal expected time (for the appropriate

---

[5] The second occurrence of $T_0(1)$ in this formula should strictly speaking be replaced by $T_0'(1)$, the elapsed time of a *failed* transmission. In practice, the difference is minor and can be subsumed by slightly adjusting the value of T_r.

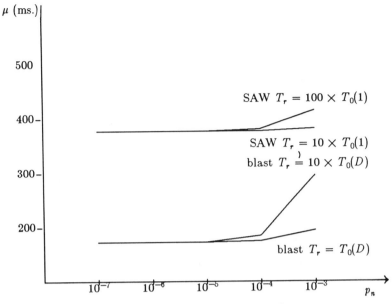

Fig. 5.   Expected time for 64 kbyte transfers.

range of p_n values), no significant improvements in expected time can be achieved by more sophisticated retransmission strategies. In the next section, we show that such strategies can significantly improve the standard deviation.

At this point, an observation is in order about the size of the data transfers used in a blast protocol. Clearly as the size of the data transfer increases, errors are more likely and retransmission becomes more costly. For such very large sizes, we suggest the use of multiple blasts, whereby the transfer is broken up in a number of different blasts, each of which proceeds according to the definition of the blast protocol.

B. Standard Deviation

We now analyze the standard deviation of different retransmission strategies that can be used in conjunction with a blast protocol. We assume that we operate under error conditions such that the expected time of the transfer is nearly identical to the error-free transmission time (i.e., we operate in the flat region of the curves in Fig. 5).

Consider a given transmission strategy and denote by $T_0(D)$ the error-free transmission time. Furthermore, let $T_0^k(D)$ be the elapsed time for the kth transmission attempt, let $T_r^k(D)$ be the interval between the kth and the $(k + 1)$th transmission attempt, and finally let $s(i + 1)$ be the probability of success on the $(i + 1)$th transmission attempt. Then, if the transfer succeeds on the $(i + 1)$th transmission attempt, the total elapsed time for this transfer is

$$\sum_{k=0}^{i} T_0^{k+1}(D) + \sum_{k=0}^{i-1} T_r^{k+1}(D).$$

Assuming we are operating under low error conditions and that, thus, the expected time is constant and approximately equal to $T_0(D)$, we get for the variance

$$\sigma^2 = \sum_{i=0}^{\infty} \left[\left(\sum_{k=0}^{i} T_0^{k+1}(D) + \sum_{k=0}^{i-1} T_r^{k+1}(D) \right)^2 \times s(i+1) \right] - T_0^2(D).$$

This formula indicates three potentially fruitful avenues for reducing the variance.

1) Reduce the retransmission intervals $T_r^k(D)$: this can be accomplished either by choosing a small timeout value or by providing a negative acknowledgment when the transfer fails.

2) Reduce the transmission time $T_0^k(D)$ for retransmissions: this can be done by reducing the number of packets to be sent on retransmission. A negative acknowledgment packet can carry information as to which packets were successfully received.

3) Reduce the probability of failure of the retransmissions: since we are assuming independent failures, this probability is only dependent on the number of packets transmitted. Thus, here also reducing the number of packets sent has a beneficial effect.

Clearly, a combination of these different approaches is optimal. However, we analyze the different methods in isolation to assess their relative benefits. The crudest retransmission strategy is full retransmission on error after the retransmission interval T_r has expired, without the use of a negative acknowledgment. The standard deviation for this strategy is easily shown to be

$$\sigma = (T_0(D) + T_r) \times \left(p_{e,B}^{1/2} \times \frac{(1 + p_{e,B})^{1/2}}{1 - p_{e,B}} \right)$$

with

$$p_{e,B} = 1 - (1 - p_n)^{D+1}.$$

A slightly more sophisticated strategy still uses full retransmission but also employs a negative acknowledgment. In particular, when the destination receives the last packet, it sends either a positive or a negative acknowledgment depending on whether or not it received all packets in the sequence. If the sender gets a negative acknowledgment, or if the sender does not receive any acknowledgment within a time interval T_r, it retransmits the whole sequence of packets. The characteristics of this strategy can be derived by an approximate argument [21] leading to

$$\sigma \approx T_0(D) \times \left(p_{e,B}^{1/2} \times \frac{(1 + p_{e,B}^{1/2})}{1 - p_{e,B}} \right)$$

with

$$p_{e,B} = 1 - (1 - p_n)^{D+1}.$$

The final two strategies we consider are partial retransmission and selective retransmission. These are implemented as follows. In order to execute a D-packet transfer, $(D - 1)$ packets are transmitted without acknowledgment. The last packet is sent reliably, i.e., it is retransmitted periodically until an acknowledgment is received. The acknowledgment to the last packet indicates which is the first of the $D - 1$ unreliably transmitted packets that was not received (in the case of partial retransmission) or which of the $D - 1$ unreliably transmitted packets did not get to their destination (in the case of selective retransmission). If D' did not get there, they need to be retransmitted using the same method: transmit D' $- 1$ packets unreliably and the last packet reliably. This procedure continues until all packets get to their destination. The standard deviations associated with these retransmission strategies are difficult to derive analytically. We have simulated the procedures by computer and determined both the expected time and the variance from the simulation.

Figure 6 presents a comparison of the standard deviation of the four retransmission strategies that we consider. Full retransmission without a negative acknowledgement produces unacceptable variations in the elapsed times of the transfers (for realistic retransmission intervals). Use of a negative acknowledgement reduces these variations drastically. Given the presence of such negative acknowledgment, the extension to partial retransmission starting from the first packet not successfully received is trivial and provides further reduction of the variance. It would seem that the additional complexity of selective retransmission is not warranted in view of the minimal improvement in performance resulting from it. However, several authors have argued that selective retransmission is desirable to make the protocol more robust against different processing speeds at the sender and the receiver and to provide a smooth extension to an internetwork environment [4], [7].

IV. RELATED WORK

Protocols to support network interprocess communication have been the subject of a number of recent research papers. The protocol supporting the V kernel interprocess communication has been described in [3], [4], [6], [20]. Another interesting example appears in Cedar RPC, although this design refrains from using blast protocols for large

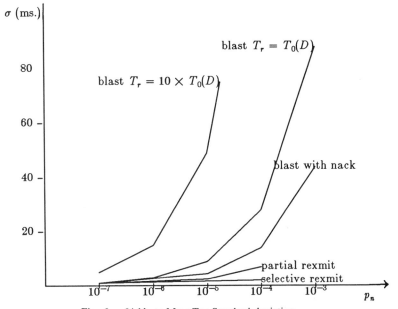

Fig. 6.   64 kbyte MoveTo: Standard deviation.

transmissions [2]. The relative importance of the cost of copying data in a local network protocol implementation is clearly pointed out by a recent paper by Kanakia and Tobagi [9]. The author first became aware of the name blast protocol in conjunction with protocols developed at M.I.T. for downloading screen images from a VAX to an Alto. More recent work on the NETBLT protocol at M.I.T. addresses the issue of large data transfers in an internetwork environment [7]. The idea of blast protocols has been mentioned by various other authors, including Spector who calls it a multipacket transfer and suggests using an overall software checksum on the entire data segment [17]. Needham mentions the use of a transmit-and-pray protocol for file transfers on the Cambridge ring: it is essentially a disk-to-disk (rather than machine-to-machine) blast protocol with full retransmission on error [14].

A large body of work is concerned with the performance of various transmissions strategies such as stop-and-wait, go-back-n, and selective retransmission [18]. Most of these analyses assume that the network is a scarce resource, to be shared in an efficient way by a large number of users, and therefore use throughput under high offered load as a measure of performance. The networks studied usually have high error rates (and frequently high latency, such as satellite networks). Although some of them consider the use of cumulative acknowledgments, few consider delaying the acknowledgment altogether until the end of the transmission. Their analysis needs to be reconsidered in a local network environment, where network bandwidth is plentiful, errors are rare, and low delay under low load is more important than high throughput under high load. In fact, most of this work ignores the software cost of generating and receiving the packets, which dominates the transmission cost in a local network environment.

V. Conclusions

The V interkernel protocol has been designed to aggressively take advantage of local network characteristics such as low error rate, high bandwidth, and low latency. In order to do so, the software overhead involved in dealing with network interprocess communication must be minimized. As a result, the protocol has been implemented at the network interrupt level and assuming communication partners that are more or less matched in speed. For large data transfers, client buffers are made available prior to the transfer, so that no intermediate copies need to be made.

In such a "tight" implementation of the protocol, we have shown that the overhead of copying data in and out of the network interfaces is a dominating factor in the overall elapsed time. Since blast protocols and sliding window protocols allow these copies to occur in parallel on the source and the destination machine, they perform substantially better than stop-and-wait protocols.

We have also considered the effect of transmission errors on the performance of various protocols. Experimental evidence suggests that network errors are relatively rare, but that interface errors occur more frequently, especially if the devices are driven at full speed. Given the network error rate, it would be acceptable to use full retransmission on error in conjunction with a blast protocol. However, the frequency of errors in the interface causes such a strategy to have unacceptable variations in the elapsed times.

Acknowledgment

The original V kernel protocol was developed by the author at Stanford University under the direction of D. Cheriton. The author wishes to thank G. Almes, D. Cheriton, A.

Porterfield, and F. Tobagi for their comments on earlier versions of this chapter. This work was supported in part by the National Science Foundation under Grant DCR-8511436 and by an IBM Faculty Development Award.

REFERENCES

[1] 3-COM Corporation, Multibus Ethernet (ME) Controller Model 3C4000, Reference Manual, May 1982.

[2] A. D. Birrell and B. J. Nelson, "Implementing remote procedure calls," *ACM Trans. Comput. Syst.*, vol. 2, pp. 39–59, Feb. 1984.

[3] D. R. Cheriton, "The V kernel: A software base for distributed systems," *IEEE Software*, vol. 1, no. 2, pp. 19–42, Apr. 1984.

[4] D. R. Cheriton, "VMTP: A transport protocol for the next generation of communication systems," in *Proc. '86 ACM SigComm Conf.*, Aug. 1984, pp. 406–415.

[5] D. R. Cheriton and P. J. Roy, "Performance of the V storage server: A preliminary report," in *Proc. 1985 ACM Comput. Sci. Conf.*, Mar. 1985, pp. 302–308.

[6] D. R. Cheriton and W. Zwaenepoel, "The distributed V kernel and its performance for diskless workstations," in *Proc. 9th Symp. Operating Syst. Principles*, Oct. 1983, pp. 129–140.

[7] D. D. Clark, M. L. Lambert, and L. Zhang, "NETBLT: A bulk data transfer protocol," RFC 969, Defense Advanced Research Projects Agency, Dec. 1985.

[8] Digital Equipment Corporation, Intel Corporation, and Xerox Corporation, "The Ethernet: A local area network-data link layer and physical layer," Specifications, Version 2.0.

[9] H. Kanakia and F. Tobagi, "Performance measurements of a data link protocol," in *Proc. ICC 86*, June 1986.

[10] E. D. Lazowska, J. Zahorjan, D. R. Cheriton, and W. Zwaenepoel, "File access performance of diskless workstations," *ACM Trans. Comput. Syst.*, vol. 4, pp. 238–268, Aug. 1986.

[11] P. J. Leach, P. H. Levine, B. P. Douros, J. A. Hamilton, D. L. Nelson, and B. L. Stumpf, "The architecture of an integrated local network," *IEEE J. Select. Areas Commun.,* vol. SAC-1, pp. 842–857, Nov. 1983.

[12] M. K. McKusick, W. N. Joy, S. J. Leffler, and R. S. Fabry, "A fast file system for UNIX," *ACM Trans. Comput. Syst.*, vol. 2, pp. 181–197, Aug. 1984.

[13] J. Nabielsky, "Interfacing to the 10 Mbps Ethernet: Observations and conclusions," in *Proc. '84 ACM SigComm Conf.*, June 1984, pp. 124–131.

[14] R. M. Needham, "Systems aspects of the Cambridge ring," in *Proc. Seventh ACM Symp. Operating Syst. Principles*, Dec. 1979, pp. 82–85.

[15] J. Ousterhout, H. Da Costa, D. Harrison, J. A. Kunze, M. Kupfer, J. G. Thompson, "A trace-driven analysis of the UNIX 4.2BSD file system," Computer Science Division, Univ. California at Berkeley, Tech. Rep.

[16] J. Shoch and J. A. Hupp, "Measured performance of an Ethernet local network," *Commun. Ass. Comput. Mach.*, vol. 23, pp. 711–721, Dec. 1980.

[17] A. Z. Spector, "Multiprocessing architectures for local computer networks," Dep. Comput. Sci., Stanford Univ., Stanford, CA, Aug. 1981, Tech. Rep. STAN-CS-81-874.

[18] A. S. Tanenbaum, *Computer Networks.* Englewood Cliffs, NJ: Prentice-Hall, 1981.

[19] C. P. Thacker, E. M. McCreight, B. W. Lampson, R. F. Sproull, and D. R. Boggs, "Alto: A personal computer," *Computer Structures: Principles and Examples*, D. P. Siewiorek, C. G. Bell, and A. Newell, Eds. New York: McGraw-Hill, 1982, pp. 549–572.

[20] W. Zwaenepoel, "Message passing on a local network," Ph.D. dissertation, Stanford Univ., Stanford, CA, Tech. Rep. STAN-CS-85-1083, Oct. 1984.

[21] ——, "Protocols for large data transfers on a local network," Dep. Comput. Sci., Rice Univ., Houston, TX, Tech. Rep. COMP TR 85-23, May 1985.

34
A Comparison of Two Network-Based File Servers

JAMES G. MITCHELL AND JEREMY DION

This chapter compares two working network-based file servers, the Xerox Distributed File System (XDFS) implemented at the Xerox Palo Alto Research Center, and the Cambridge File Server (CFS) implemented at the Cambridge University Computer Laboratory. Both servers support concurrent random access to files using atomic transactions, both are connected to local area networks, and both have been in service long enough to enable us to draw lessons from them for future file servers.

We compare the servers in terms of design goals, implementation issues, performance, and their relative successes and failures, and discuss what we would do differently next time.

I. INTRODUCTION

The increasing number of local area networks is leading to an increasing interest in the various services needed to support a distributed computing environment. This has resulted in a number of implementations and proposals for file servers providing shared access to secondary storage [2], [6], [17], [19], [24], [26]. One or more server computers can be dedicated to the control of large disk units for the benefit of the remaining client computers attached to the network. This not only allows the economies of sharing expensive mechanical storage devices among cheaper processors, but also provides the file sharing which is extremely important in a distributed environment. Without some form of file sharing, users are forced to copy files from machine to machine explicitly, distributing program updates to all users can be a nightmare, and concurrent database access by several users is impossible.

This chapter compares and contrasts two working file servers in terms of their design goals, implementation issues, and service experience. Both file servers support concurrent random access to files and an atomic transaction mechanism covering modifications to files. One server, the Xerox Distributed File System (XDFS) [24], was built at the Xerox Palo Alto Research Center; the other, the Cambridge File Server (CFS) [2], [6], [7], was built at the Cambridge University Computer Laboratory. One author (JGM) was a member of the team that built the XDFS, and the other author (JD) was the primary implementor of the CFS.

574

II. UNDERLYING HARDWARE AND SOFTWARE

The CFS was written using the BCPL language [22] and runs on a Computer Automation LSI4/30 minicomputer with 64K 16-bit words of memory and an execution rate of approximately 1 Mips (millions of instructions per second). The CFS program occupies about 50K words, leaving 14K for data and disk buffering. The Cambridge ring [29] serves as the communication medium between the CFS and its clients. It has a raw bandwidth of 10 Mbits/s and a maximum point-to-point data bandwidth of about 1 Mbit/s.

The XDFS was written using the Mesa language [15] and runs on an Alto minicomputer [27] using 164K 16 bit words, 64K of which is data and 100K of which is code. When running Mesa, the Alto executes at approximately 0.25 Mips. For communicating with its clients, the XDFS uses an Ethernet-1 communications system [14] with a raw bandwidth of 2.94 Mbits/s, which results in an effective point-to-point data bandwidth of 2.82 Mbits/s.

Both servers use disk units with average access times of 35 ms and transfer rates of about 1 Mbyte/s. Those of the CFS have an 80 Mbyte capacity, while the XDFS can also use 300 Mbyte disks.

Thus, the two servers use roughly comparable hardware: the CFS processor is four times as fast as the XDFS processor; the Alto has 2.5 times as much memory as the Computer Automation LSI4/30; and the Ethernet's point-to-point data bandwidth is three times as high as the Cambridge ring's.

III. GENERAL DESIGN CHOICES

Although the CFS and the XDFS both provide a general filing service, they were designed with different uses in mind and differ in several major aspects.

A. Background and Goals

1) CFS Background and Goals: The CFS was originally conceived as a replacement for the backing store management of the CAP computer [28]. From the outset it was required to provide rapid access in a style suited to a virtual memory system which would swap entire segments across the network. These segments were expected to be fairly small. The average size of the CAP's segments in the implementation using a local disk was 7000 bytes. The resulting interface, although not directly tailored to the CAP's convenience, is biased towards the requirements of operating systems: rapid access to files, multiplexing of bandwidth among competing clients, and a high transfer rate are characteristic of the CFS. It operates in bursts, concentrating its full bandwidth on one particular client for the duration of a file read or write, before attending to transfers for other clients.

This concentration on serving operating system clients efficiently has led to restrictions in the interest of simplicity. For example, the CFS locks entire files at a time with multiple-reader/single-writer interlocks for the duration of a transaction. It also allows only one file to be updated atomically in a single transaction. These restrictions are acceptable for most operating systems since files are not usually read and written simultaneously, and the consistency constraints between different files tend to be rather loose.

2) XDFS Background and Goals: The XDFS, by contrast, was intended to provide a basis for database research. An XDFS transaction can cover updates to a number of files so that the atomicity of a higher level database operation can be maintained. In a database environment, a few highly interrelated and often large files may be accessed concurrently by a number of clients. To reduce the degree of serialization, the XDFS provides fine-grained locking at the byte level.

One of the main design goals of the XDFS was to allow a flexible allocation of computing and storage resources to the filing service. For each local network, the choice of the number of server processors and the amount of disk storage given to each server can be made by matching desired performance and cost. The "glue" which is used to assemble the different servers into a single file service is the atomic transaction mechanism which is designed to allow several servers to change files in a single atomic update.

B. Access Control

Shared filing systems need to provide some form of access control, and the CFS and the XDFS illustrate the two main approaches to this problem. The CFS uses a capability-based mechanism while the XDFS uses identity-based access control.

1) CFS Access Control: The CFS provides access control based on capabilities. Access to a file depends solely on the ability of a client to present a valid capability for it, rather than on the identity of the client. The CFS must prevent clients from obtaining the capabilities of files to which they should not have access, and, in a local network, this may be done by including random information in capabilities. The CFS constructs these capabilities in a particularly simple way; when a file is created, it is given a 64 bit unique identifier (UID) consisting of its disk address concatenated with a 32 bit random number. Each time a client request arrives, the server checks the validity of the UID presented but does not concern itself with the identity of the client. The degree of protection is, of course, probabilistic and proportional to the difficulty of guessing a valid UID.

A consequence of capability-based access control is that multiple-client transactions require no extra mechanisms. Since the server does not concern itself with the identity of its callers, but only with the UID's they present, a client is free to pass a UID to another client for its use. The two clients may then cooperate in an atomic transaction without any special actions on the part of the server. In the current implementation of the CFS, this can only be done if the clients need the same access rights on the objects in the transaction because CFS UID's implicitly allow both reading and writing. If the CFS allowed several UID's for every object, each having the same disk address but a different random part, then different access rights could be associated with different UID's.

2) XDFS Access Control: Clients access XDFS files using UID's, in a manner similar to the CFS. However, most access is preceded by looking up a file's name in a directory to obtain its UID. Directories contain identity-based access control, modeled loosely after that of the Tenex operating system [3]. Names and passwords are used to authenticate users. Authentication—which is actually done by calling an authentication server on the network [12]—is performed when the client program operating on the user's behalf first connects to the XDFS and lasts for the duration of the connection. This form of protection was provided primarily because the potential user community was used to it and because the goals of the XDFS project did not include novel protection schemes.

The XDFS identity-based protection necessitates multiclient transactions, i.e., transactions which explicitly have more than one client. For example, the XDFS's default directory service must participate in the client's transaction, so that both the directory structures and the client's files will revert to their previous state should an abort occur, but it needs write access to the files containing the directory information while its clients have no access at all. However, the directory service appears as an ordinary client to the XDFS, so the only way to give it different access privileges than its client is to note somehow which one is commanding the XDFS at a given moment. This is done by creating an XDFS *worker agent* process for each client involved in a transaction; it encapsulates knowledge of the client and his access rights (as well as other information discussed later).

C. Storage Reclamation

A straightforward interface to a file server's storage is that of an unstructured set of files identified only by UID's. Some of the files might be used by clients as file directories to hold the names of other files, but the server would be unaware of any relationships between them. The files would appear simply as a "flat" collection with no structure. Unfortunately, this sample approach leads to the possibility for lost and undeletable files, since clients must be trusted to delete files explicitly.

1) XDFS Storage Reclamation: In the XDFS, lost files can exist because the directory service which the XDFS provides need not be used by clients. The directory service is itself simply a client like any other, and can, but need not be used to keep track of clients' files. Any client can create an XDFS file. However, the possibility of a file being lost is small. If a transaction fails, for instance, then any files created during it are deleted automatically. There is, however, the possibility that incorrect client programs can create files but omit to record their UID's, and under these circumstances, the server will never be directed to delete the file.

2) CFS Storage Reclamation: The CFS takes a different approach, proposed initially in [2], which enables it to reclaim lost files. The CFS provides two abstractions to its clients, *files* and *indexes.* An index is an array of UID's whose entries are accessed using numbered offsets from the start of the array, and operations are provided to read, erase, and replace the individual entries in an index.

The UID's retained in an index must be valid capabilities for existing objects. Except for this constraint, however, any file or index UID may be retained in an index. The storage maintained by the CFS thus appears as a directed graph to its clients. Files are terminal nodes in this graph, and indexes hold links to other nodes—cycles are allowed. There is one distinguished *root index* with in-degree zero, whose UID is never distributed to clients. A file or index is only kept so long as it may be reached by a series of retrieve operations starting from the root index.

An index is not a directory, in the sense that the XDFS provides default directories, but a building block which can be used to construct directory services. The two operating system clients of the CFS [26], [28] each represent a directory by an index. The first entry in the index contains the UID of a file which holds a mapping from textual names to offsets in the directory index. There is no requirement to provide such a mapping, and simpler microprocessor-based client programs use indexes directly to record the UID's of files which they have created.

In practice, this structured storage is simple for clients to manage. A new client is given a new index, whose UID is placed in a free slot in the root index. The UID of the new index is then given to the client and will form the root of its storage. New files and indexes may be created at will and interconnected in an arbitrarily complex graph. To prevent premature deletion of new objects, the create-file and create-index operations specify an offset in an existing index where the UID of the new object is to be placed before being returned to the client.

Objects shared among clients require no special precautions; a client receiving a UID from some source need only retain it in an index which is known to be reachable from the root. After using the object, the client should delete the index entry. No explicit cooperation between clients is required to delete the object which will be destroyed when the last index entry for it is overwritten.

Because the directed graph maintained by the CFS can contain cycles, periodic garbage collection is needed to detect objects which are no longer reachable from the root index. The garbage collector which is used for this purpose is asynchronous and runs in a different processor in the network [9]. The CFS starts a garbage collection by requesting a network *resource manager* to find a free processor and start the asynchronous collector running in it. The CFS itself contains a process which communicates with the collector, performing synchronization with client requests as needed, and deleting unreachable objects on instruction from the collector. The garbage collector is described in more detail in [6].

D. Transactions

A shared file server with pretensions to generality must provide some means for maintaining the consistency of the data it stores. The server cannot, of course, prevent the client from making apparently correct but semantically nonsensical changes to files. It can, however, help to prevent inconsistencies arising owing to events beyond the client's control such as machine or communications failures or concurrent access to files by other clients. This can be done by enclosing a sequence of simple operations requested by a client in a transaction.

Two essential requirements of transactions are that they be atomic with respect to concurrent access, appearing to execute either before or after other conflicting transactions, and that they be atomic with respect to failures, all changes to files involved in the transaction occurring or none at all. Both the CFS and the XDFS provide such *atomic transactions* to their clients. The major difference between CFS and XDFS transactions is that the CFS restricts an atomic update to involve only a single file while the XDFS permits atomic updates to multiple files—possibly residing on multiple servers.

1) CFS Transactions: Atomic transactions were added to the CFS design as a result of examining how client operating systems might keep their file directories in a consistent state. A characteristic of most operating systems is that files tend to be relatively independent. A file directory, for instance, may have a complicated internal structure, but this does not usually depend on data stored in other files or directories. Because it was not initially clear that a general transaction mechanism would be used by CFS clients, or how such a mechanism might be implemented efficiently, a single-object transaction scheme was implemented. This allows single files or indexes to be updated atomically but cannot be used for atomic updates to structures spanning several files and indexes.

In the CFS, a transaction is started by *opening* a file or an index. Supplying the UID of the object to be updated, the client obtains in return a temporary unique identifier (TUID). A TUID may be thought of as a capability for an interlocked object; while there is a TUID outstanding, further requests to establish conflicting interlocks on the same object are rejected. Again, because the CFS clients are mainly operating systems, interlocks cover entire files or indexes and are of the conventional multiple-reader/single-writer variety. There may be several outstanding TUID's for reading any object, but only one TUID if the interlock is for writing.

As well as defining an interlock, a TUID also defines a transaction; in case of a communication error or machine failure, the object will revert to its state at the time the TUID was established. Thus, the open request combines the function of starting a transaction and setting an interlock on the object to be updated.

Once in possession of a TUID, a client can perform the appropriate operations—reading and writing for a file, and retrieving, retaining, or deleting entries for an index. The TUID can also be distributed to other clients, so that several may participate in the transaction. At the end of the transaction, the *close* request is sent, and a Boolean argument determines whether the transaction is to be committed or aborted. This either makes all updates performed by the transaction permanent, or restores the object to the state it was in when the TUID was created. In either case, the interlock on the object is also removed.

Two optimizations were made to this interface. Most CFS transactions consist of a single file read or write, and in this case the necessity to open and close the file would represent unnecessary traffic. Therefore, if the CFS receives a request which contains an ordinary UID rather than an explicit TUID, it surrounds the request with the appropriate open and close requests. Thus, single operation transactions are performed efficiently.

Secondly, clients may explicitly opt out of the transaction mechanism. At the time of creating a file, the client declares it to be *normal* or *special*, according to whether or not the file will be used to hold critical data. A special file will always revert to its initial state if a transaction aborts, but a normal file might not. There is no difference in the way normal and special files are used, and indeed, a client will be unable to decide whether a UID is for a normal or a special file without causing a transaction to abort. However, for normal files, the open and close requests provide only concurrency control without the atomic update guarantee, and the server gains a performance advantage from the knowledge that updates to a normal file need not be made in a reversible fashion.

To detect client crashes, the CFS sets timeout values on TUID's. Whenever a TUID is received in a client request, this value is reset. If it ever expires, however, the CFS deems the transaction to have died and aborts it. This very simple mechanism has proved adequate in practice, even though it will not detect looping client programs.

2) XDFS Transactions: The XDFS's transaction mechanism is more general than the CFS's. Many files on different servers may be involved in an atomic update and several clients can participate in a single transaction. A transaction is begun by an explicit *start transaction* request which returns a transaction identifier. Each subsequent request contains both the transaction identifier and the UID of the file to be read or written. A transaction is ended by an explicit *end transaction*, which performs the same function as the CFS close operation.

If a client needs to access files on more than a single server, it must send an *add server* request to the new server, supplying the transaction UID. A request to read or write data is sent to the server holding the relevant file. The only communication among servers involved in the transaction occurs when the *add server* request is made and when the transaction commits.

Unlike CFS locks, XDFS locks are set implicitly as side effects of read and write requests. These locks are at the byte level and have an associated timeout period; a client implicitly locks ranges of bytes in the files that are accessed during a transaction. After the timeout period has elapsed, a lock is considered *vulnerable* and may be broken if another transaction is waiting to acquire a lock that overlaps the same range of bytes.

XDFS locks are *not* of the single-writer/multiple-reader variety. Zero or more transactions may read a byte of a file *along with* (at most) one transaction writing the same byte. However, when a transaction with one of these ''soft'' write locks commits, the lock must become a "hard" write lock. If there are any vulnerable read locks on the same byte, they are then broken and the hard write lock is granted. If, however, the soft write lock is vulnerable and at most one read lock is not, then it cannot be changed to a hard write lock and the transaction is aborted instead. This more elaborate mechanism was implemented to counter a deadly embrace problem that can readily occur with the combination of concurrent access, breakable locks, and atomic transactions (for details the reader is referred to [10]).

To enable clients to maintain local caches of file data in the presence of concurrent access, the XDFS notifies a client when any of its read locks are broken. Normally, if a lock is broken in a transaction and the client attempts to commit the transaction, the commit request will be rejected (because his transaction has not seen a consistent view of the data). However, if the client, on receiving notice of one or more broken *read* locks, informs the XDFS that it voluntarily releases those locks, it may then commit the transaction. Essentially, by so informing the XDFS the client is stating that the correctness of its transaction does not depend on the data covered by those broken locks. Using this, a client may maintain a local cache and update it when informed of broken read locks: by releasing the locks and then rereading the data it will again see a consistent state (because its new read will not complete until the transaction that wrote the data has finished).

E. Network Protocols

The networks used by the CFS and the XDFS are quite different at the lowest level. On the Cambridge ring, the basic transmission unit is a "mini-packet" containing local source and destination addresses and two data bytes. The Ethernet, on the other hand, deals in variable-sized packets with source and destination addresses and up to 128K data bytes. What differences are induced in the two servers by these low-level communications protocols?

Because of the small data capacity of a mini-packet, the CFS converses with its clients using the *basic block protocol* (BBP) which forms messages from sequences of mini-packets. Except for the inclusion of a *port number* to identify a process in the destination machine, a basic block contains essentially the same information as an Ethernet packet. However, the Pup protocol [4] on which the XDFS layers its protocols, does contain port numbers, so the CFS and the XDFS actually have very similar interfaces to their respective lower communication levels.

1) CFS Protocol Issues: The two problems that any protocol must solve are error control and flow control. Errors in the transmitted data must be detected and there must be a means for matching the speed of transmission to the speed of reception. The CFS exploits hardware features of the ring to simplify transmission error control and flow control during file transfers. For example, because of the inherent reliability of the ring (one bit error in $5*10^{11}$), the CFS only reports reception errors to a transmitting client after a complete write operation, which is implemented simply as a sequence of basic blocks flowing from the client to the server.

For flow control, the CFS uses the hardware response bits of a mini-packet that are set when the mini-packet arrives at its destination and read when it returns to its source. To reject a basic block for which there is no waiting buffer, the CFS rejects one of its early mini-packets. Conventionally, a transmitter detecting this "rejected" response on a mini-packet restarts the basic block transmission after a suitable interval. This method of flow control is not intended to be used heavily. It is "policy" that a file transfer occurs at ring speed, a client only reading as much data as can be stored immediately in memory, and the server being able to accept indefinite amounts of material at full ring speed.

The operations provided at the CFS interface were carefully designed to be repeatable. Thus, file reads and writes specify the starting offset in the file absolutely rather than relative to a current offset maintained by the server. This means that it is safe for a client to retry a command in the absence of a reply from the server. It also means that the server can discard its state as soon as it has sent a reply and need not wait for a client acknowledgment of the reply. Thus, almost all CFS operations consist of a single request followed by a single reply; reading or writing a file additionally involves an exchange of basic blocks containing pure data.

Finally, the CFS assumes purely local network communication, so problems associated with larger, long-haul networks such as duplication of packets or packets arriving out of order can be ignored. Of course this assumption will have to be revisited if the CFS ever has to be used over a larger internetwork.

2) XDFS Protocol Issues: The protocol used by XDFS is somewhat more complicated than the CFS's. This results from operating in an internetwork [4] with nonlocal as well as local communications and from assuming that the communications medium is *mostly* reliable rather than *ultra*-reliable. (This is not entirely separable from the nonlocal assumption since long-distance communications are generally less than ultra-reliable.)

The protocol used by the XDFS has the following structure.

1) The client sends a request (e.g., ReadData).

2) The XDFS processes the request and sends one or more responses (e.g., the requested data).

3) The client sends an acknowledgment upon receipt of the response.

A client that does not receive a response to a request within a few hundred milliseconds normally assumes that the request was somehow lost and retransmits it. When the server sends a response to a client it behaves similarly in the absence of an acknowledgment from the client. Once it has received the acknowledgment, the server can free any resources it might have been holding for that request (e.g., data buffers).

Error control on packets is handled by the Ethernet itself and the XDFS protocol adds additional error detection to ensure total end-to-end error detection. The control exercised is simply to discard bad packets and to let the client retransmit. Additionally, requests are sequentially numbered by the client to enable the server to discard packets that have been routed differently and arrived out of phase, or to suppress duplicates. (These phenomena are known to occur in the Arpanet [8].)

Network flow control is handled by the Pup level, and does not impact the XDFS directly. However, the server must be able to exercise flow control to help manage its own resources, especially main memory. Two mechanisms are used. It may decide not to begin processing a request at all, in which case it will not send the acknowledgment expected by the client, who will then retry in a few hundred milliseconds. Alternatively, the server can abort an already in-process client request if it needs resources held by that request; the same client retransmission scheme handles this case.

Like the CFS, most XDFS operations are repeatable, and a client can simply retry an operation if it does not receive a reply within a reasonable period of time. Unlike the CFS, the XDFS allows reading and writing of at most 512 bytes at a time—the amount of data that will fit in a single Pup packet—because it was designed primarily for random access with no optimization for sequential reading or writing of entire files.

IV. COMPARISON OF IMPLEMENTATIONS

A. File Representation

Both the CFS and the XDFS use tree structures to record the pages of files, although the exact structures are quite different.

1) CFS File Representation: In the CFS, the information needed to map a (file identifier, page number) pair into the disk address of the page is recorded in a tree of disk pages per file. The upper levels of these trees are disk pages containing arrays of disk addresses, and only the leaf pages contain the actual data of the file or index. To economize on space, the CFS creates each object (file or index) as a single empty disk page, and adds indexing levels to the tree only as the object expands. In this way, small objects occupy a single disk block, while larger objects may grow to occupy trees with an additional one or two levels of indexing. An object with two levels of pointer pages and one of data pages allows a maximum size of about 28 Mbytes.

To allow rapid access to the tree describing a file, each CFS UID directly contains the disk address of the root page of the tree. A small object, therefore, is accessible in a single disk read. For larger objects, the initial read will return a page containing disk addresses, and care is taken to ensure that an object tree is allocated on a small number of adjacent cylinders. For these objects, the first disk access will tend to position the read/write heads for rapid file transfers. An inevitable consequence of this strategy is that, once created, files and indexes cannot be moved by the CFS. This does not mean that the disk pack on which they are allocated cannot be moved to a different drive or a different machine, because CFS UID's contain a pack number which is translated into a drive number at each access. The root page of a file tree, however, cannot be moved within the pack or to another pack. In practice, this has not caused difficulties.

2) XDFS File Representation: The XDFS uses a B-tree [1] to translate a (file identifier, page number) pair into a disk address. There is a single B-tree per disk pack, and it records the allocations of pages to files for all files on the pack. Near the center of each pack is stored a bit map that is used to record the allocation state (*free* or *allocated*) of each page on the disk.

B. Disk Redundancy

The atomic transactions provided by both the CFS and the XDFS guarantee the indivisibility of transactions over client and server failures, but to compare the disk representation of the servers' files, the nature of these failures requires closer examination. It is essential to distinguish the failures that are recovered from automatically from those rarer and more serious failures which are catastrophic. This may be done by making assumptions about the information that will be destroyed during a failure. In a service failure, for instance, increasingly serious errors may destroy the contents of the processor's volatile memory, corrupt a single disk block, or destroy an entire disk due to a mechanical failure in the drive. In more serious failures, more information may be lost than can be reconstructed during automatic recovery. How much information is to be automatically recoverable, therefore, is an important design decision.

The CFS and the XDFS take similar approaches to this problem. Neither server attempts the degree of redundancy necessary for automatic recovery from disk head crashes. Both servers restrict their recovery algorithms to failures that, at worst, corrupt a single disk page during a disk transfer, such as might be caused by a power failure or a fault in the disk's writing electronics. Neither places any reliance on the contents of the processor's volatile memory after such a failure, and the construction of lost information depends solely on the state of the server's disks.

Although the two servers use quite different representations for the information on disk (as will be described below), both obey two rules when performing disk writes so that the consistency of disk information can be maintained across failures:

1) Any page which will be returned to the free pool in the event of a failure can be written without precautions. All data pages of client files fall into this category; rather than overwriting the current page of a file with changed data, both the CFS and the XDFS allocate a new *shadow* page for the data and record the fact that a modification to the file accessing structures will be needed if the transaction completes successfully. In the event of a failure, these shadow pages are released. The management of shadow pages and the steps of the transaction commit sequence will be described in the next section.

2) All other pages must be redundant at the time of writing: either their old contents or their intended contents must be reconstructible only by examining other disk blocks. In this category fall all the server's structural pages: the XDFS B-tree and free page map, and the CFS object trees and cylinder maps to be described below.

1) XDFS Disk Redundancy: The XDFS provides this structural redundancy using an abstraction called *stable storage* [24]. Pages of essential information, such as those of the B-tree or the page-allocation bit map, are recorded twice on disk. A write to a page of stable storage must be done carefully: writing on the second page must not start until it has been verified that the first has been written successfully. It is assumed that a crash while the write heads are actually turned on will leave a page *detectably bad*; i.e., future attempts to read it will fail because of CRC or ECC checksumming.

On restarting after a crash, all pages of stable storage are checked by comparing the pairs of disk pages. Usually, both pages of a pair will be identical; however, if either page is bad, then it is overwritten by the contents of the good page. If the pages are both readable but disagree, then a crash must have occurred after writing the first but before writing the second. Under these circumstances the contents of the first page overwrites the second. With this recovery algorithm, writes to pages of stable storage can be considered as atomic actions which either occur successfully or have no effect.

2) CFS Disk Redundancy: In the CFS structural redundancy is built into the disk representation at a higher level. On each disk, one block per cylinder is reserved as a *cylinder map*, an array of entries indexed by sector number, with one entry for each disk page on the cylinder. Each entry contains both the allocation state of the page, and, if it is currently in use, the UID of the object to which it belongs and the tree address it occupies within that object.

Cylinder maps and the pointer pages of object trees are mutually redundant. The current use of each disk page is described both by its cylinder map entry and by its presence in an object tree. As long as the server is careful to write a cylinder map only when the set of object maps is consistent and an object map only when the set of cylinder maps is consistent, the redundancy of each disk page of structural information is maintained. The CFS is able to rebuild its structural information after a crash using this redundancy.

If a pointer page is corrupted during a server crash, the set of cylinder maps can be scanned to find all pages belonging to its object. The tree addresses of some of these pages will show them to be children of the page whose contents were lost, and their addresses can be reinserted in it. At the end of the scan, all the addresses in the corrupted page will have been reconstructed.

Conversely, the cylinder maps can be reconstructed by starting at the root index of the file server graph and examining the contents of each index to find all object trees. These can then be examined to see whether they owned any pages on the cylinder map which has been lost. If so, the cylinder map entry can be reconstructed. This scan is appreciably longer than the linear scan of cylinder maps needed to reconstruct a pointer page. With the current 80 Mbyte disks, the linear scan takes about 30 s to read one page from each cylinder, while the graph scan takes about 30 min.

C. Dynamic Storage of a Transaction

While a transaction is in progress, and therefore subject to failure, its updates must be recorded in a reversible manner. This means that the server must maintain two states of its storage during each transaction. One is the state from which the transaction started, which must be restored in the event of a machine crash, communication failure, or explicit abort request. The other is the new incomplete state to which the client adds progressively. Only when the server is told that this new state is complete and correct can it commit the transaction by discarding its initial state.

As mentioned above, both the CFS and the XDFS have chosen to record this new accumulating state as a set of shadow pages. These pages are inserted into the appropriate positions in the tree only if the transaction commits and are returned to the free pool otherwise. While the transaction is in progress, the accumulating list of shadow pages must, of course, be maintained as the dynamic storage of the transaction. (Note that in the case of transactions involving multiple XDFS servers, there will in general be a set of shadow pages for each disk holding files involved in the transaction.) This list describes the precise changes to the file server tree which must be made to reflect the final state of the transaction.

There are two implementation problems to be faced in the management of this set. First, there is a simple question of space; if there is a limitation on the space available to hold shadow page addresses, then this may impose a limit on the amount of data which can be updated atomically. Second, when the server commits a transaction, the set of shadow pages must be recorded safely on disk; even if the server crashes immediately after recording the committal of a transaction, it must be able to find the set of shadow pages which are to be converted into "real" pages. Thus, the server should be able to write the set to disk quickly when the request to commit arrives.

1) CFS Dynamic Storage for Transactions: In the CFS, cylinder map entries record shadow pages. Cylinder map entries have four allocation states; in addition to the *allocated* and *free* states, there are two intermediate states *intending-to-allocate* and *intending-to-free*. When a shadow page is to be created for a transaction, the new page is marked intending-to-allocate in its cylinder map entry, and the page which currently occupies the tree position is marked intending-to-free. As a transaction progresses, it will mark a number of cylinder maps in this way, and a list of cylinder map addresses is kept in local storage. This list contains not the disk addresses of shadow pages, but the list of cylinder maps in which the intentions reside, which is a significant compression. Normally, even a CFS transaction which alters hundreds of pages will have created its shadow pages on only a few cylinders in the vicinity of the object tree. As each new shadow page is created, a local copy of the appropriate pointer page in the tree is changed to hold the new page address. The CFS will not commit a transaction until it has written these marked cylinder maps to disk; when this is done, the necessary alterations to the object tree have been safely recorded on disk. To commit a transaction, a *commit bit* is set in the cylinder map entry for the root of the object tree, and this cylinder map is also written to disk. At this point, the client can be informed that the transaction is complete.

Once the commit bit is set, the CFS must replace the old pages in the file structure by the corresponding shadow pages and then free the old pages. First, all the local copies of the pointer pages for the object tree are written to disk, so that the disk copy of the tree reflects the new state of the object. Then, all the pages which have been marked intending-to-allocate must be changed to allocated, and all those marked intending-to-free must be marked free. The cylinder maps which are changed are precisely those which were written just prior to committing the transaction, so they must be written again. Finally, with both cylinder maps and the object tree showing the object's new state, the commit bit can be turned off, and the cylinder map in which it is recorded written to disk.

Restarting after a service crash involves a simple linear scan of each disk's cylinder maps. If all maps are found to be readable, then they define the authoritative description of the server's storage. If a cylinder map is found to be broken, however, then it is rebuilt by performing a much more costly scan of all object trees, as described above. In either case, however, at the end of the cylinder map scan, some pages may have been found in one of the intermediate allocation states. The UID's of the object concerned are recorded in the cylinder map entries, so it is a simple matter to reconstruct the state of the transaction, consisting of the UID of the object, the list of cylinder maps holding intentions, and the value of the commit bit. The transaction can then be completed or aborted in the normal way according to the value of the commit bit.

2) XDFS Dynamic Storage for Transactions: In the XDFS, shadow pages are recorded in a data structure associated with each *worker agent* (there is one such agent per disk pack per transaction) called its *local map*, which records the changes to the B-tree map (the *global map*) as the result of writes during the transaction. To commit a transaction, the B-tree is updated in a bottom-up fashion with shadow, stable storage pages of its own until the highest level B-tree page requiring change is encountered (this is usually not the root of the tree, but some node lower down). The page is atomically updated (this is why the B-tree is implemented using stable pages) which causes the tree below it to include atomically all lower level changed pages, including the client's changed file pages. At this point the transaction is essentially done; all that remains is to free the original pages for which file or B-tree shadow pages were created.

To ensure against service interruptions, the XDFS does not consider a transaction committed until it has written a list of *intentions* recording the shadow file pages in an *intentions log*. This log is recorded in stable storage so that it can be written atomically. Once it has been, the transaction is considered committed, the client may be so informed, and the B-tree update described above may begin.

If there is an XDFS service interruption, the server scans the intentions log during restart and reconstructs worker agents and their local maps for each committed transaction. The agents then proceed to commit their transactions again. Because of the careful ordering of the B-tree update, this will work even if the intentions have been partly carried out before the crash (because the shadow B-tree pages are simply forgotten after restart and will be created anew in carrying out the intentions again). Once the intentions have been successfully carried out, the intentions log is updated atomically to reflect this and the transaction is done.

What happens to shadow pages of in-progress, but uncommitted transactions after a service interruption? Basically they are returned to the pool of free pages (recorded in a bit map on the disk) because they do not occur in the intentions log or in the B-tree, both of which are scanned during crash recovery. An aborted transaction during normal running returns any shadow pages recorded in its local map to the free pool.

In addition to single-server transactions, the XDFS must handle multiserver transactions and guarantee them even in the face of service interruptions of one or more of the servers involved or of the communications among them. It does so by employing a two-phase commit protocol, which is similar to the tree-updating algorithm used internally by each server [25]. In the first phase the coordinator for the transaction commands all its workers to write their intentions marked tentative; once they have all reported back, it writes their identities in its own intentions log. The second phase involves the coordinator commanding its workers to mark their intentions confirmed. After doing so, each worker carries out its intentions, reports success to the coordinator, and erases its intentions. Once all its workers have reported back successfully the coordinator marks its intentions done and vanishes.

All this careful sequencing is to ensure that transactions will be atomic even if workers or the coordinator suffer service interruptions. For example, if some worker does not report back at the end of the first phase, the coordinator can decide to command the workers to abort instead of committing. Even if one of them crashes after writing its tentative intentions but before receiving the abort command, it will be able to abort correctly once it has restarted and the coordinator has commanded it once more. Analyzing the algorithm for correctness in all cases is complex and outside the scope of this chapter; for details see [11].

V. EVALUATION

A. XDFS Successes

Transactions covering multiple files, servers, and clients have been a functional success: they enable database transactions that would otherwise have to be managed by client code; this would be extremely difficult to accomplish with the same level of robustness and resiliency as provided by the XDFS. They allow the system to grow smoothly by adding whatever mix of processors and disks is appropriate for a given environment. They enable separate clients, possibly in separate machines, to participate in a single transaction, which is highly desirable for distributed computing. On the negative side, multiclient/file-server transactions are more expensive than the CFS's simpler transactions, and ways must be found to reduce the overhead further.

Basing the atomic transaction guarantee on the notion of stable storage made much of the implementation of the critical parts of the XDFS simple, but at the expense of extra disk writes. Some cheaper form of stable storage would help considerably (see Section VI).

B. XDFS Shortfalls

It was a mistake not to provide normal as well as special files in the XDFS. There are often situations in which they are highly valuable, e.g., for keeping a transcript of an editing session which can be "replayed" should the editor, the client machine, or the XDFS crash. In these cases, it is not necessary that the file be absolutely correct all the time (that would require a transaction per write on it, which is not warranted by the circumstances), but it is necessary that the file not revert to its state at the beginning of the transaction.

In a system whose basic file access methods involve only UID's rather than user-sensible names, it is easy for client programs to "forget" about files they created, especially during the period they are being debugged. Although only files that survive to a successful transaction commit can become extant but forgotten, the XDFS should have provided some means of collecting this garbage or at least of recording its existence in a manner that would allow it to be collected by clients. The CFS's indexes fill this need nicely.

C. The XDFS B-Tree

The XDFS's B-tree provides a single means for organizing both the file structures on a disk pack and for providing the primary data structure for implementing atomic transaction. Is it a success or not? It is hard to say. On the positive side, it is efficient as a means for accessing file pages on large disks, and it is economical to make one structure serve two purposes. On the negative side, it is a very complex data structure when used for this particular purpose. Any corruption of its structure will, in general, cause distinctly nonlocal damage to the file system—a single node points to about 200 lower-level nodes!— and it is not clear that it provides as much locality of reference for accessing files as pointer-page mechanisms like the CFS's.

Despite these misgivings, there has not been a single file lost or damaged in the XDFS at the file system level as the result of B-tree software problems. This is due primarily to the care and skill of the implementors of the XDFS B-tree, H. Sturgis and K. Kolling, and to the strong typing of the Mesa language.

D. CFS Successes

The CFS has been helped substantially by the fairly stringent performance requirements imposed on it from the outset. A file server which provided a slow backing store service for a virtual memory machine like the CAP [5] would not have been a disappointment, but a failure. This limitation helped to keep the design simple. Particular examples of this are the extremely simple file transfer protocol used. As a result, it has become a practical proposition to write a file server interface for simple microprocessors. It must be pointed out, however, that the assumptions on which this protocol is based do not allow it to be extended easily to long-haul networks; the CFS is a local network server, and exploits this fact. Also, the distinction between normal and special files has allowed clients to avoid the expense of atomic transactions where they are not required. Client operating systems, for instance, tend to use special files to contain file directory information, but normal files for most other purposes.

The interface that the file server presents to its clients, in the form of a directed graph with capability access to files and implicit storage reclamation, must be judged a success. Capability access control is simple to implement, and avoids the question of client identity, which may be difficult to determine reliably in the local network. The embedding of disk addresses directly in these capabilities is to be recommended as a means of speeding up the access to files. The graph structure of indexes maintained by the CFS has worked out well in practice, and the index abstraction is a useful building block for operating systems; the client operating systems of the CFS construct their file directories from an index and an associated file which contains string names and access rights. Two quite different filling systems built in this way coexist on the CFS storage [5], [21].

The automatic garbage collection of the CFS has also worked well in practice, and the local network environment lends itself to asynchronous garbage collection from another machine in the network. Currently, a reference count mechanism deals with most deletions, an object being deleted immediately whenever the count of index references to it falls to zero. No particular precautions are taken by the CFS to ensure the accuracy of these reference counts, and certain types of server crashes may leave them high. Any objects for which this occurs will be found at the next garbage collection; these are currently performed once every few days.

E. CFS Shortcomings

Perhaps the most obvious shortcomings of the CFS is that atomic transactions are restricted to updating a single file or index only. This was largely due to implementation uncertainties with a more general mechanism and to doubts as to whether the style of use envisaged for the CFS would actually require multiple-file transactions. The experience of converting two operating systems to use the CFS indicates that more general transactions would have been useful. For example, since file directories are implemented as an index with an associated file, it is currently impossible to update both structures in a single transaction. An extension to the basic CFS transaction mechanism has been designed, however, which allows multiple-file and multiple-server transactions with a simultaneous reduction in the per-transaction cost in disk transfers [7].

The disk redundancy designed into the CFS is also open to criticism because it is more complex than the XDFS stable storage abstraction. As described above, the actions needed to rebuild a corrupted disk page depend on the kind of page it is; a different algorithm is needed for the index pages of object trees and for the cylinder maps.

It is interesting to note that the CFS cylinder maps are used for three different functions. In the XDFS, there is an allocation bit map for free blocks and an intentions log for transactions. Both these functions are performed by CFS cylinder maps, which record not only free pages, but also the list of changes that a transaction has accumulated on an object. Further, the XDFS uses the duplicate pages of stable storage to maintain B-tree redundancy; in the CFS the cylinder maps provide the equivalent redundancy for object trees. This economy of structure is attractive, and leads to good disk locality, since all the tree and cylinder map pages which a transaction will need tend to be grouped in a small number of cylinders. On balance, however, the redundancy function of cylinder maps does not seem to be as successful as those of page allocation and intentions logging; the program to reconstruct a corrupted block is not trivial.

F. Performance Analyses

To give some indication of the relative performance of the two file servers, we ran some simple experiments. The client machines used were of the same types as their respective servers, and the operations below were measured from the time that the client program issued the request until it had received notification of completion. Hence, they include communication time, any disk time, and the nonoverlapping software costs on the client and server machines. The CFS times in parentheses are for operations performed on normal files rather than on special files.

	CFS	XDFS
Basic communication overhead	12 ms	38 ms
Open transaction/close transaction	48 ms	360 ms
Read 256 bytes (average of 100 random reads)	41 ms	76 ms
Write 256 bytes (average of 100 random writes)	73 ms (64 ms)	142 ms
Open transaction Write 262 144 bytes in existing file Close transaction	7.1 s (5.1 s)	49.5 s

1) Basic Communication Overhead: The basic communication overhead is the time from a client's sending a null request to its being able to proceed after receipt of a reply. The actual transmission time is less than 0.5 ms for both systems assuming strictly local communications.

For the CFS, the software overhead amounts to 11.5 ms, or about 11000 instruction times (5500 instructions per basic block). For the XDFS, the software overhead is 37.5 ms, or about 9400 instruction times.

2) Open Transaction/Close Transaction: This is the time for the null transaction. It involves the communication overhead of two requests plus the time for the server to commit the transaction.

The CFS transaction overhead exclusive of communication costs is $48 - 2*12 = 24$ ms. The XDFS overhead is $360 - 2*38 = 284$ ms. It is not easy to normalize these numbers to instruction times because the XDFS algorithms involve disk transfers (to the intentions log in stable storage), with the attendant uncertainties of seek times, rotational latencies, etc. It is clear, however, that the CFS scheme of recording commit information with changed objects on disk makes this basic overhead much less because no disk transfers are required at all. The XDFS makes no attempt to optimize this case and so goes through the entire overhead of a two-phase commit with the phases recorded in stable storage.

3) Reading 256 Bytes: This operation was chosen to represent the time that a client would see when reading a small amount of data randomly from a file. We chose 256 bytes as the amount because it does not match the pages size used by either server (2048 bytes/ page for the CFS and 1024 bytes/page for the XDFS). It should not be affected by any transaction-associated overheads.

It is difficult to compare these results precisely. The times include seeks and rotational latency of the disks plus the times to find a file page using the file structures described earlier for the two systems. They are further affected by information cached by the two systems to speed up just such requests. If we exclude the basic communication overhead, the CFS time is $(41 - 12) = 29$ ms, and the XDFS time is $(76 - 38) = 38$ ms, which, given the relative processor speeds, seem roughly comparable.

4) Writing 256 Bytes: This operation represents the average time that a client would see when writing a small amount of data randomly to a file. Because 256 bytes does not match either server's disk page size, the write will generally involve finding the relevant page on the disk, reading it to insert the changed data, and rewriting it to the disk. Sometimes a write operation will be the first done in that particular page in the transaction, in which case it must include the cost of allocating a shadow page; sometimes it will not be the first time a particular page is written, and there should be no allocation of a shadow page, since one already exists. In the CFS, if a normal page is written, then no allocation cost is incurred because a shadow page is never created.

For pages of special files, the CFS and the XDFS times are, as in the case of reading a random page, roughly comparable given the speed ratios of the two machine types involved. The cost of writing a random page of a normal file in the CFS gives some indication of the extra cost seen by a client during a transaction for using a special file; it is small, about 9 ms, and is taken up by allocating shadow pages and marking their cylinder map entries.

5) Writing 262 144 Bytes in an Existing File: The last experiment involves the complete cost of opening a transaction, writing 262 144 bytes sequentially into an existing file, and closing the transaction. The times include the basic transaction overhead, the time to write the pages (and allocate shadow pages for that purpose), plus the cost of committing the transaction. The file data occupies 128 disk pages in the CFS and 256 pages in the XDFS.

For normal files, the CFS accomplishes this extremely quickly, which it was optimized to do. The bytes of the file flow from the client to the server as a sequence of basic blocks and are written on the disk. Because they are being written to an already existing file, there are no allocation costs for them or the file's index structure. Seek times are almost zero because of the sequentiality of the request, and there is virtually no work to be done at the end of writing the file. The communication overhead c for each page is 12 ms or 1.54 s for the 128 page file. This leaves 3.56 s for writing all of the pages, or about 30 ms per page.

What are the significant cost components for writing a special file under the protection of a transaction? Each page of the file must be written and a shadow page created for it, the basic transaction overhead must be paid, and the shadow pages created during the transaction must be recorded on disk as part of its commitment. For each page written we must pay the basic communication overhead c and for the entire transaction we must pay the basic transaction overhead t. From the remaining time we can calculate a per page cost w for writing a page of a special file in this sequential case.

For the CFS, the communication and basic transaction overheads are 128*0.012 + 0.048 = 1.58 s. The rest of the time, 5.52 s = 128*w s, or 43 ms per page, represents the cumulative overhead for allocating a shadow page, writing it, and recording its state at commit time. Comparing it to the 30 ms per page for the case of a normal file gives an overhead of 13 ms per special page.

For the XDFS, the communication and basic transaction overheads are 512*0.038 + 0.36 = 19.82 s. The number of requests is 512 rather than 256 because the size of a single Pup packet limits the amount of data that can be sent to 512 bytes. The remaining 29.68 = 256*w s, or 116 ms per page, represents the cumulative overhead for allocating a shadow page, writing it, recording its state at commit time, and then deallocating the previous version of the page. This additional deallocation overhead is paid by the CFS also, but is done as a background task after the client is notified of commitment. The same strategy would work in the XDFS, but has not been implemented.

One of the lessons from this measurement (which probably holds true for any file system) is that a larger disk page size lowers the cost per byte per action correspondingly. For example, if the XDFS used a page size the same as the CFS's but was otherwise unchanged, the expected time for this transaction would be 19.82 + 128*0.116 = 34.67 s, i.e., doubling the page size would reduce the cost of writing this large file by 30 percent (in fact, this was verified by earlier experiments with the XDFS). If the packet size were increased to match this larger page size, c would be reduced by 14.6 s. Thus, the result of increasing the page and packet size to be the same as the CFS's 2048 bytes would be a total time of 20.07 s, less than half the current 49.5 s. Of course, life is not so simple, and other considerations such as the expected granularity of random access must also influence which page size is chosen. Nevertheless, using a larger page/packet size is clearly better for sequential access, provided it does not overburden clients.

VI. Suggestions for Future File Servers

There is one obvious area for investigation in the design of future file servers. The requirement to survive the failure of a disk transfer has exacted a substantial cost in complexity and in actual transfers per transaction in both the CFS and the XDFS. The problem may be briefly summarized: whenever a page of structural information is to be written to disk, either its old contents or its new contents must be completely reconstructible from the contents of other disk blocks. Therefore, between every two disk transfers to a page, at least one other page must be written to maintain redundancy. Maintaining this level of robustness requires a doubling of the number of disk writes to structural pages.

An attractive solution to this problem is to make some of the server's memory nonvolatile, so that it will survive all arbitrary halts by the processor, even a power failure during a disk write [16]. This part of the memory could be used to buffer disk pages, and each buffered page would have an associated "ready-to-write" bit. On restarting after a crash, the processor could scan its nonvolatile buffer, and write out all pages which were marked in this way. Such an organization would not only eliminate the need for structural disk redundancy, but would also give a performance advantage, since a page could be considered written by the processor as soon as it had marked it ready-to-write; crashes might delay the operation, but would not prevent it.

Both the CFS and the XDFS present a "flat" view of transactions, in that a transaction cannot contain any others. Reed has proposed a scheme which allows nested transactions [22]. In many circumstances, the failure of one of the simple steps in a transaction will normally cause the entire transaction to fail in turn. Nested transactions may turn out to be advantageous, however, if the failure of a particular subtransaction can be dealt with by trying an alternative subtransaction which might lead to eventual success. More experience is needed to decide which of these two views is most generally appropriate.

A small point for future designers regards the design of internal interfaces in a file server interface. In both the CFS and the XDFS, procedures such as "allocate disk page" have evolved into "allocate many pages" as a result of experience with the working server. Wherever possible, batching of disk operations should be exploited in the internal interfaces in the interests of economy; there are never enough processor cycles.

Acknowledgment

The CFS design was inspired by ideas from A. Birrell and R. Needham, who were major contributors to the design. C. Dellar also made valuable contributions, and R. Needham and M. Johnson debugged the first version of the program.

The XDFS was also a group effort. B. Lampson, P. Baudelaire, C. Simonyi, and H.

Sturgis did the original design. H. Sturgis, J. Israel, K. Kolling, J. Mitchell, and J. Morris implemented the system.

In both cases, pioneering users, by providing client programs, gave the systems the stamp of reality that comes with actual use.

REFERENCES

[1] R. Bayer and E. M. McCreight, "Organization and maintenance of large ordered indexes," *Acta Inform.*, vol. 1, pp. 173–189, 1972.

[2] A. D. Birrell and R. M. Needham, "A universal file server," *IEEE Trans. Software Eng.*, vol. SE-6, pp. 450–453, Sept. 1980.

[3] D. G. Bobrow, J. D. Burchfiel, D. L. Murphy, and R. S. Tomlinson, "TENEX, a paged time sharing system for the PDP-10," *Commun. Ass. Comput. Mach.*, vol. 15, pp. 135–143, Mar. 1972.

[4] D. R. Boggs, J. F. Shoch, E. A. Taft, and R. M. Metcalfe, "Pup: An internetwork architecture," Xerox PARC, Palo Alto, CA, Rep. CSL-79-10, July 1979.

[5] C. N. R. Dellar, "Removing backing store administration from the CAP operating system." *Op. Syst. Rev.*, vol. 14, pp. 41–49, Oct. 1980.

[6] J. Dion, "The cambridge file server," *Op. Syst. Rev.*, vol. 14, pp. 26–35, Oct. 1980.

[7] ——, "Reliable storage in a local network," Ph.D. dissertation, Cambridge University, Cambridge, England, Feb. 1981.

[8] E. Feinler and J. Postel, Eds., *ARPANET Protocol Handbook*. NIC 7104, Network Information, SRI International, Menlo Park, CA, Jan. 1978.

[9] N. H. Garnett and R. M. Needham, "An asynchronous garbage collector for the Cambridge file server," *Op. Syst. Rev.*, vol. 14, pp. 36–40, Oct. 1980.

[10] D. K. Gifford, "Violet, an experimental decentralized system," Integrated Office System Workshop, INRIA, Rocquencourt, France, Nov. 1979, Xerox PARC, Palo Alto, CA, Rep. CSL-79-12.

[11] B. W. Lampson and H. E. Sturgis, "Crash recovery in a distributed data storage system," to be published.

[12] R. Levin and M. D. Schroeder, "Transport of electronic messages through a network," Xerox PARC, Palo Alto, CA, Rep. CSL-79-4, Apr. 1979.

[13] B. Liskov, A. Snyder, R. Atkinson, and C. Schaffert, "Abstraction mechanisms in CLU," *Commun. Ass. Comput. Mach.*, vol. 20, pp. 564–576, Aug. 1977.

[14] R. M. Metcalfe and D. R. Boggs, "Ethernet: Distributed packet switching for local computer networks." *Commun. Ass. Comput. Mach.*, vol. 19, pp. 395–404, July 1976.

[15] J. G. Mitchell, W. Maybury, and R. E. Sweet, "Mesa language manual," Xerox PARC, Palo Alto, CA, Rep. CSL-79-3, Apr. 1979.

[16] R. M. Needham, J. G. Mitchell, and A. J. Herbert, "How to connect stable memory to a computer," to be published.

[17] W. H. Paxton, "A client-based transaction system to maintain data integrity," in *Proc. 7th Symp. Operating Syst. Principles,* Asilomar, CA, Dec. 1979, pp. 18–23.

[18] G. J. Popek, J. J. Horning, B. W. Lampson, J. G. Mitchell, and R. L. London, "Notes on the design of EUCLID," in *Proc. Conf. Language Design for Reliable Software, SIGPLAN Notices,* vol. 12, Mar. 1977, pp. 11–18.

[19] D. P. Reed and L. Svobodova, "SWALLOW: A distributed data storage system for a local network," in *Proc. Int. Workshop on Local Networks,* Zurich, Switzerland, Aug. 1980.

[20] D. P. Reed, "Naming and synchronization in a decentralized computer system," Ph.D. dissertation, Dep. Elec. Eng. Comput. Sci., Mass. Inst. Technol., Sept. 1978; also in MIT Laboratory for Comput. Sci., Tech. Rep. TR-205, Sept. 1978.

[21] M. Richards, A. R. Aylward, P. Bond, R. D. Evans, and B. J. Knight, "TRIPOS: A portable operating system for mini-computers," *Software Practice and Experience,* vol. 9, pp. 513–526, July 1979.

[22] M. Richards, "BCPL: A tool for compiler writing and system programming," *AFIPS SJCC Conf. Proc.,* vol. 35, pp. 557–566, 1969.

[23] M. Shaw, W. A. Wulf, and R. London, "Abstraction and verification in Alphard: Defining and specifying iteration and generators," *Commun. Ass. Comput. Mach.*, vol. 20, pp. 553–563, Aug. 1977.

[24] H. E. Sturgis, J. G. Mitchell, and J. Israel, "Issues in the design and use of a distributed file system," *Op. Syst. Rev.*, vol. 14, pp. 55–69, July 1980.

[25] H. E. Sturgis, "A post mortem for a time-sharing system," Xerox PARC, Palo Alto, CA, Rep. CSL-74-1, Jan. 1974.

[26] D. Swinehart, G. McDaniel, and D. Boggs, "WFS: A simple shared file system for a distributed environment," in *Proc. 7th Symp. Operating Syst. Principles,* Asilomar, CA, Dec. 1979, pp. 9–17.

[27] C. P. Thacker, E. M. McCreight, B. W. Lampson, R. F. Sproull, and D. R. Boggs, ''Alto: A personal computer,'' Xerox PARC, Palo Alto, CA, Rep. CSL-79-11, Aug. 1979.

[28] M. V. Wilkes, and R. M. Needham, ''The Cambridge CAP computer and its operating system,'' *Operating and Programming System Series.*   Amsterdam, The Netherlands: North Holland, 1979.

[29] M. V. Wilkes and D. J. Wheeler, ''The Cambridge digital communications ring,'' in *Proc. Local Area Commun. Network Symp.,* Boston, MA, May 1979, Nat. Bur. Standards Special Publication.

Subject Index

Credit List

Chapters 3, 5 through 11, and 26 were adapted from papers in the November 1983 issue of the IEEE JOURNAL ON SELECTED AREAS IN COMMUNICATIONS. The other chapters were specially written for this book or were adapted, with permission, from other sources, as shown below.

Chapter	Source
1	Specially written.
2	*Lecture Notes in Computer Science*, pp. 1–35, 1982.
4	*Mini-Micro Systems*, pp. 265–274, June 1982.
12	*Bell System Technical Journal*, pp. 1413–1440, September 1982.
13	Specially written.
14	*IEEE Communications Magazine*, pp. 22–35, August 1984.
15	Specially written.
16	*Journal of Lightwave Technology*, pp. 556–559, June 1986.
17	*IEEE Journal on Selected Areas in Communications*, pp. 890–896, November 1985.
18	*Journal of Lightwave Technology*, pp. 479–489, June 1985.
19	*IEEE Communications Magazine*, pp. 6–14, March 1981.
20	*Computer Networks*, pp. 245–259, October 1980.
21	*IEEE Transactions on Communications*, pp. 763–774, June 1983.
22	*IEEE Transactions on Communications*, pp. 1465–1473, October 1981.
23	*ACM, Sigmetrics '85*, August 1985.
24	Specially written.
25	*AT&T Bell Laboratories Technical Journal*, pp. 33–55, January 1984.
27	*British Telecom Technology*, pp. 27–35, October 1985.
28	*Journal of Telecommunications Networks*, pp. 116–130, Summer 1984.
29	*IEEE Transactions on Communications*, pp. 1058–1066, October 1985.
30	*Proceedings of Globecom '85*, December 1985, pp. 1019–1023.
31	*IEEE Journal on Selected Areas in Communications*, pp. 1070–1075, December 1983.
32	*Proceedings of the 8th ACM Symposium on Operating Systems Principles, ACM SIGOPS Operating Systems Review*, December 1981, pp. 160–168.
33	*Proceedings of the 9th Communications Symposium*, September 1985, pp. 22–32.
34	*Communications of the ACM*, pp. 233–245, April 1982.

Editors' Biographies

Karl Kümmerle (M'81) received the M.S. and Ph.D. degrees in electrical engineering from Stuttgart University, Stuttgart, Federal Republic of Germany, in 1963 and 1969, respectively.

From 1963 to 1969 he was Research Assistant with the Institute for Switching Techniques and Data Processing at Stuttgart University, where he was primarily engaged in investigations in the field of telephone-traffic theory, mathematical statistics, and time-sharing systems. From 1970 to 1972 he was Research Associate of the National Research Council of the Computation Laboratory of NASA's Marshall Space Flight Center, Huntsville, AL. There his work focused on the performance analysis of large-scale computer systems. In 1972 he joined the IBM Zurich Research Laboratory, where he worked in the field of computer and data communication networks, particularly on various aspects of integrating circuit- and packet-switching into a single network. As Manager for Systems and Applications he had responsibility for investigations on architecture, transmission, and performance of a token-ring system for local area communication, its prototype implementation, and for the development of file and print servers. This work provided the basis for the IBM Token Ring System. From 1984 to 1985 he was on international assignment from Zurich to the IBM T. J. Watson Research Center, Yorktown Heights, NY, where he headed the Department of Communication Systems. On his return, he was appointed Manager of Telecommunication Systems at the IBM Zurich Research Laboratory..In 1986, he was promoted to Department Head of Communications and Computer Science. He served the IEEE Communications Society as Vice-President, International Affairs, for the period 1982–1983 and has been Editor for Local Area Networks of the IEEE TRANSACTIONS ON COMMUNICATIONS since 1982. He was Coeditor of the Special Issue on Local Area Networks of the IEEE JOURNAL ON SELECTED AREAS IN COMMUNICATIONS in November 1983.

Dr. Kümmerle was co-recipient of the 1981 Stephen O. Rice Prize Paper Award in the field of communication theory for the paper ''Balanced HDLC procedures: A performance analysis.''

John O. Limb (SM'72–F'78) received the B.E.E. and Ph.D. degrees in electrical engineering from the University of Western Australia in 1963 and 1967, respectively.

From 1966 to 1967 he was with the Research Laboratories of the Australian Post Office, Melbourne, Australia. He then became a Member of the Opto-Electronics Department of Bell Laboratories, Holmdel, NJ. In 1975 he was a Visiting Professor in the Department of Theoretical Communications and Information Processing at the Technical University of Hanover, Germany. From 1971 to 1978 he was Department Head of the Visual Communications Research Department at Bell Laboratories, Holmdel, NJ. He was Department Head of the Distributed Computer Systems

Research Department at Bell Laboratories, Murray Hill, NJ, from 1978 to 1983. In 1983 he was a Visiting Professor at the University of Sydney, Sydney, Australia. From 1983 to 1985 he was Division Manager in the Communications Sciences Research Division, Bell Communications Research, Murray Hill, NJ. At present he is Laboratory Director at Hewlett Packard Laboratories, Bristol, England. He has published 52 technical papers in refereed journals and has 24 patents in the fields of picture coding, image processing, visual perception, office automation, and local area networks. He was an Editor of the IEEE TRANSACTIONS ON COMMUNICATIONS from 1979 to 1981 and on the Board of Governors of the Communications Society from 1982 to 1985. In 1984 he was Editor-in-Chief of the IEEE TRANSACTIONS ON COMMUNICATIONS. Since 1984 he has been Editor-in-Chief of the IEEE JOURNAL ON SELECTED AREAS IN COMMUNICATIONS. In 1982 he was Founding Editor-in-Chief of the ACM *Transactions on Office Information Systems* and Conference Chairman of the ACM Conference on Office Information Systems.

Dr. Limb is a Fellow of the IEEE and a member of the Association for Computing Machinery and the Optical Society of America. He was the recipient of the Cable Makers of Australia Award in 1962, the L. G. Abraham IEEE Prize Paper Award in 1973, and the D. G. Fink IEEE Prize Paper Award in 1982.

Fouad A. Tobagi (M'77–SM'83–F'85) received the engineering degree from Ecole Centrale des Arts et Manufactures, Paris, France, in 1970 and the M.S. and Ph.D. degrees in computer science from the University of California, Los Angeles, in 1971 and 1974, respectively.

From 1974 to 1978, he was a Research Staff Project Manager with the ARPA project in the Department of Computer Science, University of California, Los Angeles, where he engaged in modeling, analysis, and measurements of packet radio systems. In June 1978, he joined the faculty of the School of Engineering at Stanford University, Stanford, CA, where he is currently Associate Professor of Electrical Engineering. His research interests include local area networks, packet switching in ground radio and satellite networks, modeling and performance evaluation of computer communications systems, and VLSI implementation of network components.

Dr. Tobagi is a Fellow of the IEEE for his contributions to the field of computer communications and local area networks, a member of the Association for Computing Machinery, and has served as an ACM National Lecturer for the period 1982–1983. He is the winner of the 1981 Leonard G. Abraham Prize Paper Award in the field of communications systems for his paper "Multiaccess protocols in packet communications networks" and co-winner of the IEEE Communications Society 1984 Magazine Prize Paper Award for the paper "Packet radio and satellite networks." He has served as Associate Editor for Computer Communications of the IEEE TRANSACTIONS ON COMMUNICATIONS for the period 1984–1986 and Editor for Packet Radio and Satellite Networks of the *Journal of Telecommunications Networks* for the period 1981–1985. He was Coeditor of the Special Issue on Local Area Networks of the IEEE JOURNAL ON SELECTED AREAS IN COMMUNICATIONS in November 1983 and the Special Issue on Packet Radio Networks of the PROCEEDINGS OF THE IEEE in January 1987.